Administering
Windows Server® 2008
Server Core

Administering

Windows Server® 2008 Server Core

John Paul Mueller

Wiley Publishing, Inc.

Acquisitions Editor: Tom Cirtin

Development Editor: David Clark

Technical Editor: Russ Mullen

Production Editor: Elizabeth Campbell

Copy Editor: Cheryl Hauser

Production Manager: Tim Tate

Vice President and Executive Group Publisher: Richard Swadley

Vice President and Executive Publisher: Joseph B. Wikert

Vice President and Publisher: Neil Edde

Book Designers: Bill Gibson and Judy Fung

Compositor: Craig W. Johnson, Happenstance Type-O-Rama

Proofreader: Rachel Gunn

Indexer: Nancy Guenther

Cover Designer: Ryan Sneed

For general information on our other products and services or to obtain technical support, please contact our Customer Care Department within the U.S. at (800) 762-2974, outside the U.S. at (317) 572-3993 or fax (317) 572-4002.

Wiley also publishes its books in a variety of electronic formats. Some content that appears in print may not be available in electronic books.Mueller, John, 1958-

Library of Congress Cataloging-in-Publication Data

       Administering Windows server 2008 server core / John P. Mueller. -- 1st ed.
         p. cm.
      ISBN 978-0-470-23840-0 (paper/website)
      1. Microsoft Windows server. 2. Operating systems (Computers) I. Title.
      QA76.76.O63M8442 2008
      005.7'1376--dc22
                      2007048497

Sybex®
An Imprint of
 WILEY

Dear Reader,

Thank you for choosing *Administering Windows Server 2008 Server Core*. This book is part of a family of premium quality Sybex books, all written by outstanding authors who combine practical experience with a gift for teaching.

Sybex was founded in 1976. More than thirty years later, we're still committed to producing consistently exceptional books. With each of our titles we're working hard to set a new standard for the industry. From the paper we print on, to the authors we work with, our goal is to bring you the best books available.

I hope you see all that reflected in these pages. I'd be very interested to hear your comments and get your feedback on how we're doing. Feel free to let me know what you think about this or any other Sybex book by sending me an email at nedde@wiley.com. Or, if you think you've found a technical error in this book, please visit http://sybex.custhelp.com. Customer feedback is critical to our efforts at Sybex.

Best regards,

Neil Edde
Vice President and Publisher
Sybex, an Imprint of Wiley

This book is dedicated to my good friend Jim Earp—a friend for all seasons and all reasons. We have known each other for many years, but not nearly as much as the past year and I hope our friendship continues to grow.

Acknowledgments

Thanks to my wife, Rebecca, for working with me to get this book completed. I really don't know what I would have done without her help in researching and compiling some of the information that appears in this book. She also did a fine job of proofreading my rough draft and page proofing the result. Rebecca also helps a great deal with the glossary and keeps the house running while I'm buried in work.

Russ Mullen deserves thanks for his technical edit of this book. He greatly added to the accuracy and depth of the material you see here. Russ is always providing me with great URLs for new products and ideas. However, it's the testing Russ does that helps most. He's the sanity check for my work. Russ also has different computer equipment from mine, so he's able to point out flaws that I might not otherwise notice. I also felt that Russ had to do a lot of extra work for this book because Server Core really is hard to get used to at first.

Matt Wagner, my agent, deserves credit for helping me get the contract in the first place and taking care of all the details that most authors don't really consider. I always appreciate his assistance. It's good to know that someone wants to help.

A number of people read all or part of this book to help me refine the approach, test the coding examples, and generally provide input that all readers wish they could have. These unpaid volunteers helped in ways too numerous to mention here. I especially appreciate the efforts of Eva Beattie, who read the entire book and selflessly devoted herself to this project.

Finally, I would like to thank Tom Cirtin, Pete Gaughan, Elizabeth Campbell, Cheryl Hauser, Craig Johnson, and the rest of the editorial and production staff at Sybex for their assistance in bringing this book to print. It's always nice to work with such a great group of professionals and I very much appreciate the friendship we've built over the few years.

About the Author

John Mueller is a freelance author and technical editor. He has writing in his blood, having produced 77 books and over 300 articles to date. The topics range from networking to artificial intelligence and from database management to heads down programming. Some of his current books include a Windows command line reference book, books on VBA and Visio 2007, and programmer's guides for Web development with Visual Studio 2007 and Visual Web Developer. His technical editing skills have helped over 52 authors refine the content of their manuscripts. John has provided technical editing services to both *DataBased Advisor* and *Coast Compute* magazines. He's also contributed articles to magazines like *DevSource, InformIT, SQL Server Professional, Visual C++ Developer, Hard Core Visual Basic, asp.netPRO, Software Test and Performance,* and *Visual Basic Developer.* Be sure to read John's blog at `http://www.amazon.com/gp/blog/id/AQOA2QP4X1YWP`.

When John isn't working at the computer, you can find him in his workshop. He's an avid woodworker and candle maker. On any given afternoon, you can find him working at a lathe or putting the finishing touches on a bookcase. He also likes making glycerin soap and candles, which comes in handy for gift baskets. You can reach John on the Internet at `JMueller@mwt.net`. John is also setting up a Web site at `http://www.mwt.net/~jmueller/`. Feel free to look and make suggestions on how he can improve it. One of his current projects is creating book FAQ sheets that should help you find the book information you need much faster.

Contents at a Glance

Contents

Introduction

Imagine my surprise when I installed Windows 2008 for the first time and was faced with a decision of installing the Full version or the Server Core version. My initial question was "What precisely is a Server Core version?" Microsoft had kept this product quiet and, as a beta tester, I was taken completely off guard. So I installed Server Core and found myself faced with a command prompt and nothing else. Server Core doesn't include a Taskbar, desktop (as we know it), or a Start menu. You won't find a plethora of GUI gizmos that can make life easier, but can also to slow your work down to a crawl. Here was an interface that reminded me of a supercharged-DOS or NetWare of days past. I just had to try it out.

Many months later, I'm still pleased by what I see and I'm sure you will be, too. *Administering Windows Server 2008 Server Core* shares all of the new skills I've learned while investigating Server Core, researching online, talking with Microsoft, and gathering the results of testing by interested individuals. Imagine having a Web server that isn't constantly bogged down with a wealth of tasks that have nothing to do with serving content. As a file and print server, you'll find that Server Core provides very perky response times and that it's amazingly reliable. You get all of these perks with just a few cons that may or may not make Server Core a good choice for your organization. However, you'll want to try it out to see. You have everything to gain and only a little experimentation time to lose.

Server Core Really Is Worth the Effort!

I've tested Server Core sorely while writing this book. Of course, I made more than the usual number of mistakes as I worked through some of the arcane command line sequences I needed to know. Naturally, I thought past experience at the command line would be enough, but Server Core throws a lot of new things your way—tasks that you probably performed using the GUI in the past. Despite the hard use, errant entries, mistaken configurations, and a wealth of other things that would have taken any other version of Windows down, Server Core kept running and it continued to run quickly. You should definitely consider using this product because it provides better performance, a higher level of security, and improved reliability over Windows Server 2008 Full version. To help you avoid some of the issues that I encountered, *Administering Windows Server 2008 Server Core* provides a number of procedures that will help you get Server Core up and running quickly.

If your command line skills are rusty, *Administering Windows Server 2008 Server Core* provides complete documentation of all of the command line commands and utilities you need to work with this product. You'll also discover techniques for working with Server Core from the client and even reusing setups you may have used in the past so that you don't have to re-create them from scratch in Server Core. This book helps you understand precisely what you're getting when you install Server Core on your system, both the positive and the negative.

That's right, there are some negatives when working with Server Core and *Administering Windows Server 2008 Server Core* tells you all about them. There are some issues you can't fix. For example, Server Core doesn't support the .NET Framework and there really isn't much you can do about it (although, you'll find some handy tips in Appendix A that may ease the pain). It also isn't possible to use Server Core as an application server in some respects. Yes, you can run certain kinds of web applications, but, no, you can't install SQL Server. Discover more about what you can expect by reading this book.

Goals for Writing This Book

There are many reasons you should read this book. One of the most important reasons I had for writing it is that Server Core represents a major change in direction for Microsoft. Here's a company that produces the most bloated software that ever existed and they've pared down their server to a diminutive size. Instead of a clunky bull raging in the china shop, you now have a lithe and adaptable server. As an added bonus, Server Core will actually save you money by using considerably less power to perform the same tasks you can perform using Windows Server 2008 Full version. That's right, I wanted to see whether Server Core uses less power to perform a certain level of work and it does. I wanted to explore power consumption, reliability, security, speed, and all of the other things that Server Core brings to the table.

Server Core, unfortunately, doesn't come with as many instructions as you might like. My first server configuration required nearly a week because I wasn't used to working entirely at the command line. This book shows you how to use commands that you may never have heard of in the past. So, my second goal was to get you up and running quickly. No one should have to spend an entire week getting their operating system going. Given the newness of this Microsoft approach, I would imagine that many administrators are scratching their heads right now.

A third reason to read the book is that this is a new topic that no one has really covered before. OK, we're still talking Windows here, but Windows without windows? Seldom does an author get a chance to cover new ground—something really interesting. Because I think that Server Core is such a great product, I want to share my enthusiasm for it with you. This book is also about knowing that Server Core is precisely the right choice for a number of tasks—far better than the full version of Windows. By employing what you discover here in your work environment, you can create a system that is fast, reliable, secure, and uses less power as well.

Who Should Read This Book?

This book is designed to meet the needs of administrators who have heard something about Server Core, but want to see more before they deploy it. The beginning of the book is quite basic because it has to be in order to get you up and running quickly. However, by the time you reach the end of the book, you'll be working on considerably more advanced topics. Everything you need to set up a Server Core environment appears in this book, including the information needed to configure IIS 7 under Server Core.

I'm assuming that you already know how to use Windows quite well and that you've performed administration tasks in the past. In some respects, everyone is starting over with Server Core, but knowledgeable administrators have gained some skills that I simply don't have space to discuss in this book. The complete novice won't be able to keep up with the pace of this book.

What You Need to Use this Book

You'll very likely want to set up a test server when working through the examples in this book. A production server simply isn't the right environment in which to learn the vagaries of Server Core. I used the Enterprise Edition of Server Core for the book. If you have some other edition, you may find that you system doesn't have some of the features I discuss. You'll still find plenty to interest you.

I recommend that you set up the hardware required for a two-machine network as part of your test setup. Otherwise, you really won't see how some of the client-side tasks are supposed to work. Remember that Server Core isn't a resource hog, so you may find that you don't need nearly as much machine as you think to get a working installation. In fact, that old server sitting in a corner of your office may actually do the job—try it out and see.

The book contains descriptions of numerous utilities that you can download and use free for the most part. You may prefer other utilities, but I used these utilities to create the content for the book. If you find a technique useful, trying downloading the utility that goes with it and try it too. I'm always on the lookout for new utilities, so please be sure to tell me about your Server Core utilities at `JMueller@mwt.net`.

Conventions Used in This Book

It always helps to know what the special text means in a book. The following table provides a list of standard usage conventions. These conventions make it easier for you to understand what a particular text element means.

TABLE 1:   Standard Usage Conventions

CONVENTION	EXPLANATION
`Inline Code`	Code appears in the text of the book to help explain application functionality. The code appears in a special font that makes it easy to see. This monospaced font also makes the code easier to read.
`Inline Variable`	As with source code, variable source code information that appears inline also appears in a special font that makes it stand out from the rest of the text. When you see monospaced text in an italic typeface, you can be sure it's a variable of some type. Replace this variable with a specific value. The text will always provide examples of specific values that you might use.
`User Input`	Sometimes I'll ask you to type something. For example, you might need to type a particular value into the field of a dialog box. This special font helps you see what you need to type.
`Filename`	A variable name is a value that you need to replace with something else. For example, you might need to provide the name of your server as part of a command line argument. Because I don't know the name of your server, I'll provide a variable name instead. The variable name you'll see usually provides a clue as to what kind of information you need to supply. In this case, you'll need to provide a filename. Although the book doesn't provide examples of every variable that you might encounter, it does provide enough so that you know how to use them with a particular command.

TABLE 1:   Standard Usage Conventions *(CONTINUED)*

CONVENTION	EXPLANATION
[*Filename*]	When you see square brackets around a value, switch, or command, it means that this is an optional component. You don't have to include it as part of the command line or dialog field unless you want the additional functionality that the value, switch, or command provides.
File ➤ Open	Menus and the selections on them appear with a special menu arrow symbol. "File ➤ Open" means "Access the File menu and choose Open."
italic	You'll normally see words in italic if they have special meaning or if this is the first use of the term and the text provides a definition for it. Always pay special attention to words in italic because they're unique in some way. When you see a term that you don't understand, make sure you check the glossary for the meaning of the term as well. The glossary also includes definitions for every nonstandard acronym in the book.
Monospace	Some words appear in a monospaced font because they're easier to see or require emphasis of some type. For example, all filenames in the book appear in a monospaced font to make them easier to read.
URLs	URLs will normally appear in a monospaced font so that you can see them with greater ease. The URLs in this book provide sources of additional information designed to improve your development experience. URLs often provide sources of interesting information as well.

➡	This is the code continuation arrow. It tells you when a single line of code in a file actually appears on multiple lines in the book. You don't type the code continuation arrow when you use the code from the book in your own code. Rather, you continue typing the code in the book on a single line in your code. For example, you would type the following code on a single line, even though it appears on multiple lines here.
	
	`<add connectionString=`
	    ➡`"Server=MAINVISTA\SQLEXPRESS;`
	    ➡`Database=ReportServer$SQLExpress;`
	    ➡`Integrated Security=true"`
	    `name="MySQLConnection" />`

Part 1

Discovering Windows in a Command Prompt

Chapter 1

Understanding Windows Server 2008 Server Core

For anyone who's worked with computers for a long time, Windows Server 2008 Server Core seems like a step into the past. After all, this new operating system is Windows without the Windows features—it's essentially a decorated command prompt. In fact, you can change the appearance of Windows Server 2008 Server Core to look just like the command prompt applications you may have used in the past. Of course, it's not quite that simple or you could just buy one of the ancient tomes on DOS to find your way around. All of the features you expect from Windows Server still appear in Windows Server 2008 Server Core—the only difference is that you must use the command prompt to manage them, which means using a different administration method than you probably use today.

Eliminating the graphical user interface (GUI) has certain security benefits. It's a lot harder to infect a machine that lacks a browser such as Internet Explorer. In fact, it's not too hard to imagine that infecting such a system from the inside would be very difficult indeed. In addition, using a command line interface can be faster than using the GUI once you have some basic management tools in place. Of course, not having the GUI tools also presents a number of problems. Many administrators have never worked at the command line so they don't have the skills required to manage a server that has only a command prompt for input.

This chapter presents a starting point for working with Windows Server 2008 Core Services. For many people, it's going to be very shocking to start Windows Server and see nothing but a command prompt (even the Start menu is missing). The overriding goal of this chapter is to make you feel more comfortable in such an environment and help you discover that nothing's really missing—it's just different from what you've used in the past to manage Windows.

In this chapter, you'll learn how to do the following:

- Define the Server Core difference in command prompt management

- Describe how to access operating system configuration without the Control Panel

- Configure your server for initial use

- Perform tasks at the Logon screen

- Manage applications and the environment using the Task Manager

- Use a few GUI utilities to help manage the operating system

- Run DLLs using RunDLL32 to perform tasks at the command prompt

Considering the Command Prompt

For many people, moving to the command prompt after relying on a GUI for so long is going to be a big change. When working with Windows Server 2008 Server Core, you perform all tasks at the command prompt, which may seem impossible, but is really quite doable. Administrators with more experience may remember using the command prompt exclusively in the past and for them returning to Windows Server 2008 Server Core is simply a return to what they've done before. In fact, many experienced administrators will welcome the change because working at the command prompt can be considerably faster than trying to locate features in a GUI. Working at the command prompt trades flexibility and speed for ease of use and fewer errors.

Of course, the main question for most administrators is why create what essentially amounts to a command prompt version of Windows—a Windows without windows. The following list describes the reasons that Microsoft apparently decided to create the Windows Server 2008 Server Core version.

NOTE Because this book doesn't discuss any other version of Windows, I'll use the shorter Server Core to refer to Windows Server 2008 Server Core from this point. Whenever the book discusses some other version of Windows, it will include the full name. In addition, when the book discusses Windows in general, you'll see Windows by itself.

Fewer Maintenance Requirements A graphical interface costs you when it comes to maintenance because you have to maintain the graphical applications in addition to all of the essential operating system files. Server Core contains only the software required to create a server that has the Active Directory (domain controller), Active Directory Lightweight Directory Services (AD LDS) (formerly known as Active Directory Application Mode), Domain Name System (DNS), Dynamic Host Configuration Protocol (DHCP), File, Media Services, or Print roles. You obtain a fully functional server, but because the server doesn't include a lot of baggage, it requires a lot less time to maintain. Notice that this list doesn't include a database server. Some server roles still require a GUI and you have to consider that issue when installing Server Core.

Reduced Security Risks Security is a major problem for most companies today. Microsoft is promoting the idea of a reduced attack surface in many of their products. You only install what you actually need to perform a task. By reducing the amount of software on a system, you also reduce the number of items that someone can attack. A successful attack requires a security hole and, with fewer pieces of software, there are fewer holes to exploit. Because it lacks a GUI, Server Core has the potential to significantly reduce the security risks for your server—in fact, given that today most security holes rely on a graphical utility such as a browser, you may find that Server Core has almost no security threats to consider.

WARNING A reduced security risk doesn't translate into no security risk. Poor passwords, an unfriendly employee, a determined outsider, and even faulty hardware still offer ports of entry to attack. Server Core reduces risk but can't eliminate it, and never fool yourself into thinking that any product can eliminate security threats. You must always remain vigilant in looking for unwanted entries.

Fewer Management Requirements You may be surprised to learn that the GUI applications on a server require far more management than a command line application ever will. By removing the GUI, you also remove many of the management requirements for a server. Using Server Core makes administration considerably less time consuming, which translates into reduced costs. Of course, the administrator is going to need a good knowledge of the command line.

Consequently, even though you have fewer management requirements, performing the actual management tasks is going to be more difficult because you won't have a GUI to provide those little reminders of what to do next.

Improved Resource Usage   If you're tired of upgrading your server every five minutes to meet some new requirement, you'll really like Server Core. The GUI elements of the operating system chew memory like candy and drink hard drive space like soda. When you eliminate the graphic applications that insist on running in the background and all of the other eye candy of the operating system, you find that system resources go considerably further. Of course, you don't get the benefits of the GUI either. For example, it's much easier to track performance using a GUI than it is to view the same information using a scrolling display of numbers. In some respects, the reduced resource requirements come with a price of potentially harder management in some situations (such as tuning server performance).

You may wonder about Internet Information Server (IIS) support in Server Core. As of this writing, it's possible to run a subset of standard IIS applications on Server Core. However, the Server Core version of IIS will have severe restrictions due to lack of .NET Framework functionality. In fact, IIS won't have the following features.

- ASP.NET
- The IIS Management Console version 7 (since it requires a graphical interface)
- The IIS Management Service
- The IIS Legacy Snap-In or IIS Management Console version 6, for managing legacy Web sites
- IIS FTP Management
- The Windows Activation Service

In short, you'll be able to use IIS to run static and some scripted applications, but that's about it. For example, you can use IIS to run Active Server Pages (ASP), but not ASP.NET applications. Anything with JavaScript should also run fine and you can use technologies such as Asynchronous JavaScript and XML (AJAX). The Common Gateway Interface (CGI) application support will still work fine, which means you could also run implementations of Practical Extraction and Report Language (PERL) and so on. Consequently, the loss of functionality isn't as bad as you may initially think, but IIS under Server Core isn't going to be the platform of preference for many people. Whether you can use IIS depends on the kinds of application support you require.

The biggest problem with IIS support in Server Core, however, is management. IIS is an example of an application that really does work better with a GUI than it does at the command line. Although you can manage IIS at the command line, this functionality is probably limited to smaller Web sites where you don't have to coordinate the efforts of multiple servers. Chapter 25 details how to manage IIS with Server Core.

Life without the Control Panel

It's important to remember that the Control Panel applets are a graphical feature of Windows. Most of these applets rely on the Microsoft Management Console (MMC), a host application. You'll find that nothing in the Control Panel appears with Server Core. At first, this omission may make it seem impossible to manage Windows. However, just about everything you need to mange Windows does appear as part of the command prompt, as you'll discover as the book progresses. For example, if you want to add or remove users, you can use the NET USER utility to do it, or create a VBScript script to perform the task. You'll find a discussion of these techniques in the "Creating, Deleting, and Managing Users" section of Chapter 20.

However, the command line isn't quite complete. For example, you can't change some characteristics of the GUI display using the command line feature. Of course, given that the GUI isn't a big part of the Server Core feature, this may not even be a consideration for you. To change the GUI display, should you need to do so, you'll have to rely on registry hacks. You'll find a number of these hardware modifications provided in the "Modifying the Hardware Setup" section of Chapter 4. The point is that the omissions generally affect something that you won't use a lot in Server Core and you probably won't notice they're missing.

One omission you'll definitely notice is that it's harder to install applications in Server Core. You won't find the familiar Add or Remove Programs applet in Server Core, but you still have a number of methods of working with applications at your disposal using the command line in this case. The "Performing Application Installations" section of Chapter 3 provides everything you need to install applications in Server Core. In fact, the entire chapter is useful reading when you know a GUI method exists for performing a common configuration task, but you don't see it anywhere in Server Core.

The Control Panel admittedly contains a number of applets you'll never need in Server Core, so it's impossible to miss them. For example, you won't have to worry about managing your game controller because Server Core isn't suited to the task. In addition, you can't really use Server Core for database management, so the lack of a Data Sources (ODBC) applet in the Administrative Tools folder of the Control Panel isn't much of a concern. (ODBC stands for Open Database Connectivity.) Because Server Core lacks any form of Internet Explorer, you also won't need to worry about the Automatic Updates applet. All of these omitted applets don't have a use in Server Core, so Microsoft doesn't provide any means to perform the related tasks at the command line either.

Configuring the Server for Initial Use

Installing Server Core is only part of the installation process. When you start Server Core the first time, you'll need to perform some configuration that you might not have had to perform in the past. The first step is getting logged in. You'll see the Press Ctrl+Alt+Del to Log On message as usual. However, after you press Ctrl+Alt+Del, all you'll see is an entry for Other User—leaving you to wonder where the Administrator account is. Click Other User and type Administrator in the User Name field (do not include a password). Click the Right Arrow icon. It's only at this point that Server Core finally decides to tell you that you must change the administrator password before you use the account the first time. Click OK and follow the prompts to change the password. At this point, you finally see the messages that the setup program normally displays when configuring a new operating system. At some point, you'll see a command prompt as shown in Figure 1.1 and that's it.

No, your system isn't broken. You won't see a Start menu or any of the other usual GUI features of Windows. Unlike other versions of Windows, you perform all configuration tasks at the command prompt. (If you want to get a quick look at some of the available commands, try the Help command described in the "Obtaining Command Line Help with the Help Utility" section of Chapter 5.) The following steps will help you get started setting up the server.

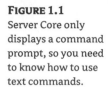

FIGURE 1.1
Server Core only displays a command prompt, so you need to know how to use text commands.

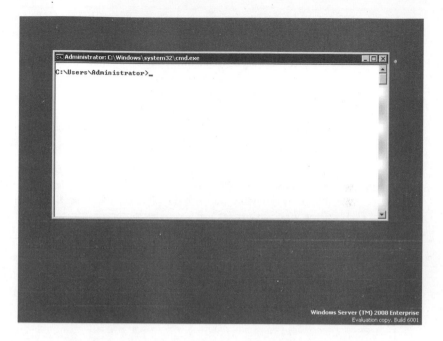

1. Type **Net User** *YourLoginName* *YourPassword* **/Add** and press Enter. (The Net utility is one of the more useful utilities at your disposal and you'll find it fully documented in the "Managing the Network with the Net Utility" section of Chapter 10.) This step sets up an account for you. Of course, you won't have administrator level privileges. I'm assuming that you're not using this setup on a domain, so you'll need to add your account to the Administrator group using a LocalGroup. If you're working on a domain, then you'll need to add your account to the Administrator group using a Group instead.

2. Type **Net LocalGroup** "**Administrators**" *YourLoginName* **/Add** and press Enter. You now are part of the Administrator group and can log in under your own name to the system. More importantly, you've just gained the ability to access the server remotely using Remote Desktop without having to perform a significant amount of configuration. You'll want to know what to call the computer, so you need to change the name of it next.

3. Type **WMIC ComputerSystem Where Name="%COMPUTERNAME%" Call Rename Name="***NewName***"** and press Enter. Make sure you choose a name that will work with your workgroup or domain setup. Of course, the computer isn't part of the workgroup or domain yet, so that's what you need to do next.

NOTE The WMIC command is one of the most powerful configuration features of Server Core. You'll find the main documentation for this command in the "Configuring Server Core Using the WMIC Command" section of Chapter 3. However, be sure to check the "Working with the WMIC Job Alias" section of Chapter 8, the "Managing Directory Services Using the WMIC NTDomain Alias" section of Chapter 19, and the "Making Modifications Using the WMIC Utility" section of Chapter 20 as well for additional WMIC information.

4. Type `WMIC ComputerSystem Where Name="%COMPUTERNAME%" Call JoinDomainOrWorkgroup Name="NameOfWorkgroup"` and press Enter. At this point, you have an account on the system and you're part of the Administrator group. Your computer has an easy-to-type name that you know and it's part of your workgroup. At this point, you need to set it up for remote access.

5. Type `WMIC RDToggle Where ServerName="%COMPUTERNAME%" Call SetAllowTSConnections AllowTSConnections="1"` and press Enter. After you reboot the system, it provides Remote Desktop capability. However, the firewall prevents you from making a connection, so you need to open a port for the Remote Desktop.

6. Type `NetSH Firewall Set PortOpening TCP 3389 "Remote Desktop"` and press Enter. (You'll use the NetSH utility for more than just the firewall configuration; see the "Scripting Networking Solutions with the NetSH Utility" section of Chapter 6 for more details.) The firewall now permits you access to the server. It's important for some tasks to have access to the C drive as well, so you need to create a share. The default share automatically provides the required permissions.

7. Type `Net Share "Drive_C"=C:\ /Grant:Everyone,Full` and press Enter. Everyone now has access to the C drive. You can refine the permissions later. However, now you have the required account, permissions, computer name, workgroup, remote access, and drive access. Many of the commands you'll work with in this book are actually scripts. The default scripting engine is WScript—Microsoft uses the graphical engine for compatibility purposes, but the graphical engine doesn't work very well in a command line environment. The next step changes the default scripting engine to the command line equivalent.

NOTE   In most cases, even if the Server Core partition isn't the first partition on the drive, it will appear as the C drive when you boot it. Server Core reconfigures the drive designations as needed to make Server Core the C drive in most cases. As with anything Microsoft, you'll find exceptions to this rule, but be sure you know which drive Server Core actually uses when you boot it before you start issuing any commands.

8. Type `CScript //H:CScript` and press Enter. (The CScript utility always uses a double slash for its own command line arguments; learn more about this utility in the "Running Scripts with the CScript and WScript Utilities" section of Chapter 6.) You'll see a message telling you that the default scripting engine is now CScript. You should activate your copy of Server Core using the next step. However, you can skip this step and go right to step 10 if you prefer.

9. Type `SLMGR -ATO` and press Enter. The activation process seems to take forever. However, get a cup of coffee, and when you get back, you should see a confirmation message like the one shown in Figure 1.2. (When using WScript instead of CScript, you'll see a confirmation dialog box that you'll need to dismiss by clicking OK.) It's time to reboot the system to ensure all of the changes occur.

10. Type `Shutdown /r` and press Enter. (The Shutdown command provides a number of useful command line switches that you can discover in the "Shutting the System Down with the ShutDown Command" section of Chapter 3.) You'll see a message telling you that the system will shut down in a few seconds. The system will reboot and you'll find all of the changes you've made in place. You should also be able to access the system using Remote Desktop at this point.

FIGURE 1.2

Activate your copy of Server Core as soon as possible so you don't forget to perform this task.

NOTE Sometimes the `WMIC RDToggle` command won't work properly with older clients. In this case, type **`SCRegEdit /CS 0`** and press Enter. You'll see a message that the script has changed the proper registry entry. You must reboot the system after making this change using the `Shutdown /r` command.

It's important to note that Server Core won't let you log into the host machine and into Remote Desktop at the same time. If you plan to use Remote Desktop, don't log into Server at the host machine. You may also notice some operational differences when working at the Remote Desktop and you'll see a slight pause when Remote Desktop obtains updates from the server. All of these issues are normal and you don't need to worry about them.

NOTE This book assumes that you're using Remote Desktop to perform all tasks, so your screen-shots may appear slightly different from the ones shown in the book. In addition, this book assumes that you'll use CScript to execute scripts. The script output may appear different from the output shown in the book when you use WScript.

CHANGING SHARE PERMISSIONS AT THE COMMAND LINE

You may wonder how to change share permissions at the command line. Apparently, Microsoft over-looked this need as part of the default configuration. You need to download a tool called RmtShare from `http://www.petri.co.il/download_free_reskit_tools.htm` to accomplish the task. This utility makes it possible to manage share information on a local or remote drive.

Whenever you use RmtShare, you must provide the name of the server at a minimum and a share name as well, in many instances, using the standard Universal Naming Convention (UNC) format. For example, if you want to determine the shares on a particular system, you'd type **`RmtShare \\ServerName`** and press Enter. The output shows all of the share names, associated resources, and comments for the specified server.

Of course, you won't simply want to view the shares on a system; you'll want to modify them in many cases. You can use RmtShare to perform any required task. The following list describes each of the RmtShare command line switches.

`/USERS:number` Specifies the number of users that can use the share at once. In some cases, you need to limit the number of users to reduce the load on the server. Typing **`RmtShare \\MainXP\Drive_D /USERS:5`** and pressing Enter would limit the number of users using the Drive_D share on MainXP to 5. You can't use this command line switch with the `/UNLIMITED` com-mand line switch.

/UNLIMITED Allows an unlimited number of users to access a share at once. To use this command line switch to change the Drive_D share on MainXP to unlimited, you'd type `RmtShare \\MainXP\Drive_D /UNLIMITED` and press Enter. You can't use this command line switch with the /USERS command line switch.

/REMARK:"text" Adds a comment to the specified share. For example, if you wanted to add a comment of "This is Drive D" to the Drive_D share on MainXP, you'd type `RmtShare \\MainXP\Drive_D /REMARK:"This is Drive D"` and press Enter.

/GRANT [user[:{READ | CHANGE | FULL}]] Allows a user or group to perform specific tasks using the share. For example, if you wanted to allow a user named George full control of the Drive_D share on MainXP, you'd type `RmtShare \\MainXP\Drive_D /GRANT George:FULL` and press Enter.

/REMOVE user Denies a user or group the right to use a particular share. For example, if you wanted to remove the rights of a user named George from the Drive_D share on MainXP, you'd type `RmtShare \\MainXP\Drive_D /REMOVE George` and press Enter.

/DELETE Removes an existing share. For example, if you wanted to stop using the Drive_D share on MainXP, you'd type `RmtShare \\MainXP\Drive_D /DELETE` and press Enter.

Working with the Logon Screen

The Logon screen is one of the few GUI elements that Microsoft provides with Server Core. You may very well have ignored it in previous versions of Windows because most of the tasks you can perform at the Logon screen are also available using other methods. These methods aren't available any longer in Server Core. For example, you can't right-click the Taskbar and choose Task Manager from the context menu to display the Task Manager because there isn't any Taskbar. Consequently, the Logon Screen takes on a higher priority in Server Core.

The initial Logon screen displays just the name and password fields you've always seen. After you log onto the system, you can press Ctrl+Alt+Del to display the Logon screen where the real work takes place. The following sections describe each of the options in the Logon screen. If you find that the Ctrl+Alt+Del key combination actually brings up the local Logon screen, rather than the remote Logon screen, you need to change the Remote Desktop Connection application settings using the information found in the "Working with the Remote Desktop Connection Application" section of Chapter 2.

Locking the Computer

Clicking Lock the Computer displays the Press CTRL + ALT + DELETE to Unlock this Computer screen. It lets you remain logged into the system while you leave to perform other work. To unlock the system, press Ctrl+Alt+Del, type your password as normal, and press Enter. The system will display the desktop as it was when you locked the system. Consequently, this feature isn't quite the same as logging off, where the system resets everything as if you hadn't logged in before. In addition, any tasks you have running continue to run while you have the computer locked. Only the user input features are locked.

Switching Users

Selecting this option lets you switch to another user. This feature doesn't work as you expect from the graphical version of Windows. You can't switch between users—Server Core logs off the existing user and switches to a new user. The only difference is that you save a few clicks using this approach. Switching users when using a Remote Desktop session is the same as logging off—the Remote Desktop session ends the moment the system logs off the current user.

Logging Off

You use this feature to log off of the current session. It's important to note that logging off will end any Remote Desktop session as well. If you want to log off and log back into the server as another user, then you need to start another Remote Desktop session to perform the login. You can also use the Logoff command to perform this task (see the "Terminating a Session Using the Logoff Utility" section of Chapter 5 for details on using the Logoff command).

Changing a Password

Microsoft recommends that you change your password using this option, rather than using the Users folder in the Computer Management console. Since the Computer Management console isn't available in Server Core, this option is your only way to change your password using a graphical interface at the server. You can also change the password using the Computer Management console from a remote machine, but using this approach can cause problems when you have encrypted files or other resources since the Computer Management console technique doesn't change the encryption (in other words, the files become unavailable). In fact, you'll see several warnings if you try to use the Computer Management console technique.

Of course, your server may be located in a closet somewhere and you may not even have a keyboard or monitor attached to it. Another way to change the password is to type **Net User *UserName*** * and press Enter. You'll see prompts for entering a password and confirming it. The characters you type for the password won't appear on screen. In fact, you won't see anything on the screen at all.

Invoking the Task Manager

Start Task Manager is probably the most often used option in the list because it helps you track running applications, end those that aren't working properly, and start new applications as needed. It's also possible to check on users with this utility and log them off when necessary. You'll see this feature described in detail in the next section. You can also start the Task Manager by typing **TaskMgr** and pressing Enter.

Using the Windows Task Manager to Your Advantage

The Task Manager takes on new importance in Server Core because it provides a convenient method of performing basic tasks quickly. For example, you can use it to manage applications, start or stop services, track basic system health, and manage user sessions. You can always start Task Manager by selecting the Start Task Manager option on the Logon screen. It's also possible to start Task Manager by typing **TaskMgr** and pressing Enter. The following sections describe the Task Manager features.

Working with Applications

Obviously, you won't have many applications running when you work with Server Core. In fact, it's quite possible that you'll only see the one application shown in Figure 1.3 running when you use this version of Windows. The command prompt is typically the only application you need to work with in Server Core with any frequency.

FIGURE 1.3
See the applications
running in the current
session on the
Applications tab.

You can use the options in the Applications tab to create, end, and switch tasks. In fact, you use the Applications tab to re-create a command prompt should you end the CMD.EXE application (the command prompt) accidentally. Simply use the techniques described in the Creating a New Task session to start a new copy of CMD.EXE as needed to work through system problems.

CREATING A NEW TASK

The Task Manager lets you create new tasks as needed, including CMD.EXE, the most important application for Server Core (see the "Starting the Command Interpreter" section of Chapter 5 for details on working with CMD.EXE). Use these steps when you want to start a new application.

1. Click New Task. You'll see the Create New Task dialog box.

2. Type the name of the application you want to start in the Open field. Make sure you include path information for the application as needed. The Browse button is inoperative in Server Core, so you must know the name and location of the application you want to start. Fortunately, any application that already exists in the Windows path, such as CMD.EXE, requires that you only type the application name.

3. Click OK. Task Manager starts the application for you.

ENDING A TASK

Sometimes you may have to end a task manually. For example, an application may experience an error and not end as normal. When this problem occurs, highlight the task in the list you want to end and click End Task. Task Manager won't display any confirmation message, so make sure you end the correct task.

WARNING Ending a task using Task Manager can cause data loss or other problems. Always use the standard application features to end the application whenever possible.

SWITCHING TO A TASK

Task Manager lists all of the applications currently running on your system. To select a new task, double-click its entry in the list. Task Manager selects the task and automatically minimizes itself on the desktop (since there isn't a Taskbar in Server Core to use for minimized applications). You can also press Alt+Tab to perform the same task. If you find that the Alt+Tab key combination actually switches between local applications, you need to change the Remote Desktop Connection application settings using the information found in the "Working with the Remote Desktop Connection Application" section of Chapter 2.

Working with Processes

Every application running on your system, whether it appears as a foreground task or a background task, is a process. Foreground tasks are those that you start and interact with, such as the command prompt. Background tasks are often started for you by the system and provide valuable services such as letting you log into the system. You'll find that Server Core uses far fewer processes than a similar setup in the GUI version of Windows Server 2008. Figure 1.4 shows a typical list of processes.

FIGURE 1.4
See the processes running for all sessions on the Processes tab.

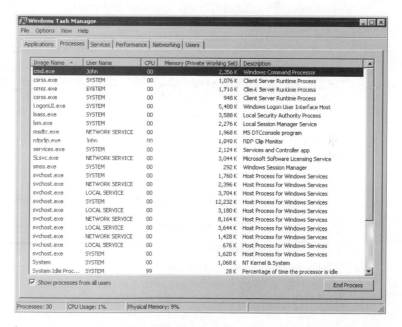

The default setting shows processes from all users. If you only want to see your own processes, clear the Show Processes from All Users option near the bottom of the Task Manager dialog box. However, given the way in which you're using this feature, you'll probably want to see all processes. To access a particular user process quickly, right-click its entry in the Applications tab and choose Go To Process from the context menu. Task Manager highlights the entry in the Processes tab.

As with applications, you can choose to end a malfunctioning process. This act is dangerous unless you know precisely how the ending the process will affect the system. Task Manager actually supports two levels of interaction in this case. You can choose to end an individual process by highlighting its entry and clicking End Process. In some cases, a process will spawn (create) other processes. In this case, if you end only the host process, the child processes may continue to run. To end the host process and all its child processes, you should right-click the host process and choose End Process Tree from the context menu.

Processes also have two properties that you need to consider. The first is *priority*, which affects the order Windows runs the processes. Windows executes all higher priority processes first. When it runs out of high priority processes to execute, then it begins executing those of a normal priority and, finally, those of a low priority. You must avoid giving a user process a high priority in hope that it will execute faster because you could prevent essential system tasks from running. To change the process priority, right-click the process and choose an option from the Set Priority menu of the context menu.

The second process property is *affinity*, which is the group of processors used to execute an application. The default setting lets the process execute on all of the processors that a machine supports. In some cases, you might want to let one process use a particular processor, but not others, to ensure the process doesn't monopolize machine resources. To change the process affinity, right-click the process and choose Set Affinity from the context menu. You'll see the Set Affinity dialog box where you can clear or check processor entries. A process can only use the processors that you have checked in the list.

The Processes tab shown in Figure 1.4 shows the default information that Microsoft feels most administrators will need. However, you can change the amount of information that the Processes tab displays by choosing View ➤ Select Columns. You'll see a Select Process Page Columns dialog box where you can choose additional information to display on screen. Of course, these columns tell you about the operational statistics of the process for the most part. The process also has file characteristics that you may need to know, such as file version number. In this case, you right-click the process entry and choose Properties from the context menu. The associated file Properties dialog box appears behind Task Manager. Minimize Task Manager to review the file properties, including the details such as file version shown on the Details tab of the Properties dialog box.

TIP   Because of the way you work with Server Core, you may want to add the Process Identifier (PID) column to the display. The PID is important because every process has a unique PID. Consequently, many command line utilities that work directly with processes require a PID as input so that Windows knows which process to work with. Even if you start multiple copies of a particular application, each copy has a unique PID, so knowing the PID helps you tell Windows precisely which application copy to work with.

Working with Services

The Services tab of Task Manager shows all of the services currently installed on the machine, not just those that the system is currently running. You can see the entire list of services, their Process Identifier (PID), description, status, and group as shown in Figure 1.5.

You can also use the Task Manager to start and stop services as needed. Simply right-click the service of interest and choose Start Service or Stop Service from the context menu as needed.

Services normally don't run independently on Windows. A special application named Service Host (SvcHost.EXE) provides a home for services. Consequently, when you see a SvcHost.EXE on the Processes tab, you know that it has something to do with a service, but not which service. To see which services the SvcHost.EXE entry affects, you can right-click the entry and choose Go To Service(s) from the context menu. Task Manager opens the Services tab with all of the services hosted by that process highlighted. You can perform the opposite task as well. When you want to see the SvcHost.EXE entry that hosts a service, right-click the service entry and choose Go To Process from the context menu.

Checking Performance

The Performance tab shown in Figure 1.6 doesn't tell you a lot about the system, but it can provide a quick overview of system health. For example, if all of the processors on a system are sitting at 100 percent all of the time, then you have a problem. Likewise, you can make a quick check of memory to ensure the server isn't running out.

FIGURE 1.5
View, start, and stop services on the Services tab.

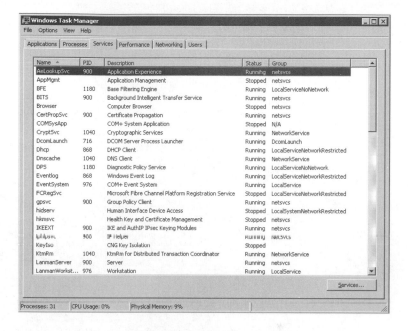

FIGURE 1.6
See basic system performance statistics on the Performance tab.

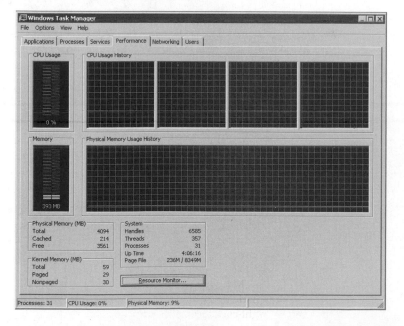

The display doesn't have many configuration options—you can't change the display to show you other statistics. The View ➤ Update Speed menu has entries that let you change how fast the display updates the statistics. You can also choose how to display the CPU information using the View ➤ CPU History menu. Finally, you can choose whether to display user times or kernel times for the CPU history. When you check the View ➤ Show Kernel Times option, the display shows how much CPU processing time the operating system is using. This statistic appears as a red line on the display (in addition to the green line that shows overall CPU usage).

Observing Network Statistics

The default Networking tab shown in Figure 1.7 shows the total network usage for each Network Interface Card (NIC) on the server. This graph gives you an idea of how well the network is performing and lets you make changes to the system setup to improve network health.

FIGURE 1.7
See basic network performance statistics on the Networking tab.

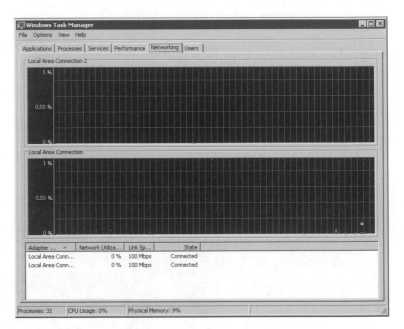

As with the Performance tab, you don't have many configuration options for this display, but you can change it in more ways than the Performance tab. The View ➤ Update Speed menu has entries that let you change how fast the display updates the statistics. The View ➤ Network Adapter History menu contains options that let you change the graphical display to show other network statistics. You can see the bytes sent (red), bytes received (yellow), and total bytes (green) on the display.

Notice that the bottom third of Figure 1.7 contains text information about the network. You can change the amount of information that you see in this area by choosing View ➤ Select Columns. The resulting Select Networking Page Columns dialog box lets you choose the statistics you see in this text data area. For example, you can choose to display the number of bytes sent or bytes received in this area.

Managing Users

The Users tab tells you about the users currently logged into the system as shown in Figure 1.8. You can determine the user's ID, status, client machine name, and session information. This information is important when using certain command line utilities because you need to identify a particular user. In fact, a single user can log in more than once, but the machine information is different for each login. All session numbers are unique, so you often need to know this information when working with active user sessions. Unlike many of the other tabs described so far, the default setup for Task Manager shows all of the available user information columns and it's usually not a good idea to remove columns from the display.

FIGURE 1.8
View and manage users on the Users tab.

You can modify the state of a particular user as needed. To disconnect a current user session, you can right-click the user entry and choose Disconnect from the context menu. Disconnecting a user doesn't end their session, but it does make server resources temporarily unavailable to them. If you want to log off a user, right-click the user's entry and choose Log Off from the context menu.

A List of Helpful GUI Utilities

Server Core comes with a number of helpful GUI utilities. These utilities don't rely on the common dialog boxes to perform tasks and they're generally simple in nature. Even so, the utilities do provide useful functionality. The following sections describe a few of the utilities that you'll find in Server Core. Other utilities appear throughout the book.

NOTE   As previously mentioned, any utility that requires use of graphical features such as the common dialog boxes or the managed .NET interface won't work completely. They may appear to work for a while, but you won't be able to complete tasks with them. For example, you won't be able to display the Save As dialog box because it doesn't exist in Server Core. Only utilities, such as Notepad, that provide built-in dialog boxes will work.

Notepad

Most people are aware they can use Notepad to modify simple text files. For example, you could use Notepad to write up basic notes for your server. However, you may not be aware that Notepad can also help you perform basic administration chores. For example, many of the settings for Windows now exist in XML files. You can use Notepad to modify these settings because XML files are simple text.

Interestingly enough, the lack of common dialog box support in Server Core doesn't affect any of the Notepad features. You can open and save files as you normally do. All of the other Notepad features work as expected. For example, you can perform a find and replace without any problem. It's also possible to use Notepad to print files. Of course, you have all of the normal Notepad limitations as well, such as an inability to work with graphics files.

RegEdit

The RegEdit utility lets you make changes to the registry. In many cases, you'll need to make direct registry changes in Server Core if you want to make local changes to configuration items. For example, you can't right-click the desktop and choose Properties to change the color of the screen. If you want to change any of the display colors, you must perform the task in the registry using the RegEdit utility. The older `RegEdt32` utility now displays the RegEdit utility, so using either command displays the same utility. Because the RegEdit utility has taken on so much new importance, you'll find it discussed in detail in Chapter 4.

WinHelp

The WinHelp utility is still available to provide access to HLP files. Unfortunately, most applications don't use HLP files any longer and rely on CHM files instead. To view a CHM file, you must use the HTML Help (`HH.EXE`) utility, which doesn't come with Server Core. When you need to view CHM files, the best option is to open them on the client machine. You can do this at the command line by typing **HH** *MappedDrive:\FilePath\FileName* and press Enter. The file opens as usual, but you'll be looking at it from the host system. Copying the required help files to your local system is also an option to improve help performance.

Accessing DLLs Using the RunDLL32 Utility

It's easy to think of a command as a built-in function within `CMD.EXE` and a utility as an external application that you run. However, the command line presents a third alternative, one that you might not have ever considered. The `RunDLL32.EXE` file is a utility that you can't run directly. Instead, you feed it a DLL that contains one or more externally accessible functions and add any arguments that the function requires as part of your input. For example, let's say you want to add a beep to your batch file. You can use the `MessageBeep()` function found in the `User32.DLL` file by adding this command to a batch file or script.

```
RunDLL32 User32.DLL,MessageBeep
```

Notice that you type the utility name, **RunDLL32**, followed by the name of the DLL, **User32.DLL**, and the name of the function, **MessageBeep()**. Note that the capitalization of the function you call is important; MessageBeep isn't the same as messagebeep.

You have many resources for learning how to use this particular command line feature. The best place to begin learning is the registry. Simply open the RegEdit utility and search for RunDLL32 entries by selecting the Edit ➢ Find command and typing **RunDLL32** in the Find What field. Figure 1.9 shows a typical entry. In this case, the example shows how to install a new screen saver using the RunDLL32 utility (a handy thing to know since there isn't any way to do it from the user interface).

Notice that, in this case, you pass the name of the screen saver file to the function. Replace any variable entries, %1 in this case, with the actual filename you want to use when working at the command line. You'll find a wealth of RunDLL32 tips online, including suggested commands. Make sure you always understand what a command will do and verify its functionality before you actually use it. Some wannabe comedians use their Web sites to get you to do odd and dangerous things to your computer. One of the better Web sites to try is Using Rundll at `http://www.ericphelps.com/batch/rundll/`.

FIGURE 1.9
DLLs provide a lot of
hidden functionality
that you can access
with RunDLL32.

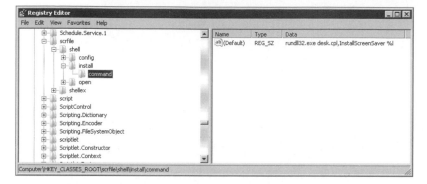

The registry might not contain a solution for every need. You can look at the DLLs directly using an application such as Depends (Dependency Walker). You can't use the Dependency Walker at the Server Core console, but you can use it at a client machine. This particular utility is used so often by developers that it has its own Web site at `http://www.dependencywalker.com/` with appropriate download links for various platforms. Figure 1.10 shows a typical view of a DLL opened in the Depends utility. Most of the information displayed in this figure has nothing to do with the command line and you can ignore it. However, the second window on the right side of the display shows the list of functions in the DLL.

FIGURE 1.10
Look for interesting
functions to run
in DLLs using the
Depends utility.

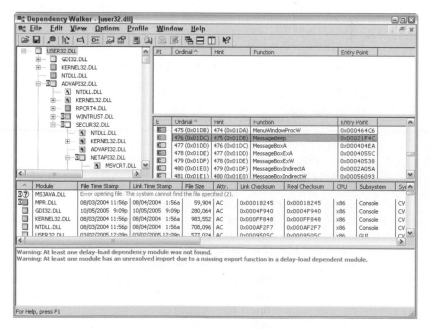

Of course, Depends won't tell you what task the function performs or how to use it. To an extent, you're left on your own as far as usage details and you'll definitely want to spend time online looking for suggestions. However, you can get complete details on the function when working with any

Microsoft DLL on the MSDN Library Web site at `http://msdn.microsoft.com/library/`. Simply type the function name in the Search For field and click Search. Other vendors usually provide similar documentation that you can use to learn more about the functions on their Web sites within DLLs.

WARNING   Server Core (and most newer versions of Windows) places significant security restrictions on users. Consequently, some RunDLL32 solutions that worked in the past might not work today. Always test a RunDLL32 solution using the same privileges as the anticipated user, rather than your own privileges, which are likely more inclusive.

Managing Windows in a New Way

Even though this chapter isn't very long and it's the first chapter in the book, you've already discovered some essential facts about Windows Server 2008 Server Core. The most important fact is that the command line actually provides faster access to many server resources as long as you know the required command. In addition, the simple interface reduces your need to look for something—you can concentrate on work. Of course, this chapter is only a peek into a much larger world for administrators. This chapter helps you build these skills:

◆ Define the Server Core difference in command line management

◆ Describe how to access operating system configuration without the Control Panel

◆ Configure your server for initial use

◆ Perform tasks at the Logon screen

◆ Manage applications and the environment using the Task Manager

◆ Use a few GUI utilities to help manage the operating system

◆ Run DLLs using RunDLL32 to perform tasks at the command prompt

It's important that you get started working with the command prompt immediately. Otherwise, you'll find that Windows Server 2008 Server Core can be an unfriendly place. Start by shutting down your system. Type **ShutDown** **−S** and press Enter to shut down your system. After you restart the system, type **ShutDown** **-?** and press Enter to display a list of other command line switches for this command. Now try working with some of the other command line utilities described in this chapter. Make sure you try using some of the RunDLL32 commands described in the chapter.

Chapter 2 provides the next step in discovering the command prompt. You'll discover how to configure the command prompt and perform a number of new tasks with it. In addition, Chapter 2 helps you understand the difference between internal and external commands. Because the "Understanding Internal and External Commands" section of the chapter is so important, you'll want to read it even if you skip the rest of the chapter.

Chapter 2

Using the Command Line Effectively

At one time, everyone worked at the command line. In fact, when you started the computer, you saw a command prompt and you never really left it the entire time you worked with the computer. I'm dating myself, of course, because no one's worked exclusively at the command line for many years. Microsoft is changing that, of course, with Windows Server 2008 Server Core. When working with this operating system, you're effectively limited to working at the command line. You can perform certain tasks from a client machine using a standard console, but in many cases, these graphical tools won't work and you'll need to perform any configuration tasks right at the command line. Certainly, you'll need to use the command line long enough to enable the Remote Desktop (see the "Configuring the Server for Initial Use" section of Chapter 1 for details).

Working at the command line doesn't mean that you have to perform tasks manually or memorize arcane syntax. It's true that you had to do that in the past to an extent, but even in the past, people created batch files so all they needed to remember was the batch file name and not the difficult series of command line switches for executing a command. Windows makes working at the command line a lot easier. You can even automate tasks so that you don't work at the command line as often; you can tell Windows to perform the mundane tasks for you. (Any unique task still requires you to enter individual commands at the command line.) Consequently, working at the command line could mean putting a batch file together and then telling Windows to execute it for you. Working at the command line need not be time consuming or difficult.

Something to consider about the command line is that it contains a lot more than you might think. Many savvy administrators and power users know that Windows provides a number of command line utilities. However, few people realize just how many utilities there are. Would you believe that this book discusses more than 300 command line utilities of various types for all Windows users? In fact, after performing the research for this book, I concluded that many of the most interesting Windows features aren't in the graphical user interface (GUI); they're at the command line, so you're actually getting the best part of Windows in Server Core. By the time you finish this book, you'll have gained an understanding of just how capable Windows is at the command line.

In this chapter, you'll learn how to do the following:

◆ Describe when to use the command line and the command line alternatives

◆ Configure the command window so that you can use it effectively

◆ Define the difference between internal and external commands

◆ Use the Remote Desktop Connection application to connect to the server

The Command Line Made Easy

Some people are of the opinion that the command line works one way. You type in a command and hope that you got all of the information right and received the correct result, which you then have to interpret. This entire activity sounds quite difficult, somewhat boring, and error prone to say the least. You have to wonder why someone would put themselves through all that pain. However, the command line isn't anything like the scenario just mentioned. Actually, if you know a few simple rules, using the command line doesn't have to be hard at all. The following sections describe some of the methods you can use to work at the command line.

 Real World Scenario

ALTERNATIVES TO EXCLUSIVE COMMAND LINE MANAGEMENT

After you perform the initial Server Core setup, you have several ways to work with Server Core without using the command line exclusively. One technique is to create a Remote Desktop connection. Using this approach, you can use the features of your local client to reduce the work required at the command line. You can learn more about this technique in the "Working with the Remote Desktop Connection Application" section of the chapter.

A second method is to rely on Windows PowerShell. You can't run Windows PowerShell in Server Core because Windows PowerShell requires a managed environment. Microsoft is actually working on a smaller version of the .NET Framework that lacks the graphical features of the full version so you can run Windows PowerShell in Server Core, but for now, you need to run Windows PowerShell from the client against Server Core instead of the local machine. You're limited to using the Windows Management Instrumentation (WMI) features of Windows PowerShell when working with Server Core.

The third method is to rely on the standard consoles that you've always used. These consoles appear in the Administrative Tools folder of the Control Panel. Not all of the consoles will work with Server Core and some of the consoles will have limited functionality. For example, the Computer Management console shown here contains fewer entries for Server Core because not all of the entries apply. In addition, when you select some entries, the console tells you that it can't display the information. For example, if you click on Performance Logs and Alerts, Device Manager, any of the Storage features, or SQL Server Configuration Manager, the Computer Management console will tell you that these features aren't available.

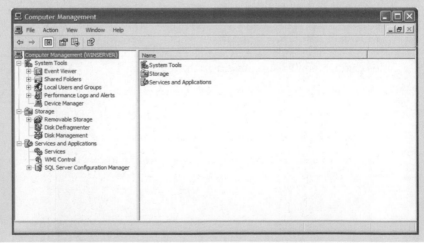

To access Server Core from a console, right-click the root node and choose Connect to Another Computer from the context menu. You'll see a Select Computer dialog box. Type the name of the other computer (or click Browse to select it) and click OK. The console makes the connection to the server and displays its contents. Depending on your network connection speed and the load on the server, you may notice a significant delay between actions. Just be patient and the console will provide the information you need.

Using Utilities Directly

Generally, you'll begin using the command line by working with the utilities directly. After all, it's a little hard to create a batch file or script if you don't know how the command works. However, using a command doesn't have to be hard. All you need to remember are two simple characters, /?. That command line switch says, "Help me!" The command usually will help by presenting you with some options for using it.

Let's begin by working with one of the more useful commands to determine how much of a load the server is carrying. Type **TaskList /?** and press Enter. Figure 2.1 shows what you'll see. (I've scrolled back to the top so you can see the major entries.)

FIGURE 2.1

Make things simple; ask the command for usage instructions.

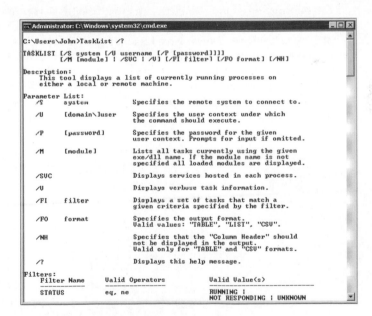

The first piece of information is the usage instructions for the command. A set of square brackets ([]) tells you about an optional input. In this case, everything is optional; you can use TaskList by itself.

A slash (/) tells you about a command line switch. Sometimes command line switches appear with a dash (-) instead. In either case, a command line switch configures the command to perform a task in a specific way. For example, TaskList doesn't normally display services, but you can tell it to display services by adding the /SVC command line switch.

NOTE Most command line switches are case insensitive, which means you can type them in either uppercase or lowercase (or even a mix). A few command line switches are case sensitive, which means you must type them as shown. In fact, a few command line switches appear in both uppercase and lowercase—/A may mean sort in alphabetical order, while /a may mean to ignore binary information. This book will always tell you when the command line switch case matters. Otherwise, you can assume that the command line switches are case insensitive and you can type them using any case that you wish.

Some command line switches depend on other command line switches. You'll see the command line switches nested within multiple layers of square brackets in this situation. For example, if you want to supply a password for logging into a remote system to view the tasks running on it, you must also supply the /System and /Username command line switches.

In other cases, command line switches are mutually exclusive. The command line separates these switches with the pipe (|) symbol. The TaskList command won't allow you to use the /M command line switch with the /SVC switch; you must select one or the other.

After the usage information, you'll normally see a description section for newer commands. The description tells you what task the command performs and why you would want to use it. Sometimes this information is quite complete, as it is with the TaskList command, and in other cases, you'll still be scratching your head after you read the description. Older commands don't provide a description at all; you just have to know what task they perform, which is why many people don't use them.

A description of the individual parameters (or arguments and inputs) comes next. These entries tell you how to use the individual command line switches. You'll also discover other kinds of information you must provide. For example, the Dir (directory) command information shown in Figure 2.2 tells you that you can provide a drive letter, followed by a colon, followed by a directory path, and ending with a filename specification. None of these entries is a command line switch, but they're all important parameters.

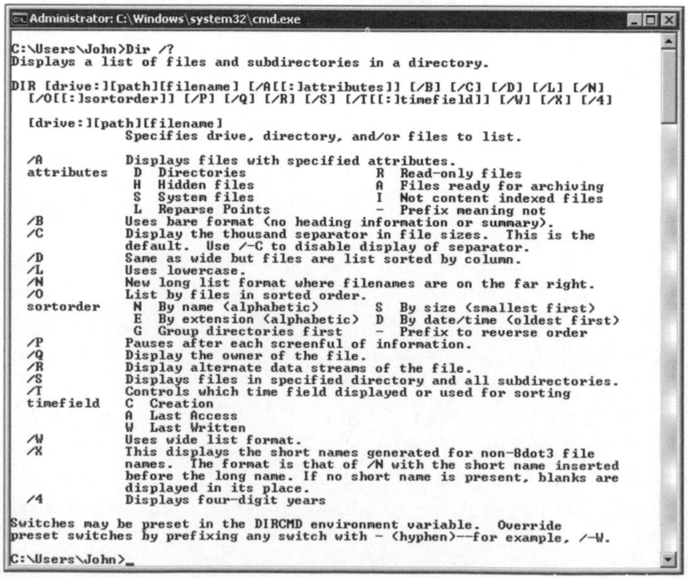

FIGURE 2.2
Sometimes you provide text input as well as command line switches.

The final section is a list of examples. Only a few commands provide this kind of information, but it's always helpful when they do. The examples come in many forms. The TaskList command provides a list of filters first, so you can see how to get the output you want. It provides actual usage examples next so you can see what to type at the command line. The point is that most people could use a command at the command prompt if they knew the simple /? command line switch. Go ahead and try it out now with the TaskList and Dir commands. You'll want to keep the /? command line switch in mind as you read about other commands in this book. Try it out with every one of them and you'll find that most commands provide some information, usually enough to jog your memory when you need to use the command.

 Real World Scenario

STORING COMMANDS IN BATCH FILES

I've worked at the command line for years, so you might assume that I have all of these commands memorized by now. However, like many people, I find that memorizing all of the commands, their parameters, and their command line switches is just too much work. However, discovering the required parameters one time isn't too much work. That's where batch files come to my aid. I use batch files to remember specific command sequences for me.

When you need to store one or more commands so you don't have to remember them every time you want to use them, a batch file can do the job. In fact, you can create batch files that have a limited amount of intelligence so they don't perform the same task in the same way every time. Batch files are the first method that many people use to automate the command line. I have batch files that I wrote over 18 years ago when I started with computers and I'm still using them today. In short, a good batch file can last a very long time. The thing to remember about batch files is that they're very easy to write, only have a little intelligence (so there isn't any heavy coding), and don't require anything special to execute. You'll discover how to work with batch files in Chapter 5.

Writing Scripts

Scripts are the next step up in complexity. A script uses a simple programming language to accomplish tasks. You can't create complex applications using a script. For example, you wouldn't want to write a word processor application using a script. However, scripting languages provide more intelligence than a batch file can. In addition, you can access some of the functionality that Windows provides. Consequently, rather than rely on utilities for every action, you can ask Windows for some help in automating your tasks.

A script requires a special environment to run. Windows provides this environment in the form of a script interpreter. The interpreter reads every line of code you write in your script and performs the task it requests. Writing scripts is a little harder than writing batch files, but not nearly as difficult as writing an application with a full-fledged programming language. Consequently, scripts are exactly what many people need to automate tasks when they don't want to learn a full-fledged programming language, yet find batch files less robust than they'd like. You'll discover how to work with scripts in Chapter 6.

Most of the tasks you perform using scripts have standard requirements and need to execute successfully. Active Directory, the Windows enterprise database, requires some special handling to work correctly. Chapter 19 discusses the scripting requirements for this special environment and helps you create scripts that make working with Active Directory a lot easier. Remember to use

CScript for your scripting needs whenever possible; the "Configuring the Server for Initial Use" section of Chapter 1 tells you how to set CScript as the default script engine.

Scheduling Tasks

No matter how you work with the command line, whether you use individual commands, batch files, or scripts, you can schedule a task to run at a specific time. For example, if you want to defragment your hard drive every night, you can schedule the `Defrag` command described in Chapter 9 to run automatically. Of course, you'd better be certain that everything is set up correctly before you assume the computer can perform the task on its own. Many people begin using the Task Scheduler to run tasks that they could forget during normal work hours and then progress to after-hours tasks. You'll find a discussion of after-hours task scheduling in Chapter 8.

Relying on Third-Party Utilities

The tools that Microsoft provides for working at the command line are basic, simple, and not always the best tools at your disposal. However, Microsoft is actually spending a lot of time trying to upgrade their offerings with new features such as the OCList utility provided with Server Core. Third-party tools for working at the command prompt have been around for a long time. Most of these products are mature, fully tested, and quite capable of making your command line experience everything it should be. You'll find third-party utilities discussed throughout this book. For example, you'll find utilities you can use to edit and compile your batch files in Chapter 7. Part 6 of the book contains two chapters packed with helpful third-party utilities you should know about when working at the command line.

Configuring the Command Window

Many users start the command window, see the typical command prompt, and just assume that they'll never see anything else. Since the command window is your main tool in Server Core, you should know how to configure it to meet your needs. Fortunately, you can easily configure the command window to appear as you want, at least within limits. You can access these features by clicking the box in the upper left corner and choosing Properties from the context menu. You'll see a properties dialog box with four tabs. Each of these tabs is described in the sections that follow.

Setting the Window Options

The Options tab shown in Figure 2.3 defines how the command window reacts when you open it. The Cursor Size option controls the size of the cursor, with small being the default. The Large option provides a block cursor that is very easy to see. The Display Options determine whether you see the command window full screen or as a window. Using the full screen mode when you have a number of tasks to perform is easier on the eyes.

NOTE Older versions of Windows let you change the display mode through a property setting. However, Server Core doesn't let you run the command window in full screen mode by changing the Display Options setting. This particular option is missing when you view the dialog box shown in Figure 2.3. In most cases, you don't want to run the command window in full screen mode when working with Server Core because the few graphical elements it provides can become inaccessible and it's already possible to maximize the screen real estate by maximizing the window. Without a Start menu, taskbar, or other graphical elements to consume space, using Window shouldn't cause any problems. (If you really must work in full screen mode, you must modify the registry to do it.)

FIGURE 2.3
The Options tab helps you control the appearance and behavior of the command window.

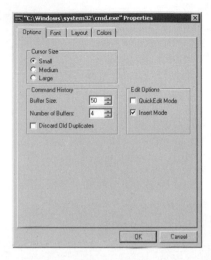

The Command History is especially important. The Buffer Size option determines the number of commands the buffer will store. Every command requires memory, so increasing this number increases the amount of memory the command prompt requires. Increase this number when you plan to perform a number of complex commands. A smaller number will save memory for larger command line applications. The Number of Buffers option controls the number of individual histories. You need one history for each process (application environment) you create. Generally, the four shown work fine.

The Edit Options determine how you interact with the command window. Check the QuickEdit Mode when you want to use the mouse to work with the entries directly. The only problem with using this feature is that it can interfere with some commands such as Edit that have a mouse interface of their own. The Insert Mode option lets you paste text into the command window without replacing the text currently there. For example, you might copy some information from a Windows application and paste it as an argument for a command.

Changing the Font

The Font tab shown in Figure 2.4 controls the font used to display text. The font size automatically changes when you resize the window, but you can also control the font size directly using this tab. The raster fonts give the typical command line font appearance that works well for most quick tasks. The Lucida Console font works better in a windowed environment. It's easier on the eyes because it's smoother, but you might find that some applications won't work well with it if they create "text graphics" using some of the extended ASCII characters. The extended ASCII characters include corners and lines that a developer can use to draw boxes and add visual detail.

Choosing a Window Layout

The Layout tab shown in Figure 2.5 has the potential to affect your use of the command window greatly when working in windowed mode. The Screen Buffer Size controls the width and height of the screen buffer, the total area used to display information. When the Window Size setting is smaller than the Screen Buffer Size, Windows provides scroll bars so you can move the window around within the buffer area and view all it contains. Some commands require a great deal of space for display purposes. Adjusting the Screen Buffer Size and Window Size can help you view all of the information these commands provide.

FIGURE 2.4
Use the Font tab to control the size of the text in the command window.

FIGURE 2.5
Change the size and positioning of the command window using the Layout tab.

The Window Position determines where Windows places the command window when you first open it. Some people prefer a specific position on the screen so they always know where a new command window will appear. However, it's generally safe to check Let System Position Window to allow Windows to place the command window on screen. Each command window will appear at a different, randomly chosen, position on screen.

Defining the Text Colors

Microsoft assumes that you want a black background with light gray letters for the command window. Although DOS used this setting all those years ago, many people today want a choice. The Color tab lets you choose different foreground, background, and pop-up colors for the command window (even though Figure 2.6 doesn't show the colors, it does present the dialog box layout). You can modify the window to use any of the 16 standard color combinations for any of the text options. Use the Select Color Values options to create custom colors.

FIGURE 2.6

Modify the text colors for an optimal display using the Colors tab.

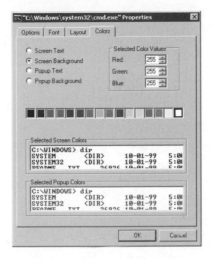

Understanding Internal and External Commands

This chapter has used the term *command* for everything you execute at the command line. In reality, you need to view the command line as having multiple command types. Some commands, such as TaskList.EXE, appear as separate files. This book will use the term *utility* for these kinds of commands from now on. A utility always resides in a separate file and you can look it up using the Dir command.

Some commands don't exist in separate files; they reside in the host program that you use to interact with the computer. The host program for the command prompt is CMD.EXE. If you want to try it out, type **CMD** and press Enter. You'll see a command prompt. CMD.EXE doesn't end after it opens the command prompt; it remains in the background to receive and react to your keystrokes.

The CMD.EXE file also has a number of internal commands. These special keystrokes tell CMD.EXE to perform a task for you. For example, the Dir command is an internal CMD.EXE command. You won't find Dir listed as an executable anywhere on your hard drive. This book lists all internal commands as commands. Consequently, you'll see the TaskList utility and the Dir command discussed later in the book. If you want to see the full list of commands that CMD.EXE supports, type **Help** and press Enter. You'll see the list shown in Figure 2.7 (the list in the screenshot isn't complete—it continues past the bottom of the command window).

Compare the list of commands provided by the Server Core version of CMD.EXE and those provided by other versions of Windows and you'll find some differences. For example, the Server Core version of CMD.EXE doesn't support the AT command (it supports AT as a utility). This makes sense since Server Core doesn't support the Task Scheduler either, since the Task Scheduler is a GUI tool. Chapter 8 provides strategies to help you work around this particular omission. Most of the changes are additions. Here are the additional commands that CMD.EXE supports (some used to appear as separate utilities) and you'll find all of them discussed in this book.

- ◆ BCDEdit (Chapter 16)
- ◆ DiskPart (Chapter 9)
- ◆ DriverQuery (Chapter 13)

◆ FSUtil (Chapter 9)

◆ GPResult (Chapter 20)

◆ ICACLS (Chapter 15)

◆ MKLink (Chapter 9)

◆ OpenFiles (Chapter 15)

◆ RoboCopy (Chapter 14)

◆ SC (Chapter 3)

◆ SchTasks (Chapter 8)

◆ Shutdown (Chapter 3)

◆ SystemInfo (Chapter 16)

◆ TaskList (Chapter 21)

◆ TaskKill (Chapter 21)

◆ WMIC (Chapter 3)

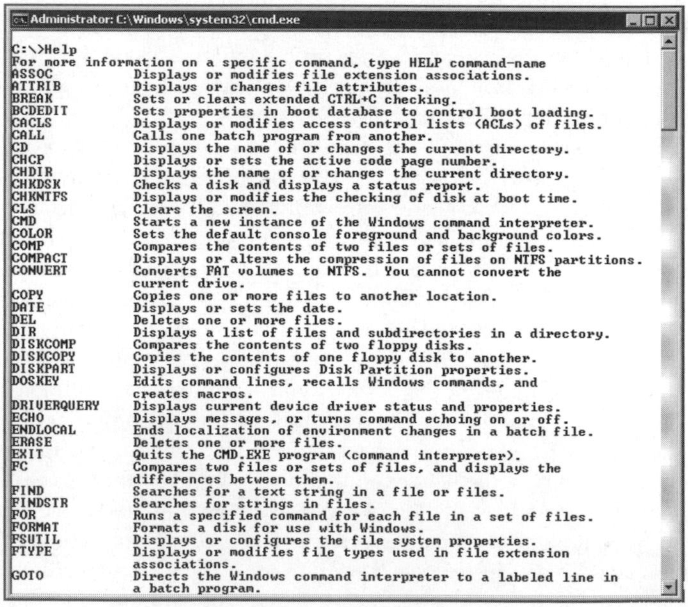

FIGURE 2.7
CMD.EXE supports a number of additional commands in Server Core.

Other utilities create a host environment and you'll discover the commands in those host environments as you read the book. For example, the TelNet utility discussed in Chapter 4 provides a host environment where you'll type commands. These commands don't exist outside TelNet, just as the Dir command doesn't exist outside of CMD.EXE.

Working with the Remote Desktop Connection Application

The Remote Desktop Connection application provides the means to connect to Server Core for remote management. You only need this application when you want to access the command prompt on Server Core. For example, you won't need this application when you want to use a console to create a remote connection or when you want to use a command line utility from a local machine to make the connection. The Remote Desktop Connection application is exceptionally useful because it does let you create a direct connection to the server. You can monitor events and manage the system directly, which reduces one potential cause of failure (making the remote connection every time you want to perform a task). Select Start ➢ Programs ➢ Accessories ➢ Communications ➢ Remote Desktop Connection to start the Remote Desktop Connection application. The following sections describe how to use this application.

TIP You must make any changes you want to the Remote Desktop Connection application configuration before you connect to the remote server. Once you make the connection, you can't change the configuration. Consequently, it's always a good idea to create a complete configuration first, save it to disk, and then reopen it as needed for a particular server. Otherwise, you'll spend a lot of time reconfiguring Remote Desktop Connection every time you want to use it.

Creating a Connection

Before you can use the Remote Desktop Connection application (I'll refer to it simply as Remote Desktop from this point on), you need to set up Server Core to provide Terminal Server connectivity. The "Configuring the Server for Initial Use" section of Chapter 1 tells you how to perform this task. Once the server is ready for a connection, you must configure Remote Desktop to make the connection. The following procedure helps you make the connection.

1. Start the application and click Options. The General tab shows the connection options as shown in Figure 2.8.

2. Type the server name or select it from the drop-down list in the Computer field.

3. Type your account name on the server in the User Name field.

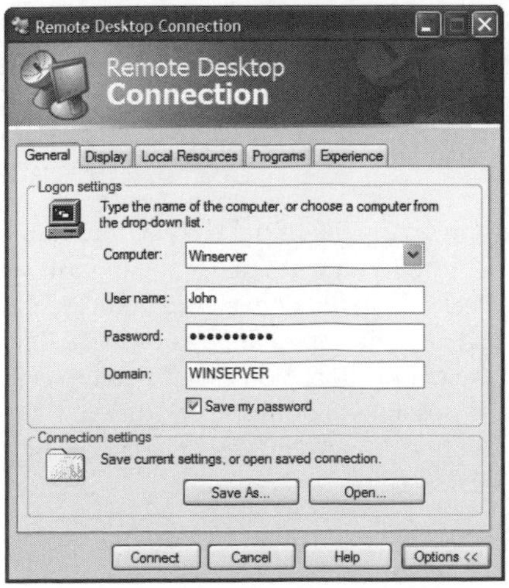

FIGURE 2.8
Set the connection parameters for the connection you want to normally make.

4. Type your password in the Password field. Make sure you use the password for your account on the remote system.

5. Type the name of the server in the Domain field when using a workgroup setup. If you're using a domain setup, then type the name of the domain in the Domain field.

6. Optionally, check Save My Password if you want Remote Desktop to save your password for future use.

7. Optionally, click Save As. You'll see a Save As dialog box. If you want to save this setup as the default connection, then click Save. Otherwise, type a name for the setup in the File Name field and click Save. You can save as many setups as needed for the servers you want to access. Use the default setup for the server you access most often.

8. Click Connect. You'll see Remote Desktop performing all of the required connection tasks. Eventually, you'll see a Remote Desktop window like the one shown in Figure 2.9.

FIGURE 2.9
The remote connection appears in a special Remote Desktop window.

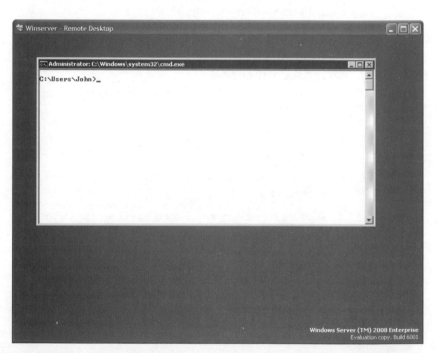

After you create the initial connection, Remote Desktop opens with the default connection already set up. If you want to use the default connection, all you need to do is click Connect when Remote Desktop starts. Otherwise, you can click Options, click Open, choose the connection you want to use from the Open dialog box, click Open in the Open dialog box, and finally click Connect to make the connection. You won't need to create a setup more than once if you save it to disk.

It's also possible to double-click the RDP file containing a connection in Windows Explorer to make the connection to the server, so you can simply place the RDP file on your desktop to make the connection instantly accessible.

Setting the Display

The display settings you use affect how much screen real estate you have for performing tasks and also affect performance. Using a larger screen size gives you more space to work. However, a larger screen size also requires more network bandwidth to transmit the data. Consequently, you must weigh the need to see as much as possible on the remote server against the performance requirements for your task. Figure 2.10 shows the display settings.

FIGURE 2.10
Define a display size that works best for the task you need to perform.

The Remote Desktop Size slider lets you change the size of the window, with the smallest size being 640 × 480 pixels, which is normally too small to work with a GUI system, but can work just fine with Server Core. If you want to use your entire display to work with Server Core, move the slider all the way to the right. The size will change to Full Screen and the display will take up your entire display area. In fact, it will look like you're working directly at the remote console, rather than using Remote Desktop.

NOTE   If you want to continue working with your local system while managing the remote system, make sure you check the Display the Connection Bar When in Full Screen Mode option. Otherwise, you may need to log out every time you want to regain access to the local system.

Performance isn't only affected by screen size. Notice that you can also modify the number of colors that Remote Desktop displays. More colors translate into a better display, but also reduce performance because Remote Desktop has to transfer more data for the additional colors. Since Server Core lacks much in the way of a GUI, you'll experience a performance gain by setting the number of colors to 256. In most cases, you won't even notice the difference in appearance, but you will notice the difference in performance.

Accessing Local Resources

Remote Desktop makes it possible to map your local hardware to respond to events on the remote machine. Figure 2.11 shows the settings you can use to map resources as needed. The following list describes each of the resource mapping areas.

FIGURE 2.11

Perform automatic resource mapping to make local resources available for use.

Remote Computer Sound   Lets you bring sounds from the remote machine to your local machine. This setting has three options. You can choose to play the remote sound locally, not play the remote sound at all (effectively muting the remote system), or play the sound at the remote location.

Keyboard   Controls the use of control key combinations. For example, when you press Alt+Tab, this setting controls whether you switch between applications on the local machine or the remote machine. This setting only affects Remote Desktop when you have it selected when working in windowed mode. If you press Alt+Tab when Remote Desktop is working in a window and you don't have Remote Desktop selected, then the Alt+Tab combination always affects the local machine, even when you choose the On the Remote Computer option. Normally, any control key combinations only go to the remote machine when you use Remote Desktop in full screen mode.

Local Devices   Determines which local devices you can access from the remote machine. This may sound like a very odd consideration, but when you're working with the remote machine, Remote Desktop shuts off access to local resources such as disk drives, printers, and serial ports. Only your display, keyboard, and mouse are active on the remote machine unless you tell Remote Desktop to perform the required mapping. Check any of these options to make the resources on your local machine available when working at the remote machine.

Running a Configuration Program

You may find that you want to run a configuration program on the remote machine when you create the connection. This program can perform any task and you can use both batch and script files, in addition to standard applications. Figure 2.12 shows the Programs tab. The options work very much like a remote profile. When you want to use a remote program, check Start the Following Program on Connection, type the name of the application you want to use (including full path), and tell Remote Desktop which folder you want to use as a starting point.

Optimizing Performance

The connection you use to create a Remote Desktop is important. You can't expect the same performance from a dial-up connection that you do from a high-speed internal network. Consequently, Remote Desktop provides a method for telling it what to expect in the way of connection in order to optimize connection performance as shown in Figure 2.13.

FIGURE 2.12
Use a configuration
application as needed
to automate Remote
Desktop tasks.

FIGURE 2.13
Use only the resources
you actually need
to obtain good
performance.

Choosing one of the default options, such as LAN (10 Mbps or Higher), automatically sets the options that Remote Desktop uses—you don't need to do anything else. As an alternative, you can choose Custom from the list and configure the options you want to use. Server Core actually works best with the Custom setting, even if you're working across a LAN. For example, Server Core doesn't provide Menu and Window Animation, so you can clear this option. You'll probably want to clear the Themes and Show Contents of Window While Dragging options as well.

Managing Windows in a New Way

If you're anything like me, you're a little overwhelmed by now at what the command line can do for you. I've always used the command line. In fact, I've had some batch files hanging around since the days of DOS—yes, really, that long. However, until you take time to look at what the command line has to offer, you don't know what's there. Microsoft certainly doesn't make the command line the centerpiece of its advertising. In fact, the command line is one of the least understood and explored parts of Windows. Consequently, this book is your doorway to a new world. Not only will you perform tasks faster, with less effort, and more precisely, but you'll have a distinct edge over those around you as well. While they fiddle with an excessively time-consuming GUI, you're speeding along at the command line and making yourself look quite good in the process.

This chapter helps you build these skills:

◆ Describe when to use the command line and the command line alternatives

◆ Configure the command window so that you can use it effectively

◆ Define the difference between internal and external commands

◆ Use the Remote Desktop Connection application to connect to the server

Of course, before you can begin working at the command line, it pays to make sure that your system is ready. One of the first things you need to know is the differences between internal and external commands. Otherwise, you may not be able to locate commands and utilities you used in the past. Make sure you get your command line prompt set up as well because you'll use it extensively in Server Core. Once you have everything set up, create a Remote Desktop connection. Using Remote Desktop can save you considerable time when the server is located in a different room.

Chapter 3 begins showing you how to perform essential maintenance tasks—the things you must do in order to get Server Core functional and keep it that way. For example, you'll discover how to perform updates, which is an important first task for your server if you want to keep it virus free. You'll also discover all of the command line switches you can use to shut down your server. Chapter 3 is also where you'll learn some of the essentials of the WMIC command—an important utility for configuring and maintaining your server.

Chapter 3

Performing Essential Maintenance Tasks

Most administrators quickly realize that they don't really understand the ramifications of working without a Graphical User Interface (GUI) in Server Core. Yes, many configuration tasks proceed without any trouble. However, once you get past the basic configuration, you need to start installing applications and performing other tasks that are quite easy when working with a GUI, but may become quite hard when working with a character-mode interface. This chapter helps reduce the pain of configuration tasks.

In addition to application installation and other configuration tasks, you must also consider how best to secure and maintain your server. Chapter 1 has already shown you some of the security configuration by telling you how to create a new user and assign that user to a particular group. However, you'll find that you need to perform many other tasks to secure your server. Although this chapter doesn't provide details on all of the security commands and utilities, you'll discover how to perform essential tasks. Maintenance in this chapter follows along the same lines as security—you'll discover the essentials you need.

One of the more important parts of the configuration, security, and maintenance picture is the Windows Management Instrumentation Command line (WMIC) command. This command helps you perform many essential tasks without having to resort to the complex commands and utilities needed for lower-level tasks. This chapter provides complete coverage for the WMIC command so you can use it for any of the tasks you must perform daily.

Server Core also comes with a number of scripts that you can use to speed configuration tasks. The scripts reduce the complexity of working at the command line and make it less likely that you'll encounter errors from incorrect input. Of course, scripts come with limited functionality and they can only do so much to protect your system from harm. You still need a good understanding of how the scripts work in order to use them properly.

In this chapter, you'll learn how to do the following:

◆ Install applications

◆ Perform maintenance

◆ Update the server

◆ Create LNK files

◆ Set security

◆ Use the WMIC command to configure the server

◆ Use maintenance commands and utilities

◆ Activate your copy of Windows

Performing Application Installations

One of the first issues that administrators encounter when performing an application installation is that the AutoRun feature no longer works. You can't simply stick the CD or DVD into the drive and expect it to do anything, because it won't. It stays there until you tell it to do something. Fortunately, Microsoft has helped vendors standardize their setups over the years. You can normally set the drive to the drive with the setup program on it by typing something like **D:** and pressing Enter, and then typing **Setup** and pressing Enter. The only problem is that this method doesn't always work.

When the setup program starts but doesn't complete, it may mean that the setup program relies on graphical features not found in Server Core. You don't have to worry too much in many cases. The vendor may very well provide a command line interface where you can configure the application setup using command line switches. The command line switches may actually appear as part of a README or other file provided on the installation media. Use these steps to learn more about the potential setup options provided on the media:

1. Select the drive that contains the installation media by typing **C:** or **D:** or whatever drive the media is using and pressing Enter.

2. If necessary, change directories to the installation media directory by typing **CD** *SetupDirectory* (where SetupDirectory is the setup directory) and pressing Enter. Often, the installation program is in a directory named Setup.

3. Type **Setup /?** and press Enter to determine whether the vendor provides localized help. If none of these options work, contact the vendor or search online for the command line instruction when you can't find help locally.

Assuming that the application uses Setup.EXE isn't always going to work—some vendors use another setup application name or might not provide the required setup interface as part of Setup.EXE. The most common alternative is Install.EXE, but the number of application variants is limitless. Fortunately, you can open the AutoRun.INF file and examine it by typing **Notepad AutoRun.INF** and pressing Enter. (As with the setup program, make sure you select the proper drive for accessing the AutoRun.INF file.) What you'll see is an INI file that contains all of the commands the application commonly used to start the setup. You can simply use these commands as a starting point for your own setup. Of course, you'll want to use command line switches to configure the application, rather than allow it to run in GUI mode (since that option has already failed).

Some vendors don't provide an AutoRun.INF file. In this case, you can type **Dir *.EXE** and press Enter. The setup disk usually contains only a few executable files and the filenames normally tell you what tasks the executable performs. If this fails, then you can type **Dir /AD** and press Enter. This command displays a listing of the subdirectories on the disk. One of the subdirectories normally has a name that indicates that it has something to do with installation or setup. You can type **CD** *DirectoryName* and press Enter to look though the files found in the installation directory—one of them generally provides the setup functionality you require.

After you get a product installed, you can use WMIC to manage it. For example, you can choose to change the application configuration if necessary by typing **WMIC Product Where Name=** **"*ProductName*" Call Configure** and pressing Enter. Likewise, you can remove a product that you no longer need by typing **WMIC Product Where Name="*ProductName*" Call Uninstall** and pressing Enter. Only the methods that the setup program supports will work. You can also use the WMIC Install method when you want to install an advertised product—one that was previously advertised using the Advertise method.

Some applications you attempt to install are doomed from the outset. Any application that lacks a command line interface is likely a poor candidate for Server Core. If the application also relies on the common dialog boxes and you need to save settings or perform other file-related tasks, you shouldn't consider using the application with Server Core because it's unlikely to work. The whole point of using Server Core is to cut down on the potential sources of contamination and to reduce the Windows bulk in a measurable way. In attaining these goals, Microsoft has made it impossible to use certain classes of applications with Server Core and you should never consider Server Core as a candidate for an application server (at least, not in an environment where you must interact directly with the application within a GUI environment).

 Real World Scenario

WORKING WITH ZIP FILES IN SERVER CORE

Many administrators maintain downloaded applications in ZIP files because the ZIP file is common and it does compress the application setup files. More importantly, the ZIP file keeps all of the setup files together, making it less likely that you'll lose one or more required setup files. Unfortunately, Server Core doesn't come with the ZIPFldr.DLL file that makes it possible to view ZIP files as folders in Windows Explorer. Of course, Server Core doesn't have Windows Explorer either, so the omission makes sense. Even so, you now have a problem with those ZIP files you've used for so long.

Fortunately, WinZIP (http://www.winzip.com/index.htm) has a command line interface, and you can purchase an add-on (http://www.winzip.com/prodpagecl.htm) that makes it a lot easier to use WinZIP at the command line. Of course, you can simply use the documentation at http://www.memecode.com/docs/winzip.html if desired. It's a little hard to follow, but the command line switches listed on the Web site all work fine. For example, if you wanted to extract the files from MyZIP.ZIP to the \MyFiles folder, you'd type **WinZIP32 -min -e MyZIP.ZIP \MyFiles** and press Enter. Make sure you provide the command line switches in the order shown or WinZIP may not work correctly. This command line works fine with versions of WinZIP 8.0 and above (it may work for older versions as well, but 8.0 was the earliest version tested for this book).

The command prompt won't have a path to the WinZIP folder, so you must add the application to the path. To perform this task, type **Path=C:\Program Files\WinZIP;%path%** and press Enter. Make sure you substitute the correct drive letter for the WinZIP installation.

You may also want to consider other alternatives for Server Core. Over the years, many vendors have made their command line interface optional or not included one at all because they assumed the GUI was here to stay. However, a few vendors have continued providing command line interfaces with their products. For example, 7-Zip provides a good command line interface and you can download it free. You can learn more about 7-Zip at http://www.7-zip.org/.

Deciding How to Perform Maintenance

The approach you take to maintenance in Server Core is important. You must weigh the cost of various methods. For example, when you work at the command line, you see an efficient command line interface. All of the commands execute quickly and you don't need to worry about a Remote Desktop connection. Of course, you also have to know the command you want to type. Unfortunately, many of the maintenance commands are quite unforgiving and you may find yourself wasting time fixing problems instead of saving time using the command line interface.

Some maintenance actions can occur in Server Core's GUI environment. Any maintenance application that doesn't require you to save settings to disk using a common dialog box could work. Testing is the best way to determine whether the application works as intended.

You can also use the Boot menu options or the installation CD repair options to perform certain kinds of maintenance. All of the Safe Mode options work, as does the Windows Memory Diagnostics tool. You can also use the installation CD to perform a restore of your hard drive as necessary. All of the normal Windows boot and install diagnostics work fine with Server Core.

It's also possible to create a connection between a client machine and the Server Core installation. You can use this connection in three ways to perform maintenance tasks.

- ◆ At the command prompt with utilities that support a remote connection
- ◆ Using Remote Desktop to manage the server from a client system
- ◆ Connecting with consoles that support a remote connection

You'll see many examples of the first technique in this book. Many utilities provide a method for creating a remote server connection and performing a task on that connection, rather than using the local machine. The second technique of working with a Remote Desktop is very much like working at the machine directly. The "Working with the Remote Desktop Connection Application" section of Chapter 2 discusses using Remote Desktop in detail. The third technique won't receive a lot of attention in this book, but you use the consoles as you would with the local machine. Here are the steps for setting up a remote connection with a console.

1. Open the console you want to use in the Administrative Tools folder of the Control Panel or by using the Run dialog box accessed using the Start ➢ Run command. (The Group Policy Editor, GPEdit.MSC, requires the Run dialog box since it doesn't appear in the Administrative Tools folder.)

2. Right-click the root node of the console tree. For example, when working with Computer Management, you would right-click the Computer Management (Local) node. When the console supports a remote connection, you'll see a Connect to Another Computer entry on the context menu.

3. Choose the Connect to Another Computer entry on the context menu and you'll see a Select Computer dialog box.

4. Type the name of the remote computer in the Another Computer field or use the Browse button to locate the computer.

5. Click OK. The console attempts to make the connection to the remote computer. If you need to provide additional credentials, you'll see a dialog box for entering them.

Not all of the console features will work. For example, you'll find that none (or sometimes most) of the Storage group features work in the Computer Management console when accessing a remote machine. Because you can't complete some processes from a remote location, Microsoft blocks the console feature. In some cases, the lack of a feature prevents you from using a console entry. For example, you can't manage SQL Server on a machine that doesn't have SQL Server installed.

Performing Server Updates

Automatic server updates would seem impossible with Server Core because it lacks Internet Explorer. Yes, you can download the update and install it manually, but this technique hasn't worked well in the past and it probably won't work well now. Most administrators are quite busy and forget to apply the required patches. Of course, if you have just one server and a dedicated administrator, downloading the patches and applying them manually can work. After all, applying patches manually is how most administrators have worked for years (just not very successfully in larger organizations).

Fortunately, you don't need Internet Explorer to perform automatic updates for Server Core. One of the features that comes with Server Core is the Windows Update AutoUpdate Client (WUAUClt) utility. This utility performs automatic updates of your server, but Microsoft doesn't enable it by default and you don't have a convenient GUI method of activating it. Use any of these techniques to enable the WUAUClt utility.

◆ Type **CScript %SYSTEMROOT%\system32\SCRegEdit.WSF /AU 4** and press Enter to set Windows Update to start every time you start the computer.

◆ Type **Net Start WUAUServ** and press Enter to start Windows Update for this session only.

Either of these commands starts Windows Update using the default parameters, which tell the server to update automatically each morning at 3:00 AM. Unlike other versions of Windows, Server Core lacks the interface requirements to notify you about anything. Consequently, the only mode available is to download the updates and install them automatically without telling you, which is mode 4.

Fortunately, you can control the time at which Windows Update performs its work. However, you must use the Registry Editor to make the change. Start the Registry Editor by typing **RegEdit** and pressing Enter. Locate the HKEY_LOCAL_MACHINE\SOFTWARE\Microsoft\Windows\CurrentVersion\ WindowsUpdate\Auto Update key shown in Figure 3.1. Change the ScheduledInstallTime value to the update hour you want to use. For example, if you enter 13 (0x0000000d), the update will take place at 1:00 PM. The maximum value is 23 (0x00000017)—use a value of 0 for midnight. The ScheduledInstallDay value determines when the update occurs. If you set this value to 0, then the update occurs every day. Otherwise, the update occurs on the day of the week you choose starting with 1 for Sunday. The maximum value is 7 for Saturday.

FIGURE 3.1

Some settings changes must occur within the Registry Editor because Server Core lacks a GUI.

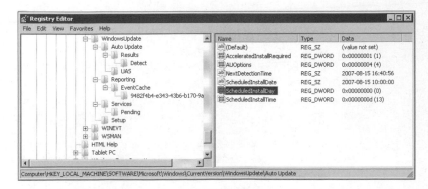

Since Server Core lacks the interface required to obtain status information, you must obtain it at the command prompt. To obtain Windows Update status, type **CScript %SYSTEMROOT%\system32\ SCRegEdit.WSF /AU /V** and press Enter. The script outputs a simple status indicator as shown in Figure 3.2. You may find that you want to perform the update immediately. In this case, you type **WUAUClt /DetectNow** and press Enter. The server uses its Internet connection to perform an immediate update.

FIGURE 3.2
Verify that Windows Update is actually set to run on the server.

If you choose at a later time not to perform an update, you can tell the Windows Update server to stop by typing **Net Stop WUAUServ** and pressing Enter. The Windows Update server stops immediately. If you want to disable Windows Update completely, type **CScript %SYSTEMROOT%\ system32\SCRegEdit.WSF /AU 1** and press Enter. The "Working with Services" section of Chapter 1 tells you more about working with services from Task Manager. Make sure you also review the "Controlling Services with the SC Command" of this chapter to discover how to control services from the command line.

Of course, you'll want to know which updates you have installed. After all, you want to be sure that the server really does have the required updates. To check the list of current updates, type **WMIC QFE List** (where QFE stands for Quick Fix Engineering) and press Enter. When the server has no updates installed, you'll see a message stating, "No Instance(s) Available."

ALTERNATIVES TO USING THE COMMAND LINE FOR UPDATES

Microsoft provides two alternatives to using the command line for Windows Update. The first is to use Windows Server Update Services (WSUS). WSUS is a mini-version of Windows Update that you can set up on a local server. Instead of requiring all of the machines on your network to update using Windows Update directly, you can load the updates onto the WSUS server. You then use a group policy to point all of the systems on the network to use the WSUS server instead of Windows Update. The WSUS server doesn't ship with Server Core, but you can find step-by-step instructions for setting it up at http:// technet2.microsoft.com/windowsserver/en/library/a68a19d2-630e-45d6-b596- d24dac987b641033.mspx.

The second alternative is to use a group policy setting. Windows Server 2008 (including Server Core) comes with a new group policy setup for Windows Update. These settings appear in an ADMX file, rather than the ADM files of old and the settings are in XML format. The XML formatting means that you can use something as simple as Notepad to make changes to group policy. The Windows Update settings appear in the WindowsUpdate.ADMX file, which supersedes the WUAU.ADM file used in the past. Microsoft has provided a reference document for the new group policy settings at http:// www.microsoft.com/downloads/details.aspx?familyid=2043b94e-66cd-4b91-9e0f- 68363245c495.

Creating LNK Files

Up until now, you may have taken LNK (link) files for granted in Windows because they're exceptionally easy to create. Unfortunately, without a GUI in Server Core, it's become significantly harder to create LNK files. You'll find a ton of references to an elusive Shortcut utility for Windows online, but you won't find the actual executable on your hard drive, which may leave you puzzling for a long time. It's possible to create LNK files using scripts. Listing 3.1 shows a script that places a LNK file on your Desktop for Notepad. Now you can double-click this LNK file and open a copy of Notepad (menu not required).

TIP Server Core may not display links on the Desktop. In this case, you can still place links in a common folder, such as %USERPROFILE%, which points to your user folder. You can still type the LNK filename and press Enter to use the link file from the command line. In short, LNK files are still useful, even if you can't see their physical manifestation in the form of an icon.

LISTING 3.1:   Creating a New LNK File

```
' Create the shell object.
Set WshShell = WScript.CreateObject("WScript.Shell")

' Define the location of the LNK file.
LinkFilename = WshShell.ExpandEnvironmentStrings("%USERPROFILE%")
LinkFilename = LinkFilename + "\Desktop\Notepad.LNK"

' Create the LNK file object.
Set LNKFile = WshShell.CreateShortcut(LinkFilename)

' Set the LNK file contents.
LNKFile.TargetPath = "%SYSTEMROOT%\System32\Notepad.EXE"
LNKFile.Arguments = ""
LNKFile.Description = "Open Notepad"
LNKFile.HotKey = ""
LNKFile.IconLocation = "%SYSTEMROOT%\System32\Notepad.EXE, 1"
LNKFile.WindowStyle = "1"
LNKFile.WorkingDirectory = "C:\"

' Save the LNK file to disk.
LNKFile.Save
```

The code begins by creating a Windows Script shell. This shell provides access to features such as environment strings and the function for creating a shortcut. The next step creates a location name based on the user's profile—the \Users\UserName folder for the user. You may use any of the environment variables that Windows supports to obtain information for your scripts. It then adds the actual LNK file location to the path.

Now that the code has a path to use for creating the LNK file, it uses the CreateShortcut() function to create it. At this point, the script sets the various LNK file contents. Any field you can change in a LNK file, you can also change using a script. Finally, the script saves the results to the hard drive. It's essential to perform this final step or LNK file won't work. Simply type the LNK filename and press Enter to execute it at the command line. For example, in this case you would type **Notepad.LNK** and press Enter at the command line to start a copy of Notepad. You'll find complete coverage of scripts in Chapter 6.

TIP You can find a downloadable version of the Shortcut command at http://www.optimumx .com/download/. The Shortcut command provides the means to create a LNK file without resorting to using a script. In addition, you can use it to create an INI file that contains all of the LNK file configuration information. The ReadMe.TXT file that comes with the Shortcut command tells you about all of the command line parameters you need to use it.

Setting Security

Security occurs at a number of levels in Windows. This section isn't a comprehensive treatment of the topic—it only gets you started. Of course, the first task you'll complete is to add users to the server and use shares to make resources available. The "Configuring the Server for Initial Use" section of Chapter 1 describes how you'll perform this task. Of course, making a resource available as a share isn't always enough to make it available to the user. The user must have both share and physical permission to use a resource.

Because you created your user account as an Administrator in Chapter 1, you already have access, but your users won't be administrators. Consequently, you also need to use the ICACLS command to provide physical access (see the "Changing File and Directory Access with the *ICACLS* Command" section of Chapter 15 for complete details). You can determine the existing rights for a directory or file by typing the directory or filename with its complete path. For example, if you want to determine who has access to the root directory of the C drive, you'd type **ICACLS C:** and press Enter. The results appear as shown in Figure 3.3.

The letters beside each of the entries tells you which rights the specified user or group has to the file or directory. For example, the letter F denotes full access, while M denotes modify access. Chapter 15 describes all of these security indicators in detail. When an entry has more than one letter after it, that entry has all of those rights. To grant access to a particular user or group, you use the grant syntax for the ICACLS command. For example, to grant user John full access to the C:\Users directory, you'd type **ICACLS C:\Users /Grant John:(F)** and press Enter. If the system can't allow access due to User Access Control (UAC) or other reasons, then you'll see an Access Denied error message. Otherwise, you'll see a Successfully Processed message, along with the number of entries that the command has processed.

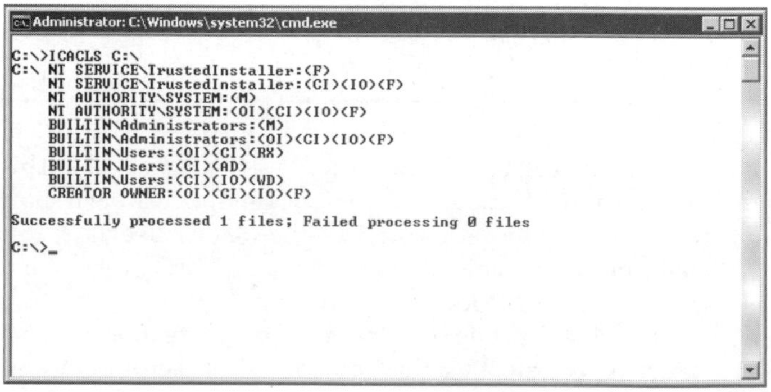

FIGURE 3.3
Determine who has access to a particular file or directory as part of creating a share for it.

It's important to set security policies for the server. Of course, you could always open the GPEdit console in a client machine and use it to connect to the remote server. Any group policies that you set at the server affect everyone who logs into the server. Set any local policies at the machine the policies affect. If you have Active Directory installed, Chapter 19 tells you how to manage policies, users, and resources using Active Directory.

Along with user and resource security, you'll need to consider communication and network security. For example, the "Managing the IPv6 Policies and Security with the IPSec6 Utility" section of Chapter 11 describes how to set IPv6 communication security. Make sure you check Chapter 21 for additional information on security commands and utilities.

Configuring Server Core Using the WMIC Command

You may wonder what Windows Management Instrumentation (WMI) is all about and it's important to know a little about it. In 1996, BMC Software, Cisco Systems, Compaq Computer, Intel, and Microsoft sponsored the Web-Based Enterprise Management (WBEM) initiative. The whole purpose of WBEM is to make it possible to manage systems across a network even if those systems aren't normally compatible. For example, using WBEM, you could manage Linux and Windows servers from the same location with equal ease—at least, that's the theory. For the most part, the theory does work and many companies have adopted WBEM as a base for performing management tasks without platform considerations. In fact, the Distributed Management Task Force (DMTF) has a number of standards for WBEM and you can see them at `http://www.dmtf.org/standards/wbem/`.

NOTE   This book does provide enough information about WMIC to help you perform most common tasks. It doesn't document WMI or WMIC completely because the application is large and complex enough to warrant a book of its own. If you find that you need additional information about WMI, check out *Understanding WMI Scripting* by Alain Lissoir (Digital Press, 2003). This book contains 579 pages on the topic of WMI scripting, including use of WMIC.

WMI is Microsoft's next step for WBEM. Even though this is still supposedly an open standard, WMI builds on WBEM and implements it at a lower level. The instrumentation takes place through device drivers, services, and other software, making the entire structure of a system appear more as a hierarchical database than a collection of statistics that someone could use for management tasks. As a result, WMI lets you do more than WBEM, but the added functionality also makes WMI considerably more complex. The point is that WMI looks like a hierarchical database of any system you wish to manage that supports WMI. You can learn more about WMI at `http://www.microsoft.com/whdc/system/pnppwr/wmi/default.mspx`.

The Windows Management Interface Command line (WMIC) command is an extremely powerful command that you'll see demonstrated throughout the book. This utility is the command line interface for WMI. You'll probably need to spend some time working with WMIC before you can make it do everything you want. Because WMI reflects the setup of your machine and not mine, it's impossible to provide detailed particulars of every element of WMIC in this book. However, WMIC does work well for many common tasks where you know that most machines will have essentially the same configuration. In fact, you've already seen it used in Chapter 1 to change the computer name and toggle the Remote Desktop access. The following sections describe WMIC in detail.

Understanding the SQL Syntax of WMIC

The basic use for WMIC isn't hard. You have access to a number of global command line arguments, some aliases for particular parts of the system, and alias-specific command line switches. The difficulty comes when you begin using the WMIC command for real work. In most cases, you'll need to use a Structured Query Language (SQL)-like syntax that tells WMIC precisely what element of your system to work with. Given that WMIC makes your system look like a hierarchical database, the use of a SQL-like syntax works well. The actual name for this syntax is WMI Query

Language (WQI) and you can find detailed information about it at http://msdn2.microsoft .com/en-us/library/aa394552.aspx. As an example of WQI at work, the **WMIC ComputerSystem Where Name="%COMPUTERNAME%" Call Rename Name="*NewName*"** command defines a new name for your computer. The rest of this section takes this command apart.

The term ComputerSystem is an alias. It references the computer system elements of WMI. You need an alias to locate the particular branch of the database that contains the element that you want to work with.

The Where clause tells WMIC which property to access within the alias. In this case, the name of the property must match the %COMPUTERNAME% expansion variable. This system environment variable appears with every copy of Windows and it always contains the name of the local system. Consequently, you can create command that will run on any system simply by referencing the expansion variable. The ComputerSystem alias supports a number of properties including the following (to see this list for yourself, type **WMIC ComputerSystem** and press Enter):

AdminPasswordStatus	NumberOfProcessors
AutomaticResetBootOption	OEMLogoBitmap
AutomaticResetCapability	OEMStringArray
BootOptionOnLimit	PartOfDomain
BootOptionOnWatchDog	PauseAfterReset
BootROMSupported	PowerManagementCapabilities
BootupState	PowerManagementSupported
Caption	PowerOnPasswordStatus
ChassisBootupState	PowerState
CreationClassName	PowerSupplyState
CurrentTimeZone	PrimaryOwnerContact
DaylightInEffect	PrimaryOwnerName
Description	ResetCapability
Domain	ResetCount
DomainRole	ResetLimit
EnableDaylightSavingsTime	Roles
FrontPanelResetStatus	Status
InfraredSupported	SupportContactDescription
InitialLoadInfo	SystemStartupDelay
InstallDate	SystemStartupOptions
KeyboardPasswordStatus	SystemStartupSetting
LastLoadInfo	SystemType
Manufacturer	ThermalState
Model	TotalPhysicalMemory
Name	UserName
NameFormat	WakeUpType
NetworkServerModeEnabled	Workgroup

ASSOC   Displays a list of the associators of the current alias. Think again about the hierarchical nature of the WMI database. An *associator* would be a WMI element that appears as a child of the current node in the database.

CALL   Calls the specified method with the arguments you provide. Every alias provides special methods for configuration tasks. In the case of the example, the command calls on the Rename method. The ComputerSystem alias also provides the JoinDomainOrWorkgroup and the `UnJoinDomainOrWorkgroup` methods. To see the list of calls for a particular alias, type **WMIC *Alias* Call /?** and press Enter. The methods normally include input and output arguments. The help listing tells you about each of these arguments, but you don't necessarily need to use all of them. For example, the example call only uses the `Name` argument, but it also includes the `UserName` and `Password` arguments when you work on a remote system. To use an argument, provide its name, followed by an equals sign, followed by the value of that argument in double quotes as shown in the example.

CREATE   Creates a new instance of a particular element. You must provide the arguments required to create the element. The element also has optional arguments that you don't have to provide. If you don't supply enough arguments, then WMIC displays an error message that normally tells you what arguments are missing.

DELETE   Removes an existing element. Make sure you use a `Where` clause that defines the element completely. Otherwise, you might delete something you really wanted to keep.

GET   Obtains all of the details for a particular alias. However, the true power of this action is retrieving individual property values. For example, if you want to determine the current startup delay for your system, you'd type **WMIC ComputerSystem Where Name="%COMPUTERNAME%" GET SystemStartupDelay** and press Enter. In this case, `SystemStartupDelay` is one of the properties that the `ComputerSystem` alias supports.

LIST   Obtains all of the details for a particular alias. You can specify how much information to provide using the `Brief` and `Full` settings. For example, if you type **WMIC ComputerSystem LIST Brief** and press Enter, WMIC only provides the `Domain`, `Manufacturer`, `Model`, `Name`, `PrimaryOwnerName`, and `TotalPhysicalMemory` properties as output.

SET   Sets the value of a property directly. You must include a `Where` clause that specifies which element to change. For example, if you wanted to change the system startup delay (at the boot manager) to 35 sections, you'd type **WMIC ComputerSystem Where Name="%COMPUTERNAME%" SET SystemStartupDelay=35** and press Enter. Type **WMIC Alias SET /?** and press Enter to see a list of properties you can change. The `ComputerSystem` alias includes the following writeable properties.

- ◆ `AutomaticResetBootOption`
- ◆ `CurrentTimeZone`
- ◆ `EnableDaylightSavingsTime`
- ◆ `Roles`
- ◆ `SystemStartupDelay`
- ◆ `SystemStartupOptions`
- ◆ `SystemStartupSetting`
- ◆ `Workgroup`

An Overview of WMIC Aliases

As mentioned in the "Understanding the SQL Syntax of WMIC" section of the chapter, much of your work with WMIC involves using aliases. Using an alias means that you don't have to worry about the physical structure of WMI—you can access the information you need quickly and easily (or at least easier than if you also had to worry about the path to a particular WMI element). The following list tells you about the aliases that WMIC supports.

Alias   Provides access to a list of all of the aliases available on the local system.

Baseboard   Provides access to features on the motherboard (system board). For example, if you type **WMIC Baseboard GET Manufacturer** and press Enter, you'll see the name of the manufacturer of your motherboard.

BIOS   Provides access to the Basic Input/Output System (BIOS) management features. For example, if you type **WMIC BIOS GET BIOSVersion** and press Enter, you'll see the version of the BIOS installed in the system. This isn't the same as the firmware update. To obtain the firmware version, type **WMIC BIOS GET SMBIOSBIOSVersion** and press Enter.

BootConfig   Provides access to boot configuration information. Microsoft may not support this feature with Server Core—always use the BCDEdit utility instead for making changes to the boot configuration.

CDROM   Provides access to all of the CD and DVD devices on the system. For example, if you want to obtain the name and volume of each of your CD or DVD devices, you would type **WMIC CDROM GET Name, VolumeName** and press Enter (notice that you must separate the individual properties with commas).

ComputerSystem   Manages the computer system configuration.

CPU   Provides access to the CPU. You'll see one entry for each CPU. If the CPU is dual (or more) processing, the output displays one entry for each processor in the CPU. One of the more important properties is the status indicator, which provides a simple indication of whether the CPU is currently operating within designed parameters (the output is a simple OK when the CPU is functioning properly). Type **WMIC CPU GET Status** and press Enter to obtain the status information.

CSProduct   Provides access to the computer system product information. For example, you'd use this alias to determine the system's Universally Unique Identifier (UUID), which is actually better than a serial number since it's unique across all systems.

Datafile   Manages information about data files on the system. This alias locks up the machine if you don't use it correctly. You must provide specific data file criteria in order to achieve good results. For example, if you want to locate all of the executable files in the Windows directory, type **WMIC DataFile Where "Path='\\Windows\\' and Extension='exe'"** and press Enter. Notice the use of double quotes to encompass the search criteria and single quotes to encompass values. In addition, notice the use of double backslashes in the path variable. You can't use expansion variables in this case.

DCOMApp   Manages the Distributed Component Object Model (DCOM) applications on the system. You can use this feature to start, stop, install, and remove DCOM applications as needed using a simple batch file. Because DCOM applications can become quite complex, make sure you understand how to configure DCOM applications using the Component Services console first.

Desktop   Manages the user's desktop. Unfortunately, this alias assumes that the user's desktop includes a GUI. Consequently, this alias doesn't work well with Server Core. You can obtain information such as the screen saver that the user is employing and what the desktop has for a background image.

DesktopMonitor   Provides access to statistics about the configuration of the desktop on the specified system.

DeviceMemoryAddress   Provides access to the memory ranges used by physical devices installed on the system. You'll see one entry for each memory range used by a device. The output of this alias is somewhat useless because it doesn't provide names for each of the devices, but you can still use it to detect specific memory range.

DiskDrive   Provides access to hard drives and hard drive-like devices, such as USB flash drives. The output includes formatting, status, and other statistics that are helpful for managing the hard drive. For example, if you want to quickly determine drive status, type **WMIC DiskDrive GET Name, Caption, NeedsCleaning, Status** and press Enter.

DiskQuota   Manages disk space usage on Windows NT File System (NTFS) volumes. You must have the disk quota feature enabled to use this alias. Otherwise, when you type **WMIC DiskQuota** and press Enter, you'll see a list of the partitions on the current drive, but none of the drives will show that they have any space used. Setting a disk quota is somewhat complex, partly because you have to provide so much information to do it. A disk quota is a combination of a user account and a disk, so you normally specify both. For example, you may want to set a disk quota for a user named John on the C drive of 600,000,000 bytes. In this case, you'd type **WMIC DiskQuota Where (User="Win32_Account.Domain='MAINXP',Name='John'" And QuotaVolume="Win32_LogicalDisk.DeviceID='C:'") SET WarningLimit=600000000** and press Enter. As you can see, the Where clause is complex. The User property includes both a domain and a name value. The QuotaVolume property must reflect the actual C drive entry, which includes all of the additional text shown. Once you know how to select the user and drive, you use the SET verb to change the WarningLimit property as shown. The best way to learn how to form this particular command is to spend time selecting users and drives first, and then using what you learn to set the property values.

DMAChannel   Provides access to Direct Memory Access channel information on the system. You'll see one entry for each DMA channel. The output of this alias is somewhat useless because it doesn't really tell you anything about DMA channel usage.

Environment   Manages environment variable information. This alias provides extensive information about the environment variables and makes it easy to query them from a remote system. For example, you'd type **WMIC Environment Where Name="Path" GET VariableValue** and press Enter to determine the path for a system.

FSDir   Provides specifics about a particular directory or file on a hard drive. This alias locks up the machine if you don't use it correctly. You must provide double backslashes for the path. For example, if you want to determine the statistics for the Windows directory on the D drive, then you would type **WMIC FSDir Where Name="D:\\Windows"** and press Enter. You can't use expansion variables in this case.

Group   Manages groups on the specified system. Make sure you differentiate between the Caption and Name properties. The Caption property requires that you provide a realm or domain with the group name. To see the difference between the two, type **WMIC Group LIST Brief** and press Enter.

IDEController   Provides access to information about the Integrated Device Electronics (IDE) controllers on the system.

IRQ Provides access to information about the Interrupt Request (IRQ) lines on the system. You'll see one entry for each IRQ line. The output of this alias is somewhat useless because it doesn't really tell you anything about IRQ usage.

Job Manages jobs on the system through the Task Manager. This alias is exceptionally helpful with Server Core since you don't have direct access to Task Manager (it requires a GUI). Learn more about this particular alias in the "Working with the WMIC Job Alias" section of Chapter 8.

LoadOrder Manages the order in which system services load. Normally, you won't want to change these entries because a change in order could prevent a service from starting. However, this feature is helpful when you suspect a service isn't starting as anticipated (make sure you create a copy of the order when the system is in a known good working state). To create a copy of the current load order, type **WMIC LoadOrder > LoadOrder.TXT** and press Enter. The load order will appear in LoadOrder.TXT.

LogicalDisk Provides access to information about the logical disks on the system. The information includes only local drives.

Logon Provides access to information about the current logon sessions. Unfortunately, the output isn't very useful because it doesn't contain logon names—it provides logon identifiers instead, so you need to perform additional processing.

MemCache Provides access to the cache memory information for a system. To check the status of the Static Random Access Memory (SRAM) on a system, type **WMIC MemCache GET Purpose, InstalledSize, Status** and press Enter.

MemoryChip Provides information about memory chips installed on the system. Most systems don't support this alias.

MemPhysical Provides information about the physical memory installed on a system.

NetClient Provides information about Terminal Services and the Remote Desktop functionality the service provides.

NetLogin Provides information about logins for the specified system. This alias requires a little extra work to use because you must provide a more complex WQI statement. To obtain information about any particular user, type **WMIC NetLogin Where (Name Like "%UserName")** and press Enter. Once you get past the initial requirement to provide additional information, you can use the standard actions to obtain specific data.

NetProtocol Manages the network protocols used on the current system. When working with this protocol to obtain information, use the Caption property instead of the Name property to access particular protocols. For example, the Caption property may display NetBIOS, while the Name property displays MSAFD NetBIOS [\Device\NetBT_Tcpip_{2CFD1858-4741-4AD2-AD9B-E00D23BF8ED9}] DATAGRAM 2. Use the Name property when you want to modify a specific protocol to ensure you change the correct protocol.

NetUse Manages network connectivity information on the specified system. For example, you would use this alias to discover mapped network drives. In this case, you'd type **WMIC NetUse Where ResourceType="Disk" GET LocalName, RemoteName** and press Enter.

NIC Provides access to information about the Network Interface Controllers (NICs) installed on the specified system.

NICConfig Manages the NIC setup. Unlike most of the aliases, this alias doesn't include a Name property, so you must use the Caption property. To obtain a list of NICs on the target system, type **WMIC NICConfig GET Caption** and press Enter.

NTDomain   Manages Windows domain information, including several useful Active Directory settings. You can learn more about this alias in the "Managing Directory Services Using the WMIC NTDomain Alias" section of Chapter 19.

NTEvent   Displays the entries in the Windows event log. This alias locks up the machine if you don't use it correctly (even if you do use it correctly, the required search can require several minutes). For example, if you want to discover any System event log entries with a type greater than 4, type **WMIC NTEvent Where "LogFile='system' and Type>'4'"** and press Enter. You can't use this alias to add new event entries to the log. Use the EventCreate utility described in the "Managing System Events with the EventCreate Utility" section of Chapter 18 for this purpose instead.

NTEventLog   Manages the Windows event logs. Unlike the NTEvent alias, which helps you manage the actual event log entries, this alias controls the actual logs. For example, you can use this alias to manage the event log size. This is also the alias you use to clear the event log. To clear the System event log, you'd type **WMIC NTEventLog Where LogFileName="System" CALL ClearEventLog** and press Enter. If you choose to save the log before clearing it, add the ArchiveFileName argument.

OnBoardDevice   Provides access to adapter devices built onto the motherboard. At least, it should provide this access. Testing on several systems shows that support for this feature is sketchy at best. You'll generally manage adapters on the motherboard using the same techniques that you use to manage stand-alone adapters.

OS   Provides access to statistics about the current operating system. For example, to obtain the operating system name and build, you'd type **WMIC OS GET Caption, BuildNumber** and press Enter.

Pagefile   Provides information about the Windows page file. You can't use this alias to control the page file size.

PageFileSet   Manages the Windows page file. However, instead of using a method to set the page file, you use properties. For example, to set the page file on drive C to an initial size of 2 GB and a maximum size of 2 GB, you'd type **WMIC PageFileSet Where Name="C:\\PageFile.SYS" SET InitialSize=2048,MaximumSize=2048** and press Enter. Notice that you separate the SET arguments with commas and that you have to use a double backslash for the page file entry, even though the Name property displays with a single backslash.

Partition   Provides statistics about the partitions on the hard drive. You can't use this alias to change the partition sizes.

Port   Provides information about the I/O ports on the system. For example, if you wanted to detect any failed ports, you could type **WMIC Port Where(NOT Status="OK") GET Caption,Description** and press Enter. Notice the use of the word NOT to indicate that the ports aren't OK. You'll see one entry for each port. The output of this alias is somewhat useless because it doesn't tell you the name of each port; you must correlate the address range to the actual port.

PortConnector   Provides access to the physical ports on the system. You can use this feature to find the physical port names (such as LPT1), their connection type, and port type. The listing includes both internal and external connectors. It even includes the motherboard ports, such as fan connectors. To obtain a listing of the most commonly used port information type **WMIC PortConnector GET ConnectorType,InternalReferenceDesignator,PortType** and press Enter.

Printer Manages the logical printer characteristics for the system. The list of printers includes any mapped printer connections. Use the CALL verb to access any of these management methods: AddPrinterConnection, CancelAllJobs, Pause, PrintTestPage, RenamePrinter, Reset, Resume, SetDefaultPrinter, and SetPowerState. For example, if you wanted to resume printing on a networked printer named HP LaserJet 5 located on WinServer, you'd type **WMIC Printer Where Caption="\\\\WinServer\\HP LaserJet 5" CALL Resume** and press Enter. Notice that you must use four backslashes to begin the UNC location of the printer.

PrinterConfig Provides information about the physical characteristics of both local and networked printers. The statistics include the printer resolution, any driver information, and whether the printer prints in color (along with other useful information).

PrintJob Manages individual print jobs for the local machine. You can also use methods to pause and resume individual jobs.

Process Manages processes on the local machine. You can obtain a wealth of information about each process, including memory statistics. The methods associated with this alias let you attach a debugger to a process, create a new process, obtain process owner information, set the process priority, and even terminate the process. Normally, you'll want to perform all tasks using the ProcessID property. To obtain a list of Process Identifiers (PIDs) and their associated application names, type **WMIC Process GET Name,ProcessID** and press Enter. Once you have the ProcessID, you can perform tasks such as terminating the process. To terminate a process with a PID of 688, you'd type **WMIC Process Where ProcessID=688 CALL Terminate** and press Enter.

Product Manages products on the local machine. This alias provides the equivalent of all of the information you'd find in the Add/Remove Programs applet in the Control Panel, so it's an essential aid on Server Core. In addition to the product name and vendor support information, you can also find the product uninstall information, which helps you perform the uninstall at the command line, rather than use the GUI as normal. Special methods let you configure, install, uninstall, reinstall, or upgrade application packages as needed. See the "Performing Application Installations" section of the chapter for additional information.

QFE Provides a listing of all of the Quick Fix Engineering (QFE) patches for the Windows system. This alias only lists the fixes and you can't use it to manage them in any way.

QuotaSetting Manages the quota settings on the local hard drive. You must use the SET verb to change the settings. For example, if you want to configure the C drive default quota limit to 1 GB, you would type **WMIC QuotaSetting Where Caption="C:" SET DefaultLimit=1073741824** and press Enter. To enable the quota you just set, type **WMIC QuotaSetting Where Caption="C:" SET State=1** and press Enter. If you also want to deny disk space to users who exceed their quota, you can set the State to 2. Combine this alias with the DiskQuota alias to create a complete disk quota solution.

RDAccount Manages the accounts that can access a server using Remote Desktop. This alias assumes that the Remote Desktop Listener is active (see the RDToggle alias for details). You need not add users to the account listing to see some users have access by default. Type **WMIC RDAccount GET AccountName**, press Enter, and you'll see this list of standard users.

- BUILTIN\Administrators

- NT AUTHORITY\LOCAL SERVICE

- NT AUTHORITY\NETWORK SERVICE

◆ NT AUTHORITY\SYSTEM

◆ BUILTIN\Remote Desktop Users

Remote access actually depends on two features, the account name and the terminal name (console or Remote Desktop Protocol-Transmission Control Protocol, RDP-TCP, in most cases). To remove a user from the list, you must include both the account name and the terminal name to ensure you delete the right account. To remove the administrators account from console access, type **WMIC RDAccount where "TerminalName='console' and AccountName like '%Administrators%'" CALL Delete** and press Enter. Interestingly enough, you can't add new accounts using the RDAccount alias, you must use the RDPermissions alias to do it.

RDNIC Manages the NIC associated with the Remote Desktop connection. You can configure items such as the number of connections allowed.

RDPermissions Manages permissions for Remote Desktop connections. To add a user to the Console terminal, you type **WMIC RDPermissions Where TerminalName="Console" CALL AddAccount "*Domain\UserName*",2** and press Enter. You must provide a domain and a username as shown. The second value is the permission preset. It uses the following values:

0 Guest access, the user can only log into the system.

1 User access, the user has the following permissions: Logon, Query Information, Send Message, and Connect.

2 Full access, the user has full system access.

RDToggle Manages the Remote Desktop listener settings. See the "Configuring the Server for Initial Use" section of Chapter 1 for an example of how to use this alias.

RecoverOS Manages the system recovery options, including the memory dump feature.

Registry Provides access to the physical features of the registry such as size and location. You can also provide a proposed registry size.

SCSIController Provides information about any Small Computer System Interface (SCSI) devices on the selected computer. In addition, this alias provides information about Redundant Array of Inexpensive Disk (RAID) controllers. You can use calls to set the power state and to reset the controller.

Server Provides statistics about the server such as the logon errors and number of bytes received.

Service Manages the services running on the target system. You can use calls to start, stop, pause, continue, and perform other tasks with services. To determine the status of the services, type **WMIC Service GET Name,State** and press Enter. To start a particular service, type **WMIC Service Where Name="*ServiceName*" CALL StartService** and Press Enter.

ShadowCopy Provides information about volumes with shadow copy management. You can also use this alias to add shadow copy management to a volume.

ShadowStorage Provides information about the shadow copy storage areas for the target system. This alias lets you set the maximum storage area size through a property and create new storage areas using a method.

Share Shares the specified resource on the target system. You can read more about this alias in the "Configuring the Server for Initial Use" section of Chapter 1.

NOTE The Microsoft documentation provides entries for the `SoftwareElement` and `SoftwareFeature` aliases. However, these aliases don't appear to provide any functionality. In fact, during testing they output an error code of 0x80041010. You should probably avoid using these aliases until Microsoft makes them functional and provides better documentation for them.

SoundDev Provides statistics about any sound devices on your system. You can't use this alias to change any sound system features.

Startup Provides information about the applications and services that run automatically when the computer starts. This feature works similarly to the Startup tab of the System Configuration Utility (`MSConfig.EXE`), except that you can't make any changes to the setup.

SysAccount Provides a list of the system accounts that includes account statistics such as their global Security Identifiers (SIDs).

SysDriver Provides a list of the system drivers. The methods provided with this alias let you pause and resume the service. You can also interrogate the service for additional information.

SystemEnclosure Provides statistics about the system enclosure, such as whether it provides a hot swappable disk feature.

SystemSlot Provides information about the system slot configuration of the motherboard. Theoretically, this alias also provides information about other motherboard connections such as port, peripheral, and proprietary connection points, but normally you won't actually see this information provided.

TapeDrive Provides information about any tape drives installed on the target system.

Temperature Provides information about any temperature sensors installed on the system. Unfortunately, this feature doesn't work at all on older systems and may not work on newer systems either. When this alias does work, you obtain a considerable amount of information about the sensor—everything you could ever want except the temperature. The `CurrentReading` property should contain the current temperature, but it often doesn't.

TimeZone Provides complete information about the time zone settings on the target machine. However, you can't use this alias to change any of the settings.

UPS Provides complete statistics about the Uninterruptible Power Supply (UPS) attached to the target system. The statistics you receive depend, in part, on the capabilities of the UPS. Newer UPSs tend to provide more information than older setups. In some cases, you can even detect the operating temperature of the UPS. The UPS must rely on the UPS service in Windows for this feature to work. You can't change any of the UPS feature settings using this alias.

UserAccount Manages user account information. You can add, delete, or modify user entries as needed. The modifications include the ability to rename the user account, disable the account, and set account password requirements. For example, if you want to set the user's full name, you would type `WMIC UserAccount Where Name="UserName" SET FullName="FullName"` and press Enter.

Voltage Provides information about any voltage sensors installed on the system. Unfortunately, this feature doesn't work at all on older systems and may not work on newer systems either. When this alias does work, you obtain a considerable amount of information about the sensor—everything you could ever want except the power supply voltages. The `CurrentReading` property should contain the current voltage readings, but it often doesn't.

Volume   Manages the volumes on the target system. You obtain detailed statistics about the volume in question. In addition, you can use methods to add a mount point, start ChkDsk, defragment the drive (or exclude it from defragmentation), obtain a fragmentation analysis, mount and dismount the drive, and format the drive. The properties let you change the volume letter, the volume label, or enable or disable indexing for the volume.

VolumeQuotaSetting   Associates a disk quota setting with the specified volume. See the QuotaSetting alias for additional details.

VolumeUserQuota   Associates a per user storage setting with the specified volume. See the DiskQuota alias for additional information.

WMISet   Manages the WMI settings for the target system. You'll use properties to change the writeable settings. For example, if you wanted to change the maximum log file size to 64 KB, you would type **WMIC WMISet SET MaxLogFileSize=65536** and press Enter.

Using Maintenance Commands and Utilities

Maintaining your server is a big part of working with Windows. You'll perform many types of performance, but some maintenance tasks occur more often than others do. For example, you'll find that you need to start and stop services to perform certain tasks, so knowing how to start and stop services at the command line is essential. The following sections don't describe every maintenance command, but you'll find most of the common maintenance commands (those that you'll use regularly) in these sections.

Controlling Services with the SC Command

The Service Control (SC) command helps you control services on your machine. The control is at a low level. Although you can start, stop, pause, and continue services using other utilities, this utility lets you perform additional tasks, such as query the service for detailed status information, send it a change of configuration message, or enumerate the services that the target service depends on. This utility uses the following syntax:

```
sc [\\server] [command] [service name] [<option1> [<option2>...]]
```

The following list describes each of the command line arguments.

\\server   Specifies the server that runs the service you want to manage. The default assumes that you want to use the local machine.

command   Specifies the command you want to execute. For example, if you want to stop a service, you issue the stop command. Some commands can work alone or with a service name. To obtain a list of all of the services installed on a machine, type **SC Query** and press Enter at the command line.

service_name   Specifies the name of the service that you want to manage. This name isn't the same as the name that you see displayed in the Services console located in the Administrative Tools folder of the Control Panel. The name also isn't the executable name for the service. This entry is the name that the service used for registration purposes. For example, to access the Event Log, you would use the eventlog service. However, the display name for this service is Event Log and the executable name is Services.EXE. Use the SC Query command to obtain a list of registered service names on the target system.

option1 [option2...]   Provides additional information required by some commands.

The focus of this section is the command that you issue to a service. The command determines what tasks the service performs. For example, when you issue a stop command, the service stops whatever it's doing at the time. The following list describes the common commands for all services. Theoretically, a vendor could (and many do) introduce custom commands for a particular service. You'll need to refer to the vendor documentation to discover these custom commands.

query   Queries the status of a service or enumerates the services installed on the computer. The output from this command includes service name, type, state, Win32 exit code, service exit code, checkpoint, and wait hint. You don't need to provide a service name with this command. You can filter the output of this command by adding optional information described in the following list (make sure you include the space between the equals sign (=) and the setting).

   type={driver | service | all}   Specifies the kind of service to query. The default setting is a service.

   state={inactive | all}   Defines the state of the service to enumerate. The default setting is active.

   bufsize=*size*   Defines the size of the enumeration buffer in bytes. The default size is 4,096 bytes.

   ri=*index*   Specifies the resume index at which to begin the enumeration. This number starts the enumeration at a location other than the first entry. The default setting is 0.

   group=*group*   Defines which service groups to enumerate. The default setting is all groups.

queryex   Queries the extended status of a service or enumerates the services installed on the computer. You can filter the output of this command by adding optional information as explained for the query command. The output from this command includes service name, type, state, Win32 exit code, service exit code, checkpoint, wait hint, PID, and flags. You don't need to provide a service name with this command.

start   Starts the specified service.

pause   Pauses the specified service. Pausing the service differs from stopping it. When you stop a service, the service returns all resources to the operating system and removes itself from memory. Pausing the service lets it maintain status information and the service remains in memory.

interrogate   Queries the status of a specific service. The output from this command includes service name, type, state, Win32 exit code, service exit code, checkpoint, and wait hint.

continue   Restarts the service after a pause. You can't issue this command for a stopped service; use the start command instead.

stop   Stops the requested service. Stopping the service differs from pausing it. When you stop a service, the service returns all resources to the operating system and removes itself from memory. Pausing the service lets it maintain status information and the service remains in memory.

config   Changes the service configuration. You must specify these changes using the options in the following list. Make sure you include the space between the equals sign (=) and the value.

   type={own | share | interact | kernel | filesys | rec | adapt}   Defines the service type. Change this setting only if the vendor requests that you do so.

   start={boot | system | auto | demand | disabled}   Defines the method the system uses to start the service. The auto option always starts the service when the system starts, while the disabled option prevents the service from ever starting.

error={normal | severe | critical | ignore}   Defines the method used to report service errors in the event log. Using the ignore option means that the system never reports errors for the service.

binPath=*BinaryPathName*   Specifies the location of the service's executable on the hard drive.

group=*LoadOrderGroup*   Specifies the service's group, which defines the order in which the service loads, among other things.

tag={yes | no}   Specifies whether the system obtains a tag identifier from the CreateService() function call. The system only uses tag identifiers for the boot-start and system-start drivers.

depend=*Dependencies*   Defines one or more dependencies for this service to start. The requested service must start before this service can start. Separate each of the dependencies with a slash (/).

obj=*AccountName* | *ObjectName*   Specifies an account name or a driver object name to use to run the service. This entry defines the security for the service. The default setting is the LocalSystem driver object.

DisplayName=*display_name*   Defines the name that the user sees in the Services console.

password=*password*   Specifies a password the service must use to log into the system. You don't need to provide a password for the LocalSystem driver object.

description   Changes the description of a service.

failure   Specifies the action the system should take in case of a service failure. You specify these actions using the following options.

reset=*interval*   Defines the length of time in seconds that the service must wait before the system can reset the failure count to 0. You may specify a value of INFINITE to keep the failure count from ever resetting. Use this setting with the actions option.

reboot=*message*   Defines the message to broadcast before rebooting the system due to a failure.

command=*command*   Defines the command you want to run after a failure.

actions={run | reboot | restart}/delay   Specifies an action to take, along with the delay time, for executing the action in milliseconds. For example, run/5000 would attempt to run the service again after 5,000 milliseconds. You must also specify a reset interval when using an action.

failureflag [*ServiceName*] [*Flag*]   Modifies the failure flag to a new value. You can use this command to set special failure flags that define the special circumstances of a failure (such as environmental factors). The default value of 0 tells the Service Control Manager (SCM) to use the configured failure actions on the service only when the service terminates in a state other than SERVICE_STOPPED. When you set this value to 1, the SCM performs the configuration failure actions whenever the service terminates with an exit code other than 0 (in addition to the actions performed with a flag value of 0). The system ignores this flag when the service lacks configured failure actions.

sidtype [*ServiceName*] [{Unrestricted | Restricted | None}]   Changes the service Security Identifier (SID) type of the service. This change affects the service's ability to interact with the system by increasing or decreasing its privileges. In all three cases, the setting affects the content of the process token. When you specify a value of `Unrestricted`, the service's SID appears as part of the process token without restrictions. You can only use this level for Win32 user mode services. The `Restricted` setting also places the service's SID in the process token, but as a restricted token. You can learn more about restricted tokens at `http://msdn2.microsoft .com/en-us/library/aa379316.aspx`. Finally, the `None` setting doesn't add the service's SID to the process token.

privs [*ServiceName*] [*Privileges*]   Modifies the privileges required to run the service. This command can keep unwary users from starting the service (even accidentally or through an application). You can see a listing of common privilege constants at `http://msdn2.microsoft .com/en-us/library/aa375728.aspx`.

qc   Queries the specified service for configuration information. The output from this command includes service name, type, start type, error control, binary path name, load order group, tag, display name, dependencies, and service start name.

qdescription [*BufferSize*]   Queries the description for a service. You can specify an optional buffer size argument for this command that defines the size of the buffer you've set aside for the description. When the buffer is too small, the utility returns a value that tells you the minimum buffer size.

qfailure [*BufferSize*]   Queries the actions taken by a service when a failure occurs. You can specify an optional buffer size argument for this command that defines the size of the buffer you've set aside for the description. When the buffer is too small, the utility returns a value that tells you the minimum buffer size.

qfailureflag [*ServiceName*]   Queries the failure actions flag of the service. You use this option for diagnostic purposes.

qsidtype [*ServiceName*]   Queries the service's SID type.

qprivs [*ServiceName*] [*BufferSize*]   Queries the privileges required to run the service. You can see a listing of common privilege constants at `http://msdn2.microsoft.com/en-us/ library/aa375728.aspx`.

delete   Removes a service from the registry, which means that the system won't activate it and that the service won't appear in the Services console.

create *ServiceName* binPath= *Path*   Creates a service by querying the executable and adding any required entries to the registry. The creation process requires that you supply a service name and the path to the binary (executable) file. In addition, you can provide configuration options for the service as defined in the following list. Make sure you include the space between the equals sign (=) and the value.

    type={own | share | interact | kernel | filesys | rec | adapt}   Defines the service type. Change this setting only if the vendor requests that you do so.

    start={boot | system | auto | demand | disabled}   Defines the method the system uses to the start the service. The auto option always starts the service when the system starts, while the disabled option prevents the service from ever starting.

    error={normal | severe | critical | ignore}   Defines the method used to report service errors in the event log. Using the ignore option means that the system never reports errors for the service.

binPath=*BinaryPathName* Specifies the location of the service's executable on the hard drive.

group=*LoadOrderGroup* Specifies the service's group, which defines the order in which the service loads, among other things.

tag={yes | no} Specifies whether the system obtains a tag identifier from the `CreateService()` function call. The system only uses tag identifiers for the boot-start and system-start drivers.

depend=*Dependencies* Defines one or more dependencies for this service to start. The requested service must start before this service can start. Separate each of the dependencies with a slash (/).

obj={*AccountName* | *ObjectName*} Specifies an account name or a driver object name to use to run the service. This entry defines the security for the service. The default setting is the LocalSystem driver object.

DisplayName=*display_name* Defines the name that the user sees in the Services console.

password=*password* Specifies a password the service must use to log into the system. You don't need to provide a password for the LocalSystem driver object.

control *Value* Sends a control code to a service. Control codes generally ask the service to perform a task. The control code can be a standard value such as `paramchange`, `netbindadd`, `netbindremove`, `netbindenable`, or `netbinddisable`. Many services also provide custom control codes. You must obtain these custom codes from the vendor documentation.

sdshow Displays the security descriptor for a service in Security Descriptor Definition Language (SDDL) format. You can learn more about SDDL at `http://msdn2.microsoft.com/en-us/library/aa379567.aspx`.

sdset *SD* Sets the service's security descriptor. You must provide the security descriptor in SDDL format. You can learn more about SDDL at `http://msdn2.microsoft.com/en-us/library/aa379567.aspx`.

showsid *Name* Displays the SID string associated with a service based on the arbitrary name you provide as input. The name can be of an existing service or a service that doesn't exist on the local machine. The resulting string lets you query the security of a service.

GetDisplayName *KeyName* [*BufferSize*] Obtains the display name (the one shown in the Services console) for a service based on its key name. For example, when you enter a key name of eventlog, you receive a display name of Event Log. You can specify an optional buffer size argument for this command that defines the size of the buffer you've set aside for the description. When the buffer is too small, the utility returns a value that tells you the minimum buffer size.

GetKeyName "*DisplayName*" [*BufferSize*] Obtains the key name (the one used for most SC utility commands) for a service based on its display name. For example, when you enter a display name of Event Log, the utility returns a key name of event log. Make sure you enclose the display name in quotes. You can specify an optional buffer size argument for this command that defines the size of the buffer you've set aside for the description. When the buffer is too small, the utility returns a value that tells you the minimum buffer size.

EnumDepend [*BufferSize*]   Enumerates the dependencies (the list of services that must be running before the service can start) for a service. You can specify an optional buffer size argument for this command that defines the size of the buffer you've set aside for the description. When the buffer is too small, the utility returns a value that tells you the minimum buffer size.

The SC utility has three special commands that affect the services as a whole, so they don't require a service name. The following list describes the three commands.

boot {ok | bad}   Determines whether the system saves the last boot information into the last-known-good boot configuration.

Lock   Locks the SCManager database. The command line displays a prompt that shows that the system has locked the database. The database remains locked until you press **u** to remove the lock.

QueryLock   Returns the locked status of the SCManager database.

Shutting Down the System with the ShutDown Command

The ShutDown command lets you shut down a system in a controlled manner. In addition, the utility helps you document the reason for the shutdown and can even provide the user with a specific level of control over the shutdown process. You can even shut down other machines on the network, such as after the completion of an application installation. This utility uses the following syntax:

```
shutdown [/i | /l | /s | /r | /g | /a] [/f] [/m \\computername] [/t xx]
    [/c "comment"] [/d [u][p:]xx:yy]
shutdown [/i | /l | /s | /r | /g | /a | /p | /h | /e] [/f] [/m
    \\ComputerName] [/t XXX] [/d [p:] XX:YY/c"Comment"]
```

The first version is for Windows XP users, while the second is for Windows 2003 users. The following list describes each of the command line arguments.

/i   Displays the GUI version of the utility. You must supply this command line switch as the first option.

/l   Logs off, rather than rebooting the system. You can't use this command line switch with the -m switch.

/s   Shuts down the computer. In most cases, this means turning off the computer.

/r   Shuts down and restarts the computer. This command line switch performs a soft boot of the system, which is all you need to ensure application changes take place as intended.

/g   Shuts down and restarts the computer. After the system reboots, the operating system automatically restarts any registered applications.

/a   Aborts the system shutdown. Although you can stop a pending shutdown, it's usually difficult to stop a shutdown that's already in progress.

/m *computername*   Specifies a remote computer to shut down, restart, or abort. You must have the rights required to perform these actions on the remote computer.

/t *xx*   Specifies a timeout to perform the shutdown. The system defaults to a value of 30 seconds.

/c "*comment*"   Provides a shutdown comment for the event log that details why you shut the system down. The comment can contain a maximum of 127 characters. You must use this command line switch with the -d switch. Always place the comment in quotes.

/f   Forces any running applications to close without warning. Normally, the system warns the user of the shutdown and provides time for the user to react. Use this option with extreme caution because it can result in data loss.

/d [u][p]:*xx:yy*   Specifies a reason for the shutdown. This reason appears as part of the event log entry. The u argument defines the shutdown as user related. If you don't provide the u argument, the system assumes that the shutdown somehow relates to a system need. The p argument defines the shutdown as planned. If you don't provide the p argument, the system assumes the shutdown was unplanned—part of an emergency. The p argument is important because it affects whether the ShutDown utility is successful. If you provide the p argument and then use an unplanned reason code, the utility registers an error. Likewise, if you omit the p argument and use a planned reason code, the utility registers an error. The xx argument is the major reason code. You may use any value between 0 and 255. The yy argument is the minor reason code. You may use any value between 0 and 65,535. Unfortunately, Microsoft doesn't document reason codes for this utility. However, your reason codes should match those of System Shutdown Reason Codes Web page at `http://msdn2.microsoft.com/en-us/library/aa376885.aspx`. If you want to use some other reason for shutting down a system, you must register the reason in the registry so the ShutDown utility can provide the correct text within the registry entry.

/p   Turns off a local computer (you can't use this command line switch with a remote system) without a timeout period of user warning. You can only use this command line switch with the /d command line switch. If your computer doesn't support power off functionality, the system will shut down, but the computer will remain running.

/h   Places the computer in the hibernation state when you have hibernation enabled. You can only use this command line switch with the /f switch. Since hibernation isn't the same as shutting down the computer, the utility doesn't allow you to provide a reason code using the /d command line switch or a comment using the /c command line switch.

/e   Enables you to document the reason for an unexpected shutdown on the target computer. You must be part of the administrators group to document an unexpected shutdown.

TIP   Many users complain about the amount of time spent waiting for Windows to shut down. You can greatly improve the shutdown speed by creating a new shortcut and adding this entry to the Target field, `%windir%\System32\shutdown.exe  -s  -t  0`. Set the Start In field to `%windir%` as well. Using this command line doesn't affect the shutdown in any way whatsoever. You won't lose data or anything of that nature. The only change is that Windows won't wait for applications to end before it begins the shutdown process. Since the default wait period is 30 seconds (even if the computer isn't doing anything), you can save 30 seconds by using this technique.

Replicating COM+ Applications with the COMRepl Utility

Use the COMRepl utility to replicate all of the COM+ applications on the current machine to one or more remote machines. This utility doesn't replicate system applications, COM+ utilities, COM+ QC Dead Letter Queue Listener, IIS in-process applications, IIS utilities, or all applications created for isolated or pooled virtual roots. You won't find this utility in the normal `\Windows\System32` directory. To add this command to the path, use the `path = %PATH%;%windir%\system32\Com` set command. This utility uses the following syntax:

```
COMREPL <source> <targetList> [/n [/v]]
```

The following list describes each of the command line arguments.

source   Specifies the name of the source computer.

targetList   Specifies the names of the target computers. Separate each target computer with a space.

/n   Performs the replication without displaying any confirmation prompts.

/v   Echoes the log output to the console so that you can see every event that occurs during replication.

Managing Type Libraries with the RegTLib Utility

Use the RegTLib utility to register a type library on your system. You won't find this utility in the normal `\Windows\System32` directory. To add this command to the path, use the `path = %PATH%;%windir%\system32\URTTemp` set command. Vista doesn't support this utility and there isn't any replacement provided. This utility uses the following syntax (the first form registers a type library; the second form unregisters a type library):

```
RegTLib [-q] Library
RegTLib [-q] -u Library
```

The following list describes each of the command line arguments.

-q   Performs a quiet registration or unregistration of a type library. The user doesn't see any prompts.

Library   Specifies the drive, path (absolute or relative), and filename of the type library you want to register.

-u   Unregisters the type library by removing its entries from the registry.

Saving and Restoring System Restore Data with the SRDiag Utility

The System Restore Diagnostic (SRDiag) utility helps you recover from system damage. The system uses CAB files to store the information required to restore the system. You supply this CAB file as input to the utility, and the utility then performs a diagnostic to restore the system. You won't find this utility in the normal `\Windows\System32` directory. To add this command to the path, use the `path = %PATH%;%windir%\system32\Restore` set command. This utility uses the following syntax:

```
SRDiag [/CabName: cab] [/CabLoc:"path"]
```

The following list describes each of the command line arguments.

/CabName:cab   Specifies the full name of the CAB file that you wish to use for system restoration. When you don't supply a CAB file as input, the system creates a CAB file that uses the following format: `<machine_name>_mmddyy_hhss.cab`. This file appears in whatever directory you choose to use for restoration file storage.

/CabLoc:"*path*"   Specifies the location of the CAB file on disk. The path must include a final backslash (\). The default setting is the current directory.

Performing Web-Based Enterprise Management Tasks

Microsoft has worked hard to introduce more techniques for remote management of systems on large networks, including use of the Internet. Web-Based Enterprise Management (WBEM) is one of several attempts to make Windows friendlier for large organizations. You'll find that WBEM is the term that many vendors use for this kind of management and there are some de facto standards for implementing it.

WMI is Microsoft's technology for implementing WBEM on Windows. Consequently, you'll often see the two terms used almost interchangeably in the Microsoft documentation. The Windows Management Instrumentation service provides the server functionality for working with WMI on a computer system. Although the following sections tell you about the command line utilities that you can use to work with both WBEM and WMI, they don't provide you with administration information for these technologies. You'll find a good overview of both WBEM and WMI on the Microsoft Web site at http://www.microsoft.com/whdc/system/pnppwr/wmi/WMI-intro.mspx. If you must maintain older systems and want to use the WMI functionality described in this chapter, make sure you download the update at http://www.microsoft.com/downloads/details .aspx?displaylang=en&FamilyID=AFE41F46-E213-4CBF-9C5B-FBF236E0E875.

TIP   One of the newer graphical utilities that Microsoft has introduced to make working with WMI easier is the Windows Management Instrumentation Tester. Microsoft also calls this utility Web-Based Enterprise Management Test in some literature. (Realizing the confusion they were causing, some Microsoft documentation actually uses both terms now.) You can get an overview of this utility, along with usage instructions, at http://technet2.microsoft.com/ windowsserver/en/library/9d99ec04-e386-4120-8dd0-47d4e2cccbdd1033.mspx.

ADMINISTERING MANAGED OBJECT FORMAT FILES WITH THE MOFCOMP UTILITY

The Managed Object Format (MOF) Compiler (MOFComp) utility parses files that contain WMI scripting information and adds the result to the WMI repository where you can access the classes. You can see an example of a script that relies on MOF to add Simple Network Management Protocol (SNMP) functionality to a computer system at http://msdn2.microsoft.com/en-us/library/ aa393621.aspx. This utility uses the following syntax:

```
mofcomp [-check] [-N:<Path>] [-class:updateonly|-class:createonly]
    [-instance:updateonly|-instance:createonly] [-B:<filename>]
    [-P:<Password>] [-U:<UserName>] [-A:<Authority>] [-WMI] [-AUTORECOVER]
    [-MOF:<path>] [-MFL:<path>] [-AMENDMENT:<Locale>]
    [-ER:<ResourceName>] [-L:<ResourceLocale>] <MOF filename>
```

The following list describes each of the command line arguments.

-check   Performs a syntax check of the script only.

-N:*path*   Loads the result into the specified namespace.

-class:updateonly   Performs class updates, rather than creating a new class.

-class:safeupdate   Performs a class update only when there aren't any conflicts.

-class:forceupdate Forces the system to update the class by resolving conflicts if possible.

-class:createonly Creates new classes only; the compiler won't update existing classes.

-instance:updateonly Performs instance updates, rather than creating new instances.

-instance:createonly Creates new instances only; the compiler won't update existing instances.

-U:*UserName* Specifies the username.

-P:*Password* Specifies the user password.

-A:*Authority* Specifies the authority for verifying the account information. For example, you might specify a domain using NTLMDOMAIN:Domain, where Domain is the domain name of the system.

-B:*filename* Creates a MOF file as output, rather than adding the compiled result to the database.

-WMI Performs the Windows Driver Model (WDM) checks on the results. You must use the -B command line switch with this switch.

-AUTORECOVER Adds MOF to the list of files compiled during a database recovery.

-Amendment:*LOCALE* Divides the MOF into language-neutral and language-specific versions.

-MOF:*path* Specifies the name of the language-neutral output.

-MFL:*path* Specifies the name of the language-specific output.

-ER:*ResourceName* Extracts a binary MOF from the named resource.

-L:*ResourceLocale* Specifies the number of the locale you want to extract from a named resource when using the -ER switch.

Interacting with the WBEM Server with the WinMgmt Utility

The WinMgmt utility is a special application for interacting with the Windows Management Instrumentation service. It provides better management than the SC utility because it addresses specific WMI requirements. This utility uses the following syntax:

```
Winmgmt [/exe] [/kill] [/regserver] [/unregserver] [/backup <filename>]
    [/restore <filename><mode>] [/resyncperf <winmgmt service process
    id>] [/clearadap]
```

The following list describes each of the command line arguments.

/exe Runs WinMgmt.EXE as an application, rather than as a service. The Windows Management Instrumentation entry won't appear in the Services console. The main reason to use this command line switch is to allow debugging of providers using the standard Microsoft debuggers. When you run WinMgmt.EXE as an application, it runs in the user's security context. Normally, you should run this program as a service so that it receives the proper rights.

/kill Terminates all instances of WinMgmt.EXE on the local system including any processes started as a service by the Service Control Manager. You must have administrative rights to use this command line switch.

/regserver Registers the Windows Management Instrumentation service by adding entries to the registry.

/unregserver   Removes the registry entries for the Windows Management Instrumentation service. This act makes the service unavailable for use, which can result in a loss of operating system functionality.

/backup *filename*   Backs up the WMI repository to the specified filename. The filename argument can contain a drive and path specification, along with the actual backup filename. The backup process requires a write lock on the repository, which means that the operating system suspends any write operations to the repository until the backup process completes.

/restore *filename mode*   Restores the WMI repository from the specified file. The filename argument can contain a drive and path specification, along with the actual backup filename. The utility deletes the existing repository when you restore a backup. It writes the specified backup file to the automatic backup file, and then connects to WMI to perform the restoration. The restoration process requires exclusive access to the repository, which means that the utility disconnects any existing clients from WMI before it begins the restoration process. You must set the mode argument to 1 to force user disconnection and begin the restoration or 0 to restore only when there aren't any users connected. Newer versions of Windows ignore the mode argument and always disconnect users to perform the restoration.

/resyncperf *winmgmt_service_process_id*   Invokes the WMI AutoDiscovery / AutoPurge (ADAP) mechanism.

/clearadap   Removes all of the ADAP information from the registry. This effectively resets the state of each performance library. The ADAP utility stores state information about the system performance libraries in the registry.

Tracing WinSxs Behavior with the SxsTrace Utility

The SxSTrace utility helps you trace side-by-side execution on versions of Windows, Vista and above. The side-by-side execution feature lets you maintain multiple versions of DLLs. Each application can use its own DLL to perform tasks, which means you'll encounter fewer problems. However, the WinSxS folder can eventually become full of DLLs that you don't use, which is why tracing application DLL use is so helpful. This utility uses the following syntax:

```
SxSTrace Trace -logfile:FileName [-nostop]
SxSTrace Parse -logfile:FileName -outfile:ParsedFile
    [-filter:AppName]]
SxSTrace StopTrace
```

The following list describes each of the command line arguments.

Trace   Begins the trace of side-by-side DLL usage on the system.

Parse   Transforms the log file created during a trace into output. The standard method is to output the data to a file. You can then supply the name of a filter application to view the data.

StopTrace   Stops the current trace and closes the log file.

-logfile:*FileName*   Defines the name of the file to use for logging purposes.

-nostop   Specifies that the utility shouldn't prompt you before it stops a trace. Normally, the utility asks whether you're sure that you want to stop a trace.

-outfile:*ParsedFile*   Defines the name of an output file that contains the translated log file data.

-filter:*AppName*   Specifies the name of an application to filter the data. The data is in a specific text format, which makes it relatively easy to parse by third-party applications.

Managing Activation with SLMGR

The Windows Software License Manager (SLMGR) tool is one of those tools that you'll use a few times, but you must use it at least once to activate your copy of Windows. Otherwise, you'll find that your copy becomes useless at some point. You can also use this utility to install a product key, display the activation information (in case a support person needs it), and reset the licensing status of the system. This script uses the following syntax:

```
CScript SLMGR.VBS [MachineName [User Password]] [<Option>]
```

The following list describes each of the command line arguments.

MachineName   Specifies the name of a remote system. The default setting performs tasks on the local system. Make sure the remote system is accessible to the local system. You only need to provide the machine name—this input isn't in Universal Naming Convention (UNC) format.

User   Specifies the name of the user making the changes. Use the user account name as it appears on the remote system.

Password   Specifies the user password for the remote system.

-ipk *Product_Key*   Installs the specified product key. The product key is the number provided as part of the installation CD. Make sure you type this number precisely, including the dashes between number groups, just as you would when installing the product.

-ato   Activates your copy of Windows. You only need to use this command line switch once. Type **CScript SLMGR.VBS -ato** and press Enter to activate the local machine. If you attempt to use this command more than once, the script will display an error message telling you that the system is already activated.

-dli [*Activation_ID* | All]   Displays standard licensing information including the license name, description, partial product key, and the current licensing status. The default setting displays the licensing information for the currently installed license. You may also display the licensing information for a particular activation identifier or display the licensing information for all possible activation identifiers (even those not currently licensed for the machine).

-dlv [*Activation_ID* | All]   Displays detailed licensing information for the machine as shown in Figure 3.4. The default setting displays the licensing information for the currently installed license. You may also display the licensing information for a particular activation identifier or display the licensing information for all possible activation identifiers (even those not currently licensed for the machine).

-xpr   Displays the expiration date for the current license. If you have used the -ato command line switch to activate the machine, the output of this command displays "The machine is permanently activated."

-cpky   Clears the product key from the registry, which means that no one will be able to obtain your product key by hacking the registry. Of course, the product key also becomes unavailable for your use and you'll have to refer to the product key on the installation CD when asked.

-ilc *License_File*   Installs the specified license file.

-rilc   Reinstalls the license files that you previously installed using the -ilc command line switch.

-rearm   Resets the licensing state of the machine. Many people have used this command line switch to extend the Windows evaluation period. The command line switch normally works a fixed number of times.

FIGURE 3.4
Obtain complete
activation information
for your server using
the –dlv command
line switch.

-upk   Uninstalls the product key. This command line switch differs from the –cpky in that the product is no longer licensed. You'd need to install a new product key and activate Windows again after using this command line switch.

-dti   Displays the installation ID for offline activation.

-atp *Confirmation_ID*   Activates Windows using the confirmation identifier that you receive from the Microsoft support staff after calling to activate using the telephone method. Make sure you type the confirmation identifier precisely as supplied by Microsoft or your copy of Windows won't activate. It's normally easier and less error prone to activate your copy of Windows using the –ato command line switch.

Managing Windows in a New Way

This chapter has gotten you started performing essential maintenance tasks. The tasks actually fall into three categories: application installation, security, and system maintenance. The material in this chapter is purposely simple—it helps you get started with the essentials and doesn't bog you down in complexities that you need to know later. The focus of this chapter is to help you get started with the tasks you'll perform daily. This chapter helps you build these skills:

- Install applications

- Perform maintenance

- Update the server

- Create LNK files

- Set security

- Use the WMIC command to configure the server

- Use maintenance commands and utilities

- Activate your copy of Windows

Now that you have some idea of what tasks you'll need to perform, it's time to continue configuring your server. Of course, you'll start by adding the users who will use the server and adding them to groups as you did for your own account in the "Configuring the Server for Initial Use" section of Chapter 1. After you perform this task, consider adding the applications you need and configuring them. Make special note of any applications that present problematic installation. If you have an available Internet connection, update your server. Next, make sure you add any required additional security for applications, files, and folders. Use the WMIC command to examine your server and perform any additional required installation. Begin working with the commands and utilities you'll use to maintain your server. Finally, look through the list of scripts in this chapter and begin using them to help you maintain your server.

The configuration information in this chapter is helpful, but Microsoft has removed so many GUI utilities that you'll find you need to modify the registry directory to accomplish some tasks. For example, when you want to modify the server environment or change the color of the GUI elements that still exist, you must perform the task in the registry. Chapter 4 tells you about the essential registry hacks you need to use to configure your server completely. The hacks in Chapter 4 are for general use, the book doesn't discuss specific applications because it's impossible to discuss them all (or even a small subset that will satisfy anyone). Even so, you'll need these hacks at some point as you manage your Server Core setup.

Chapter 4

Essential Registry Hacks

It was actually possible to work with other versions of Windows without ever touching the registry directly—at least it was for the average user. Even administrators rarely touched the registry and did so with the proper regard for its delicacy. Working with Server Core means not having access through the Graphical User Interface (GUI) to many features that you had in the past. Now you must perform certain tasks from the client through consoles, using the Remote Desktop, through shares, and even using the registry directly. In fact, some tasks, such as reconfiguring the desktop, require that you use the Registry Editor, rather than make the change using a GUI. For this reason, you must have some exposure to the registry in order to work with Server Core competently.

This book can't provide you with a blow-by-blow description of the entire registry. The registry is a huge hierarchical database that contains the settings for your hardware, all of the users that work with the machine, and most of the applications that you've installed. In short, it contains many settings that are common to both Server Core and other versions of Windows. The purpose of this chapter is to acquaint you with some of the registry settings that you've probably always set using the GUI and may not even know exist in the registry. In other words, this chapter covers some ground that you may not have even considered in the past.

NOTE There are many sources of information for the registry online and you'll probably want to have a book or two on the topic as well.

This chapter looks at the registry in two ways. First, you'll discover the various utilities that Microsoft provides for altering the registry. Not only will you see the familiar RegEdit utility (and its relatively unknown command line component), you'll discover the new SCRegEdit utility provided with Server Core. Of course, you'll want to know about scripting with the RegIni utility as well. Second, you'll discover some settings that you commonly change using the GUI, but must make by altering the registry directly in Server Core. Some of these settings may look familiar, but the purpose is to ensure that you know where to change a common setting when you need to. This chapter won't discuss application or other settings that you'd normally read about in a book dedicated to the registry.

In this chapter, you'll learn how to do the following:

◆ Start and configure both RegEdit and SCRegEdit

◆ Script registry entries using RegIni

◆ Configure the console

◆ Configure the environment

◆ Manage hardware settings

◆ Manage software settings

Starting and Configuring the Registry Editor

As previously mentioned, the registry is a huge hierarchical database and like most databases, you need tools to modify it. Applications modify portions of the registry all of the time. For example, when you save your user settings, they very often appear in the registry and the application makes the appropriate changes. However, you also need generic tools to work with the registry. Although you'll find third-party tools on the market to work with the entire registry, you also have access to two tools in Windows to perform the work.

The first tool is RegEdit, which provides both a command line interface and a GUI. Interestingly enough, the RegEdit GUI works in Server Core so you can use either interface or both as needed.

The second tool is SCRegEdit and it's new for Windows 2008. This tool provides only a command line interface that lets you modify registry entries as needed without opening a registry editor. You've already seen a use for this tool in the "Configuring the Server for Initial Use" section of Chapter 1. It appears again in the "Performing Server Updates" section of Chapter 3. The following sections describe both tools.

Working with the RegEdit Utility GUI

You'll commonly use the Registry Editor (RegEdit.EXE) utility in GUI mode. To start this utility in GUI mode, simply type **RegEdit** and press Enter. You'll see an initial display like the one shown in Figure 4.1. The left pane shows hives and keys, while the right pane shows values associated with the hives and keys that you select in the left pane. Anyone who's worked with the registry already knows about hives, keys, and values.

FIGURE 4.1
The /CLI command line switch is useful because it provides information on performing common tasks.

NOTE A *hive* is a major data storage unit—think of it as an equivalent of a table within a database because the purpose is the same. *Keys* are entries within the hive—you can view them as individual records within the database. *Values* contain the actual registry information—you can view them as fields. If you don't already know these three terms, then you don't have enough knowledge to begin working with the registry and should probably not use the information in this chapter until you do have a good working knowledge of the registry. Making changes to the registry without the required registry knowledge will almost certainly damage the database at some point and could even cause Server Core to stop working.

This chapter only provides a refresher course for the GUI portion of the RegEdit utility. It assumes that you've already worked with RegEdit and may simply need to obtain quick information on performing a particular task. Table 4.1 contains a listing of common tasks and a short description of how to perform them.

TABLE 4.1:   Common RegEdit Tasks

TASK	DESCRIPTION
Locating a key, value name, or data.	Press Ctrl+F. The Registry Editor displays a Find dialog box. Type the information you want to find in the Find What field. Choose any or all of the Look At options. Check Match Whole Strings Only when you want to locate a particular piece of information. Click OK. The Registry Editor looks for the information you specified and highlights it as appropriate.
Finding a key, value name, or data again.	Press F3.
Setting a bookmark for a particular registry entry.	Highlight the location you want to bookmark in the registry. Choose Favorites ➤ Add to Favorites. You'll see an Add to Favorites dialog box. Type a name for the location and click OK. The Registry Editor adds this location and its name to the Favorites menu so you can locate the entry quickly later.
Change a value.	Double-click the entry in the right pane. The Registry Editor displays the correct editor to modify the value. Click OK when you've finished editing the value.
Add a key.	Right-click the parent that will hold the new key and choose New ➤ Key from the context menu. You'll see a new key. Type the key name and press Enter.
Add a value.	Right-click the key that will hold the new value and choose one of the value options from the New menu on the context menu. The value options include String Value, Binary Value, DWORD (32-bit) Value, QWORD (64-bit) Value, Multi-String Value, and Expandable String Value. The Registry Editor displays the correct editor to modify the value. Click OK when you've finished editing the value.
Save a registry branch to disk.	Right-click the starting location for the area of the registry that you want to save in the left pane and choose Export from the context menu. You'll see an Export Registry File dialog box. Type a name for the file that will hold the registry information in the File Name field and click OK. If you want to save the entire registry, right-click the Computer entry.
Import existing registry data from disk.	Choose File ➤ Import. You'll see an Import Registry File dialog box. Locate the registry file you want to import and click OK. When the Registry Editor completes the process, it displays a success message.
Loading a hive from another location.	Select either the HKEY_LOCAL_MACHINE or HKEY_USERS hive. Choose File ➤ Load Hive. You'll see a Load Hive dialog box. Locate the hive file that you want to load and click OK. The Registry Editor asks which key to load. Type the name of one of the keys within the hive when you want to load a particular key and press Enter. The Registry Editor displays the new hive in the left pane.
Removing an unneeded hive.	Select the hive that you no longer need to modify in the left pane. Choose File ➤ Unload Hive. The Registry Editor removes the hive from the left pane.

TABLE 4.1:   Common RegEdit Tasks *(CONTINUED)*

TASK	DESCRIPTION
Connecting to a remote system.	Choose File ➤ Connect Network Registry. You'll see a Select Computer dialog box. Type the name of the computer that will provide the connection and click OK. If you have permission to access the remote computer and the Remote Registry service is running on that computer, then the Registry Editor provides access to the other machine.
Disconnecting from a remote system.	Select the remote computer's entry in the left pane. Choose File ➤ Disconnect Network Registry. The Registry Editor terminates the connection to the remote computer.
Setting registry permissions.	Right-click the registry hive, key, or value you want to secure and choose Permissions from the context menu. You'll see a Permissions dialog box. Set the security features using the same techniques you use for a directory or file on the hard drive. Click OK to set the permission.
Removing an entry from the Favorites menu.	Choose Favorites ➤ Remove Favorite. You'll see a Remove Favorites dialog box. Choose the favorite you want to remove and click OK. If you want to remove multiple favorites, use the Ctrl+Click or Shift+Click methods you use in Windows Explorer to make multiple selections. Click OK. The Registry Editor removes the entries from the Favorites menu.

Working with the RegEdit Utility at the Command Line

The RegEdit utility is extremely powerful, yet it's one of the most undocumented utilities available on your machine. The Microsoft-recommended command line switches for the RegEdit utility appear in the Knowledge Base article at `http://support.microsoft.com/kb/q82821/`. The Knowledge Base article limits you to the /V and /S command line switches. The RegEdit utility itself doesn't display any helpful information when you try the /? command line switch. The Windows help file just barely discusses using the utility in GUI mode. In short, not only is this utility extremely powerful, you also won't get much help from Microsoft in using it. This utility uses the following syntax:

```
RegEdit [Filename] [-v] [-s] [-e RegFilename [Key]] [-l:Path] [-r:Path]
    [-c RegFilename] [-d Key]
```

The following list describes each of the command line arguments.

Filename   Specifies the name of a file that contains registry information. A registry file normally has a REG file extension. You can use a batch file to restore previously saved registry entries. For example, you might use this technique to set up a new system with user settings that you saved earlier.

-v   Opens RegEdit in advanced (verbose) mode. If you're familiar with the standard registry appearance, you'll suddenly notice some registry keys that RegEdit didn't display before. Use this option with care; all of the registry settings are editable if you have the proper permissions and the new settings tend to have dramatic system results.

-s   Suppresses any informational messages. You can use this feature to make a batch file installation work in the background.

-e *RegFilename* **[*Key*]**   Exports the requested key to the specified registry file. You can use this command line switch within a batch file to save user settings prior to a system change. For example, typing **Regedit -e Test.REG "HKEY_CURRENT_USER\Software\Nico Mak Computing"** and pressing Enter at the command prompt saves the WinZIP application settings to a file named Test.REG. Notice that you must enclose keys with spaces in the name in double quotes to ensure the RegEdit utility interprets them correctly.

-l:*Path*   Specifies the path for the System.DAT file to edit in the registry. The system database contains systemwide settings such as the HKEY_LOCAL_MACHINE hive. You can use this option to edit a registry on another machine as long as that machine allows remote editing. Use this option with the -c command line switch to create a new user based on an existing setup.

-r:*Path*   Specifies the path for the User.DAT file to edit in the registry. The user database appears in the individual user directories and contains the HKEY_CURRENT_USER hive. You can use this option to edit a registry on another machine as long as that machine allows remote editing. Use this option with the -c command line switch to create a new user based on an existing setup.

-c *RegFilename*   Creates a new registry based on the content of the registry entries in RegFilename. This command line switch is destructive. It completely destroys the System.DAT and User.DAT files for the affected user and reconstructs them using the contents of the supplied registry file. With this in mind, you must use this command line switch with a registry file containing a full registry backup. Otherwise, you'll leave the system in an unbootable state.

-d *Key*   Deletes the specified key. This switch appears to work fine on Windows 9*x* systems, but doesn't work with Windows NT and above. The command line switch deletes the requested key from the registry.

It's unfortunate that the -d command line switch doesn't work on newer systems. One way around this problem for Windows XP and above users is to create a negative key registry file and then register it as normal. To create such a file, open Notepad or any other text editor. Enter the following code into the file.

```
REGEDIT4
[-HKEY_CLASSES_ROOT\Test]
```

The negative key entry deletes a key named Test from the HKEY_CLASSES_ROOT hive. Try creating the HKEY_CLASSES_ROOT\Test key and then running this file. You'll find that RegEdit removes the key without any problem.

Saving and Restoring the Registry

Before you make any changes to the registry, you should always create a copy of the registry section you plan to change. The easiest way to perform this task is to use the GUI to export or import the entire registry hive or simply a registry branch. Use these steps to export your registry using the GUI method.

1. Type RegEdit. You'll see the Registry Editor window.

2. Select the My Computer entry.

3. Choose File ➢ Export to display the Export Registry File dialog box.

4. Verify that All is selected in the Export Range area.

5. Type a name for the export file in the File Name field.

6. Click Save. The Registry Editor will save a copy of the entire registry in the location you specified using the filename you provided.

You can accomplish this task at the command line by typing **RegEdit -e RegSave.REG** and pressing Enter. Notice that you don't supply the name of a hive or branch when you want to save the entire registry. When you want to restore the entire registry, simply type the name of the REG file. For example, if you type **RegSave.REG** and press Enter, then the system will display a dialog box asking if you want to add the information to the registry. Click Yes and the system will complete the task.

If you decide to save just a particular hive or branch of the registry, choose that hive or branch in the RegEdit utility. When you choose File ➢ Export, the Export Registry File dialog box will automatically choose the Selected Branch option for you and show the hive or branch you've selected. The –e command line switch description in the previous section shows how to perform this task at the command line. To restore this file, you simply type the name of the REG file and press Enter.

Working with the SCRegEdit Script

Microsoft has begun using a new scripting file format called the Windows Scripting File (WSF). The SCRegEdit.WSF file on your system is just one of many WSF files you should expect to see at some point. The purpose of this script is to make it easier to perform certain types of registry edits. The following sections detail the kinds of registry edits you can perform and the command line switches you use to perform the tasks.

NOTE The "Understanding the WSF" section of Chapter 6 tells you more about WSF files. You can't execute WSF scripts on older versions of Windows because the WScript and CScript utilities aren't set up to support them. You can discover how to create your own WSF scripts in the "Editing Script Files with Script Editor 2.1" section of Chapter 7.

SETTING AUTOMATIC UPDATES

This feature of the SCRegEdit script lets you set the automatic update feature for Windows without relying on the GUI. You've already seen this feature in action in the "Performing Server Updates" section of Chapter 3. This script feature uses the following syntax:

```
/AU [/v][1 | 4]
```

The following list describes each of the command line arguments:

/v Displays the current Automatic Update settings.

1 Disables the Automatic Update feature.

4 Enables the Automatic Update feature.

ENABLING TERMINAL SERVICES

Because Server Core lacks a GUI, it's often helpful to use Remote Desktop to administer the server. Using this approach lets you combine the benefits of both the command line and the GUI to get work done faster. You've already seen this feature in action in the "Configuring the Server for Initial Use" section of Chapter 1.

There are two forms of this particular script feature. The first form is for newer versions such as Vista. This form provides additional security not provided with previous versions of Windows, so it's more secure, but also limits connectivity. This script feature uses the following syntax:

```
/AR [/v][0 | 1]
```

The following list describes each of the command line arguments:

/v   Displays the Terminal Services connection settings.

0   Enables the Terminal Services connection.

1   Disables the Terminal Services connection.

The second form lets older versions of Windows make a connection to Server Core. Except for the amount of security provided, this form works just like the other form of this feature. When working in secure mode, Terminal Services relies on the Credential Security Support Provider (CredSSP) to provide security. Read more about CredSSP at http://blogs.msdn.com/windowsvistasecurity/archive/2006/08/25/724271.aspx. You may also want to review the group policy settings for this feature at https://msdn2.microsoft.com/en-us/library/bb204773.aspx. This script feature uses the following syntax:

```
/CS  [/v][0 | 1]
```

The following list describes each of the command line arguments:

/v   Displays the CredSSP setting.

0   Allows previous versions of Windows to connect to the server using non-CredSSP techniques.

1   Requires that all Terminal Services remote connections use CredSSP.

CONFIGURING THE IP SECURITY (IPSEC) MONITOR

You may need to provide remote management capability for the IPSec feature of Windows. Use this script feature to modify the remote management capability as needed. This script feature uses the following syntax:

NOTE   The Internet Engineering Task Force (IETF) created the Internet Protocol (IP) Security Protocol Working Group to look at the problems of IP security, such as the inability to encrypt data at the protocol level. It's currently working on a wide range of specifications that will ultimately result in more secure IP transactions. For example, IPSec is used in a variety of object-based group policy schemes. Windows currently uses IPSec for network-level authentication, data integrity checking, and encryption.

```
/IM [/v][0 | 1]
```

The following list describes each of the command line arguments:

/v   Displays the IPSec Monitoring setting.

0   Prevents remote management of IPSec Monitoring.

1   Allows remote management of IPSec Monitoring.

MANAGING DNS SERVICE PRIORITY AND WEIGHT

The Domain Name System (DNS) service is one of the more important features of Windows because it helps set the addresses for each node on the network. In fact, the services provided are standardized across all operating systems as part of RFC 2782 (see `http://www.faqs.org/rfcs/rfc2782 .html` for details). You'll normally use this script feature on domain controllers only. The DNS Service (SRV) records have both a priority and a weight. The priority affects the LdapSrvPriority registry setting (see `http://www.microsoft.com/technet/prodtechnol/windows2000serv/ reskit/regentry/55945.mspx` for details). When two DNS servers have the same priority setting, Windows relies on the weight setting to determine which server to use. You set the priority using the /DP command line switch. This script feature uses the following syntax:

```
/DP [/v][Value]
```

The following list describes each of the command line arguments:

/v Displays the current DNS SRV priority setting.

Value A value between 0 and 65,535 that defines the server priority. Microsoft recommends a value of 200.

As previously mentioned, when two DNS servers have the same priority, Windows relies on the weight value to determine which server to use. Use the /DW command line switch to modify the DNS SRV record weight. This setting affects the LdapSrvWeight registry setting. You can read more about the LdapSrvWeight setting at `http://www.microsoft.com/technet/prodtechnol/ windows2000serv/reskit/regentry/55945.mspx`. This script feature uses the following syntax:

```
/DW [/v][value]
```

The following list describes each of the command line arguments:

/v Displays the current DNS SRV weight setting.

Value A value between 0 and 65,535 that defines the server weight. Microsoft recommends a value of 50.

USING THE COMMAND LINE REFERENCE

The SCRegEdit script also includes a command line reference for performing some common command line tasks. This script feature uses the following syntax:

```
/CLI
```

When you type **CScript SCRegEdit.WSF /CLI** and press Enter, you'll see a display similar to the one shown in Figure 4.2. The command line information tells you how to perform common tasks using the current version of the server. Since Microsoft will likely keep this file updated as it provides revisions, you should refer to this information when it appears that an update has made an older configuration technique incomplete. Unfortunately, the information only tells you how to perform the most basic tasks and not in any particular order. The "Configuring the Server for Initial Use" section of Chapter 1 provides a procedure you can use in lieu of the help provided by Microsoft.

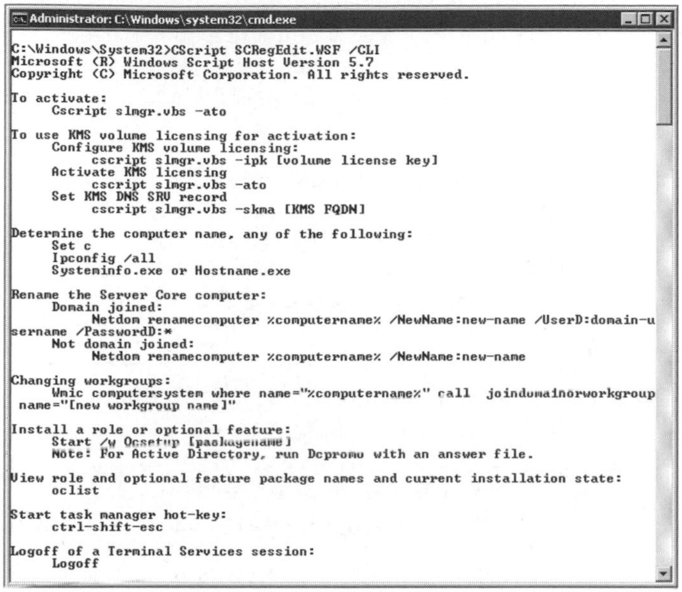

FIGURE 4.2

The /CLI command line switch is useful because it provides information on performing common tasks.

Scripting Registry Entries with the RegIni Utility

The RegIni utility lets you perform registry manipulations that involve security or other configurations. You can also use it to perform a list of registry modifications as a script, rather than individually using RegEdit. The most common use of this utility is to modify the security settings for the registry as explained by the Knowledge Base article at `http://support.microsoft.com/?kbid=245031`. The Knowledge Base article at `http://support.microsoft.com/?kbid=237607` has additional information on using this utility for security purposes. You can find a more complete discussion of how to use RegIni, including creating scripts using a number of techniques, on the Windows IT Library site at `http://www.windowsitlibrary.com/Content/237/2.html`. This utility uses the following syntax:

```
RegIni [-m \\computername] scriptname
```

The following list describes each of the command line arguments:

scriptname Specifies the name of the file containing the registry script.

-m \\computername Specifies the name of the computer on which to perform the modifications. The default is the local computer.

Performing Console Configuration

Many people are used to right-clicking their desktop and choosing Properties from the context menu to display the Display Properties dialog box. You can use this dialog box to perform all kinds of tasks, including configuring the console. For example, you may choose to use a larger active border or change the color to red to make it more visible. Right-clicking the Server Core desktop doesn't display a context menu, not to mention the Display Properties dialog box. Consequently, you need to use the Registry Editor to modify the registry to provide any new color combinations that you want. As with any change, you'll locate the hive, then the key you want to modify, and finally, the value you need to change. Table 4.2 contains a list of common color values that you can change.

NOTE   The color values are actually Red Green Blue (RGB) tuplets (a group of three numbers). The values can range from 0 for no color to 255 for maximum color. For example, a value of 255 0 0 (255 for red, 0 for green, and 0 for blue) displays bright red on screen. By combining different RGB values, you can create nearly any color imaginable. Always keep the numbers between 0 and 255 and be sure to include a space between each color.

TABLE 4.2:   Common Windows Color Settings

KEY NAME	VALUE NAME	VALUE TYPE	DEFAULT VALUE
HKEY_CURRENT_USER\Control Panel\Colors	ActiveBorder	REG_SZ	212 208 200
HKEY_CURRENT_USER\Control Panel\Colors	ActiveTitle	REG_SZ	10 36 106
HKEY_CURRENT_USER\Control Panel\Colors	AppWorkSpace	REG_SZ	128 128 128
HKEY_CURRENT_USER\Control Panel\Colors	ButtonAlternateFace	REG_SZ	181 181 181
HKEY_CURRENT_USER\Control Panel\Colors	ButtonDkShadow	REG_SZ	64 64 64
HKEY_CURRENT_USER\Control Panel\Colors	ButtonFace	REG_SZ	212 208 200
HKEY_CURRENT_USER\Control Panel\Colors	ButtonHilight	REG_SZ	255 255 255
HKEY_CURRENT_USER\Control Panel\Colors	ButtonLight	REG_SZ	212 208 200
HKEY_CURRENT_USER\Control Panel\Colors	ButtonShadow	REG_SZ	128 128 128
HKEY_CURRENT_USER\Control Panel\Colors	ButtonText	REG_SZ	0 0 0
HKEY_CURRENT_USER\Control Panel\Colors	GradientActiveTitle	REG_SZ	166 202 240
HKEY_CURRENT_USER\Control Panel\Colors	GradientInactiveTitle	REG_SZ	192 192 192
HKEY_CURRENT_USER\Control Panel\Colors	GrayText	REG_SZ	128 128 128
HKEY_CURRENT_USER\Control Panel\Colors	Hilight	REG_SZ	10 36 106
HKEY_CURRENT_USER\Control Panel\Colors	HilightText	REG_SZ	255 255 255
HKEY_CURRENT_USER\Control Panel\Colors	HotTrackingColor	REG_SZ	0 0 128
HKEY_CURRENT_USER\Control Panel\Colors	InactiveBorder	REG_SZ	212 208 200

TABLE 4.2:   Common Windows Color Settings *(CONTINUED)*

KEY NAME	VALUE NAME	VALUE TYPE	DEFAULT VALUE
HKEY_CURRENT_USER\Control Panel\Colors	InactiveTitle	REG_SZ	128 128 128
HKEY_CURRENT_USER\Control Panel\Colors	InactiveTitleText	REG_SZ	212 208 200
HKEY_CURRENT_USER\Control Panel\Colors	InfoText	REG_SZ	0 0 0
HKEY_CURRENT_USER\Control Panel\Colors	InfoWindow	REG_SZ	255 255 225
HKEY_CURRENT_USER\Control Panel\Colors	Menu	REG_SZ	212 208 200
HKEY_CURRENT_USER\Control Panel\Colors	MenuText	REG_SZ	0 0 0
HKEY_CURRENT_USER\Control Panel\Colors	Scrollbar	REG_SZ	212 208 200
HKEY_CURRENT_USER\Control Panel\Colors	TitleText	REG_SZ	255 255 255
HKEY_CURRENT_USER\Control Panel\Colors	Window	REG_SZ	255 255 255
HKEY_CURRENT_USER\Control Panel\Colors	WindowFrame	REG_SZ	0 0 0
HKEY_CURRENT_USER\Control Panel\Colors	WindowText	REG_SZ	0 0 0
HKEY_CURRENT_USER\Control Panel\Colors	Background	REG_SZ	29 95 122

The Value Type column in Table 4.2 shows how the value appears in the Registry Editor. Of course, this value type isn't very readable. Table 4.3 shows all of the common registry data types, their value type equivalents, and provides a description of how that value type is used.

TABLE 4.3:   Common Registry Value Types

DATA TYPE	VALUE TYPE	DESCRIPTION
String Value	REG_SZ	Contains a simple string value. Sometimes the string looks like other kinds of data, but it's always in string format. Make sure you type any string in the correct format. For example, the individual numbers in a color tuple should have a single space separating them.
Binary Value	REG_BINARY	Contains binary data that can include both computer and human-readable numeric data. You type the input as numbers. However, the editor translates any numbers into human-readable form when possible. For example, type 34 and you'll see the number 4 displayed in the human-readable area.
DWORD (32-bit) Value	REG_DWORD	Contains a 32-bit numeric value.

TABLE 4.3: Common Registry Value Types *(CONTINUED)*

DATA TYPE	VALUE TYPE	DESCRIPTION
QWORD (64-bit) Value	REG_QWORD	Contains a 64-bit numeric value.
Multi-String Value	REG_MULTI_SZ	Contains multiple strings separated by a carriage return/line feed combination. The strings appear in a single line in the Registry Editor value pane. Double-click the entry to see the individual strings.
Expandable String Value	REG_EXPAND_SZ	Contains a string that includes expansion variables, such as %SYSTEMROOT%, that translate into specific computer data such as a directory location.
Custom Value	N/A	Custom values are uncommon, but you'll see them. Whenever you encounter a custom value, refer to the vendor data to determine how to set the value. In some cases, you'll be able to use an existing entry as a pattern for setting your own value.

The Display Properties dialog box provides access to considerably more information than simply the GUI colors. You can also set other desktop features using this dialog box. Table 4.4 provides a list of common Desktop settings that you might want to change when working with Server Core.

TABLE 4.4: Common Windows Desktop Settings

KEY NAME	VALUE NAME	VALUE TYPE	DEFAULT VALUE
HKEY_CURRENT_USER\Control Panel\Desktop	ActiveWndTrackTimeout	REG_DWORD	0x0
HKEY_CURRENT_USER\Control Panel\Desktop	BlockSendInputResets	REG_SZ	0
HKEY_CURRENT_USER\Control Panel\Desktop	CaretWidth	REG_DWORD	0x1
HKEY_CURRENT_USER\Control Panel\Desktop	ClickLockTime	REG_DWORD	0x4b0
HKEY_CURRENT_USER\Control Panel\Desktop	CoolSwitchColumns	REG_SZ	7
HKEY_CURRENT_USER\Control Panel\Desktop	CoolSwitchRows	REG_SZ	3
HKEY_CURRENT_USER\Control Panel\Desktop	CursorBlinkRate	REG_SZ	530
HKEY_CURRENT_USER\Control Panel\Desktop	DragFullWindows	REG_SZ	1
HKEY_CURRENT_USER\Control Panel\Desktop	DragHeight	REG_SZ	4
HKEY_CURRENT_USER\Control Panel\Desktop	DragWidth	REG_SZ	4
HKEY_CURRENT_USER\Control Panel\Desktop	FocusBorderHeight	REG_DWORD	0x1

TABLE 4.4: Common Windows Desktop Settings *(CONTINUED)*

KEY NAME	VALUE NAME	VALUE TYPE	DEFAULT VALUE
HKEY_CURRENT_USER\Control Panel\Desktop	FocusBorderWidth	REG_DWORD	0x1
HKEY_CURRENT_USER\Control Panel\Desktop	FontSmoothing	REG_SZ	2
HKEY_CURRENT_USER\Control Panel\Desktop	FontSmoothingGamma	REG_DWORD	0x0
HKEY_CURRENT_USER\Control Panel\Desktop	FontSmoothingOrientation	REG_DWORD	0x1
HKEY_CURRENT_USER\Control Panel\Desktop	FontSmoothingType	REG_DWORD	0x2
HKEY_CURRENT_USER\Control Panel\Desktop	ForegroundFlashCount	REG_DWORD	0x3
HKEY_CURRENT_USER\Control Panel\Desktop	ForegroundLockTimeout	REG_DWORD	0x30d40
HKEY_CURRENT_USER\Control Panel\Desktop	LeftOverlapChars	REG_SZ	3
HKEY_CURRENT_USER\Control Panel\Desktop	MenuShowDelay	REG_SZ	400
HKEY_CURRENT_USER\Control Panel\Desktop	PaintDesktopVersion	REG_DWORD	0x0
HKEY_CURRENT_USER\Control Panel\Desktop	Pattern	REG_DWORD	0x0
HKEY_CURRENT_USER\Control Panel\Desktop	RightOverlapChars	REG_SZ	3
HKEY_CURRENT_USER\Control Panel\Desktop	TileWallpaper	REG_SZ	0
HKEY_CURRENT_USER\Control Panel\Desktop	WallpaperOriginX	REG_DWORD	0x0
HKEY_CURRENT_USER\Control Panel\Desktop	WallpaperOriginY	REG_DWORD	0x0
HKEY_CURRENT_USER\Control Panel\Desktop	WallpaperStyle	REG_SZ	2
HKEY_CURRENT_USER\Control Panel\Desktop	WheelScrollChars	REG_SZ	3
HKEY_CURRENT_USER\Control Panel\Desktop	WheelScrollLines	REG_SZ	3
HKEY_CURRENT_USER\Control Panel\Desktop	ScreenSaveActive	REG_SZ	1
HKEY_CURRENT_USER\Control Panel\Desktop	ScreenSaverIsSecure	REG_SZ	1
HKEY_CURRENT_USER\Control Panel\Desktop	ScreenSaveTimeOut	REG_SZ	600
HKEY_CURRENT_USER\Control Panel\Desktop	SCRNSAVE.EXE	REG_SZ	C:\Windows\system32\logon.scr
HKEY_CURRENT_USER\Control Panel\Desktop\WindowMetrics	BorderWidth	REG_SZ	-15

TABLE 4.4: Common Windows Desktop Settings *(CONTINUED)*

KEY NAME	VALUE NAME	VALUE TYPE	DEFAULT VALUE
HKEY_CURRENT_USER\Control Panel\ Desktop\WindowMetrics	CaptionFont	REG_BINARY	LOGFONT
HKEY_CURRENT_USER\Control Panel\ Desktop\WindowMetrics	CaptionHeight	REG_SZ	-270
HKEY_CURRENT_USER\Control Panel\ Desktop\WindowMetrics	CaptionWidth	REG_SZ	-270
HKEY_CURRENT_USER\Control Panel\ Desktop\WindowMetrics	IconFont	REG_BINARY	LOGFONT
HKEY_CURRENT_USER\Control Panel\ Desktop\WindowMetrics	IconTitleWrap	REG_SZ	1
HKEY_CURRENT_USER\Control Panel\ Desktop\WindowMetrics	MenuFont	REG_BINARY	LOGFONT
HKEY_CURRENT_USER\Control Panel\ Desktop\WindowMetrics	MenuHeight	REG_SZ	-270
HKEY_CURRENT_USER\Control Panel\ Desktop\WindowMetrics	MenuWidth	REG_SZ	-270
HKEY_CURRENT_USER\Control Panel\ Desktop\WindowMetrics	MessageFont	REG_BINARY	LOGFONT
HKEY_CURRENT_USER\Control Panel\ Desktop\WindowMetrics	ScrollHeight	REG_SZ	-240
HKEY_CURRENT_USER\Control Panel\ Desktop\WindowMetrics	ScrollWidth	REG_SZ	-240
HKEY_CURRENT_USER\Control Panel\ Desktop\WindowMetrics	SmCaptionFont	REG_BINARY	LOGFONT
HKEY_CURRENT_USER\Control Panel\ Desktop\WindowMetrics	SmCaptionHeight	REG_SZ	-180
HKEY_CURRENT_USER\Control Panel\ Desktop\WindowMetrics	SmCaptionWidth	REG_SZ	-180
HKEY_CURRENT_USER\Control Panel\ Desktop\WindowMetrics	StatusFont	REG_BINARY	LOGFONT
HKEY_CURRENT_USER\Control Panel\ Desktop\WindowMetrics	Shell Icon Size	REG_SZ	32

Creating the LOGFONT data structure is a complex undertaking. It contains 14 data fields that you must define as part of the data entry. Constructing the required binary data by hand isn't impossible, but it can be quite difficult. You can find a description of the LOGFONT data structure at `http://msdn2.microsoft.com/en-us/library/ms533931.aspx`.

You could also modify the console (command prompt) settings in the registry if desired by changing the values under the `HKEY_CURRENT_USER\Console` key. However, the process described in the "Configuring the Command Window" section of Chapter 2 is significantly easier and less error prone. You may see additional keys under the `HKEY_CURRENT_USER\Console` key. These additional keys will have the titles of command prompts that you open and contain the settings for those command prompts. Each unique command prompt title can have its own settings. Consequently, you can do things like create command prompts with different colors for specific tasks.

Setting the Environment

Normally you use the Environment Variables dialog box to set both user and system environment variables. However, this option isn't available in Server Core, so you must either set the environment variables in the registry directly or use a command line utility to perform the task.

When working at the command line, you can choose between creating session or permanent environment variables. Use the `Set` and `SetX` commands to create session environment variables (see the "Managing Environment Variables with the Set Command" and "Managing Environment Variables with the SetX Utility" sections of Chapter 5 for details). Use the `WMIC Environment` command to create permanent environment variables for the current user (see the "Configuring Server Core Using the WMIC Command" section of Chapter 3 for details). You can't create permanent system-level environment variables at the command line.

Permanent environment variables are those that exist between reboots. Once you set them, you can depend on them remaining in place until you change them. A user-level environment variable affects only the current user. You'll find these environment variables in the `HKEY_CURRENT_USER\Environment` key. The default environment variables include `Path`, `TEMP`, and `TMP`.

A system-level environment variable affects everyone that uses the system. You'll find these environment variables in the `HKEY_LOCAL_MACHINE\SYSTEM\CurrentControlSet\Control\Session Manager\Environment` key. The default environment variables include `comspec`, `FP_NO_HOST_CHECK`, `lib`, `NUMBER_OF_PROCESSORS`, `OS`, `Path`, `PATHEXT`, `PROCESSOR_ARCHITECTURE`, `PROCESSOR_IDENTIFIER`, `PROCESSOR_LEVEL`, `PROCESSOR_REVISION`, `TEMP`, `TMP`, and `windir`.

Each environment variable appears as a separate value under its respective key. Use the following procedure to add a new environment variable.

1. Right-click the appropriate key.

2. Choose New ➢ String Value from the context menu.

3. Type the name of the environment variable you want to create and press Enter.

4. Double-click the new environment variable. You'll see the Edit String dialog box.

5. Type the value you want in the Value Data field of the Edit String dialog box.

6. Click OK to complete the process.

At this point, you can use the environment variable as you would any other environment variable. You can also export your environment variables and import them into the registry on a similarly configured machine. Of course, you'll want to be sure that you format the environment variables correctly to ensure they aren't drive letter or hardware specific.

Modifying the Hardware Setup

Many of the settings you need to change to control the hardware on your system appear as part of the console or software settings. For example, if you want to control the appearance of the text on your display, you actually need to change the console settings and not the hardware settings. Likewise, if you want to change how the system handles languages, then you need to change the international settings instead of the keyboard settings. With this in mind, you'll want to check the "Performing Console Configuration" and "Modifying the Software Setup" sections of the chapter as needed when you don't see what you want in this section.

The hardware settings fall into two categories. First, vendors provide specific settings for their hardware. Because there are so many hardware vendors on the market, it's impossible to provide a comprehensive list of vendor-specific settings, so you won't find them in this chapter. Second, generic settings affect Server Core as a whole and they're part of the generic drivers that affect all hardware. The following sections describe this second category of hardware setting. You won't find every generic setting here, but you'll find many that you normally need to set as part of the GUI, rather than access them directly in the registry.

Video

The video settings are a bit tough to set. It's not a matter of finding the settings, so much as figuring out which settings to change. The best way to proceed is to locate the Globally Unique Identifier (GUID) for your adapter. Locating this information means knowing the name of the display adapter. For example, on one system I own, I have a Gigabyte RADEON X300 installed. Searching for this string in the registry netted several hits, but the one that I want is under the HKEY_LOCAL_MACHINE\ SYSTEM\CurrentControlSet\Enum\PCI\ key. In this case, the information appears as part of the VEN_1002&DEV_5B60&SUBSYS_21021458&REV_00\4&243d7bd0&1&0070 key, but your setup is likely different from mine.

The Device Parameters subkey is the one you want. It contains a VideoID value. The data value contains the GUID for the display adapter. Double-click the value. Press Ctrl+C to copy of the GUID to the clipboard. In my case, the GUID is {2E9CD519-7E88-4189-9745-5389D6D145CF}—your GUID will likely differ from mine. Press Ctrl+F to display the Find dialog box. Press Ctrl+V to paste the GUID into the Find What field of the Find dialog box. If you leave just the Keys option checked in the Look At field, you'll locate the information you need faster. Press OK to begin the search.

Your search should take you to the HKEY_LOCAL_MACHINE\SYSTEM\CurrentControlSet\Hard-ware Profiles\0001\System\CurrentControlSet\Control\VIDEO key. The Registry Editor actually highlights the adapter GUID for which you searched. The 0000 subkey contains the settings you want to change. If you have the ability to attach multiple monitors to your system, you'll see an additional subkey for each monitor and you'll need to change the settings there. For example, the complete key path for the first monitor on my system is HKEY_LOCAL_MACHINE\SYSTEM\ CurrentControlSet\Hardware Profiles\0001\System\CurrentControlSet\Control\VIDEO\ {2E9CD519-7E88-4189-9745-5389D6D145CF}\0000\Mon10000084.

Table 4.5 contains a list of the settings you can modify in most cases. After you make a change, you'll need to restart the system to see the difference because Windows doesn't know to incorporate the settings for you.

TABLE 4.5:   Common Video Adapter Settings

VALUE NAME	VALUE TYPE	DEFAULT VALUE
Attach.ToDesktop	REG_DWORD	00000001
DefaultSettings.BitsPerPel	REG_DWORD	00000010
DefaultSettings.XResolution	REG_DWORD	00000500
DefaultSettings.YResolution	REG_DWORD	00000400
DefaultSettings.VRefresh	REG_DWORD	0000003c
DefaultSettings.Flags	REG_DWORD	00000000
DefaultSettings.XPanning	REG_DWORD	00000000
DefaultSettings.YPanning	REG_DWORD	00000000
DefaultSettings.Orientation	REG_DWORD	00000000
DefaultSettings.FixedOutput	REG_DWORD	00000000
Attach.RelativeX	REG_DWORD	00000000
Attach.RelativeY	REG_DWORD	00000000

Keyboard

Keyboards are pretty much generic from a configuration perspective, so you don't have to spend a lot of time looking for the values you need. In general, you can set all of the hardware configuration settings that you find in the Keyboard applet of the Control Panel. Table 4.6 shows the settings you can change.

TABLE 4.6:   Generic Keyboard Settings

KEY NAME	VALUE NAME	VALUE TYPE	DEFAULT VALUE
HKEY_CURRENT_USER\Control Panel\Keyboard	InitialKeyboardIndicators	REG_SZ	2147483648
HKEY_CURRENT_USER\Control Panel\Keyboard	KeyboardDelay	REG_SZ	1
HKEY_CURRENT_USER\Control Panel\Keyboard	KeyboardSpeed	REG_SZ	31

Mouse

The mouse has some differences based on the features you obtain for it. For example, you might have a three-button mouse instead of a two-button mouse. In addition, you have to consider differences for left- and right-handed users. Even so, Windows provides many generic settings for the mouse. You'll find all of the generic settings in Table 4.7. Most of these settings also appear in the Mouse applet of the Control Panel. Refer to your vendor documentation for specialized settings for your mouse.

TABLE 4.7:   Generic Mouse Settings

KEY NAME	VALUE NAME	VALUE TYPE	DEFAULT VALUE
HKEY_CURRENT_USER\Control Panel\Mouse	ActiveWindowTracking	REG_DWORD	0
HKEY_CURRENT_USER\Control Panel\Mouse	Beep	REG_SZ	No
HKEY_CURRENT_USER\Control Panel\Mouse	DoubleClickHeight	REG_SZ	4
HKEY_CURRENT_USER\Control Panel\Mouse	DoubleClickSpeed	REG_SZ	500
HKEY_CURRENT_USER\Control Panel\Mouse	DoubleClickWidth	REG_SZ	4
HKEY_CURRENT_USER\Control Panel\Mouse	ExtendedSounds	REG_SZ	No
HKEY_CURRENT_USER\Control Panel\Mouse	MouseHoverHeight	REG_SZ	4
HKEY_CURRENT_USER\Control Panel\Mouse	MouseHoverTime	REG_SZ	400
HKEY_CURRENT_USER\Control Panel\Mouse	MouseHoverWidth	REG_SZ	4
HKEY_CURRENT_USER\Control Panel\Mouse	MouseSensitivity	REG_SZ	10
HKEY_CURRENT_USER\Control Panel\Mouse	MouseSpeed	REG_SZ	1
HKEY_CURRENT_USER\Control Panel\Mouse	MouseThreshold1	REG_SZ	6
HKEY_CURRENT_USER\Control Panel\Mouse	MouseThreshold2	REG_SZ	10
HKEY_CURRENT_USER\Control Panel\Mouse	MouseTrails	REG_SZ	0
HKEY_CURRENT_USER\Control Panel\Mouse	SmoothMouseXCurve	REG_BINARY	00 00 00 00 00 00 00 00 15 6e 00 00 00 00 00 00 00 40 01 00 00 00 00 00 29 dc 03 00 00 00 00 00 00 00 28 00 00 00 00 00

TABLE 4.7: Generic Mouse Settings *(CONTINUED)*

KEY NAME	VALUE NAME	VALUE TYPE	DEFAULT VALUE
HKEY_CURRENT_USER\Control Panel\Mouse	SmoothMouseYCurve	REG_BINARY	00 00 00 00 00 00 00 00 b8 5e 01 00 00 00 00 00 cd 4c 05 00 00 00 00 00 cd 4c 18 00 00 00 00 00 00 00 38 02 00 00 00 00
HKEY_CURRENT_USER\Control Panel\Mouse	SnapToDefaultButton	REG_SZ	0
HKEY_CURRENT_USER\Control Panel\Mouse	SwapMouseButtons	REG_SZ	0

The SmoothMouseXCurve and SmoothMouseYCurve settings control the acceleration of your mouse. Given that Server Core isn't a mouse-intensive operating system, you probably won't need to change these settings. However, if you do find that the mouse doesn't work as well as expected in Remote Desktop, where you'll often cut and paste text in the command prompt, you may need to change the settings. One of the better adjustments appears at http://www.softwaretipsandtricks .com/windowsxp/articles/69/1/Mouse-Permanent-Acceleration-Fix/print/69. However, a search online for either SmoothMouseXCurve or SmoothMouseYCurve will likely turn up a wealth of settings you can try.

Power Configuration

The power configuration settings control how your computer works with power. For example, you can set the power policy to shut off the monitor after a specific time frame or turn off the hard drives when they aren't being used. The problem is that these policies are set using binary values, which means that you can't do much more than select a particular policy using the Registry Editor unless you have documentation for that binary data. Consequently, you'll normally use the PowerCfg utility described in the "Managing Power Settings with the PowerCfg Utility" section of Chapter 12 to perform power configuration. That said, Table 4.8 shows typical registry settings for the power configuration. Most of these settings normally appear in the Power Options applet of the Control Panel.

TABLE 4.8: Typical Power Configuration Settings

KEY NAME	VALUE NAME	VALUE TYPE	DEFAULT VALUE
HKEY_CURRENT_USER\ Control Panel\PowerCfg	CurrentPowerPolicy	REG_SZ	8

TABLE 4.8: Typical Power Configuration Settings *(CONTINUED)*

KEY NAME	VALUE NAME	VALUE TYPE	DEFAULT VALUE
HKEY_CURRENT_USER\ Control Panel\PowerCfg\ GlobalPowerPolicy	Policies	REG_BINARY	01 00 00 00 00 00 00 00 03 00 00 00 10 00 00 00 00 00 00 00 03 00 00 00 10 00 00 00 02 00 00 00 03 00 00 00 00 00 00 00 02 00 00 00 03 00 00 00 00 00 00 00 02 00 00 00 01 00 00 00 00 00 00 00 02 00 00 00 01 00 00 00 00 00 00 00 01 00 00 00 03 00 00 00 02 00 00 00 04 00 00 c0 01 00 00 00 04 00 00 00 01 00 00 00 0a 00 00 00 00 00 00 00 03 00 00 00 01 00 01 00 01 00 00 00 00 00 00 00 00 00 00 00 00 00 00 00 00 00 00 00 00 00 00 02 00 00 00 00 00 00 00 00 00 00 00 00 00 00 00 00 00 00 00 00 00 00 00 00 03 00 00 00 00 00 16 00 00 00
HKEY_CURRENT_USER\ Control Panel\PowerCfg\ PowerPolicies\0	Name	REG_SZ	Home/Office Desk
HKEY_CURRENT_USER\ Control Panel\PowerCfg\ PowerPolicies\0	Description	REG_SZ	This scheme is suited to most home or desktop computers that are left plugged in all the time.
HKEY_CURRENT_USER\ Control Panel\PowerCfg\ PowerPolicies\0	Policies	REG_BINARY	01 00 00 00 02 00 00 00 01 00 00 00 00 00 00 00 02 00 00 00 00 00 00 00 00 00 00 00 00 00 00 00 00 2c 01 00 00 32 32 00 03 04 00 00 00 04 00 00 00 00 00 3d 77 2e f2 07 00 b0 04 00 00 2c 01 00 00 00 00 00 00 58 02 00 00 00 00 64 64 64 64 91 7c

The CurrentPowerPolicy setting is the one of interest. Changing this value changes the preconfig-ured power policy. Table 4.8 only shows one PowerPolicy key setting. A typical computer contains at least five subkeys and you can choose any of them as a power configuration for the computer.

Network

Network drive mappings are important because they provide access to other resources on the network such as disk drives. Generally, you'll use the Net Use command to map a network drive as described in the "Managing the Network with the Net Utility" section of Chapter 10. However, you can perform tweaks of existing drive mappings or even create new mappings using the registry as well. Table 4.9 shows typical settings for a network drive mapping. Your drive mapping contains the same keys, but has different data from the data shown in Table 4.9. A drive mapping doesn't have any default data—only the specific data required to create the drive mapping. The I key in this example is the local drive letter for the mapping.

TABLE 4.9:   Typical Network Mappings

Key Name	Value Name	Value Type	Typical Value
HKEY_CURRENT_USER\Network\I	RemotePath	REG_SZ	\\\\Winserver\\Drive C
HKEY_CURRENT_USER\Network\I	UserName	REG_DWORD	00000000
HKEY_CURRENT_USER\Network\I	ProviderName	REG_SZ	Microsoft Windows Network
HKEY_CURRENT_USER\Network\I	ProviderType	REG_DWORD	00020000
HKEY_CURRENT_USER\Network\I	ConnectionType	REG_DWORD	00000001
HKEY_CURRENT_USER\Network\I	DeferFlags	REG_DWORD	00000004

Modifying the Software Setup

The software on your system requires configuration. While this section can't tell you how to configure your favorite third-party utility, you can see how some of the Server Core software works. One of the more important settings is determining how the accessibility features work. Table 4.10 shows the common accessibility settings that you'd see in the Accessibility applet of the Control Panel.

TABLE 4.10:   Common Accessibility Settings

Key Name	Value Name	Value Type	Default Value
HKEY_CURRENT_USER\Control Panel\ Accessibility	MessageDuration	REG_DWORD	0x5
HKEY_CURRENT_USER\Control Panel\ Accessibility	MinimumHitRadius	REG_DWORD	0x0
HKEY_CURRENT_USER\Control Panel\ Accessibility\On	On	REG_DWORD	0x0

TABLE 4.10: Common Accessibility Settings *(CONTINUED)*

KEY NAME	VALUE NAME	VALUE TYPE	DEFAULT VALUE
HKEY_CURRENT_USER\Control Panel\ Accessibility\On	Locale	REG_DWORD	0x0
HKEY_CURRENT_USER\Control Panel\ Accessibility\Blind Access	On	REG_SZ	0
HKEY_CURRENT_USER\Control Panel\ Accessibility\HighContrast	Flags	REG_SZ	126
HKEY_CURRENT_USER\Control Panel\ Accessibility\HighContrast	High Contrast Scheme	REG_SZ	High Contrast Black (large)
HKEY_CURRENT_USER\Control Panel\ Accessibility\Keyboard Preference	On	REG_SZ	0
HKEY_CURRENT_USER\Control Panel\ Accessibility\Keyboard Response	AutoRepeatDelay	REG_SZ	1000
HKEY_CURRENT_USER\Control Panel\ Accessibility\Keyboard Response	AutoRepeatRate	REG_SZ	500
HKEY_CURRENT_USER\Control Panel\ Accessibility\Keyboard Response	BounceTime	REG_SZ	0
HKEY_CURRENT_USER\Control Panel\ Accessibility\Keyboard Response	DelayBeforeAcceptance	REG_SZ	1000
HKEY_CURRENT_USER\Control Panel\ Accessibility\Keyboard Response	Flags	REG_SZ	126
HKEY_CURRENT_USER\Control Panel\ Accessibility\MouseKeys	Flags	REG_SZ	62
HKEY_CURRENT_USER\Control Panel\ Accessibility\MouseKeys	MaximumSpeed	REG_SZ	80
HKEY_CURRENT_USER\Control Panel\ Accessibility\MouseKeys	TimeToMaximumSpeed	REG_SZ	3000
HKEY_CURRENT_USER\Control Panel\ Accessibility\ShowSounds	On	REG_SZ	0
HKEY_CURRENT_USER\Control Panel\ Accessibility\SoundSentry	Flags	REG_SZ	2

TABLE 4.10: Common Accessibility Settings *(CONTINUED)*

KEY NAME	VALUE NAME	VALUE TYPE	DEFAULT VALUE
HKEY_CURRENT_USER\Control Panel\ Accessibility\SoundSentry	FSTextEffect	REG_SZ	0
HKEY_CURRENT_USER\Control Panel\ Accessibility\SoundSentry	WindowsEffect	REG_SZ	1
HKEY_CURRENT_USER\Control Panel\ Accessibility\StickyKeys	Flags	REG_SZ	510
HKEY_CURRENT_USER\Control Panel\ Accessibility\TimeOut	Flags	REG_SZ	2
HKEY_CURRENT_USER\Control Panel\ Accessibility\TimeOut	TimeToWait	REG_SZ	300000
HKEY_CURRENT_USER\Control Panel\ Accessibility\ToggleKeys	Flags	REG_SZ	62

The input method settings shown in Table 4.11 actually affect the techniques used to work with other human languages. For example, if you configure Windows to support multiple languages, you need a way to switch between those languages. To see these settings in the GUI setup, open the Regional and Language Options applet of the Control Panel. Select the Languages tab and click Details. Choose any secondary language you have installed and Windows enables the Key Settings button. Click this button and you'll see the shortcuts described in Table 4.11.

TABLE 4.11: Common Windows Desktop Settings

KEY NAME	VALUE NAME	VALUE TYPE	DEFAULT VALUE
HKEY_CURRENT_USER\Control Panel\ Input Method	Show Status	REG_SZ	1
HKEY_CURRENT_USER\Control Panel\ Input Method\Hot Keys\00000010	Key Modifiers	REG_BINARY	02 c0 00 00
HKEY_CURRENT_USER\Control Panel\ Input Method\Hot Keys\00000010	Target IME	REG_BINARY	00 00 00 00
HKEY_CURRENT_USER\Control Panel\ Input Method\Hot Keys\00000010	Virtual Key	REG_BINARY	20 00 00 00

TABLE 4.11: Common Windows Desktop Settings *(CONTINUED)*

KEY NAME	VALUE NAME	VALUE TYPE	DEFAULT VALUE
HKEY_CURRENT_USER\Control Panel\ Input Method\Hot Keys\00000011	Key Modifiers	REG_BINARY	04 c0 00 00
HKEY_CURRENT_USER\Control Panel\ Input Method\Hot Keys\00000011	Target IME	REG_BINARY	00 00 00 00
HKEY_CURRENT_USER\Control Panel\ Input Method\Hot Keys\00000011	Virtual Key	REG_BINARY	20 00 00 00
HKEY_CURRENT_USER\Control Panel\ Input Method\Hot Keys\00000012	Key Modifiers	REG_BINARY	02 c0 00 00
HKEY_CURRENT_USER\Control Panel\ Input Method\Hot Keys\00000012	Target IME	REG_BINARY	00 00 00 00
HKEY_CURRENT_USER\Control Panel\ Input Method\Hot Keys\00000012	Virtual Key	REG_BINARY	be 00 00 00
HKEY_CURRENT_USER\Control Panel\ Input Method\Hot Keys\00000070	Key Modifiers	REG_BINARY	02 c0 00 00
HKEY_CURRENT_USER\Control Panel\ Input Method\Hot Keys\00000070	Target IME	REG_BINARY	00 00 00 00
HKEY_CURRENT_USER\Control Panel\ Input Method\Hot Keys\00000070	Virtual Key	REG_BINARY	20 00 00 00
HKEY_CURRENT_USER\Control Panel\ Input Method\Hot Keys\00000071	Key Modifiers	REG_BINARY	04 c0 00 00
HKEY_CURRENT_USER\Control Panel\ Input Method\Hot Keys\00000071	Target IME	REG_BINARY	00 00 00 00
HKEY_CURRENT_USER\Control Panel\ Input Method\Hot Keys\00000071	Virtual Key	REG_BINARY	20 00 00 00
HKEY_CURRENT_USER\Control Panel\ Input Method\Hot Keys\00000072	Key Modifiers	REG_BINARY	03 c0 00 00
HKEY_CURRENT_USER\Control Panel\ Input Method\Hot Keys\00000072	Target IME	REG_BINARY	00 00 00 00
HKEY_CURRENT_USER\Control Panel\ Input Method\Hot Keys\00000072	Virtual Key	REG_BINARY	bc 00 00 00
HKEY_CURRENT_USER\Control Panel\ Input Method\Hot Keys\00000200	Key Modifiers	REG_BINARY	03 c0 00 00

TABLE 4.11: Common Windows Desktop Settings *(CONTINUED)*

Key Name	Value Name	Value Type	Default Value
HKEY_CURRENT_USER\Control Panel\ Input Method\Hot Keys\00000200	Target IME	REG_BINARY	00 00 00 00
HKEY_CURRENT_USER\Control Panel\ Input Method\Hot Keys\00000200	Virtual Key	REG_BINARY	47 00 00 00
HKEY_CURRENT_USER\Control Panel\ Input Method\Hot Keys\00000201	Key Modifiers	REG_BINARY	03 c0 00 00
HKEY_CURRENT_USER\Control Panel\ Input Method\Hot Keys\00000201	Target IME	REG_BINARY	00 00 00 00
HKEY_CURRENT_USER\Control Panel\ Input Method\Hot Keys\00000201	Virtual Key	REG_BINARY	4b 00 00 00
HKEY_CURRENT_USER\Control Panel\ Input Method\Hot Keys\00000202	Key Modifiers	REG_BINARY	03 c0 00 00
HKEY_CURRENT_USER\Control Panel\ Input Method\Hot Keys\00000202	Target IME	REG_BINARY	00 00 00 00
HKEY_CURRENT_USER\Control Panel\ Input Method\Hot Keys\00000202	Virtual Key	REG_BINARY	4c 00 00 00

You may need to change the regional settings for your computer. These settings normally appear on the Regional Options tab of the Regional and Language Options dialog box. Table 4.12 lists all of the common settings.

TABLE 4.12: Common International Settings

Key Name	Value Name	Value Type	Default Value
HKEY_CURRENT_USER\Control Panel\ International	Locale	REG_SZ	409
HKEY_CURRENT_USER\Control Panel\ International	LocaleName	REG_SZ	en-US
HKEY_CURRENT_USER\Control Panel\ International	s1159	REG_SZ	AM
HKEY_CURRENT_USER\Control Panel\ International	s2359	REG_SZ	PM

TABLE 4.12: Common International Settings *(CONTINUED)*

KEY NAME	VALUE NAME	VALUE TYPE	DEFAULT VALUE
HKEY_CURRENT_USER\Control Panel\ International	sCountry	REG_SZ	United States
HKEY_CURRENT_USER\Control Panel\ International	sCurrency	REG_SZ	$
HKEY_CURRENT_USER\Control Panel\ International	sDate	REG_SZ	/
HKEY_CURRENT_USER\Control Panel\ International	sDecimal	REG_SZ	.
HKEY_CURRENT_USER\Control Panel\ International	sGrouping	REG_SZ	3;0
HKEY_CURRENT_USER\Control Panel\ International	sLanguage	REG_SZ	ENU
HKEY_CURRENT_USER\Control Panel\ International	sList	REG_SZ	,
HKEY_CURRENT_USER\Control Panel\ International	sLongDate	REG_SZ	dddd, MMMM dd, yyyy
HKEY_CURRENT_USER\Control Panel\ International	sMonDecimalSep	REG_SZ	.
HKEY_CURRENT_USER\Control Panel\ International	sMonGrouping	REG_SZ	3;0
HKEY_CURRENT_USER\Control Panel\ International	sMonThousandSep	REG_SZ	,
HKEY_CURRENT_USER\Control Panel\ International	sNativeDigits	REG_SZ	123456789
HKEY_CURRENT_USER\Control Panel\ International	sNegativeSign	REG_SZ	-
HKEY_CURRENT_USER\Control Panel\ International	sPositiveSign	REG_SZ	
HKEY_CURRENT_USER\Control Panel\ International	sShortDate	REG_SZ	M/d/yyyy
HKEY_CURRENT_USER\Control Panel\ International	sThousand	REG_SZ	,

TABLE 4.12: Common International Settings *(CONTINUED)*

KEY NAME	VALUE NAME	VALUE TYPE	DEFAULT VALUE
HKEY_CURRENT_USER\Control Panel\ International	sTime	REG_SZ	:
HKEY_CURRENT_USER\Control Panel\ International	sTimeFormat	REG_SZ	h:mm:ss tt
HKEY_CURRENT_USER\Control Panel\ International	sYearMonth	REG_SZ	MMMM, yyyy
HKEY_CURRENT_USER\Control Panel\ International	iCalendarType	REG_SZ	1
HKEY_CURRENT_USER\Control Panel\ International	iCountry	REG_SZ	1
HKEY_CURRENT_USER\Control Panel\ International	iCurrDigits	REG_SZ	2
HKEY_CURRENT_USER\Control Panel\ International	iCurrency	REG_SZ	0
HKEY_CURRENT_USER\Control Panel\ International	iDate	REG_SZ	0
HKEY_CURRENT_USER\Control Panel\ International	iDigits	REG_SZ	2
HKEY_CURRENT_USER\Control Panel\ International	NumShape	REG_SZ	1
HKEY_CURRENT_USER\Control Panel\ International	iFirstDayOfWeek	REG_SZ	6
HKEY_CURRENT_USER\Control Panel\ International	iFirstWeekOfYear	REG_SZ	0
HKEY_CURRENT_USER\Control Panel\ International	iLZero	REG_SZ	1
HKEY_CURRENT_USER\Control Panel\ International	iMeasure	REG_SZ	1
HKEY_CURRENT_USER\Control Panel\ International	iNegCurr	REG_SZ	0
HKEY_CURRENT_USER\Control Panel\ International	iNegNumber	REG_SZ	1

TABLE 4.12: Common International Settings *(CONTINUED)*

KEY NAME	VALUE NAME	VALUE TYPE	DEFAULT VALUE
HKEY_CURRENT_USER\Control Panel\ International	iPaperSize	REG_SZ	1
HKEY_CURRENT_USER\Control Panel\ International	iTime	REG_SZ	0
HKEY_CURRENT_USER\Control Panel\ International	iTimePrefix	REG_SZ	0
HKEY_CURRENT_USER\Control Panel\ International	iTLZero	REG_SZ	0
HKEY_CURRENT_USER\Control Panel\ International\Geo	Nation	REG_SZ	244

Managing Windows in a New Way

You haven't seen everything there is to see about the registry in this chapter, but you've discovered some registry elements that you may not have seen in the past because you'd normally change these features using the Windows GUI. Using the registry to change these elements may seem a bit counterproductive, but since the focus of Server Core is the command line, you may actually find that you use these special tweaks less often than you thought. Even so, it's nice to know the tweaks are available when you need them. This chapter helps you build these skills:

◆ Start and configure both RegEdit and SCRegEdit

◆ Script registry entries using RegIni

◆ Configure the console

◆ Configure the environment

◆ Manage hardware settings

◆ Manage software settings

Server Core probably hasn't felt very comfortable to this point because you can't easily customize it to meet your needs. In addition, drivers that normally require a right-click for configuration purposes, don't have that capability in Server Core, so things like setting your mouse for left-handed use are very tough. Now that you know the registry keys you need to use, take time to configure your system so it does feel more comfortable. Not only will your productivity improve, but you'll probably find that you like Server Core a lot better too.

Chapter 5 begins looking at automation. Microsoft doesn't really intend for you to spend all of your time typing single commands at the command prompt. Otherwise, you might never get any work finished. The batch file is an automation solution that's far older than you might expect, but it still works fine today. In addition, batch files are incredibly easy to create because you use the same commands that you normally use when you work at the command line. Chapter 5 tells you all about batch files and shows how to create efficient batch files for Server Core.

Part 2

Automation Essentials

Chapter 5

Creating CMD and BAT Files

So far, you've performed all of the Server Core configuration tasks manually, by typing individual commands at the command prompt. Performing tasks manually makes sense when you'll only perform a task once or when you want to learn something new about a command or utility. However, performing repetitive tasks manually is boring, error prone, and inefficient. One of the easiest ways to automate command line tasks is to use batch files. A batch file works just as if you'd typed the commands manually, but you're asking the computer to type them.

Users have relied on batch files of various sorts for many years because they're quick to create, easy to understand, and painless to modify. Testing a batch file is simple—you don't need any fancy tools or a debugger. In fact, as far as any kind of programming goes, working with batch files represents the least difficult way to get started. You literally enter the commands in the same order as you do at the command prompt. With a little effort in Windows, you can cut and paste your way to a completed batch file.

One of the most interesting uses of batch files are the AutoExec.NT and Config.NT files used to configure the command line. These two files represent a significant opportunity to configure the command environment to meet specific needs without doing much more than selecting a menu option, yet most people miss this opportunity. This chapter demonstrates that a little code mixed with some simple instructions really can do a lot to make the command line environment a pleasure to work with.

Although you won't spend a lot of time debugging your batch files, they can become complex enough that you'll need to do some debugging. The last section of this chapter provides you with some techniques for debugging your batch file as necessary. This last section completes the batch file picture for you and provides you with a complete set of batch file tools.

In this chapter, you'll learn how to do the following:

- ◆ Create a new command interpreter and configure it
- ◆ Perform basic command line tasks
- ◆ Create batch files
- ◆ Test batch files

Starting the Command Interpreter

The command interpreter is a special kind of application. When you open a command window, what you're really doing is starting the command interpreter. The command interpreter accepts your commands and does something with them. The command interpreter for Windows is CMD.EXE. This application is responsible for creating the command window, accepting your configuration commands, and providing access to the built-in commands such as the Dir command.

You can configure the command interpreter using five techniques in Windows. The first is to add command line switches to the CMD.EXE. This approach configures the command interpreter as a whole and you don't have much control over this particular change once the command interpreter is running. Of course, you can have a shortcut for each occasion that relies on different command line switch setups for each task.

The second configuration method is to change the content of Config.NT. The Config.NT file appears in the \Windows\System32 directory and the command interpreter calls on it to configure the command window environment. The Config.NT file changes the device drivers, number of files, the loading of the Virtual DOS Machine into upper memory, and other configuration issues.

TIP The Windows directory can appear in many locations on a system. For example, it may not install on the C drive, but could use the D drive instead. In addition, the name can change some systems used Windows, some Win, some WinNT, and others still other names. To find the Windows directory on the local system, type **Echo %SYSTEMROOT%** and press Enter. You'll see the location of the Windows directory displayed at the command prompt. Once you know this information, you can find all of the other resources you need on the local machine because the Windows directory setup doesn't change much from system to system.

The third configuration method is to change the content of AutoExec.NT. This file is actually a batch file that you can modify as you would any other batch file. All of the techniques described in the "Creating Batch Files" section of the chapter apply to this file. You can create any environment you want using the proper programming techniques. In fact, you could present the user with choices and act on those choices as part of configuring the environment.

The fourth configuration method is the Program Information File (PIF). The configuration information you provide for DOS applications using this file directly affect their execution. In fact, the PIF provides a means of specifying alternative Config.NT and AutoExec.NT files. Consequently, when your command line application requires a special environment in which to run, you can create it.

The fifth configuration method is manual command line changes. The "Managing Environment Variables with the *Set* Command" section of the chapter discusses some of the changes you can make. However, you can make other changes using common command line utilities that you'll find in the sections that follow.

Using the CMD Switches

The command interpreter, CMD.EXE, is the most important part of the command line because it affects everything you do at the command line. A small change in the command interpreter can make a significant change in the way your applications run. The default command prompt setup assumes that you don't want to use any of the command line switches and that you want to start in your home directory.

If you used the Disk Operating System (DOS) at some point, it's important to remember that the command line switches that Windows supplies for the CMD.EXE command interpreter in no way match what you used in the past. Microsoft does make some command line switches available for compatibility purposes. For example, the /X command line switch is the same as /E:ON, /Y is the same as /E:OFF, and /R is the same as /C. The command interpreter ignores all other old switches; you need to use the command line switches described in this section instead.

You might also remember a few convenience features from the days of DOS that no longer appear as part of Windows. For example, at one time you could create a setup menu by using the [MENU] entry in Config.SYS. The Config.NT file doesn't support this setup. The only alternative is to create multiple Config.NT files and assign them to applications as needed. In short, even though the command interpreter does many of the same things that the DOS version does, this command interpreter is different and you need to proceed with caution about any assumptions you want to make. This application uses the following syntax:

```
CMD [{/A | /U}] [/Q] [/D] [/E:{ON | OFF}] [/F:{ON | OFF}] [/V:{ON |
     OFF}] [[/S] [{/C | /K}] string] [/T:FG]
```

The following list describes each of the command line arguments.

/C *string*   Performs the command specified by *string* and then terminates the command interpreter session. Generally, you won't get to see any application output using this technique unless the application provides graphical output or you use redirection to save the results in a file.

NOTE   When using either the /C or /K command line switches, you can specify multiple commands by creating a single string that contains all of the commands. Separate each command using a double ampersand (&&). You must enclose the entire string in double quotes. For example, "Dir *.DOC&&Dir *.TXT" would perform two Dir commands. The first would search for any file with a DOC extension, while the second would search for any file with a TXT extension.

/K *string*   Performs the command specified by *string*. The command window remains after execution ends so that you can see the application results.

/S   Modifies the treatment of the command string used with the /C and /K command line switches. The command interpreter provides two methods for processing the command string. When you use the /S command line switch, the command processor views the string associated with the /C and /K command line switch. It verifies that the first character is a quote and removes it from the string. The command processor then looks for the closing quote and removes it as well. You can use this option when the presence of quotes causes problems executing the command. The command interpreter also strips the quotations marks when you:

- ♦ Use any of the following special characters within the string: & < >( ) @ ^ |
- ♦ Include one or more white space characters
- ♦ Include an executable filename as part of the string
- ♦ Use more than one set of quotes in the string

/Q   Turns off echo. Echo is the output of the command interpreter that tells you which command is running.

/D   Disables the execution of AutoRun commands from the registry. This registry entry appears later in this section of the chapter.

/A   Specifies the output of internal commands to a pipe or file using American National Standards Institute (ANSI) characters.

/U   Specifies the output of internal commands to a pipe or file using Unicode characters.

/E:ON   Enables the command extensions. The command extensions provide added functionality for these commands: Assoc, Call, ChDir (CD), Color, Del (Erase), EndLocal, For, FType, GoTo, If, MkDir (MD), PopD, Prompt, PushD, Set, SetLocal, Shift, and Start (also includes changes to external command processes). The "Understanding Command Extensions" section of the chapter tells you how the command extensions affect these commands.

NOTE You might notice that some commands appear in parentheses. For example, the ChDir command appears before the (CD) command in parentheses. The two commands are equivalent. You can use whichever form you want. The parentheses don't show a preference, simply an alternative.

/E:OFF Disables command extensions.

/F:ON Enables file and directory name completion characters. File and directory completion allow speed typing at the command line. For example, if you want to type Dir Temp, using directory or file completion, you could type Dir T, and then press Ctrl+D (for a directory) or Ctrl+F (for a file). The command interpreter automatically completes the directory or filename for you. If you type in a partition string that doesn't match any entries, the command interpreter beeps to signify that the entry is incorrect. When the command interpreter sees multiple entries that could match the entry you provide, it displays the first entry in the list. You cycle through the entries by pressing Ctrl+D or Ctrl+F again. Use the Shift+Ctrl+D and Shift+Ctrl+F control key combinations to move backward through the list of choices. You can change the control characters that this feature uses by changing the associated registry entry. You must enclose any file or directory names that begin with special characters in quotes. These characters include <space> & ( ) [ ] { } ^ = ; ! ' + , ` ~.

/F:OFF Disables file and directory name completion characters (see the /F:ON command line switch for details).

/V:ON Enables delayed environment variable expansion. The expansion relies on the exclamation mark (!) as the delimiter. Consequently, supplying !MyVar! at the command line would expand (display the value of) MyVar at execution time.

/V:OFF Disables delayed environment variable expansion.

NOTE Vista and Server Core continue to support the /T command line switch, even though it doesn't appear with the CMD executable help. It's important to realize that Microsoft often gets rid of undocumented command line switches, so you might not have access to this feature in a future release.

/T:FG Sets the foreground (F) and background (G) colors. You must place the values together, without any space between. The following list tells you which colors you can use at the command prompt, along with their associated color number.

0—Black

1—Blue

2—Green

3—Aqua

4—Red

5—Purple

6—Yellow

7—White

8—Gray

9—Light blue

A—Light green

B—Light aqua

C—Light red

D—Light purple

E—Light yellow

F—Bright white

Combine the command line interpreter with the Start command to create additional windows as you need them. To create an additional basic command interpreter, type **Start /Separate CMD.EXE** and press Enter. Notice the positioning of the /Separate command line switch—it belongs to Start, so you place it with Start. If you wanted to create a new command line interpreter with a blue background and green lettering, you'd type **Start /Separate CMD.EXE /T:1A** and press Enter. Again, notice the positioning of the /T command line switch—it belongs to CMD.EXE, so you place it there. When you finish using the new command line interpreter, type **Exit** and press Enter.

WORKING WITH THE COMMAND INTERPRETER IN THE REGISTRY

Many of the command line behaviors depend on registry settings. You can find these settings in the HKEY_CURRENT_USER\Software\Microsoft\Command Processor key for the local user and HKEY_LOCAL_MACHTNE\SOFTWARE\Microsoft\Command Processor for everyone using the same machine. The command interpreter looks for these registry settings when you don't provide an appropriate command line switch. If you don't see the registry entry, then the command interpreter uses a default setting. Local user settings always override the machine settings, and command line switches always override the registry settings. Here are the registry settings and their meanings.

AutoRun   Defines the command that you want the command interpreter to run every time you open a command prompt. This value is of type REG_SZ or REG_EXPAND_SZ. Simply provide the executable name along with any command line switches that the executable may require. As with the string for the /C and /K command line switches, you can separate multiple commands using a double ampersand (&&).

EnableExtensions   Specifies whether the command interpreter has extensions enabled. See the /E:ON command line switch description for a list of the applications that this entry affects. This value is of type REG_DWORD. Set it to enabled using a value of 0x1 and disabled using a value of 0x0.

CompletionChar   Defines the file completion character (see the /F:ON command line switch for details). The default character is Ctrl+F (0x06). Use a value of a space (0x20) to disable this feature since the space isn't a valid control character. This value is of type REG_DWORD.

PathCompletionChar   Defines the directory completion character (see the /F:ON command line switch for details). The default character is Ctrl+D (0x04). Use a value of a space (0x20) to disable this feature since the space isn't a valid control character. This value is of type REG_DWORD.

DelayedExpansion   Specifies whether the command interpreter uses delayed variable expansion. See the /V:ON command line switch description for additional information. This value is of type REG_DWORD. Set it to enabled using a value of 0x1 and disabled using a value of 0x0.

UNDERSTANDING COMMAND EXTENSIONS

Command extensions are additional processing that the command interpreter provides for certain commands. The effects vary by command, but generally the commands receive additional functionality. In some cases, such as the del (erase) command, the extensions simply change the way the command works. The following list describes the command extension changes to each of the affected commands.

Assoc   Microsoft hasn't documented how command extensions change the Assoc command. Even though Microsoft lists it as one of the commands that changes with command extensions, there isn't any obvious difference at the command line.

Call   Accepts a label as the target for a call (rather than a filename as normal). This feature means that you can transfer control from one portion of a batch file to another. Using extensions means that you can call the label using call :Label Arguments. Notice that you must precede the label with a colon.

Chdir (CD)   Displays the directory names precisely as they appear on your hard drive. For example, if a directory name has a space, you'll see the space when you change directories. Capitalization is also the same. A directory name that appears with an initial capital letter in Windows Explorer also appears that way at the command prompt. In addition, when you turn off the command extensions, the command doesn't treat spaces as delimiters. Consequently, you don't need to surround directory names with spaces or with quotes in order to obtain the correct results from this command.

Color   Microsoft hasn't documented how command extensions change the Color command. Even though Microsoft lists it as one of the commands that changes with command extensions, there isn't any obvious difference at the command line.

Del (Erase)   Changes the way the /S command line switch works. The command shows you just the files that it deletes, rather than showing you all of the files, including those that it couldn't find.

EndLocal   Restores the command extension settings to their state before calling the SetLocal command. Normally, the SetLocal command doesn't save the state of the command extensions.

For   Implements an expanded number of For command options. When working with directories, you process directories, rather than a list of files within a directory, using this call: for /D {%% | %}Variable in (Set) do Command [CommandLineOptions]. You can also perform recursive processing of a directory tree. Using this feature means that a single command can process an entire tree, rather than using individual commands to process a branch. Use the for /R [[Drive:]Path] {%% | %}Variable in (Set) do Command [CommandLineOptions] command line syntax to perform recursion. It's also possible to iterate through a range of values, similar to the functionality of the For loop used in higher level languages, using this command syntax: for /L {%% | %}Variable in (Start#,Step#,End#) do Command [CommandLineOptions]. Variable substitution is another useful feature that using command extensions provides (see the "Using Variable Substitution" section of the chapter for details). Finally, you can perform complex file parsing and iteration with the command extension in place (see the "Performing Complex File Iteration" section of the chapter for details).

FType Microsoft hasn't documented how command extensions change the FType command. Even though Microsoft lists it as one of the commands that changes with command extensions, there isn't any obvious difference at the command line.

Goto Defines a special label called :EOF. If you define a Goto command in a batch file with the :EOF label, the system transfers control to the end of the current batch file and exits. You don't need to define the label in the batch file to make this feature work.

If Defines additional comparison syntax that makes the If command considerably more flexible. See the "Using the *If* Command" section of the chapter for details.

MkDir (MD) Lets you create intermediate directories with a single command. For example, you could define an entire subdirectory structure using MD MyDir/MySub1/MySub2. If MyDir doesn't exist, the system creates it first, then MySub1, and, finally, MySub2. Normally, you'd need to create each directory separately and use the CD command to move to each lower level to create the next subdirectory.

PopD Removes any drive letter assignment made by the PushD command.

Prompt Supports additional prompt characters. The $+ character adds one or more plus signs (+) to the command prompt for every level of the PushD command. Using this feature lets you know how many levels of redirection the PushD command has saved on the stack and how many more times you can use the PopD command to extract them. The $m character adds the remote name associated with a drive to the command prompt. The command prompt doesn't display any additional information for local drives.

PushD Allows you to push network paths onto the stack as well as local drive letters and path information.

Set Displays all currently defined environment variables when you use the Set command alone. Displays the specified environment variable when you supply an environment variable name, but not an associated value. If you supply only a partial variable name, the Set command displays all of the variables that could match that name.

SetLocal Allows the SetLocal command to enable or disable command extensions as needed to meet specific language requirements.

Shift Supports the /N command line option, which lets the Shift command shift variables starting with the *n*th variable. For example, if you use Shift /2 at the command line, then variables %0 and %1 are unaffected by the shift, but variables %3 through %9 receive new variable input.

Start Microsoft hasn't documented how command extensions change the Start command. Even though Microsoft lists it as one of the commands that changes with command extensions, there isn't any obvious difference at the command line.

Modifying *Config.NT*

The Config.NT file contains a number of entries that affect how the system works at the command prompt. At one time, the configuration file contained a wealth of device drivers and statements that defined how the command prompt used files and buffers. However, the Config.NT file rarely contains device drivers and these driver entries are normally defined by third-party software for you. Given that Server Core lacks the functionality required for an application server (which means providing complex server-based applications such as a database-based application), you may never see a driver entry in Config.NT. The following sections describe common additions you can make to the Config.NT file.

NOTE   Some people may remember Config.SYS, the file that DOS uses to perform the same configuration that Windows performs with Config.NT. In fact, some people try to move Config.SYS to the Windows environment. Fortunately, the 32-bit version of Windows accepts many older DOS commands even when it doesn't use them. For example, the FastOpen utility provides a caching feature in DOS to make directory searches faster. Even though Windows provides this file, too, it doesn't actually use the functionality and FastOpen doesn't actually perform any task. Once you move to the 64-bit versions of Windows, much of this functionality is missing completely. For example, you can't create a Config.NT file that contains a reference to the FastOpen utility.

USING *ANSI.SYS* TO CONTROL THE ENVIRONMENT

The ANSI.SYS device driver provides added functionality for applications at the command prompt. By using special escape codes, you can create a character-based user interface for your batch files. You can find a good listing of ANSI escape codes at http://www.evergreen.edu/biophysics/technotes/program/ansi_esc.htm and on the Microsoft Web site at http://www.microsoft.com/technet/archive/msdos/comm1.mspx?mfr=true. This utility uses the following syntax:

```
device=[Drive:][Path]ANSI.SYS [/X] [/K] [/R]
```

As with all device drivers that you add to the Config.NT file, you begin the ANSI.SYS entry using device= entry, followed by the drive and path to the ANSI.SYS file. The following list describes each of the command line arguments.

/X   Remaps the extended keys on 101-key keyboards independently. Actually, this feature works no matter how many extra keys your keyboard has.

/K   Forces ANSI.SYS to treat a 101-key (or more) keyboard like an 84-key keyboard by ignoring the extended keys.

/R   Changes the line scrolling functionality to improve readability when working with screen reader programs. A screen reader program interprets the screen content and presents it using some other form of output. Normally, screen reader applications say what's on screen to help those with special sight needs understand the content.

SETTING THE DOS LOCATION

This utility uses the following syntax:

```
DOS=[{HIGH | LOW}] [{,UMB | ,NOUMB}]
```

The following list describes each of the command line arguments.

HIGH | LOW   Determines whether the command environment attempts to load part of itself into the High Memory Area (HMA) (HIGH) or keep all of the code in conventional memory (LOW). The default setting is LOW. Generally, you want to load the command environment into high memory to preserve more conventional memory for applications.

UMB | NOUMB   Determines whether the command environment should manage the Upper Memory Blocks (UMBs) created by a UMB provider. Windows provides a UMB provider as a default. DOS users used to rely on a special program named EMM386.EXE to perform this task. The UMB argument tells the command environment to manage the UMBs, which frees additional memory for loading applications in areas other than conventional memory. The default setting is NOUMB.

RUNNING DOS APPLICATIONS ONLY

You can execute any kind of application you want from the command prompt. If you want to start Notepad, simply type Notepad and press Enter. However, mixing Windows and older DOS applications can sometimes cause problems. Developers wrote DOS applications with the expectation that these applications controlled the entire machine, which can cause myriad problems with Windows applications. If you have one of these older applications (and they're quite rare), you can help the DOS application execute properly by adding the NTCMDPROMPT entry to Config.NT. This entry tells the operating system to disallow Windows application execution at the command prompt, which means that the DOS application continues to feel that it owns the machine. Of course, you can start your Windows applications from another command prompt or by using any of the usual techniques, such as the Start menu.

DISPLAYING THE *CONFIG.NT* COMMANDS

Normally, you won't see any information about the commands that execute before the command window opens; all you see is a command prompt. Adding an ECHOCONFIG to the Config.NT file displays each of the commands as they execute. Using this feature can help you diagnose problems with the Config.NT file contents.

CONTROLLING THE EXPANDED MEMORY EMM ENTRY

Older applications, especially character mode (DOS) games, rely on the Expanded Memory Specification (EMS) memory to overcome command prompt memory limitations. It's important to remember that the command line effectively limits the amount of memory available to DOS applications to 640 KB minus any memory that the operating system uses. Normally, you set the amount of this memory as part of the application's PIF. However, the PIF doesn't let you control the Expanded Memory Manager (EMM), which is the application that actually makes the memory accessible. The EMM entry lets you change how the EMM works. This option uses the following syntax:

```
EMM = [A=AltRegSets] [B=BaseSegment] [RAM]
```

The following list describes each of the command line arguments.

A=AltRegSets   Defines how many alternative mapping register sets the EMM has available for mapping memory between extended memory and conventional memory. You can provide any value between 1 and 255. The default setting of 8 works fine in most cases. Check your application documentation for additional requirements.

B=BaseSegment   Defines the base segment, the location where the EMM places code within the DOS conventional memory area from extended memory as needed. Generally, any setting you choose works fine. However, some applications use specific segments for their use. Using the same memory segment for two purposes causes memory corruption and can cause the application to fail. The application documentation should tell you about any requirements. You can set the base segment to any hexadecimal value between 0x1000 and 0x4000. The default setting is 0x4000.

RAM   Specifies that the EMM should only use 64 KB of address space from the UMB area for the EMM page. Normally, the EMM uses the entire UMB for the EMM page to improve EMM performance. However, your application may require more conventional memory than this practice allows. Using the RAM option reduces the EMM page size, which makes it easier for the command environment to load more applications in upper memory—freeing conventional memory for application use.

SETTING THE NUMBER OF ACCESSIBLE FILES

The Files setting may not seem very important, but every file handle you provide to the command environment uses conventional memory. Remember that conventional memory is already quite small and many older applications barely load in the space provided. The default Files=40 setting usually provides a good compromise. This setting means that the command environment can open 40 files, which is more than sufficient for most older applications. You can increase the number to as many as 255 when your application complains that it's out of file handles or decrease the number to as little as 8 when the application complains about a lack of memory.

CONTROLLING EXTENDED MEMORY WITH *HIMEM.SYS*

The HIMEM.SYS driver provides extended memory support at the command prompt. The eXtended Memory Specification (XMS) is a method that applications use to overcome the DOS memory limitations. You set the amount of available XMS using the PIF for the application. However, you can further refine XMS functionality by relying on the command line switches described in this section. As with all device drivers that you add to the Config.NT file, you begin the HIMEM.SYS entry using the device= entry, followed by the drive and path to the HIMEM.SYS file. This driver uses the following syntax:

```
DEVICE=[drive:][path]HIMEM.SYS [/HMAMIN=m] [/INT15=xxxx]
    [/NUMHANDLES=n] [/TESTMEM:{ON|OFF}] [/VERBOSE]
```

The following list describes each of the command line arguments.

NOTE   HIMEM.SYS includes a number of command line switches, many of which are archaic. For example, even though HIMEM.SYS still supports the /A20CONTROL command line switch, you'd have to have a very old computer (over 10 years old) to need it. In short, unless you have a very old system, you'll never have a use for these older command line switches. In addition to the /A20CONTROL command line switch, I haven't discussed the /CPUCLOCK, /EISA, /MACHINE, and /SHADOWRAM command line switches. This section contains descriptions of the command line switches that are still useful.

/HMAMIN=*m* Specifies how many kilobytes of HMA memory an application must request in order for HIMEM.SYS to fulfill the request. Some applications ask for small pieces of the HMA area, which fragments an already small memory area and makes it unavailable for other applications. It becomes a question of efficient memory use. An application that can use a larger piece of the HMA will likely free more conventional memory for use by other applications. You can specify any value between 0 and 63. The default value is 0. Setting this command line switch to 0 or omitting it from the command line lets HIMEM.SYS allocate the HMA memory to the first application that requests it, regardless of how much HMA memory that application will use.

/INT15=*xxxx* Specifies the amount of extended memory in kilobytes that HIMEM.SYS should reserve for the Interrupt 15h interface. You may wonder what the Interrupt 15h interface is all about; it's the method that applications use to interact with XMS. The only time you need to use this command line switch is if you have an older DOS application, very likely a game or graphics application, that relies on XMS memory. The application will very likely display a nebulous error message that specifically mentions the Interrupt 15h interface. Make sure you set the amount of XMS memory to 64 KB larger than the amount required by the application. You can specify any value from 64 KB to 65,535 KB. However, you can't specify more memory than your system has installed. When you specify a value less than 64, HIMEM.SYS sets the value to 0. The default value is 0.

/NUMHANDLES=*n* Specifies the maximum number of Extended Memory Block (EMB) handles that the system can use simultaneously. Every time an application requests more memory, it needs a handle to access that memory. Generally, you don't need to provide this command line switch unless you have an older graphics-intensive application. You can specify a value from 1 to 128. The default setting is 32, which is more than enough for most applications. Changing the number of handles uses more memory for housekeeping chores, so you'll want to use this command line switch with care.

/TESTMEM:{ON|OFF} Determines whether HIMEM.SYS performs a memory check when you open the command prompt. Most people don't actually know whether the memory they're using is good, so checking it from time to time is a way to reduce unwelcome surprises. However, running the test takes time. You'll see a noticeable delay in displaying the command prompt when you use this command line switch. In most cases, it's far better to test your memory using a third-party diagnostic program that works outside of Window's influence. Otherwise, you can't be sure that you're testing all of the memory and won't know which surprises Windows has hidden from view. The HTMEM.SYS test is more thorough than the test that runs when you start your computer, so you can use it when you don't have any other means of testing available.

/VERBOSE Displays additional status and error messages while HIMEM.SYS is loading. The system normally doesn't display any messages unless it encounters a problem loading or initializing HIMEM.SYS. Adding this command line switch can point out potential problems in your system setup and aid in diagnosing application problems that you wouldn't normally detect. You can abbreviate this command line switch as /V. Unfortunately, despite the documentation for HIMEM.SYS online, you can't display the verbose messages by pressing the Alt key as the system loads HIMEM.SYS into memory; you must use the /VERBOSE command line switch to see the extended messages.

Modifying *AutoExec.NT*

Although Config.NT offers some interesting low-level methods of changing the command line environment, the AutoExec.NT file provides far more opportunities. Any application that you can access from the command line is also a candidate for inclusion in the AutoExec.NT file. Adding applications that you always use can set up the command line from the outset, so you see what you need without entering any commands at all. You can also program the AutoExec.NT file as you would any other batch file. This means you can add menus to your setup so you can choose the options you want to see. See the "Creating Batch Files" section of the chapter for details on creating a programmed interface to your AutoExec.NT file. The sections that follow describe some utilities that you'll use most often from within the AutoExec.NT file. These utilities tend to configure the command environment, in some way, to make your computing experience better. However, don't limit yourself to these selections—any command or utility described in the book is a candidate for inclusion.

NOTE You'll find some older utilities that Windows installs for compatibility purposes and then doesn't support. The KB16 utility should provide keyboard support, but you'll find that the command line provides this support automatically, so you don't actually need to use the KB16 utility. Even though the KB16 utility loads into memory and appears to perform a task, it doesn't do anything. In addition to the KB16 utility, you'll find that Windows doesn't support the MSCDex utility. This chapter doesn't discuss these compatibility commands and utilities.

SETTING THE CODE PAGE NUMBER WITH THE CHCP UTILITY

A code page defines language support at the command prompt. In the days of DOS, you needed to provide a code page to obtain proper language support at the command prompt, but Windows doesn't usually require you to set a code page. You might need to set a code page for older character-mode applications. Only the OEM font you installed as part of Windows displays properly when you use a raster font in a windowed command prompt. However, you can use any of the supported code pages in full screen mode or with a TrueType font. This utility uses the following syntax:

```
CHCP [nnn]
```

The following describes the command line argument.

nnn Defines the code page to use. The standard code page numbers appear in Table 5.1. Code pages 874 through 1258 are both OEM and ANSI implementations that are only available in Windows. You can install additional code pages as needed. The Web site at http://www.i18nguy.com/unicode/codepages.html#msftdos shows how these code pages appear.

TABLE 5.1:   Standard OEM and OEM/ANSI Code Pages

CODE PAGE	COUNTRY OR LANGUAGE
437	United States
850	Multilingual (Latin I)
852	Slavic (Latin II)
855	Cyrillic (Russian)
857	Turkish
860	Portuguese
861	Icelandic
863	Canadian-French
865	Nordic
866	Russian
869	Modern Greek
874	Thai
932	Japanese Shift-JIS
936	Simplified Chinese GBK
949	Korean
950	Traditional Chinese Big5
1258	Vietnam

ADDING DPMI SUPPORT USING THE DOSX UTILITY

The DOS Protected Mode Interface (DPMI) is one method for a DOS application to access more than the 640 KB that DOS (the command line) typically allows. In addition, this interface provides protected memory access, so the DOS application doesn't interfere with Windows operation. You can read about DPMI at http://whatis.techtarget.com/definition/0,,sid9_gci213913,00.html. To use this interface, an application developer needs to provide special support in the application; usually as part of a third-party add-on library. All you need to know is whether the application (typically a game) supports DPMI to use this feature. This utility uses the following syntax:

```
DosX
```

As you can see, this utility doesn't require any command line switches and it doesn't display any messages after you install it. You can use the MEM utility described in the "Determining Memory Status with the Mem Utility" section of Chapter 12 to determine whether the utility loaded into memory as anticipated.

ENABLING GRAPHICS CHARACTER SUPPORT WITH THE GRAFTABL UTILITY

Normally, the system displays any extended characters your application needs to display as plaintext. In some cases, this means the extended characters won't display correctly because your system may lack the capability required to display the extended characters properly. The GrafTabl utility helps Windows display extended characters as graphics, which means they always display correctly as long as you have the proper code page support loaded. The GrafTabl utility only affects extended character display; you need to use the Mode or CHCP utilities to change the console input. This utility uses the following syntax:

```
GRAFTABL [xxx]
GRAFTABL /STATUS
```

The following list describes each of the command line arguments.

xxx Specifies the code page number to use for display purposes. Table 5.1 lists the common code pages for Windows.

/STATUS Displays the code page that the GrafTabl has loaded for display purposes. This command line switch doesn't reflect the Mode or CHCP utility settings.

NOTE The GrafTabl utility won't work with Windows Itanium or Windows 64-bit versions.

PRINTING COMMAND LINE GRAPHICS WITH THE GRAPHICS UTILITY

Server Core isn't supposed to do anything when you try to use the Graphics utility, according to the Windows help file. However, the Graphics utility does load and apparently has some functionality. With this in mind, using the Graphics utility is an "at your own risk" kind of utility that you should only try as a last resort to obtain required application functionality. The \WINDOWS\system32 directory contains the GRAPHICS.COM and GRAPHICS.PRO files mentioned in the Knowledge Base article at http://support.microsoft.com/default.aspx?scid=kb;en-us;Q78123.

WARNING Using the Graphics utility can produce some unexpected side effects when working at the command prompt. For example, you may find that the command history buffer no longer works. In addition, you might not be able to scroll through the buffer to see older information. The Graphics utility tends to restrict you to a single command mode and only one screen at a time.

Use the Graphics utility to load support for printing graphics at the command line. Some older applications may require this support, but generally, you don't need to load the Graphics utility. For example, you may need to load the graphics utility to print a screenshot of an older game. Press Shift+Print Screen to print a graphics image with this utility loaded. This utility uses the following syntax:

```
GRAPHICS [type] [[drive:][path]filename] [/R] [/B] [/LCD]
    [/PRINTBOX:STD | /PRINTBOX:LCD]
```

The following list describes each of the command line arguments.

type   Specifies the printer type. In most cases, you'll want to use the default type unless you experience problems getting the default type to work. The printer types include: COLOR1, COLOR4, COLOR8, HPDEFAULT, DESKJET, GRAPHICS, GRAPHICSWIDE, LASERJET, LASERJETII, PAINTJET, QUIETJET, QUIETJETPLUS, RUGGEDWRITER, RUGGEDWRITERWIDE, THERMAL, and THINKJET.

[drive:][path]filename   Specifies a file containing printer support information. You must obtain this file from the printer vendor in most cases.

/R   Prints the output as white letters on a black background as normally displayed on screen. Normally, the utility reverses the colors to save ink.

/B   Prints the background in color for the COLOR4 and COLOR8 printers.

/LCD   Outputs the screen using the Liquid Crystal Display (LCD) aspect ratio so the output looks like the screen.

/PRINTBOX:STD | /PRINTBOX:LCD   Displays a print box around the output. The options specify the print box size. You can choose between the standard (STD) or LCD aspect ratios.

SAVING MEMORY USING THE *LH* COMMAND

The Load High (LH) command attempts to load a utility into high memory, instead of using application memory. Loading the utility high saves memory that memory-hungry applications can use to load. Generally, you should try to load high all of the utilities that you can, including DosX and ReDir. Windows 64-bit editions don't support this command. This command uses the following syntax:

```
LH
```

You don't need to provide any command line switches with this command. Simply add the command or utility that you want to load high after LH on the command line. The system won't display an error message if the command fails. However, you can verify the utility's location in memory using the Mem utility.

ADDING CD SUPPORT WITH MSCDEXNT UTILITY

Windows provides all of the CD and DVD support that you need. The name of this support under DOS is Microsoft Compact Disk (or CD-ROM) Extensions (MSCDEX). However, you still need access to this support from the command prompt. Loading the MSCDexNT utility loads several additional applications including VCDEX.DLL, which is the 32-bit MSCDEX Virtual Device Driver. This utility uses the following syntax:

```
MSCDexNT
```

You don't need to supply any command line switches when using this utility.

INSTALLING THE NETWORK REDIRECTOR USING THE REDIR UTILITY

Use this utility to load the VDM Virtual Device Driver (VDD) redirector. The redirector provides virtual device access from the command prompt. Essentially, it provides network access. This utility uses the following syntax:

```
ReDir
```

You don't need to supply any command line switches when using this utility.

SERVER CORE AND THE PIF

The Program Information File (PIF) is an addition to a DOS application that controls how Windows interacts with the application. You don't start the application using the PIF (although double-clicking the PIF will start the application), but the PIF always affects how Windows works with the application. From a command line perspective, you can use a PIF to perform two special tasks. First, you can create custom AutoExec.NT and Config.NT for the application so you can control the application environment. Second, you can add command line switches to the application command line so that the application starts with the features you want to use.

When working with a graphical version of Windows, you simply right-click the DOS application you want to modify and choose Properties from the context menu. This act actually creates the PIF. Unfortunately, Server Core lacks Windows Explorer, which means you don't have access to the usual graphical means of creating a PIF. At one time, Microsoft also provided the PIFEdit utility. However, this utility disappeared with Windows NT because users found it too difficult to use and there isn't a place to download this utility any longer online (if you find a reliable location to download the utility, please contact me at JMueller@mwt.net). Consequently, if you want to work with PIF files in Server Core, you'll have to perform the task at the client machine using the same techniques you've always employed.

Defining Application Compatibility with the SetVer Utility

Some older applications expect a specific version of DOS (the command interpreter) when they execute and won't execute with any other version. Usually, these applications won't even start; they simply display an error message telling you to get the right version of DOS. You can overcome this particular problem by adding an entry for the application to the Set Version (SetVer) utility table. When you try to execute the application, the command interpreter tells it that it's executing with the specific version of DOS that the application needs. This utility uses the following syntax:

```
Display the SetVer Information
      SETVER [drive:path]
Add a New Application
      SETVER [drive:path] filename n.nn
Delete an Application
      SETVER [drive:path] filename /DELETE [/QUIET]
```

The following list describes each of the command line arguments.

[drive:path]   Specifies the location of the SetVer.EXE file.

filename   Specifies the name of the program to add to or delete from the SetVer table.

n.nn   Specifies the DOS version to report to the application.

/DELETE or /D   Deletes the application listing from the SetVer table.

/QUIET   Performs the specified task without displaying any prompts. Use this option when working with batch files to prevent the utility from interrupting the user.

NOTE   You must load SetVer.EXE as a device driver in Config.NT to obtain the version-setting feature that it provides. You can check the SetVer status at the command prompt by typing SetVer and pressing Enter. The command displays a list of applications that appear in the SetVer table, and then displays the SetVer status. You'll see an error message when the device isn't loaded into memory.

Using Common DOS Utilities

You'll find a number of common DOS utilities on your hard drive. Most of these utilities appear with every version of DOS, even those that Microsoft didn't produce (such as the IBM version). For the most part, these utilities perform maintenance tasks that you could perform in a batch file. For example, many people had batch files for working with the DiskCopy utility when floppy disks were popular. The following sections describe these utilities in detail.

COMPARING THE CONTENTS OF DISKS WITH THE DISKCOMP UTILITY

You can use this utility to compare the contents of two floppy disks. Because of the way the utility works, the two floppies must have precisely the same format and you can't compare two newer forms of media, such as CDs. A better alternative for modern media is the FC utility described in the "Performing Advanced File Comparison with the FC Utility" section of Chapter 14. This utility uses the following syntax:

```
DISKCOMP [drive1: [drive2:]]
```

The following list describes each of the command line arguments.

drive1:   Specifies the source drive.

drive2:   Specifies the destination drive. If you don't specify a destination drive, the utility assumes that you'll use one drive for the comparison and prompts you to replace the source disk with the destination disk as needed.

COPYING ONE DISK TO ANOTHER WITH THE DISKCOPY UTILITY

You can use this utility to copy the contents of one floppy disk to another floppy disk. Because of the way the utility works, the two floppies must have precisely the same format. A better alternative for modern media is the XCopy utility described in the "Performing Bulk File Transfers with the XCopy Utility" section of Chapter 14. This utility uses the following syntax:

```
DISKCOPY [drive1: [drive2:]] [/V]
```

The following list describes each of the command line arguments.

drive1:   Specifies the source drive.

drive2:   Specifies the destination drive. If you don't specify a destination drive, the utility assumes that you'll use one drive for the comparison and prompts you to replace the source disk with the destination disk as needed.

/V   Verifies that the files copied correctly. Always use this option to ensure maximum copy reliability.

MODIFYING DATA FILES WITH THE EDIT UTILITY

The Edit utility is a very useful application to know about because it works when most other editors don't. The Edit utility is quite small, so you can place it on a floppy if you want or a CD that contains your diagnostic software. In addition, you don't need a graphical interface to use Edit, so it works at the DOS prompt, the Windows recovery console, or just about anywhere else you might need an editor. However, even with these limits, Edit supports a robust interface for a text editor, as shown in Figure 5.1. From a Server Core perspective, however, the Edit utility is best because it has no reliance on Windows functionality, so you don't need to worry about issues such as common dialog box usage.

FIGURE 5.1

Use Edit wherever you need a fully functional text editor.

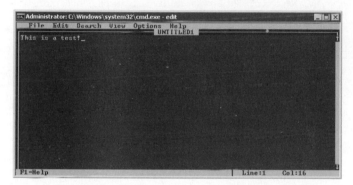

As you can see, the utility sports many of the same features as Notepad, but without the Notepad requirements. This utility uses the following syntax:

```
EDIT [/B] [/H] [/R] [/S] [/<nnn>] [/?] [file(s)]
```

The following list describes each of the command line arguments.

/B   Sets Edit to start in monochrome mode.

/H   Sets Edit to start with the maximum number of lines of text for your hardware. The default setup displays 25 lines of text.

/R   Loads files in read-only mode. Use this option when you want to view the file content without accidentally changing it.

/S   Forces Edit to use short filenames.

/nnn   Loads a binary file and displays the content by wrapping any long lines to the specified number of characters.

file   Specifies the name of the file to load. You can use wildcard characters and multiple file specifications to load multiple files. This argument must appear as the last argument on the command line.

FORMATTING A DISK WITH THE FORMAT UTILITY

The Format utility formats a drive and prepares it for use. The utility removes any existing data from the volume you select. This section discusses the command line version of the Format utility.

The recovery console offers a slightly different version of this utility. You must be a member of the Administrators group to use this utility. The utility always displays a warning message before it formats a hard drive; you must specifically accept the warning message content before the format will start. This utility uses the following syntax:

```
FORMAT volume [/FS:file-system] [/V:label] [/Q] [/A:size] [/C] [/X]
    [/P:Passes]
FORMAT volume [/V:label] [/Q] [/F:size] [/P:Passes]
FORMAT volume [/V:label] [/Q] [/T:tracks /N:sectors] [/P:Passes]
FORMAT volume [/V:label] [/Q] [/P:Passes]
FORMAT volume [/Q]
```

The following list describes each of the command line arguments.

WARNING   The Format utility has caused people more woe than any other utility ever created. Simply stated, the Format utility will format your hard drive. In many cases, you can recover files that the Format utility removes from the hard drive using a special utility, but the process is time consuming and error prone at best. Use this utility with extreme caution.

volume   Specifies the drive letter, mount point, or volume name to format. Always include this argument because the default value is the current drive.

/FS:filesystem   Specifies the file system to use to format the volume. You have the option of using the FAT (older 16-bit), FAT32, or NTFS file systems when working with a hard drive. Floppy media only accepts the FAT file system.

/V:[label]   Specifies the volume name. If you use this command line switch without specifying a volume name, the Format utility prompts you for a volume name on completion of the format.

/Q   Performs a quick format of the media. A quick format deletes the file table and the root directory of the media. It doesn't perform a sector-by-sector scan of the media to locate bad sectors. You should only use this option with known good media.

/C   Creates an NTFS volume that the system compresses by default. Consequently, you won't need to perform this step separately later.

/X   Forces the system to dismount the drive before formatting if necessary. Dismounting the drive closes all open handles.

/A:size   Overrides the default allocation unit size for the hard drive. You can use this feature to optimize storage for specific tasks. For example, if you plan to store many small files, you might want to use a small allocation size. The size argument can include 512 bytes, 1,024 bytes, 2,048 bytes, 4,096 bytes, 8,192 bytes, 16 KB, 32 KB, and 64 KB cluster sizes for NTFS drives. You can't use compression on NTFS drives with a cluster size larger than 4,096. A FAT- or FAT32-formatted drive can use cluster sizes of 512 bytes, 1,024 bytes, 2,048 bytes, 4,096 bytes, 8,192 bytes, 16 KB, 32 KB, 64 KB, 128 KB, and 256 KB. You can only use the 128 KB and 256 KB options for a sector size greater than 512 bytes.

NOTE   FAT and FAT32 file systems impose a limit on the number of clusters per volume. A FAT-formatted drive can have 65,526 or fewer clusters. A FAT32-formatted drive can have any number of clusters between 65,526 and 4,177,918. The Format utility stops immediately when it detects that a drive can't meet the number of cluster requirements using the specified cluster size.

/F:*size* Specifies the size of the floppy disk to format. The default setting is 1.44 MB. You can specify this value as 1,440, 1,440k, 1,440kb, 1.44, 1.44m, or 1.44mb. The Format utility will also format 720 KB floppies. None of the Microsoft documentation specifies whether the utility formats 2.88 MB floppies. Theoretically, you can also format the very old 5¼-inch floppies with sizes of 640 KB and 1.2 MB. Use this option, whenever possible, instead of the /T and /N command line switches.

/T:*tracks* Specifies the number of tracks per side of the disk.

/N:*sectors* Specifies the number of sectors per track.

The format command provides a number of exit codes that you can use when working with batch files. The following list describes each of the exit codes.

0 The format completed successfully.

1 The format failed because you provided incorrect arguments.

4 A fatal error occurred. For example, the utility couldn't format the drive because the system has it locked for use. The Format utility uses this error when the 0, 1, or 5 codes don't apply.

5 The user pressed N when the utility asked whether it should proceed with the disk format. Pressing N always stops the formatting process.

/P:*Passes* Zeroes every sector on the hard drive the number of times defined by Passes. The /P command line switch makes it possible for you to erase the data on a hard drive more completely. However, the only certain way to ensure the data is gone is to destroy the hard drive completely and magnetically erase the media.

Loading Older DOS Applications with the LoadFix Utility

Some older applications don't load correctly. You'll see a "Packed file corrupt" error message when you try to load them. The LoadFix utility modifies the loading process for these applications so they load above the 64 KB area of memory used for operating system needs. This utility uses the following syntax:

```
LOADFIX [drive:][path]filename
```

The following describes the command line argument:

[*drive:*][*path*]*filename* Specifies the name and location of the file to modify.

Terminating a Session Using the Logoff Utility

The Logoff utility ends a user session and logs off the user. The advantage of this utility is that you can find it in older versions of Windows, so you can use the same script on just about any machine. The disadvantage of this utility is that it provides limited functionality. The ShutDown utility, described in the "Shutting Down the System with the ShutDown Command" section of Chapter 3, is far more capable and you should use it whenever possible. This utility uses the following syntax:

```
LOGOFF [sessionname | sessionid] [/SERVER:servername] [/V]
```

The following list describes each of the command line arguments.

sessionname Defines the name of the session that you want to log off. Older versions of the tool don't provide this argument. The default is to log off the current session.

sessionid Defines the identifier of the session that you want to log off.

/SERVER:*servername* Specifies the server containing the user session to log off. Some documentation implies that you need Terminal Server to use this command line switch, but it appears to work just as well without it.

/V Displays detailed information about the actions the system performs during the logoff cycle.

CONFIGURING SYSTEM DEVICES WITH THE MODE UTILITY

The Mode utility configures system devices for use. In addition, you can use it to display the status of a single device or all devices in the system. To display the status of all accessible devices type Mode and press Enter. If you want the status of just one device, type Mode followed by the device name, such as LPT1:, and press Enter. This utility uses the following syntax:

```
Serial Port
      MODE COMm[:] [BAUD=b] [PARITY=p] [DATA=d] [STOP=s] [to={on |
          off}] [xon={on | off}] [odsr={on | off}] [octs={on | off}]
          [dtr={on | off | hs}] [rts={on | off | hs | tg}] [idsr={on |
          off}]
Device Status
      MODE [device] [/STATUS]
Redirect Printing
      MODE LPTn[:]=COMm[:]
Select Code Page
      MODE CON[:] CP SELECT=yyy
Code Page Status
      MODE CON[:] CP [/STATUS]
Display Mode
      MODE CON[:] [COLS=c] [LINES=n]
Typematic Rate
      MODE CON[:] [RATE=r DELAY=d]
```

The following list describes each of the command line arguments.

COM*m*[:] Defines the COM port to configure. The Mode utility recognizes any COM port for which it can find a device name. Generally, this means it will support COM1: through COM9: unless you have special hardware to make additional COM ports available.

NOTE As you work with utilities at the command prompt, you'll find that different utilities support different numbers of ports. Most utilities support at least LPT1: through LPT3:, but you'll find a few that support up to LPT9:. Support for the COM (serial) ports is even more diverse. A few utilities only support COM1: through COM3:. More common is support for COM1: through COM4: for utilities. However, you'll find a few that support up to COM9: and a few that support as many COM ports as your machine has installed. One device is a constant: every workstation supports the CON: (console) device.

BAUD=*b* Determines the transmission rate of the COM port in bits per second (bps). Note that bps isn't always equivalent to baud; see the definition at http://webopedia.internet.com/TERM/B/baud.html for details. Table 5.2 shows numbers you must use to specify a desired rate.

TABLE 5.2:   Baud Rates Supported by the Mode Utility

NUMERIC VALUE	EQUIVALENT BAUD RATE
11	110 baud
15	150 baud
30	300 baud
60	600 baud
12	1,200 baud
24	2,400 baud
48	4,800 baud
96	9,600 baud
19	19,200 baud

PARITY=*p* Determines how the system checks for transmission errors. The mode command supports the values shown in Table 5.3.

TABLE 5.3:   Parity Types Supported by the Mode Utility

PARITY VALUE	PARITY CHECKING TYPE
n	none
e	even
o	odd
m	mark
s	space

DATA=*d* Specifies the number of data bits per character. You may use any value between 5 and 8. The default setting of 7 provides support for standard ASCII characters. Use 8 for extended ASCII characters (the 256-character set). Not all computers support 5 or 6 bits per character.

STOP=*s* Specifies the number of stop bits after each character. You may specify 1, 1.5, and 2 as stop bit values. The default setting for 110 baud is 2. All other data transfer rates use 1 as a default value. Not all computers support 1.5 stop bits.

to={on | off} Specifies whether the computer uses infinite timeout processing. The default value is off. Setting this value to on means that the computer will wait literally forever to receive a response from a host or client computer.

xon={on | off} Specifies whether the system enables XON/XOFF protocol. The XON/XOFF protocol provides flow control for serial communications, making them more reliable, but also exacting a performance penalty. You can learn more about the XON/XOFF protocol at http://docs.hp.com/en/32022-90051/ch09s08.html.

odsr={on | off} Specifies whether the system enables the Data Set Ready (DSR) output handshaking.

octs={on | off} Specifies whether the system enables the Clear to Send (CTS) output handshaking.

dtr={on | off | hs} Specifies whether the system enables the Data Terminal Ready (DTR) output handshaking. The on mode provides a constant signal showing the terminal is ready to receive data. The hs mode provides a handshaking signal between the two terminals.

rts={on | off | hs | tg} Specifies whether the system enables the Request to Send (RTS) output handshaking. The on mode provides a constant signal showing the terminal is ready to send data. The hs mode provides a handshaking signal between the two terminals. The tg mode provides a toggling feature between ready and not ready states.

idsr={on | off} Specifies whether the system enables DSR sensitivity. You must enable this feature to use DSR handshaking.

device Defines the name of the device that you want to work with. Standard names include LPT1: through LPT3:, COM1: through COM9:, and CON:.

/STATUS Specifies that you want to obtain the status of a specified device or of all accessible devices on the system.

LPT*n*[:] Defines the number of the LPT port to configure. Generally, this means supplying a name from LPT1: through LPT3: unless your system includes special parallel port support.

CON[:] Defines the console as the target for configuration or a status check.

NOTE The Mode utility only supports physical devices. You can't use it to configure virtual devices. For example, if you redirect a network printer to use LPT1:, the Mode utility won't display any status information about it and you won't be able to configure the device in any way. However, if you have a physical LPT1 port on your machine, you can use the Mode utility to configure it. Because every workstation computer has a physical console, you can always use the Mode utility to configure the CON device and obtain status information about it.

CP Configures or queries the code page information for the selected device. Table 5.1 contains a list of the code pages that Windows supports natively. You can add support for additional code pages.

SELECT=*yyy* Determines the number of the code page to use with the selected device.

COLS=*c* Determines the number of columns displayed on screen. The default setting is 80 columns. Although you can configure the number of columns to any value, other standard values include 40 and 135. Using a nonstandard value can result in command line application problems.

LINES=*n* Determines the number of lines in the screen buffer. The default value is 25 (the other standard value is 50). You can use any value for the number of lines.

RATE=*r* Determines the typematic rate for the keyboard. The typematic rate determines how fast Windows will repeat a character when you press the associated key on the keyboard. You may use any value in the range from 1 through 32. The default setting is 20 characters per second. If you set the typematic rate, you must also set the delay.

DELAY=d Determines the delay between the time you press a key and the time Windows begins repeating the associated character on screen. Valid values for d are 1 (0.25 seconds), 2 (0.50 seconds), 3 (0.75 seconds), and 4 (1 second). The default value is 2.

MANAGING ENVIRONMENT VARIABLES WITH THE *SET* COMMAND

The term *environment variable* is foreign to many users because environment variables work in the background to make life easier for both GUI users and those who work at the command line. Admittedly, someone working at the command line is more likely to see the effects of environment variables directly. For example, without a proper path environment variable, you can't execute many applications. The path points to the locations where the command processor should look for applications.

Windows supports two forms of environment variables: permanent and session. The session environment variables only affect the current command line session. As soon as you close the command window, these environment variables are gone. You create session environment variables using the Set command. Permanent environment variables exist for all Windows GUI applications as well as the command prompt. Unless you change them, permanent environment variables exist between reboots of your system as well. You set permanent environment variables using the WMIC Environment alias (see Chapter 3 for details on the WMIC command). For example, if you want to set the permanent path variable to include the C:\Temp directory, you would type **WMIC Environment Where Name="Path" SET VariableValue="C:\Temp;%PATH%"** and press Enter. Notice that you include the %PATH% expansion variable to preserve the existing path information.

NOTE   Many administrators know that they can set environmental variables using the Environment Variables dialog box. To access this dialog box in a GUI version of Windows, right-click My Computer and choose Properties from the context menu. Select the Advanced tab of the System Properties dialog box. Click Environment Variables to display the Environment Variables dialog box. Unfortunately, Server Core lacks the interface elements required to use this option.

When you work at the command line, you often need environment variables in addition to those Windows uses. For example, the COPYCMD environment variable affects the Copy, Move, and XCopy utilities. You can set the command line switches you want to use with these utilities by setting the COPYCMD environment variable. Of course, you can always override your selections by specifying a different set of command line switches at the command line. For example, if you set the /Y command line switch in the COPYCMD environment variable, you can override it by specifying the /-Y command line switch.

Many environment variables only affect one application. For example, you can set the MORE environment variable to set the command line switches for the More utility. Every time you use the More utility, it searches for this environment variable and sets itself up accordingly.

Command line environment variables need not impose on those used in Windows. Besides setting environment variables in the Environment Variables dialog box and at the command line using the Set command, you can add environment variables to the AutoExec.NT file. Windows executes the commands within AutoExec.NT every time it opens a command prompt for you. These environment variables appear every time you open a command prompt, but won't appear within Windows. You use the Set command within the AutoExec.NT file, just as you would at the command prompt. The "Modifying *AutoExec.NT*" section of the chapter describes the AutoExec.NT file in more detail.

For all of the tasks that it performs, the Set command is relatively simple. This command uses the following syntax:

```
SET [variable[=[string]]]
SET /A expression
SET /P variable=[promptString]
```

The following list describes each of the command line arguments.

variable   Specifies the environment variable name. The name can't contain spaces or most special characters. You can split words in a variable name using the underscore (_) or dash (-).

string   Defines the value of the environment variable. If you type the environment variable, followed by an equals sign (=), but without a value, the Set command deletes the environment variable. Type the Set command followed by the environment variable without an equals sign to determine the current environment variable value. In fact, you can type as little as a single letter to see a list of environment variables and their associated values that begin with that letter.

/A expression   Creates an environment variable based on an expression, such as a math equation or the concatenation of multiple environment variables, instead of a standard string.

/P variable=[promptString]   Prompts the user to assign a value to an environment variable, rather than assigning the value directly. You must supply a variable name. The optional prompt string lets you provide a specific prompt to the user. Otherwise, the display doesn't show any prompt at all.

Server Core comes with a number of standard environment variables. These hard-coded environment variables perform essential tasks, such as displaying the current directory for you. You can see a list of these environment variables on the Microsoft Web site at http://www.microsoft.com/resources/documentation/windows/xp/all/proddocs/en-us/ntcmds_shelloverview.mspx. Typing **Set** by itself and pressing Enter displays the list of environment variables set for your machine as shown in Figure 5.2. This list doesn't include the hard-coded environment variables such as CD.

You can use the /A command line switch to combine existing environmental variables or even perform math with them. For example, you could use the following Set command to create a new environment variable based on the existing %NUMBER_OF_PROCESSORS% environment variable.

```
SET /A TwiceTheProcessor=%NUMBER_OF_PROCESSORS% * 2
```

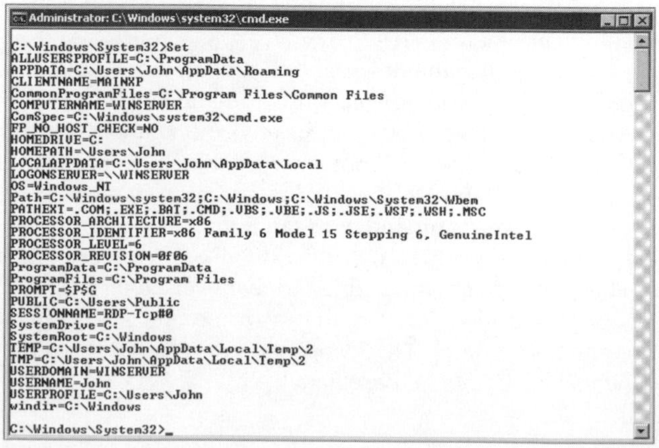

FIGURE 5.2
The Set command displays the list of environment variables defined for your machine.

You can use any of the operators shown in Table 5.4 when creating your expression. The operators appear in order of precedence.

TABLE 5.4: Set Expression Operators

OPERATOR	DESCRIPTION
( )	Group expression elements
! ~ -	Not, negate, and negative unary operators
* / %	Multiply, divide, and modulus arithmetic operators
+ -	Add and subtract arithmetic operators
<< >>	Right and left logical shift
&	Bitwise AND
^	Bitwise exclusive OR
|	Bitwise OR
= *= /= %= += -= &= ^= |= <<= >>=	Assignment operators
,	Expression separator

Any expressions you create can also contain octal, decimal, or hexadecimal numbers. All octal values begin with a 0 (zero) and hexadecimal values begin with a 0x. The Set command is quite handy when you create batch files, so you'll see additional coverage for it in the "Creating Batch Files" section.

MANAGING ENVIRONMENT VARIABLES WITH THE SETX UTILITY

The SetX utility performs essentially the same tasks as the Set command described in the "Managing Environment Variables with the *Set* Command" section of the chapter. However, it offers considerably more flexibility because you can use SetX over a network to interact with variables on other machines. In addition, it offers considerable flexibility in setting variables, such as letting you choose between the current user and the system as a whole. Rather than repeat all of the common information for using SetX, please refer to the Set command as a starting point. This command uses the following syntax:

```
SETX [/S system [/U [domain\]user [/P [password]]]] var value [/M]
SETX [/S system [/U [domain\]user [/P [password]]]] var /K regpath [/M]
SETX [/S system [/U [domain\]user [/P [password]]]] /F file {var
    {/A x,y | /R x,y string}[/M] | /X} [/D delimiters]
```

The following list describes each of the command line arguments.

/S *system* Specifies the remote system that you want to check. In most cases, you'll also need to supply the /U and the /P command line switches when using this switch.

/U [*domain*]*user* Specifies the username on the remote system. This name may not match the username on the local system. You'll need to supply a domain name when working with a domain controller.

/P [*password*] Specifies the password for the given user. You can provide the command line switch without specifying the password on the command line in cleartext. The system prompts you for the password. Using this feature can help you maintain the security of passwords used on your system.

var Contains the name of the variable you wish to change.

value Sets the specified variable to the supplied value. You don't have to provide the equals sign (=) as you do when working with the Set command. Place values with spaces within double quotes.

/M Sets the value as a system-wide (machine-level) variable that appears in HKEY_LOCAL_MACHINE. The default setting places the variable within the current user's environment.

/K *regpath* Sets the specified variable using the content of a registry key. You must provide the fully qualified registry value (including all of the keys), such as KEY_LOCAL_MACHINE\System\CurrentControlSet\Control\TimeZoneInformation\StandardName.

/F *file* Specifies the name of a text file to use for settings. You must also provide the position of the setting within the file as an absolute or relative coordinate (line number and character position). In addition, if the setting is delimited, you must provide the delimiter used for it.

/A *x,y* Provides the absolute position of the setting within the file. You must provide the position as a line number and character number.

/R *x,y string* Provides a relative position of the setting within the file. SetX first searches for the string you specify within the file. It then moves relative to that string the number of lines and characters within the line that you specify.

/X Displays the file contents using x and y coordinates. This argument doesn't actually set any variables. What it does is display the position of each potential setting within the file so that you can use the /A and /R arguments with greater ease.

/D *delimiters* Defines the delimiters used to begin and end settings entries within the file. The default settings include space, tab, carriage return, and linefeed. You can use any ASCII character as a delimiter. The maximum number of delimiters, including the default delimiters, is 15.

EXECUTING APPLICATIONS USING THE *START* COMMAND

Many of the commands and utilities discussed so far in this book wait until they complete a task before they return control of the command prompt to the user. A common way to handle this problem, when the application supports it, is to ask it to return immediately and continue working in the background. The only problem with this approach is that you aren't sure that the command or utility completed successfully. The Start command helps you overcome this problem by creating a new window for the command or window to run in. The command or utility still controls the command prompt until it completes, but since it runs in another window, the user can continue working.

Another use for this utility is to start the command or utility in a window with a specific title. You can apply settings to a window that rely on the window title (see the "Configuring the Command Window" section of Chapter 2 for details). Whenever you open a window with that title, it also has the special formatting that you specified. In short, you can create custom environments in which to run a utility. This utility uses the following syntax:

```
START ["title"] [/Dpath] [/I] [/MIN] [/MAX] [/SEPARATE | /SHARED] [/LOW
    | /NORMAL | /HIGH | /REALTIME | /ABOVENORMAL | /BELOWNORMAL] [/WAIT]
    [/B] [{command | program}] [parameters]
```

The following list describes each of the command line arguments.

"*title*"   Defines the title of the command window title bar.

/D*Path*   Specifies the starting directory for the command window. This value doesn't have to be the same as the path for the command that you want to execute. For example, it might be the path to the data directory for the command.

/B   Starts the application without creating a new window. The application executes as a background task and doesn't display a user interface. The lack of user interface means that the application won't provide Ctrl+C handling, so you would need to stop the application using the Task Manager or an application such as the TaskKill command described in the "Terminating Tasks with the TaskKill Command" section of Chapter 21. Some applications may also allow termination using Ctrl+Break.

/I   Passes the standard command environment to the new window, rather than using any changes made to the command environment by the current command window. Using this command line switch ensures that the application won't run in a contaminated environment where an environmental setting could adversely affect the way the application runs.

/MIN   Starts the application with the command window minimized.

/MAX   Starts the application with the command window maximized.

/SEPARATE   Starts 16-bit Windows applications in a separate memory space. Normally, Windows uses a separate memory space for all 32-bit applications, but a single memory space for all 16-bit applications. Older applications don't always use memory correctly, resulting in memory corruption that can cause other applications to fail. Using this command line switch eliminates shared memory corruption problems. However, this feature comes at the cost of performance and overall system resource usage. Unlike 32-bit memory spaces, 16-bit memory spaces remain fixed in memory, which uses the memory inefficiently and causes memory fragmentation. Memory fragmentation can cause Windows to perform inefficiently, leading to performance problems. In short, use this command line switch only when you actually experience problems.

/SHARED   Starts the 16-bit Windows application in a shared memory space. This is the default setting and you should normally use it unless you experience memory corruption problems while running the application.

/LOW   Starts the application in the IDLE priority class. Use this priority setting for applications that only run when other applications don't require the processor. This command line switch helps the system function more efficiently when you want to run the application as a background task and don't care when it completes its work.

/BELOWNORMAL   Starts the application in the BELOWNORMAL priority class. Use this priority setting for background applications that you want to complete in a timely manner, but not at the expense of foreground applications.

/NORMAL   Starts the application in the NORMAL priority class. This is the default setting. Foreground applications normally start at this priority. You should only use this setting for applications that you want to complete at a normal pace. This setting does affect all foreground application responsiveness.

/ABOVENORMAL   Starts the application in the ABOVENORMAL priority class. This setting places the application at a slightly higher priority than standard applications. The other foreground tasks continue to run, but at a noticeably slower pace. Use this setting for priority applications that must complete tasks quickly.

/HIGH   Starts the application in the HIGH priority class. You won't normally have a good reason to use this priority for any application. Using this priority level can affect system functionality and definitely slows other foreground applications to a crawl. Always use this setting with extreme caution.

/REALTIME   Starts the application in the REALTIME priority class. Using this priority level stops execution of other foreground tasks and some system tasks as well. In addition, system functionality degrades noticeably. In some circumstances, the system could actually freeze and require a reboot. Generally, you don't want to use this priority for any reason.

/WAIT   Starts the application and waits for it to terminate. This setting ensures that you know when an application completes its task.

{*command* | *program*}   Specifies the internal command/batch file or the external utility/ application to run. The command window remains visible after you run an internal command or batch file because the system executes the command processor (CMD.EXE) with the /K switch. (See the "Using the CMD Switches" section of this chapter for details on the CMD.EXE command line switches.) The system runs external utilities and applications in a window or in a full-screen console. Unless you change the default behavior using a command line switch, the window or full-screen console closes when the application completes execution.

parameters   Specifies the parameters (arguments) passed to the command or program.

DETERMINING THE OPERATING SYSTEM VERSION WITH THE *VER* COMMAND

The Ver command is one of the easier commands to use. It doesn't require any arguments and provides only one type of output. Whenever you use the Ver command, you receive the operating system version information. The version information contains the operating system name in human-readable form, the major version number, the minor version number, and the build number. For example, the current Windows XP version at the time of this writing is Microsoft Windows XP [Version 5.1.2600]. Server Core displays something like Microsoft Windows [Version 6.0.6001].

GETTING VOLUME INFORMATION WITH THE *VOL* COMMAND

The Vol command displays the volume information for the current or selected drive. The information includes the drive letter, the drive volume name, and the serial number. This command uses the following syntax:

```
VOL [drive:]
```

The following describes the command line argument.

drive   Specifies the letter of the drive for which you want to obtain volume information. The default is the current drive.

Using Debugging Utilities

The command line is an admittedly simple place to work from a programming perspective. In fact, using batch files is more along the lines of working with a very simple kind of script, rather than a complex application. Even so, you'll eventually need to perform some kind of debugging. The debugging may involve checking inside a file to ensure you aren't going to execute a virus. You may also have to perform some low-level tasks with very old applications to get them to run in the Server Core environment. The following sections describe the debugging utilities that Server Core makes available for your use.

EXAMINING, MODIFYING, AND DEBUGGING FILES WITH THE DEBUG UTILITY

Microsoft originally intended the Debug utility to help developers debug assembly language applications. You can still use the utility for that purpose, but the number of assembly language programs still in use is very small. In fact, it's likely that you'll never see an application originally written in assembler.

Fortunately, the Debug utility does have other purposes. For example, you can use it to view hidden information in executable files. Application developers leave many notes inside applications and it's often helpful to view these messages when deciding on the alternative uses of a utility. You can also locate copyright information in files when you want to know more about the file. Sometimes, you can also use the Debug utility to locate information in data files or make quick fixes to damaged data files. Most people refer to this other use for Debug as hex (short for hexadecimal) editing. However, the Debug utility interface is archaic and many people find it hard to use. If you need low-level access to files regularly, you might want to invest in a third-party utility for the task such as XVI32 (see the "Using XVI32 to View Files in Depth" section of Chapter 22 for details). This utility uses the following syntax:

```
DEBUG [[drive:][path]filename [testfile-parameters]]
```

The following list describes each of the command line arguments.

[*drive:*][*path*]*filename* Specifies the name of the file that you want to view, edit, or debug.

testfile-parameters Specifies the command line arguments required by the application you want to test. You never use this second argument to simply view or edit a file.

CONVERTING EXECUTABLES WITH THE EXE2BIN UTILITY

The Exe2Bin utility converts an application from the Portable Executable (PE) format to the binary format. The main difference is in how the executable loads. At some time in the past, you needed to use this utility quite often to convert executable files because the linkers of the time didn't provide the required functionality, but now it's a relic that you might never use. The resulting binary file is smaller than the executable and may execute slightly faster. At a time when developers counted individual bits, this utility served an important purpose. This utility uses the following syntax:

```
EXE2BIN [drive1:][path1]input-file [[drive2:][path2]output-file]
```

The following list describes each of the command line arguments.

[*drive1:*][*path1*]*input-file* Specifies the location and name of the EXE file you want to convert. If you don't provide drive and path information, the utility assumes that you want to use the current drive and path.

[drive:][path]output-file Specifies the location and name of the binary file (usually with a COM extension) that you want to output. If you don't provide drive and path information, the utility assumes that you want to use the current drive and path.

Working at the Command Prompt

Some commands and utilities help you create a better working environment at the command prompt. In many cases, these commands are aesthetic; they don't do any useful work in the sense of modifying a file or the system state. The following sections describe these efficiency commands and utilities.

 Real World Scenario

CREATING A NICE WORK ENVIRONMENT

You might wonder why you would spend time learning about commands and utilities that don't do any useful work. For me, it's the same reason for having carpeting on the floor or a remote for the television; it's all about comfort. For example, you'll find that the display buffer eventually becomes full of extraneous data you don't really want to see any longer. Sure, you could ignore the garbage on your screen, but it's a lot better to get rid of it so you can work in comfort. Using the CLS command clears the display buffer for you so you can continue working efficiently.

Users of your batch file and script applications want a nice working environment too. You'll often use these commands and utilities in your batch files to provide special effects. The CLS command clears the display so the user viewing the output of the batch file doesn't become confused.

Redirecting Command Line Output to the Clipboard with the Clip Utility

Anyone who has used redirection knows the benefits of sending output data to another location, such as a file, or getting input from another location, such as the COM port. The Clip utility lets you perform redirection using the Windows Clipboard. You use redirection or the pipe command as you normally do. For example, Dir | Clip sends the output for the directory command to the clipboard. This command uses the following syntax:

```
Clip
```

You don't need to supply any command line switches when using this command. It works much like the More command. For example, if you want to place the output of the Dir command on the clipboard, you would type **Dir | Clip** and press Enter. At this point, you can type **Notepad** and press Enter to start the Notepad utility. Select Edit ➤ Paste and you'll see the output of the Dir command in Notepad, where you can edit the information to suit your needs.

Clearing the Display with the *CLS* Command

The Clear Screen (CLS) command clears the screen buffer and presents you with a clean display. All that remains is the command prompt. This command uses the following syntax:

```
CLS
```

You don't need to supply any command line switches when using this command.

Managing Usernames and Passwords with CmdKey

The CmdKey utility helps you manage username and passwords. Using this utility, you can display, create, and delete credentials as needed. However, this utility only works with the current user. In other words, the credentials you manage are for the current user, not for another user on the same system. To work with other users, you must first log in as that user. Consequently, this command works well with login batch files that perform tasks on the user's behalf, but not necessarily as a good tool for administering users at the command line.

A system can have two kinds of passwords managed by CmdKey. The first is generic passwords that you can use anywhere. For example, you might create a username and password to access a remote system using a Virtual Private Network (VPN). The second is domain passwords that you use to access a domain server. These password types appear in the Type field output when you list credentials for your system.

DISPLAYING

The /list command line switch lets you list all of the credentials associated with the current account. This mode uses the following syntax:

```
cmdkey /list
cmdkey /list:targetname
```

The following list describes each of the command line arguments.

/list Displays all of the entries or only those that you specify with a target name.

targetname Defines a target credential. You use the name of the credential as the target. This command line argument doesn't allow wildcard characters, so you can only use it to list one credential at a time.

CREATING

Creates a new domain or generic credential based on a username and password. Use the /add command line switch to create domain credentials and the /generic command line switch to create generic credentials. This mode uses the following syntax:

```
cmdkey /add:targetname /user:username /pass:password
cmdkey /add:targetname /user:username /pass
cmdkey /add:targetname /user:username
cmdkey /add:targetname /smartcard
cmdkey /generic:targetname /user:username /pass:password
cmdkey /generic:targetname /user:username /pass
cmdkey /generic:targetname /user:username
cmdkey /generic:targetname /smartcard
```

The following list describes each of the command line arguments.

/add Creates a domain credential.

/generic Creates a generic credential.

targetname Defines a target credential. You use the name of the credential as the target. This command line argument doesn't allow wildcard characters, so you can only use it to list one credential at a time.

/user:*username* Specifies the username used for login purposes. The username can include any qualifiers required to perform the login.

/pass or **/pass:*password*** Specifies the password used for login purposes. If you specify /pass without the password, the system prompts you for a password to use on the remote system. Unlike many password prompts, this prompt doesn't display the password characters as asterisks (*), so it's easy to make mistakes. Make sure you type the password carefully.

/smartcard Creates a password based on the content of a smartcard. The system prompts you to provide the smartcard as part of the input.

DELETING

You can't change a credential using the CmdKey utility. To change a credential, you must first delete the old credential and then create a new one. In addition, you'll likely find that you need to delete old credentials when you don't need them any longer. This mode uses the following syntax:

```
cmdkey /delete:targetname
cmdkey /delete /ras
```

The following list describes each of the command line arguments.

/delete:*targetname* Removes the specified credential. You must provide a target name unless you're deleting a Remote Access Server (RAS) credential.

/ras Specifies that you want to remove a RAS credential.

Changing Screen Colors with the *Color* Command

The Color command changes the foreground (text) and background colors of the command window. This command uses the following syntax:

```
COLOR [FG]
```

The following describes the command line argument.

FG Sets the foreground (F) and background (G) colors. You must place the values together, without any space between. If you use the Color command without specifying color values, the command changes the colors to the default values used when you opened the command window. The following list tells you which colors you can use at the command prompt, along with their associated color number.

0—Black

1—Blue

2—Green

3—Aqua

4—Red

5—Purple

6—Yellow

7—White

8—Gray

9—Light blue

A—Light green

B—Light aqua

C—Light red

D—Light purple

E—Light yellow

F—Bright white

Working with the System Date Using the *Date* Command

The `Date` command displays or sets the system date. This command uses the following syntax:

```
DATE [{/T | date}]
```

The following list describes each of the command line arguments.

/T   Displays the date without prompting for a new date. This command line switch only works when you enable command extensions.

date   Specifies the new system date.

Tracking Command Line Actions with the DosKey Utility

The DosKey utility performs three tasks. First, it provides the history feature that most people use to scroll through existing command line entries. Press Down Arrow to see the next command, Up Arrow to see the previous command, Page Down to see the most recent command, and Page Up to see the oldest command in the history.

Second, you can use this command to edit previous commands. The following list describes the editing features.

LEFT ARROW   Moves to the previous character in the command.

RIGHT ARROW   Moves to the next character in the command.

CTRL+LEFT ARROW   Moves to the previous word in the command.

CTRL+RIGHT ARROW   Moves to the next word in the command.

HOME   Moves to the beginning of the line.

END   Moves to the end of the line.

ESC   Clears the command from the display.

F1   Copies the next character from the same column in the command that you previously issued.

NOTE   The system places the previous command in a special area of memory called the template and lets you work with that command based on the current column position. For example, if you typed `Dir *.BAK` as the previous command, executed it, and then typed `Dir` at the command line, pressing F1 would type a space. Pressing F1 again would type the asterisk (*) and so on. Using the same example, pressing F2 and then the letter A would display `Dir *.BA` at the command prompt. Using the combination of the template and function keys helps you reduce the number of keystrokes you make to type a command.

F2   Searches forward in the previous command for the next key you type after pressing F2.

F3   Copies the remainder of the previous command to the command line.

F4   Deletes characters from the current cursor position up to a character you specify. For example, if the command line currently displays `Dir *.BAK` and the cursor is blinking under the asterisk (*), pressing F4 and the letter B would change the command prompt to read `Dir BAK`.

F5   Copies the previous command into the current command line.

F6   Places an end-of-file character (Ctrl+Z) at the current cursor position. You typically use this feature when using the console to create a file.

F7   Displays all of the commands stored in the command history in a dialog box. Select a command using the Up Arrow and Down Arrow. Press Enter to select the command. DosKey types the selected command at the command prompt. Press Enter again to execute the command. You can also note the sequential number in front of the command and use this number with the F9 key.

ALT+F7   Deletes all commands stored in the current command history buffer.

F8   Displays a single command from the command history that starts with the characters in the current command. Press F8 multiple times to cycle through the list of matching commands.

F9   Prompts you for a history buffer command number, and then displays the command associated with the number you specify. Press Enter to run the command. Press F7 to display a list of commands in the command history buffer, along with their associated command number.

ALT+F10   Deletes all macro definitions.

Third, you can use this command to create macros. The macros automate some command line tasks, similarly to batch files, but far more inconveniently. You can also use these macros to interact with applications. However, the number of applications that can use DosKey macros is extremely limited. For example, you could use a DosKey macro with the FTP utility described in the "Managing FTP Servers with the FTP Utility" section of Chapter 17. To qualify for use with the DosKey utility, the application must run at the command prompt and provide buffered input. Because of the limitations posed by DosKey macros, this book won't discuss them. However, you can find many examples of DosKey macros online. For example, the Web page at `http://www.palmtoppaper.com/ptphtml/17/pt170037.htm` shows a number of helpful macros you can create. You'll find a good how-to article at `http://www.atarimagazines.com/compute/issue137/S18_How_to_create_keyboa.php`. The article at `http://www.melbpc.org.au/pcupdate/9405/9405article7.htm` provides step-by-step creation process for DosKey macros. This utility uses the following syntax:

```
DOSKEY [/REINSTALL] [/LISTSIZE=size] [/MACROS[:ALL | :exename]]
    [/HISTORY] [/INSERT | /OVERSTRIKE] [/EXENAME=exename] [/MACROFILE=filename]
    [macroname=[text]]
```

The following list describes each of the command line arguments.

/REINSTALL   Installs a new copy of DosKey. Use this feature when your current copy has become corrupted or simply filled with extraneous data.

/LISTSIZE=size   Determines the number of commands that will fit within the command history buffer. The default setting is 10.

/MACROS   Displays a list of all of the DosKey macros. The output includes command line macros, as well as those associated with an application.

/MACROS:ALL Displays a list of all the DosKey macros for all executables that have DosKey compatibility. For example, if you create a DosKey macro for the FTP utility, this command line switch would display it.

/MACROS:*exename* Displays a list of all the DosKey macros associated with the specified application.

/HISTORY Displays a list of all of the commands in the command history buffer.

/INSERT Places DosKey in insert mode. Any new text you type at the command line appears in addition to the existing text.

/OVERSTRIKE Places DosKey in overstrike mode. Any new text you type at the command line replaces (overwrites) existing text.

/EXENAME=*exename* Specifies the name of an executable to use when creating a macro. The resulting macro runs within that application. The application must support DosKey to use this functionality. If you don't specify this command line switch, any macro you create or install runs at the command line and not as part of an application.

/MACROFILE=*filename* Specifies a file containing macros that you want to install.

macroname Specifies the name for a macro you create. Typing the macro name, followed by an equals sign, and pressing Enter deletes a macro from the list.

text Contains the text of the macro you want to record. You must include a macro name, followed by an equals sign, followed by the macro text to use this argument. For example, you can define a macro named MyDir that displays a directory by typing `DosKey MyDir=Dir *.ᴬ /P` and pressing Enter. After you create this macro, you can type **MyDir** at the command prompt, press Enter, and DosKey will execute the MyDir macro.

Obtaining Command Line Help with the Help Utility

In most cases, you'll type the name of a utility, followed by the /? command line switch to learn more about it. However, Microsoft decided to make things difficult in some cases. For example, some utilities require that you use the /Help command line switch instead or you might have to use the Help utility to learn more about the command or utility in question. To see a list of commands and utilities that Help supports, type `Help` and press Enter. This utility uses the following syntax:

```
HELP [command]
```

The following describes the command line argument.

command Specifies the name of the command for which you want to obtain more information. If you type **Help** by itself and press Enter, you'll see a list of all of the available commands. You can then choose a specific command to learn more about with the Help utility.

Working with the System Time Using the *Time* Command

The Time command displays or sets the system time. This command uses the following syntax:

```
TIME [/T | time]
```

The following list describes each of the command line arguments.

/T Displays the date without prompting for a new time. This command line switch only works when you enable command extensions.

time Specifies the new system time.

Changing the Command Window Title with the *Title* Command

The title that a command window displays might not seem important at first, but it can be important for two reasons. First, if you have multiple command windows open, using a descriptive title can make it easier to locate the correct command window on the Windows Taskbar. Second, it's important to remember that Windows associates settings changes you make with the command window title. Changing the title affects how Windows stores the settings changes you make. The Title command can change the title of a command window. This command uses the following syntax:

```
TITLE [string]
```

The following describes the command line argument.

string   Contains the text for the command window.

Creating Batch Files

Batch files are a type of simple programming that can help you store a series of commands that you want to execute more than once. The batch file normally appears within a file with a BAT extension. In most cases, you won't need to perform any programming to create a batch file; simply create a file that contains the commands you want to execute one after the other.

NOTE   Windows doesn't support the Break command found in many older batch files. The original purpose of the Break command was to provide control over the Ctrl+Break key. Setting Break ON would let someone press Ctrl+Break to stop execution of a batch file. Windows ignores this command line switch. In addition, Server Core changes support for some batch commands from previous versions of Windows and adds new commands. Consequently, batch files that worked fine in Windows XP may suddenly stop working in Server Core. (If you've already updated your batch files to work in Vista, they'll also work fine in Server Core.)

Even with the limitations of a batch file, however, you might be surprised at the number of ways that people use them. For example, if you find that you're constantly forgetting how to perform tasks at the command line, create a menu system with your favorite commands. That way, you only have to look up the command information one time. The following sections describe the programming features of batch files and provide you with some sample batch files.

 Real World Scenario

FINDING CODE ONLINE

I'm a code hound. I have more links to online code than I care to think about because all of these links are useful in some way. This chapter contains batch file examples that help you understand basic principles and perform some essential tasks at the command line. However, if you're like me, you'll want more; you'll want examples that show you how to perform more tasks than I could ever include in a single book. You can find a wealth of batch files for performing administrative or other essential tasks at the Rob van der Woude Web site at http://www.robvanderwoude.com/batchfiles.html. If you want to see some very complex examples, including using math within a batch file (something most people will say you can't do) then go to Tom Lavedas' Batch File Applications Web site at http://members .cox.net/tglbatch/.

Using the *Call* Command

You use the `Call` command to call another location with the current batch file or to start another batch file. When you want to call another location in the same batch file, you use the label formatting shown here:

```
Call :MyLabel
```

Calling another batch file is similar. You provide the drive, path, and filename of the batch file. In addition, you can provide command line arguments for the external batch file as shown here:

```
Call C:\MyBatchFiles\MyBatch.BAT CommandArg1
```

A call is different from going to another location. When a call completes, the batch file returns to the calling location and executes the next instruction. In contrast, when you use the `Goto` command, the batch file actually transfers control to the new location. The return feature of the `Call` command lets you create an advanced programming construct called recursion. Recursion occurs when a batch file calls itself. You must provide an exit strategy, however, or the batch file will enter an endless loop.

The easiest way to see the effect of the `Call` command is to create two batch files named `Batch1.BAT` and `Batch2.BAT`. Here's the content for `Batch1.BAT`.

```
@ECHO OFF
Call Batch2.BAT
Call Batch2.BAT Passed %1 %PATH%
ECHO In Batch 1
GOTO :EOF
ECHO Goodbye
```

Here's the content for `Batch2.BAT`.

```
ECHO In Batch 2, Goodbye
IF NOT [%1]==[] ECHO String: %1
IF NOT [%2]==[] ECHO Batch 1 Input: %2
IF NOT [%3]==[] ECHO Environment Variable: %3
```

Looking at the `Batch1.BAT` content, the example begins by turning off echo. You'll normally add this code to your batch files so the user doesn't see a lot of confusing text that has nothing to do with the current task. Preceding the `ECHO` command with the @ symbol tells the system not to display the `ECHO` command either. The first call to `Batch2.BAT` doesn't pass any information, so `Batch2.BAT` only displays the message, "In Batch 2, Goodbye." The second call to `Batch2.BAT` passes the three kinds of information you can include with a batch file: a string, a local variable (argument), and a global variable. The code then proceeds to display "In Batch 1," and then it exits. The `GOTO :EOF` statement is special; it tells the batch file to end now. You don't have to define a label, in this case, because EOF is built into the command process. (See the "Using the *Goto* Command" section of this chapter for details.)

The `Batch2.BAT` file always echoes "In Batch 2, Goodbye." In this case, the `IF` statements verify that the caller has passed information to the batch file. When the caller doesn't pass the required variables, then the batch file doesn't display any information for that input. The `[%1]==[]` construct is one way to check for an empty input. Figure 5.3 shows the output from this application. Notice the sequence of events. The first batch file calls the second batch file. When the second batch file is finished, execution continues with the next statement in the first batch file.

FIGURE 5.3
Calls provide a means of performing subtasks in a batch file and then continuing with the main task.

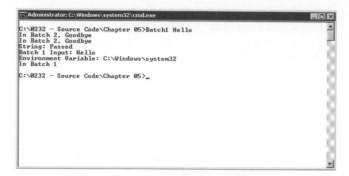

Windows provides enhanced methods of working with variables in batch files. These enhanced expansions help you pass specific variable information to a callee from your batch files. See the "Using Variable Substitution" section of the chapter for details on using this technique.

Using the *Choice* Command

The Choice command lets you add interactive processing to batch files. Whether you use this option depends on the kind of automation you want to add to your processing tasks. Most of the automation you create for optimization tasks won't require any kind of interactivity because you already know how you want the task performed based on experience you obtained performing the task manually. However, sometimes you do need to add some interactivity. For example, you might run the command one way on Friday and a different way the rest of the week. The Choice command can also help you add safeguards that ensure the user understands the ramifications of performing a certain task before they actually do it. Vista and Server Core change the Choice command significantly, breaking many batch files. The Vista and Server Core form of the Choice command differs not in arguments, but in how you combine those arguments at the command line. Here's the command line for Vista and Server Core:

```
CHOICE [/C choices] [/N] [/CS] [/T timeout /D choice] [/M text]
```

The changes make the command clearer, but they break existing batch files in a way that you can't easily fix. The new /CS command line switch lets you make choices case sensitive, so you can have 26 additional menu choices. However, notice that /T no longer takes both a default option and a timeout value. The new form requires that you provide a choice using the /D command line switch instead. You must also provide the /M command line switch to specify optional text. The following sample code performs the same task, but the first form works in Windows XP and earlier, while the second form works in Vista and Server Core.

```
Old Choice Command Form
CHOICE /C:N /N /T:N,15
Vista and Server Core Choice Command Form
CHOICE /C N /N /T 15 /D N
```

NOTE Vista and Server Core provide alternatives for the Choice command. The TimeOut utility provides a specific timeout value without requiring the user to make a choice. You can learn more about this utility in the "Using the TimeOut Utility" section of the chapter. The WaitFor utility lets you use signaling between systems or applications on the same system. One application sends a signal and another reacts when it receives the signal. You can learn more about this utility in the "Using the WaitFor Utility" section of the chapter.

When you use Choice by itself, it displays a simple [Y,N] prompt that doesn't accomplish much unless you also provide an Echo command to describe what the user should say yes or no to. Normally, you'll combine the Choice command with one or more arguments. Listing 5.1 shows a simple example of the Choice command at work. You can obtain this example on the Sybex Web site at http://www.sybex.com/WileyCDA/.

LISTING 5.1:   Using the *Choice* Command

```
Echo Off

REM Keep repeating until the user enters E.
:Repeat

REM Display the choices.
Choice /C DCE /N /T 15 /D E /M "Choose an option (D)isplay, (C)opy, ⏎
   or (E)nd."
REM Act on the user choice.
If ErrorLevel 3 Goto End
If ErrorLevel 2 Goto Copy
If ErrorLevel 1 Goto Display

REM Copy the file.
:Copy
Echo You chose to copy the file.
Goto Repeat

REM Display the file.
:Display
Echo You chose to display the file.
Goto Repeat

REM End the batch processing.
:End
Echo Goodbye
Echo On
```

The code begins by creating a repeat label so the batch file continues working until the user specifically stops it. Next, the code uses the Choice command to display the choices to the user. The /C switch tells Choice that the valid options are D, C, or E instead of the default Y or N. Because the text specifically defines the characters that the batch file expects, the batch file uses the /N switch to suppress displaying the valid key choices on the command line. The /T command line switch tells Choice to automatically choose E after 10 seconds. The /D command line switch provides the default choice of E. Finally, the /M command line switch provides the message displayed to the user.

Although this batch file doesn't actually do anything with a file, it shows how you'd set up the batch file to process the user choice. Notice that the batch file uses the ErrorLevel clause of the If statement to detect the user choice. The ErrorLevel clause detects every choice lower than the user selection, so you must place the values in reverse order, as shown. In addition, you must specifically set the batch file to go to another location because it will process all other statements after the current error level.

The processing code simply displays a string telling you what choice the user made. Normally, you'd add tasks that the batch file should perform based on the user's selection. Notice that the copy and display selections tell the batch file to go back to the Repeat label. This is the most common technique for creating a menu loop in a batch file. The batch file ends by telling the user goodbye and turning echo back on.

Using the *Echo* Command

The command line uses the term *echo* to describe the process where the system echoes (repeats) every command in a batch file to the command line. Echo provides a means of seeing which command the system is processing. However, echo can become confusing for users who aren't aware of or don't care about the commands that are executing. In addition, echo can disrupt visual effects, such as menu systems, that you create. The Echo command has two forms. The first form

```
ECHO [{ON | OFF}]
```

displays the echo status when you don't include any arguments. The ON argument turns on echo so you can see the commands, and the OFF argument turns off echo so you can create visual effects. You can precede the Echo command with the @ sign so it doesn't appear as one of the commands. @Echo OFF would turn echo off without displaying the echo command at the command prompt.

The second form of echo

```
ECHO [message]
```

lets you display a message. Simply type the text you want to see after the Echo command. In this case, the system won't display the Echo command, just the message you want to display. Don't use the @ sign with this form of the Echo command or the user won't see the message.

Using the *Exit* Command

Most people associate the Exit command with closing the current command window. Using Exit alone will close the command window. However, you can also use this command within a batch file to exit the batch file. To perform this task, you must use one or both of the following optional Exit arguments.

/B   Specifies that you want to exit a batch file, rather than the current command line session. If you don't specify this command line switch, the command window closes, even when you issue the Exit command from a batch file.

ExitCode   Defines an exit code for the batch file. The default exit code is 0, which normally signifies success. You can use exit codes to alert the caller to errors or special conditions. The exit codes aren't defined by the system, so you can define any set of exit codes that you deem necessary for your application.

Using the ForFiles Utility

The ForFiles utility provides a means of looping through a list of files and performing actions on those files one at a time. For example, you might want to process all files that someone has changed since a certain date. In most respects, this loop method works precisely the same as the For command described in the "Using the *For* Command" section of the chapter. This command uses the following syntax:

```
FORFILES [/P pathname] [/M searchmask] [/S] [/C command]
[/D [+ | -] {MM/dd/yyyy | dd}]
```

The following list describes each of the command line arguments.

/P *pathname*   Specifies the starting point for a search. The path is the starting folder in the search. The default setting uses the current directory as the starting point.

/M *searchmask*   Defines a search mask for the files. You can use the asterisk (*) and question mark (?) as wildcard characters, just as you would when using the Directory command. The default setting searches for all files in the target directory.

/S   Searches all of the subdirectories of the specified directory.

/C *command*   Specifies the command you want to execute for each file. Always wrap the command in double quotes to ensure it isn't interpreted as part of the ForFile command. The default command is "cmd /c echo @file". Always precede internal command processor command with cmd /c. The following list describes the variables that you can use as part of the command.

@file   Returns the name of the file, including the file extension.

@fname   Returns the name of the file without the extension.

@ext   Returns only the file extension.

@path   Returns the full path of the file. This information includes the drive as well as the actual path.

@relpath   Returns the relative path of the file. The relative path begins at the starting folder.

@isdir   Specifies whether the file type is a directory. True indicates a directory entry.

@fsize   Indicates the size of the file in bytes.

@fdate   Indicates the date that someone last modified the file.

@ftime   Indicates the time that someone last modified the file.

TIP   You can include special characters in a command by using the 0xHH format where HH is a hexadecimal number. For example, you can specify a tab by typing 0x09.

/D *date*   Selects files that have a last modified date within the specified range. You specify a specific date using the month/day/year (mm/dd/yyyy) format. Add a plus sign if you want files after the specified date or a minus sign if you want files before the specified date. For example, /D -01/01/2008 would select all files modified before January 1, 2008. You can also specify a relative date by providing a positive or negative number. For example, /D -7 would select all files modified within the last seven days. The /D command line switch accepts any number between 0 and –32,768.

Using the *For* Command

The For command fulfills a special niche in batch file programming. The "Working with Wildcard Characters" sidebar in Chapter 14 tells you how you can use wildcard characters to make multiple file selections when needed. Unfortunately, using wildcard characters won't always work. Sometimes you need to know the name of the file. A command line utility might not support wildcard characters or the file argument doesn't easily fit within the wildcard method of description. That's where the For statement comes into play for batch files. This command takes the form:

```
FOR %%variable IN (set) DO command [command-parameters]
```

You can also use this command at the command prompt to process files manually. Instead of using a single percent (%) symbol, you use two in front of the variable. Here's a sample of how you can use this command in a batch file.

```
Echo Off
For %%F In (*.BAT *.TXT) Do Dir %%F /B
Echo On
```

In this case, the For command processes all of the files that have a BAT or TXT extension in the current directory. The command processes the files in the order in which they appear in the directory and you have no guarantee what the order is. The %%F variable contains the name of an individual file. The Dir command is called once for each file with the %%F variable as an input. In this case, the command outputs the filenames using the bare format, so you could use this batch file to create a text file containing a list of files that match the criteria. Additional processing could archive the files or do anything else that you might like. The For command provides the following arguments.

{%Variable | %%Variable}   Specifies a replaceable parameter; the argument that will receive the individual members of a set. The replaceable parameter takes two forms. Use the %Variable form when you want to use the replaceable parameter as input to another command or utility. Use the %%Variable form when you want to use the replaceable parameter for activities within the batch file. The variable names are case sensitive, so %f isn't the same as %F. In addition, you must use an alphabetical variable name, such as %A, %B, or %C.

(Set)   Defines the set to process. The set can include one or more files, directories, range of values, or text strings that you want to process with the specified command. For example, you can use environment variables as the set. The command For %%P In (%PATH%) Do ECHO %%P would display the members of the PATH environment variable as individual strings.

Command   Specifies the command you want to perform for each entry in the set.

CommandLineOptions   Defines the command line options for the command that you want to perform for each entry in the set. The command line options are command or utility specific; see the other entries in this book for details.

PERFORMING COMPLEX FILE ITERATION

You can use the For command to process command output, strings, and the content of files. In this case, the For command begins by breaking the input into individual lines of content and discarding any blank lines. It then breaks whatever input you provide into specific tokens based on the rules you specify. A token can be a control character, a special word, or anything else you can define as part of the simple syntax for this command. The For command passes the token to a command you specify as input. Here's the command line syntax for this form of the For command.

```
for /F ["ParsingKeywords"] {%% | %}Variabe lin (FileNameSet) do Command
    [CommandLineOptions]
```

```
for /F ["ParsingKeywords"] {%% | %}Variable in ("LiteralString") do
    Command [CommandLineOptions]
for /F ["ParsingKeywords"] {%% | %}Variable in ('Command') do Command
    [CommandLineOptions]
```

Notice that you need to use a different command line syntax for each kind of input. A filename appears without quotes, while a string appears in double quotes and a command appears in single quotes. The small differences in command format determines how the For command views the input.

The ParsingKeywords input is a quoted string that specifies the rules for parsing the input into tokens. These keywords always appear in double quotes, as shown. The following list describes the keywords you can use.

eol=c Specifies an end of line character. The For command only allows you to specify one character.

skip=N Specifies the number of lines to skip at the beginning of the file.

delims=xxx Specifies a delimiter set. The delimiter set defines which characters the For command views as elements between tokens. The default setting relies on the space and tab. Consequently, the For command produces a new token every time it sees a space or tab within the input.

tokens=X,Y,M-N Defines which tokens to retrieve from each line of text to pass to the For command body for each iteration. The For command allocates one variable for each of the tokens. The M-N format defines a range of tokens to use as input. Whenever the last character in a processed string is an asterisk (*), the For command creates an additional variable to receive the additional text on the line after the For command parses the last token.

usebackq Specifies that you can use quotation marks to quote filenames in FileNameSet, a back quoted string is executed as a command, and a single quoted string is a literal string command.

You need to use a slightly different command line syntax with the For command when you rely on the usebackq keyword. Here are the three command lines using this syntax.

```
for /F ["usebackqParsingKeywords"] {%% | %}Variable in ("FileNameSet")
    do Command [CommandLineOptions]
for /F ["usebackqParsingKeywords"] {%% | %}Variable in
    ('LiteralString') do Command [CommandLineOptions]
for /F ["usebackqParsingKeywords"] {%% | %}Variable in ('Command') do
    Command [CommandLineOptions]
```

USING VARIABLE SUBSTITUTION

Variable substitution is the act of exchanging a variable name for the content of that variable. However, unlike expansion, you don't necessarily use all of the variable content. For example, instead of using the entire path for a file, you might just use the drive letter, the path, or the filename. The following list describes the basic forms of variable substitution available with the For command. (The list assumes that you're using a variable named I, which translates into %I at the command line.)

%~I Removes any surrounding quotation marks from the variable content.

%~fI Expands %I to a fully qualified pathname.

%~dI   Expands %I to a drive letter only.

%~pI   Expands %I to a path only.

%~nI   Expands %I to a filename only.

%~xI   Expands %I to a file extension only.

%~sI   Creates a path variable, and then changes any long directory names into their short name equivalents.

%~aI   Obtains the file attributes of the input file.

%~tI   Obtains the date and time of the input file.

%~zI   Obtains the size of the input file.

%~$PATH:I   Searches the directories listed in the PATH environment variable for the file specified by I. The system then expands the first match that it finds to a fully qualified filename, which includes the drive, path, and filename. This variable substitution returns an empty string when the PATH environment variable is undefined or if the system can't find a match for the filename.

You can use these variable substitutions in combination to produce specific results. For example, you might want to create a directory-like listing of files. The following list provides some ideas on how to use the variable substitution arguments in combination.

%~dpI   Outputs just the drive letter and path of a file, without including the filename.

%~nxI   Outputs the filename and extension, but leaves out the drive letter and path.

%~fsI   Outputs the file information using the short name (8.3 format) form only.

%~dp$PATH:I   Locates the file using the PATH environment variable. The system outputs just the drive letter and path of the first match found.

%~ftzaI   Creates the same output as the Dir command. However, the output is different from the Dir command because the file listing could span multiple directories. The focus of the listing is different.

Using the *Goto* Command

The Goto command transfers control from one part of a batch file to another. You can't use the Goto command to transfer control to other batch files. For this task, you use the Call command described in the "Using the *Call* Command" section of the chapter. The Goto command takes a simple form: Goto Label, where Label is a keyword used to define the transfer point in the batch file. Labels are always preceded by a colon, such as :MyLabel. Listings 5.1 and 5.2 both show the Goto command in action.

Using the *If* Command

To write any reasonably complex batch file, you need to perform flow control—the active selection of code to run based on current conditions. For example, you might want to know that the previous task succeeded before you begin the next task. In some cases, you'll look for a specific file or act on user input to the batch file. You can also verify that the user provided a certain input string. The point is that you can exercise some control over how the batch files react to system and environmental conditions. Batch files don't provide extensive decision-making support, but you can use these three forms of the If statement to increase the flexibility of your batch files.

```
If [Not] ErrorLevel number command
If [Not] string1==string2 command
If [Not] Exist filename command
```

In all three cases, you can add the word "Not" to perform the reverse of the check. For example, you can perform a task when a given file doesn't exist, rather than when it does exist. By combining both versions of the If statement, you can create the equivalent of an If...Else statement found in most programming languages.

The ErrorLevel argument requires special consideration. Whenever you run an application, batch file, or script, the system provides a numeric error level as output. By convention, an error level of 0 always represents success. Other numbers represent an error or special condition. A special condition isn't always an error; it's simply not complete success. In fact, you might expect an application, batch file, or script to exit with a special condition. For an example of a command that exits with special conditions, review the Choice command in the "Using the *Choice* Command" section of the chapter. Error conditions can represent a user, system, or application failure. For example, consider the XCopy error levels shown in Table 5.5.

TABLE 5.5:   XCopy Error Levels

ERROR LEVEL	MEANING
0	Success, no error occurred.
1	The system didn't find any files to copy.
2	The user stopped XCopy by pressing Ctrl+C.
4	The application experienced an initialization error. The system doesn't have enough memory or disk space. You may have entered an invalid drive name or used invalid syntax at the command line.
5	The system experienced a disk write error.

As you can see, the cause of an error varies greatly depending on conditions. In all cases, you could rightfully say that the application has experienced an error. However, notice that error level 2 could actually occur by design. The user recognizes an error and presses Ctrl+C to stop the copying process before it completes. In this case, you have to consider whether the error level defines a special condition or an error by prompting the user and handle it appropriately. Listing 5.2 shows examples of the various If statement forms at work. You can obtain this example on the Sybex Web site at http://www.sybex.com/WileyCDA/.

LISTING 5.2:   Using the *If* Statement in Batch Files

```
Echo Off

REM Verify the user has provided an action.
If %1Err==Err GoTo ProcessError

REM Simulate an error when the file doesn't exist.
Copy MyFile.TXT MyFile2.TXT
If Not ErrorLevel 1 Goto CheckFile
   Echo The File doesn't exist so the batch file can't copy it.
```

```
REM Check for a specific file and process it when it does exist.
:CheckFile
If Exist MyFile.TXT Goto ProcessFile

REM If the file doesn't exist then create it. Display a message with
REM instructions and then let the user type the text.
Echo Type some text for the test file. Press Ctrl+Z when you finish.
Pause
Copy CON MyFile.TXT

REM This is a label for processing the file.
:ProcessFile

REM Determine whether the user wants to display the file.
If Not %1==display Goto Process2
    Echo MyFile.TXT Contains:
    Type MyFile.TXT
    Goto TheEnd

REM Determine whether the user wants to delete the file.
:Process2
If Not %1==delete Goto ProcessError
    Erase MyFile.TXT
    Echo Deleted MyFile.TXT
    Goto TheEnd

REM The user didn't define a processing action.
:ProcessError
Echo You didn't tell the batch file what to do!
Echo Type UseIf Display to display the file or
Echo UseIf Delete to delete the file.

:TheEnd
Echo On
```

The first line of this example demonstrates a principle that you should always use in batch files that you expect someone else will use—check for errors within the limits of the batch file to do so. In this case, the batch file expects the user to provide an input value of delete or display. When the user doesn't provide any input value, then the first input value, %1, is blank so the string Err equals Err and the code goes to a label named ProcessError. Batch files can work with up to nine input values at a time using %1 through %9 as variables. The Goto statement always tells the code to go to a label within the batch file. You define a label by preceding the label name with a colon such as :ProcessError.

The next segment of code attempts to copy a temporary file to another file. The operation results in an error that you can trap using the ErrorLevel statement when the file doesn't exist. When the ErrorLevel value matches the value you provide, then the If statement executes the command. In this case, because the code uses the Not clause, the reverse is true, the If statement only executes the Goto command when the error level is not 1. Notice that, in this case, the code uses the Echo command to display an error message to the user—Echo works not only for turning messages on or off, but for displaying custom messages to the user that the Echo setting doesn't hide as well.

Once the code performs these initial steps, it determines whether the MyFile.TXT file does exist using the Exit clause of the If statement. When the file exists, the code immediately begins processing it. Otherwise, the code displays a message prompting the user to type information for such a file. Notice the Pause command, which pauses the batch file execution until the user presses a key. The Copy command sends whatever the user types at the console (CON) to the MyFile.TXT file until it detects an end of file character, which the user creates by pressing Ctrl+Z.

Now that you know the file exists, the batch file can process it. This batch file provides two options: displaying the file and deleting it. The problem with batch files is that they use case-sensitive string comparisons—the word delete is different from the word Delete so error trapping can cause false problems. Some developers resolve this problem by using single character command line switches for batch files. That way, all you need to do is perform two checks, one for uppercase and another for lowercase. The example uses a full word for the purpose of demonstration. To see how this works, type Delete at the command line instead of delete—the code displays a failure message. When the user does type delete, the batch file erases the file and displays a success message. Likewise, when the user types display, the code sends the content of MyFile.TXT to the display. In both cases, the code goes to TheEnd where the batch file turns Echo back on.

So far, the chapter has discussed the standard form of the If command that you can execute even at the DOS prompt. The If command has the following additional syntax forms when you use command line extensions.

```
if [/i] String1 CompareOp String2 Command [else Expression]
if CMDEXTVERSION Number Command [else Expression]
if DEFINED Variable Command [else Expression]
```

The following list describes each of the command line arguments.

/I Performs a case-insensitive comparison of the two strings. This feature is handy when you expect the user to input a string, but don't know how the user will capitalize it. These comparisons are generic, in that if both String1 and String2 are composed of numbers, the system converts the strings to numbers and performs a numeric comparison.

String1 Specifies the input string; the first half of the comparison.

CompareOp Defines the comparison operator. Each three-letter comparison operator performs a different comparison as described in the following list.

> **EQU** Equal to
>
> **NEQ** Not equal to
>
> **LSS** Less than
>
> **LEQ** Less than or equal to
>
> **GTR** Greater than
>
> **GEQ** Greater than or equal to

String2 Specifies the comparison string—the second half of the comparison.

Command Specifies the command that you want to execute when the comparison is true.

else *Expression* Defines the else expression for the If command. When you use this syntax, you must surround the If and Else portions of the statement in parentheses. In addition, the entire statement must appear on a single line. You can't separate the various elements to provide a neater appearance. Here's an example of this form of the If command.

```
IF [%1] EQU [] (ECHO String Empty) ELSE (ECHO String Has Data)
```

In this case, the If command checks whether the input has a string for the first variable. When the input is available, the output tells the user that the string has data. Otherwise, the input displays, "String Empty" as output.

CMDEXTVERSION *Number* Tests for a specific version of the command extensions feature. When the command extension version number is equal to or greater than the specified number, the condition is true. This form of If command never returns true when you disable command extensions.

DEFINED *Variable* Tests whether you have a specific environment variable defined. The DEFINED argument works just like the EXISTS argument. The If command returns true when the variable is defined.

Using the *Pause* Command

The Pause command stops batch file execution to give the user time to react to a particular need. For example, if you need the user to change media to complete the batch file, you could use the Echo command to tell the user about the need and then use the Pause command to tell the user to press any key when the media exchange is complete.

Using the *Prompt* Command

The Prompt command changes the command line prompt. For example, instead of the usual drive letter, directory, and greater than sign, you could use the time and date as a prompt. In fact, the prompt can contain any text you want. To change the prompt, simply type Prompt, followed by the text you want to display, and press Enter. The following list defines the special characters you can use as part of the command prompt.

$A & (Ampersand)

$B | (Pipe)

$C ((Left parenthesis)

$D Current date

$E Escape code (ASCII code 27)

$F) (Right parenthesis)

$G > (Greater than sign)

$H Backspace (erases previous character)

$L < (Less than sign)

$N Current drive

$P Current drive and path

$Q = (Equals sign)

$S (Space)

$T Current time

$V Windows version number

$_ Carriage return and linefeed

$$ $ (Dollar sign)

You can access two additional formatting characters when you have command extensions enabled. The following list describes these two additions.

$+ Displays zero or more plus sign characters depending on the depth of the PushD utility directory stack. The display shows one character for each level you've pushed onto the stack.

$M Displays the remote name associated with the current drive letter. If this is a local drive, then the system displays an empty string.

Using the *Rem* Command

The Rem (Remark) command lets you add comments to your batch files. Given that batch files often use difficult to read coding sequences and that you'll probably want to modify them at some point, lots of comments are advisable. In fact, you'll want to add at least one comment for each complex line of code in your batch file. Many people have lost use of interesting and helpful batch files because they contain complex code that becomes unreadable after the initial writer forgets what the code means.

Using the *Shift* Command

A batch file supports a maximum of 10 command line arguments numbered %0 through %9. However, you might run into situations where you need more than 10 command line arguments. The Shift command can help you shift in these additional arguments. The new arguments replace existing arguments. In fact, all of the arguments are shifted one position, so the argument in %1 now appears in %0. Unfortunately, the argument in %0 is shifted out so that it's no longer accessible.

You can retain some older arguments in memory when you have command extensions enabled. The Shift command will accept a numeric argument that tells where to begin shifting arguments. For example, when the command appears as Shift /2, the values in %0 and %1 are unaffected. However, Shift will shift the arguments starting with %2 so that %2 now contains the value from %3.

Using the TimeOut Utility

The TimeOut utility provides a unique feature in that you can tell it to wait for a specified time period no matter what the user does. Consequently, unlike the Choice command, when you tell TimeOut to wait 30 seconds, it waits the entire time period even if the user presses a key. In addition, the TimeOut utility doesn't display a message for the timeout, so you can use this utility where silence is necessary (such as a background task). This command uses the following syntax:

```
TIMEOUT [/T] timeout [/NOBREAK]
```

The following list describes each of the command line arguments.

/T *timeout* Specifies the timeout value. The command line switch is optional. You may specify any value from –1 to 99999 seconds. A value of –1 means that the utility waits indefinitely for a key press. The utility won't allow you to combine a value of –1 with the /NOBREAK command line switch since that would effectively lock the system.

/NOBREAK Prevents the utility from recognizing key presses. The TimeOut utility waits for the specified time period before it exits.

Using the WaitFor Utility

The WaitFor utility enables communication between processes. You can send a signal from one application to another. In fact, you can use this feature for signaling between batch files. When using this utility, you start the receiving application first and tell it to wait for the signal. The sender then sends the signal when it's ready. This command uses the following syntax:

```
Sender Syntax:
WAITFOR [/S system [/U [domain\]user [/P [password]]]] /SI signal

Receiver Syntax:
WAITFOR [/T timeout] signal
```

The following list describes each of the command line arguments.

/S *system* Specifies the remote system that you want to check. In most cases, you'll also need to supply the /U and the /P command line switches when using this switch.

/U [*domain\]user* Specifies the username on the remote system. This name may not match the username on the local system. You'll need to supply a domain name when working with a domain controller.

/P [*password]* Specifies the password for the given user. You can provide the command line switch without specifying the password on the command line in clear text. The system prompts you for the password. Using this feature can help you maintain the security of passwords used on your system.

/SI Sends the requested signal across the network.

signal Specifies the signal to send or receive. The signal is a simple string value such as StartSetup. A system can wait for multiple unique signals. The maximum signal name length is 255 characters. You may use a–z, A–Z, 0–9, and any ASCII character code in the range 128–255 for the string value. The string value can't contain special characters or spaces.

/T *timeout* Defines the amount of time to wait for the signal. You can specify any value from 1 to 99,999 seconds. The default setting waits an infinite amount of time.

Testing Batch Files

It's important to remember the place that batch files occupy in the hierarchy of automation. A batch represents a fast and simple way of executing a series of tasks using applications, commands, and utilities. The batch file possesses basic programming structures and you can perform amazing tasks at times with those structures, but in the end, batch files are somewhat limited. Something as simple as a disk being full or a lack of rights to create a file in a specific location can cause the batch file to fail. Error trapping in such cases is difficult because you have to check for error levels from the errant application, command, or utility and not every one of them supports output error levels. The "Providing Fault Tolerance for an After Hours Batch or Script" section of Chapter 8 discusses fault tolerance, including error handling, in detail. The following sections describe some batch file techniques you should consider using, especially when working with large systems.

Real World Scenario

REAL ADMINISTRATORS USE BATCH FIYLES

At one time, I thought I held the title for the number of batch files used for daily activities. That's until I ran into one network administrator who had more batch files than I'd ever seen before. He had batch files for every occasion. In fact, one of the batch files was simply there to track all of the other batch files (so he didn't reinvent the wheel at some point). The entire collection required two CDs, a considerable amount of space when you consider that many of the batch files in this book are less than 1 KB in size.

Of course, he didn't build this huge source of batch files in a day. In fact, he had been building and refining them over a period of years. This administrator customized many of the batch files to his way of working with systems and the network as a whole. In fact, that's the point of batch files. You can do things your way. Because batch files are simplicity itself, you can add, remove, and rebuild them as needed.

However, batch files are important for administrators for another reason. The examples in this book demonstrate that batch files can be quite powerful. Yet, the time required to develop a batch file is short and you don't need to become a programmer to use one. These are the two reasons that most administrators I've talked with give for using batch files instead of scripts. Although batch files can't replace scripts or full-fledged programming languages, over the years I've found that batch files serve the purpose for most administrator needs.

Adding Debug Information to Batch Files

Developers of most applications know how to add debugging statements to their code. The debugging statements aren't for general use; they simply make it easier to check the application for flaws. In addition, the debugging statements make it possible to track program flow and generally help the developer understand the application better. A batch file can also include debugging information, even though there aren't specific statements to perform the task. The following code shows one method you can use.

```
@IF NOT DEFINED DEBUG @ECHO OFF
ECHO
@ECHO ON
```

In this case, the debug trigger is an environment variable named DEBUG. You can set this environment variable to any value desired by using the Set command. Type **Set DEBUG=** and press Enter to turn off debugging. The purpose of this debugging statement is to keep echo on when you're debugging the batch file. During the debugging cycle, you want to see all of the statements, so you display them by keeping the echo on. When the batch file runs normally, the user won't have an environment variable named DEBUG, and the batch file turns off echo so the user doesn't see all of the intervening commands. Using the ECHO command by itself displays the current echo state so you can easily test this technique for yourself.

Notice that the batch file doesn't include anything special for the @ECHO ON statement. It's bad practice to use conditional statements with commands that set the system back to a default state. In this case, you can set echo on without considering the current echo state because having echo on is the default setting.

You can extend debugging to other activities. For example, you might want to know the current value of a variable within the batch file. Because you don't have a debugging environment that you can rely on to perform such tasks, you'll need to use other methods with a batch file. Listing 5.3 shows one technique you can use to extend a batch file to output debugging information about an internal variable (note that this example also uses the DEBUG environment variable). You can obtain this example on the Sybex Web site at http://www.sybex.com/WileyCDA/.

LISTING 5.3:   Adding Simple Debugging to a Batch File

```
@ECHO OFF

REM Locate all of the temporary files on your hard drive.
@ECHO Locating temporary files to delete.
FOR /F %%F IN (DelFiles.TXT) DO CALL :GetFile %%F
GOTO :NextStep

REM This is the actual code for handling the temporary file
REM processing.
:GetFile
IF DEFINED DEBUG @ECHO Adding %1 to the list.
Dir %1 /B /S >> DeleteMe.TXT
GOTO :EOF

REM You would normally place the next step of the processing
REM task here.
:NextStep

@ECHO ON
```

This is actually a batch file within a batch file. The code begins by displaying information to the user that it's collecting a list of temporary files. At this point, the user normally waits while the batch file does its job in complete silence. However, as a developer, you really need to know what's going on within the batch file. To make this work, you need to execute multiple commands. Consequently, the batch file calls a label named :GetFile and passes it to the %%F argument.

Now, look at the :GetFile label and you'll see two statements. The first displays the current %%F value when you create an environment variable named DEBUG. However, notice that it's called %1 here, not %%F. Whenever you employ a Call command to pass control to a label within a batch file, you create a new batch file context. As far as the :GetFile label is concerned, it exists in a different batch file from the original that called it. The first batch file passes %%F as an input value, so it appears as %1 to the :GetFile label code. The second statement in :GetFile is the Dir command that locates the files you want to delete based on the file specification.

Notice that the :GetFile section ends with GOTO :EOF, which should end the batch file. It does, in fact, end the :GetFile batch file and returns control to the FOR command that called it. Now the FOR command can process the next file extension in the list. Figure 5.4 gives you a better idea of how this batch file works with and without DEBUG defined. Notice the batch file doesn't display the file extensions the first time because DEBUG isn't defined yet.

The examples in this section have only shown a single level of debugging so far. However, you can create as many levels of debugging as you want by adding some additional code. Listing 5.4

shows the example in Listing 5.3 with a second level of debugging added. You can obtain this example on the Sybex Web site at `http://www.sybex.com/WileyCDA/`.

LISTING 5.4:   A Batch File with Multiple Debug Levels Defined

```
IF NOT DEFINED DEBUG2 @ECHO OFF

REM Set the second level of debugging.
IF DEFINED DEBUG2 SET DEBUG=TRUE

REM Locate all of the temporary files on your hard drive.
@ECHO Locating temporary files to delete.
FOR /F %%F IN (DelFiles.TXT) DO CALL :GetFile %%F
GOTO :NextStep

REM This is the actual code for handling the temporary file
REM processing.
:GetFile
IF DEFINED DEBUG @ECHO Adding %1 to the list.
Dir %1 /B /S >> DeleteMe.TXT
Goto :EOF

REM You would normally place the next step of the processing
REM task here.
:NextStep

REM Always remember to remove additional debugging levels.
IF DEFINED DEBUG2 SET DEBUG=

@ECHO ON
```

The two levels of debugging for this example are DEBUG and DEBUG2. When you define the DEBUG2 level, the batch file automatically defines DEBUG for you and then removes the DEBUG definition when the batch file ends. As shown in the code, the DEBUG2 level displays all of the batch code as it executes. Although this display can be handy, as shown in Figure 5.5, it can also become quite messy. You don't always need it to locate a problem in your batch file. In fact, displaying the code can sometimes hide problems in plain sight.

FIGURE 5.4
Batch files can output as little or much debugging information as needed.

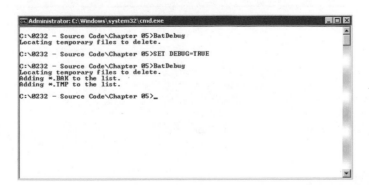

FIGURE 5.5
Display code statements in batch files with care to avoid overwhelming yourself with too much content.

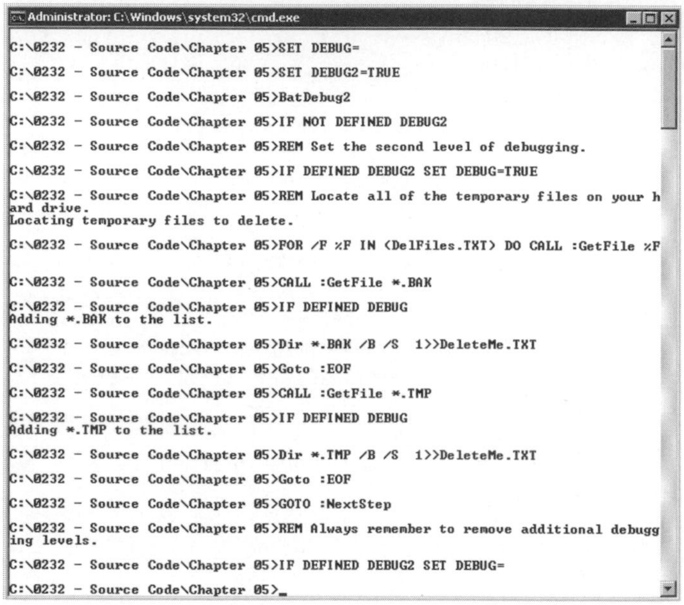

Many people claim that batch files don't offer any form of debugging. Admittedly, batch files don't provide the robust debugging features that full-fledged programming languages do, but batch files don't require these advanced levels of debugging either since they normally perform simple tasks. Using the techniques found in this section, you can provide at least a modicum of debugging functionality for your batch files.

Identifying Batch Files and Their Actions

If you work on a large system, you know that automation isn't just a nicety; it's a requirement if you want to stay on top of maintenance actions. However, automation brings with it all kinds of problems. One of the more critical problems is identifying which machine produced a particular data file. After all, if a machine encounters an error, you want to know which machine to fix. The same concept holds true for other kinds of data. No matter what data you collect, data without an attached context is worthless. With this in mind, you can use code as shown in Listing 5.5 to create a descriptive data file. You can obtain this example on the Sybex Web site at `http://www.sybex.com/WileyCDA/`.

LISTING 5.5: Creating a Descriptive Data File Header

```
@ECHO OFF

REM Add identifying information.
@ECHO Computer: %COMPUTERNAME% > Temps.TXT
@ECHO User: %USERNAME% >> Temps.TXT

REM Add the date and time.
Date /T >> Temps.TXT
Time /T >> Temps.TXT
```

```
REM Create a header for the data.
@ECHO. >> Temps.TXT
@ECHO Temporary Files: >> Temps.TXT
@ECHO. >> Temps.TXT


REM Locate all of the temporary files on your hard drive.
@ECHO Locating temporary files to delete.
FOR /F %%F IN (DelFiles.TXT) DO Dir %%F /B /S >> Temps.TXT


@ECHO ON
```

This example uses several techniques to output descriptive data. First, it combines standard text with environmental variable expansion. Every Windows machine will include the %COMPUTERNAME% and %USERNAME% environment variables (or you can define them in the unlikely event that they don't exist). Notice the first output contains just a single > redirection symbol, so this first line always erases any existing file.

Second, the example uses the Date and Time utilities to output the date and the time. Notice the use of the /T command line switch to prevent these utilities from prompting the user for the date or time. It's a common error not to include the /T command line switch, so you should watch for the error in your own code.

Third, the example creates a header for the data. Notice the use of the special ECHO. command to create a blank space in the output. The addition of the period prevents echo from displaying its status. Because there isn't any other data to display, the ECHO command simply displays a blank line. The remainder of this example outputs a temporary file listing. Figure 5.6 shows typical output from this example.

FIGURE 5.6

It's important to create identifying information for the data files you produce with a batch file.

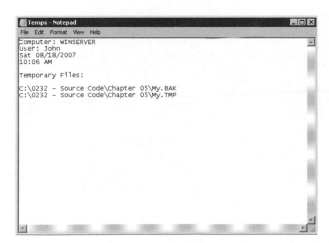

Adding the identifying information to the data file is fine when you don't want to maintain backups of previous data and when the data resides on the original machine. Of course, things change when you want to create a historical view of the data or store the information in a centralized location. In this second instance, you need a unique filename for every submission. Listing 5.6

shows how to add the information to the filename, rather than the data file. You can obtain this example on the Sybex Web site at `http://www.sybex.com/WileyCDA/`.

LISTING 5.6:   Adding Descriptive Information to a Data File

```
@ECHO OFF

REM Create a new environment variable with the identifying
REM information for this file. Start with the computer and
REM user name.
SET DataStore=%COMPUTERNAME%
SET DataStore=%DataStore%_%USERNAME%

REM Add the date.
SET DataStore=%DataStore%_%DATE:~4,2%
SET DataStore=%DataStore%_%DATE:~7,2%
SET DataStore=%DataStore%_%DATE:~10,4%

REM Add the time.
SET DataStore=%DataStore%_%TIME:~0,2%
SET DataStore=%DataStore%_%TIME:~3,2%
SET DataStore=%DataStore%_%TIME:~6,2%

REM Add the file extension.
:SetExtension
SET DataStore=%DataStore%.TXT

REM Locate all of the temporary files on your hard drive.
@ECHO Locating temporary files to delete.
@ECHO Saving files to "%DataStore%".
FOR /F %%F IN (DelFiles.TXT) DO Dir %%F /B /S >> "%DataStore%"

@ECHO ON
```

In this example, the batch files build up an environment variable named `DataStore` that contains the computer and usernames, along with the date and time. Obtaining the computer and usernames are simply a matter of using the existing %COMPUTERNAME% and %USERNAME% environment variables. However, the date and time prove more interesting.

Even though the Set command doesn't show them, Windows dynamically generates several environment variables each time you request them, including %DATE% and %TIME%. When working at DOS, you had to generate these environment variables yourself, which is a time-consuming and error-prone process (see the examples at `http://www.robvanderwoude.com/datetime.html` for details). Unfortunately, these environment variables contain characters that you can use for a filename including the slash (/) and colon (:). Consequently, you can't use the variables directly. The solution is to extract the numbers you need. For example, to extract the first two numbers of the time, you use %TIME:~0,2%, where the first number is the starting point in the string and the second number defines the number of characters to use. Strings in batch file always rely on a 0-based starting point.

TIP   When extracting characters from a string, the system assumes that you want to start on the left side of the string and move to the right. You can reverse this process by using a negative number. For example, %TIME:~-2% would extract the last two characters in the TIME environmental variable.

The %DATE% environment variable requires a little more manipulation than %TIME%. In this case, the string contains the day of the week, so you must extract that information from the string as well. Consequently, the month always appears at position 4, rather than 0.

Now that the batch file has built a unique filename based on the machine name, username, date, and time, it adds a file extension of .TXT to it. The result appears in place of the standard filename in the FOR command for this example. Notice that you must enclose the filename with quotes because it could contain a space.

Using a Centralized Data Store

One problem that none of the examples in the book have addressed so far is the use of a centralized data store. Overcoming this problem with scripts is relatively easy because you have access to standard database objects. With the proper code, you can simply send the data from a client machine to a server and never have to worry about it again except for analysis purposes. However, batch files don't support database objects and the individual machine records discussed so far in the book are ill suited for import into a database. If you have a large network, it's unlikely that you'll want to view every one of those individual records.

You have options at your disposal when working with individual commands. For example, many commands and utilities support the Comma Separated Value (CSV) format. When working with one of these utilities, you simply specify that you don't want headers and that the system should use the CSV format. Unfortunately, these utilities won't address special needs, such as error reports or a listing of interesting files on a machine (perhaps an unacceptable or unsupported application, temporary files, viruses, adware, or spyware). For all of these needs and many more, you must create the output in a form that lends itself to use with a database. Fortunately, creating your own CSV output (a data form commonly accepted by databases) isn't difficult. Listing 5.7 shows one way to do it with a list of temporary files. You can obtain this example on the Sybex Web site at http://www.sybex.com/WileyCDA/.

LISTING 5.7:   Creating Output for a Database

```
@ECHO OFF

REM Clean up any existing output file.
IF EXIST Output.CSV Del Output.CSV

REM Create a new environment variable to hold the static
REM data for this session.
SET DataEntry="%COMPUTERNAME%"
SET DataEntry=%DataEntry%,"%USERNAME%"
SET DataEntry=%DataEntry%,"%DATE%"
SET DataEntry=%DataEntry%,"%TIME%"

REM Locate all of the temporary files on your hard drive.
@ECHO Locating temporary files to delete.
```

```
FOR /F %%F IN (DelFiles.TXT) DO CALL :AddValue %%F
GOTO :Finished

REM Work with the individual directory entries as a set
REM and process them as part of a FOR command.
:AddValue
@ECHO Adding database values for %1.
FOR /F "delims==" %%E IN ('Dir %1 /B /S') DO @ECHO %DataEntry%,"%%E" >> Output.CSV
GOTO :EOF

:Finished
@ECHO ON
```

The idea behind CSV is that you encapsulate the individual data values in quotes and separate them with commas. This example works as most batch files that create CSV will work. You begin by creating one or more static data values that provide a snapshot of this particular session. When you combine this data with other snapshots, the static information provides the means for separating the individual data entries.

The example requires two FOR loops in this case. The first FOR command parses the file specifications located in the DelFiles.TXT file and passes them to a secondary routine.

The secondary FOR loop processes the individual file entries returned by the Dir command. Notice the two additions to the FOR command. First, you must provide the "delims==" option so that the FOR loop doesn't cut off the paths at the first space. Second, notice that this FOR loop doesn't process the data as a file; it uses the command representation instead. Remember that single quotes are for commands and double quotes are for strings. The resulting Output.CSV file contains a pure string representation that you could open in Notepad if desired. However, the power of this particular routine is that you can also open it as a database in a database application or even in Excel. Figure 5.7 shows typical output presented in Excel.

FIGURE 5.7

CSV files make it very easy to move data to a spreadsheet or database.

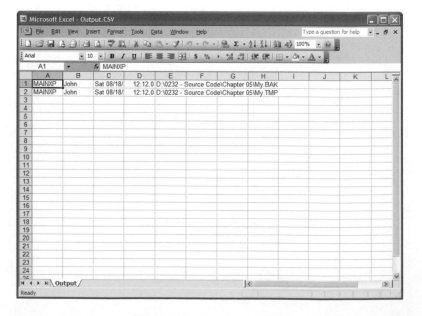

Managing Windows in a New Way

This chapter has demonstrated the functionality that batch files can provide. If you work at the command line very often, you should have a full set of batch files to augment your toolkit. Batch files are a very simple form of programming that can produce dramatic results because they rely on the power of the commands that Windows provides at the command prompt. This chapter introduces what anyone can do with batch files because everyone has access to these features. Batch files can be quite powerful. This chapter helps you build these skills:

- ◆ Create a new command interpreter and configure it
- ◆ Perform basic command line tasks
- ◆ Create batch files
- ◆ Test batch files

It's your turn to try writing batch files. Start simply. Try writing batch files to configure the command line to meet specific needs. You might try something as simple as changing the color of the command line to match your mood on a given day. The point is to try simple concepts first and work your way up to more complex goals. With the right tools, you can automate a considerable number of the tasks you need to perform each day to administrate a network or even work with a single machine.

As powerful as batch files can be in the right hands, they can't perform some basic programming tasks. A batch file limits you to the resources of the commands and utilities available from the command prompt. Chapter 6 shows the next step in automating the command prompt—the use of scripts. A script can provide better programming support and you can even obtain a certain level of debugging for scripts. A script also provides an essential that a batch file can't—a nice user interface. Although batch files work just fine for experienced users and administrators, they aren't a very good choice for novice users. The scripting techniques demonstrated in Chapter 6 help you improve the command line experience for everyone, even—with the proper additions—novice users.

Chapter 6

Working with Scripts

The batch files described in Chapter 5 do provide a reasonable amount of flexibility and they're very easy to produce. However, batch files aren't the same as using an actual programming language. Scripts provide a happy medium between the complexity of a full-fledged programming language that you can compile into an executable and the ease of using batch files. You gain access to more of the system functionality through scripts and have better access to programming constructs, such as flow control. Error trapping is also better with scripts. In fact, you'll be amazed at what scripts can do. People have even developed games in them and most of the Web pages on the Internet rely on scripts to perform tasks in the background.

This chapter isn't going to make you a scripting guru. In fact, it assumes that you already know something about scripting or are willing to look at online resources if you don't. However, you'll discover how scripting can make you extremely effective at the command line. The following sections help you understand scripting languages, learn how to execute them at the command line, and then create scripts under a variety of conditions. Finally, you'll learn how to overcome security problems that using scripts might incur in today's complex workstation environment.

In this chapter, you'll learn how to do the following:

◆ Work with scripting languages

◆ Execute scripts using CScript and WScript

◆ Script network solutions using the NetSH utility

◆ Write a basic script

◆ Use scripting objects

◆ Change the environment using a script

◆ Test a script for errors

Understanding Scripting Languages

There are many scripting languages on the market today. Space won't allow me to discuss them all, even if I knew them all. The following sections discuss JavaScript and VBScript for one reason—they're the languages that Windows supports out of the box so you don't need to install anything special to use them. Of the two, JavaScript enjoys greater popularity and you can use it on more than one platform. Consequently, the scripting examples in the book rely on JavaScript.

🌐 Real World Scenario

SCRIPTS, NOT JUST FOR THOSE WHO TINKER

There's a perception that scripting languages are so limited that you can only use them to create small programs and that only people who like to tinker need consider using them. However, scripting languages today are more powerful that you might think. For example, it's quite easy to write applications that interact with Web services using scripts. I've personally written scripts to interact with all of the major online Web services including Amazon.com, Google, and eBay. Of course, Web service support is really just the tip of the iceberg and not everyone is working with Web services today.

Scripting languages provide access to a number of the features that developers consider essential for complex applications. For example, you can access most COM controls and components using a scripting language. The ability to create objects means that you can rely on code other developers created to produce complex applications. For example, most developers would argue that eXtensible Markup Language (XML) support is essential today. You can gain access to XML by creating the correct objects using a scripting language. In fact, the "Using the Scripting Objects" section of the chapter describes specialized scripting objects you can use.

Don't get the idea that scripting languages are a replacement for full-fledged programming languages, however. They do have limitations. For example, you'll find that debugging, while available, is limited. You also won't gain access to all of the features that an Integrated Development Environment (IDE) can provide. Scripts are procedural and many developers feel that classes are the best way to approach some programming problems. In short, scripts really are that halfway point between batch files and full-fledged programming languages.

NOTE You'll find that JavaScript comes in several slightly different forms and names. Besides JavaScript, you'll see this language as LiveScript, JScript, and ECMAScript. You can find an interesting language history at `http://www.webmasterworld.com/forum91/68.htm` (may require a log in).

Learning the Basics of JavaScript

This chapter doesn't provide a nuts and bolts discussion of JavaScript. I'm assuming you have some experience using this language. Because this language is used in so many ways, you can find great JavaScript resources online. Many sites include tutorials, a reference, and sample code. If you want to be sure your code runs in as many environments as possible, make sure you download a copy of European Computer Manufacturer's Association (ECMA) standard 262 from `http://www.ecma-international.org/publications/standards/Ecma-262.htm`, which is the standard for JavaScript.

If you've never used JavaScript before, you'll need a good tutorial. The W3Schools.com site at `http://www.w3schools.com/js/default.asp` provides an excellent tutorial for first-time users. Webmonkey provides several JavaScript tutorials including a basic tutorial at `http://www.webmonkey.com/98/03/index0a.html` and an advanced tutorial at `http://www.webmonkey.com/98/29/index0a.html`. You might also want to view their crash course index at `http://www.webmonkey.com/programming/javascript/tutorials/jstutorial_index.html`.

It's important to have a good JavaScript reference. One of the best places to find a JavaScript reference is at `http://developer.mozilla.org/en/docs/JavaScript_Language_Resources`.

If you want to learn about the Microsoft perspective on JavaScript, the Windows Script 5.6 Documentation site at `http://www.microsoft.com/downloads/details.aspx?FamilyId=01592C48-207D-4BE1-8A76-1C4099D7BBB9` has a downloadable reference that contains a wealth of helpful information. You may also want to check out Microsoft's Scripting technology site at `http://msdn2.microsoft.com/en-us/library/ms950396.aspx`.

 Real World Scenario

VERIFYING YOUR JAVASCRIPT SETUP

You may run into a problem where the scripts in this book don't work. Double-clicking the script file doesn't work and it appears that you can't do anything else with the file either. In fact, Windows might not know anything about the file at all. Although it does happen with VBScript, most people have problems getting their JavaScript (JS) files to run correctly after they install certain kinds of software or perform actions with virus detection software. If you double-click on a JS file and nothing happens, the problem might be in the registry. For whatever reason (and I wasn't able to verify a single specific reason), sometimes people find Windows or another external application removes their JavaScript settings.

The main problem is that the registry lacks entries for the .JS extension handler. Verify that you have the handler installed by viewing the `HKEY_CLASSES_ROOT\.JS` key first. This key should say JSFile as the (Default) value. Now, look at the `HKEY_CLASSES_ROOT\JSFile` entry. It should have JScript Script File as the (Default) value and `@%SystemRoot%\System32\wshext.dll,-4804` as the FriendlyTypeName value. You should see two open verbs. The first is at `HKEY_CLASSES_ROOT\JSFile\Shell\Open\Command` and should have a (Default) value of `%SystemRoot%\System32\WScript.exe "%1" %*`. The second is at `HKEY_CLASSES_ROOT\JSFile\Shell\Open2\Command` and should have a (Default) value of `%SystemRoot%\System32\CScript.exe "%1" %*`. If you're not seeing these entries, it means that something has gone awry with your registry. When this problem occurs, you can usually restore your JavaScript and VBScript settings by typing **RegSvr32 WSHExt.DLL** in the `\Windows\System32` folder and pressing Enter.

Learning the Basics of VBScript

As with JavaScript, this chapter doesn't provide a VBScript tutorial. Unfortunately, VBScript is also less popular than JavaScript, so you won't find as many resources online for using it. However, a few developers still use VBScript for their application needs. The main VBScript Web site is at `http://msdn2.microsoft.com/en-us/library/t0aew7h6.aspx`. This Web site includes a VBScript user's guide and language reference. You can find another good reference on the W3Schools Web site at `http://www.w3schools.com/vbscript/vbscript_ref_functions.asp`.

You can find a number of good tutorials online. One of the better tutorials is at `http://www.w3schools.com/vbscript/vbscript_intro.asp`. Make sure you try the Learn by Example resource on the W3Schools Web site at `http://www.w3schools.com/vbscript/vbscript_examples.asp`. A basic tutorial appears on the IntranetJournal Web site at `http://www.intranetjournal.com/corner/wrox/progref/vbt/` and `http://www.intranetjournal.com/corner/aitken/vbs-1.shtml`. Once you learn the basics, try the tutorials on the ComputerTechnicalTutorials Web site at `http://www.techtutorials.info/vbscript.html`. You can find a browser perspective of VBScript tutorial at `http://www.tizag.com/vbscriptTutorial/`.

Sometimes you need additional help using VBScript. The VisualBasicScript.com Web site at `http://www.visualbasicscript.com/` provides a forum for asking questions about VBScript.

You also find a complete, albeit somewhat outdated, book on VBScript at http://docs.rinet.ru/VB/. If you haven't found what you wanted in this section, try the centralized Web site of VBScript links at http://www.cetus-links.org/oo_vbscript.html. If you don't find what you want with one of the sources listed in this section, try the list of resources found at http://searchvb.techtarget .com/generic/0,295582,sid8_gci1158017,00.html?track=NL-283&ad=539962.

Understanding the WSF

The Windows Scripting File (WSF) isn't a new scripting language. Instead, it's a new way to package your scripts. Current script technology doesn't make it easy to create certain kinds of scripts. For example, if you have code written in VBScript that you want to combine with code writing in JavaScript, you can't do it. The WSF technology provides a significant number of advantages to the script developer including:

♦ Using Include statements to add external code to your script.

♦ Using more than a single language per scripting file (of course, you must have all of the required scripting engines installed on your system).

♦ Adding type libraries to your script, which means you have access to type library features such as constants.

♦ Adding XML components to your code by using an XML editor to create the file.

♦ Including multiple applications in a single file.

Microsoft has only recently begun using the WSF. In fact, you can't execute WSF files in older versions of windows such as Windows XP—you need either Vista or Windows Server 2008 (any version) to use this technology. The main WSF script for Server Core is SCRegEdit.WSF (see the "Working with the SCRegEdit Script" section of Chapter 4 for details). Another WSF script, Manage-BDE.WSF, helps you manage the BitLocker setup on your Server Core system.

TIP   You can find a wealth of information about Windows scripting technologies online. However, one of the more interesting places to look is the Batch Scripts for Windows site at http:// www.wilsonmar.com/1wsh.htm. If you want to learn about WSF files in a hurry, you may want to obtain the video found at http://www.onscript.com/training-videos/titles/windows-script-files-unmasked.asp. You can see some WSF examples at http://msdn.microsoft .com/archive/en-us/wsh/htm/wsAdvantagesOfWs.asp.

The best way to edit a WSF file is to use an editor designed for the purpose. You may find the combination of XML and scripting code a little disorienting at first and a good editor can help you overcome that problem. The "Editing Script Files with Script Editor 2.1" section of Chapter 7 tells you about one such editor, but you'll likely find many other editors on the market.

A WSF file begins with a <job> element. The <job> element can contain an id attribute that you can use later to execute a specific job within a file. For example, if the source code file contains the following <job> element:

```
<job id="MyJob">
```

and the name of the file is MyScript.WSF, you can execute it by typing **CScript //Job:MyJob MyScript.WSF** and pressing Enter. Of course, as with any good XML, you must include the ending </job> element.

Having the `<job>` element isn't enough to create a script, however. You must also include the `<script>` element. The `<script>` element defines the beginning of a scripting area and a job can include more than one scripting area. Each scripting area can include a single language. Consequently, the `<script>` element normally has the `language` attribute. When you want to execute a VBScript, you set the `language` attribute to VBScript. The `<script>` element can also include the `scr` attribute, which defines the location of external code. Consequently, if your script is in VBScript and it relies on the `MyExternal.VBS` file, the `<script>` element would include both entries like this:

```
<script language="VBScript" src="MyExternal.VBS">
```

The final essential WSF element is the `<reference>` element. You use it to reference external code. The type library must appear in the registry before you can use it. The RegSvr32 utility described in the "Adding and Removing Servers with the RegSvr32 Utility" section of Chapter 13 tells you how to perform this task. The `<reference>` element accesses the external code using its `progid` attribute. The actual usage of the external code looks similar to how you might have worked with it in earlier versions of Visual Basic. Here's an example of external code access in a WSF file.

```
<job id="ExternalCodeAccess">
   <reference progid="MyComponent.MyClass">
   <script language="VBScript">
      Dim ObjRef
      Set ObjRef = CreateObject("MyComponent.MyClass")
      Result = ObjRef.MyMethod
      If Result = 0 then
         WScript.Echo "An Error Occurred"
      End If
   </script>
</job>
```

The `<reference>` element makes it possible to load the external code contained in the `MyComponent` file. You access a particular class, `MyClass`, within that object and instantiate by setting `ObjRef` equal to the output of `CreateObject()`. Now that the code has an object to use, it can call the `MyMethod()` method. The output of this call appears in `Result`. When `Result` contains an unexpected value, the code can display an error message to the user. Although this feature is very simple, it does provide you with access to a wealth of additional resources and makes your scripts considerably more flexible.

Executing Scripts

All you need to create a standard script is a text editor, such as Notepad, and a little time. (If you want to create a WSF, then you really should use an editor designed for the purpose.) You can also use script-specific tools such as the Visual Basic Editor or Microsoft Script Editor provided with Microsoft Office, but not when working directly with Server Core. A number of third parties also produce products that can help you create and even compile your script. Chapter 7 discusses a few of these products and you'll find more online.

No matter what you do to create your script, however, it's useless unless you can run it. Windows provides two interpreters—applications that run scripts—for you to use. The first, CScript, works at the command line and the second, WScript, works from within Windows. Interestingly enough, Server Core can execute scripts with WScript, but because you can't be sure how the script will interact with the GUI, using CScript is always a better idea. The following sections describe both options.

Running Scripts with the CScript and WScript Utilities

Windows supports two methods of starting scripts. The CScript application works at the command prompt, while the WScript application works from within the graphical user environment. Both applications accomplish the same task—they provide a means for interpreting a script file you create.

CScript and WScript use the same command line. You must provide a script name as the first command line argument. Most scripts have a VBE or JS file extension, but any extension is acceptable. For example, you can still use VBS files with Windows Script Host (WSH), but the icon won't look right, in some cases, and you can't double-click it to start the execution with newer Windows products. The VBS extension is the right choice for older versions of Windows. The icon is yellow for VBE files and blue for JS and WSF files. These utilities use the following syntax:

```
CScript <Script Name> [<WSH Command Line Switches>] [<Script Arguments>]
WScript <Script Name> [<WSH Command Line Switches>] [<Script Arguments>]
```

The following list describes each of the command line arguments.

//?   Displays the currently documented command line switches. The newest versions of WSH tend to reject older switches, even those of the undocumented variety.

//B   Limits user interaction with the script. Batch mode suppresses all non–command line console user interface requests from the script. It also suppresses error message display (a change from previous versions).

//D   Activates debugging mode so you can fix errors in a script.

//E:*Engine*   Specifies the engine to use to execute the script. You use this feature when a script has something other than the default extension (such as .JS or .VBS). The common settings are //E:JScript for JavaScript and //E:VBScript for VBScript. However, you can use any compatible scripting engine.

//H:CScript   Makes CSCRIPT.EXE the default application for running scripts. (WScript is the default engine.)

//H:WScript   Makes WSCRIPT.EXE the default application for running scripts.

//I   Allows full interaction with the user. Any pop-up dialog boxes wait for user input before the script continues.

//Job:*JobName*   Executes a WSH job. A WSH job has a Windows Scripting File (WSF) extension. This file enables you to perform tasks using multiple scripting engines and multiple files. Essentially, this allows you to perform a "super batch" process.

//Logo and //NoLogo   WSH normally prints out a logo message. You'd use the //NoLogo switch to prevent WSH from displaying this message.

//S: This command line switch allows you to save current command line options for a user. WSH saves the following options: //B, //I, //Logo, //Nologo, and //T:n.

//T:*TimeLimit*   Limits the maximum time the script can run to the number of seconds specified. Normally, there isn't any timeout value. You'd use this switch in situations where a script might end up in a continuous loop or is unable to get the requested information for other reasons. For example, you might use this switch when requesting information on a network drive.

//X   Starts the script in the debugger. This allows you to trace the execution of the script from beginning to end.

//U   Outputs any console information using Unicode instead of pure ASCII. You use this switch on systems where you need to support languages other than English. This is a CScript-only option.

Notice that all of these command line switches start with two slashes (//) to differentiate them from switches you may need for your script. WSH passes script arguments to your script for processing. Script arguments can be anything including command line switches of your own or values needed to calculate a result.

NOTE   Users of older versions of CScript and WScript may remember the //C and the //W switches used to switch the default scripting engines. Newer versions of CScript and WScript replace these switches with the //H switch. You'll also find the //R (reregister) and //Entrypoint switches missing from WSH because script developers no longer need the functionality. Always use the correct command line switches for the version of Windows and WSH installed on your machine.

You can work with WSH in either interactive or batch mode. Use batch mode when you need to perform tasks that don't require user input. For example, you might want to run Scan Disk every evening, but use different command line switches for it based on the day. You could use Task Scheduler to accomplish this task, but using it in conjunction with a WSH script improves the flexibility you get when running the task.

Another kind of batch processing might be to send log files to your supervisor or perhaps set up a specific set of environment variables for a character-mode application based on the current user. On the other hand, interactive mode requires user interaction. You'd use it for tasks such as cleaning the hard drive because you don't always know whether the user needs a particular file. Such a script could ask the user a set of general questions, and then clean excess files from the hard drive based on the user input. The cleaning process would follow company guidelines and save the user time.

TIP   Because batch processing doesn't require any form of user input, it's usually a good idea to include the //T switch with the //B switch. This combination stops the script automatically if it runs too long. In most cases, using this switch setup stops an errant script before it corrupts the Windows environment or freezes the machine. However, you can't time some tasks with ease. For example, any Web-based task is difficult to time because you can't account for problems with a slow connection. In this case, you'll need to refrain from using the //T switch or provide a worst-case scenario time interval.

The next set of command line switches to consider is //Logo and //NoLogo. There isn't any right or wrong time to use these switches, but you usually use the //Logo switch when testing a script and the //NoLogo switch afterward. The reason is simple. During the testing process, you want to know about every potential source of problems in your script environment, including an old script engine that might cause problems. On the other hand, you don't want to clutter your screen with useless text after you debug the script. Using the //NoLogo switch keeps screen clutter to a minimum.

Configuring the Host and Property Page Options

You don't have to rely exclusively on command line switches to configure WSH; you can configure two WSH options from the Windows Script Host Settings dialog box shown in Figure 6.1. Run WScript by itself and you'll see the Windows Script Host Settings dialog box.

FIGURE 6.1
Configure WSH to
meet specific needs.

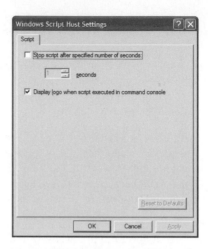

The Stop Script after Specified Number of Seconds check box tells WSH to stop executing a script after a certain time interval has elapsed. The edit box below it contains the number of seconds to wait. Setting this option is like adding the //T command line switch to every script that you run.

The Display Logo When Script Executed in Command Console check box determines whether WSH displays WSH logo when running scripts from the DOS prompt. Normally, Windows checks this option, which is the same as adding the //Logo command line switch to every script that you run. Clearing this option tells WSH that you don't want to display the logo, which is the same as using the //NoLogo command line switch.

You can also display the Windows Script Host Settings dialog box for individual scripts. Simply right-click the script file and select Properties from the context menu. Select the Script tab to see the options. These settings only affect the individual script file; the options for WSH in general remain the same.

Scripting Networking Solutions with the NetSH Utility

Many of the utilities discussed in this book are mini-command processors. For example, the FTP utility described in the "Managing FTP Servers with the FTP Utility" section of Chapter 17 describes such an environment. The Network Command Shell (NetSH) utility extends this idea by providing an extensible command processor. You access the functionality that this utility provides by loading a helper Dynamic Link Library (DLL). Each helper DLL places the NetSH utility into a different context. The use of helper DLLs theoretically makes it possible for third-party vendors to add NetSH functionality as part of their network product installation. One of the essential commands to know for NetSH, since it's so flexible, is NetSH Show Helper. This command displays a list of helper DLLs installed on your machine, which may differ from the list shown in Figure 6.2 based on the operating system features you have installed.

Notice the hierarchy of contexts displayed in Figure 6.2. To access the IP context at the command line, you must type **NetSH Interface IP** and then the command you wish to use. Likewise, if you want to access the 6To4 context, you must type **NetSH Interface IPv6 6To4** at the command line. Typing any context by itself (or followed by a question mark (?) or Help) displays the list of commands for that context.

FIGURE 6.2

Obtain a list of helper DLLs for your setup using the NetSH Show Helper command.

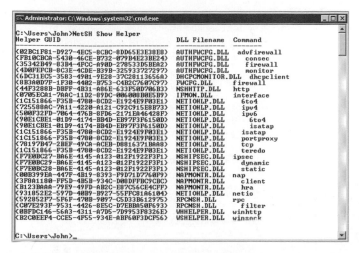

Type a command to see the list of subcommands or the instructions for using that command. Type a subcommand to see the instructions for using that subcommand. For example, to discover how to add a new IP address, type **NetSH Interface IP Add Address** at the command prompt and press Enter. You'll see a help display explaining the command, as shown in Figure 6.3. Figure 6.3 shows the Server Core view of the help for this command. If you're familiar with previous versions of Windows, you'll notice that the Server Core help is an improvement.

FIGURE 6.3

The multilevel command structure provided by NetSH provides you with help at each step.

NOTE This chapter doesn't discuss the specifics of each context because they vary according to operating system version and the helpers you have installed. Unfortunately, there isn't any documented resource from Microsoft for standard contexts in Windows Server 2008, but you can use the Windows 2003 resource as a guideline. The contexts for Windows 2003 appear at `http://technet2.microsoft.com/WindowsServer/en/Library/552ed70a-208d-48c4-8da8-2e27b530eac71033.mspx`. You can find additional NetSH utility documentation in the Microsoft Knowledge Base article at `http://support.microsoft.com/?kbid=242468` and The Cable Guy article at `http://www.microsoft.com/technet/community/columns/cableguy/cg1101.mspx`.

The NetSH utility provides access to a broad range of networking functionality using contexts. Each context represents a different functional network area such as configuring the firewall or modifying security. You can interact with NetSH at the command line, in an interactive environment, and using scripts. In this case, a script file is simply a list of commands that you want NetSH to perform. You place these commands in a text file and pass them to NetSH to execute. This utility uses the following syntax:

```
netsh [-a AliasFile] [-c Context] [-r RemoteMachine]
[-u [DomainName\]UserName] [Command | -f ScriptFile]
```

The following list describes each of the command line arguments.

-a *AliasFile* Specifies the alias file to use. An alias file contains a set of strings and their associated NetSH equivalents. You can use the alias in place of the corresponding `NetSH` command. This feature also allows you to map older commands to the appropriate `NetSH` command.

-c *Context* Defines the context of the command that you want to run. A context refers to a specific helper DLL.

Command Specifies the `NetSH` command to execute. The command is helper DLL specific.

-f *ScriptFile* Specifies the name of a file that contains NetSH commands. A script file is simply a text file that contains NetSH commands one after another. You can use the pound (#) symbol followed by text to create script file comments. Use the NetSH Dump command to display a sample script. Because the script is long, you might want to use redirection to send the output to a file (see the "Employing Data Redirection" section of Chapter 14 for details).

-r *RemoteMachine* Defines the name or IP address of a remote machine to use to execute NetSH commands. This feature helps you manage remote systems.

-u [*DomainName*]*UserName* Specifies the credentials to use to log into a system. Server Core prompts you for a password when logging into another system.

The various helper DLLs provide contexts that you can use to perform specific tasks. You can access some of these contexts directly from the command line using a command. Table 6.1 describes each of the top-level contexts.

TABLE 6.1:   Standard NetSH Contexts

CONTEXT NAME	WINDOWS VERSION	DESCRIPTION
Bridge	Windows XP and above	Shows configuration information for network adapters that are part of a network bridge. You can also use this context to enable or disable Level 3 compatibility mode.
Diag	Windows XP and above	Performs network diagnostic commands. For example, you can use this context to display network service status information or perform diagnostics similar to the Ping utility described in the "Checking Connections with the Ping Utility" section of Chapter 11. A special NetSH Diag GUI command displays a Web page in the Help and Support Center that provides access to the network diagnostics.
Firewall	Windows XP and above	Provides complete access to the Windows firewall. You can use this context to add and remove configuration information, as well as display the current firewall state.
Interface	Windows 2000 and above	Provides access to the network interfaces installed on your machine, which normally include IP, IPV6 (Windows XP and above), and standard port proxies. You can use this context to configure the TCP/IP protocol including addresses, default gateways, DNS servers, and WINS servers.
RAS	Windows 2000 and above	Provides access to the Remote Access Server (RAS) and all of its configuration information. For example, this context provides access to the Authentication, Authorization, Accounting, and Auditing (AAAA) subcontext where you perform security setups.
Routing	Windows 2000 and above	Helps you configure the routing features of the system using a command line interface, rather than rely on the Routing and Remote Access console. The biggest advantage of the command line interface, in this case, is speed. You can access and manage remote servers over a large network, especially wide area networks (WANs) much faster using NetSH than you can the graphical equivalents. In addition, since these configuration tasks can become quite complex, you gain the advantage of scripting them once, rather than going through every required step each time you perform the task.
WinSock	Windows XP and above	Shows Windows Socket (WinSock) information for the current system. You can also use this context to dump the WinSock configuration script.

The default context is the root context, the NetSH utility itself. You can use specific commands from this context to perform configuration tasks or access other contexts. The following list describes the command line arguments, which differ according to the version of Windows that you use and the networking features you have installed.

add   Adds a configuration entry to the list of entries. When working at the root context, you can add new helper DLLs to the list.

delete   Deletes a configuration entry from the list of entries. When working at the root context, you can remove a helper DLL from the list.

dump   Displays a configuration script. The script is quite long, so you'll want to use redirection to store the script to a file.

exec   Executes the specified script file.

interface   Sets NetSH to use the interface context.

ras   Sets NetSH to use the RAS context.

routing   Sets NetSH to use the routing context.

set   Updates the configuration settings. Most versions of NetSH only allow you to set the machine name when working at the root context.

show   Displays NetSH configuration information. Most versions of NetSH provide commands to display both the list of aliases and the list of helpers installed on the system.

Windows XP and above provide additional functionality to support items such as the firewall. Here are the Windows XP additions.

bridge   Sets NetSH to use the bridge context.

diag   Sets NetSH to use the diag context.

firewall   Sets NetSH to use the firewall context.

winsock   Sets NetSH to use the WinSock context.

Windows 2003 and above supports still more commands. The following list describes the Windows 2003 additions.

cmd   Creates a command window where you can enter NetSH commands manually.

comment   Executes any commands accumulated in offline mode.

flush   Discards the commands accumulated in offline mode.

online   Sets the current mode to online. In online mode, which is the default for all previous versions of NetSH, the utility executes immediately any command you issue. Use the show mode command to display the current mode.

offline   Sets the current mode to offline. In offline mode, which was new for Windows 2003, the utility accumulates any commands you issue and executes them as a batch. Using this second approach on remote servers can greatly enhance performance without any loss of functionality. Use the show mode command to display the current mode.

pushd   Pushes a context onto the NetSH stack. Earlier versions pushed context onto the system stack by using the PushD command described in the "Storing and Retrieving Directories with the *PushD* and *PopD* Commands" section of Chapter 9.

popd Removes a context from the NetSH stack. Earlier versions popped the context from the system stack using the PopD command described in the "Storing and Retrieving Directories with the *PushD* and *PopD* Commands" section of Chapter 9.

 Real World Scenario

NEWER UTILITIES CAN REPLACE OLDER EQUIVALENTS

One of the tricks of the trade when working at the command line is to look for efficient replacements of old bulky commands. The NetSH utility is such a replacement. You can use it in place of a number of older utilities and graphical tools. For example, the NetSH utility replaces the older RouteMon utility. Even though you'll find the RouteMon executable on Windows XP and newer systems, the executable now tells you to use NetSH instead.

As part of keeping track of utility functionality, you must also monitor the services that Microsoft supports. For example, Windows 2000 supports the ReSerVation Protocol (RSVP), but Microsoft no longer supports this service on Windows XP and newer systems. The loss of this service affects the method you use to reserve network resources and, consequently, the use of utilities. See the MSDN article at `http://msdn2.microsoft.com/en-us/library/aa374137.aspx` for details. Of course, even if the latest version of Windows supports a particular service, you'll want to ensure the service runs automatically. As an example, Windows XP originally enabled the TelNet service, but disabled it for the SP2 release. You'll often need to rely on third-party resources, such as the Web site at `http://www.ss64.com/ntsyntax/services.html`, to obtain information about services because Microsoft tends to hide this information (or not publish it at all).

Creating a Basic Script

Scripts can make the command line significantly easier to automate and can improve the reliability of command line tasks by helping you perform tasks in the same sequence every time. This section shows how to create basic scripts in both VBScript and JavaScript so you can see the differences between the two languages. You'll also see how to use some of the objects described in the "Using the Scripting Objects" section of the chapter. The following code shows a basic example in VBScript.

```
' Test1.VBS shows how to use functions and subprocedures
' within a WSH script.

WScript.Echo("The value returned was: " + CStr(MyFunction(1)))

function MyFunction(nSomeValue)
    WScript.Echo("Function received value of: " + CStr(nSomeValue))
    Call MySubprocedure(nSomeValue + 1)
    MyFunction = nSomeValue + 1
end function

sub MySubprocedure(nSomeValue)
    WScript.Echo("Subprocedure received value of: " + CStr(nSomeValue))
end sub
```

As you can see, the sample code uses the WScript object to send information to the screen. The WScript object is always available at the command line, even though you have probably never used it as part of a browser application. As shown in the example, it's important to know how to use both functions and subs, the two building blocks of VBScript. The following code shows a similar example for JavaScript.

```javascript
// Test1.JS shows how to use functions within a WSH script.

WScript.Echo("The value returned was: " + MyFunction(1));

function MyFunction(nSomeValue)
{
   WScript.Echo("The value received was: " + nSomeValue);
   return nSomeValue + 1;
}
```

JavaScript only provides functions, so that's all this example demonstrates. It's also important to notice that VBScript requires you to convert numeric values to a string, while JavaScript performs the conversion automatically. The following sections show how to perform certain command line–oriented tasks using scripting.

Scripting the Command Line and System Environment

Many of your scripts require access to the command line. The command line is where you type switches to modify the behavior of the script, as many of the utilities described in this book do. The system environment contains user, application, and operating system values, such as the user's name or the version of the operating system. The JavaScript code in Listing 6.1 retrieves information from the command line. It also retrieves information about the application environment. You can obtain this example on the Sybex Web site at `http://www.sybex.com/WileyCDA/`.

LISTING 6.1:   Working with the Command Line and System Environment

```javascript
// ProgInfo.JS determines the specifics about your program and then
// displays this information on screen.

// Create some constants for display purposes (buttons and icons).
var intOK = 0;
var intOKCancel = 1;
var intAbortRetryIgnore = 2;
var intYesNoCancel = 3;
var intYesNo = 4;
var intRetryCancel = 5;
var intStop = 16;
var intQuestion = 32;
var intExclamation = 48;
var intInformation = 64;

// Create some popup return values.
var intOK = 1;
```

```javascript
var intCancel = 2;
var intAbort = 3;
var intRetry = 4;
var intIgnore = 5;
var intYes = 6;
var intNo = 7;
var intClose = 8;
var intHelp = 9;

// Create a popup display object.
var WshShell = WScript.CreateObject("WScript.Shell");

// Create a variable for holding a popup return value.
var intReturn;

// Get the program information and display it.
WshShell.Popup("Full Name:\t" + WScript.Fullname +
        "\r\nInteractive:\t" + WScript.Interactive +
        "\r\nName:\t\t" + WScript.Name +
        "\r\nPath:\t\t" + WScript.Path +
        "\r\nScript Full Name:\t" + WScript.ScriptFullName +
        "\r\nScript Name:\t" + WScript.ScriptName +
        "\r\nVersion:\t\t" + WScript.Version,
        0,
        "Program Information Demonstration",
        intOK + intInformation);

// Ask if the user wants to display the argument list.
intReturn = WshShell.Popup("Do you want to display the argument list?",
            0,
            "Argument List Display",
            intYesNo + intQuestion);

// Determine if the user wants to display the argument list and
// display an appropriate message.
if (intReturn == intYes)

    // See if there are any arguments to display.
    DisplayArguments();
else
    WScript.Echo("Goodbye");

function DisplayArguments()
{

    // Create some variables.
    var strArguments = "Arguments:\r\n\t";     // Argument list.
    var intCount = 0;             // Loop counter.
```

```
    // See if there are any arguments, if not, display an
    // appropriate message.
    if (WScript.Arguments.Length == 0)
        WshShell.Popup("There are no arguments to display.",
            0,
            "Argument List Display",
            intOK + intInformation);

    // If there are arguments to display, then create a list
    // first and display them all at once.
    else
    {
        for (intCount = 0;
             intCount < WScript.Arguments.Length;
             intCount++)

            strArguments = strArguments +
                        WScript.Arguments.Item(intCount) + "\r\n\t";

        WshShell.Popup(strArguments,
                    0,
                    "Argument List Display",
                    intOK + intInformation);
    }
}
```

When you run this script, you'll see a dialog box containing all of the information about the script engine. When you click OK, the program asks if you want to display the command line arguments. If you say yes, then you'll see anything you typed at the command line. Otherwise, the script displays a Goodbye message.

You should notice a few things about this example. First, I created an object in this code. You need access to the WshShell object for many of the tasks you'll perform with scripts. The code also shows how to use the Popup() method to obtain information from the user. Finally, the code uses the Arguments object to access the command line information. Notice the object hierarchy used in this example.

Scripting the Registry

Many of the utilities described in this book rely on the registry to store and retrieve data about the machine, the operating system, the user, and the application itself. Knowing how to access the registry from your script is important because you also need to access these values in order to discover how a particular utility will react or how the user had configured the system. You can also use the registry to store and retrieve values for your script. The example in Listing 6.2 shows how to use VBScript to access information in the registry. You don't want to change information unless you have to, but seeing what's available in the registry is a good way to build your knowledge of both scripting and the registry. Note that this example uses the command line argument to determine which file extension to look for in the registry. The example uses the TXT file extension when you don't supply one. You can obtain this example on the Sybex Web site at http://www.sybex.com/WileyCDA/.

LISTING 6.2:   Working with the Registry

```
` RegRead.VBE will display the application extension information
` contained in the registry.

` Create an icon and button variable for Popup().
intOK = 0
intInformation = 64

` Create a popup display object.
set WshShell = WScript.CreateObject("WScript.Shell")

` Create variables to hold the information.
strExtension = ""     ` File extension that we're looking for.
strFileType = ""     ` Holds the main file type.
strFileOpen = ""     ` File open command.
strFilePrint = ""     ` File print command.
strDefaultIcon = ""   ` Default icon for file type.

` See if the user provided a file extension to look for.
` If not, assign strExtension a default file extension.
if (WScript.Arguments.Length > 0) then
    strExtension = WScript.Arguments.Item(0)
else
    strExtension = ".txt"
end if

` Get the file type.
strFileType = WshShell.RegRead("HKEY_CLASSES_ROOT\" +_
                strExtension + "\")

` Use the file type to get the file open and file print
` commands, along with the default icon.
strFileOpen = WshShell.RegRead("HKEY_CLASSES_ROOT\" +_
                strFileType +_
                "\shell\open\command\")
strFilePrint = WshShell.RegRead("HKEY_CLASSES_ROOT\" +_
                strFileType +_
                "\shell\print\command\")
strDefaultIcon = WshShell.RegRead("HKEY_CLASSES_ROOT\" +_
                strFileType +_
                "\DefaultIcon\")

` Display the results.
WshShell.Popup "File Type:" + vbTab + vbTab + vbTab + strFileType +_
        vbCrLf + "File Open Command:" + vbTab + strFileOpen +_
        vbCrLf + "File Print Command:" + vbTab + vbTab + strFilePrint +_
```

```
                 vbCrLf + "Default Icon:" + vbTab + vbTab + strDefaultIcon,_
                 0,_
                 "RegRead Results",_
                 intOK + intInformation
```

When you run this script, it reads the command line. If you haven't supplied a value, the script assigns a default extension of TXT. The script uses the extension to locate information in the registry such as the file open and print commands. Finally, the script uses the Popup() method to display the output.

You should notice several differences between this example and the JavaScript example in Listing 6.1. First, the method for creating an object requires the use of a set—you can't simply assign the object to a variable. You'll also notice that VBScript has access to all of the standard Visual Basic constants such as vbTab and vbCrLf. Finally, VBScript handles many of the method calls as subs, not as functions. You need to exercise care when working in a mixed environment.

Using the Scripting Objects

A section of a chapter can't provide you with a complete tutorial on scripting. Some developers require months to learn everything there is to know about the scripting language and the objects the language controls. This section helps you understand the various objects that WSH supports. You won't become a guru overnight, but you could create some simple scripts immediately after you work through this chapter. As you learn more, you'll be able to create scripts of increasing complexity. Scripting isn't hard to learn, but you need to take your time and learn it a bit at a time.

TIP   Windows XP and above don't include any sample scripts. However, earlier versions of Windows do include a sample directory for scripts that you can use to learn more about the scripting process. You can still download the script samples from Microsoft's site at http://msdn2 .microsoft.com/en-us/library/ms950396.aspx. You can find examples of scripts in Server Core. For example, change directories to the root directory of the Server Core drive (use CD \), type **Dir *.VBS /S**, and press Enter. You'll see a number of VBScript examples that you can examine (don't execute them unless you know what task they perform).

WSH depends on objects that Microsoft supplies as part of Windows to perform tasks such as outputting text to the display. This chapter demonstrates the latest version of WSH. Every version of Windows has similar objects, but you might not find some objects in older versions of Windows.

NOTE   An object consists of three elements: properties, methods, and events. A property describes the object and determines its functionality. For example, you can say an apple is red. In this case, red is a property of the apple. However, you can also paint the apple blue. In this case, you changed the color property of the apple to another value. Methods are actions you can perform with an object. For example, looking at an apple again, you can say that it has a grow method. As the tree applies the grow method, the apple becomes larger. Events are responses to specific object actions. For example, when the apple becomes mature, it raises the "color" event to tell you that it's ripe.

Writing scripts in Windows means knowing the object you want to work with, the properties that object provides, and the methods you can use with that object. You don't have to know about every object. In fact, you'll find it easier to learn about one object at a time. The following sections tell you about the main scripting object, WScript, and some of the supporting objects it contains.

TIP   The combination of WSH and a scripting engine form an interpreter that accepts a script file as input and outputs application data from the computer. Of course, WSH and its associated scripting engines are more complex than any previous interpreter. The Internet includes many useful WSH resource sites. Of the more interesting sites is the Scripting Guide for Windows site at http://www.pctools.com/guides/scripting/. You can find books about WSH at http://ourworld.compuserve.com/homepages/Guenter_Born/WSHBazaar/USBook.htm. You'll find quite a few other resource sites throughout the sections. Make sure you check them out to get the most out of the material presented in this chapter.

Working with the *WScript* Object

The WScript object is the main object for WSH. You'll access every other object through this one. The following list tells you about the properties that the WScript object supports.

Application   Provides you with access to a low level interface for WScript. An interface is a pointer to a list of functions that you can call for a particular object. Only advanced programmers need this property because WSH exposes all of the basic functions for you.

Arguments   Provides a complete list of the arguments for this script. Applications pass arguments on the command line. WSH passes the argument list as an array. You create a variable to hold the argument list, and then access the individual arguments as you would any array. The Arguments.Count property contains the total number of array elements.

FullName   Contains the full name of the scripting engine along with the fully qualified path to it. For example, if you were using CScript, you might get C:\WINDOWS\SYSTEM32\CSCRIPT.EXE as a return value.

Interactive   Returns true if the script is in interactive mode.

Name   Returns the friendly name for WScript. In most cases, this is Windows Script Host.

Path   Provides just the path information for the host executable. For example, if you were using CScript, you may get a return value of: C:\WINDOWS\SYSTEM32\.

ScriptFullName   Contains the full name and path of the script that's running.

ScriptName   Provides just the script name.

Version   Returns the WSH Version number.

Remember that all of these properties tell you about the WScript object. You can also use methods to perform tasks with the WScript object. The following list provides a brief overview of the more important methods you'll use with the WScript object. Note that most of these methods require you pass one or more parameters as input. A parameter is a piece of data the method uses to perform a task.

CreateObject(*strProgID*)   Create the object specified by strProgID. This object could be WSH specific like "WScript.Network" or application specific like "Excel.Application".

GetObject(*strPathname* [, *strProgID*])   Retrieves the requested object. strPathname contains the filename for the object you want to retrieve. In most cases, this is going to be a data file, but you can retrieve other kinds of objects as well. As soon as you execute this command, WSH starts the application associated with that object. For example, if you specified C:\MyText.TXT as the strPathname, then WSH may open Notepad to display it. The optional strProgID argument allows you to override the default processing of the object. For example, you may want to open the text file with Word instead of Notepad.

Real World Scenario

WORKING WITH OBJECTS

Scripts have a definite advantage over batch files because you can use objects in scripts. An object can be anything. For example, you can create an object that contains an Excel worksheet and use the functionality of Excel to perform tasks at the command line. A worksheet could hold a directory listing, and you can use the database features of Excel to perform a customized sort. All you need to do is create the object using the WScript.CreateObject() method. If you already have a data file available to use for your application, then use the WScript.GetObject() method to open the data file directly. In most cases, you don't even need to worry about which application to use because the system uses the correct application by default.

Applications are an obvious kind of object. Your machine contains literally thousands of objects, all of which are available for use. For example, you can load an XML document by using the Msxml2 .DOMDocument.5.0 object. Once you create this object, you can load the XML document using the Load() method and then process it using the various methods that the object provides. For example, use the TransformNode() method to use XML Stylesheet Language Transformation (XSLT) to transform the XML from one presentation to another.

Make sure you spend time looking at all of the objects described in the script resource Web pages provided in this chapter. You might be surprised at how much work a script can perform with only a modicum of work on your part. Even though the WScript objects described in this section are your most important resource, don't neglect the other resources at your fingertips.

Echo(*AnyArg*) Displays text in a window (WScript) or to the console screen (CScript). *AnyArg* can contain any type of valid output value. This can include both strings and numbers. Using Echo without any arguments displays a blank line.

GetScriptEngine(*strEngineID*) Registers an alternative script engine such as PerlScript (see the PerlScript site at http://www.xav.com/perl/Components/Windows/PerlScript .html or the Windows Script Host Resources site at http://labmice.techtarget.com/ scripting/WSH.htm for details on this alternative). strEngineID contains the identifier for the script engine that you want to retrieve. You'll need to register the engine using the GetScriptEngine .Register() method before you can actually use it. A script engine also requires you to provide a default extension.

Quit(*intErrorCode*) Exits the script prematurely. The optional intErrorCode argument returns an error code if necessary. You can test for this value using the ErrorLevel clause in batch files.

Working with the *WScript.WshArguments* Object

Whenever you start a script, you have the option of passing one or more arguments to it on the command line. That's where the WshArguments object comes into play. It helps you determine the number of arguments, and then retrieve them as needed. You'll always use the WScript.Arguments property to access this object; it's not directly accessible. The following list describes the properties for this object.

Item(*intIndex*)   Retrieves a specific command line argument. intIndex contains the index of the argument that you want to retrieve. The array used to hold the arguments is 0 based, so the first argument number is 0.

Count()   Returns the number of command line arguments.

Length()   Returns the number of command line arguments. WSH provides this property for JScript compatibility purposes.

Working with the *WScript.WshShell* Object

You'll use the WScript.WshShell object to access the Windows shell (the part of Windows that interacts with applications and creates the user interface) in a variety of ways. For example, you can use this object to read the registry or to create a new shortcut on the desktop. This is an exposed WSH object, which means you can access it directly. However, you need to access it through the WScript object like this: WScript.WshShell. The following list describes the WshShell methods.

CreateShortcut(*strPathname*)   Creates a WSH shortcut object. strPathname contains the location of the shortcut, which will be the Desktop in most cases.

DeleteEnvironmentVariable(*strName* [, *strType*])   Deletes the environment variable specified by strName. The optional strType argument defines the type of environment variable to delete. Typical values for strType include System, User, Volatile, and Process. The default environment variable type is System.

GetEnvironmentVariable(*strName* [, *strType*])   Retrieves the environment variable specified by strName. Default environment variables include NUMBER_OF_PROCESSORS, OS, COMSPEC, HOMEDRIVE, HOMEPATH, PATH, PATHEXT, PROMPT, SYSTEMDRIVE, SYSTEMROOT, WINDIR, TEMP, and TMP. The optional strType argument defines the type of environment variable to delete. Typical values for strType include System, User, Volatile, and Process. The default environment variable type is System.

Popup(*strText* [,*intSeconds*] [,*strTitle*] [,*intType*])   Displays a message dialog box. The return value is an integer defining which button the user selected including the following values: OK (1), Cancel (2), Abort (3), Retry (4), Ignore (5), Yes (6), No (7), Close (8), and Help (9). strText contains the text that you want to display in the dialog box. intSeconds determines how long WSH displays the dialog box before it closes the dialog box and returns a value of –1. strTitle contains the title bar text. The intType argument can contain values that determine the type of dialog box you'll create. The first intType argument determines button type. You have a choice of OK (0), OK and Cancel (1), Abort, Retry, and Ignore (2), Yes, No, and Cancel (3), Yes and No (4), and Retry and Cancel (5). The second intType argument determines which icon Windows displays in the dialog box. You have a choice of the following values: Stop (16), Question (32), Exclamation (48), and Information (64). Combine the intType argument values to obtain different dialog box effects.

RegDelete(*strName*)   Removes the value or key specified by strName from the registry. If strName ends in a backslash, then RegDelete removes a key. You must provide a fully qualified path to the key or value that you want to delete. In addition, strName must begin with one of these values: HKEY_CURRENT_USER, HKEY_LOCAL_MACHINE, HKEY_CLASSES_ROOT, HKEY_USERS, HKEY_CURRENT_CONFIG, or HKEY_DYN_DATA.

RegRead(*strName*)   Reads the value or key specified by strName from the registry. If strName ends in a backslash, then RegRead reads a key. You must provide a fully qualified path to the key or value that you want to read. In addition, strName must begin with one of these values: HKEY_ CURRENT_USER, HKEY_LOCAL_MACHINE, HKEY_CLASSES_ROOT, HKEY_USERS, HKEY_CURRENT_CONFIG, or HKEY_DYN_DATA. RegRead can only read specific data types including REG_SZ, REG_EXPAND_SZ, REG_DWORD, REG_BINARY, and REG_MULTI_SZ. Any other data types will return an error.

RegWrite(*strName*, *anyValue* [, *strType*])   Writes the data specified by anyValue to a value or key specified by strName to the registry. If strName ends in a backslash, then RegWrite writes a key. You must provide a fully qualified path to the key or value that you want to write. In addition, strName must begin with one of these values: HKEY_CURRENT_USER, HKEY_LOCAL_ MACHINE, HKEY_CLASSES_ROOT, HKEY_USERS, HKEY_CURRENT_CONFIG, or HKEY_DYN_DATA. RegRead can only write specific data types including REG_SZ, REG_EXPAND_SZ, REG_DWORD, and REG_BINARY. Any other data types will return an error.

Run(*strCommand* [, *intWinType*] [*lWait*])   Runs the command or application specified by strCommand. You can include command line arguments and switches with the command string. intWinType determines the type of window that the application starts in. You can force the script to wait for the application to complete by setting lWait to True; otherwise, the script begins the next line of execution immediately.

SetEnvironmentVariable(*strName*, *strValue* [, *strType*])   Sets the environment variable named strName to the value specified by strValue. The optional strType argument defines the type of environment variable to create. Typical values for strType include System, User, Volatile, and Process. The default environment variable type is System.

Working with the *WScript.WshNetwork* Object

The WshNetwork object works with network objects such as drives and printers that the client machine can access. This is an exposed WSH object, which means you can access it directly using the WScript.WshNetwork object. The following list describes properties associated with this object.

ComputerName   Returns a string containing the client computer name.

UserDomain   Returns a string containing the user's domain name.

UserName   Returns a string containing the name that the user used to log on to the network.

As with any other WSH object, the WshNetwork object uses methods to work with network resources. The following list describes the methods associated with this object.

AddPrinterConnection(*strLocal*, *strRemote* [, *lUpdate*] [, *strUser*] [, *strPassword*])   Creates a new printer connection for the local machine. strLocal contains the local name for the printer specified by strRemote. The strRemote value must contain a locatable resource and usually uses a UNC format such as \\Remote\Printer. Setting lUpdate to True adds the new connection to the user profile, which means Windows makes the connection available each time the user boots their machine. strUser and strPassword contain optional username and password values required to log onto the remote machine and create the connection.

EnumNetworkDrives()   Returns a WshCollection object containing the list of local and remote drives currently mapped from the client machine. A WshCollection object is essentially a 0-based array of strings.

EnumPrinterConnections()   Returns a WshCollection object containing the list of local and remote printers currently mapped from the client machine. A WshCollection object is essentially a 0-based array of strings.

MapNetworkDrive(*strLocal***, ***strRemote*** [, ***lUpdate***] [, ***strUser***] [, ***strPassword***])**
Creates a new drive connection for the local machine. `strLocal` contains the local name for the drive specified by `strRemote`. The `strRemote` value must contain a locatable resource and usually uses a UNC format such as \\Remote\Drive_C. Setting `lUpdate` to True adds the new connection to the user profile, which means Windows makes the connection available each time the user boots their machine. `strUser` and `strPassword` contain optional username and password values required to log onto the remote machine and create the connection.

RemoveNetworkDrive(*strName*** [, ***lForce***] [, ***lUpdate***])** Deletes a previous network drive mapping. If `strName` contains a local name, Windows only cancels that connection. If `strName` contains a remote name, then Windows cancels all resources associated with that remote name. Set `lForce` to True if you want to disconnect from a resource whether that resource is in use or not. Setting `lUpdate` to True removes the connection from the user profile so that it doesn't appear the next time that the user logs onto the machine.

RemovePrinterConnection(*strName*** [, ***lForce***] [, ***lUpdate***])** Deletes a previous network printer connection. If `strName` contains a local name, Windows only cancels that connection. If `strName` contains a remote name, then Windows cancels all resources associated with that remote name. Set `lForce` to True if you want to disconnect from a resource whether that resource is in use or not. Setting `lUpdate` to True removes the connection from the user profile so that it doesn't appear the next time that the user logs onto the machine.

Impersonating a User with the RunAs Utility

It's important to set security on your machine to prevent outside sources, especially those from email or Web sites, to run scripts on your machine. Of course, setting security to prevent others from executing virus-laden code also tends to keep your scripts from running—at least with the credentials of the current user. The RunAs utility provides a way for you to have great security and still allow script execution too. You use this utility to run a particular application with credentials other than those used by the current user. This utility uses the following syntax:

```
RUNAS [ [/noprofile | /profile] [/env] [/netonly] ] /user:<UserName> program
RUNAS [ [/noprofile | /profile] [/env] [/netonly] ] /smartcard
     [/user:<UserName>] program
```

The following list describes each of the command line arguments.

/noprofile Specifies that you don't want to load the RunAs user's profile when running the application. The benefit of using this setting is that the application loads more quickly. In addition, this setting acts as a safety feature because the application you want to run is less likely to corrupt the RunAs user's settings. However, using this feature can prevent some applications from running, especially when they rely on settings in the user profile to perform certain tasks.

/profile Specifies that you want to load the RunAs user's profile when running the application. This is the default setting.

/env Specifies that you want to use the current environment, instead of the RunAs user's environment, to run the application. This feature is useful when the local environment differs from the environment that the RunAs user normally relies on to run applications.

/netonly Specifies the credentials supplied for the RunAs user apply to remote access only.

/savecred   Uses the credentials previously saved by the RunAs user, rather than obtaining a new copy of the credentials.

/smartcard   Specifies that the RunAs user credentials appear on a smart card.

/user:*UserName*   Specifies the username. You must supply the username in one of two forms, User@Domain or Domain\User.

program   Specifies the application you want to run as well as any command line switches the application requires to run.

Changing the Environment

Server Core provides the means to control the user's environment with greater accuracy through command line utilities. You can define whether the user can install applications, enable or disable session logons, and modify port configurations. The Change utility is the most powerful of the three because you can use it to perform any of these tasks. The remaining three utilities provide subsets of the Change functionality. The following sections describe these environment-changing utilities.

Changing Logons, Ports, and Users with the Change Utility

The Change utility helps you control the user's ability to install applications, enable or disable session logons, and control ports. You could consider each of these actions a specific utility mode, but the utility is quite simple, so this section describes all three tasks. This utility uses the following syntax:

```
CHANGE USER {/EXECUTE | /INSTALL | /QUERY}
CHANGE LOGON {/QUERY | /ENABLE | /DISABLE}
CHANGE PORT [portx=porty | /D portx | /QUERY]
```

The following list describes each of the command line arguments.

USER {/EXECUTE {Enable | Disable} | /INSTALL {Enable | Disable} | /QUERY}   Specifies whether the user has execute or install privileges. Follow the privilege with the word *enable* to enable the privilege or *disable* to disable the privilege. Use the /Query command line switch to determine the user's current capabilities.

LOGON {/QUERY | /ENABLE | /DISABLE}   Determines whether Server Core enables or disables session logons. The /Query command line switch displays the current session logon status.

PORT [portx=porty | /D portx | /QUERY]   Redefines the port configuration. You can assign a port to a particular device. Use the /D command line switch to remove the port assignment. The /Query command line switch displays the current port assignments.

Enabling or Disabling Session Logons with the ChgLogon Utility

Use the ChgLogon utility to enable or disable session logons. This utility uses the following syntax:

```
CHGLOGON {/QUERY | /ENABLE | /DISABLE}
```

Usage is the same as the CHANGE LOGON {/QUERY | /ENABLE | /DISABLE} utility form described in the "Changing Logons, Ports, and Users with the Change Utility" section of the chapter.

Listing COM Port Mappings Using the ChgPort Utility

The ChgPort utility controls port assignments on the current system. This utility uses the following syntax:

```
CHANGE PORT [portx=porty | /D portx | /QUERY]
```

Usage is the same as the `CHANGE PORT [portx=porty | /D portx | /QUERY]` utility form described in the "Changing Logons, Ports, and Users with the Change Utility" section of the chapter.

Modifying the Install Mode with the ChgUsr Utility

The ChgUsr utility controls the user's execute and install privileges on the system. This utility uses the following syntax:

```
CHGUSR {/EXECUTE | /INSTALL | /QUERY}
```

Usage is the same as the `CHANGE USER {/EXECUTE | /INSTALL | /QUERY}` utility form described in the "Changing Logons, Ports, and Users with the Change Utility" section of the chapter.

Testing Scripts

Scripting languages provide far more than batch files do in the way of flow control and error handling support. In addition, you can debug your scripts with greater ease because Microsoft includes a script debugger with Windows. If you find this script debugger a tad limited (many people do), you can also use third-party utilities to debug your scripts. You can learn more about the Microsoft Script Debugger at `http://msdn2.microsoft.com/en-us/library/ms875975.aspx`. The following sections discuss some script techniques you can use to create robust script applications in a command line environment.

Mapping a Network Drive

You can map a network drive using a batch file, but it's more difficult and error prone than using a script. A script can provide one thing that a batch file can't in this case, great interactivity. Using a script lets you interact with the user in a way that would be difficult using a batch file. In addition, the script provides a modicum of additional error handling support that makes error handling easier. Listing 6.3 shows a typical example of how you can implement this functionality using JavaScript. You can obtain this example on the Sybex Web site at `http://www.sybex.com/WileyCDA/`.

 **Real World Scenario**

USING SCRIPTING EFFECTIVELY

Sometimes you do need to use scripting techniques to ensure you get the right results from your command line activities. The best rule of thumb to follow is that anything that requires direct application access through something other than command line switches requires a script, rather than a batch file. In addition, if you've just spent five hours trying to get a batch file to work and feel that you still haven't made any progress, then perhaps you're not using the right tool for the job.

It's this second point where many people get into endless discussions about the suitability of one technique over another. In many cases, it's part personal preference and part skill or special need. For example, at one time some people tried to use spreadsheets in place of word processors (it really was common in the 1980s). However, anyone who has used both products today knows that each tool has a particular job to perform and it's better to use the right tool for the job. The same rule applies to scripts versus batch files. You might be able to use batch files to meet most of your needs, but eventually, you'll run into a complex task that simply requires a script to perform adequately.

LISTING 6.3:   Mapping a Network Drive with JavaScript

```javascript
// Define the network object used to map the drive.
var oNetwork = new ActiveXObject("WScript.Network");

// Detect a request for command line help.
if (WScript.Arguments.length == 1)
   if (WScript.Arguments(0) == "/?")
      {
         // Display the help information
         WScript.Echo("Usage: MapNetwork <letter> <UNC target>\n");

         // Exit the script and provide an error level of 1 to
         // indicate a help request.
         WScript.Quit(1);
      }
   else
      {
         // Display an error message.
         WScript.Echo("Input argument is unknown.");
         WScript.Echo("Usage: MapNetwork <letter> <UNC target>\n");

         // Exit the script and provide an error level of 2 to
         // indicate  a data entry error.
         WScript.Quit(2);
      }

// Create variables to hold the drive letter and the UNC location.
var DriveLtr;
var UNCName;

// Detect the correct number of input arguments.
if ( WScript.Arguments.length < 2 )
{
   // Ask whether the user wants to continue.
   WScript.Echo("No input provided! Provide it interactively? [Y | N]");
   var Answer = WScript.StdIn.ReadLine();
```

```
      // If the user doesn't want to continue, display help and exit.
      // Use an exit code of 2 to indicate a data entry error.
      if (Answer.toUpperCase() == "N")
      {
         WScript.Echo("Usage: MapNetwork <letter> <UNC target>\n");
         WScript.Quit(2);
      }

      // Input the drive letter.
      WScript.Echo("Type the local drive letter (X:).");
      DriveLtr = WScript.StdIn.ReadLine();

      // Input the UNC drive on the remote machine.
      WScript.Echo("Type the UNC location (\\MyServer\MyDrive).");
      UNCName = WScript.StdIn.ReadLine();
   }
   else
   {
      // Obtain the required inputs from the command line.
      DriveLtr = WScript.Arguments(0);
      UNCName = WScript.Arguments(1);
   }

   // Tell the user which drive is mapped.
   WScript.Echo("Mapping drive " + DriveLtr + " to " + UNCName);

   // Attempt to create the connection.
   try
   {
      // Perform the drive mapping function.
      oNetwork.MapNetworkDrive(DriveLtr, UNCName);
   }
   catch(e)
   {
      // Display an error when the task fails.
      WScript.Echo("Couldn't map the drive!\n" + e.description);
      WScript.Quit(3);
   }
```

The example begins by creating a network object to create the connection. In this case, the code uses the new ActiveXObject() method. You can also use WScript.CreateObject() to perform the same task. The method you use depends on personal taste in most cases. This example uses the ActiveXObject() method for the sake of completeness. If you want to use the other method, you would replace this line of code with var oNetwork = WScript.CreateObject("WScript.Network");.

The next section of code addresses the need to handle the /? command line switch. The help displayed in this example is decidedly weak. You'd provide a lot more help in a fully functional production script. The command and utility examples in this book provide you with a good idea of the kind of information you need to provide to make a script useful for everyone. Notice how the code detects the number of arguments first, and then handles the special case of the /? command line switch. Notice how the code exits with an error level of 1, so you can trap the help request in a batch file if desired.

Of course, you also need to handle the case where someone provides a single input, but it isn't the /? command line switch. The code displays a special error message along with the same help that you would normally display for the /? command line switch. Notice that in this case the script exits with an error level of 2. Using a different error level lets you trap this particular problem in a batch file.

At this point, the code begins looking at the input. The input must provide two arguments to map a network drive to a local drive letter. Consequently, when the script detects two input arguments, it places them in the appropriate variables and attempts to map the network drive. You might wonder why the script doesn't perform all kinds of odd error checking on the input arguments. The try...catch statement is the secret in this case. If the user provides incorrect input, the oNetwork.MapNetworkDrive(DriveLtr, UNCName) call fails and the catch part of the statement traps the error. The script displays an error message in this case and exits again. Because this is another kind of error, the script sets the error level to 3. Notice that the script conveniently disregards any more than two inputs.

At this point, all the code needs to handle is the case where the user doesn't provide any input arguments. This is where the interactive features of scripting pay off. The script begins by asking the user whether they want to provide the input interactively. If so, the code asks some simple questions and tries to map the drive. If not, the code exits with a help message and an error level of 2. The reason the script uses an error level of 2 is that this is the same kind of error as providing a single input that isn't the /? command line switch.

Creating a CSV File

Sometimes it's important to see the same example using two different techniques. The example in this section performs the same task as the batch file example in the "Using a Centralized Data Store" section of Chapter 5. When you compare the code in Listing 6.4 with the code in 5.7, you'll notice that Listing 6.4 is significantly longer, even though it produces the same output. In addition, the code in Listing 6.4 is significantly more complex. However, if you perform just these two comparisons, you'll miss some of the reasons to use scripts. Mostly notably, the script version demonstrates the flexibility that this form of coding can provide. For example, you have more control over the files. The input files are read only, which means that the code can't damage them, even accidentally. Consequently, the files are safer than when you use a batch file to manipulate them. Listing 6.4 shows the script version of the CSV output example. You can obtain this example on the Sybex Web site at http://www.sybex.com/WileyCDA/.

LISTING 6.4:   Creating CSV Output Using a Script

```
// Create a File System Object to work with files.
var FSO = WScript.CreateObject("Scripting.FileSystemObject");

// Determine whether the Output2.CSV file exists and delete it.
if (FSO.FileExists("Output2.CSV"))
   FSO.DeleteFile("Output2.CSV", false);
```

```javascript
// Create a WshShell object to obtain environment variables.
var Shell = WScript.CreateObject("WScript.Shell");

// Create variables to hold the static data.
var CompName = Shell.ExpandEnvironmentStrings("%COMPUTERNAME%");
var UserName = Shell.ExpandEnvironmentStrings("%USERNAME%");
var DateTime = new Date();

// Obtain the list of file specifications.
WScript.Echo("Locating temporary files to delete.");
var DirSpec = FSO.OpenTextFile("DelFiles.TXT", 1);

// Process each entry in the file.
while (!DirSpec.AtEndOfStream)
{
   // Get a single file specification.
   var ThisSpec = DirSpec.ReadLine();

   // Process the directory specification.
   WScript.Echo("Adding database values for " + ThisSpec);
   Shell.Run(
      "Cmd /C Dir " + ThisSpec + " /B /S > TmpDirFiles.TXT", 0, true);

   // Open the file containing the individual file entries.
   var Files = FSO.OpenTextFile("TmpDirFiles.TXT", 1);

   // Open the CSV file to accept the file entries.
   var Output = FSO.OpenTextFile("Output2.CSV", 8, true);

   // Process each of the file entries in turn.
   while (!Files.AtEndOfStream)
   {
      // Get an individual file entry.
      var File = Files.ReadLine();

      // Create the CSV file entry. Begin with the computer name and
      // the username.
      Output.Write("\"");
      Output.Write(CompName);
      Output.Write("\",\"");
      Output.Write(UserName);
      Output.Write("\",\"");

      // Processing the date requires a little additional work. You
      // must extract the individual elements and put them together as
      // desired. Begin by converting the day number to a day string.
      var DayNum = DateTime.getDay();
      switch (DayNum)
      {
```

```
            case 0:
                Output.Write("Sun ");
                break;
            case 1:
                Output.Write("Mon ");
                break;
            case 2:
                Output.Write("Tue ");
                break;
            case 3:
                Output.Write("Wed ");
                break;
            case 4:
                Output.Write("Thu ");
                break;
            case 5:
                Output.Write("Fri ");
                break;
            case 6:
                Output.Write("Sat ");
                break;
        }

        Output.Write(DateTime.getMonth() + 1);
        Output.Write("/" + DateTime.getDate() +
                    "/" + DateTime.getFullYear());
        Output.Write("\",\"");

        // Extract the time from DateTime.
        Output.Write(DateTime.getHours() + ":" +
                    DateTime.getMinutes() + ":" +
                    DateTime.getSeconds());
        Output.Write("\",\"");

        // Finally, add the filename to the output.
        Output.Write(File);
        Output.WriteLine("\"");
    }

    // Close the working files.
    Files.Close();
    Output.Close();
}

// Close the file containing the file specifications.
DirSpec.Close();
```

The code begins by removing any existing output file. JavaScript and VBScript lack file support. However, you have access to the `Scripting.FileSystemObject` object, which does provide full file system support. You can use this object to perform a multitude of tasks with files, including creating, deleting, and editing them. The `FileSystemObject` also includes functionality for working with folders.

The next step is to retrieve the username, computer name, date, and time. In many cases, you can simply use the `ExpandEnvironmentStrings()` method to obtain the information you need from the system. Notice that the example code uses the `Date` object in place of obtaining the date from the environment variables using the `Shell.ExpandEnvironmentStrings("%DATE%")` method. When working with JavaScript, you can only access the environment variables that you can see with the `Set` command. JavaScript doesn't support the extended functionality that's available at the command line. In fact, you'll find that this general rule applies to both VBScript and JavaScript; neither scripting language supports the extensions that you can access from a batch file at the command prompt. The `Date` object also provides time support, so you don't need a separate `Time` variable.

At this point, it's time to begin collecting a list of temporary files on the system. This example, like its batch file counter, relies on an external file to hold the file specifications. The code opens the file and begins processing it one line at a time. The use of a constant value of 1 for the `FSO.OpenTextFile()` method opens the file in read-only mode. The code processes the file one line at a time (one file specification at a time) using the `DirSpec.ReadLine()` method. You can read one character at a time using the `DirSpec.Read()` method instead.

This example points out a very special feature of the scripting languages. Notice the use of the `Shell.Run()` method. You can use this method to run any application. To use this feature at the command prompt, you have to begin by creating a command processor using the CMD utility as shown. In this case, the code runs the `Dir` command with the file specification obtained from `DelFiles.TXT`. This line of code begs the question of why the code doesn't use the `FileSystemObject`. In this particular case, you can perform the task faster and without any loss of functionally by using the `Dir` command. The point is that you don't always have to use a scripting object; sometimes a command line tool works just as well or even better.

The code now has two files to work with. The first is an input file, `TmpDirFiles.TXT`, which contains the list of temporary files. The second is an output file, `Output2.CSV`, which contains the database of file entries. The `FSO.OpenTextFile()` constant of 8 opens the file in append (read/write) mode. If the file doesn't exist, the code raises an error unless you also set the third argument to True, which tells the method to create the file when it doesn't exist.

Now all the code needs to do is process the data and output it. The user and computer names are straightforward. Processing the date requires the most code because the code has to put the date string together. The downside of all this code is that it makes the example harder to read than the batch file. The plus side is that you can create a date string in any format required, even nonstandard formats.

As a final note on this example, make sure you close files when you finish working with them. Otherwise, the script raises an error when you try to open the file again. In some cases, the file could remain open until you reboot the system, making it inaccessible to everyone.

Managing Windows in a New Way

This chapter has shown you how to work with scripts at the command prompt. Of course, this is merely the tip of the iceberg. Scripting can become quite addictive and profitable as well, because it represents an easy way to create applications that run on multiple platforms. In short, if this chapter is your introduction to scripting, it's a good one, but you can do a lot more. Of course, what you've seen might seem like quite a lot already because scripting at the command line gives you complete access to your system in a way that batch file programming can't. This chapter helps you build these skills:

◆ Work with scripting languages

◆ Execute scripts using CScript and WScript

◆ Script network solutions using the NetSH utility

◆ Write a basic script

◆ Use scripting objects

◆ Change the environment using a script

◆ Test a script for errors

It's your turn. If you don't already know how to work with scripting languages, make sure you use the resources at the beginning of the chapter to learn. These tutorials and online references will greatly enhance your ability to begin working with scripts immediately. Of course, you'll want to go slowly when scripting anything that could cause damage to your system. The best general rule is to try one thing at a time, perfect your knowledge, and go on to the next item you want to learn.

Chapter 7 takes the next logical step when it comes to working with batch files and scripts. This chapter contains information about a number of third-party tools you can use to make your programming experience significantly easier. You'll also discover techniques for protecting your code investment. If you plan to work with Server Core a lot, you'll want these tools to ensure you can get the work you need done quickly.

Chapter 7

Editing and Compiling Batch Files and Scripts

Any full automation effort at the command line will likely require batch files and scripts. You can use any technique that you want to write the batch file or script. For example, you can use the simple command **Copy CON: C:MyBatch.BAT** and press Enter to start an editing session right there at the command prompt. The "Modifying Data Files with the Edit Utility" section of Chapter 5 demonstrates how you can use the Edit utility to perform batch and script file editing as well. If the batch file is small and simple enough, either of these environments may be all that you need.

Most batch files and scripts aren't small, however, so most people use an editor of some kind. In fact, Notepad is one of the more popular options. You can even use Notepad within Server Core, but it's likely that you'll edit complex batch files and scripts at the client system and transfer them to Server Core. Of course, you can find more powerful editors than Notepad and this chapter examines a few of those choices. The chapter assumes that you'll perform any editing tasks at the client system. (If you do plan to work at Server Core, then your choices may only include the Copy CON method, the Edit utility, and Notepad.) The point is that you should use the editor that feels comfortable to you and achieves any task that you want to complete. You don't need the IDE of a full-fledged programming language to complete most tasks at the command line.

Nothing says that you must do anything more than write the lines of instructions to create a perfectly usable solution. In fact, for many years, this is all that people did. They wrote their batch files and used them as is. However, you can obtain some additional efficiencies by compiling your batch file or script. In some cases, you might see slightly faster executing speeds. Compiling your batch file or script also hides the content from prying eyes, so your coding secrets remain safe. In addition, compiling the batch file or script makes it difficult to edit; you don't have to worry about someone else modifying the content of the file. Editing is a major concern in the corporate environment where an administrator might have hundreds of machines to manage and an equal number of curious users.

In this chapter, you'll learn how to do the following:

◆ Edit all file types with WinVi

◆ Use Notepad+ to perform editing tasks

◆ Create executable batch files with Batch File Compiler 5.2

◆ Develop and compile batch files with Quick Batch File Compiler

◆ Understand JavaScript and VBScript compilers

◆ Create and edit WSF and other script files using Script Editor 2.1

Real World Scenario

LOCATING SCRIPTING EXAMPLES

Many people will look at the scripting examples provided as part of a product and then not get any further because the examples are limited or don't meet their needs. However, you don't have to learn every aspect of scripting before you can become productive with it. You can find many scripting Web sites online. Many of them have coding samples you can use. Others provide tools, tips, or techniques you can use when working with scripts.

One of the most interesting of these Web sites is Rob van der Woude's Scripting Pages at http://www.robvanderwoude.com/index.html. This particular Web site not only provides a wealth of scripts in various languages (most of which haven't appeared in this book), and the explanations provided are unusually clear and easy to understand. Because of the diversity of these scripts, you can often find what you need and use it without writing a single line of code yourself. In other cases, you can make simple changes to adapt the script to meet your specific needs.

Editing All File Types with WinVi

When working at the command line, you often require a versatile editor that does more than simply edit text. Unfortunately, most low-cost editors on the market either edit text or edit binary information, but not both. Normally, to obtain an editor that does both, you have to buy a full-fledged programming language such as Visual Studio. Obviously, buying Visual Studio to write batch files is significant overkill. If you find you need both text and binary editing capabilities in a single editor, WinVi might provide everything you need. As shown in Figure 7.1, this editor features a full binary editing mode. It edits text equally well. You can download this product at http://www.winvi.de/en/.

The WinVi editor has a few interesting features that make it exceptionally useful to administrators. One of the more interesting features is that it supports multiple character sets. You can choose between the American National Standards Institute (ANSI), Disk Operating System (DOS), or Extended Binary Coded Decimal Interchange Code (EBCDIC) character sets. The third character set comes in handy for examining older mainframe data.

Unlike many low-cost editors on the market, WinVi also supports multiple language options. You can choose between English, French, German, or Spanish as your language. The automatic selection feature chooses a language based on the current system setup. Consequently, if you use multiple languages, you can change language setups and start a new copy of WinVi. The editor automatically changes languages for you as long as it supports the language you're using.

Printing might not seem like such an important issue, but developers often print out their code listings. The printing features of WinVi match those of Notepad in many respects. However, it includes a two-column printout feature that can save a significant number of pages. You can also have the editor add line numbers to the printout so you can discuss the code with someone else over the telephone or email with greater ease.

If you want support for automation for your editor, WinVi includes keyboard macro support. You can create short macros of tasks that you want performed and assign them to a key combination. Whenever you use that key combination, the editor automatically performs the preprogrammed series of steps. Overall, you'll find this feature is less capable than a full-fledged editor such as Microsoft Word, but definitely better than most low-cost editors provide.

The editor also supports a number of programmer features. You can set it to support automatic indenting and define the number of characters for each indent. In addition, you can select the end of line sequence. WinVi supports the standard carriage return/line feed combination for Windows, the line feed–only character used by Unix, or the carriage return–only character used by the Macintosh. Best of all, you can save all of your settings as a profile. The editor supports multiple profiles so you can switch between them as needed for your editing needs. All of these settings appear in one location—the Settings dialog box shown in Figure 7.2.

FIGURE 7.1
You can use WinVi
to edit text files and
binary files with
equal ease.

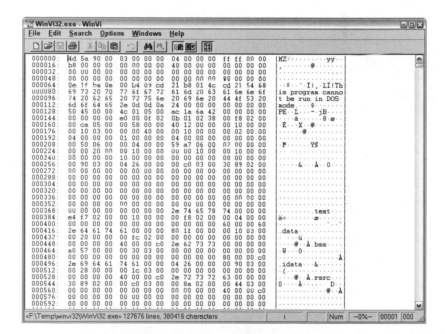

FIGURE 7.2
Use the WinVi
Settings dialog box to
access all of the fea-
tures of this highly
configurable editor.

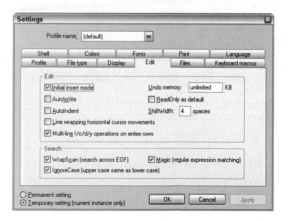

Obtaining a Better Notepad with Notepad+

Many people use Notepad for all of their development needs. After all, you really don't need anything fancy when working on a batch file or a simple script. Of course, it would be nice if Notepad had some additional features. For example, you can only open one file at a time in Notepad. Notepad+ looks strikingly similar to Notepad at first. It even has the same name. The vendor envisions this freeware utility as a replacement for Notepad and gives it the same name for that reason. However, one look at this utility as shown in Figure 7.3 tells you that it's different from Notepad. Notice that the figure shows two documents opened and the editor supports more. You can download Notepad+ at http://www.mypeecee.org/rogsoft/.

FIGURE 7.3

Notepad+ looks very much like the Windows Notepad, but with important differences.

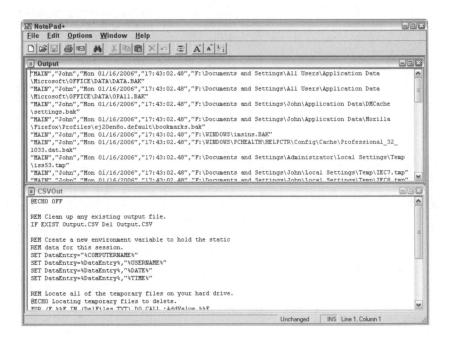

Real World Scenario

EXPLORING THE ALTERNATIVES TO APPLICATION DEFICIENCIES

Most applications have deficiencies. The deficiency is something that you perceive the application is lacking. When enough people feel that the application has a deficiency, the vendor normally does something about it. However, many deficiencies reflect a personal requirement that the vendor will never address. Consequently, either you continue to use the application or you obtain another application that addresses the concern.

The applications in this chapter address various deficiencies in Windows applications. However, you should also consider the alternatives. For example, Notepad only opens one file at a time, but you can open multiple copies of Notepad. Sure, it's a little inconvenient moving between copies of Notepad to compare files, but it works. Whether this alternative addresses the deficiency of not opening multiple files depends on your particular tastes and needs. The important issue is to consider options before you obtain a third-party alternative that might have other deficiencies that you must address.

Make sure that when you do look at the third-party application alternatives, that you review enough products to ensure the new selection meets all of your needs. For example, you might find that EditPlus (`http://www.softwarerate.com/EditPlus-Version-2-download-9666.htm`) meets your needs more effectively than Notepad+ does. Only you can decide when an application meets enough of your needs and provides enough functionality that any required workarounds are minor.

Notepad+ includes a number of interesting features. If you ever ran into the file size barrier when using older versions of Windows, you don't have to worry about this issue with Notepad+. In fact, I was able to open very large files quickly and without any problems.

Besides opening rather large files, Notepad+ supports one feature that many administrators find saves considerable time. You can click a single button to send the content of the file that you're editing to someone else. This makes it very easy to communicate with other administrators without ever leaving the editing environment.

Notepad+ includes a number of interesting configuration options, some of which appear in the Preference dialog box shown in Figure 7.4. The Dialogs tab lets you set the filters used for the Open and Save dialog boxes—an unusual feature that you probably won't see in many other utilities. Having this feature means that you can set up Notepad+ to edit text files of any kind. You can choose the filter for that file directly from the Open or Save dialog boxes as needed. This support is very important when you need a flexible editing environment.

FIGURE 7.4
Configure Notepad+ to open and save any file type using these options.

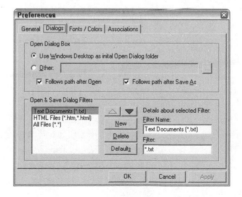

You can also associate Notepad+ with any file using the features on the Association tab of the Preferences dialog box. This feature means that you can double-click the file in Windows Explorer and have Notepad+ open it for you automatically. Notepad+ includes a number of other helpful configuration options, such as the ability to use proportional fonts that should make your editing experience nicer. Generally, this is a very helpful update for a utility that most people have used at one time or another to create or edit batch or script files.

Creating Executable Batch Files with Batch File Compiler 5.2

The main reason to use the Batch File Compiler is to create an executable from your batch file—a task this utility performs very well. However, this utility does a lot more. The Batch File Compiler is a shareware product that works with pure batch files, but it can also augment batch files so that they do more. For example, you can perform math within your batch file when you compile it using this utility. You can download the Batch File Compiler at `http://www.topshareware.com/Batch-File-Compiler-download-45.htm`.

The feature I like best about this product is that it's very simple. Figure 7.5 shows the interface for this product. The main window lets you access and edit your batch files. Select an option from the Extended Commands menu when you want to add more functionality to your batch file. You can find a complete list of these features in the `bfcped.HTM` file provided as part of the application.

FIGURE 7.5
Batch File Compiler supports a simple interface that makes it easy to create batch file executables.

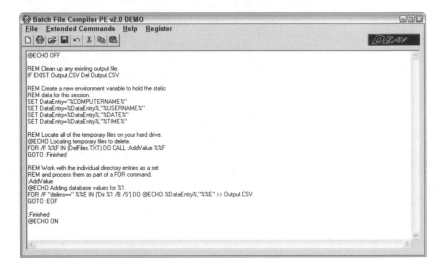

To compile your application, edit the batch file code and then click Compile. The utility opens a dialog box where you type the name of the executable you want to create. After you provide the name, the utility asks which operating system you're using to execute the batch file (the choices are essentially DOS or Windows). Once you select an operating system, the utility completes the compilation and displays a success message. A few odd things happened when I used the resulting application. First, it seemed to assume that I would use some of the extended features to place the cursor on screen. Second, the output didn't use the colors I selected for the command prompt—it used the default command prompt colors instead. Otherwise, the batch file worked precisely as it should. When using the demonstration version of the product, you also have to live with the developer's commercial messages.

Develop and Compile Batch Files with Quick Batch File Compiler

The Quick Batch File Compiler has all the look and feel of a development platform. This isn't the kind of utility that you use for a quick application—it's an environment you can use to perform in-depth coding with your batch files. Everything about this product feels solid. For example, when you load your batch file for editing, you'll immediately notice that the editor uses color coding to make the code more readable. In addition, I found that the help file was an easy read and put together in a way that made accessing the various topics fast. You can download this utility at http://www.abyssmedia.com/quickbfc/index.shtml.

The best way to use the Quick Batch File Compiler is with the IDE shown in Figure 7.6. However, you can also use it in batch mode by supplying an input filename and an output (executable) filename. The IDE has an upper window where you edit the code and a lower window where you can see the results of any tasks you perform. For example, the utility uses this window when it compiles the application for you.

FIGURE 7.6

Color coding and great help features make Quick Batch File Compiler easy to use.

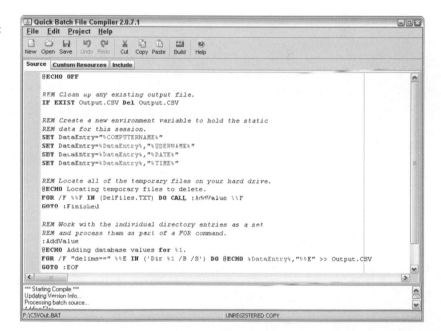

Unlike most utilities, this one includes a number of customizations that you need to produce a professional looking executable. The Custom Resources tab shown in Figure 7.7 shows the customizations you can perform. You can include a file description, company name, version, and an icon. Everything works as it should. Displaying the executable's Properties dialog box shows the results of these entries.

FIGURE 7.7
The Custom Resources tab helps you customize your application as needed.

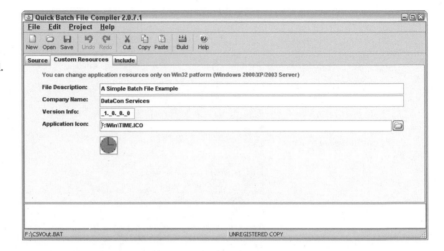

Understanding JavaScript and VBScript Compilers

Generally, you aren't going to find a JavaScript or a VBScript compiler that works at the command line. The problem is that you need to have the support of the Windows Scripting Host (WSH) at the command line and WSH only provides an interpreted environment. Consequently, what you'll find is a vast array of JavaScript and VBScript editors, some of which are extremely complex and provide just about anything you could ask for, except WSH support. For example, the C-Point Antechinus JavaScript Editor (http://www.c-point.com/javascript_editor.php) shown in Figure 7.8 provides all of the functionality that you would expect from a full-fledged programming language at a fraction of the cost. Unfortunately, while this editor provides everything you need, including IntelliSense support, to build a Web application, it won't help you create a JavaScript application that relies on WSH. Yes, it will help you write the code, but you can't compile it.

An important issue to remember is that any time you see HTML Application (HTA), what you're really talking about is a Web application of some sort. Yes, you can create stand-alone HTA versions for the local machine with the right editor, but an HTA can't rely on the functionality that WSH provides, which means that you'll lose a lot of functionality. The best place to look for tools that will work at the command line is on the Microsoft site at http://www.microsoft.com/technet/scriptcenter/createit.mspx. Another great place to look is the Asp4Hs: Add-On's: ActiveScripts / WSH Scripts Web site at http://www.wilk4.com/asp4hs/list5.htm.

Fortunately, you can find editors that make your task significantly easier. For example, the AdminScriptEditor described at http://www.adminscripteditor.com/editor/ provides you with a number of features that make working with WSH easier. For example, you can use it to create scripts that use Windows Management Instrumentation (WMI). This Windows feature provides access to various Windows management functions that you can control from your script. This particular product isn't shareware and it doesn't come with a fully functional demonstration program. The 45-day trial version does give you a good idea of how the product works though.

FIGURE 7.8
Most JavaScript editors and compilers focus their attention on Web pages.

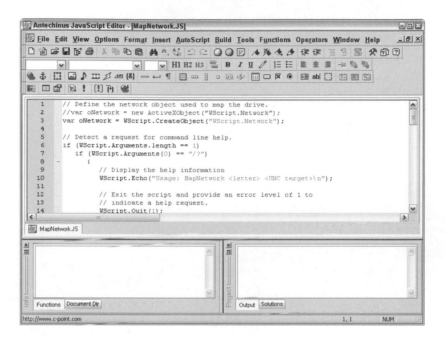

Real World Scenario

CONSIDERING THE WSH ALTERNATIVES

Microsoft created WSH many years ago. It's amazing that this interpreted environment still meets so many needs and will continue to meet them well into the future. However, you still need to consider what WSH offers as part of your application-building task. At some point, you might need to consider giving up the convenience that WSH provides and using an entirely different environment. You can find a wealth of third-party utilities such as OnScript (`http://www.onscript.com/en/home.asp`) and ExeScript (`http://www.hide-folder.com/overview/hf_7.html`) online. The important consideration is finding the right tool for your particular needs.

Editing Script Files with Script Editor 2.1

You can edit almost any kind of script using Script Editor 2.1 (`http://www.brinesoft.com/ScriptEditor.asp`) from BrineSoft. However, the main reason that this editor is different from the others in this chapter is that it provides the means to edit the Windows Script File (WSF) scripts on your system. You can use any text or XML editor to work with WSF, but it's better to have an editor specifically designed for the task. In addition to the material in this chapter, you'll also find a review of this product at `http://rbytes.net/software/script-editor-review/`.

The first time you start Script Editor 2.1, it asks whether you want to add existing scripts to a workspace. You can also create new workspaces as needed using the Workspace ➤ New command. Storing your scripts in workspaces makes them easier to manage. You can separate scripts by type and purpose. Choose any existing workspace by selecting its entry in the Workspace field.

Script Editor comes with a number of sample scripts as shown in Figure 7.9. To open a package, simply click its entry in the Files tab. Opened packages appear in red, while unopened packages appear in black. The selected package appears in bold type to differentiate it from other opened packages.

FIGURE 7.9
Select any of the sample scripts and run them to see how the scripting technology works.

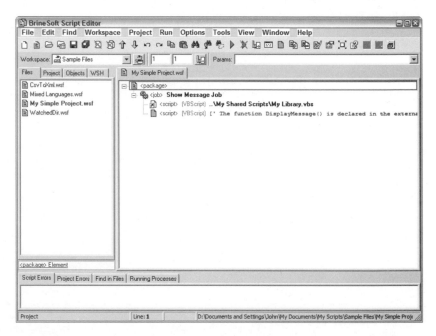

The "Understanding the WSF" section of Chapter 6 emphasizes the XML structure of WSF files. Notice that you can see this structure clearly in Figure 7.9. Script Editor 2.1 makes it very easy to work with the XML data structure of WSF files as shown in Figure 7.10. All you need to do to work with a particular element is right-click it. The context menu shows what you can do with that element, so you don't have to guess about the rules. In addition, the editor automatically creates opening and closing tags as necessary and asks questions about the element when necessary to define it.

Debugging a script is also easier in Script Editor 2.1 than it is in some other editors. All you need to do is click the Run Project/Script button (the right-pointing red arrow) on the toolbar to start the script. When Script Editor 2.1 sees an error, it flags it and offers solutions on fixing the problem.

You can use bookmarks to make it easy to locate the code you want to work with. The bookmarks stay in place between sessions, so you can set them as needed to maintain your place in the code between sessions. The Toggle Bookmark, Next Bookmark, and Previous Bookmark buttons on the toolbar make it easy to move between locations quickly.

One of the features you'll like best is the ability to drag and drop statements as needed from the left pane. Figure 7.11 shows the VBScript statements, but you'll also find statements for WScript objects (see the "Using the Scripting Objects" section of Chapter 6 for details) and WSH statements. To use any of these aids, simply drag and drop it from the left pane to the location you want in the right pane. Using this approach helps you create error-free code quite quickly.

When you find that you don't completely understand a bit of code, you can place the cursor on it and then click the help links in the left pane as shown in Figure 7.11. You'll see a copy of Help open with the appropriate help information selected. The help information is equivalent to what Microsoft provides, so it does provide enough information to look for further information should the help file itself prove unhelpful.

FIGURE 7.10

Script Editor 2.1 makes it easy to manipulate the structure of WSF scripts.

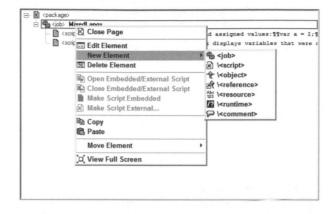

FIGURE 7.11

Drag-and-drop coding makes it easier to produce error-free code.

This is a quick overview of Script Editor 2.1. As you can see, it provides the means to create and edit WSF scripts quickly, which means you'll spend less time trying to figure out the WSF technology and more time getting your work done. The free download provides a considerable array of features, but you can also choose to purchase the product to obtain support and updates.

Managing Windows in a New Way

This chapter has discussed a number of products you can use to edit or compile your batch or script files. The important issue to remember about editors is that most of them have a feature that makes them special. Whether the feature is actually useful to you determines whether the editor is a good choice for your particular needs. For example, the binary file editing features of WinVi are only useful if you perform editing on binary files. Otherwise, you might want the added functionality provided by an editor such as Notepad+. The important issue is that there aren't any right choices— only the choice that works best for you. Remember that compiling your batch file or script is optional. These programs work just fine at the command prompt even if you don't compile them. The three essential reasons for compiling your batch file or script are hiding the content from others, keeping others from changing the content, and getting a small performance gain. This chapter helps you build these skills:

- Edit all file types with WinVi
- Use Notepad+ to perform editing tasks
- Create executable batch files with Batch File Compiler 5.2
- Develop and compile catch files with Quick Batch File Compiler
- Understand JavaScript and VBScript compilers
- Create and Edit WSF and other script files using Script Editor 2.1

One of the problems with looking for new utilities is the need to focus on what you need, rather than what looks interesting. The interesting features might make you aware of other possibilities, but more often than not, they only serve to distract you from the task at hand (not that this is always bad, even administrators need play time). The best way to begin looking for a new utility is to define the goal of that utility before you do anything else. Write down the tasks the utility must perform and then search for the utility that performs those tasks. Of course, sometimes you'll find several utilities that perform the required tasks and you'll need to test them out. The important thing is to find an editor and compiler that do the kinds of things that you need to perform at the command line.

At this point in the book, you know how to perform a basic setup and automate tasks using both batch files and scripts. In addition, you now have a host of tools at your disposal for editing and compiling your batch files and scripts as needed. You may think you have it all, but you don't. The problem is that you still have to run those batch files and scripts manually—you can tell the computer to run them for you automatically if you want. Chapter 8 discusses the next step in your management of Server Core—getting Server Core to perform some tasks automatically for you. All you need to do is tell Server Core when and how to run the task. The content in Chapter 8 takes you to that next step where the computer becomes an assistant—one that runs tasks automatically and without question so you can get on to those tasks that you can't address using automation.

Chapter 8

Performing Task Automation

Using batch files or scripts represents one level of automation. You can issue a single command and expect a number of things to take place. In addition, you don't have to remember all of those arcane command line switches. However, you still have to be present at your desk to execute the command. Executing the batch file or script manually isn't such a big deal when you aren't doing anything that will interrupt anyone else, but staying the weekend so you can execute a command is undesirable to say the least. That's where the Task Scheduler comes into play. You can use the Task Scheduler to execute reliable batch files or scripts automatically. In essence, you're asking your computer to do the work for you—imagine that, the computer working for you for once.

This chapter describes how the Task Scheduler performs its job, shows how you can schedule tasks from the command line, and explores some productivity techniques you can use with this form of optimization. You'll also discover a few problems with using the Task Scheduler and gain an understanding of the kinds of tasks that work best with the Task Scheduler. Finally, you'll see some new utilities that make the Task Scheduler easy to use from the command line. This chapter doesn't explore the graphical utilities you can use to work with Task Scheduler because Server Core doesn't support them.

In this chapter, you'll learn how to do the following:

◆ Manage the Task Scheduler, applications, and associated service

◆ Provide automation fault tolerance

 Real World Scenario

THE TASK SCHEDULER NIGHTMARE

Some people just don't get it when it comes to Task Scheduler. A customer once had a "virus" on their machine. The only problem is that the virus didn't show up with Task List, none of the virus checkers could find it, and it didn't have any of the usual virus symptoms. The virus simply showed up at what appeared at first random intervals. After many hours of searching, I discovered that the user had added a buggy script to Task Scheduler. The buggy script was the virus of my nightmares. My client ended up paying for quite a few hours worth of consulting time to have me remove the buggy script from Task Scheduler. My actual repair time, once I located the problem, was less than 5 minutes.

You can easily misuse Task Scheduler. It's a tool like any other tool—valuable in the hands of someone who knows how to use it, dangerous for everyone else. Never use Task Scheduler to run batch files, scripts, or applications that aren't reliable. If you think there's even a small chance that the Task Scheduler entry will fail to work as anticipated, don't create it because locating the problem can require a substantial investment in time and effort. In addition, it's essential to test every Task Scheduler entry the first time while you're at the office. You don't want an errant entry to ruin the chances of a perfectly reliable batch file, script, or application running as anticipated.

Scheduling and Managing Tasks

The Task Scheduler consists of multiple elements. The Task Scheduler application is actually a Windows service. Because Task Scheduler is a service, it's always present in the background so it can run applications automatically for you. You use the SC command described in the "Controlling Services with the *SC* Command" section of Chapter 3 to configure the Task Scheduler.

As a safety precaution, it's a good idea to set the service to manual and manually start it as needed. To set the Task Scheduler to start manually, type **SC Config Schedule Start= Demand** and press Enter. Notice the space between the equals sign (=) and the value. Of course, if you're running tasks every day, the automatic start option makes more sense. In this case, you type **SC Config Schedule Start= Auto** and press Enter. When you want to determine the Task Scheduler status, type **SC QueryEx Schedule** and press Enter. Use QueryEx, rather than Query, so that you obtain the Process Identifier (PID) as part of the output—many command line utilities require the PID as input. To start the Task Scheduler, type **SC Start Schedule** and press Enter.

The Task Scheduler logs on using the Local System account. Normally, this account provides more than sufficient rights for local activities. However, when you automatically perform tasks on remote machines, you might need to change the account to handle the increased security requirements. Always make sure you have the Task Scheduler service running when you need to execute applications automatically. To change the password to another account, type **SC Config Schedule Obj= "*.\AccountName*" Password= "*AccountPassword*"** and press Enter. Notice that the account name includes both the domain and the username. The use of a period indicates the location machine. To change the service account back to Local System, type **SC Config Schedule Obj= ".\LocalSystem" Password= ""** and press Enter. It's important to note that Server Core tightens security considerably, so you need to consider the effect of the new security measures on any tasks you want to perform. In many cases, you'll need to change the security settings of any jobs that you want to move from other servers to Server Core to ensure they'll run correctly.

The second part of Task Scheduler is a graphical utility called Scheduled Tasks that you'll normally find in the Start ➤ Programs ➤ Accessories ➤ Systems Tools folder on a GUI system. This utility displays all of the tasks you've scheduled. You can also use it to create new tasks, either directly or by using the supplied wizard. This second part of the Task Scheduler doesn't exist in Server Core, so you won't see it discussed in any detail in this book.

WARNING   Standard Server Core tasks aren't visible to previous versions of Windows (they are visible to Vista users). To create a scheduled task in Server Core that's visible to previous versions of Windows, you must use the SchTasks utility with the /V1 command line switch (see the "Managing Tasks with the SchTasks Commands" section of the chapter for details). You can also modify the Configure For field found on the General tab of any standard task you create to support other Windows versions. The Configure For field only contains Vista as an option when you create a basic task.

The third part of the Task Scheduler is a number of related utilities that are discussed in the sections that follow. These utilities make it considerably easier to schedule multiple tasks or to schedule tasks for multiple users. You can use these utilities from a remote location to ensure user machines perform required maintenance tasks automatically at a time that's convenient for the user. Because operation is automatic, you don't have to worry about users performing the task incorrectly, inconsistently, or not at all.

TIP   Scripts can have payoffs other than increased personal productivity. For example, Microsoft regularly offers incentives for submitting scripts to the Community-Submitted Scripts Center at `http://www.microsoft.com/technet/scriptcenter/csc/default.mspx`. At the time of this writing, you can obtain a free e-learning course.

Managing Tasks with the *SCHTasks* Command

The Schedule Tasks (SchTasks) Command helps you schedule tasks at the command line. The basic command line requires that you provide a parameter (an action or command) and any arguments that the parameter requires. The list of recognized parameters includes /Create, /Delete, /Query, /Change, /Run, and /End. The following sections describe each of these parameters.

/CREATE

The /Create parameter helps you create new tasks. Never use this parameter to change an existing task; use the /Change parameter instead. This parameter uses the following syntax:

```
SCHTASKS /Create [/S system [/U username [/P password]]] [/RU username
    [/RP password]] /SC schedule [/MO modifier] [/D day] [/I idletime]
    /TN taskname /TR taskrun [/ST starttime] [/M months] [/SD startdate]
    [/ED enddate] [/RI interval] [ {/ET endtime | /DU duration} [/K]
    [/XML xmlfile] /V1]] [/IT | /NP] [/Z] [/F]
```

The following list describes each of the standard command line arguments.

/S system   Specifies the remote system that you want to check. In most cases, you'll also need to supply the /U and the /P command line switches when using this switch.

/U [domain]user   Specifies the username on the remote system. This name may not match the username on the local system. You'll need to supply a domain name when working with a domain controller.

/P [password]   Specifies the password for the given user. You can provide the command line switch without specifying the password on the command line in cleartext. The system prompts you for the password. Using this feature can help you maintain the security of passwords used on your system.

/RU username   Specifies the user account or user context that you want to use to run the task. Use "", "NT AUTHORITY\SYSTEM", or "SYSTEM" to use the system account to run the task.

/RP password   Specifies the password of the user account or user context you want to use to run the task. Use an asterisk (*) or a blank (nothing after the command line switch) in place of the password when you want the system to prompt you for the password. This command line switch has no effect when you use the system account to run the task.

/SC schedule   Defines the frequency at which the system runs the task. The valid frequencies include MINUTE, HOURLY, DAILY, WEEKLY, MONTHLY, ONCE, ONSTART, ONLOGON, and ONIDLE.

/MO modifier   Refines the schedule type to provide finer control over the schedule frequency. The modifier you use depends on the scheduling frequency. The following list describes each of the modifiers.

MINUTE   Every 1–1,439 minutes

HOURLY   Every 1–23 hours

DAILY   Every 1–365 days

WEEKLY   Every 1–52 weeks

ONCE   No modifiers

ONSTART   No modifiers

ONLOGON   No modifiers

ONIDLE   No modifiers

MONTHLY   Every 1 to 12 months, or FIRST, SECOND, THIRD, FOURTH, LAST, or LASTDAY

/D days   Specifies the day of the week to run the task. Acceptable values include MON, TUE, WED, THU, FRI, SAT, and SUN. When working with a monthly schedule, you can specify date numbers between 1 and 31.

/M months   Specifies the month of the year to run a task. The default setting is the current month. Acceptable values include JAN, FEB, MAR, APR, MAY, JUN, JUL, AUG, SEP, OCT, NOV, and DEC.

/I idletime   Specifies the amount of time to wait before running a scheduled ONIDLE task. Idle time is when no other application on the system is running (the system idle process is using all of the computer resources). The acceptable range of values is 1 to 999 minutes.

/TN taskname   Specifies the name of the task. The utility requires a unique name for the purpose of identification.

/TR taskrun   Specifies the full path and filename of the task that you want to run. Never assume that the task will run based on a PATH environment variable because you can't guarantee the user will have the environment variable defined. You can also specify any command line arguments that the task requires. Enclose tasks with spaces in quotes.

/ST starttime   Specifies the time that you want the task to run. The time format is HH:MM:SS (24-hour time). Don't use a 12-hour time format that includes AM and PM. The default setting is the current time.

/SD startdate   Specifies the first date on which to run the task. The date format is mm/dd/yyyy. Always include a 4-digit year. The default setting is the current day.

/ED enddate   Specifies the last date that you want to run the task. The date format is mm/dd/yyyy. Always include a 4-digit year. The default is not to use an end time, so the task continues to run indefinitely.

/RI interval   Specifies the repetition interval of the task in minutes. You can't use this feature with schedule types of MINUTE, HOURLY, ONSTART, ONLOGON, ONIDLE, and

ONEVENT. The valid range for this argument is 1 to 599,940 minutes. If you specify either the /ET or /DE command line arguments, then the default interval is 10 minutes.

/ET *endtime*   Specifies the end time of the task. The time format is HH:MM:SS (24-hour time). Don't use a 12-hour time format that includes AM and PM. You can't use this feature with schedule types of ONSTART, ONLOGON, ONIDLE, and ONEVENT. It also isn't possible to use this feature with the /DU option.

/DU *duration*   Specifies the duration of the task. The time format is HH:MM (a time interval in hours and minutes, not a specific time). You can't use this feature with schedule types of ONSTART, ONLOGON, ONIDLE, and ONEVENT. It also isn't possible to use this feature with the /ET option. When you specify the /RI argument with a /V1 task, the default duration is 1 hour.

/K   Automatically terminates the task at the end time or after the duration interval expires. You can't use this feature with schedule types of ONSTART, ONLOGON, ONIDLE, and ONEVENT. This argument is only applicable when you specify either the /ET or /DU command line arguments.

/XML *xmlfile*   Creates a task based on the task XML in the specified file. Combine this command line switch with the /RU and /RP command line switches to specify a complete entry (including security). The task XML can also contain the principal, which means that you only supply the /RU command line switch.

/V1   Creates a task that's compatible with pre-Vista versions of Windows. If you don't use this command line switch on a Vista system, then other versions of Windows can't see the task you create. You can't use this command line switch with /XML.

/IT   Forces the task to run interactively only. The job runs when the user is logged on, but Vista and above ignores it when the user is logged out.

/NP   Disables password storage. The job runs noninteractively using the credentials of the specified user. The job can only access local resources. Using this command line switch improves security by not storing the password and by reducing task access to external resources.

/Z   Marks the task for deletion after its final run (as specified in the schedule you provide). The job isn't actually deleted—Vista only marks it for deletion.

/F   Forces task creation even if a task by that name already exists on the system. Vista and above doesn't display any warning messages, it simply overwrites the existing job.

/DELETE

The /Delete parameter deletes tasks that you no longer want to run. This parameter uses the following syntax:

```
SCHTASKS /Delete [/S system [/U username [/P password]]] /TN taskname [/F]
```

The following list describes each of the command line arguments.

/S *system*   Specifies the remote system that you want to check. In most cases, you'll also need to supply the /U and the /P command line switches when using this switch.

/U *[domain\]user*   Specifies the username on the remote system. This name may not match the username on the local system. You'll need to supply a domain name when working with a domain controller.

/P [*password*] Specifies the password for the given user. You can provide the command line switch without specifying the password on the command line in cleartext. The system prompts you for the password. Using this feature can help you maintain the security of passwords used on your system.

/TN *taskname* Specifies the name of the task you want to delete. You can delete all tasks using the asterisk (*) wildcard.

/F Forces the utility to delete the task and suppress any warnings when the task is currently running. Use this command line switch only when the task is frozen or unresponsive. Using this command line switch can result in data loss or other unexpected system behavior.

/QUERY

The /Query parameter requests information about any tasks you've created. This parameter uses the following syntax:

```
SCHTASKS /Query [/S system [/U username [/P password]]]
    [/FO format | /XML] [/NH] [/V] [/?] [/TN taskname]
```

The following list describes each of the command line arguments.

/S *system* Specifies the remote system that you want to check. In most cases, you'll also need to supply the /U and the /P command line switches when using this switch.

/U [*domain*]*user* Specifies the username on the remote system. This name may not match the username on the local system. You'll need to supply a domain name when working with a domain controller.

/P [*password*] Specifies the password for the given user. You can provide the command line switch without specifying the password on the command line in cleartext. The system prompts you for the password. Using this feature can help you maintain the security of passwords used on your system.

/FO {TABLE | LIST | CSV} Defines the output provided by the utility. The table format is normally the easiest to view on screen. The table columns define the values for output, while each row contains one driver entry. The CSV output provides the best method for preparing the data for entry in a database. Use redirection (see the "Employing Data Redirection" section of Chapter 14 for details) to output the CSV data to a file and then import it to your database. The list format provides one data element per line. Each group of data elements defines one driver. The utility separates each driver by one blank line. Some people find the list format more readable when working in verbose mode since the table format requires multiple lines for each entry (the lines wrap).

/XML Displays the output in XML format. This command line switch is useful when you want to learn more about creating jobs using XML files.

/NH Forces the utility to display the data without a column header. You can only use this command line switch with the table and CSV formats. Omitting the header makes it easier to incorporate the data in a report or import it into a database.

/V Displays detailed data about each of the defined tasks. The standard display shows only TaskName, Next Run Time, and Status. In addition to this basic information, the verbose display shows HostName, Last Run Time, Last Result, Creator, Schedule, Task To Run, Start In, Comment, Scheduled Task State, Scheduled Type, Start Time, Start Date, End Date, Days,

Months, Run As User, Delete Task If Not Rescheduled, Stop Task If Runs X Hours and X Mins, Repeat: Every, Repeat: Until: Time, Repeat: Until: Duration, Repeat: Stop If Still Running, Idle Time, and Power Management.

/TN *taskname* Specifies the name of the task you want to query. Vista and above displays all of the tasks when you don't supply this parameter.

/CHANGE

The /Change parameter changes an existing task. You can't use this parameter to create a new task. However, this parameter does work well to indicate a change in task location. This parameter uses the following syntax:

```
SCHTASKS /Change [/S system [/U username [/P [password]]]] [/RU
    runasuser] [/RP runaspassword] [/TR taskrun] /TN taskname [/ST
    starttime] [/RI interval] [ {/ET endtime | /DU duration} [/K] ]
    [/SD startdate] [/ED enddate] [/ENABLE | /DISABLE] [/IT] [/Z] }
```

The following list describes each of the command line arguments.

/S *system* Specifies the remote system that you want to check. In most cases, you'll also need to supply the /U and the /P command line switches when using this switch.

/U *[domain\]user* Specifies the username on the remote system. This name may not match the username on the local system. You'll need to supply a domain name when working with a domain controller.

/P *[password]* Specifies the password for the given user. You can provide the command line switch without specifying the password on the command line in cleartext. The system prompts you for the password. Using this feature can help you maintain the security of passwords used on your system.

/RU *username* Specifies the user account or user context that you want to use to run the task. Use "", "NT AUTHORITY\SYSTEM", or "SYSTEM" to use the system account to run the task.

/RP *password* Specifies the password of the user account or user context you want to use to run the task. Use an asterisk (*) or a blank (nothing after the command line switch) in place of the password when you want the system to prompt you for the password. This command line switch has no effect when you use the system account to run the task.

/TR *taskrun* Specifies the full path and filename of the new task that you want to run. The new task need not be a new execution; it may simply be a new version or a version of the same executable in a different location. Never assume that the task will run based on a PATH environment variable because you can't guarantee the user will have the environment variable defined. You can also specify any command line arguments that the task requires. Enclose tasks with spaces in quotes.

/TN *taskname* Specifies the name of the task to change.

/ST *starttime* Specifies the time that you want the task to run. The time format is HH:MM:SS (24-hour time). Don't use a 12-hour time format that includes AM and PM. The default setting is the current time.

/RI *interval* Specifies the repetition interval of the task in minutes. You can't use this feature with schedule types of MINUTE, HOURLY, ONSTART, ONLOGON, ONIDLE, and

ONEVENT. The valid range for this argument is 1 to 599,940 minutes. If you specify either the /ET or /DE command line arguments, then the default interval is 10 minutes.

/ET *endtime*   Specifies the end time of the task. The time format is HH:MM:SS (24-hour time). Don't use a 12-hour time format that includes AM and PM. You can't use this feature with schedule types of ONSTART, ONLOGON, ONIDLE, and ONEVENT. It also isn't possible to use this feature with the /DU option.

/DU *duration*   Specifies the duration of the task. The time format is HH:MM (a time interval in hours and minutes, not a specific time). You can't use this feature with schedule types of ONSTART, ONLOGON, ONIDLE, and ONEVENT. It also isn't possible to use this feature with the /ET option. When you specify the /RI argument with a /V1 task, the default duration is 1 hour.

/K   Automatically terminates the task at the end time or after the duration interval expires. You can't use this feature with schedule types of ONSTART, ONLOGON, ONIDLE, and ONEVENT. This argument is only applicable when you specify either the /ET or /DU command line arguments.

/SD *startdate*   Specifies the first date on which to run the task. The date format is mm/dd/yyyy. Always include a 4-digit year. The default setting is the current day.

/ED *enddate*   Specifies the last date that you want to run the task. The date format is mm/dd/yyyy. Always include a 4-digit year. The default is not to use an end time, so the task continues to run indefinitely.

/ENABLE   Enables the scheduled task (so it can run).

/DISABLE   Disables the schedule task (it can't run, even when scheduled).

/IT   Forces the task to run interactively only. The job runs when the user is logged on, but Vista and above ignores it when the user is logged out.

/Z   Marks the task for deletion after its final run (as specified in the schedule you provide). The job isn't actually deleted—Vista and above only marks it for deletion.

/RUN

The /Run parameter runs an existing task, even if the task isn't scheduled to run. Running a task using this method doesn't change the task schedule; the task runs using the schedule you set for it. You can use this feature to test your tasks to ensure they work as anticipated. Check the \Windows\SchedLgU.TXT file for the results of any task you run, especially on remote machines. This parameter uses the following syntax:

```
SCHTASKS /Run [/S system [/U username [/P password]]] /TN taskname
```

The following list describes each of the command line arguments.

/S *system*   Specifies the remote system that you want to check. In most cases, you'll also need to supply the /U and the /P command line switches when using this switch.

/U *[domain\]user*   Specifies the username on the remote system. This name may not match the username on the local system. You'll need to supply a domain name when working with a domain controller.

/P *[password]*   Specifies the password for the given user. You can provide the command line switch without specifying the password on the command line in cleartext. The system prompts you for the password. Using this feature can help you maintain the security of passwords used on your system.

/TN *taskname*   Specifies the name of the task you want to run. Running a task at the command line is different from having the Task Scheduler run it for you. Using this option forces the utility to use your credentials, rather than the Task Scheduler credentials, which means that an executable that normally works could fail when used in this way.

TIP   You can use the RunAs utility described in the "Impersonating a User with the RunAs Utility" section of Chapter 6 to test run a task using another person's credentials. In fact, you can use this technique to run the task using the system account. Because people have differing rights, you need to test the task using the credentials of the person who normally runs it.

/END

The /End parameter forces a task to stop, even if the task is in the middle of processing data. Consequently, you should use this parameter with care to avoid data loss or odd system behavior. You can only use this parameter to end programs started with the Task Scheduler. Use the TaskKill utility described in the "Terminating Tasks with the TaskKill Command" section of Chapter 21 to end other processes. This parameter uses the following syntax:

```
SCHTASKS /End [/S system [/U username [/P password]]] /TN taskname
```

The following list describes each of the command line arguments.

/S *system*   Specifies the remote system that you want to check. In most cases, you'll also need to supply the /U and the /P command line switches when using this switch.

/U *[domain\]user*   Specifies the username on the remote system. This name may not match the username on the local system. You'll need to supply a domain name when working with a domain controller.

/P *[password]*   Specifies the password for the given user. You can provide the command line switch without specifying the password on the command line in cleartext. The system prompts you for the password. Using this feature can help you maintain the security of passwords used on your system.

/TN *taskname*   Specifies the name of the task you want to end.

Working with the AT Utility

The AT command line utility is an older utility that many longtime Windows users are comfortable using to create tasks. This is an alternative (albeit, less capable) to the SchTasks utility described in the "Managing Tasks with the SchTasks Command" section of the chapter. The advantage of this utility is that it's very easy to use. In addition, because this utility has been around since Windows NT, you'll find many scripts already written to use it. Use the AT utility alone to display a list of tasks that you've created using the AT utility (the AT utility won't display any tasks created using the graphical tools). This utility uses the following syntax:

```
Remove a Task:
AT [\\Computer] [[<Id>] [/DELETE] [/YES]]
Add a Task:
AT [\\Computer] <Time> [/INTERACTIVE] [/EVERY:<Dates> | /NEXT:<Dates>] <Command>
Query the Task List:
AT
```

The following list describes each of the command line arguments.

\\\Computer   Specifies the name of a remote computer used to run the AT utility.

Id   Specifies the identifying number of the job. The AT command begins at 1 and increments the count as needed. Every job must have a unique identifier.

/DELETE   Removes a job from the list. If you omit the Id argument, AT removes all jobs that it created from the list. This command doesn't affect jobs that you create using the graphical utilities. AT requests confirmation before it deletes a job unless you specify the /YES switch.

/YES   Prevents AT from asking whether it should delete each job in the list.

Time   Determines the starting time of the job.

/INTERACTIVE   Determines whether the user can interact with the job (and vice versa). The default setting runs the job in the background without any interaction.

/EVERY:Dates   Runs the job during the specified day of the week or month. The valid values for days of the week include Monday, Tuesday, Wednesday, Thursday, Friday, Saturday, and Sunday. The month values are a number between 1 and 31. Adding more than one entry runs the job on multiple days of the week or month. If you omit the date argument, AT assumes you want to run the job monthly during the current day of the month. Vista doesn't allow you to use abbreviations for this argument.

/NEXT:Dates   Runs the job during the next occurrence of the day of the week or month. The valid values for days of the week include Monday, Tuesday, Wednesday, Thursday, Friday, Saturday, and Sunday. The month values are a number between 1 and 31. Adding multiple dates runs the job during each of the specified dates. If you omit the date argument, AT assumes you want to run the job during the current day. Server Core doesn't allow you to use abbreviations for this argument.

Command   Specifies the command that you want to run. This entry must include the path of the command you want to run and any command line switches. You must enclose the command in quotes.

Working with the WMIC Job Alias

The WMIC Job alias works much the same as any other WMIC command. You have access to a number of verbs and use those verbs to perform specific tasks, such as creating a new Task Scheduler job, deleting a job, or simply checking on the status of an existing job. The "Configuring Server Core Using the WMIC Command" section of Chapter 3 provides details on how the WMIC command works in Server Core. This utility uses the following syntax:

```
WMIC Job ASSOC [<format specifier>]
WMIC Job CALL <method name> [<actual param list>]
WMIC Job CREATE <assign list>
WMIC Job DELETE
WMIC Job GET [<property list>] [<get switches>]
WMIC Job LIST [<list format>] [<list switches>]
```

WMIC does have a significant oddity in this case—it doesn't appear to support jobs created using the SchTasks utility. The only jobs that appear on the list are the ones that you create using WMIC or the AT utility.

Listing jobs is as easy as typing **WMIC Job** and pressing Enter. You'll see all of the jobs created using the AT utility. Of course, this output is a little unreadable. If you want to see the output in readable form, use the GET or LIST verbs instead. One of the features of WMIC that Chapter 3 doesn't really discuss is the ability to format the output using an XSL file. You'll find a number of these files in the \WINDOWS\system32\wbem directory of your system. For example, if you type **WMIC JOB GET /Format:TextValueList.XSL** and press Enter, you'll see a listing where each property and value pair appears on a single line—making it much easier to determine which property has what value. Figure 8.1 shows an example of the output.

FIGURE 8.1
Use formatting to make the output of the WMIC command easier to read.

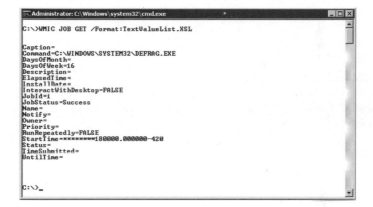

TIP You can use the /Format switch with any WMIC GET verb output. In fact, you can create your own formats using the instructions at http://technet2.microsoft.com/windowsserver/en/library/5d434da3-666d-434a-b259-0f0da0cfaff11033.mspx. If you want to edit an existing format, check out the instructions at http://technet2.microsoft.com/windowsserver/en/library/f4612816-4131-4e6d-999a-bda8c9a373491033.mspx.

Creating a new job is an interesting task with WMIC because you have to know several bits of information to do it. First, all of the input arguments are required, even if you don't need them for the job. Consequently, you'll need to type something like **WMIC JOB Call Create "C:\WINDOWS\SYSTEM32\DEFRAG.EXE",0,16,FALSE,FALSE,"********180000.000000-420"** and press Enter to create a job that defragments the hard drive at 6 P.M. every Friday. The list of create arguments includes:

◆ Command

◆ DaysOfMonth

◆ DaysOfWeek

◆ InteractWithDesktop

◆ RunRepeatedly

◆ StartTime

Several of these values are easy to obtain. The Command argument is a simple string that defines the command you want Task Scheduler to execute. Make sure you include the full path to the executable to ensure the Task Scheduler can locate it on the hard drive. The InteractWithDesktop (determines whether the job only executes in the background) and RunRepeatedly (the job only executes once when set to false) arguments are Boolean (true/false) values.

The DaysOfMonth and DaysOfWeek arguments are positional. These arguments determine when to run the job. They use binary flags to set them. If you set the value to 0, then the task isn't scheduled for that time frame. When working with DaysOfMonth, you create a number based on the day's position in the calendar. The value can become quite large. If you want the task to run each day of the month (from days 1 through 31), then you use a value of 2147483647, which is the maximum value allowed. Here's the list of numbers you use with the day of the month listed first and the value for the call second.

Day of the month	Value	Day of the month	Value	Day of the month	Value	Day of the month	Value
1	1	9	256	17	65536	25	16777216
2	2	10	512	18	131072	26	33554432
3	4	11	1024	19	262144	27	67108864
4	8	12	2048	20	524288	28	134217728
5	16	13	4096	21	1048576	29	268435456
6	32	14	8192	22	2097152	30	536870912
7	64	15	16384	23	4194304	31	1073741824
8	128	16	32768	24	8388608		

Using this table, if you want to perform a particular task on day 1 (a value of 1), 5 (a value of 16), and 7 (a value of 64) of each month, then you would use a value of 81. When working with DaysOfWeek, you create a number based on the day of the week's position. These numbers include:

Day of the Week	Value
Monday	1
Tuesday	2
Wednesday	4
Thursday	8
Friday	16
Saturday	32
Sunday	64

Consequently, if you want to run a task Monday, Wednesday, and Friday, you'd add 1 (for Monday), 4 (for Wednesday), and 16 (for Friday) for a total of 21. Setting the DaysOfWeek value to 0 means that the job won't run on a particular day of the week. You must include either a DaysOfMonth or DaysOfWeek as part of the input or the call will fail.

The StartTime variable is as a DATETIME data type and it determines when the job will begin running the first time. This data type relies on the Universal Time Coordinated (UTC) time. In most cases, you'll simply want a time value, so you'll display the date values as eight asterisks (*) as shown in the example. The hours, minutes, and seconds come next. In the case of the example, you're looking at a value of 6 P.M.

If you want to include the date in your start time, it appears in year, month, and day format. For example, 20080130073001.100000-420 would indicate January 1, 2008, 7:30:01.1 A.M. The –420 is the bias for the time—it indicates the difference between local time and UTC time in minutes. To set this value correctly, check the time zone information for your area. For example, the Eastern United States is at the GMT –05:00 time zone according to the Windows time zone properties. Multiply –05 * 60 to obtain a value of –300 for the bias. Of course, you have to take daylight savings time into account when you perform your calculation. California has a bias of –420 in the summer, but –480 in the winter.

The output of the call, as shown in Figure 8.2, is a `JobId` value. You can't assign this value, the Task Scheduler assigns it for you. When you view the WMIC job in the Task Scheduler, it appears the same as a job you create using the AT utility. The `JobId` value is unique, so you can use it to access any job you create.

FIGURE 8.2

Creating a new job defines a new JobId value as well.

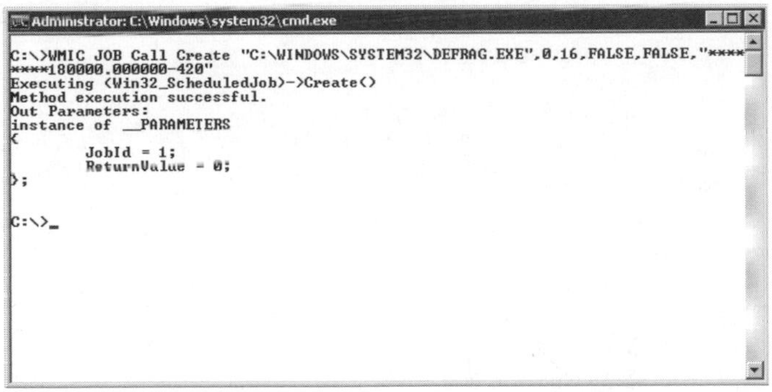

Removing a job you no longer need is relatively simple. All you need is the `JobId` value, which you can obtain by listing the jobs. The `JobId` value is unique, so it guarantees that you remove the correct job. Once you have this number, you can use the DELETE verb to remove the job. For example, if you want to remove job 3, you'd type **WMIC JOB Where JobID=3 DELETE** and press Enter.

Combining the AT Utility with Batch Files

Before you can begin using the AT utility within a batch file, you need to know how to use it at the command line. Creating a job with AT is relatively easy. Imagine that you want to defragment your hard drive. You could create a defragmenter job that runs at 6 P.M. every Friday, immediately after you leave work to go home for the weekend. You can create the job using the following command line.

```
AT 6pm /Every:FRIDAY "C:\WINDOWS\SYSTEM32\DEFRAG.EXE"
```

The same job using the SchTasks utility would require a longer command line, as shown here.

```
SchTasks /Create /RU SYSTEM /SC WEEKLY /D FRI /TN "ST Defrag Hard
    Drive" /TR "C:\WINDOWS\SYSTEM32\DEFRAG.EXE" /ST 18:00:00
```

Of course, you can also create the same job using WMIC, as shown here.

```
WMIC JOB Call Create "C:\WINDOWS\SYSTEM32\DEFRAG.EXE",
    0,16,FALSE,FALSE,"********180000.000000-420"
```

NOTE Server Core doesn't let you abbreviate day or month names. Previous versions of Windows would let you use an abbreviation such as FRI for Friday. In some cases, you'll find that this change breaks macros in Server Core that work fine in other Windows versions.

You don't obtain the same level of configuration features using AT that you would using the graphical or SchTasks method. Many of the special configuration features that the graphical utility supports are unavailable (they're available when you use the SchTasks utility).

The Scheduled Tasks window tracks jobs created using both the graphical and the command line method. AT only tracks jobs that it creates. If you type **AT** at the command prompt and press Enter, all you'll see are the AT jobs (including those created using the WMIC command). Figure 8.3 shows a typical example of the same jobs created using the graphical utility, SchTask, and AT. (The graphical utility only works with the versions of Windows with a graphical interface, not with Server Core.) Notice that the AT job name has "At" plus the number of the job. The top screenshot shows the Windows XP/Windows 2003 version of Task Scheduler, while the bottom screenshot shows the Vista/Windows Server 2008 version. The entries are essentially the same in both views, but the Windows XP/Windows 2003 view is simpler, while the Vista/Windows Server 2008 view provides more details.

FIGURE 8.3
AT jobs appear in the Scheduled Tasks window as "at" jobs (Windows XP/ Windows 2003 appears at the top and Vista/Windows Server 2008 appears at the bottom).

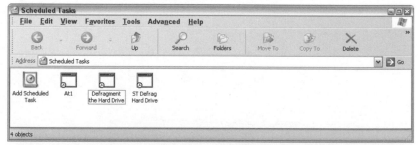

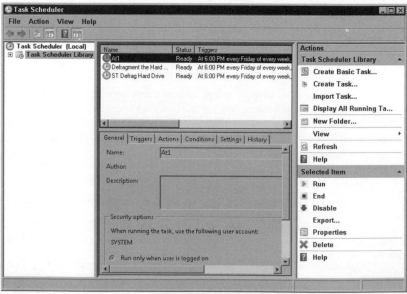

As you can see, from a Scheduled Tasks window perspective, all three jobs are the same. The only two differences are the job name and the creator name. Unless you change the default setting, the system creates all AT jobs. Any job created using the Scheduled Tasks window appears under the user's name.

The limitations of the AT utility do bring up one additional useful feature for batch files. You can schedule a number of temporary tasks using one batch file, and remove all of those tasks from the Scheduled Tasks window using another, all without disturbing the original scheduled tasks. Because the AT utility only operates on the tasks that it creates, you can use it to create temporary tasks and simplify the method required to remove those tasks later.

USING THE AT UTILITY EFFECTIVELY

The AT utility is still useful, but many would say that it's outdated. If you're working at the command prompt, the AT utility probably is outdated; the SchTasks utility provides more functionality. However, the AT utility still provides good functionality for other purposes. One of the main reasons to use the AT utility is that there are already a wealth of scripts on the Internet for using it.

Another reason to use the AT utility is that it's compatible with WMIC, which is more of an advantage than many administrators realize, especially when working with Server Core. Using WMIC provides additional flexibility over remote connections that you don't realize when working with the SchTasks utility.

Sometimes you don't require complexity to get the job done at the command line. The AT utility tends to be simpler to use than the SchTasks utility. Sure, all you can do is query, add, and delete tasks, but sometimes that's all you really need to do. You don't want all of the details; a simple task scheduling will do just fine. Even though the AT utility might look outdated, it really does have some very useful features that make it a worthwhile utility to consider.

Creating Script-Based Scheduler Activities

You might wonder how you can use the Task Scheduler to improve productivity without expending a lot of energy. Some of the best Task Scheduler tasks are those that you normally perform manually or using a batch file, but don't perform consistently. For example, everyone knows that your hard drive eventually fills up with garbage if you don't remove all of those temporary files. However, many people don't get the job done because it simply isn't convenient, ever.

If you've ever tried to locate all of the temporary files on your hard drive, you know that it's a time-consuming task. In fact, I would go so far as to say that some people would rather hear fingernails screeching across a chalkboard or walk barefooted across broken glass than have to locate all of their temporary files. Fortunately, you don't have to go to such extreme measures because you can tell the computer to do all of the work for you. You can't perform this task easily using Windows Explorer because it won't find all of the files for you (many people have tried). However, the Dir command always tells the truth, you just need to put it to work. The batch file shown in Listing 8.1 will remove all of your temporary files. It's fully configurable and you'll find that it's quite reliable.

LISTING 8.1: Deleting Temporary Files Using a Batch File

```
@ECHO OFF

REM Verify that the file specifications file exists.
IF NOT EXIST DelFiles.TXT GOTO :NoFileError
GOTO :GetFiles

REM Display an error message that shows how to correct the problem.
:NoFileError
@ECHO This utility depends on the presence of a file named Delfiles.TXT
@ECHO that contains all of the file specifications you want to delete.
@ECHO All the file need contain is a list of entries such as *.BAK.
@ECHO Place each entry on a separate line.
GOTO :EOF

:GetFiles
REM Remove any existing list of temporary files.
REM This file is retained after the previous cleaning so you have
REM a record of the deletions.
@ECHO Removing old DeleteMe.TXT.
IF EXIST DeleteMe.TXT Del DeleteMe.TXT

REM Locate all of the temporary files on your hard drive.
@ECHO Locating temporary files to delete.
FOR /F %%F IN (DelFiles.TXT) DO Dir %%F /B /S >> DeleteMe.TXT

REM Delete the temporary files.
@ECHO Removing the temporary files.
FOR /F "delims==" %%D IN (DeleteMe.TXT) DO Del "%%D" /Q > Errors.TXT

@ECHO Deletion of Temporary Files Completed!
@ECHO ON
```

This batch file uses three basic steps. First, it ensures that you've defined a file that contains the file extension specifications to delete. Second, it uses these file specifications to locate the files you want to delete. Third, it deletes the file using the accumulated list of files. Notice that the batch file automatically erases any old file lists before it begins generating the new one.

The trickiest piece of code in this example is the second FOR command. Notice the "delims==" entry. Because the DeleteMe.TXT file contains filenames with spaces, you need to use this option. Otherwise, the FOR command only outputs the filenames up to the first space and the deletion will fail. The batch file outputs any files that failed to delete to Errors.TXT, so you can check on them later.

Once you create and fully test this batch file, you can create a second batch file for installing it as a scheduled task on every machine on the network. Of course, you want to do all this without working with each machine individually, so it's just as well that you can tell the batch file to generate the list of machines for you. Listing 8.2 shows how to create such a list as batch file. Note that some of the long lines are broken in the book. All of the FOR commands must appear on a single line.

LISTING 8.2:   Defining Tasks on Every Machine on a Network

```
@ECHO OFF

REM Obtain a list of machines from the system.
Net View > Temp.TXT

REM Remove any existing list of machines.
@ECHO Removing old Machines.TXT.
IF EXIST Machines.TXT Del Machines.TXT

REM Make the list usable by removing extraneous material.
@ECHO Generating a New Machine List
FOR /F "skip=3" %%M in (Temp.TXT) DO IF %%M NEQ The @ECHO %%M >> Machines.TXT

REM Copy the required files to each machine.
@ECHO Copying the File Specification and Deletion Batch Files
FOR /F %%M in (Machines.TXT) DO Copy DelFiles.TXT "%%M\Drive_D" /Y
FOR /F %%M in (Machines.TXT) DO Copy MyBatch.BAT "%%M\Drive_D" /Y

REM Schedule the task on each machine.
@ECHO Creating the Scheduled Task
FOR /F %%M in (Machines.TXT) DO SchTasks /Create /S %%M /RU SYSTEM
   /SC WEEKLY /D FRI /TN "Remove Temporary Files"
   /TR "D:\MyBatch.BAT" /ST 18:00:00

@ECHO ON
```

The example begins by using the Net View utility to create a list of machines. Unfortunately, the output from this utility isn't very useful for a batch file, as shown in Figure 8.4. The first three lines contain a header that you can't get rid of and the output ends with "The command completed successfully." In addition, some machines in the list contain a comment.

FIGURE 8.4

Some utilities produce helpful output, but you can't use it for a batch file.

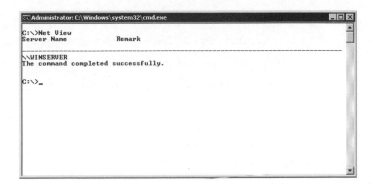

The first FOR command gets rid of this extraneous material using three techniques. First, it relies on the "skip=3" option to remove the top three lines from the file. The FOR command doesn't even

process these lines. At this point, the FOR command does process the three lines with machine names. Because there's a space after each machine name, the result only contains the machine name and not the comment. This is one case where the natural FOR command behavior works in your favor. The FOR command passes the file output to an IF command. Remember that the first word of the last line of the file is "The." By using the code IF %%M NEQ The, you can remove the offending line. The final step copies only the good input to a new file named Machines.TXT by redirecting the output of the ECHO command.

The batch file shown in Listing 8.1 requires two files. The first is a text file containing a list of file specifications. The second is the batch file itself. The next two FOR commands copy these two files to every machine on the network. Because the file could already exist (this could be an update), you use the /Y command line switch with the Copy utility.

The final step creates the required scheduled task on every machine. Notice the use of the /S command line switch to access each machine in turn. The resulting task runs every Friday at 6 P.M. using the system account.

Providing Fault Tolerance for an After Hours Batch or Script

The Task Scheduler provides an effective way to manage jobs on your system. With the AT utility, WMIC command, and SchTasks command at your disposal, you have considerable flexibility in creating and managing automated jobs. Of course, creating and managing the jobs doesn't ensure they'll run as expected. In most cases, you'll find that Task Scheduler is as reliable as the commands that you automate with it. In other words, Task Scheduler will start the command on time as long as no outside influence prevents it and you consider any local requirements (such as setting the computer clock correctly). However, starting the application is the least of your worries.

Using the Task Scheduler assumes that you'll leave your computer to run independently at some point—usually after hours, when you've gone home for the day or even left town for a vacation. Even though the computer is following your instructions (to the letter mind you), you aren't there to monitor it. This chapter discusses a number of techniques you can use to reduce risk, but not eliminate it. Assuming that Task Scheduler starts the task on time and with all of the required information, you still have to consider failure of the application itself. When all or part of an after hours processing task fails, you have four choices:

♦ Let the task fail gracefully and fix it when you arrive the next morning.

♦ Create a batch file or script loop that automatically restarts the processing after a failure.

♦ Add a Task Scheduler task to check for a failure condition and attempt to execute the application again when Task Scheduler detects an error.

♦ Provide administrator notification so that the administrator can restart the application.

Each of these options has advantages. For example, letting the task fail gracefully means that the system will be in a known state the next morning and you can try to discover what error occurred. Unfortunately, letting the task fail gracefully is no longer an option for many enterprises where 24/7 operation is the standard and you must provide five 9's of reliability (in short, an average of 5 minutes of downtime during an average year). Including a loop in the batch file or script has the advantage of automatically restarting the task without bothering anyone. The application can attempt to succeed all night long. Unfortunately, you can still arrive at work the next morning to a nasty surprise and now you won't have that first failure to examine—the reason the application failed can remain a mystery. Having Task Scheduler check for the error is a great idea, but now you have to create a batch file or script to check for the error and act on it by starting the application. In addition, you have to schedule the task once for each attempt, which means added complexity in managing Task Scheduler. Of all the options, the one least likely to fail is alerting the administrator, but now you have to disrupt someone's evening and possibly get them out of bed to restart an application that would have run the second time using a simple batch file or script loop. In short, there aren't any perfect solutions, but you should decide on a policy for handling errors at the outset.

Make sure you also have policies in place for machines that perform after hours processing. Task Scheduler can't run if someone turns off the machine. Well-intentioned people can cause all kinds of problems for your system. Imagine what would happen if someone decided to work late on a report that requires the database and your batch file or script requires exclusive access to that database. As part of your strategy, you might want to broadcast a message across the network telling everyone about the outage. Make sure you include an automated broadcast message with Task Scheduler as well. You don't want to have to come into work just to send a message telling everyone that your automated software is about to begin its task.

Fault tolerance can consume a lot of ground. A reliable environment is one that doesn't change. For example, you might think that applying a patch to your software will make it more reliable because the vendor has fixed the problem. Like the human body, every networked system is different. Just as you can't guarantee that a new medication won't have disastrous side effects, you can't guarantee that a patch will do anything other than make your system stop working. Even though the hope is that things will go well and the application will run better than before, you don't know about side effects until you've thoroughly tested the new setup. Testing takes the guesswork out of the system, makes it stable, and therefore more reliable.

As a final consideration for making your after hours processing more robust and reliable, think about training several people to take over repairing the problem should you become unavailable. In many cases, protectionist policies by those with knowledge (making them theoretically indispensable) also serve to make the system completely unreliable. A reliable system requires redundancies in every area, including the humans who run the system. Cross-training other people to perform the tasks that you perform actually makes the system more reliable. In addition, if you really want to have some evenings at home, rather than babysit a sick system, having a backup is required. Generally, you want to consider every possible contingency before you start up that automated system the first time. Expecting it to work without help isn't going to be effective; remember that Murphy fellow who seems obliged to make our lives interesting in the worst possible way.

 Real World Scenario

THINK ABOUT THE SMALL STUFF

I use checklists for everything. In fact, the book you're reading now relied on many checklists to ensure I didn't miss any details (at least not purposely). Checklists aren't perfect, but by documenting the process you use to accomplish a task, you can reduce errors and fix any procedural errors as you continue to work with the checklist. In many cases, checklists also help you avoid common, silly errors. The type of error where you wonder what you were thinking about later. Often, these errors occur when you're in a rush, such as at the end of the day when you're setting up the after hours processing for the night.

Someone once complained that the automation they'd set up didn't work. After going through all of the usual problems, I thought to ask about the computer clock. The user checked the clock and found it was set incorrectly; problem solved. However, small errors are often the cause of problems with automation. Creating and using a checklist can mean the difference between sleeping well at night knowing your computer is working hard for you and coming in the next morning to a nasty surprise.

Managing Windows in a New Way

This chapter has shown that you have to use Task Scheduler to automate the applications, batch files, and scripts you use from the command line further. Instead of being present to execute these entities, you can ask the system to do it for you. The one thing you can depend on is that the system will execute the task when you ask, using the input data you requested, unless it's unable to do so. Of course, this means that you have to make certain that the Task Scheduler entry is correct or you might get some unanticipated results. This chapter helps you build these skills:

◆ Manage the task scheduler, applications, and associated service

◆ Provide automation fault tolerance

It's time for you test this new form of automation. The best route to pursue is to experiment with a number of simple entries to see how Task Scheduler works. Try something simple and non-destructive, such as the Dir command. As you gain proficiency with Task Scheduler, move up to other kinds of commands—those that actually do some work you need to perform offline. When you know beyond any doubt that the entry works as anticipated, you can move on to executing the commands when you aren't sitting at your machine.

Chapter 9 begins a new section that describes how to work with hardware within Server Core. You won't have the Control Panel applets you used in the past to manage hardware; everything must occur at the command line or through remotely connected consoles (when available—they often aren't). In Chapter 9, you'll discover how to work with the hard drives on your system in a new way. The command line utilities provided by Server Core help you perform a vast array of hard drive tasks and even manage tasks in remote locations using new technologies such as the Internet Small Computer System Interface (iSCSI).

Part 3

Working with the Hardware

Chapter 9

Managing the Hard Drive

The hard drive is a special piece of hardware because it provides permanent storage for all of your data. At the same time, the hard drive is more vulnerable than many other parts of the system and easier to damage. Compounding the problem are the multiple formats that Microsoft has supported over the years and the myriad ways in which you can work with a hard drive today, even when you choose to work with the Windows NT File System (NTFS). Consequently, the hard drive requires special treatment.

This chapter views the hard drive as the operating system. In other words, you won't find any detailed description of how the hardware works in the chapter and you won't see any detailed discussions of track layout. For the most part, Windows hides the intricacies of the hard drive from you.

The computer industry has also muddied the term *hard drive* in recent years. Most people think of a hard drive as a box containing spinning disks and several read heads. A hard drive today can include flash drives, those little solid-state devices you plug into a Universal Serial Bus (USB) slot. Hard drives can also take on a virtual form with Internet Small Computer System Interface (iSCSI). This chapter views the hard drive in the same way that the computer industry does within the limitations of Windows. A hard drive need not contain spinning disks or even appear as part of your system to use many of these utilities, but the device must adhere to the basic principles of hard drives. In most cases, that means using a track layout, partitioning scheme, provide random access, use File Allocation Table (FAT) or NTFS as a formatting scheme, and all of the other criteria you've used in the past.

In this chapter, you'll learn how to do the following:

◆ Manage an existing hard drive configuration

◆ Convert FAT partitions to use NTFS

◆ Create and manage hard drive partitions

◆ Work with RAID configurations

◆ Work with iSCSI configurations

◆ Improve hard drive performance

Opening Remote Directories with the Append Utility

The Append utility lets you open multiple directories as if they exist in the current directory. In short, this utility lets you consolidate several directories into a single directory on the hard drive. The other directories don't actually appear in the current directory; the Append utility only makes them appear that they do. This utility uses the following syntax:

```
APPEND [[drive:]path[;...]] [/X[:ON | :OFF]] [/PATH:ON | /PATH:OFF] [/E]
```

The following list describes each of the command line arguments.

drive: Specifies the drive you want to use to append directories. The drive is always a letter. If you want to use a drive on another machine, you must first map the drive using Windows and then use the mapped drive letter for access.

path   Contains one or more paths on the drive that you specify. Separate multiple paths using a semicolon (;). If you want to append paths from multiple drives, you must execute the Append utility multiple times, once for each drive.

/X:ON or X:OFF   Defines whether you can use the appended path to perform file searches and application execution or just to open files. The default setting is X:OFF, which only allows you to use the appended path to open files.

/PATH:ON or /PATH:OFF   Determines whether the appended path is included with commands that rely on a path. For example, if you have C:\Temp included within the path statement and use /PATH:ON with the Append utility, any requests to C:\Temp automatically include the appended path as well. However, if you select /PATH:OFF, the appended paths aren't included as part of the path. The default setting is /PATH:ON.

/E   Stores all of the appended directories in an environment variable named APPEND. You can only use this command line switch the first time you execute Append within a particular command line window. However, other command line windows aren't affected by this command line switch; the APPEND environment variable only exists within the command line window in which you executed the Append utility and only for the time the command line window is open.

Executing Append with just a semicolon clears all of the appended paths for a particular directory. Running Append by itself lists the appended paths for a particular directory.

NOTE   Windows XP and above ignores the results of the Append utility. Microsoft supplies the Append command in these versions of Windows for DOS batch file compatibility. When the appended directory feature is important, store the appended directories in the APPEND environment variable using the /E command line switch and then use the environment variable to search for files in other directories. As an alternative, you can employ data redirection (see the "Employing Data Redirection" section Chapter 14 for details). The Subst utility can also help by assigning long paths to a drive letter. You can also employ some direct substitutes for the Append utility, such as the shared folder redirection technique discussed at http://windowsxp.mvps.org/ sharedfolders.htm (the TweakUI utility provided by Microsoft at http://www.microsoft .com/windowsxp/downloads/powertoys/default.mspx makes this process easier by providing a graphical interface). Consider modifying the path as described in the "Setting and Viewing Application Paths with the *Path* Command" section to make executables accessible.

Determining the Current Directory and Changing Directories with the CD and *ChDir* Commands

The CD and ChDir commands perform the same two tasks. First, you can use these commands to establish your current location at the command line. Second, you can use these commands to move to another directory. You can display the current directory by typing CD or ChDir without any arguments and pressing Enter. These commands use the following syntax:

```
CHDIR [/D] [drive:][path]
CHDIR [..]
```

```
CD [/D] [drive:][path]
CD [..]
```

The following list describes each of the command line arguments.

drive   Specifies the new drive. The default is the current drive.

path   Specifies the relative or absolute path of the new directory. The default is the current directory. You can use a double period (. .) to specify the parent directory of the current directory.

/D   Changes the current drive as well as the directory.

Converting FAT Partitions to NTFS with the Convert Utility

At some point, you may need to convert a hard drive formatted using the FAT format into one that uses NTFS. However, this task is becoming less common as people move from Windows 9x to Windows NT–based operating systems. Newer machines usually come with NTFS installed. In fact, the number of existing systems with FAT installed diminishes every day, so you'll eventually be able to forget about the Convert utility as a relic of some bygone era. However, for now, you'll still need to convert hard drives from one format to another.

The Convert utility is unique in that it relies on three other utilities to perform its work: AutoConv (automates the file system conversion during reboots), AutoFmt (automates the file formatting process during reboots), and AutoLfn (automates the conversion of long filenames). These executables exist in the \Windows\System32 directory, but you can't use them at the command prompt. When you try to execute them, you'll see an error message, such as "The C:\WINDOWS\ system32\autolfn.exe application cannot be run in Win32 mode." The reason you need to know about these three utilities, even though you'll never use them from the command line, is that some misguided individuals have marked them as viruses and will attempt to tell you that these files are a source of infection. Not all of the utilities in the \Windows\System32 directory execute from the command line.

NOTE   Convert can't update the boot drive of your system immediately because the drive is locked by the operating system. However, the Convert utility will offer to mark the drive for conversion during the next boot cycle when the system hasn't locked the drive. Your system must have access to the AutoConv, AutoFmt, and AutoLfn utilities to perform the conversion during a boot or the conversion will fail. The system normally recovers from this error, but it's better to check for the presence of the required utilities at the outset.

You actually control the activities of the AutoConv, AutoFmt, and AutoLfn utilities through the Convert utility. The Convert utility helps you set up everything, and then you let the system handle the details automatically. This utility uses the following syntax:

```
CONVERT volume /FS:NTFS [/V] [/CvtArea:filename] [/NoSecurity] [/X]
```

The following list describes each of the command line arguments.

volume   Specifies the drive letter (include the colon), mount point, or volume name to convert.

/FS:NTFS   Specifies that you want the volume converted to NTFS.

/V   Performs the conversion in verbose mode. Normally, the utility only displays initialization and error messages. The verbose mode provides a number of supplemental messages.

/CvtArea:*filename* Specifies a contiguous file (one that isn't fragmented) in the root directory that you want to use as a placeholder for the NTFS system files. Using this technique can help avert some of the performance degradation that normally occurs with a converted drive.

/NoSecurity Sets the converted files and directories to give the Everyone group full access. This setting means that everyone can access the files and circumvent the security features that NTFS can provide. Make sure you set security to reasonable levels of access after the conversion.

/X Forces the volume to dismount (become inaccessible) prior to conversion if necessary. The system closes all handles to the volume, which means any open files become inaccessible as well.

Converted drives don't always perform as well as drives that you created as NTFS drives from the outset. The main problem is that the Convert utility may not be able to place the Master File Table (MFT) in the same location as it would appear on a drive that's formatted with NTFS at the outset. The additional head movement causes the drop in performance. The converted drive security setup may differ from the original drive as well. Make sure you read the Knowledge Base article at `http://support.microsoft.com/kb/237399` for additional information about security changes that can occur as the result of a conversion.

Improving Disk Access Performance with the Defrag Utility

As your hard drive processes files, it becomes fragmented; a file may appear in several segments on the hard drive. Moving the disk head to read each of these file segments is time consuming and hurts the performance of your system. Windows provides a graphical interface for defragmenting your hard drive, but using the command line interface can be more efficient, especially when you automate the process so that it starts automatically. This utility uses the following syntax:

```
defrag <volume> -a [-v]
defrag <volume> [{-r | -w}] [-f] [-v]
defrag        -c [{-r | -w}] [-f] [-v]
```

The following list describes each of the command line arguments.

volume Specifies the drive letter or mount point to defragment.

-a Performs only an analysis of the drive. The analysis tells you whether the drive requires defragmentation, but doesn't actually perform the task. The output information includes the fragmentation percentage, which you can use as an indicator of drive condition. Don't use this command line option when you want to automate the defragmentation process.

-f Forces a defragmentation, even if the drive or mount point free space is low. Normally, the Defrag utility requires 15 percent free space to perform a complete defragmentation. Using this command line switch lets you perform a partial defragmentation when the free space is less than optimal.

-v Displays additional information about the defragmentation process.

-r Performs a partial defragmentation, which runs faster, but doesn't assure the hard drive will run at peak efficiency. Defrag only consolidates fragments smaller than 64 MB. This is the default setting under Server Core.

-w Performs a full defragmentation of the drive regardless of fragment size. Although this option can improve performance on heavily fragmented drives, you pay a penalty in additional defragmentation time.

-c   Performs defragmentation of all drives on the system. Combine this command line switch with the -w or -r command line switch to specify the level of defragmentation.

Managing Partitions with the DiskPart Command

The DiskPart command lets you manage partitions on your hard drive without relying on the graphical utilities. In some cases, this utility is your only resource when the graphical environment isn't running and you need to make a repair. You can use DiskPart with direct command line input or supply a text file containing a script of actions for DiskPart to perform. You'll usually have a better experience with DiskPart if you create a script to perform the required tasks. Using a script reduces the potential for error. To use a script, type **DiskPart /s *ScriptName*** and press Enter. Otherwise, start the command line version of DiskPart by typing **DiskPart** and pressing Enter. You'll see the DISKPART> prompt where you enter the specific subcommands described in the following list.

active   Marks the partition with focus as active. Making a partition active informs the Basic Input/Output System (BIOS) or Extensible Firmware Interface (EFI) that the partition is a valid system partition that the system can use to boot. If you mark a partition that doesn't contain system files active, the system may not boot. DiskPart doesn't check your partition selection for accuracy.

add disk=*n* [noerr]   Mirrors a simple volume with the focus set to the specified disk. The disk must contain enough unallocated space to match the size of the simple volume that you want to mirror.

NOTE   Use the noerr option only with scripts. Normally, a script ends when it encounters an error. Using the noerr option lets the script continue running.

assign [{letter=D | mount=Path}] [noerr]   Assigns a drive letter or mount point to the volume with focus. If you don't specify a drive letter or mount point, the utility uses the next available drive letter. The utility generates an error when you attempt to assign an existing drive letter to the volume. The system won't allow you to assign drive letters to system volumes, boot volumes, or volumes that contain the paging file. In addition, you can't assign a drive letter to an Original Equipment Manufacturer (OEM) partition or any GUID Partition Table (GPT) partition other than a basic data partition.

attributes *volume* [{set | clear}] [{hidden | readonly | nodefaultdriveletter | shadowcopy}] [noerr]   Displays, sets, or clears attributes on the specified volume. This command is only available on Windows 2003 and above systems. Use attributes with a volume specification alone to see the attributes for that volume. The set option adds an attribute, while the clear option removes the attribute. The hidden attribute hides the volume from view, while the readonly attribute makes it impossible for the user to write to the volume. The nodefaultdriveletter attribute prevents the drive from receiving a drive letter during the boot cycle. Generally, there isn't a good reason to use this feature unless you want to create an invisible drive for a specific reason, such as a ghost backup of the system. The shadowcopy attribute defines the drive as a shadow copy of another drive. You can obtain a good overview of the Windows Volume Shadow copy Service (VSS) at http://computerperformance.co.uk/w2k3/disaster_volume_shadow.htm.

automount [enable] [disable] [scrub] [noerr]   Defines the automatic mounting functionality that Windows provides. Normally, Windows automatically mounts any new basic disks that it finds during the boot cycle. The enable option enables automatic basic disk mounting. The disable option disables the automatic mounting feature. The scrub object removes any mount point directories and registry settings for volumes that are no longer in the system. This feature ensures that each new drive that you mount or remount receives a clean setup and that Windows doesn't attempt to use old and possibly incorrect settings. This command is only available on Windows 2003 and above systems.

break disk disk=N [nokeep] [noerr]   Breaks mirrored volumes into two simple volumes. You can only use this command with dynamic disks. The first disk in the set retains the current drive letter and any mount points. The second disk receives the focus so that you can assign it a new drive letter. The nokeep option tells the utility to free any data on the second disk. The second disk becomes a new empty disk that you can format and use as a simple volume.

clean [all]   Removes the partition and volume formatting on the disk with focus. The system overwrites the Master Boot Record (MBR) partitioning information and hidden section information on MBR disks. The system overwrites the GPT partitioning information, including the Protective MBR, on GPT disks. A GPT disk doesn't include hidden sector information. The system completely erases the disk when you use the all option.

convert basic [noerr]   Converts an empty dynamic disk into a basic disk.

NOTE   The system won't convert a disk that has data on it. Back up the hard drive data and remove the partitions and volumes before you perform a conversion. This same note holds true for any conversion you want to perform.

convert dynamic [noerr]   Converts an empty basic disk into a dynamic disk.

convert gpt [noerr]   Converts an empty basic disk that relies on the MBR partition style into an empty basic disk that relies on the GPT partition style.

TIP   The GPT partition style has significant advantages over the MBR partition style. See the Microsoft article at http://technet.microsoft.com/en-us/library/bb457110.aspx for a comparison of the two technologies.

convert mbr [noerr]   Converts an empty basic disk that relies on the GPT partition style into an empty basic disk that relies on the MBR partition style.

create partition efi [size=N] [offset=N] [noerr]   Creates an EFI partition on a GPT disk. You must have an Itanium computer to use this feature. The utility gives the new partition the focus once the system creates it. The size argument defines the size of the partition in megabytes. The utility uses all of the free space on the disk when you don't specify this option. The offset argument defines the byte offset of the new partition. If you don't specify an offset, the utility creates the partition at the beginning of the first disk extant that's large enough to hold it.

create partition extended [size=N] [offset=N] [noerr]   Creates an extended partition on the current drive. The utility gives the new partition the focus once the system creates it. A disk can only have one extended partition. You must create an extended partition before you can create logical drives. The size argument defines the size of the partition. For example, if you specify a size of 500 MB, the system rounds the size of the partition up to 504 MB. The system uses all of the free space on the disk when you don't define a partition size. The offset only affects MBR disks. The offset defines the byte offset of the partition. If you don't specify an offset, the partition begins at the beginning of the free space on the disk. The system snaps the partition size to the cylinder size; it rounds the offset to the closest cylinder boundary. For example, if you specify an offset that's 27 MB and the cylinder size is 8 MB, the system rounds the offset to the 24 MB boundary.

`create partition logical [size=N] [offset=N] [noerr]` Creates a logical disk within an extended partition. The utility gives the new partition the focus once the system creates it. The system snaps the partition size to the cylinder size. For example, if you specify a size of 500 MB, the system rounds up the size of the partition to 504 MB. The system uses all of the free space on the disk when you don't define a partition size. The offset only affects MBR disks. The offset defines the byte offset of the partition. If you don't specify an offset, the partition begins at the beginning of the extended partition. The offset you specify must allow enough room for the partition defined by the size argument. If the offset won't allow enough space, the system changes the offset so that the logical disk can fit within the extended partition.

`create partition msr [size=N] [offset=N] [noerr]` Creates a Microsoft Reserved (MSR) partition on a GPT disk. The size argument defines the size of the partition in MB. The utility uses all of the free space on the disk when you don't specify this option. The offset argument defines the byte offset of the new partition. If you don't specify an offset, the utility creates the partition at the beginning of the first disk extant that's large enough to hold it. The offset is sector snapped. The system rounds up the value of the offset to fill an entire sector.

WARNING MSR partitions can cause a number of problems. The most significant problem is that Itanium computers won't mount an MSR partition. This means you can't store data on the partition or delete it; the partition ends up wasting space on the disk. In addition, GTP disks require a specific partition layout. Adding an MSR partition could disrupt the layout and make the disk unreadable. On GPT disks used to start Windows XP 64-bit Edition (Itanium), the EFI System partition is the first partition on the disk, followed by the MSR partition. GPT disks used only for data storage don't have an EFI System partition; the MSR partition is the first partition.

`create partition primary[size=N] [offset=N] [ID={Byte | GUID}] [align=N] [noerr]` Creates a primary partition on a disk. The utility gives the new partition the focus once the system creates it. The system snaps the partition size to the cylinder size. For example, if you specify a size of 500 MB, the system rounds up the size of the partition to 504 MB. The system uses all of the free space on the disk when you don't define a partition size. The offset only affects MBR disks. The offset defines the byte offset of the partition. If you don't specify an offset, the partition begins at the beginning of the extended partition. The offset you specify must allow enough room for the partition defined by the size argument. Microsoft sets the ID argument aside for OEMs. Never specify an ID for a GPT disk. Use the create partition EFI and create partition MSR as needed to set up GPT disks. When working with an MBR disk, you can use the ID to set the disk type. The MBR values include C12A7328-F81F-11D2-BA4B-00A0C93EC93B (EFI system partition), E3C9E316-0B5C-4DB8-817D-F92DF00215AE (MSR partition), EBD0A0A2-B9E5-4433-87C0-68B6B72699C7 (basic data partition), 5808C8AA-7E8F-42E0-85D2-E1E90434CFB3 (LDM Metadata partition on a dynamic disk), and AF9B60A0-1431-4F62-BC68-3311714A69AD (LDM Data partition on a dynamic disk). The `align` argument specifies the alignment of the primary partition on a disk that isn't cylinder aligned. You normally use this value for hardware Redundant Array of Inexpensive Disks (RAID) setups to improve performance. The value is the number of kilobytes from the beginning of the disk to the closest alignment boundary.

`create volume raid [size=N] disk=N,N,N[,N,...] [noerr]` Creates a RAID-5 volume based on three or more dynamic disks. The utility automatically changes focus to the new volume once the system creates it. The `size` argument specifies the amount of space that the

RAID-5 volume consumes on each drive. When you don't specify the size, the utility creates the largest possible RAID-5 volume by using the maximum space on the smallest volume (or the maximum available space when the drives are the same size). The RAID-5 volume consumes the same amount of space on each disk. The `disk` argument defines which disks to use in the RAID-5 volume. The volume must contain at least three drives simply because of the way that RAID-5 works (you can find an overview of the various RAID levels at `http://www.microsoft.com/technet/ prodtechnol/exchange/guides/E2k3HighAvGuide/02ed19b2-d2b3-4f77-8835-b4b0dd2f68f5 .mspx`).

`create volume simple [size=N] [disk=N] [noerr]`   Creates a simple volume. The utility automatically changes focus to the new volume once the system creates it. The size argument defines the size of the volume in megabytes. The utility uses the entire free space on the disk when you don't specify the size argument. The disk argument specifies the disk to receive the new volume. The utility uses the current disk when you don't specify the disk option.

`create volume stripe [size=N] disk=N,N[,N,...] [noerr]`   Creates a striped volume using two or more dynamic disks. The utility automatically changes focus to the new volume once the system creates it. The `size` argument defines the amount of space the volume consumes on each drive. Every drive provides precisely the same amount of space toward the total volume size. The system uses all of the free space on the smallest drive when you don't provide the `size` argument. The `disk` argument specifies the drives to use to create the striped set. You must provide a minimum of two drives for a striped set.

`delete disk [noerr] [override]`   Removes a missing dynamic disk from the disk list. The override option enables DiskPart to remove all of the simple volumes on a disk. When the disk contains half a mirrored volume, the system removes the half of the mirrored volume. This command fails on RAID-5 volumes.

`delete partition [noerr] [override]`   Removes the partition with focus from the drive. You can't delete the system partition, boot partition, or any partition that contains the active paging file or crash dump (memory dump). Use the override argument to allow DiskPart to remove partitions of any type on a drive. Normally, DiskPart removes only data partitions from the drive.

WARNING   Deleting a partition on a dynamic disk could delete all of the volumes on the disk and leave the disk in an unusable state. Always remove volumes on a dynamic disk using the `delete volume` command.

`delete volume [noerr]`   Deletes the volume with focus from the drive. You can't delete the system volume, boot volume, or any volume that contains the active paging file or crash dump (memory dump).

`detail disk`   Displays the properties of the disk with focus. In addition, this command shows any volumes on the disk.

`detail partition`   Displays the properties of the partition with focus.

`detail volume`   Displays the disks on which the current volume resides. You can use this command with a volume that spans multiple disks, such as a mirrored, striped, or RAID-5 volume.

`exit`   Terminates the DiskPart session.

extend [size=*N***] [disk=***N***] [noerr]**   Extends the currently selected volume into the next contiguous unallocated space. The unallocated space must appear on the same disk. The unallocated space must also appear after the current partition; the sector number of the unallocated space must be higher than the sector number of the currently selected volume. This command only works for NTFS-formatted volumes. The size argument defines the amount of space to add to the current partition. If you don't specify the size argument, the system uses all of the contiguous unallocated space. The disk argument applies to dynamic disks. Use this argument to specify the dynamic disk to use to extend the volume. If you don't specify the disk argument, the system uses the current disk.

gpt attributes=*N***   Applies the specified attributes to a GPT disk. The GPT attribute field is 64-bits long and contains two subfields. The higher subfield applies only to partition identifiers; the lower subfield applies to all identifiers. Currently, the file system only supports two attributes. The 0x0000000000000001 attribute defines a required partition. Adding this attribute means that disk utilities won't delete the partition for any reason. The 0x8000000000000000 attribute tells the system not to automatically assign the drive a drive letter. The main purpose for this attribute is to ensure the system won't automatically assign a drive letter when you move the drive to another machine. Using this feature allows the user of the other machine to assign a drive letter based on that machine's configuration. This command is only available on Windows 2003 and above systems.

help   Displays a list of DiskPart commands.

import [noerr]   Imports a foreign disk group into the local computer's disk group. This command imports every disk that's in the same group as the disk that has focus.

inactive   Marks the current MBR disk partition inactive, which means you can no longer boot from the partition. When the computer reboots, the system starts using the next available boot option specified in the BIOS, such as a CD-ROM drive or a Pre-Boot eXecution Environment (PXE)–based boot environment. A PXE can include Remote Installation Services (RIS). Some computers won't restart without an active partition, so use this command with care. If you're unable to start your computer after marking the system or boot partition as inactive, insert the Setup CD in the CD-ROM drive, restart the computer, and repair the partition using the FixMBR and FixBoot utilities from the Recovery Console.

list disk   Lists the disks installed and detected for the current machine. The output includes the disk number, disk status, total disk size, amount of free space, whether the disk is basic or dynamic, and the GPT style. The disk with the asterisk (*) is the one with focus.

list partition   Lists the partitions for the currently selected disk. The output includes the partition number, the partition size, the partition type, and the offset of the partition from the beginning of the disk. On dynamic disks, these partitions may not correspond to the dynamic volumes on the disk. This discrepancy occurs because dynamic disks contain entries in the partition table for the system volume or boot volume (if present on the disk). The partition with the asterisk (*) is the one with focus.

list volume   Lists the volumes on all disks for the current machine. The output includes the volume number, the volume drive letter, the volume label, the file system used to support the volume, the volume type (such as partition, DVD-ROM, or CD-ROM), the volume size, the volume status, and information about the volume purpose (such as a system or a boot drive). The volume with the asterisk (*) is the one with focus.

online [noerr]   Brings the offline volume with focus online. This command also resynchronizes the mirrored or RAID-5 volume.

rem   Provides a means for making comments in scripts. You won't use this command in interactive mode.

remove [{letter=D | mount=Path | all}] [dismount] [noerr]   Removes a drive letter or mount point from the drive with focus. If you don't specify a drive letter or mount point, the utility removes the first drive letter or mount point that it encounters. The letter option specifies the drive letter that you want to remove. The mount option specifies the path of the mount point that you want to remove. Use the all option to remove all of the drive letters and mount paths for a drive. The dismount option takes the drive offline when it no longer has any drive letters or mount points assigned to it. You can't access a dismounted drive. You can't remove the drive letters on system, boot, or paging volumes, OEM partition, any GPT partition with an unrecognized GUID, or any of the special, nondata, GPT partitions such as the EFI system partition.

repair disk=N [noerr]   Repairs the RAID-5 volume with focus by replacing a failed RAID-5 member with the specified dynamic disk. The new disk must have free space equal to or greater than the disk that it replaces.

rescan   Locates any new disks that you've added to the computer.

retain   Prepares an existing simple volume for use as a boot or system volume. When working with an MBR disk, the utility adds the partition entry to the MBR. The dynamic system volume must begin at a cylinder-aligned offset and be an integral number of cylinders in size. When working with a GPT disk, the utility creates a partition entry in the GPT.

select disk[=n]   Selects the specified disk and gives it focus. If you don't provide a number, the utility lists the drive that has the focus.

select partition[=n]   Selects the specified partition and gives it focus. If you don't provide a number, the utility lists the partition that has the focus.

select volume[={n | d }]   Selects the specified volume and gives it focus. You may provide either a volume number or a drive letter as input. If you don't provide a number or letter, the utility lists the volume that has the focus.

Managing Disk Performance with the DiskPerf Utility

The original purpose of the DiskPerf utility was to help you control monitoring of disk performance on your computer. However, systems later than Windows 2000 keep the counters used to monitor performance enabled permanently. Consequently, the main purpose this utility serves on later systems is to let you see which performance counters Windows provides, which is still a useful function when you want to monitor these counters at the command line.

The DiskPerf utility can also temporarily disable the performance counters. You can use this feature with older applications that rely on the Windows Application Programming Interface (API) IOCTL_DISK_PERFORMANCE() function to retrieve raw counter information (see the description of this function at http://msdn2.microsoft.com/en-us/library/aa365183.aspx). Don't reboot the system when you disable the counters because the effect is temporary; rebooting the machine simply removes the effect. This utility uses the following syntax:

```
DISKPERF [-Y[D|V] | -N[D|V]] [\\computername]
```

The following list describes each of the command line arguments.

-Y Sets the system to start all performance counters when you start the system on older systems. This command line switch restarts all of the disk performance counters on Windows 2000 and above systems. The performance counters always start automatically on these systems after a reboot.

-YD Enables the disk performance counters for physical drives when you start the system.

-YV Enables the disk performance counters for logical drives or storage volumes when you start the system.

-N Sets the system to disable all performance counters when you start the system on older systems. This command temporarily disables all of the disk performance counters on Windows 2000 and later systems.

-ND Disables the performance counters for physical drives.

-NV Disables the disk performance counters for logical drives.

\\\computername Specifies the name of the computer. Using this argument alone lets you see the list of disk performance counters. Adding a command line switch changes the performance counter setting.

Managing RAID Setups Using the DiskRAID Utility

The DiskRAID utility helps you work with any Redundant Array of Inexpensive Disks (RAID) hardware on your system. However, there are some caveats for using this utility. The biggest problem is that your system must have the appropriate Virtual Disk Service (VDS) drivers installed—something not all vendors support. In addition, except for the command line syntax, the VDS software apparently has vendor-specific commands. Consequently, you'll need to refer to the vendor documentation to use this utility fully. This utility uses the following syntax:

```
DISKRAID [/? | [/s <file-path>] [/v]]
```

The following list describes each of the command line arguments.

/? Displays the DiskRAID usage instructions.

/s _file-path_ Specifies the location of a file containing commands that DiskRAID should execute. The instructions found in this script file depend on the vendor implementation.

/v Executes all DiskRAID commands in verbose mode. You'll see additional output. The amount and type of information depends on the vendor implementation.

Managing the File System with the FltMC Utility

The Filter Manager Control (FltMC) utility tracks minifilters attached to your hard drive or other storage system (such as a DVD drive). You'll often see this utility included as part of a Windows service pack. However, it usually does its work and ends. A minifilter controls what a drive sees, which means that a minifilter could help control viruses by rejecting virus content. Here are the types of filters that Microsoft provides support for in storage applications.

- Activity Monitor
- Undelete
- Antivirus
- Replication

- Continuous Backup
- Content Screener
- Quota Management
- System Recovery
- Cluster File System
- Hierarchical Storage Manager (HSM)
- Compression
- Encryption
- Physical Quota Management
- Open File
- Security Enhancer
- Copy Protection

Generally, you won't need to use this utility unless you want to see which minifilters are running on your system or your storage vendor provides an update that you must install manually. You can use the FltMC in several modes to load, unload, attach, detach, and list filters. The following sections describe the modes that FltMC supports.

Load

Use this mode to load a filter driver. Loading the driver doesn't activate it. This mode uses the following syntax:

```
FltMC Load [driverName]
```

The following describes the command line argument.

driverName Specifies the name of the file that contains the driver that you want to load.

Unload

Use this mode to unload an inactive driver. The utility won't unload a driver that's in use. This mode uses the following syntax:

```
FltMC Unload [driverName]
```

The following describes the command line argument.

driverName Specifies the name of the file that contains the driver that you want to unload.

Filters

Use this mode to list the filters installed on your machine. These filters are loaded, but not necessarily active. Use the Instances mode to see which filters are active. This mode uses the following syntax:

```
FltMC Filters
```

Instances

Use this mode to list the active filters on your machine. These filters are loaded and have at least one instance attached to a particular volume. A filter may have multiple instances. This mode uses the following syntax:

```
FltMC Instances
```

Volumes

Use this mode to list the volumes that have a filter instance attached. This mode uses the following syntax:

```
FltMC Volumes
```

Attach

Use this mode to attach a filter that you've loaded into memory to a particular volume. You can assign the instance (the attachment of a filter to a volume) a specific name. In addition, you can also specify an altitude when you obtain this information from the minifilter vendor. The altitude determines the minifilter's order in the minifilter attachment stack, which determines when the minifilter sees data sent to the storage device. This mode uses the following syntax:

```
FltMC Attach [filterName] [volumeName] [[-i instanceName ][-a altitude]]
```

The following list describes each of the command line arguments.

filterName Specifies the name of the filter that's been loaded into memory using the Load mode.

volumeName Specifies the name of the volume, such as C:, that will have the filter attached.

-i *instanceName* Specifies the name of the instance. When the utility is successful in attaching the minifilter to the volume, it displays the resulting instance name.

-a *altitude* Specifies the altitude of the minifilter when compared to other minifilters in the stack. Microsoft controls the altitude information and you'll receive this information (when required) from the minifilter vendor. Normally, this information appears as part of the registry entries for the minifilter.

Detach

Use this mode to detach a minifilter from a storage device that you previously attached using the Attach mode. This mode uses the following syntax:

```
FltMC detach [filterName] [volumeName] [instanceName]
```

The following list describes each of the command line arguments.

filterName Specifies the name of the filter that's been loaded into memory using the Load mode.

volumeName Specifies the name of the volume, such as C:, that will have the filter detached.

instanceName Specifies the name of the instance to remove. If you don't supply an instance, the utility removes the default instance.

Monitoring the File System with the *FSUtil* Command

Many people take the file system for granted. After all, it just stores data on disk. However, the file system is a lot more complex than you might initially think. Not only does it have to read and write data, it also must create, delete, and edit files. The file system has to track directories and perform a number of other management tasks. It has to do all this without losing a single bit. It isn't until you start working with a utility such as File System Utility (FSUtil) that you begin to understand just how complex the file system is. FSUtil provides several modes of operation including:

- Behavior
- Dirty
- File
- FSInfo
- Hardlink
- ObjectID
- Quota
- Repair
- ReparsePoint
- Resource
- Sparse
- Transaction
- USN
- Volume

Each of these modes helps you manage a different aspect of the file system. For example, the behavior mode queries and sets the file system behavior parameters and controls how the file system reacts in a given situation. The following sections describe each of these operational modes in detail.

Behavior

The Behavior mode controls how the file system works. For example, you can modify the use of the older DOS 8-character filename, with 3-character file extension. This mode uses the following syntax:

```
FSUtil Behavior Query [allowextchar] [disable8dot3]
    [disablecompression] [disableencryption] [disablelastaccess]
    [encryptpagingfile] [mftzone] [memoryusage] [quotanotify]
    [SymlinkEvaluation]
FSUtil Behavior Set [allowextchar {1 | 0}] [disable8dot3 {1 | 0}]
    [disablecompression {1 | 0}] [disableencryption {1 | 0}]
    [disablelastaccess {1 | 0}] [encryptpagingfile {1 | 0}]
    [mftzone Zone] [memoryusage Value] [quotanotify Value]
    [SymlinkEvaluation [L2L:{0|1}] | [L2R:{0|1}] | [R2R:{0|1}] |
    [R2L:{0|1}]]
```

When querying a value, all you supply is the option name. However, when you set an option, you must also provide a new value. The following list describes each of the command line arguments.

allowextchar {1 | 0} Determines whether you can use extended characters, including diacritic characters used for languages other than English, in the short filenames on NTFS volumes. The default setting doesn't provide a value for this option. Setting the value to 1, or true, allows you to use the extended character set.

disable8dot3 {1 | 0} Determines whether Windows supports older DOS naming conventions or uses extended filenames exclusively. The older DOS naming conventions relied on an 8-character filename and a 3-character file extension. Disabling this support could cause some older applications to fail. The default value is 0, or false, which means that the older DOS naming convention is available.

disablecompression {1 | 0} Disables compression for the affected file system object. The default value is 0, or false, which means that compression is available.

disableencryption {1 | 0} Disables data encryption for the affected file system object. The default value is 0, or false, which means that encryption is available.

disablelastaccess {1 | 0} Determines whether Windows changes the last access time stamp for a directory or file each time you list the directory contents on an NTFS volume. The default setting doesn't provide a value for this option. Setting this option to 1, or true, will increase disk performance slightly, but then you'll lack last access time statistics when working with the drive.

encryptpagingfile {1 | 0} Encrypts the paging file to ensure third parties can't obtain information about your system by reading it. For example, it may be possible to read passwords as part of the paging file under certain conditions. Using this setting incurs a significant performance penalty. The default value is 0, or false, which means that the paging file isn't encrypted.

mftzone _Zone_ Changes the MFT zone value. Learn more about the MFT at `http://www.microsoft.com/technet/prodtechnol/windows2000serv/reskit/prork/prdf_fls_xkhv.mspx?mfr=true`. The Windows NT File System (NTFS) normally sets aside 12.5 percent of the disk (zone 1) to hold the MFT so that it doesn't become fragmented. Generally, this value provides more than sufficient space for data entries. Each zone (values 1 through 4) provides additional space for the MFT: 1 (12.5 percent), 2 (25 percent), 3 (37.5 percent), and 4 (50 percent). Any change to the MFT zone won't take effect until you reboot the system. Generally, you want to set this value before you do anything else with a new hard drive to ensure the MFT zone doesn't become fragmented.

memoryusage _Value_ Controls the amount of paged memory used for file operations. The default value of 1 uses the default amount of paged memory for file operations. Setting the value to 2 increases the amount of paged memory available for file operations. However, this feature can have unwanted side effects. The added file operation memory only nets increased performance when you don't take paged memory away from other areas of the operation system. Generally, you'll need to experiment with this setting and monitor its effect on overall system performance before you make it permanent.

quotanotify _Value_ Defines the interval between disk quota violation checks on an NTFS drive. The disk quota system ensures that a user doesn't use more resources than the administrator allows. The default setting is 3,600 seconds or 1 hour when you enable the quota system. You can supply any value between 1 second and 4,294,967,295 seconds. Longer intervals enhance system performance, but could result in more quota violations.

SymlinkEvaluation [L2L:{0|1}] | [L2R:{0|1}] | [R2R:{0|1}] | [R2L:{0|1}]
Determines the use of symbolic links within the operating system. You can individually set the use of local-to-local (L2L), local-to-remote (L2R), remote-to-remote (R2R), and remote-to-local (R2L) links. The default value for L2L and L2R is 1, or true, which means that these symbolic links are enabled. The default value for R2R and R2L links is 0, or false, which means that you can't create these link types.

Dirty

Use this mode to check or set the dirty bit for a volume. The system automatically performs an AutoChk whenever it detects the dirty bit during startup. The AutoChk utility looks for drive errors. This mode uses the following syntax:

```
FSUtil Dirty Query Volume
FSUtil Dirty Set Volume
```

The following describes the command line argument.

Volume Determines the NTFS volume to check during the next reboot. This utility only works with local volumes, so you can't query or set the dirty bit on a remote volume.

File

The file mode lets you perform tasks with files. Some of the tasks are quite mundane. For example, you can create a new file of a specific size. The file mode will even fill the file with zeros for you. Other tasks are unique. The findbysid argument lets you locate a file using its Security Identifier (SID). This mode uses the following syntax:

```
FSUtil File [findbysid UserName Directory] [queryallocranges
Offset=StartRange Length=RangeLength Filename] [setshortname Filename
ShortFilename] [setvaliddata Filename DataLength] [setzerodata
Offset=StartRange Length=RangeLength Filename] [createnew Filename Length]
```

The following list describes each of the command line arguments.

findbysid *UserName Directory* Locates a file based on the user's SID. The **username** argument contains a local user's name, which the operating system maps to the SID. FSUtil then locates the file based on this SID in the directory supplied. Unlike other command line utilities, this one lets you search for files that belong to specific users on an NTFS volume.

queryallocranges Offset=*StartRange* Length=*RangeLength* *Filename* Displays a list of allocated ranges within the specified file. The **Offset** argument defines the starting point of the search, while the **Length** argument specifies the length of the search. You can use this command to locate sparse regions within files. See the "Understanding Sparse Files" sidebar for additional information.

setshortname *Filename ShortFilename* Sets the short (DOS) filename for a file. The short filename must fall within the 8-character filename and 3-character extension limitations. The **Dir** command won't normally display the results of this command. However, using the /X command line switch with the **Dir** command displays both the long and the short filename.

setvaliddata *Filename DataLength* Sets the valid data length for a file. The Valid Data Length (VDL) is the length of the valid data within a file, rather than the actual file length as indicated by an End Of File (EOF) marker. The data between the VDL and the EOF may contain data, as in a download cache, but any query to that data returns a 0 since the data isn't valid. Because of the low-level nature of this particular argument, only administrators with the SetManageVolumePrivilege can execute it.

setzerodata Offset=*StartRange* Length=*RangeLength* *Filename* Changes the data bits within a file to 0. This is an excellent method of clearing a file before deleting it for security reasons (deleting a file retains the data on disk; Windows only removes the directory entries, making the file recoverable). The start range determines the starting point within the file for writing zeros. The start of the file is 0, but you can use any range up to the size of the file in bytes. The range length determines how many zeros to write. This value must be less than or equal to the length of the file minus the start range value.

createnew *Filename* *Length* Creates a new file that FSUtil fills with zeros. You must include a filename and the length of the file. Because these files are zeroed, they make excellent test files for other file utilities.

UNDERSTANDING SPARSE FILES

It's possible for a file to contain some data in addition to large ranges of zeros (or null data). A cache file could fall into this category. You might allocate 1 MB for the cache, but the cache file could contain only a little data; the rest of the file contains zeros. The part of the file that contains zeros wastes disk space. There's no reason to allocate an entire 1 MB storage location for a file that contains 10 KB of data. The term for such a file is *sparse*. Generally, you want to manage sparse files so they use the minimum space necessary, yet continue to provide full functionality to the application that creates the sparse file.

The most common Windows application that uses sparse files is the indexing service. You define the size of the catalogs as part of creating a new catalog. However, the catalog might not actually contain that much information. Rather than waste the disk space, the indexing service uses a sparse file to hold the catalog.

Sparse files require special handling. The FSUtil command provides a number of special commands to work with sparse files. For example, you can use the queryallocranges argument of the file mode to locate sparse files on the hard drive. Likewise, the sparse mode arguments help you manage sparse files. For example, you can use this mode to set a sparse range within a file. You can learn more about sparse files on the Microsoft Web site at http://technet.microsoft.com/en-us/library/ Bb457112.aspx.

FSInfo

This mode is one of the more interesting and immediately usable modes. It provides you with statistics regarding the file system. For example, you can use it to obtain a list of active drives on the current system. You could redirect this list to a text file for use with a script or output it to a batch file to perform a task on every attached drive. This mode uses the following syntax:

```
FSUtil FSInfo [drives] [drivetype Volume] [volumeinfo Volume]
[ntfsinfo Volume] [statistics Volume]
```

The following list describes each of the command line arguments.

drives Displays the current list of active drives on the system.

drivetype *Volume* Displays the drive information for the specified volume. The output is a generic term for the drive type such as Fixed Drive or CD-ROM Drive.

volumeinfo *Volume* Displays statistics about the specified volume including the volume name, volume serial number, maximum component length, and file system name. In addition, the output tells whether the drive supports case-sensitive filenames, Unicode in filenames, file-based compression, disk quotas, sparse files, reparse points, object identifiers, the encrypted file system, and named streams. Finally, you can determine whether the volume preserves the case of filenames, and if it preserves and enforces Access Control Lists (ACLs).

ntfsinfo *Volume* Displays the low-level statistics about the NTFS volume. This information includes NTFS version, number of sectors, total clusters, free clusters, total reserved clusters, bytes per sector, bytes per cluster, bytes per file record segment, and clusters per file record segment. In addition, you can learn the following MFT statistics: valid data length, start location (MFT1 and MFT2), zone start, and zone end.

statistics *Volume* Displays a list of the operational statistics for the specified volume. The statistics include the following user information: UserFileReads, UserFileReadBytes, UserDiskReads, UserFileWrites, UserFileWriteBytes, and UserDiskWrites. These are all standard counters, so you can also access them using the Performance console. In addition to user information, you can obtain metadata, MFT, root file, and log file statistics.

Hardlink

A hard link is a connection between two files. The new file that you create is a pointer to the existing file. In essence, you're creating another directory entry to a single file. The file continues to exist until you remove all of the directory entries pointing to it. Any change you make to the content of the new file also appears within the existing file, and vice versa. The main reason to use hard links is to create the same file in multiple locations on the hard drive. For example, you might need to use the same initialization file with multiple applications. Instead of copying the file multiple times, you can simply create multiple hard links to it. This mode uses the following syntax:

```
FSUtil Hardlink Create NewFilename Filename
```

The following list describes each of the command line arguments.

NewFilename The name of the new file to create from the existing file. The new file is simply a directory entry, not an actual copy of the file.

Filename The name of the existing file. You can include a drive and either relative or absolute path information to the file, along with the filename.

ObjectID

Files on NTFS volumes have four identifiers: object, birth volume, birth object, and domain. Each of these identifiers is a 16-byte hexadecimal number in the form of 17e0b9211e61da11879e0013d4337d7d. The first three identifiers always have a value; the fourth identifier (domain) isn't currently used. Generally, unless a file is damaged in some way, you should never need to change the identifiers. This mode uses the following syntax:

```
FSUtil ObjectID [query Filename] [set ObjectId BirthVolumeId
BirthObjectId DomainId Filename] [delete Filename] [create Filename]
```

The following list describes each of the command line arguments.

Filename Specifies the name of the file to query or modify.

ObjectId   Contains a 16-byte hexadecimal number that uniquely identifies the file on a particular volume. This identifier is extremely important because the Distributed Link Tracking (DLT) Client service and the File Replication Service (FRS) use it to identify files. This identifier can change when you move a file from one volume to another. However, the `BirthVolumeId` and `BirthObjectId` values never change, so Windows can always identify a particular file using these values no matter where you move it.

BirthVolumeId   Contains a 16-byte hexadecimal number that identifies the initial file volume. The DLT Client service uses this value to identify moved files.

BirthObjectId   Contains a 16-byte hexadecimal number that reflects the file's initial `ObjectID`. The DLT Client service uses this value to identify moved files.

DomainId   Contains a 16-byte hexadecimal value of all zeros. Windows doesn't currently use this identifier and you should always set it to 0.

query   Displays the `ObjectId`, `BirthVolumeId`, `BirthObjectId`, and `DomainId` for the specified file.

set   Changes the `ObjectId`, `BirthVolumeId`, `BirthObjectId`, and `DomainId` of the specified file.

delete   Removes the `ObjectId`, `BirthVolumeId`, `BirthObjectId`, and `DomainId` from the specified file.

create   Adds an `ObjectId`, `BirthVolumeId`, `BirthObjectId`, and `DomainId` to the specified file. Windows automatically generates unique identifiers for you.

Quota

Quotas help keep resource usage under control on systems with multiple users. Each user receives a specific amount of disk space to use for personal needs. Every file that has the user as an owner counts against the total. When the user exceeds their quota, the system informs both the user and the administrator (using a system of violation notifications). This mode uses the following syntax:

```
FSUtil Quota [disable Path] [track Path] [enforce Path]
[violations] [modify Path Threshold Limit User] [query Path]
```

The following list describes each of the command line arguments.

Path   Specifies the target path (generally an entire volume) for a particular quota action. The path can include a drive specification. It can also rely on an absolute or relative path specification.

Threshold   Defines the amount of space in bytes that the user can use on the drive before the system alerts the user to a possible limit violation. The user still has additional space on the drive, but the threshold is normally the point at which the user should consider cleaning up old files. The threshold is a warning point.

Limit   Defines the amount of space in bytes that the user can access on the drive. Generally, the system begins issuing warnings for every disk activity at this point. Depending on the quota setup, the drive could prohibit additional drive use. The user must clean up old files on the hard drive after reaching the limit.

User   Specifies the Windows account that has a quota attached to it.

disable   Stops quota tracking and enforcement for the specified resource.

track   Enables quota tracking for the specified resource. This option doesn't enable enforcement of any rules you have in place.

enforce Enables quota enforcement for the specified resource. This option doesn't enable tracking.

violations Displays a list of quota violations found in the event log. If the event log doesn't have any quota violations, the utility displays a "No quota violations detected" message. The utility checks both the system and application logs for both quota threshold and quota limit violations.

modify Changes the quota settings for a particular user. You must supply the drive, threshold, limit, and user inputs when using this option.

query Displays the query settings for the specified resource. In addition to the actual quota settings, this command displays the per user settings. This information includes the user SID, change time, quota used, quota threshold, and quota limit.

Repair

This mode lets you repair a file system object from the command line. You use it to place the system object in a known good state. In some cases, repairing the system object could mean data loss because the object is broken in such a way that repairing it means losing the data (perhaps due to a pointer or other problem). This mode uses the following syntax:

```
FSUtil Repair [query Volume] [set Volume Flags] [wait FSObject]
[initiate Volume FileReference]
```

The following list describes each of the command line arguments.

query *Volume* Determines the repair status of the specified volume. The repair status defines what kinds of repairs you can perform on the volume. The status includes any of the following values.

   1 The volume supports general repair.

   8 The volume warns about potential data loss when performing a repair.

set *Volume Flags* Changes the repair status of the specified volume. The flag contains a number that specifies the repair status. See the query keyword for a list of acceptable values.

wait *FSObject* Tells the FSUtil to wait for the specified file system object repairs before performing any other tasks.

initiate *Volume FileReference* Performs a repair of the specified file on the referenced volume. To use this feature, you must provide the segment number of the file.

ReparsePoint

The ReparsePoint mode helps you manage Windows reparse points. A reparse point is a collection of user data, usually from a remote source. An application creates the reparse point by saving the data to a file along with some special configuration information. You can learn more about reparse points on the Microsoft Web site at `http://msdn2.microsoft.com/en-us/library/Aa365503 .aspx`. Normally, you'll rely on an application to create the reparse point. However, the Knowledge Base article at `http://support.microsoft.com/?kbid=205524` tells you how to create and manipulate them manually. In this case, the reparse point creates a link between another drive and a directory on the hard drive. To gain a better understanding of how you can use reparse points on an active system, read the Knowledge Base article at `http://support.microsoft.com/default`

.aspx?scid=kb;en-us;Q262797. Because of the way the system creates reparse points, you can only use FSUtil to query and delete them. This mode uses the following syntax:

```
FSUtil ReparsePoint [query Filename] [delete Filename]
```

The following list describes each of the command line arguments.

Filename Defines the path used as a junction or the filename of the user data storage. Whether the input defines a path or a filename (with an optional path) depends on the kind of reparse point in use.

query Requests information about the specified reparse point. The information includes the reparse tag created when the system defined the reparse point. The tag information varies, but can include the reparse tag value, one or more tag values, a Globally Unique Identifier (GUID), the data length, and the actual reparse data.

TIP Directories used as reparse points normally have a special icon attached to them, rather than using the standard folder icon. In the case of a drive, the icon is a special drive symbol. In other words, even though the entity is a directory, the system is treating it as a drive attached to that directory. If you delete the reparse point, the directory remains, but the icon changes back to a standard folder icon and the remote data is no longer available.

delete Removes the specified reparse point.

Resource

This mode helps you interact with Transactional Resource Managers. A Transactional Resource Manager is a managed construct that provides a method of tracking and optionally reversing change to file system objects. You must use this mode to create, discover, and modify the folder used to hold the transaction information, including the transaction logs. Use the Transaction mode to work with the transactions contained in the log. This mode uses the following syntax:

```
FSUtil Resource [create Path] [info Path]
[setautoreset {True | False} RootPath] [setlog Options]
[start Path [RMLogPath TMLogPath]] [stop Path]
```

The setlog option requires additional explanation. The following list describes each of the other command line arguments.

create *Path* Creates a new folder that holds the logs for a Transactional Resource Manager. The path must not already exist. Creating the folder is the first step in defining a secondary Transactional Resource Manager. Once you create the folder, you must start the Transactional Resource Manager using the start option.

info *Path* Obtains information about any started Transactional Resource Manager. If the target system doesn't have any secondary Transactional Resource Managers running and you type this command without a path, then FSUtil reports the status of the default Transactional Resource Manager for the current drive. You can also access the default Transactional Resource Manager by providing the root directory for the target drive (such as C:\).

setautoreset {True | False} *RootPath* Changes the automatic reset feature for the default Transactional Resource Manager, which is always the root directory of the selected volume (such as C:\). This feature sets the default Transactional Resource Manager to reset all of its metadata each time you reboot the machine. The default setting retains the metadata across reboots to better track system state. You can use this feature to overcome problems with the transactional state of the file system.

start *Path* **[***RMLogPath TMLogPath***]**   Starts the Transactional Resource Manager specified by path. You'll normally use this option to start a secondary manager, rather than the default. In addition to the Transactional Resource Manager folder, you can also specify the path to the log files that the manager uses to track file system transactions.

stop *Path*   Stops the Transactional Resource Manager specified by path. You'll normally use this option to stop a secondary manager, rather than the default. While it's possible to stop the default manager, you can't restart it, so this action isn't advisable.

The `setlog` option of the resource mode lets you modify the log used to record transactions on the system. The log configuration affects just how much Server Core can do when it comes to monitoring transactions on your system. This option uses the following syntax:

```
FSUtil Resource setlog
[growth {NumContainers containers Path | Percentage percent Path}]
[maxextents NumContainers Path] [minextents NumContainers Path]
[mode {full Path | undo Path}] [rename Path] [shrink Percentage Path]
[size NumContainers Path]
```

The following list describes the `setlog` option–specific command line arguments.

growth {*NumContainers* **containers** *Path* **|** *Percentage* **percent** *Path***}**   Changes the container growth increment. Each container holds a specific amount of data (the default is 10 MB). Every time the Transactional Resource Manager requires additional hard drive space to store transactions, it increases the number of containers. You can set the specific number of containers or grow the number of containers as a percentage of the current total log capacity. Consequently, if you set the value to 10 percent, the default container size is 10 MB, and the total log capacity is 200 MB, then the Transactional Resource Manager adds two containers. The default growth size is two containers.

maxextents *NumContainers Path*   Defines the maximum number of containers that a Transactional Resource Manager can create. This setting helps you control hard drive usage by the Transactional Resource Manager. The default setting is 20 containers.

minextents *NumContainers Path*   Defines the minimum number of containers that a Transactional Resource Manager can create (usually created at the beginning of a session). This setting can help improve performance by forcing the Transactional Resource Manager to create the full number of containers it requires at the outset, rather than taking time out to create them one or two at a time.

mode {full *Path* **| undo** *Path***}**   Determines the mode used to log transactions. The full logging method logs every activity as a transaction. However, this mode uses considerable hard drive space. The undo mode only records transactions required to undo permanent activities, such as erasing a file. The undo mode also appears as Simple when viewing the Transactional Resource Manager statistics.

rename *Path*   Assigns a new GUID to the Transactional Resource Manager. The new GUID appears as part of the RM Identifier statistic. There isn't a good reason to use this option and many reasons you shouldn't when working with an application that may rely on the current GUID. In general, the application may cease working or work improperly.

shrink *Percentage Path* Determines the amount of hard drive space that the Transactional Resource Manager returns to the system when it no longer requires the space for transactions. The default setting doesn't return any hard drive space to the system, so the number of containers only increases until the Transactional Resource Manager reaches the maximum number of containers.

size *NumContainers Path* Sets the number of containers available to the Transactional Resource Manager. You can use this option to manually return hard drive space to the system after performing a number of file system object changes.

 Real World Scenario

HARD DRIVES AS DATABASES

Hard drives have always been a kind of database, but operating systems typically don't treat them that way. Consequently, disk drives often suffer failures that databases would never encounter. However, Microsoft steadily adds database features to Windows. Server Core is no exception. Although Microsoft's original plan for Server Core included a considerable number of other database features that it later dropped, the use of transactions to support disk activities is a significant step forward.

In the real world, the hardware that comprises a hard disk isn't the valuable commodity—it's the data. By using transactions, Server Core can reduce the possibility of damage to valuable data. However, transactions are more than a nice feature for Server Core. The code for the Transactional Resource Manager actually appears as part of the .NET Framework and developers can rely on this technology to create robust applications. You can read about the developer view of transactions at `http://msdn2 .microsoft.com/en-us/library/ms973865.aspx`. Because the application code uses the same functionality as the operating system uses, you can also rely on the Resource and Transaction modes described in this chapter to work with application-specific Transactional Resource Managers.

Sparse

Some applications create large files that contain mostly zeros. For example, an application may create a large cache to hold temporary data. Sparse file management compresses these files smaller than standard compression can. For a discussion of sparse files, see the "Understanding Sparse Files" sidebar. This mode helps you manage sparse files and uses the following syntax:

```
FSUtil Sparse [setflag Filename] [queryflag Filename]
[queryrange Filename] [setrange Filename Offset Length]
```

The following list describes each of the command line arguments.

Filename Specifies the file to manage.

Offset Defines the beginning of a sparse range.

Length Determines the number of bytes in the sparse range.

setflag Adds a sparse attribute to the file to mark it as a sparse file.

queryflag Displays status information as to the state of the sparse flag (attribute).

queryrange Displays any sparse ranges within the specified file. Each entry contains two numbers. The first number specifies the sparse range offset, while the second number defines the sparse range length.

setrange Sets a sparse range for the specified file. You must provide the offset (in bytes) for the beginning of the sparse range, as well as the number of bytes to include within the sparse range.

Transaction

The Transaction mode lets you interact with the transactions currently supported by a Transactional Resource Manager. See the "Resource" section of the chapter for additional details about working with a Transactional Resource Manager. This mode uses the following syntax:

```
FSUtil Transaction [commit GUID] [list] [fileinfo Filename]
[query [{files | all}] GUID] [rollback GUID]
```

The following list describes each of the command line arguments.

commit *GUID* Completes a transaction and makes all of the tasks specified by the entries in the log permanent. You must commit a transaction before the system considers the action completed, even though the file system objects will appear to have all of the changes.

list Displays a list of all of the current transactions.

fileinfo *Filename* Displays the transactional data about a particular file.

query [{files | all}] *GUID* Displays detailed information about the transaction specified by GUID. You can obtain just the file information or all of the transaction details. Use the **list** option to obtain a list of the current transactions and their associated GUIDs.

rollback *GUID* Undoes all of the changes made to file system objects within the current transaction since the start of the transaction. A rollback returns the file system objects to their pre-change state.

USN

You use this mode to manage the Update Sequence Number (USN) for the system. The USN provides a persistent log of all of the changes made to the files on the system. As users add, delete, and modify files and directories, NTFS makes an entry in the USN. Each volume has a separate USN. The main use of the USN for administrators is to check the changes made to one or more files. Using the USN is more efficient than relying on time stamps and you'll receive more information as well. You can find a complete description of the USN on the Microsoft Systems Journal Web site at http://www.microsoft.com/msj/0999/journal/journal.aspx. This mode uses the following syntax:

```
FSUtil USN [createjournal m=MaximumSize a=AllocationDelta Volume]
[deletejournal [/D] [/N] Volume] [enumdata FileRef LowUSN HighUSN]
[queryjounral Volume] [readdata Filename]
```

The following list describes each of the command line arguments.

Volume Specifies the NTFS volume to manage. The journal always affects an entire volume. Consequently, even though you can query statistics for an individual file, you must work with a volume when creating or deleting the journal.

Filename Specifies the name of the file to manage. The filename can include both drive and path information.

m=*MaximumSize* Defines the maximum size of the USN journal in bytes. The journal can grow larger than this value, but NTFS truncates it during the next checkpoint to less than this size. The checkpoint size is the maximum size plus the allocation delta. Consequently, if you set the journal size to 1,000 bytes and the allocation delta to 100, then NTFS automatically truncates the journal when it reaches 1,100 bytes to 900 bytes in size.

a=*AllocationDelta* Determines the delta between a full journal and a truncated journal.

/D Disables a USN journal (rather than deleting it) and returns control of the Input/Output (I/O) of the system immediately. NTFS continues to disable the journal in the background. This option takes more time to complete than the /N option, but lets the user continue working immediately.

/N Disables a USN journal (rather than deleting it) and maintains control of the I/O subsystem. The system won't read or write data to the hard drive while NTFS disables the USN journal. This option completes the process much faster, but requires that the user give up access to the system while the process completes.

FileRef Specifies the ordinal position of the file within the drive hierarchy. Each file has a unique number. This value specifies the starting point for the enumeration.

LowUSN Determines the lowest USN number within a range. Only USNs with numbers that are equal to or higher than this number appear within the range.

HighUSN Determines the highest USN number within a range. Only USNs with numbers lower than or equal to this number appear within the range.

createjournal Creates a new journal for the specified volume. If you set the m and a arguments to 0, Windows determines journal allocation sizes based on the size of the hard drive.

deletejournal Deletes or disables a USN journal. Deleting the journal removes it from the system permanently and could adversely affect applications such as Indexing Service, File Replication Service (FRS), Remote Installation Services (RIS), and Remote Storage that rely on it. Disabling the journal makes it inaccessible, but doesn't free the resources used by the journal.

enumdata Enumerates the change journal entries between two boundaries as specified by the LowUSN and HighUSN arguments for files starting with a specific reference number.

queryjournal Displays the USN journal statistics for the requested volume. This information includes the USN journal identifier, first USN number, next USN number, lowest valid USN, maximum valid USN, maximum size, and allocation delta.

readdata Displays data about the requested file. The information includes the major version, minor version, file reference number, parent file reference number, USN, time stamp, reason, source information, security identifier, file attributes, filename length, filename offset, and filename.

Volume

The Volume mode helps you work with volumes directly. This mode uses the following syntax:

```
FSUtil Volume [dismount Drive] [diskfree Drive]
```

The following list describes each of the command line arguments.

Drive Specifies the drive to query or dismount.

dismount Removes a drive from service. Dismounting a volume makes it unavailable for any activity.

diskfree   Displays the amount of free space on the drive. The output includes the number of free bytes, the total number of bytes on the drive, and the available number of free bytes (after any allocations).

Working with iSCSI Using the iSCSICli Utility

The Internet Small Computer System Interface Client (iSCSICli) utility helps you gain access to and manage virtual hard drives located on Internet sites. The utility makes it appear that the drive is local when it actually appears online. The advantage of this technology is that you can access the drive from anywhere. In addition, the driver provider performs tasks such as ensuring you have a good backup of your data. Of course, this technology also has drawbacks such as performance penalties. You can't expect to access an iSCSI drive at the same performance levels as a local drive.

 Real World Scenario

PRACTICAL USAGE TIPS FOR iSCSI

Working with iSCSI can be a complex topic. This chapter doesn't provide any actual iSCSI scenarios, nor does it tell you how to configure an iSCSI setup on your server since each connection is different. You can find tips on using iSCSI to organize your storage architecture at http://technet.microsoft.com/en-us/library/aa996710.aspx. There is also a good overview of storage technologies for use with Exchange Server at http://technet.microsoft.com/en-us/library/aa995741.aspx. If you want to know how iSCSI compares to other storage technologies, check out the comparison at http://technet.microsoft.com/en-us/library/bb123945.aspx.

You'll also want to review the Knowledge Base articles at http://support.microsoft.com/kb/870964 and http://support.microsoft.com/kb/839686. The first article tells you how to overcome some of the file sharing problems with iSCSI, while the second discusses Exchange Server support for iSCSI. The Knowledge Base article at http://support.microsoft.com/kb/833770 tells you about iSCSI support for SQL Server. In fact, Microsoft provides a considerable number of Knowledge Base articles about iSCSI and you can Google them using the http://www.google.com/search?hl=en&q=iSCSI+site%3Asupport.microsoft.com&btnG=Search search URL.

Every system that requires iSCSI support must have access to an iSCSI initiator (the software that makes the connection). You can download the latest version of the iSCSI initiator at http://www.microsoft.com/downloads/details.aspx?familyid=12cb3c1a-15d6-4585-b385-befd1319f825 to support iSCSI on older versions of Windows (a must for a complete iSCSI solution). Microsoft provides other support information for iSCSI at http://www.microsoft.com/windowsserver2003/technologies/storage/iscsi/default.mspx.

An iSCSI connection requires support from an Internet Storage Name Service (iSNS) server. You can install this server as one of the roles for the GUI version of Windows Server 2008. It's also available on a significant number of other platforms (including Linux). You can obtain a good overview of iSNS and its relation to iSCSI at http://www.san-ip.com/iSCSI/techoverviewart.htm. Another good overview appears at http://en.wikipedia.org/wiki/ISNS. The actual iSNS standard appears at http://www.ietf.org/rfc/rfc4171.txt.

Starting the iSCSI Initiator

Before you can use an iSCSI drive, you must start the iSCSI initiator service by typing **SC Start MSiSCSI** and pressing Enter. To ensure that the iSCSI initiator service starts in the future, type **SC Config MSiSCSI Start= Auto** and press Enter (remember the space between the = and the word Auto). In addition, you must allow the iSCSI initiator through the firewall. Unfortunately, you can't use the NetSH utility to perform this task because Windows Server 2008 uses a new technique to set some features. You must use the Registry Editor (`RegEdit.EXE`) to perform this task. The following steps tell you how to perform the configuration change.

1. Type **RegEdit** and press Enter. You'll see the Registry Editor window.

2. Locate the `HKEY_LOCAL_MACHINE\SYSTEM\CurrentControlSet\Services\SharedAccess\Parameters\FirewallPolicy\FirewallRules` key.

3. Find the MsiScsi-In-TCP value and double-click its entry. You'll see an Edit String dialog box. The Value Data field contains
`v2.0|Action=Allow|Active=FALSE|Dir=In|Protocol=6|Profile=Domain|Profile=Private|Profile=Public|App=%SystemRoot%\system32\svchost.exe|Svc=Msiscsi|Name=@FirewallAPI.dll,-29003|Desc=@FirewallAPI.dll,-29006|EmbedCtxt=@FirewallAPI.dll,-29002|Edge=FALSE|`.

4. Change the Active value to TRUE, so that it reads `Active=TRUE`. Do not change anything else in this string or you'll find that the Windows Firewall won't work. Click OK to save the entry.

5. Find the MsiScsi-Out-TCP value and double-click its entry.

6. Change the Active value to TRUE, so that it reads `Active=TRUE`. Do not change anything else in this string. Click OK to save the entry.

7. Locate the `HKEY_LOCAL_MACHINE\SYSTEM\CurrentControlSet\Services\SharedAccess\Defaults\FirewallPolicy\FirewallRules` key.

8. Perform steps 3 through 6 to change these Active values to TRUE.

Working with the iSCSI Client (iSCSICli) Utility

As with many of the complex utilities in this book, the iSCSICli utility supports an interactive mode. Type **iSCSICli** and press Enter to access this mode. You can use any of the commands that you can use at command line in interactive mode without typing iSCSICli first. For example, if you want to obtain a list of initiators, type **ListInitiators** and press Enter. This utility uses the following syntax for each supported command:

```
Manually Configured Targets:

iSCSICli AddTarget TargetName TargetAlias TargetPortalAddress
   TargetPortalSocket TargetFlags Persist LoginFlags HeaderDigest
   DataDigest MaxConnections DefaultTime2Wait DefaultTime2Retain
   Username Password AuthType MappingCount MappingEntries
iSCSICli QAddTarget TargetName TargetPortalAddress
iSCSICli RemoveTarget TargetName
iSCSICli ListTargets [ForceUpdate]
```

Target Portals:

```
iSCSICli AddTargetPortal TargetPortalAddress TargetPortalSocket
    [HBAName] [PortNumber] SecurityFlags LoginFlags HeaderDigest
    DataDigest MaxConnections DefaultTime2Wait DefaultTime2Retain
    Username Password AuthType
iSCSICli QAddTargetPortal TargetPortalAddress [CHAPUsername]
    [CHAPPassword]
iSCSICli RemoveTargetPortal TargetPortalAddress TargetPortalSocket
    [HBAName] [PortNumber]
iSCSICli RefreshTargetPortal TargetPortalAddress TargetPortalSocket
    [HBAName] [PortNumber]
iSCSICli ListTargetPortals
```

iSNS Commands:

```
iSCSICli AddiSNSServer iSNSServerAddress
iSCSICli RemoveiSNSServer iSNSServerAddress
iSCSICli RefreshiSNSServer iSNSServerAddress
iSCSICli ListiSNSServers
```

Target Operations:

```
iSCSICli TargetInfo TargetName [DiscoveryMechanism]
iSCSICli LoginTarget TargetName ReportToPNP TargetPortalAddress
    TargetPortalSocket InitiatorInstance PortNumber SecurityFlags
    LoginFlags HeaderDigest DataDigest MaxConnections DefaultTime2Wait
    DefaultTime2Retain Username Password AuthType Key MappingCount
    MappingEntries
iSCSICli QLoginTarget TargetName  [CHAPUsername] [CHAPPassword]
iSCSICli LogoutTarget SessionId
iSCSICli PersistentLoginTarget TargetName ReportToPNP
    TargetPortalAddress TargetPortalSocket InitiatorInstance PortNumber
    SecurityFlags LoginFlags HeaderDigest DataDigest MaxConnections
    DefaultTime2Wait DefaultTime2Retain Username Password AuthType Key
    MappingCount MappingEntries
iSCSICli ListPersistentTargets
iSCSICli RemovePersistentTarget InitiatorName TargetName PortNumber
    TargetPortalAddress TargetPortalSocket
iSCSICli AddConnection SessionId InitiatorInstance PortNumber
    TargetPortalAddress TargetPortalSocket SecurityFlags LoginFlags
    HeaderDigest DataDigest MaxConnections DefaultTime2Wait
    DefaultTime2Retain Username Password AuthType Key
iSCSICli QAddConnection SessionId InitiatorInstance TargetPortalAddress
    [CHAPUsername] [CHAPPassword]
iSCSICli RemoveConnection SessionId ConnectionId
```

```
SCSI Commands:

iSCSICli ScsiInquiry SessionId LUN EvpdCmddt PageCode [Length]
iSCSICli ReadCapacity SessionId LUN
iSCSICli ReportLUNs SessionId
iSCSICli ReportTargetMappings

Internet Protocol Secure (IPSec) Commands:

iSCSICli TunnelAddr InitiatorName InitiatorPort DestinationAddress
    TunnelAddress Persist
iSCSICli GroupKey Key Persist
iSCSICli PSKey InitiatorName InitiatorPort SecurityFlags IdType Id Key
    Persist
iSCSICli GetPSKey InitiatorName InitiatorPort IdType Id

Volume Binding Commands:

iSCSICli BindPersistentVolumes
iSCSICli BindPersistentDevices
iSCSICli ReportPersistentDevices
iSCSICli AddPersistentDevice VolumeOrDevicePath
iSCSICli RemovePersistentDevice VolumeOrDevicePath
iSCSICli ClearPersistentDevices

Miscellaneous Commands:

iSCSICli CHAPSecret CHAPSecret
iSCSICli ListInitiators
iSCSICli NodeName NodeName
iSCSICli Ping InitiatorName Address [RequestCount] [RequestSize]
    [RequestTimeout]
iSCSICli SessionList [ShowSessionInfo]
iSCSICli VersionInfo
```

The following list describes each of the command line arguments.

Address Specifies the address of the iSNS server to ping.

AuthType Determines the kind of authentication used to verify the caller's identity. See the "iSCSICli Mappings and Flags" section of the chapter for a description of the authentication types.

CHAPPassword Contains the Challenge-Handshake Authentication Protocol (CHAP) password used to authenticate the caller. This password forms the CHAP secret that the initiator uses to create a hash value that identifies the caller. The hash value provides identification during subsequent calls.

TIP You can specify CHAP secrets, CHAP passwords, and IPSec pre-shared keys as a text string or a hexadecimal value sequence. In order to define a hexadecimal value sequence, start the command line string with 0x (a zero and an x) to designate it as a hexadecimal value. The hexadecimal values appear in pairs. For example, 0x12345678 is a 4-byte hexadecimal value.

CHAPSecret Contains the initiator CHAP secret used for mutual CHAP authentication. If the input value is an asterisk (*), then the system sets an empty initiator CHAP secret.

CHAPUsername Contains the username used for CHAP authentication. If the input value is an asterisk (*), then the initiator uses the node name as the CHAP username.

ConnectionId Represents a particular connection to the iSNS server. You use this value to define which connection to manage.

NOTE The iSCSICli utility assumes that all numbers you provide are in decimal, unless you precede them with a 0x. For example, 10 is a decimal value of ten, while 0x10 is a decimal value of 16.

DataDigest Determines the data digest setting used when logging into the target portal. A value of 0 indicates that the client won't use a data digest, while a non-zero value indicates the use of a data digest. Use an asterisk (*) to indicate that you want to set the data digest value to the value used by the initiator kernel mode driver.

DefaultTime2Retain Specifies the time that the iSCSI initiator negotiates for retaining a connection when logging into the target. When this time expires without caller activity, the server automatically terminates the session. Use an asterisk (*) to indicate that you want to set the default retention time value to the value used by the initiator kernel mode driver.

DefaultTime2Wait Specifies the time that the iSCSI initiator waits when logging into the target. When this time expires without a login, the iSCSI initiator registers an error. Use an asterisk (*) to indicate that you want to set the default waiting time value to the value used by the initiator kernel mode driver.

DestinationAddress Specifies the Internet Protocol (IP) address to associate with the tunnel address for IPSec communication.

DiscoveryMechanism Defines the method used to discover targets on the iSNS server. If you don't specify this option, then iSCSICli lists all of the discovery mechanisms without any target data. Providing a discovery mechanism value displays targets associated with that discovery mechanism.

EvpdCmddt Defines the parameter to use for the inquiry.

ForceUpdate Forces an update of the target list when set to T or t.

HBAName Defines the name of the Host Bus Adapter (HBA) used to route the SendTargets calls. If you don't specify this value, then the iSCSI initiator service chooses an HBA. Some sources call this value the InitiatorInstanceName.

HeaderDigest Specifies whether the iSCSI initiator should enable the header digest when logging into the target portal. Use a non-zero value to enable the header digest. Use an asterisk (*) to indicate that you want to set the header digest value to the value used by the initiator kernel mode driver.

Id Represents the Internet Key Exchange (IKE) ID payload.

IdType Defines the IKE ID payload type. This value can include a fully qualified domain name or an Internet Protocol version 4 (IPv4) address.

InitiatorInstance Defines the name of the iSCSI initiator used to perform the login operation. The iSCSI initiator service chooses an iSCSI initiator when you don't provide this value.

InitiatorName   Specifies the name of the iSCSI initiator normally used to login to the target (the tunnel mode outer address when used for IPSec). You must configure the iSCSI initiator for this purpose. When working with IPSec, providing a value of asterisk (*) configures all iSCSI initiators to use the caller's address.

InitiatorPort   Specifies the physical port number of the iSCSI initiator for the specified tunnel mode outer address. When working with IPSec, providing a value of asterisk (*) configures all ports to use the caller's address.

iSNSServerAddress   Represents a particular iSNS server. You may provide either an IP address or a Domain Name System (DNS) name as input. The iSCSI initiator queries the specified server to discover targets. It also registers the iSNS for State Change Notification (SCN) so that it can detect changes in server functionality, such as a change in availability. Any value you provide is persisted and the iSCSI initiator queries the server during each restart of the service or whenever an SCN occurs.

Key   Contains the IPSec pre-shared key used to establish the Transaction Control Protocol (TCP) connection when the iSCSI initiator relies on IPSec to connect with the target.

Length   Defines the allocation length to specify for an inquiry. This argument doesn't appear with some forms for the iSCSICli command. It's always optional. The default value is 0xFF (255 bytes). The maximum value is 8 KB (0x2000).

LoginFlags   Determines how the client logs into the target portal. See the "iSCSICli Mappings and Flags" section of the chapter for a description of the login flags.

LUN   Specifies the Logical Unit Number (LUN) that receives an inquiry.

MappingCount   Specifies the number of target mappings that the iSCSI initiator should use to login to the target. See the "iSCSICli Mappings and Flags" section of the chapter for a description of the target mappings.

MappingEntries   Contains one or more TargetLun, OSBus, OSTarget, or OSLun entries. The MappingCount argument determines the number of entries. See the "iSCSICli Mappings and Flags" section of the chapter for a description of the target mappings.

MaxConnections   Determines the number of connections that the system uses during the discovery session to perform tasks such as the SendTargets operation. Use an asterisk (*) to indicate that you want to set the maximum connections value to the value used by the initiator kernel mode driver.

NodeName   Changes the default iSCSI node name for the iSCSI initiator. This argument specifies the new node name. The system won't validate the name you provide as a valid iSCSI Qualified Name (IQN) or Institute of Electrical and Electronics Engineers (IEEE) EUI-64 format. You can see examples of both formats at http://docs.hp.com/en/T1452-90011/ch04s01.html. Microsoft doesn't support the Network Address Authority (NAA) naming format described at http://tools.ietf.org/html/draft-ietf-ips-iscsi-name-ext-00. See the specification at http://www.pdl.cmu.edu/mailinglists/ips/mail/msg05298.html for additional information about the IQN format and the specification at http://standards.ieee.org/regauth/oui/tutorials/EUI64.html for additional information about the EUI-64 format.

PageCode   Contains the page code to use for an inquiry.

Password   Contains the password used to authenticate the caller. This password forms the CHAP secret that the initiator uses to create a hash value that identifies the caller. The hash value provides identification during subsequent calls.

Persist Determines when the iSCSI initiator persists the specified object, such as a target or tunnel mode outer address. The iSCSI initiator re-creates persisted object each time you restart the service. Use a value of T or t to specify that you want to persist the target.

PortNumber Determines which port the iSCSI initiator uses to route SendTargets calls. If you don't specify this value, then the iSCSI initiator uses the port value provided by the initiator kernel mode drive. Some texts call this value the InitiatorPortNumber.

ReportToPNP Determines whether the iSCSI initiator exposes the LUN to a port driver so that the operating system can display it as a storage device using Plug and Play (PNP). When the target is exposed through PNP, the client can perform standard device operations such as mounting the drive, assigning it a drive letter, and formatting it. You must set this argument to T or t to obtain the PNP functionality. If you set this argument to any other value, then the operating system only allows you to perform iSCSI discovery on the target.

RequestCount Specifies the number of Ping requests to perform.

RequestSize Specifies the size of the Ping request.

RequestTimeout Determines the time that the Ping command will wait until it signifies an error condition after making a request and not receiving a response.

SecurityFlags Specifies the type of IPSec to use when creating a TCP connection to the target portal. See the "iSCSICli Mappings and Flags" section of the chapter for a description of the security flags.

SessionId Represents a particular iSNS server session. You use this value to define which session (and by extension, connection) to manage.

ShowSessionInfo Determines whether the SessionList command displays full session information. This is an optional argument that displays the full information when set to T or t. Older versions of iSCSICli don't support this argument.

TargetAlias Specifies the alias of the target. Use a value of asterisk (*) when the target doesn't have an alias defined.

TargetFlags Determines how the iSCSI initiator service manages the target. See the "iSCSICli Mappings and Flags" section of the chapter for a description of the target flags.

TargetName Specifies the name of the target.

TargetPortalAddress Defines the IP or DNS address of the target portal.

TargetPortalSocket Defines the TCP port number of the target portal. The default port setting is 3260. However, the administrator can set the TCP port number to any value.

TunnelAddress Specifies the IP address to associate with the destination address for IPSec communications.

Username Contains the username used for authentication. If the input value is an asterisk (*), then the initiator uses the node name as the username.

VolumeOrDevicePath Specifies the drive letter or mount point for the volume that you want to bind persistently or the device interface name for a device. If you specify a drive letter, mount point, or device interface name that the iSCSI initiator has already bound, the system returns an error.

iSCSICli Mappings and Flags

The iSCSICli utility requires a number of special mappings and flags. A *mapping* provides the means for the iSCSICli utility to make a connection between a physical device and its information within the operating system. In this case, the actual mapping is the Logical Unit Number (LUN). In addition, many of the arguments support specific flag values. A *flag* is a bit position or specific value that determines how iSCSICli reacts in a given situation. The following list describes the mappings and flags used by iSCSICli.

Target Mappings   Determines how the iSCSI initiator accesses a particular LUN or the techniques used to expose the LUN.

> **TargetLun**   Defines the LUN value the target uses to expose the LUN. You must provide this value in the form 0x0123456789abcdef.
>
> **OSBus**   Defines the bus number that the operating system should use to access the LUN.
>
> **OSTarget**   Defines the target number the operating system should use to access the LUN.
>
> **OSLUN**   Defines the LUN number the operating system should use to access the LUN.

Payload Id Type   Defines the technique used to provide an address for the payload.

> **ID_IPV4_ADDR**   1—Id format is 1.2.3.4
>
> **ID_FQDN**   2—Id format is ComputerName
>
> **ID_IPV6_ADDR**   5—Id format is IPv6 Address

Security Flags   Specifies the technique used to authenticate requests and responses.

> **TunnelMode**   0x00000040
>
> **TransportMode**   0x00000020
>
> **PFS Enabled**   0x00000010
>
> **Aggressive Mode**   0x00000008
>
> **Main Mode**   0x00000004
>
> **IPSec/IKE Enabled**   0x00000002
>
> **Valid Flags**   0x00000001

Login Flags   Determines the method used to log into the iSNS server.

> **ISCSI_LOGIN_FLAG_REQUIRE_IPSEC**   0x00000001 (Requires IPSec for the operation.)
>
> **ISCSI_LOGIN_FLAG_MULTIPATH_ENABLED**   0x00000002 (Enables multipathing for the target on this initiator.)

AuthType   Defines the authentication type.

> **ISCSI_NO_AUTH_TYPE**   0 (Disables iSCSI in-band authentication.)
>
> **ISCSI_CHAP_AUTH_TYPE**   1 (Relies on one-way CHAP, where the target authenticates the iSCSI initiator.)
>
> **ISCSI_MUTUAL_CHAP_AUTH_TYPE**   2 (Relies on mutual CHAP, where the target and the iSCSI initiator authenticate each other.)

Target Flags   Determines the visibility of the target on the local system.

ISCSI_TARGET_FLAG_HIDE_STATIC_TARGET   0x00000002 (The local system doesn't see the target unless it also discovers the target dynamically.)

ISCSI_TARGET_FLAG_MERGE_TARGET_INFORMATION   0x00000004 (The local system receives target information. The operating system merges this information with any existing statically configured information for the target.)

Managing Volume Labels with the Label Utility

The Label utility creates, deletes, or changes the volume label for a drive. The volume label appears at the top of the hierarchy in applications such as Windows Explorer and helps the user identify the drive. In addition to standard drives, this utility also works with mount points (see the "Reparse-Point" section of the chapter for details). This utility uses the following syntax:

```
LABEL [drive:][label]
LABEL [/MP] [volume] [label]
```

The following list describes each of the command line arguments.

drive: Specifies the letter of the drive to change.

label   Defines the new volume label. If you leave the volume label blank, then the Label utility queries you for a volume label. Pressing Enter deletes any existing label. Type a new value and press Enter to change the volume label. Press Ctrl+C to abort the action without changing the label. Volume labels for FAT-formatted drives can only have 11 characters, while NTFS-formatted drives can have volume labels up to 32 characters. You can't use these characters in a label for a FAT-formatted drive: * ? / \ | . , ; : + = [ ] < > ".

/MP   Specifies that the drive specification is a mount point or a volume, rather than a drive.

volume   Defines the mount point or volume name. If you specify a volume name, then you don't need to provide the /MP command line switch.

Creating Directories with the *MD* and *MkDir* Commands

The MD and MkDir commands are equivalent. Both of these commands create a new directory from the command line. Windows automatically recognizes the new directory, and you can see it within Windows Explorer and use it from applications. One of the more interesting ways to use this command is within a batch file to create a directory structure for some task or to set up a new user. This utility uses the following syntax:

```
MKDIR [drive:]path
MD [drive:]path
```

The following list describes each of the command line arguments.

drive   The drive to use when creating the new directory. The default is to use the current drive.

path   The absolute or relative path to use when creating the new directory. The default is to create the new directory as a subdirectory of the current directory. However, you can specify an absolute or relative path as needed. See the "Understanding Absolute and Relative Paths" sidebar for additional details. These commands create all of the directories required to provide the full path in the specification, so you might create multiple directories when specifying a long path.

UNDERSTANDING ABSOLUTE AND RELATIVE PATHS

Some people get confused by the term *path* at the command line. The path is simply the list of directories from the root (topmost) directory to the current directory. The current directory is the one that you're working in at any given time.

The command line specifies the root directory with a simple backslash (\). When you go down a level, you add the directory name to the list. For example, if you move to the MyDir directory, then the path becomes \MyDir\. You can expand this list to any level of detail required to describe the current directory. For example, when you move to the SubDir directory from the MyDir directory, then the path becomes \MyDir\SubDir\.

Many commands and utilities require path information. Most of them can use either an absolute or relative path. An absolute path always expresses the full path from the root directory to the current directory. For example, when you're in the SubDir directory, the absolute path is \MyDir\SubDir. The relative path describes the hierarchy in reference to the current directory. Consequently, the relative path for SubDir is SubDir. Notice that you don't begin a relative path with a backslash.

When working with directories using commands, you often need to specify a destination using either an absolute or a relative path. For example, if you want to create a new subdirectory in the SubDir directory, you could type **MD NewDir**. This form of the command uses a relative path. The same command using an absolute path would appear as MD \MyDir\SubDir\NewDir. You might think the absolute path form wastes time, but it's always more accurate than using a relative path and eliminates the possibility of creating a directory where you didn't expect it.

The command window also provides support for two special relative paths. The first is the current directory, which is specified as a single period (.). The second is the parent directory (the one directly above the current directory in the directory hierarchy), which is specified as a double period (..). Many commands and utilities, such as the CD, benefit from this current directory and parent directory shortcut terminology.

Creating Symbolic Links and Hard Links with the *MKLink* Command

The MKLink command helps you create symbolic or hard links. You use these links to make it appear that the link is actually part of the system. Junctions, another type of link, provide a connection between a nonexistent directory and an existing directory. For example, Windows Server 2008 uses a junction to provide support for the Documents and Settings folder that used to appear in Windows. The real directory is now the Users folder. This utility uses the following syntax:

```
MKLink [[/D] | [/H] | [/J]] Link Target
```

The following list describes each of the command line arguments.

/D Creates a directory symbol link. The default setting creates a file symbolic link. You can't use the /D command line switch with the /H or /J command line switches.

/H Creates a hard link instead of a symbolic link. You can't use the /H command line switch with the /D or /J command line switches.

/J Creates a directory junction instead of a symbolic link. You can't use the /J command line switch with the /D or /H command line switches.

Link   Specifies the new symbolic link name.

Target   Specifies the path (relative or absolute) that the new link references (points at).

NOTE   The Windows Server 2008 operating system uses symbolic links in many places. The "Behavior" section of this chapter describes how FSUtil works with symbolic links. You'll also want to discover how to work with symbolic link attributes in the "Changing File and Directory Attributes with the Attrib Utility" section of Chapter 15. The "Standard FAT and NTFS File Attributes" sidebar in Chapter 15 provides a more extensive description of the symbolic link attribute. You can use either the Copy or XCopy command to copy symbolic links as described in Chapter 14. You'll also want to consider the effects of symbolic links on directory security. Use the ICACLS command described in the "Changing File and Directory Access with the *ICACLS* Command" section of Chapter 15 to manage symbolic link security.

Mounting a Volume with the MountVol Utility

The MountVol utility helps you create, delete, and list mount points. You can use this utility to manage mount points without using a drive letter. Windows 2003 and above provides functionality that older versions of Windows don't provide. You can't use the Windows 2003 version of the utility on older Windows versions since these older versions won't provide the required support as part of the file system. This utility uses the following syntax:

```
MOUNTVOL [drive:]path VolumeName
MOUNTVOL [drive:]path /D
MOUNTVOL [drive:]path /L
MOUNTVOL [drive:]path /P
MOUNTVOL /R
MOUNTVOL /N
MOUNTVOL /E
MOUNTVOL drive:/S
```

The following list describes each of the command line arguments.

[*drive:spath*]   Specifies the existing NTFS directory to use for the mount point. When you don't specify the drive, the utility assumes you want to use the current drive. You can use an absolute or relative path.

VolumeName   Specifies the name of the volume that you want to make the target of the mount point.

/D   Removes the volume mount point from the specified directory.

/L   Lists the mounted volume name for the specified directory. If the directory doesn't include a mount point, the utility displays an "The file or directory is not a reparse point." error message.

/P   Removes the volume mount point from the specified directory. The system dismounts the basic volume at this point and takes the volume offline, which makes it unmountable. When other processes are using the volume, the system closes any open handles before dismounting the volume. The system marks volumes dismounted using this technique with the NOT MOUNTED UNTIL A VOLUME MOUNT POINT IS CREATED attribute. If the volume has additional mount points, remove them first using the /D command line switch. You can re-create the basic volume by assigning the volume a mount point.

/R   Removes the volume mount point directories. In addition, this command line switch removes the registry settings for volumes that are no longer in the system. This approach prevents the system from mounting new volumes automatically and using the previously assigned mount points.

/N   Disables automatic mounting of new basic volumes. After you use this command line switch, the system won't automatically mount new volumes when you add them to the system.

/E   Enables automatic mounting of new basic volumes. This is the default setting for a new system.

/S   Mounts the EFI system partition on the specified drive. You can use this command line switch only on Itanium-based computers.

Setting and Viewing Application Paths with the *Path* Command

The `Path` command controls a very important environment variable. The path is the environment variable that lets you access executables even if they aren't in the current directory when at the command prompt. For example, a typical path includes the `\Windows\System32` directory on your machine so you have access to the majority of Windows utilities. Without the path, you'd need to supply the path for every command you want to execute. Imagine typing `\Windows\System32\TaskList` every time you want to discover which tasks are running on your system.

The problem is that Microsoft can't anticipate every application path needed for your system. For example, when you install SQL Server on a machine, you need another path to access the SQL Server executables with ease. Fortunately, many application vendors ease the use of paths by adding them to the Windows permanent path. This registry setting contains the paths to the applications you commonly use. However, sometimes you need to add a path for just the current session. The `Path` command helps you make short-term path changes that affect a specific command window. This command uses the following syntax:

```
PATH [[drive:]path[;...][;%PATH%]
PATH ;
```

The following list describes each of the command line arguments.

drive   Specifies the drive to use for the path entry. The default is to use the current drive, current being relative to where you are at any given moment. Always define a drive when changing the path to avoid unwanted drive reference problems.

path   Specifies the absolute path to use for the entry. You can't use a relative path with the `Path` command. Separate multiple path entries with a semicolon (;).

%PATH%   Obtains the current path environment variable value. In fact, you can access any other environment variable by enclosing it within percent signs (%). The "Managing Environment Variables with the *Set* Command" section of Chapter 5 provides details on working with environment variables. Any environment variable that contains path information can appear as part of the `Path` command. The most common environment variable used for this purpose is `%WINDIR%`, which contains the location of the current Windows directory.

Typing **Path** at the command line and pressing Enter always shows you the current path. If you haven't changed the path in any way, the `Path` command shows you the permanent path for your system. When you need to add a temporary path, always type the new path information followed by the %PATH% environment variable so that you don't lose the current path information. Finally, if you really do want to clear the path, Type **Path;** followed and press Enter. This syntax clears the

Path environment variable for the current command window only; using it won't affect your system as a whole.

Storing and Retrieving Directories with the *PushD* and *PopD* Commands

Windows maintains a directory stack that you can use to store locations that you visit. You use this stack to store directory information and then retrieve it as needed. The PushD and PopD commands provide access to the directory stack and help you move around your hard drive more efficiently.

TIP Think about a stack as you would a stack of pancakes. Fry a pancake and you can add it to the top of the stack. Get hungry and you can remove a pancake from the top of the stack to eat it. The first (bottom) pancake on the stack is always the last pancake off. When the pancakes are all gone, the stack is empty.

If you move around your hard drive a lot, using the PushD and PopD commands can save you considerable typing time. However, most people use these commands to simplify batch files. No matter which way you use them, the directory stack is a handy way for tracking your movement. These commands use the following syntax:

```
PUSHD [path | ..]
POPD
```

The following list describes each of the command line arguments.

path Specifies the absolute or relative path to change to from the current location. See the "Understanding Absolute and Relative Paths" sidebar for additional details.

The PushD and PopD commands can also use command extensions to change to a network drive. When you use PushD in this manner, Windows automatically maps a drive to the network path for you. The PopD command treats the networked drive as it would any other mapped drive for your system. You can learn more about command extensions in the "Understanding Command Extensions" section of Chapter 5. Notice that you can also specify the next directory as the parent directory by using the .. syntax with the PushD command.

Removing a Directory with the *RD* and *RmDir* Commands

The RD and RmDir commands perform the same task; they remove an empty directory from your hard drive. If you attempt to remove a directory that contains any files, the command displays an error message. Removing old directories cleans up the hard drive and makes it easier to find existing data. In addition, each directory consumes a minuscule amount of space on the hard drive that removing the directory frees. These commands use the following syntax:

```
RMDIR [/S] [/Q] [drive:]path
RD [/S] [/Q] [drive:]path
```

The following list describes each of the command line arguments.

drive Specifies the drive where the directory is located.

path Specifies the absolute or relative path of the directory to remove.

/S   Removes all of the subdirectories and files in the specified directory along with the directory itself. This feature removes the safety feature that tells you when a directory contains files, but does make these commands easier to use within a batch file. This command line switch makes the RD and RmDir commands equivalent to the DelTree command.

/Q   Forces removal of the directory tree without asking the user first. You can use this option within a batch file to ensure the batch continues to run without user intervention.

Managing Removable Storage with the RSM Utility

The Removable Storage Management (RSM) utility helps you manage any portable media for your machine. Microsoft provides this utility so you can manage resources for applications that don't support the Removable Storage API through scripts or batch files. Early versions of the RSM utility relied on a simple command line and didn't provide much functionality. The following sections reflect the modes supported by newer versions of the utility.

NOTE   Like many utilities, the command line for RSM is case insensitive when you type actual arguments. However, this utility differs in that the media objects, which include media, drives, changers, libraries, media types, and slots, are case sensitive. If you have a drive named MyDrive and want to refer to it by its friendly name, then you must observe the actual case of the name when typing the command. In addition, unlike many utilities, you must type the arguments for a command line switch directly after the switch. For example, /MMyPool will work, but /M MyPool won't because it has a space between the command line switch and the argument.

Windows operating systems, Vista and above, do provide support for the RSM utility. However, you won't find it in the same location as previous versions of Windows. Depending on your system configuration, you'll likely find this utility in the \Windows\winsxs\x86_microsoft-windows-r..emanagement-service_31bf3856ad364e35_6.0.5744.16384_none_21ccd2c119fdb6d5 folder of your hard drive. In addition, you might see complaints about a missing NTMSAPI.DLL file that you'll find in the \Windows\winsxs\x86_microsoft-windows-r..management-apilayer_31bf3856ad364e35_6.0.5744.16384_none_cb8fdf31cbc6c1a7 folder. Theoretically, Microsoft will eventually work out all of these issues. In the meantime, you may have to spend some time getting the RSM utility to work. All you need to do is create a new folder and place all of the files from both directories into it to make RSM work under Server Core. Make sure you have full rights to the new folder or the copy process will fail.

ALLOCATE

Use the ALLOCATE mode to allocate existing media for a specific use. This mode uses the following syntax:

```
RSM ALLOCATE /M<MediaPoolName> [/L[G|F]<LogicalMediaID> |
    /P[G|F]<PartitionID>] /O[{ERRUNAVAIL | NEW | NEXT}] [/T{<timeout> |
    INFINITE}] [/LN<LogicalMediaName>] [/LD<LogicalMediaDescription>]
    [/PN<PartitionName>] [/PD<PartitionDescription>] [/B]
```

The following list describes each of the command line arguments.

/MMediaPoolName   Specifies the name of the media pool to use for the allocation.

/LGLogicalMediaIdentifier   Defines the logical media identifier as a GUID.

/LFLogicalMediaIdentifier   Defines the logical media identifier as a friendly name.

/PG*PartitionID*   Defines the partition identifier as a GUID.

/PF*PartitionID*   Defines the partition identifier as a friendly name.

/O[{ERRUNAVAIL | NEW | NEXT}]   Defines the removable storage allocation options. You may use more than one command line switch to define multiple options, but each option must appear as a separate command line switch. The ERRUNAVAIL option specifies that the utility submit a request for new media to the operator when the allocation fails due to a lack of media. The NEW option allocates media in such a way that another application can't use the media. You can use this option to reserve the second side of two-sided media for exclusive use of a single application. Once you set the media aside, you must actually allocate it with the NEXT option. The NEXT option allocates the next partition of media previously allocated using the NEW option.

/T{timeout | INFINITE}   Specifies the timeout value for a drive in milliseconds. The timeout value determines how long the utility waits for the media allocation to succeed. The default setting is INFINITE.

/LN*LogicalMediaName*   Defines the friendly name that the utility assigns to the LogicalMedia object of the allocated media.

/PN*PartitionName*   Defines the friendly name that the utility assigns to the Partition object of the allocated media.

/LD*LogicalMediaDescription*   Defines the description that the utility assigns to the LogicalMedia object of the allocated media.

/LD*PartitionDescription*   Defines the description that the utility assigns to the Partition object of the allocated media.

/B   Specifies the bare option that you can use with scripts. The utility displays only the GUIDs of the allocated media. You can redirect this output to another utility to perform additional media processing.

DEALLOCATE

Use the DEALLOCATE mode to deallocate previously allocated media. This mode uses the following syntax:

```
RSM DEALLOCATE /L[G|F]<LogicalMediaID> | /P[G|F]<PartitionID>
```

The following list describes each of the command line arguments.

/LG*LogicalMediaID*   Defines the logical media to deallocate as a GUID.

/LF*LogicalMediaID*   Defines the logical media to deallocate as a friendly name.

/PG*PartitionID*   Defines the partition to deallocate as a GUID.

/PF*PartitionID*   Defines the partition to deallocate as a friendly name.

MOUNT

Use the MOUNT mode to make removable media available for use. This mode uses the following syntax:

```
RSM MOUNT /L[G|F]<LogicalMediaID> /O[{ERRUNAVAIL | READ | WRITE |
    OFFLINE}] [/R[{NORMAL | HIGH | LOW | HIGHEST | LOWEST}]
    [/T{timeout | INFINITE}]]
```

```
RSM MOUNT /P[G|F]<PartitionID> /O[{ERRUNAVAIL | READ | WRITE |
    OFFLINE}] [/R[{NORMAL | HIGH | LOW | HIGHEST | LOWEST}]
    [/T{timeout | INFINITE}]
RSM MOUNT /S[G|F]<SlotID> /O[{ERRUNAVAIL | READ | WRITE | OFFLINE}]
    [/R[{NORMAL | HIGH | LOW | HIGHEST | LOWEST}] [/T{timeout | INFINITE}]
RSM MOUNT /C[G|F]<ChangerID /O[{ERRUNAVAIL | READ | WRITE | OFFLINE}]
    [/R[{NORMAL | HIGH | LOW | HIGHEST | LOWEST}] [/T{timeout | INFINITE}]
RSM MOUNT /D[G|F]<DriveID> /O[{ERRUNAVAIL | DRIVE | READ | WRITE |
    OFFLINE}] [/R[{NORMAL | HIGH | LOW | HIGHEST | LOWEST}]
    [/T{timeout | INFINITE}]
```

The following list describes each of the command line arguments.

/LG*LogicalMediaID* Defines the logical media to mount as a GUID.

/LF*LogicalMediaID* Defines the logical media to mount as a friendly name.

/PG*PartitionID* Defines the partition to mount as a GUID.

/PF*PartitionID* Defines the partition to mount as a friendly name.

/SG*SlotID* Defines the slot identifier to mount as a GUID.

/SF*SlotID* Defines the slot identifier to mount as a friendly name.

/CG*ChangerID* Defines the changer identifier to mount as a GUID.

/CF*ChangerID* Defines the changer identifier to mount as a friendly name.

/DG*DriveID* Defines the drive identifier to mount as a GUID.

/DF*DriveID* Defines the drive identifier to mount as a friendly name.

/O[{ERRUNAVAIL | DRIVE | READ | WRITE | OFFLINE}] Defines the removable storage allocation options. You may use more than one command line switch to define multiple options, but each option must appear as a separate command line switch. The ERRUNAVAIL option tells the utility to generate an error if either the media or the drive isn't available. The error normally notifies an operator of the need to fix the drive. The READ option mounts the drive for read access. The WRITE option mounts the drive for write access. This option fails when you try to mount media that's marked as completed (non-writeable). The DRIVE option is required when you use the /DG or /DF options. The OFFLINE option tells the utility to generate an error if the media isn't online.

/T{timeout | INFINITE} Specifies the timeout value for a drive in milliseconds. The timeout value determines how long the utility waits for the media allocation to succeed. The default setting is INFINITE.

[/R[{NORMAL | HIGH | LOW | HIGHEST | LOWEST}] Specifies the mount priority of the media. The system mounts higher priority media first. The default priority is NORMAL.

DISMOUNT

Use the DISMOUNT mode to remove media from service. This mode uses the following syntax:

```
RSM DISMOUNT /L[G|F]<LogicalMediaID> | /P[G|F]<PartitionID> [/O[DEFERRED]]
```

The following list describes each of the command line arguments.

/LG*LogicalMediaID* Defines the logical media to dismount as a GUID.

/LF*LogicalMediaID*   Defines the logical media to dismount as a friendly name.

/PG*PartitionID*   Defines the partition to dismount as a GUID.

/PF*PartitionID*   Defines the partition to dismount as a friendly name.

/O [DEFERRED]   Defines the removable storage allocation options. The DEFERRED option marks the media as dismountable, but keeps the media in the drive. The default setting dismounts the media immediately and ejects it from the drive.

EJECT

Use the EJECT mode to eject media from the device. When the media is virtual, then the utility performs the equivalent of ejecting the media from the device; the bottom line is that the media is no longer available for use. This mode uses the following syntax:

```
RSM EJECT /P[G|F]<PhysicalMediaID> [/A[{START | STOP | QUEUE}]]
    [/O<EjectOperation>] [/B]
RSM EJECT /S[G|F]<SlotID> /L[G|F]<LibraryID> [/A[{START | STOP |
    QUEUE}]] [/O<EjectOperation>] [/B]
RSM EJECT /D[G|F]<DriveID> /L[G|F]<LibraryID> [/A[{START | STOP |
    QUEUE}]] [/O<EjectOperation>] [/B]
```

The following list describes each of the command line arguments.

/PG*PhysicalMediaID*   Defines the physical media identifier to eject as a GUID.

/PF*PhysicalMediaID*   Defines the physical media identifier to eject as a friendly name.

/SG*SlotID*   Defines the slot identifier to eject as a GUID.

/SF*SlotID*   Defines the slot identifier to eject as a friendly name.

/DG*DriveID*   Defines the drive identifier to eject as a GUID.

/DF*DriveID*   Defines the drive identifier to eject as a friendly name.

/LG*LibraryID*   Specifies the library to eject as a GUID. Use a GUID with the /SG and /DG options. The library identifier is the specific media to eject from the drive.

/LF*LibraryID*   Specifies the library to eject as a friendly name. Use a friendly name with the /SF and /DF options. The library identifier is the specific media to eject from the drive.

/A[{START | STOP | QUEUE}]   Defines the ejection action to perform. The default action is START. The START action begins the ejection process. The system ejects the media until a timeout occurs (the timeout value appears as part of the library object for all ejects in the library) or you call this command with a STOP action. The STOP action terminates the eject operation. You must use the GUID returned when you start the ejection to perform a STOP action. The QUEUE action queues the media for ejection. The system ejects the media in turn. You can use this action to group media for multi-slot Inputs/Exports (IEPorts). The discussion at http://www.osronline.com/ddkx/storage/05chgr_59nr.htm provides IEPort details.

/O*EjectOperation*   Obtains the GUID when you use eject with the START action (or switch). Use the resulting GUID with the STOP action (or switch) to stop the eject process.

/B   Specifies the bare option that you can use with scripts. You can redirect this output to another utility to perform additional media processing.

EJECTATAPI

Use the EJECTATAPI mode to eject media from an Advanced Technology Attachment Packet Interface (ATAPI) device. This mode uses the following syntax:

```
RSM EJECTATAPI /N<AtapiChangerNumber>
```

The following describes the command line argument.

/N*AtapiChangerNumber* Specifies the number found at the end of the device name for the changer. For example, CdChanger0 has a changer number of 0. The number uniquely identifies the device.

CREATEPOOL

Use the CREATEPOOL mode to create a new media pool. This mode uses the following syntax:

```
RSM CREATEPOOL /M<MediaPoolName> [/T[G|F]<MediaPoolTypeID>]
    /A[{EXISTING | ALWAYS | NEW}] [/D] [/R]
```

The following list describes each of the command line arguments.

/M*MediaPoolName* Specifies the name of the media pool that you want to create.

/TG*MediaPoolTypeID* Defines the media pool type identifier as a GUID.

/TF*MediaPoolTypeID* Defines the media pool type identifier as a friendly name.

/A[{EXISTING | ALWAYS | NEW}] Defines the pool creation action to perform. The EXISTING action opens an existing media pool. It returns an error when an existing media pool doesn't exist. The ALWAYS action opens an existing media pool or creates a new media pool when one doesn't exist. The NEW action always creates a new media pool. It returns an error when a media pool already exists.

/D Specifies that the media pool can draw media from the free pool.

/R Specifies that the media pool can return media to the free pool.

DELETEPOOL

Use the DELETEPOOL mode to remove a media pool. This mode uses the following syntax:

```
RSM DELETEPOOL /M<MediaPoolName>
```

The following describes the command line argument.

/M*MediaPoolName* Specifies the name of the media pool that you want to delete.

VIEW

Use the VIEW mode to display one of the RSM objects on screen. You can use this mode to discover any information you need to use any of the other modes described for this utility. This mode uses the following syntax:

```
RSM VIEW /T[{DRIVE | LIBRARY | CHANGER | STORAGESLOT | IEDOOR | IEPORT
    | PHYSICAL_MEDIA | MEDIA_POOL | PARTITION | LOGICAL_MEDIA |
    MEDIA_TYPE | DRIVE_TYPE | LIBREQUEST}] [/CG<ContainerID>] [/GUIDDISPLAY] [/B]
```

The following list describes each of the command line arguments.

/T[{DRIVE | LIBRARY | CHANGER | STORAGESLOT | IEDOOR | IEPORT | PHYSICAL_MEDIA | MEDIA_POOL | PARTITION | LOGICAL_MEDIA | MEDIA_TYPE | DRIVE_TYPE | LIBREQUEST}] Defines the kind of information you want the utility to return. You may only request one media object at a time. The output always contains the object's friendly name data unless you specify the /GUIDDISPLAY command line switch. You must specify a particular object; using /T alone displays an error message.

/CG*ContainerID* Specifies the container identifier for an object as a GUID.

/GUIDDISPLAY Specifies that the output should appear as a GUID, rather than as a friendly name.

/B Specifies the bare option that you can use with scripts. You can redirect this output to another utility to perform additional media processing.

REFRESH

Use the REFRESH mode to refresh the library, physical media, or all devices of a particular media type. The refresh cycle obtains the latest device information. This mode uses the following syntax:

```
RSM REFRESH /L[G|F]<LibraryID>
RSM REFRESH /P[G|F]<PhysicalMediaID>
RSM REFRESH /TG<MediaTypeID>
```

The following list describes each of the command line arguments.

/LG*LibraryID* Specifies the library to eject as a GUID. Use a GUID with the /SG and /DG options. The library identifier is the specific media to eject from the drive.

/LF*LibraryID* Specifies the library to eject as a friendly name. Use a friendly name with the /SF and /DF options. The library identifier is the specific media to eject from the drive.

/PG*PhysicalMediaID* Defines the physical media identifier to eject as a GUID.

/PF*PhysicalMediaID* Defines the physical media identifier to eject as a friendly name.

/TG*MediaTypeID* Defines the media type identifier as a GUID.

INVENTORY

Use the INVENTORY mode to create an inventory of the specified library. The system queues the request, so it might not execute immediately. This mode uses the following syntax:

```
RSM INVENTORY /L[G|F]<LibraryID> /A[{FULL | FAST | DEFAULT | NONE | STOP}]
```

The following list describes each of the command line arguments.

/LG*LibraryID* Specifies the library to inventory as a GUID.

/LF*LibraryID* Specifies the library to inventory as a friendly name.

/A[{FULL | FAST | DEFAULT | NONE | STOP}] Defines an action to perform for the inventory. You may only choose one of the options. The FULL action performs a complete on-media inventory. The FAST action performs a differential inventory of the media (to look for changes between this inventory and a previous inventory) unless the library has a bar code reader installed. When a bar code reader is present, the utility performs a bar code inventory. The DEFAULT action uses the inventory method specified as part of the library object. The NONE action doesn't perform any inventory. The STOP action causes the current inventory, if any, to terminate.

Associating a Folder to a Drive with the Subst Utility

The Subst utility is one that just about anyone can use. It makes a directory look like a new drive to a user. In fact, this effect shows itself in Windows Explorer, so the Subst utility has a lasting impact on your system. This utility uses the following syntax:

```
SUBST [drive1: [drive2:]path]
SUBST drive1: /D
```

The following list describes each of the command line arguments.

drive1   Specifies the drive to substitute for the directory specification you provide. The default is the current drive.

drive2   Specifies the drive that contains the directory for substitution. The default is the current drive.

path1   Specifies the absolute or relative path to substitute. The default is the current directory.

/D   Terminates the directory substitution. You can also terminate the substitution using Windows Explorer.

USING THE SUBST UTILITY EFFECTIVELY

The Subst utility performs a task that you can't perform within the Windows GUI. It makes directories easily accessible to users. Instead of digging through the directory hierarchy, the user can access the directory using a drive letter. In addition, you can use the Subst utility to equalize all systems on a network, even if the various machines have different drive configurations. For example, you could set all machines to use Drive X as the word processing directory. The Subst utility can also make network reconfigurations invisible to the user. If you set Drive X as the word processing drive, it doesn't matter where the actual directory appears on the network and you can move it around at will. Here's an example of the Subst utility used to redirect the G:\Windows directory to the L drive.

```
Subst L: G:\WINDOWS
```

The substitute drive letter always appears first; the directory appears second. Type **Subst** by itself to display a list of substituted directories. You can obtain additional ideas and detailed information about this technique by reviewing the TechRepublic article at http://techrepublic.com.com/5100-10877_11-5975262.html?tag=nl.e064.

Displaying a Directory Structure with the Tree Utility

If you've ever tried to get a complete picture of the directory structure of your hard drive using Windows Explorer, you know the task is tough. Windows Explorer focuses on helping you perform tasks, so it tends to focus your attention on a specific set of directories on the hard drive. In fact, the default settings actually hide many directories from view. The Tree utility hides nothing.

It's easy to become quite overwhelmed by the amount of information it provides. This utility uses the following syntax:

```
TREE [drive:][path] [/F] [/A]
```

The following list describes each of the command line arguments.

drive   Specifies the drive to examine. The default is the current drive.

path   Specifies the absolute or relative path to examine. The default is the current directory.

/F   Displays the filenames in each directory as well as the directory names.

/A   Displays the output using standard ASCII characters, rather than extended ASCII characters that have a graphical appearance.

One of the best reasons to use the Tree utility is to explore your drive looking for places to clean out old information. This utility can also help you locate hidden directories and even provide a certain level of virus detection because most virus writers are counting on you to use Windows utilities to explore the hard drive. The fact that you can run this utility from the recovery console means that you can even use it to explore the drive for rootkits—a particularly nasty form of virus that actually hides itself from view when Windows is operating.

WARNING   Rootkits are particularly dangerous viruses because you don't even know you have one. They hide by using the operating system to trick you into not seeing the folders that store the executables. The rootkit writer doesn't want you to know the rootkit is in place, so don't expect a rootkit to do anything odd or strange. In fact, unlike common viruses, rootkits often go out of their way not to use your system to propagate because that action would expose them. Because of the level of integration a rootkit requires with the operating system, even removing a rootkit is going to cause problems because now your system is compromised at a low level. This book doesn't provide you with enough information to rid your system of a rootkit, but the Tree utility can help you detect one when used correctly. Obviously, third-party utilities specifically designed for the task will locate a rootkit faster. If you suspect your system has a rootkit installed, you'll want to spend time viewing online resources such as the Rootkit Web site at http:// www.rootkit.com/. You can learn more about rootkits at http://en.wikipedia.org/ wiki/Rootkit.

Managing the Volume Shadow Service with the VSSAdmin Utility

The VSSAdmin utility lets you view the status of the VSS, which is a method of providing a backup copy of Windows. (Learn more about how VSS works on the Microsoft Web site at http://www .microsoft.com/windowsserversystem/wss2003/techinfo/plandeploy/stormgtusingvdsvss .mspx.) This utility uses the following syntax:

```
VSSAdmin list shadows [/set={shadow copy set guid}]
VSSAdmin list writers
VSSAdmin list providers
VSSAdmin list volumes
VSSAdmin resize storage /For=ForVolumeSpec /On=OnVolumeSpec
    [/MaxSize=MaxSizeSpec]
```

The following list describes each of the command line arguments.

/set={shadow copy set guid}   Determines which shadow copy set to list based on the GUID provided as input.

shadows   Lists all of the shadow copies on the system grouped by GUID.

writers   Displays a list of shadow volume writers on the system. Common shadow writers include Internet Information Server (IIS), Windows Management Interface (WMI), and Microsoft Data Engine (MSDE). The information includes the writer name in human-readable form, writer identifier as a GUID, the writer instance identifier as a GUID, and the current writer state.

providers   Displays the current VSS provider information. This information includes the provider name, provider type, provider identifier as a GUID, and the version number.

volumes   Displays a list of volumes eligible for shadow copies. In general, you can shadow any permanent hard drive on the system.

The new resize storage mode lets you change the amount of storage set aside for shadow copies on the specified volume. The following list describes each of the command line arguments.

/For=ForVolumeSpec   Defines the volume for which you want to provide a shadow copy.

/On=OnVolumeSpec   Defines the volume that will hold the shadow copy. This volume must be different from the /For argument volume.

/MaxSize=MaxSizeSpec   Specifies the maximum size of the shadow copy. If you don't specify this value, then the shadow copy can be as large as the free space on the shadow drive. The minimum shadow copy size is 300 MB. You may include any of the following size definitions: KB, MB, GB, TB, PB, and EB. If you don't specify a size, then VSSAdmin assumes that you supplied the value in bytes.

Managing Windows in a New Way

Your hard drive is possibly the most vulnerable and valuable resources on your server. Even if the hard drive exists in a separate location, the fact that the server relies on it for all permanent storage makes it incredibly important. In this chapter, you've learned about the functionality that Server Core provides for managing the hard drive, even if the hard drive is part of a SAN or requires an iSCSI setup. The point is that you now have the tools to work with a hard drive in any way necessary to preserve data. It's important to remember that this chapter is about the hard drive and not about the data on the hard drive. To discover more about data, review Chapters 14 and 15. This chapter helps you build these skills:

- Manage an existing hard drive configuration
- Convert FAT partitions to use NTFS
- Create and manage hard drive partitions
- Work with RAID configurations
- Work with iSCSI configurations
- Improve hard drive performance

Now that you know quite a bit more about the hard drive, try using some of the utilities on a test system. Never attempt to work with these utilities on a production server unless you've worked with them extensively. A small mistake may seem minor until you try to recover the data lost on the hard drive. If you work with a test system for a while first, you can learn from any mistakes in a nonthreatening environment. Errors on a test server are easier to overcome.

Chapter 10 moves onto the next piece of hardware that will require frequent maintenance, the network. Although the network hardware doesn't have any moving parts, it's subject to a great deal of abuse. People end up crushing cabling, moving cables around, disconnecting Network Interface Cards (NICs), and generally making it difficult to maintain any kind of connection. Even though the utilities in Chapter 10 can't provide a complete solution, they do make working with the network considerably easier.

Chapter 10

Managing the Network

Networks are complex combinations of hardware and software that link systems together so they can work interactively and share data. A network can consist of static or dynamic connections. Managing these connections in Server Core can be a bit of a challenge if you're used to working exclusively with the GUI. However, a surprising number of administrators probably have some level of experience because many tasks are simply faster to perform at the command line, so Server Core may not prove as big a shock as you think in this area.

NOTE Generally, all networks follow the same rules or protocols. A *protocol* is simply a kind of rule that everyone has agreed to follow, usually through a standards organization. The most famous of these rules is the International Standards Organization/Open Systems Interconnection (ISO/OSI) seven-layer network model discussed at http://en.wikipedia.org/wiki/OSI_model.

This chapter isn't going to help you configure your network or provide you with advice on how to create a network. You'll find network configuration basics in Chapter 1. In addition, many other books can help you through that process. However, the sections in this chapter do describe the many useful utilities that Microsoft provides for navigating all seven layers of the network model. In many cases, these utilities provide you with insights about the construction of your network and how to prevent outside intrusion (or at least keep it at bay). The utilities you use depend, in part, on the combination of hardware and software you use, so you need to have some idea of what your network uses before these sections will become completely useful.

In this chapter, you'll learn how to do the following:

◆ Obtain Media Access Control (MAC) information with the GetMAC utility

◆ Manage the network configuration using the Net utility

NOTE You may notice as you progress through the book that some older network utilities such as ATMAdm and ProxyCfg are missing. Some Netware related commands, such as IPXRoute are also missing. Microsoft is taking the upgrade to Windows Server 2008, especially the Server Core version, as an opportunity to get rid of some older commands. I'd be interested in knowing whether you use any of these older commands. If you do, feel free to contact me at JMueller@mwt.net.

Getting the Media Access Control Information with the GetMAC Utility

Every network adapter has a Media Access Control (MAC) address. The address is unique for every network adapter across all vendors. The output from this utility consists of the network adapter MAC address and the transport name associated with it. You don't gain much in the way of additional information. However, the MAC address is central to all kinds of monitoring activity, including sniffing packets on your network (the act of filtering the packets and viewing the ones of interest). This utility uses the following syntax:

```
GETMAC [/S system [/U [domain\]user [/P [password]]]]
[/FO {TABLE | LIST | CSV}] [/NH] [/V]
```

The following describes the command line arguments.

/S *system*   Specifies the remote system that you want to check. In most cases, you'll also need to supply the /U and the /P command line switches when using this switch.

/U [*domain***\]***user***   Specifies the username on the remote system. This name may not match the username on the local system. You'll need to supply a domain name when working with a domain controller.

/P [*password***]**   Specifies the password for the given user. You can provide the command line switch without specifying the password on the command line in cleartext. The system prompts you for the password. Using this feature can help you maintain the security of passwords used on your system.

/FO {TABLE | LIST | CSV}   Defines the output provided by the utility. The table format is normally the easiest to view on screen. The table columns define the values for output, while each row contains one driver entry. The Comma Separated Value (CSV) output provides the best method for preparing the data for entry in a database. Use redirection (see the "Employing Data Redirection" section of Chapter 14 for details) to output the CSV data to a file and then import it to your database. The list format provides one data element per line. Each group of data elements defines one driver. The utility separates each driver by one blank line. Some people find the list format more readable when working in verbose mode since the table format requires multiple lines for each entry (the lines wrap).

/NH   Forces the utility to display the data without a column header. You can only use this command line switch with the table and CSV formats. Omitting the header makes it easier to incorporate the data in a report or import it into a database.

/V   Displays detailed data about each of the network adapters. In addition to the standard output, the utility provides the human-readable connection name and network adapter name. Using this command line switch makes it a lot easier to associate a particular MAC address with a specific network adapter (making monitoring easier as well).

Managing the Network with the Net Utility

The Net utility represents one of the most flexible and comprehensive means of controlling all aspects of your network. Given all that it does, it's not surprising that the Net utility relies on several operating modes to perform tasks. For example, you manage user accounts using the Accounts mode. The Net utility modes include Accounts, Computer, Config, Continue, File, Group, Help, HelpMsg, LocalGroup, Name, Pause, Print, Send, Session, Share, Start, Statistics, Stop, Time, Use, User, and View. The following sections describe each of these modes.

NOTE   If you find that you need help with the Net utility, you can't use the standard practice of typing /?. The /? command line switch provides extremely limited help. Instead, you need to type **Net Help Mode** at the command line and press Enter. For example, to obtain help on using the Accounts mode, type **Net Help Accounts** and press Enter.

ACCOUNTS

Use the ACCOUNTS mode to modify all user accounts on a system with specific settings. For example, you can define all user accounts to have a maximum password age of so many days. This mode only affects existing user accounts—not user accounts that you create in the future. Typing Net Accounts by itself displays the current settings. This mode uses the following syntax:

```
NET ACCOUNTS [/FORCELOGOFF:{minutes | NO}] [/MINPWLEN:length]
[/MAXPWAGE:{days | UNLIMITED}] [/MINPWAGE:days] [/UNIQUEPW:number]
[/DOMAIN]
```

The following list describes each of the command line arguments.

/FORCELOGOFF:{*minutes* | NO}   Sets the number of minutes before the system forces a user to log off after the user's account or valid logon hours expire. The default setting of NO prevents forced logoff.

/MINPWLEN:*length*   Sets the minimum number of characters in a password. The default setting is 6 characters. You may use any value between 0 and 14 characters.

/MAXPWAGE:{*days* | UNLIMITED}   Sets the maximum number of days between password changes. You may define no password change requirement by using the UNLIMITED argument. The /MAXPWAGE setting must always exceed the /MINPWAGE setting. The default setting is 90 days. You may use any value between 1 and 999 days.

/MINPWAGE:*days*   Sets the minimum number of days that must pass before a user can change their password. A value of 0 sets non-minimum time. The /MAXPWAGE setting must always exceed the /MINPWAGE setting. The default setting is 0 days. You may use any value between 0 and 999 days.

/UNIQUEPW:*number*   Specifies that the user must provide a unique password for each password change through the number specified. For example, if you specify 5, then the system tracks five of the user's passwords and allows the user to reuse a password on the sixth change. The maximum value is 24.

/DOMAIN   Performs the task on a domain control for the current domain. Otherwise, any task affects only the local computer.

COMPUTER

Use the COMPUTER mode to add a computer to the domain database or delete it from the database. You can only use this mode on a server. This mode uses the following syntax:

```
NET COMPUTER \\computername {/ADD | /DEL}
```

The following list describes each of the command line arguments.

computername   Specifies the Universal Naming Convention (UNC) name of the computer to add or delete. Always use the computer's name as it appears to the network.

/ADD   Adds the specified computer to the domain.

/DEL   Removes the specified computer from the domain.

CONFIG

Use the CONFIG mode to discover network configuration information for the current machine. When used alone, this mode displays the configurable services on a machine. This mode uses the following syntax:

```
NET CONFIG [SERVER | WORKSTATION]
```

The following list describes each of the command line arguments.

Server Displays information about the configuration of the server service. This information includes the server name, server comment, software version, network node information, whether the server is hidden, the maximum number of users that can log in, the maximum number of available file handles per session, and the idle session time.

Workstation Displays information about the configuration of the workstation service. This information includes computer UNC name, full computer name, username, network node information, software version, workstation domain, workstation Domain Name Service (DNS) name, logon domain, and COM statistics.

CONFIG SERVER

You can use the CONFIG SERVER mode to adjust a few, but not all, of the server configuration features. This mode uses the following syntax:

```
NET CONFIG SERVER [/AUTODISCONNECT:time] [/SRVCOMMENT:"text"] [/HIDDEN:{YES | NO}]
```

The following list describes each of the command line arguments.

/AUTODISCONNECT:time Sets the maximum number of minutes that a user's session remains inactive before the server disconnects it. Use a value of –1 to force the system to remain connected indefinitely. You may use any value from –1 to 65,535 minutes. The default setting is 15 minutes.

/SRVCOMMENT:"text" Adds a comment to the server information. The comment appears in all graphical displays and in the Net View mode. You may use up to 48 characters for the comment. Always enclose comments in quotes.

/HIDDEN:{YES | NO} Determines whether the server appears in the display listing for servers. Using this feature can prevent unauthorized users from finding a server on your network since the user would need to know the server name to access it. However, this setting doesn't change the server security. You still have to set security aggressively to protect your server. The default setting is NO.

CONTINUE

Use this mode to reactivate a service that you suspended using the Net Pause mode or the Services console located in the Administrative Tools folder of the Control Panel. This mode uses the following syntax:

```
NET CONTINUE service
```

The following list describes each of the command line arguments.

service Specifies the name of the service to reactivate. Always enclose services that contain a space in their name in quotes. The following list contains typical service names.

NET LOGON

NT LM SECURITY SUPPORT PROVIDER

SCHEDULE

SERVER

WORKSTATION

FILE

Use this mode to control shared files on a system. When used alone, the FILE mode displays a list of active files on the current system. This mode uses the following syntax:

```
NET FILE [id [/CLOSE]]
```

The following list describes each of the command line arguments.

id Specifies a particular open file. Queries information about a specific file when used alone.

/CLOSE Closes the specified file and removes any file locks.

GROUP

Use the GROUP mode to query, add, delete, and modify Windows groups. Use this mode alone to display a list of groups on the domain controller. This command only works on Windows domain controllers. Use the LocalGroup mode for local workstations instead. This mode uses the following syntax:

```
NET GROUP [groupname [/COMMENT:"text"]] [/DOMAIN]
NET GROUP groupname /ADD [/COMMENT:"text"] [/DOMAIN]
NET GROUP groupname /DELETE [/DOMAIN]
NET GROUP groupname username [...] /ADD [/DOMAIN]
NET GROUP groupname username [...] /DELETE [/DOMAIN]
```

The following list describes each of the command line arguments.

groupname Defines the name of the group that you want to query, add, delete, or modify. Providing just the group name displays the list of users in that group. You also see the group alias and comment (the comment normally indicates the purpose of the group).

/COMMENT:"text" Adds or modifies a comment for a new or existing group. You may use up to 48 characters to describe a group. Always enclose comments within quotes.

/DOMAIN Performs the specified task on the domain controller for the current domain. Using this command line switch lets you use a workstation for making changes to groups and users on the domain controller. The default setting performs tasks on the local machine, which means that the utility fails unless you're working at the domain controller.

username[...] Defines one or more usernames to add or remove from a group. Separate multiple entries with a space.

/ADD   Adds a group or a username to a group.

/DELETE   Removes a group or a username from a group.

HELP

The HELP mode displays detailed help about the other modes. This mode uses the following syntax:

```
NET HELP command
```

The following describes the command line argument.

command   Specifies the command (mode) for which you want help. The Help mode provides NET HELP SERVICES to show the services that you can start and stop using the Net utility. Use NET HELP SYNTAX to see help on using the various Help mode screens. Enter **NET HELP HELP** at the command line to see a complete list of Help mode screens.

HELPMSG

The Net utility displays a wealth of messages to provide information, warnings, and error indications. In addition, you can run into these messages when using Windows. For example, the event log often contains network-specific messages. Often, these messages appear as a number. The HELPMSG mode accepts a number as input and outputs the information in human readable form. This mode uses the following syntax:

```
NET HELPMSG MessageNumber
```

The following describes the command line argument.

MessageNumber   Specifies a four-digit error number that Windows displays for information, warning, or error indication. Type only the four-digit number. You don't need to provide the NET prefix that Windows displays with some messages. For example, one common error is NET2182. You'd type **Net HelpMsg 2182** and press Enter at the command prompt to display the human-readable message of "The requested service has already been started."

LOCALGROUP

Use the LOCALGROUP mode to query, add, delete, and modify Windows groups on the local machine. Use this mode alone to display a list of groups on the local machine. This mode uses the following syntax:

```
NET LOCALGROUP [groupname [/COMMENT:"text"]] [/DOMAIN]
NET LOCALGROUP groupname /ADD [/COMMENT:"text"] [/DOMAIN]
NET LOCALGROUP groupname /DELETE [/DOMAIN]
NET LOCALGROUP groupname name [...] /ADD [/DOMAIN]
NET LOCALGROUP groupname name [...] /DELETE [/DOMAIN]
```

The following list describes each of the command line arguments.

groupname   Defines the name of the group that you want to query, add, delete, or modify. Providing just the group name displays the list of users in that group. You also see the group alias and comment (the comment normally indicates the purpose of the group).

/COMMENT:"*text*"   Adds or modifies a comment for a new or existing group. You may use up to 48 characters to describe a group. Always enclose comments within quotes.

/DOMAIN Performs the specified task on the domain controller for the current domain. Using this command line switch lets you use a workstation for making changes to groups and users on the domain controller. The default setting performs tasks on the local machine.

username[...] Defines one or more usernames to add or remove from a group. Separate multiple entries with a space.

/ADD Adds a group or a username to a group.

/DELETE Removes a group or a username from a group.

NAME

The NAME mode adds and deletes aliases for users of the Windows Messenger service. Administrators commonly use this service to send network messages and other important information. Sources of aliases for messages include names added with the Net Name utility, the computer name (added as a name when the workstation service starts), and a username (added when you log into the computer). You can't delete the workstation name as a destination for messages. This mode uses the following syntax:

```
NET NAME [name [/ADD | /DELETE]]
```

The following list describes each of the command line arguments.

name Specifies the alias (name) to receive messages. The name can contain up to 15 characters.

/ADD Adds the name of the list of aliases for a computer. Using this command line switch is optional. Typing **Net Name** name and pressing Enter automatically adds the name to the list.

/DELETE Removes the name for the list of aliases for the computer.

WARNING The Net Name mode relies on the Windows Messenger service. This isn't the same as Microsoft Messenger, the online utility. Windows Messenger sends messages between machines on the network. Microsoft recommends disabling this particular service because crackers commonly target it as a way to spread a virus on a network. In general, you don't want to use this service in place of more common methods of sending messages, such as email. You can discover how to disable this service on the About Web site at http://antivirus.about.com/cs/tutorials/ht/msgsvc.htm. As one example of what can happen with Windows Messenger, see the Microsoft Knowledge Base article at http://support.microsoft.com/kb/883261.

PAUSE

Use the PAUSE mode to suspend a service temporarily. Use Net Stop when you wish to stop a service long term. Pausing a service maintains its presence in memory and therefore preserves the service's state information. Stopping a service removes it from memory and frees the resources that the service is using. This mode uses the following syntax:

```
NET PAUSE service
```

The following describes the command line argument.

service Specifies the name of the service to pause. Always enclose services that contain a space in their name in quotes. The following list contains typical service names.

- NET LOGON
- NT LM SECURITY SUPPORT PROVIDER

◆ SCHEDULE

◆ SERVER

◆ WORKSTATION

You can't pause some services. The Net utility displays an error when you try to stop some services. Here's a list of common services that you can't pause.

◆ DCOM Server Process Launcher

◆ Event Log

◆ Plug and Play

◆ Remote Procedure Call (RPC)

◆ Security Accounts Manager

PRINT

The PRINT mode controls printing on the local machine. Used with just the sharename, the Net Print command displays the status of the print queue. You can also use this mode to manage the existing print jobs. This mode uses the following syntax:

```
NET PRINT \\computername\sharename [\\computername] job#
[/HOLD | /RELEASE | /DELETE]
```

The following list describes each of the command line arguments.

\\computername   Specifies the name of the computer providing the print services as a queue.

sharename   Specifies the name of the print queue. The print queue name is the same as the sharename for the printer.

job#   Specifies the job number to modify. The system assigns the print job number when the user submits the print job. The computer provides each job with a unique number across printer queues.

/HOLD   Prevents a job from printing. All other jobs in the printer queue will bypass a job on hold and print. The job stays in the printer queue until the user releases the job or deletes it.

/RELEASE   Releases a job that a user previously placed on hold.

/DELETE   Removes a job from the printer queue.

SEND

Use the SEND mode to send a message to other users on the network with the Windows Messenger service. Unlike email, the message appears immediately on the remote system as a popup. The utility displays an error when you attempt to send a message to someone who's not active on the network. Use the Net Name utility to determine which users or systems are available to receive messages. This mode uses the following syntax:

```
NET SEND {name | * | /DOMAIN[:name] | /USERS} message
```

The following list describes each of the command line arguments.

name   Specifies the username, computer name, or messaging name to receive the message you send. Always enclose names that include spaces in quotes.

*   Sends the message to all of the names in your group. A group might only include the names in a workgroup and not the entire organization.

/DOMAIN[:name]   Sends the message to all of the names in a domain. The default is to use the current system's domain. You may also specify a domain name to send messages to other domains.

/USERS   Sends the message to all users connected to a particular server, regardless of the user workgroup and domain boundaries. Use this option when you intend to perform tasks such as shutting down a server.

message   Defines the message to send. Always enclose the message in quotes (even though the command line help for this utility doesn't mention the requirement to use quotes).

SESSION

Whenever your system acts as a server (the Server service is started) and someone uses a shared resource, the activity creates a session. The SESSION mode lists and deletes sessions associated with the specified computer. When used alone, it displays sessions for the local computer. Note that you must have the Server service started to use this mode. This mode uses the following syntax:

```
NET SESSION [\\computername] [/DELETE]
```

The following list describes each of the command line arguments.

\\computername   Specifies the name of a computer to work with when listing or deleting sessions.

/DELETE   Ends the session between the local computer and the specified computer. The utility closes all open files on the local computer for the ended session and frees any resources that the session uses. If you use this command line switch without specifying a computer, the utility ends all of the existing sessions.

SHARE

Use the SHARE mode to define resources available to other users or machines on the network. For example, you can choose to share a hard drive with other users on the network. When used alone, the SHARE mode displays a list of shared items on the local computer. Each shared item entry includes the device name, the pathname, and a descriptive comment. You must start the Server service to use this mode. This mode uses the following syntax:

```
NET SHARE sharename
NET SHARE sharename=drive:path [/USERS:number | /UNLIMITED]
[/REMARK:"text"] [/CACHE:Manual | Documents | Programs | None ]
NET SHARE sharename [/USERS:number | /UNLIMITED] [/REMARK:"text"]
 [/CACHE:Manual | Documents | Programs | None]
NET SHARE {sharename | devicename | drive:path} /DELETE
```

The following list describes each of the command line arguments.

sharename   Specifies the network name (the UNC name) of the shared resource. Type **Net Share sharename** alone and press Enter to display information about the shared resource including the sharename, path, remark, maximum users, users, and caching.

drive:path Specifies the absolute path of the drive or directory to share. The path must contain a drive letter and colon as a minimum. You share a directory by combining the drive information with an absolute path on that drive.

/USERS:number Defines the maximum number of users who can simultaneously access the shared resource.

/UNLIMITED Specifies that an unlimited number of users can simultaneously access the shared resource.

/REMARK:"text" Provides a descriptive comment about the shared resource. Always enclose the comment in quotes. It's a good idea to include a comment about the shared resource that specifies why you're sharing it. The more descriptive you make the comment, the easier it becomes for users who need the resource to find it.

devicename Defines one or more printers (LPT1: through LPT9:) by sharename.

/DELETE Stops sharing the resource.

/CACHE:Manual Enables manual client caching of programs and documents from this share. Using this option leaves the decision of whether to cache up to the user. Caching generally improves performance at the expense of local resources. Some devices might not have enough local resources to perform caching effectively.

/CACHE:Documents Enables automatic caching of documents from this share.

/CACHE:Programs Enables automatic caching of documents and programs from this share.

/CACHE:None Disables caching from this share.

START

Use this mode to start a service. You can also perform this task using the Services console located in the Administrative Tools folder of the Control Panel. Using Net Start alone displays a list of the services that are currently active on the local machine. This mode uses the following syntax:

```
NET START [service]
```

The following describes the command line argument.

service Specifies the name of the service to start. Always enclose services that contain a space in their name in quotes. The following list contains typical service names.

- ◆ NET LOGON
- ◆ NT LM SECURITY SUPPORT PROVIDER
- ◆ SCHEDULE
- ◆ SERVER
- ◆ WORKSTATION

STATISTICS

The STATISTICS mode displays the service statistics for the local workstation or Server service. When used alone, the mode displays the services for which you can obtain statistics. This mode uses the following syntax:

```
NET STATISTICS [WORKSTATION | SERVER]
```

The following list describes each of the command line arguments.

SERVER   Displays the Server service statistics, which include sessions accepted, sessions timed out, sessions errored out, kilobytes sent, kilobytes received, mean response time (msec), system errors, permission violations, password violations, files accessed, communication devices accessed, print jobs spooled, and times buffers exhausted (both big buffers and request buffers).

WORKSTATION   Displays the Workstation service statistics, which include bytes received, Server Message Blocks (SMBs) received, bytes transmitted, SMBs transmitted, read operations, write operations, raw reads denied, raw writes denied, network errors, connections made, reconnections made, server disconnects, sessions started, hung sessions, failed sessions, failed operations, use count, and failed use count.

STOP

Use this mode to stop a service that you started using the NET START mode or the Services console located in the Administrative Tools folder of the Control Panel. This mode uses the following syntax:

```
NET STOP service
```

The following describes the command line argument.

service   Specifies the name of the service to stop. Always enclose services that contain a space in their name in quotes. The following list contains typical service names.

- ◆ NET LOGON
- ◆ NT LM SECURITY SUPPORT PROVIDER
- ◆ SCHEDULE
- ◆ SERVER
- ◆ WORKSTATION

You can't stop some services. The Net utility displays an error when you try to stop some services. Here's a list of common unstoppable services.

- ◆ DCOM Server Process Launcher
- ◆ Event Log
- ◆ Plug and Play
- ◆ Remote Procedure Call (RPC)
- ◆ Security Accounts Manager

TIME

Use the TIME mode to access a time service. The essential task of this mode is to synchronize the local computer with a timeserver. Contrast this mode with the W32Tm utility discussed in Chapter 12. While the W32Tm utility interacts with the timeserver (and even creates it), the TIME mode interacts with the client and uses the timeserver as a resource. Read the Microsoft Knowledge Base article at http://support.microsoft.com/kb/q224799/ for additional Windows time service information. This mode uses the following syntax:

```
NET TIME [\\computername | /DOMAIN[:domainname]
| /RTSDOMAIN[:domainname]] [/SET] [\\computername] /QUERYSNTP
[\\computername] /SETSNTP[:ntp server list]
```

The following list describes each of the command line arguments.

\\\computername Specifies the name of the computer to check or use for synchronization.

/DOMAIN[:domainname] Specifies the domain of the PDC to use for synchronization purposes. The default is the client's current domain.

/RTSDOMAIN[:domainname] Specifies the domain of the Reliable Time Server (RTS) to use for synchronization purposes. The default is the client's current domain.

/SET Synchronizes the specified system's time (the default is the local system) with the time on the configured time source (a specific computer or domain).

/QUERYSNTP Displays the currently configured National Time Protocol (NTP) server for this computer.

/SETSNTP[:ntp server list] Sets the NTP timeservers that this computer relies on for synchronization. You may specify more than one server using IP addresses or DNS names separated by spaces. When working with multiple timeservers, you must surround the entire command line switch with quotes. Three common servers include tick.usno.navy.mil, tock.usno.navy.mil, and ntp2.usno.navy.mil.

USE

The USE mode connects a computer to a shared resource, disconnects a computer from a shared resource, or lists the shared resources. When used by itself, this mode displays the status, local drive letter, remote UNC source, and the network type of any drives the local system uses. This mode uses the following syntax:

```
NET USE [devicename | *] [\\computername\sharename[\volume]
[password | *]] [/USER:[domainname\]username] [/USER:[dotted
domainname\]username] [/USER:[username@dotted domainname] [/SMARTCARD]
 [/SAVECRED] [[/DELETE] | [/PERSISTENT:{YES | NO}]]
NET USE {devicename | *} [password | *] /HOME
NET USE [/PERSISTENT:{YES | NO}]
```

NOTE There's a lack of consistency between Windows and the Net Use utility when working with printers. If you create a connection to a drive using the standard Windows techniques, you'll see it in the list when you use the Net Use command. However, if you create a connection to a printer, the printer doesn't show up in the list, even if you ensure the printer has an LPT port connection. Any printer connections that you create using Net Use do show up in the list, but these connections don't show up in the Printers and Faxes folder. Generally, you'll want to work with printers in Windows unless you have a need for a printer connection in a batch file for script.

The following list describes each of the command line arguments.

devicename   Specifies a name to connect to the resource or specifies the device that you want to connect. The two device types are disk drives (D: through Z:) and printers (LPT1: through LPT3:). (It's theoretically possible to create printer connections up to LPT9: even though Microsoft only documents connections up to LPT3:.) Type an asterisk (*) instead of a specific device name to assign the next available device name to a device.

\\computername   Specifies the name of the computer that controls the shared resource. Make sure you enclose the computer name, including the backslashes, in double quotes when the computer name has a space in it. You may use any computer name from 1 to 15 characters long.

\sharename   Specifies the sharename for the resource you want to use. This entry is the same as the name that appears in Network Neighborhood.

\volume   Specifies a NetWare volume on the server. You must have the correct software installed on your system to access the NetWare volume. In most cases, this means you'll have Client Services for NetWare or Gateway Services for NetWare installed to connect to the NetWare servers.

password   Defines the password used to access the shared resource, which isn't necessarily the same as the local password.

*   Produces a prompt for the password. The system displays a dialog box that shows the password as a series of asterisks instead of using cleartext at the command line. Using this feature can help you maintain the security of passwords used on your system.

/USER   Specifies that the utility uses a different username than the current username to make the connection. The username can take a number of forms as shown by the command line syntax. In addition, you can provide alternative credentials, such as smart cards.

domainname   Defines the domain name to use for the logon. If you omit the domain name, then the utility uses the currently logged in domain. You may also use a dotted form of the domain name, which looks much like the domain names for the Internet, when working with Active Directory.

username   Specifies the username to use to log into the remote system.

/SMARTCARD   Specifies that the connection relies on the credentials stored on a smart card.

/SAVECRED   Specifies that the connection should save the username and password. The utility ignores this command line switch unless the connection requires a username and password for access.

/HOME   Connects the user to their home directory. This command line switch only works when the user account has a home directory specified.

/DELETE   Deletes the connection from the list of persistent connections. The connection becomes unusual as soon as the command completes.

/PERSISTENT:{YES | NO}   Sets the state of the persistent network connection. When set to YES, the utility saves all connections as you make them and restores them at the next logon. When set to NO, the utility doesn't save any new connections. However, the utility still restores any existing connections during the next logon even if you set this command line switch to NO. Use the /DELETE command line switch to remove any persistent connections you no longer need.

USER

The USER mode works with user accounts on the network. You can change local user accounts or specify that you want to change the user information on the domain. The utility displays a list of current users when you use the USER mode alone. The names appear in three columns and the output doesn't include any additional information. The USER mode only works on servers (machines that have the Server service running). This mode uses the following syntax:

```
NET USER [username [password | *] [options]] [/DOMAIN]
NET USER username {password | *} /ADD [options] [/DOMAIN]
NET USER username [/DELETE] [/DOMAIN]
NET USER username [/TIMES:{times | ALL}]
```

The following list describes each of the command line arguments.

username   Specifies the name of the user account that you want to add, delete, modify, or view. The user account name can contain up to 20 characters.

password   Specifies the password used to access the user account. A password must satisfy all logon requirements for the machine, including the minimum and maximum length requirements set with the Net Accounts command. A password can contain up to 14 characters.

*   Produces a prompt for the password. The system displays a dialog box that shows the password as a series of asterisks instead of using cleartext at the command line. Using this feature can help you maintain the security of passwords used on your system.

/DOMAIN   Performs the requested task on the domain controller of the current domain instead of the local machine. You must have the rights required to make user account changes on the domain controller to use this command line switch.

/ADD   Adds the user account to the user accounts database.

/DELETE   Removes the user account from the user accounts database.

/TIMES:{times | ALL}   Specifies the times that the user can log into the system. The option requires specific intervals or the keyword ALL, which means that the user has no time restriction.

options   Specifies one or more specialized options that the mode uses when working with a particular user.

The options require a little more explanation. You use the options to change the way that the USER mode handles specific users. The following list describes each of the options.

/ACTIVE:{YES | NO}   Activates or deactivates the account. The user can't access the server when the account is inactive. The default setting is YES.

/COMMENT:"text"   Provides a comment for the user's account. You can use a maximum of 48 characters to describe the user or the user's role. Always enclose the comment in quotes.

/COUNTRYCODE:nnn   Defines a three-digit country code for the user. The country code tells applications how to implement language support for the user. In addition, the country code affects how Windows displays help and error messages. Use a value of 0 to signify the default country code. You can find a list of standard three-digit country codes at http://www.unicode.org/onlinedat/countries.html.

/EXPIRES:{date | NEVER}   Defines an expiration date for the user account. The default setting of NEVER keeps the account active forever. The form of the date depends on the country code; it's usually mm/dd/yy or dd/mm/yy. You can use a number for months, abbreviate them with three letter codes, or spell them out. The year can appear as a two- or four-digit number. Always use slashes and not spaces to separate the date elements.

/FULLNAME:`"name"` Specifies the user's full name for the account. The full name is the user's given name, rather than the account name used for logging into the system. Enclose the name in quotes.

/HOMEDIR:`pathname` Defines a home directory for the user. The path must exist. You must supply an absolute path and it's always a good idea to include the drive letter.

/PASSWORDCHG:`{YES | NO}` Specifies whether the user can change their own password. The default setting is YES.

/PASSWORDREQ:`{YES | NO}` Specifies whether the user account must have a password associated with it. The default setting is YES. Creating a user account without a password, even on a stand-alone machine, is an invitation to invasion by a cracker. In fact, you should change your password relatively often to ensure that crackers have short-term use of your machine even if they do guess your password.

/PROFILEPATH[:`path`**]** Sets the path for the user's logon profile. You can learn more about user logon profiles at `http://www.kellys-korner-xp.com/win_xp_logon.htm`.

/SCRIPTPATH:`pathname` Defines the location of the user's logon script. The logon script controls actions the machine takes as part of setting up Windows for the user after the user logs into the system.

/TIMES:`{times | ALL}` Defines the user's logon hours. A user can't log onto the system outside of these hours. You express the times as starting day, ending day, starting time, and ending time. The system limits you to using one-hour increments for the time. You can spell days out or abbreviate them. The times can appear in 12- or 24-hour format. Supplying a value of ALL as input means that the user can always log into the system. Likewise, a blank value means the user can never log into the system. Separate the day and time values using commas. Create multiple entries by separating the day and time groups with semicolons.

/USERCOMMENT:`"text"` Defines a user comment for the user account. The comment should describe the user or the user's role within the organization. Create useful comments that describe the user in such a way that it's easier to identify the user in a large organization.

/WORKSTATIONS:`{computername[...] | *}` Defines up to eight computers that the user can use for login purposes. If this command line switch doesn't include a list, or the list is an asterisk (*), then the user can log in from any computer.

VIEW

The VIEW mode displays a list of shared resources on a computer. When you use this mode without any command line switches, it displays all of the machines on a network or domain. This mode uses the following syntax:

```
NET VIEW [\\computername [/CACHE] | /DOMAIN[:domainname]]
NET VIEW /NETWORK:NW [\\computername]
```

The following list describes each of the command line arguments.

****`computername` Specifies the computer whose resources you want to view. The default output includes the sharename, resource type, used as information, and comment.

/DOMAIN:*domainname* Specifies the domain for which you want to view the available computers. The utility displays the current domain or local network when you omit this command line switch.

/NETWORK:NW Displays the list of available servers on a NetWare network. The utility displays the resources available on a particular computer when you include the computername argument.

/CACHE Displays the offline client caching settings for the resources on the specified computer. The output includes the sharename, resource type, used as information, and the caching setting.

SHARING FOLDERS USING THE SHRPubW UTILITY

Your hard drive is probably loaded with a wealth of undocumented utilities. In many cases, these undocumented utilities are gold for anyone working at the command line. The SHRPubW is one of those undocumented Microsoft utilities that can make a difference in many cases. The command line interface for this utility is SHRPubW /s *ComputerName*, where *ComputerName* is the name of a computer on the network. You must always include the /s command line switch, which causes the utility to share a folder on the target computer. In all cases, this utility starts the Create a Shared Folder Wizard. Follow the prompts and you'll end up with a shared folder on your machine or any other machine you designate.

This utility has a number of interesting uses. One of the most interesting uses is sharing a folder on Windows XP Home machines. The graphical interface doesn't provide any means of performing this task. However, Windows XP Home does include this utility, so you can still share folder with this operating system.

Another interesting use for this utility is to share folders on other machines. For example, if you're a network administrator and want to share a folder on your server without walking over to it, you can start this utility with that server's name. The utility helps you set basic share security and the user sees the new share immediately.

Managing Windows in a New Way

Most organizations today require a network of some kind. Even the smallest business will likely require a network at some point. Consequently, it's quite possible that you'll work with a network. This chapter provides you with the tools you require to work with a network at the command line. However, it's important to remember that you can also perform network configuration using graphical tools (something you can do from a remote location with the right console). The combination of command line tools and remote graphical administration techniques assures that you'll keep your network running smoothly. This chapter helps you build these skills:

◆ Obtain Media Access Control (MAC) information with the GetMAC utility

◆ Manage the network configuration using the Net utility

The most important utility in this chapter is the Net utility. This particular utility helps you perform more network tasks than nearly any other utility on your machine. It's important to begin using the Net utility whenever you can. You'll find a few usage examples in this chapter. However, the "Configuring the Server for Initial Use" section of Chapter 1 provides a considerable number of usage examples as well. You'll also find examples in Chapters 3 (the "Performing Server Updates" section) and 4 (the "Network" section). In fact, the Net utility is important enough that you'll find it sprinkled throughout many of the chapters in this book. Make sure you spend time practicing with this utility and discovering what kinds of information it can provide. Work with the Net utility on a test system to build your skills at using it.

Chapter 11 goes to a deeper level than just the network by showing you techniques for working with TCP/IP. Because TCP/IP is the basis for most of what you do with a network, it's important to know how to work with it at the command line. Without TCP/IP, you couldn't make a connection or perform any useful work with the network. Most importantly, many of the network woes you'll encounter occur with TCP/IP. In many cases, you'll find that configuration problems are to blame. The information in Chapter 11 can help you avoid these configuration issues.

Chapter 11

Working with TCP/IP

The Transmission Control Protocol/Internet Protocol (TCP/IP) is the basis of most of the communication on modern networks and the Internet alike. As an administrator, you must know about TCP/IP or you'll never get your network working. In most respects, TCP/IP isn't a complex protocol for communicating between computers because its originators designed it to provide simple, robust, and reliable service. (Get the TCP/IP facts at http://www.networksorcery.com/enp/protocol/tcp.htm and http://www.cisco.com/univercd/cc/td/doc/cisintwk/ito_doc/ip.htm.)

The ways in which networks use TCP/IP does complicate matters. The same protocol that connects machines on the network can also connect you to any machine worldwide on the Internet. Because TCP/IP is found everywhere, you can't rely on technology differences to protect your network—you have to assume that anyone can access your network unless you provide roadblocks to that access.

In addition to the broad usage that TCP/IP enjoys, the protocol also appears on most platforms. Unfortunately, each platform seems to have its own little oddities in dealing with TCP/IP. As an administrator, you need to know how to deal with these oddities. This chapter reflects the Server Core manner of working with TCP/IP, which may not reflect the Linux or Macintosh use of TCP/IP precisely.

NOTE   You'll find differences in the way that various versions of Windows handle TCP/IP. The differences are subtle. For example, an older version of a utility, such as one found in Windows 2000, may not include support for Internet Protocol Version 6 (IPv6). Even though the command line utilities in Server Core still favor Internet Protocol Version 4 (IPv4), the version of IP that you've used all these years, it's safe to assume that Microsoft will make further changes at some point to favor IPv6. In short, you must plan to work with TCP/IP as the operating system version supports it.

Finally, TCP/IP has evolved over time. In general, some of the utilities you'll see in the sections that follow are remakes of utilities that appear on other systems. The utilities of early UNIX still appear as part of TCP/IP. Consequently, the following sections may have a few surprises for you because they include a wide variety of utilities that have a single purpose, diagnosing problems with TCP/IP connections.

In this chapter, you'll learn how to do the following:

◆ Manage both IPv4 and IPv6 addresses

◆ Discover user information

◆ Obtain specific information about the system and its configuration

- ◆ Discover how the system routes information

- ◆ Perform network diagnostics

- ◆ Obtain network statistics

- ◆ Work with remote resources

Managing the Address Resolution Protocol with the ARP Utility

The Address Resolution Protocol (ARP) utility displays and modifies the IP address to physical address translation tables that ARP relies on to make connections. This utility uses the following syntax:

```
ARP -a [inet_addr] [-N if_addr] [-v]
ARP -g [inet_addr] [-N if_addr]
ARP -d inet_addr [if_addr]
ARP -s inet_addr eth_addr [if_addr]
```

The following list describes each of the command line arguments.

-a Displays the current ARP entries by requesting the current protocol data. The output includes the interface address, Internet address, physical address, and type of connection. When used alone, the table includes all entries for all tables. If you specify the Internet address, the utility displays the IP and physical addresses for the specified computer. When more than one network interface uses ARP, the utility displays entries for each ARP table.

-g Performs the same task as -a.

inet_addr Defines an Internet address. Generally, this value is the computer that hosts the ARP table, which might not be the local computer. This utility doesn't currently support IP version 6, so the addresses are all in the form of 192.168.0.1.

-N *if_addr* Displays a list of ARP entries for the specified network interface. The N is case sensitive and the utility ignores a lowercase n.

if_addr Specifies the Internet address of the interface that the utility will modify. If you don't include this argument, the utility modifies the first applicable interface. You can normally obtain the information required for this entry using the IPConfig utility.

-d Deletes the host specified by the Internet address. You may delete just a specific interface by including the interface address. Delete all of the hosts by using the asterisk (*) wildcard.

-s Adds a new host to the ARP table and associates the Internet address with the physical (Ethernet) address. The resulting entry is permanent; you must manually delete it using the -d command line switch.

eth_addr Specifies a physical address as 6 hexadecimal bytes separated by hyphens in the form 00-AA-00-4F-2A-9C. You can obtain the physical address using the GetMAC utility.

-v Displays information in verbose mode. In addition to the standard entries, the output also includes all loopback interface entries.

Discovering User Information with the Finger Utility

Use the Finger utility to obtain information about a user with access to a remote system. The remote computer must run the Finger service or daemon, which means that it's normally a Linux or UNIX system. The standard output includes the login name, the username, the user's Terminal Type (TTY), the amount of idle time, when the user logged in, and where the user logged in. This utility uses the following syntax:

```
finger [-1] [User] [@host] [...]
```

The following list describes each of the command line arguments.

-1 Displays the user information in long list format, with one item per output line. This option makes room for long entries. However, it only displays the user's login name and username.

User Specifies the login name of the user to check. When you omit the user argument, Finger displays information about all of the users on the specified computer.

@host Specifies the identity of the remote computer running the Finger service. You must have proper rights to make the request on the remote computer. The host information can appear as a computer name or IP address.

Getting the Local Hostname with the Hostname Utility

The Hostname utility can both set and query the hostname on many operating systems. However, when using Windows, the Hostname utility can only obtain the name of the host; the utility ignores the -s command line switch. Use this utility by typing **Hostname** at the command prompt and pressing Enter. The utility still lets you query the current host when working with batch files or scripts.

Managing the Internet Protocol with the IPConfig Utility

The IPConfig utility displays information about the configuration of the IP stack (software) on the local machine. In many cases, all you need is the basic address information, so you can type **IPConfig** and press Enter. You'll see the addresses for your network adapters as shown in Figure 11.1.

FIGURE 11.1
Obtain basic information about your network adapters using IPConfig alone.

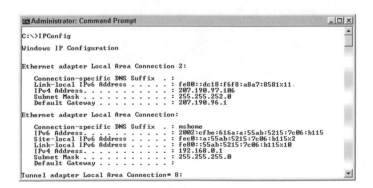

However, if you're diagnosing errors on your network, you'll need more information. In this case, you'll type **IPConfig /all** and press Enter to obtain all of the information you can as shown in Figure 11.2. Notice that in this case, the output includes all of the setting information, in addition to the basic addresses. By knowing the configuration information, you can learn more about errors on your network.

FIGURE 11.2
Using the /all command line switch displays considerably more information.

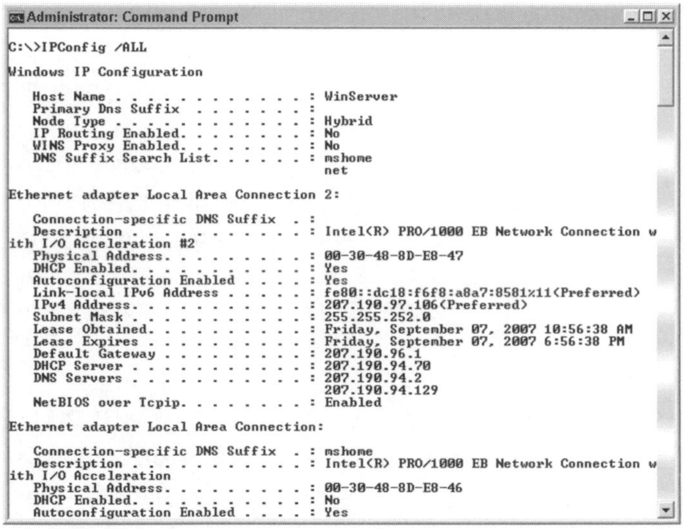

You can also use IPConfig to renew the IP address for a particular adapter, which includes both the Dynamic Host Configuration Protocol (DHCP) and Domain Name System (DNS) settings. This utility uses the following syntax:

```
ipconfig [/? | /all | /renew [adapter] | /release [adapter]
| /flushdns | /displaydns | /registerdns | /showclassid adapter
| /setclassid adapter [classid] | /renew6 [adapter] | /release6
[adapter]]
```

The following list describes each of the command line arguments.

adapter   Specifies the name of the connection. The connection name is the one that appears in the Network Connections window (accessed by right-clicking My Network Places and choosing Properties from the context menu). A common connection name for a single adapter machine is "Local Area Connection." Enclose the connection name in quotes.

/all   Displays complete configuration information for all of the adapters. The information includes all of the Windows IP configuration information, plus the Ethernet information. For example, you can use the output to discover both the physical and IP addresses of the connection. In addition, you can see the adapter's description (human-readable name) and both DNS and DHCP information.

/release   Releases the IP address for the specified adapter.

/release6   Releases the IPv6 address for the specified adapter.

TIP   You'll find that Server Core provides support for a wide range of IPv6 commands and utilities. These new features only support IPv6. You still use the older commands to work with Internet Protocol Version 4 (IPv4), which is the current standard. You can learn more about IPv6 at http://www.ipv6.org/.

/renew   Renews the IPv4 address for the specified adapter. This is one of the most common ways to fix errors with a network adapter. To renew the addresses for all adapters on the server (usually not necessary and could interrupt user tasks), type **IPConfig /renew** and press Enter. In most cases, you'll want to renew a specific adapter. Using the network shown in Figures 11.1 and 11.2 as a basis, you'd type **IPConfig /renew "Local Area Connection 2"** and press Enter to renew the address for the second adapter. You can also use the asterisk (*) wildcard character for the adapter names. For example, typing **IPConfig /renew Local*** and pressing Enter would renew the addresses for every adapter that begins with Local in its name. Notice that you don't have to include the double quotes when the adapter name doesn't include spaces.

/renew6   Renews the IPv6 address for the specified adapter.

/flushdns   Purges (clears) the DNS Resolver Cache. The cache is a memory location that stores DNS information about other machines. This cache can become corrupted, making purging the only way to clear it and start fresh. Generally, you won't need to purge the cache unless you move machines around on the network and change their IP address.

/registerdns   Refreshes all of the DHCP leases and re-registers the DNS names.

/displaydns   Displays the contents of the DNS Resolver Cache. The content depends on the machine type. For example, a server might contain a wealth of addresses for machines across the network and even machines on the Internet. A workstation might only contain the DNS information for Localhost. To use this feature for diagnostic purposes, type **IPConfig /displaydns** and press Enter. You'll see DNS information like the information shown in Figure 11.3. Notice that the output includes both IP addresses and hostnames.

/showclassid   Displays the DHCP class identifiers allowed for the adapter. In many cases, you won't find any classes defined. Use the asterisk (*) wildcard to obtain class identifiers for all of the adapters on the local machine. Most servers won't have any DHCP class identifiers defined for the installed adapters. The easiest way to detect this setup information is to type **IPConfig /showclassid *** and press Enter.

/setclassid   Modifies or sets the DHCP class identifier for the specified adapter. Use the asterisk (*) wildcard to set the class identifier for all adapters on the local machine. Using this command line switch without specifying a class identifier clears the class identifier information for the specified adapter. Using the network shown in Figures 11.1 and 11.2 as an example, if you wanted to set the DHCP class identifier for the second adapter to TEST, you'd type **IPConfig / setclassid "Local Area Connection 2" TEST** and press Enter. You'll find an article on how setting DHCP class identifiers improves security at http://articles.techrepublic.com.com/ 5100-1035_11-5498436.html.

FIGURE 11.3
Discover DNS
information for your
network using the
/displaydns switch.

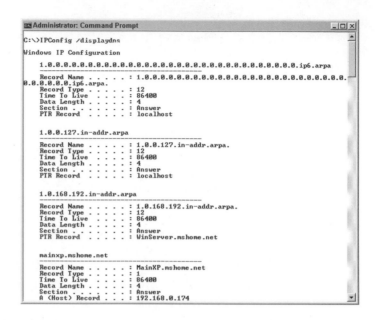

Obtaining Multicast Router Information with the MRInfo Utility

The MRInfo utility provides information about the multicast routers on a system. The output includes both the multicast router interfaces and a list of the neighboring machines. This utility uses the following syntax:

```
mrinfo [-n?] [-i address] [-t secs] [-r retries] destination
```

The following list describes each of the command line arguments.

-n Displays the IP addresses in numeric format. The output normally contains the IP addresses as DNS names.

-i *address* Defines the address of the local interface to query. The utility sends this interface information to the destination.

-t *seconds* Defines the timeout in seconds for Internet Group Multicast Protocol (IGMP) queries. The default setting is 3 seconds, which might not be long enough on large networks. You can learn more about the IGMP standard at http://www.ietf.org/rfc/rfc1112.txt.

-r *retries* Defines the extra number of times to send the Simple Network Management Protocol (SNMP) queries. The utility always sends the SNMP query at least once. The default number of extra tries is 0. You can find the SNMP specification at http://www.ietf.org/rfc/rfc1157.txt.

destination Specifies the IP address or the DNS name of the destination.

Each of the interface entries in the output contains a series of informational entries placed within square brackets and separated by slashes like this: [1/0/pim/querier/leaf]. A parent node may contain only the first three entries, but leaf nodes normally include all five pieces of data. The entries always appear in the same order and the node never skips information. The following list describes the entries in order of appearance.

Metric   Defines the cost of the link in hops. This value is used in routing calculations.

TTL *Threshold*   Defines the Time-to-Live (TTL) threshold for the multicast datagram. The router forwards the datagram when the TTL in the IP header is greater than the TTL threshold for the interface. This value limits the distances that packets can travel.

PIM   Defines the Protocol Independent Multicast (PIM) the interface uses. The PIM defines the type of routing the server uses.

Querier   Defines the designated multicast router that sends the IGMP Host Membership queries.

Leaf   Indicates that this router is on the edge of the network—that it doesn't have any child nodes.

Getting NetBIOS over TCP/IP Status with the NBTStat Utility

The NBTStat utility displays a number of NetBIOS statistics about a network, including the NetBIOS over TCP/IP (NetBT) protocol status. You can also receive information about NetBIOS name tables for both the local computer and remote computers, and the NetBIOS name cache. The utility helps you perform specific tasks such as refreshing the local NetBIOS cache or the Windows Internet Name Service (WINS). This utility uses the following syntax:

```
NBTSTAT [ [-a RemoteName] [-A IP_address] [-c] [-n] [-r] [-R]
[-RR] [-s] [-S] [interval] ]
```

It's important to note that the command line switches for this utility are case sensitive. Using the -a command line switch isn't the same as using the -A command line switch. The following list describes each of the command line arguments.

-a   Lists the remote machine's name table when you provide a machine name as input. The name table includes the NetBIOS name, the type, and the status.

-A   Lists the remote machine's name table when you provide an IP address as input. The name table includes the NetBIOS name, type, and status.

-c   List the NetBIOS Table (NBT) cache of remote machine names and their IP addresses. The table contents include the NetBIOS name, type, host address, and life in seconds.

-n   Lists the local NetBIOS names. The resulting table includes the NetBIOS name, type, and status.

-r   Lists the NetBIOS names resolved or registered by broadcast and using WINS. The output includes the resolved by broadcast, resolved by name server, registered by broadcast, and registered by name server statistics. In addition, you'll see a listing of NetBIOS names.

-R Purges and reloads the remote cache name table.

-S Lists the sessions table with the destination IP addresses. The resulting table includes the local name, state, whether the destination is used for input or output, the remote host IP address, the input buffer size in megabytes, and the output buffer size in megabytes.

-s Lists the sessions table with the destination IP addresses converted to NetBIOS names. The resulting table includes the local name, state, whether the destination is used for input or output, the remote host NetBIOS name, the input buffer size in megabytes, and the output buffer size in megabytes.

-RR Sends the name release packets to WINS, and then starts the refresh process.

RemoteName Specifies the remote host machine name.

IP_address Specifies the remote host IP address.

interval Redisplays the selected statistics at the specified interval in seconds. Press Ctrl+C to stop the output.

Performing Network Diagnostics with the NetDiag Utility

The NetDiag helps you research a number of networking problems by using specific tests. Each test outputs data about a particular network feature, and you can use the tests to assess the general health of the network. Server Core doesn't provide support for this utility by default. However, you can download a copy of the utility from http://www.microsoft.com/downloads/details.aspx? familyid=1EA70814-7E6C-46E5-8C8C-3C439A732E9F. The downloaded product will work fine on your Server Core installation, even though it is designed for Windows 2000. In some cases, you may find that you obtain better results by running this utility at a client, rather than at the server, due to Server Core's security features. This utility uses the following syntax:

```
netdiag [/q] [/v] [/l] [/debug] [/d: DomainName]
[/fix] [/DcAccountEnum] [/test: TestName] [/skip: TestName]
```

The following list describes each of the command line arguments.

/q Outputs only error information.

/v Outputs verbose information, which includes testing, general, and error information.

/l Sends the output to NetDiag.LOG. The utility creates the log file in the same directory as the NetDiag.EXE file.

/debug Outputs debugging information, which includes all of the verbose output (the /v command line switch) and detailed information required to diagnose networking errors.

/d:*DomainName* Locates a domain controller within the specified domain.

/fix Locates and fixes minor problems.

/DcAccountEnum Enumerates (lists) the domain controller computer accounts.

/test:*TestName* Executes only the requested test or tests. Generally, the utility performs all tests in an attempt to locate all networking problems on the first pass. You must bind TCP/IP to one or more adapters before running any of the tests. The utility runs any non-skippable tests.

Use this feature when you already have a good idea of which problems the utility will locate. The valid tests for this command line switch include:

Autonet
Automatic Private IP
  Addressing (APIPA)
  address test
Bindings
Bindings test
Browser
DcList
DefGw
Default gateway test
DNS
DNS test
Domain controller
  discovery test
Domain controller list
  test
Domain membership
  test
DsGetDc

IP address
  configuration testIP
address loopback
  ping test
IpConfig
IpLoopBk
IPX
IPX test
Kerberos
Kerberos test
Ldap
LDAP test
Member
Modem
Modem diagnostics
  test
NbtNm
Ndis
NetBT name test
NetBTTransports

NetBT transports test
Netcard queries test
Netstat
Netstat information
  test
Netware
Netware test
Redir and Browser test
Route
Routing table test
Trust
Trust relationship test
WAN
WAN configuration
  test
WINS
WINS service
Winsock
Winsock test

/skip:*TestName* Skips the requested test or tests. (See the /test command line switch for additional details.) The tests that you can skip include:

Autonet
Automatic Private IP
  Addressing (APIPA)
  address test
Bindings
Bindings test
Browser
DcList
Default gateway test
DefGw
DNS
DNS test
Domain controller
  discovery test
Domain controller list
  test
DsGetDc

IP address
  configuration test
IP address loopback
  ping test
IpConfig
IpLoopBk
IPX
IPX test
Kerberos
Kerberos test
Ldap
LDAP test
Modem
Modem diagnostics
  test
NbtNm
NbtNm
NetBT name test

Netstat
Netstat information
  test
Netware
Netware test
Redir and browser test
Route
Routing table test
Trust
Trust relationship test
WAN
WAN configuration
  test
WINS
WINS service test
Winsock
Winsock test

Getting Network Statistics with the NetStat Utility

The NetStat utility outputs statistics about the network. You can use this utility in a number of ways. For example, changes in a statistic could indicate the activities of a cracker or the imminent failure of a piece of hardware. The statistics can also indicate the success of performance modifications you make or the impact of security features that you install. This utility uses the following syntax:

```
NETSTAT [-a] [-b] [-e] [-f] [-n] [-o] [-p proto] [-r] [-s] [-t]
    [interval]
```

The following list describes each of the command line arguments.

-a Displays all connections and listening ports for the current machine. The output includes both TCP and User Datagram Protocol (UDP) connections. The table includes the protocol, local address, foreign address, and state of the connection. To use this feature, simply type **NetStat -a** and press Enter.

-b Displays the application that created each connection or listening port. This feature is actually one of the better ways to locate spyware, adware, and viruses on your system because these applications usually communicate outside your machine. In most cases, the cracker doesn't write the application in such a way that it disguises this information, so you can see the applications you don't want on your machine quite quickly. The output table includes the protocol, local address, foreign address, state, and Process Identifier (PID). The PID includes both the number and the translated application name in square brackets ([]). Using this feature can be time consuming and usually fails unless you're part of the Administrators group. The most useful way to work with this switch is in combination with the –a switch. Type **NetStat -a -b** and press Enter to see a connection-by-connection listing of who created a particular connection (see Figure 11.4), which is very useful in pinning down unauthorized connections.

FIGURE 11.4
Discover precisely who created each connection on a server by combining the -a and -b switches.

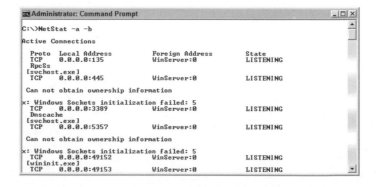

-e Displays the Ethernet statistics, which include the amount of data sent and receive for general data bytes, unicast packets, non-unicast packets, discards, errors, and unknown protocols. You can combine this command line switch with the –s switch to receive a complete picture of the Ethernet status.

-f Displays the Fully Qualified Domain Names (FQDN) for foreign addresses, which means you have better access to other domain information.

-n Displays addresses and port numbers in numerical form. The default setting displays the addresses as DNS names whenever possible.

-o Displays the owning PID for each connection. Sometimes, you can't get enough information by using a combination of the −a and −b switches to detect who is responsible for a particular connection. In this case, combine the −a and −o command line switches by typing **NetStat -a -o** and pressing Enter. The output changes as shown in Figure 11.5. Now you can use a utility such as TaskList to determine which application has started the connection.

FIGURE 11.5

Look for application identification by combining the -a and -o switches.

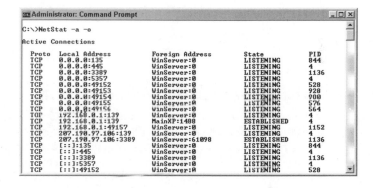

-p proto Displays the connections for the specified protocol. You may use TCP, UDP, TCPv6, or UDPv6 as the protocol names. When you use this command line switch with the −s switch to display per-protocol statistics, you may use IP, IPv6, ICMP, ICMPv6, TCP, TCPv6, UDP, or UDPv6 as the protocol name. For example, if you only want to know which applications have created a TCP/IPv4 connection, type **NetStat -a -o -p TCP** and press Enter.

-r Displays the routing table. The output includes the interfaces, as well as the active and persistent routes. The routing information includes the network destination, netmask, gateway, interface, and metric.

-s Displays per-protocol statistics for the current machine. By default, the statistics include the for IP, IPv6, ICMP, ICMPv6, TCP, TCPv6, UDP, and UDPv6 protocols. You can reduce the size of the list by using the −p command line switch to select a specific protocol. For example, if you only want to see the TCP/IPv4 statistics, type **NetStat -s -p TCP** and press Enter. Figure 11.6 shows typical output for a TCP/IPv4 connection. The statistics that the utility outputs vary by protocol.

-t Displays the current offload state for the connection. The default offload state is InHost. The offload state is part of the network protocol offload that Microsoft has introduced as part of scalable networking. The operating system actually offloads certain tasks to the Network Interface Card (NIC). Of course, your NIC has to support these features. To see the offload settings for your NIC, right-click its entry in the Network Connections window and choose Properties. Click Configure in the network connection's Properties dialog box and choose the Advanced tab. You'll see the offload settings in the list of settings that your NIC supports. If you want to display the offload state for the various TCP/IPv4 connections, you type **NetStat -a -t -p TCP** and press Enter.

interval Redisplays the selected statistics at the specified interval in seconds. Press Ctrl+C to stop the output.

FIGURE 11.6
Get the statistics for a particular protocol by combining the -s and -p switches.

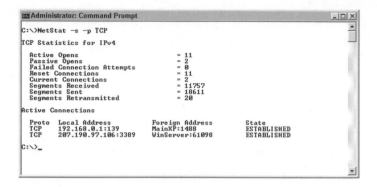

Tracking Servers with the NSLookup Utility

The NSLookup utility provides information about the DNS setup on your network. You can use this utility to perform tasks such as diagnosing DNS errors. The NSLookup utility has two modes. The interactive mode provides access a number of subcommands that you can't access from the command prompt. For example, you can't access the exit subcommand at the command prompt because you have already exited the interactive mode by being at the command prompt. You can access the QueryType and Set subcommands. This utility uses the following syntax:

```
nslookup [-Query=QueryType] [-SetOption=Value]
[-QueryType=QueryType QueryData] [ComputerToFind | [-Server]}]
```

Note that if you find the command line version of NSLookup a tad difficult to follow, you can find an online version at http://www.kloth.net/services/nslookup.php that employs an easier-to-use Web interface. In fact, using this online version can significantly ease the learning process for the command line version since you'll see how the various commands work. The following list describes each of the command line arguments.

–Query=*QueryType* Sets the type of query that the NSLookup utility performs for all subsequent commands. This command line switch affects the kind of data you must provide for the ComputerToFind argument. NSLookup supports the following query types.

A Specifies a computer's IP address.

ANY Specifies all types of data.

CNAME Specifies a canonical name for an alias.

GID Specifies a group identifier of a group name.

HINFO Specifies a computer's CPU and type of operating system.

MB Specifies a mailbox domain name.

MG Specifies a mail group member.

MINFO Specifies mailbox or mail list information.

MR Specifies the mail rename domain name.

MX Specifies the mail exchanger.

NS Specifies a DNS name server for the named zone.

PTR   Specifies a computer name if the query is an IP address; otherwise, specifies the pointer to other information.

SOA   Specifies the start of authority for a DNS zone.

TXT   Specifies the text information.

UID   Specifies the user identifier.

UINFO   Specifies the user information.

WKS   Describes a well-known service.

-SetOption=*Value*   Most versions of NSLookup use an actual -set command line switch. However, when using the Windows version of NSLookup, specify the set option as part of the command line switch. When required, you must also supply a value for the option. The timeout option requires a value as part of the input, so you might type **nslookup -timeout=30 mit.edu** and press Enter to give MIT additional time to answer a query. Some options are simply on or off values that you don't need to set specifically. For example, type **nslookup -d2 mit.edu** and press Enter to receive extensive information about the DNS configuration at MIT. If you use this feature without specifying either a query or a computer to find, then NSLookup starts in interactive mode using the settings you provided. Here's a list of standard NSLookup options.

-all   Displays a list of the option settings, current server, and the current host.

-[no]debug   Specify debug to display debugging information with the query. The nodebug option is the default. The debugging information includes the header, any queries you made, and the authority records from the computer. In some cases, the output includes an additional records section.

-[no]d2   Specify d2 to display additional debugging information with the query. The nod2 option is the default. The additional debugging information includes the header and queries for the send request, and the header, queries, and authority records for the get request.

-[no]defname   Specify nodefname when you want to refrain from sending your domain name with the query. The default setting is defname, which sends the domain name.

-[no]recurse   Specify norecurse to receive just the first answer to a query. Otherwise, the NSLookup utility makes multiple requests to obtain all of the information from the server. The default setting is recurse.

-[no]search   Specify nosearch to refrain from using the domain search list. The default setting is search.

-[no]vc   Specify novc when you don't want to use a virtual circuit. The default setting is novc. A virtual circuit can improve performance by providing a set path for data transmission. However, you must set up this feature on the server before it becomes available.

-domain=*NAME*   Sets the default domain name to the specified value. The default setting uses the current domain.

-srchlist=*N1*[/*N2*/.../*N6*]   Defines a search list. The first member of the search list also acts as the domain, unless you specify some other value using the -domain command line switch. The Windows version of NSLookup allows up to six search list elements.

-root=*NAME*   Defines the root server.

-retry=*X*   Sets the number of retries for a particular query. The default setting is 1.

-timeout=X   Sets the initial timeout interval (the amount of time that passes before NSLookup considers a query to fail) to the specified value. The default setting is 2 seconds.

-type=X or -querytype=X   Sets the query type as specified. See the -Query command line switch for a listing of valid query types.

-class={IN | CHAOS | HESIOD | ANY}   Sets the query class. The query class can be any of the following classes: IN (specifies the Internet class), CHAOS (specifies the Chaos class), HESIOD (specifies the MIT Athena Hesiod class), and ANY (specifies any of the previously listed classes).

NOTE   If you need to know more about the MIT Athena Hesiod class, check the "About Hesiod, and HS-class Resource Records" section of the article at http://www.dns.net/dnsrd/docs/ bog/bog-sh-5.html. You'll also want to review the article entitled, "The Hesiod Name Server" at ftp://athena-dist.mit.edu/pub/ATHENA/usenix/hesiod.PS (you can find the article in various other formats such as PDF as well).

-[no]msxfr   Specify nomsxfr when you want to perform a standard query using standardized techniques. The default is to use the Microsoft Fast Zone Transfer (MSXFR).

-ixfrver=X   Specifies the current version to use in the Incremental Zone Transfer (IXFR) transfer request. The default value is 1.

-QueryType=*QueryType QueryData*   Performs a query of the specified type (see the -Query command line switch for details) using the specified data. For example, if you want to determine all of the types of data that MIT handles, you would type **NSLookup -QueryType=ANY mit.edu** and press Enter.

ComputerToFind   Specifies the computer to interact with when making queries. The computer name relies on the current DNS server when you don't specify a server name. Append a period to the name to view information for a computer not in the current DNS domain. Specifying an IP address displays the name of the computer based on the DNS entry. Using a hyphen (-) in place of the DNS name places the NSLookup utility in interactive mode.

TIP   Some NSLookup commands can require an inordinate amount of time to complete due to distances and machine configurations. Press Ctrl+B to interrupt any interactive command. To exit interactive mode at any time, type **Exit** and press Enter.

The NSLookup utility relies on commands to perform various tasks. Consequently, it's important to know which commands to use to perform diagnostics or query the DNS system for some other purpose. The following list contains the NSLookup commands that Windows supports (which aren't necessarily the same as the UNIX commands for the same utility—see http://publib16 .boulder.ibm.com/pseries/en_US/cmds/aixcmds4/nslookup.htm for an example of an alternative form of this utility).

Tracing Transmission Paths with the PathPing Utility

The Path Packet Internet Groper (PathPing) utility serves an important function by showing you the path between your machine and a remote machine. In addition, it provides communication statistics for each host in the communication path. When you type **PathPing *Location*** and press Enter, you see the complete path for that connection. For example, Figure 11.7 shows the path to the main server for my ISP. Of course, you don't get this information free. PathPing requires considerably more time to run than other utilities, such as PING.

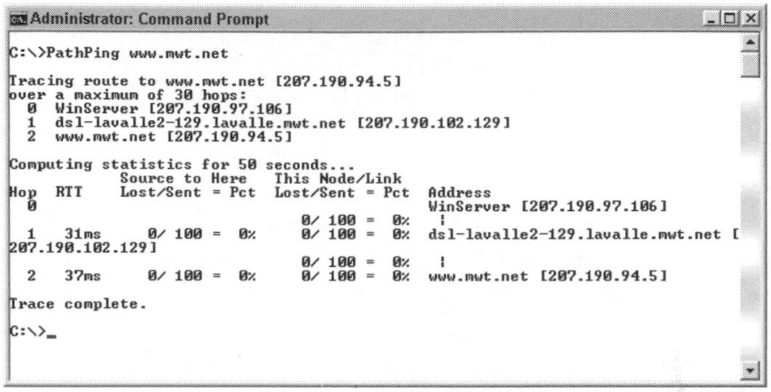

FIGURE 11.7
PathPing provides a
lot of information
about the path be-
tween connections.

Using the PathPing utility can tell you when your communication is taking an unusual route. A communication disruption and network congestion can cause a message to take an unusual route, but so can someone using a "man in the middle" attack. The man in the middle attack is one in which a cracker intercepts any communication you make, records the information for future use, and then passes the information along to the intended recipient so you don't suspect what's happening.

The PathPing utility can also tell you where communications are breaking down (so you know whether you need to call your ISP) and can help you diagnose a number of connection problems. At the very least, the PathPing utility can tell you why communications are so slow on a given day. This utility uses the following syntax:

```
pathping [-g host-list] [-h maximum_hops] [-i address] [-n] [-p period]
    [-q num_queries] [-w timeout] [-P] [-R] [-T] [-4] [-6] target_name
```

The following list describes each of the command line arguments.

-g *host-list* Specifies that the Echo Request messages used as part of defining the path between one point and another use the Loose Source Route option in the IP header with the set of intermediate destinations. The PathPing utility creates the list of servers that it outputs by extending the path between the source and destination by one machine for each call. The target machine, the one that's at the end of the line, receives an Echo Request message that requests that machine's name, which is why you receive a list of hosts as part of the output. This option lets the command use a number of intermediate routers to speed the process of defining the path between one machine and another. The results are less accurate, but you receive them faster.

NOTE The host list must use the standard dotted notation for the IP addresses and you must separate each of the hosts with a space. The PathPing utility allows a maximum of nine hosts in the host list. You can find a diagram of the affected IP header data at http://www.networksorcery .com/enp/protocol/ip/option003.htm. You can find a good discussion of this topic in the "Loose Source and Record Route" section of the Web page at http://www.freesoft.org/ CIE/Course/Section3/7.htm.

-h *maximum_hops* Defines the maximum number of hops the utility uses to search for the target. The PathPing utility automatically stops tracing the path when it reaches the specified number of hops. Using this option reduces the wait for long paths when you only need to use some of the path between your machine and the target.

NOTE A hop is an individual jump from one host to another. For example, when you communicate with the server on your network, the direct communication between client and server normally requires one hop or one connection between client and host.

-i *address* Defines a specific starting address for the path search. The default starting location is the current machine. However, by starting the path search on your ISP's machine or even further down the path, you reduce the search time. Theoretically, you can also use this command line switch to determine the path from a completely different machine to a destination. In practice, this technique tends to produce inaccurate results.

OVERCOMING DOCUMENTATION ERRORS

If you haven't run into a documentation error at some point in your career, consider yourself lucky. You'll encounter documentation problems with the PathPing utility. Depending on where you go, you might find what appear to be interesting additional command line switches, but in fact turn out to be documentation errors. Like many Windows utilities, Microsoft has made changes and documented some items inaccurately. The best place to go when you suspect a documentation error is the Microsoft Knowledge Base. For example, you can find an update for this utility at http://support.microsoft .com/default.aspx?scid=KB;EN-US;Q244602.

It's important to realize that the documentation you're viewing might not always match the utility you're using. For example, the Windows 2000 version of a utility often contains less functionality than its Windows XP or Windows 2003 counterpart. However, in the case of the PathPing utility, the Windows 2000 version includes the -P, -R, and -T command line switches, which don't appear in later versions of the utility. In addition, Microsoft often includes undocumented command line switches or discontinues a command line switch without removing it from the documentation. When you can't find what you need in the Microsoft Knowledge Base or are unsure whether you're reviewing materials for the right version of the utility, check third-party resources as well. For example, you'll find a third-party resource for the PathPing utility at http://www.pchelper.com/modules.php?name=News& file=article&sid=81&POSTNUKESID=d18f99f92e500ee411dea29a2beabd11.

-n Displays only the IP addresses of the hosts in the path, rather than displaying the hostnames. Using this technique produces faster results because the utility doesn't have to make two queries for each intermediate location. In addition, using this approach can help you trace a complete path when some intermediaries have disabled the Request Echo message handling code.

-p *period* Defines the number of milliseconds to wait between pings (or requests for information). Using a shorter ping period improves performance, but could result in a failure of PathPing to resolve the entire path. The default setting is 250 milliseconds.

-q *num_queries* Defines the maximum number of Request Echo messages per hop. Normally, the PathPing utility uses 100 requests to determine path statistics for each hop. A higher number produces statistics that are more accurate. However, if you're mainly interested in the path, then you should set this value to 1.

-w *timeout* Specifies the number of milliseconds to wait for each reply. The default setting is 3,000 milliseconds.

-4   Forces PathPing to use Internet Protocol Version 4 (IPv4) calls, even when the system normally uses IPv6.

-6   Forces PathPing to use Internet Protocol Version 6 (IPv6) calls, even when the system normally uses IPv4. Even though newer versions of Windows include some level of IPv6 support, most systems still use IPv4 and will do so for several more years.

NOTE   The path from one location to another will likely vary every time you issue the PathPing command. That's because the Internet makes connections on an as needed basis. For example, try typing **PathPing microsoft.com** at the command line and pressing Enter. Depending on your ISP and conditions on the Internet, the path might require 11 hops the first time, 17 hops the second time, and 15 hops the third time. The path varies because of the way that the Internet works. However, if you keep noticing the same host every time you issue the PathPing command and it's not your ISP, then you might have a problem (or it could simply be random chance). The point is that PathPing can help you understand trends and see potential problems, but don't depend on it as a precise tool that will display a blinking error message telling you something is wrong.

Checking Connections with the PING Utility

The Packet Internet Groper (PING) utility helps you diagnose problems on your network by sending a series of messages of a specific length from one computer to the other. You can vary a number of the PING utility features to produce specific results. In addition, you can use it to see a number of difficult to find problems, such as messages that end up going through too many intermediaries to reach a destination. This utility uses the following syntax:

```
ping [-t] [-a] [-n count] [-l size] [-f] [-i TTL] [-v TOS]
[-r count] [-s count] [[-j host-list] | [-k host-list]]
[-w timeout] [-R] [-S srcaddr] [-4] [-6] target_name
```

The following list describes each of the command line arguments.

-t   Forces the utility to continue pinging the specified host until stopped. Use this feature for diagnostic tasks so you don't have to restart the PING utility continuously. You can stop the utility in two ways. Press Ctrl+Break to stop pinging the host and generate the statistics that normally appear at the end of the PING session. Press Ctrl+C to stop the utility immediately without generating the statistics.

-a   Resolves address to hostname. Using this command line switch can require additional pings to perform a given check, but also means that the output is more readable.

-n *count*   Defines the number of Echo Request messages to send. The default setting is 4.

-l *size*   Defines the size of the buffer used to create the data field of the message. The default size is 32 bytes. The maximum size is 65,527 bytes. Larger buffers tend to reduce performance, but also create a more realistic test. Generally, you should test with the same size buffer that your application will use.

-f   Sets the Don't Fragment flag in the packets. Routers generally break down packets into smaller sizes to improve performance. In addition, some routers don't accommodate the same size packet, so the packet becomes fragmented to meet the needs of a specific router. Using this command line switch lets you check for Path Maximum Transmission Unit (PMTU) problems between machines. You can learn more about PMTU at `http://www.microsoft.com/technet/community/columns/cableguy/cg0704.mspx`.

-i *TTL*   Defines the Time-to-Live field of the message. A larger TTL value can let the packet travel a longer distance. However, a larger value also increases the time you must wait to discover an error on the network. The default value is 128. You may set this value to a maximum of 255.

-v *TOS*   Defines the type of service (level of quality) the message should receive. The default value is 0. You may use a value up to 255. You can learn more about the TOS field of the message in the standards document at `http://www.ietf.org/rfc/rfc0791.txt` in the "Type of Service" section and the standards document section at `http://www.freesoft.org/CIE/RFC/1812/111.htm`.

-r *count*   Specifies that the system use the Record Route option in the IP header to record the path the message will follow from one machine to another. This option lets you record the path and display it as part of the output. The *count* argument defines how many hops the system records. Every hop negatively affects performance, but you also obtain additional path information. The minimum value of count is 1 and the maximum value is 9.

-s *count*   Specifies that the system record the timestamp in the Internet Timestamp option in the IP header for each hop. The minimum value of count is 1 and the maximum value is 4.

-j *host-list*   Specifies that the Echo Request messages used as part of defining the path between one point and another use the Loose Source Route option in the IP header with the set of intermediate destinations. The PING utility creates the list of servers that it outputs by extending the path between the source and destination by one machine for each call. The target machine—the one that's at the end of the line—receives an Echo Request message that requests that machine's name, which is why you receive a list of hosts as part of the output. This option lets the command use a number of intermediate routers to speed the process of defining the path between one machine and another. The results are less accurate, but you receive them faster.

-k *host-list*   Specifies that the Echo Request messages used as part of defining the path between one point and another use the Strict Source Route option in the IP header with the set of intermediate destinations. When using this command line switch, PING queries the servers in the path using the precise host list that you provide. The result is more accurate than a standard path ping. However, using this technique also means that the utility will display an error and exit immediately if one of the hosts isn't directly reachable. The maximum number of hosts in the list is 9.

-w *timeout*   Specifies the number of milliseconds to wait for each reply. The default setting is 4,000 milliseconds.

-R   Tests the reverse route (from the target to your machine) as well by adding a special routing header. You can only use this option with IPv6.

-S *srcaddr*   Specifies a source address to use so that you can test from a different client to the specified target. You can only use this option with IPv6. The default source address is the current machine.

-4   Forces PING to use Internet Protocol Version 4 (IPv4) calls, even when the system normally uses IPv6.

-6 Forces PING to use Internet Protocol Version 6 (IPv6) calls, even when the system normally uses IPv4. Even though newer versions of Windows include some level of IPv6 support, most systems still use IPv4 and will do so for several more years.

 Real World Scenario

USING PING FOR DIAGNOSTICS

Many network administrators know the benefits of using PING, and those that don't often learn quite quickly. For example, a recent client call presented a problem where the network almost worked, but not quite. Using a Time Domain Reflectometer (TDR) showed that the cables were good. The diagnostics for the network card didn't show any unusual results and the systems had all of the correct setup information. By using PING, it was possible to diagnose an intermittent timing problem with the network card, which isn't a hard error and is extremely difficult to locate without the right tools.

You'll use this utility more often than you think. This command line tool helps you test TCP/IP connections with another computer, so the diagnostic benefits are apparent the first time you use it. The two command lines you'll commonly use for PING in a diagnostic mode are:

```
PING <HostName>
PING <IP Address>
```

Therefore, if you want to contact a machine named AUX, you'd type **PING AUX** and press Enter. PING outputs four messages of 32 bytes and tells you about the response to each one. You can modify the size of the packet sent to the remote computer using the -l Size command line switch. To test the computer at 192.168.0.1 with 1,024-byte packets, you can type **PING -l 1024 192.168.0.1** and press Enter. Using a different packet size often reveals problems the standard packet size won't show. The maximum packet size is 65,500 bytes.

You can also use the -n Count switch to change the number of packets sent to the other computer. You might suspect that an error won't occur until you send the fifth or sixth packet, so you can adjust the count to 5 or 6. If you use a value of 1, PING continues sending packets until you press Ctrl+C (using Ctrl+Break won't work).

Manipulating the Network Routing Tables with the Route Utility

The Route utility displays the current IP routing information for the local machine and lets you change the routing table as needed. The routing table includes a number of entries, but the most important are the active routes and the permanent routes. An active route is one that's currently connected, but might not be permanent. A permanent route is always available, even when it isn't connected (active). This utility uses the following syntax:

```
ROUTE [-f] [-p] [-4 | -6] [command [destination] [MASK netmask]
[gateway] [METRIC metric] [IF interface]
```

The following list describes each of the command line arguments.

-f   Clears the routing table of all gateway entries. Using this command line switch with one of the commands clears the routing table before the utility executes the command. For example, if you add a new entry, then the routing table will contain just that entry when the utility finishes its work. This command line switch doesn't affect host routes (those with a netmask of 255.255 .255.255), loopback routes (those with an IP address of 127.0.0.0), or multicast routes (those with an IP address of 224.0.0.0 and a netmask of 240.0.0.0).

-p   Makes a route persistent across boots of the system when used with the ADD command. The system normally doesn't preserve routes when you restart the system and rediscovers the routes during the boot process. The Route utility ignores this command line switch for all other commands. You can't use this command line switch with older versions of Windows (most notably, Windows 95). Windows stores permanent routes in the HKEY_LOCAL_MACHINE\SYSTEM\ CurrentControlSet\Services\Tcpip\Parameters\PersistentRoutes registry key.

command   Performs the required IP routing task. The Route utility supports the following four commands.

PRINT   Prints (displays) one or more routes.

ADD   Adds a new route to the routing table. You can add an IP network address (where the host bits of the network address are set to 0), an IP address for a host route (those with a netmask of 255.255.255.255), or 0.0.0.0 for the default route.

DELETE   Removes a route from the routing table. You can't remove host routes (those with a netmask of 255.255.255.255), loopback routes (those with an IP address of 127.0.0.0), or multicast routes (those with an IP address of 224.0.0.0 and a netmask of 240.0.0.0).

CHANGE   Modifies an existing routing table entry.

destination   Specifies the destination for the route. Windows supports three route types that include an IP network address (where the host bits of the network address are set to 0), an IP address for a host route (those with a netmask of 255.255.255.255), or 0.0.0.0 for the default route.

MASK netmask   Specifies the subnet mask value for this route entry. The default subnet mask is 255.255.255.255.

gateway   Specifies the next host in the communication path. The gateway is the forwarding IP address; it defines how to reach the IP address specified by this route. When working with locally attached subnet routes, the gateway address is the IP address assigned to the interface attached to the subnet. When working with a remote route, the gateway address is a directly reachable IP address assigned to a neighboring router.

IF interface   Defines the interface to use to reach the destination. You can obtain a list of interfaces using the Route Print command. The Route utility lets you define interfaces using decimal or hexadecimal values. Precede the number with 0x when working with a hexadecimal number. When you don't provide this command line switch, the utility relies on the gateway information to determine the interface.

METRIC metric   Defines the cost of using a particular route. When the system needs to transfer information, it begins with the lowest cost route and moves to the next higher cost route as needed (for example, when an error occurs). The metric value is in the range from 1 to 9,999. There aren't any absolute metric values. Generally, you determine the metric value in relation to other routes on the system and by considering the number of hops, speed of the path, path reliability, path throughput, and administrative properties.

-4 Forces Route to use Internet Protocol Version 4 (IPv4) calls, even when the system normally uses IPv6.

-6 Forces Route to use Internet Protocol Version 6 (IPv6) calls, even when the system normally uses IPv4. Even though newer versions of Windows include some level of IPv6 support, most systems still use IPv4 and will do so for several more years.

Checking Connections using RPC with the RPCPing Utility

The Remote Procedure Call (RPC) Ping (RPCPing) utility lets you check RPC connections to a server with the same efficiency as other ping variants described in this chapter. Most people associate the RPC protocol with the Component Object Model (COM). However, in today's computing environment, it's better to view RPC as application-to-application communication. For example, you might want to test the connectivity between a local copy of Outlook and Exchange Server. This utility uses the following syntax:

```
RPCPing [-t <protseq>] [-s <server_addr>] [-e <endpoint>
|-f <interface UUID>[,MajorVer]] [-O <Object_UUID]
[-i <#_iterations>] [-u <security_package_id>] [-a <authn_level>]
[-N <server_princ_name>] [-I <auth_identity>] [-C <capabilities>]
[-T {Static | Dynamic}]
[-M {Anonymous | Identify | Impersonate | Delegate}]
[-S <server_sid>] [-P <proxy_auth_identity>] [-F <RPCHTTP_flags>]
[-H <RPC/HTTP_authn_schemes>] [-o <binding_options>]
[-B <server_certificate_subject>] [-b]
[-R {None | Default | <Proxy_Name>}] [-E] [-q] [-c]
[-A <http_proxy_auth_identity>] [-U <HTTP_proxy_authn_schemes>]
[-r <report_results_interval>] [-v {1 | 2 | 3}] [-d]
```

The following list describes each of the command line arguments.

-t *protseq* Defines the protocol sequence to use. The standard protocol sequences include ncacn_ip_tcp, ncacn_np, and ncacn_http. You can find a list of all of the protocol sequences at http://support.microsoft.com/kb/325930. The default protocol sequence is ncacn_ip_tcp.

-s *server_addr* Specifies the server address. The default setting is the local machine.

-e *endpoint* Specifies the endpoint to ping. The endpoint is the target of the test. The default setting is the endpoint mapper on the local machine. You can't use this option with the -f command line switch.

-o *binding_options* Defines the RPC binding options to use during testing. This feature relies on the RpcStringBindingCompose() function of the Windows API. You can learn more about this function at http://msdn2.microsoft.com/en-us/library/Aa378481.aspx. The article at http://msdn2.microsoft.com/en-us/library/aa378705.aspx provides an example of the RpcStringBindingCompose() function. The option strings appear at http://msdn2.microsoft.com/en-us/library/Aa378691.aspx. See the article at http://msdn2.microsoft.com/en-us/library/aa375384.aspx to learn more about how the binding options affect a real-world environment.

-f *interface_UUID[,MajorVer]* Specifies which interface to ping. You identify the interface by providing its Universally Unique Identifier (UUID). The default interface version is 1.0, which you can override by providing a major version number. When you use this option, the RPCPing utility queries the endpoint mapper on the specified machine to locate the interface endpoint. The utility then uses the interface endpoint for testing purposes.

 Real World Scenario

WATCH FOR RPC SECURITY ISSUES

One possible outcome of an RPC check is that you'll find an unexpected problem. For example, the RPC service might not be running or you might not have sufficient rights to access RPC using this utility. Unfortunately, Server Core tends to provide the same error for all error sources and you need to review the output information when testing locally. The output information includes the following fields (with sample error data included).

```
Exception 5 (0x00000005)

  Number of records is: 1

  ProcessID is 3452

  System Time is: 11/13/2006 18:26:0:60

  Generating component is 2

  Status is 0x5, 5

  Detection location is 1750

  Flags is 0

  NumberOfParameters is 1

  Long val: 0x5
```

This error message tells you that you don't have the required credentials to perform the test. It's possible to overcome this particular error by including the required credentials as part of the RPCPing call. In real-world testing, it's easy to forget that Server Core locks down just about everything so tightly that running even simple tests is nearly impossible. For example, it's unlikely that you'd see this error information when working with Windows 2000 as long as you have an administrator account.

-O *Object_UUID* Specifies the object UUID to ping. The object must register an object UUID (generally, using RegSvr32 or an equivalent utility) to use this feature.

-i *#_iterations* Defines the number of calls to make. The RPCPing utility uses a default value of 1, which is sufficient to test connectivity. If you want to test for other kinds of errors, you'll normally need to specify more iterations.

-u *security_package_id* Determines which security provider RPCPing uses to make the call. You specify the security provider as a number or a name. If you use a number, then it must match the numbers used for the RpcBindingSetAuthInfoEx() function (see http://msdn2 .microsoft.com/en-us/library/Aa375608.aspx for details on this function). You must specify an authentication level other than none when using this option (otherwise, RPCPing won't use security for the test). Here's a list of the standard security providers and their associated numbers.

Negotiate 9 (You can also provide values of nego, snego, or negotiate.)

NTLM 10

> SChannel   14
>
> Kerberos   16

-a *authn_level* Determines the authentication level that RPCPing uses to make the calls during the test. You must provide the –u command line option when using this option. RPCPing doesn't provide a default value for this option. You can use any of the following authentication levels.

- connect
- call
- pkt (packet)
- integrity
- privacy

-N *server_princ_name* Defines the server principal name. You use the same arguments as you would when using the RpcBindingSetAuthInfoEx() function (see http:// msdn.microsoft.com/library/en-us/rpc/rpc/rpcbindingsetauthinfoex.asp for details on this function). You can only use this option when you also specify the –a and –u options.

-I *auth_identity* Specifies an alternative identity to use to connect to the server. You specify the identity as a string in the form "user,domain,password". Always enclose the identity information in double quotes when it contains spaces or other special characters that can cause problems at the command line. Use the asterisk (*) instead of the password when you want the system to prompt you for the identification information. Using this approach reduces the risk that someone will see your password or other identification in plain text. The default for this option is the identification of the current user. You can only use this option when you also specify the –a and –u options.

-C *capabilities* Identifies the security services the application requires. The RPCPing call requires that you provide a hexadecimal bitmask of flags. You can find these flags in the Capabilities field of the RPC_SECURITY_QOS data structure described at http://msdn2 .microsoft.com/en-us/library/aa378647.aspx. You can only use this option when you also specify the –a and –u options.

-T {Static | Dynamic} Defines the type of identity tracking that the call uses. The default value is dynamic tracking. You can only use this option when you also specify the –a and –u options. This option is the same as the IdentityTracking field of the RPC_SECURITY_QOS data structure described at http://msdn2.microsoft.com/en-us/library/aa378647.aspx.

-M {Anonymous | Identify | Impersonate | Delegate} Defines the impersonation type. The default value is impersonate. You can only use this option when you also specify the –a and –u options. This option is the same as the ImpersonationType field of the RPC_ SECURITY_QOS data structure described at http://msdn2.microsoft.com/en-us/library/ aa378647.aspx.

-S *Server_SID* Provides the expected Security Identifier (SID) of the server. This option is only usable with Windows .NET Server 2003 or higher. You can only use this option when you also specify the –a and –u options. The intended purpose of this option is to prevent a cracker from tricking the server into a Denial of Service (DoS) attack.

-P *proxy_auth_identity* Provides the identity of the RPC/HTTP proxy to use for authentication purposes. This value has the same format as the –I option. You can only use this option when you also specify the –a, –u, and -H options.

-F *RPCHTTP_flags*   Specifies the flags to pass to the RPC/HTTP front-end authentication. The flags can appear as names or numbers. You can only use this option when you also specify the −a and −u options. This option is the same as the Flags field of the RPC_HTTP_TRANSPORT_ CREDENTIALS data structure described at http://msdn2.microsoft.com/en-us/library/ aa378624.aspx. The following list describes the flags you can use.

Use SSL   1 (You can also provide ssl or use_ssl as values.)

Use first auth scheme   2 (You can also provide first or use_first as values.)

-H *RPC/HTTP_authn_schemes*   Specifies the authentication scheme to use for the RPC/HTTP front-end authentication. The flags can appear as names or numbers. You can only use this option when you also specify the −a and −u options. The following list describes the authentication schemes you can use.

Basic   1

NTLM   2

Certificate   65536 (You can also abbreviate this value as Cert.)

-B `server_certificate_subject`   Defines the server certificate subject. This entry has the same value as the ServerCertificateSubject of the RPC_HTTP_TRANSPORT_CREDENTIALS data structure described at http://msdn2.microsoft.com/en-us/library/aa378624.aspx. This option only works when you use Secure Sockets Layer (SSL) authentication. You can only use this option when you also specify the −a and −u options.

-b   Prints the server certificate subject on screen. The utility retrieves this value from the certificate sent by the server. This option only works when you use SSL authentication. You can only use this option when you also specify the −a, −u, and −E options.

-R `{None | Default | Proxy_Name}`   Specifies the HTTP proxy to use for a call. When you set this option to None, RPCPing attempts to contact the RPC proxy directly. An input value of Default uses the Internet Explorer settings on the client machine. RPCPing treats any other value as the name of a specific HTTP proxy. The utility relies on a standard value of Default. You can only use this option when you also specify the −a, −u, and -E options. In addition, you must set the −t option to ncacn_http protocol. The RPCPing utility ignores this command line switch when you specify the HTTP proxy as part of the −o option.

-E   Restricts the test to using the RPC/HTTP proxy only. The ping doesn't reach the server. Use this option when you want to test the proxy, rather than the server. You can only use this option when you also specify the −a and −u options. Use the −R option when you want to specify the HTTP proxy, rather than using the default settings.

-q   Places the RPCPing utility in quiet mode. The utility won't issue any prompts except for password and it assumes a response of Y (yes) for all other queries. This option is useful for batch files where you don't want to make the user aware of all of the underlying prompts. However, use this option with care since the default response is yes.

-c   Forces the RPCPing utility to rely on a smart card certificate in place of standard credentials. The utility prompts the user to provide a smart card for authentication purposes.

-A *http_proxy_auth_identity*   Specifies the credentials to use when authenticating with the HTTP proxy. This value has the same format as the −I option. You can only use this option when you also specify the −a, −u, and −U options.

-U *HTTP_proxy_authn_schemes*   Defines the authentication schemes to use for HTTP proxy authentication. The flags can appear as names or numbers. You can only use this option when you also specify the −a and −u options. The following list describes the authentication schemes you can use.

> **Basic**   1
>
> **NTLM**   2

-r report_results_interval   Indicates the reporting interval in seconds when you specify multiple testing iterations. The default reporting interval is 15 seconds.

-v {1 | 2 | 3}   Determines the amount of information the RPCPing utility provides as output. The default value is 1, which provides basic test information. Increasing the value enhances the amount of output information.

-d   Launches the RPC network diagnostic user interface.

Managing Files with the TFTP Utility

The Trivial File Transfer Protocol (TFTP) utility transfers data from one computer to another. The host must have the TFTP daemon service installed. Workstation versions of Windows (such as Windows XP) don't provide support for this service. Server versions of Windows provide a limited version of the TFTP daemon service, but you can only use it for booting Windows workstations. However, you can use TFTP to transfer data to UNIX and Linux systems (and other operating systems with UNIX roots). The standard at http://spectral.mscs.mu.edu/RFC/rfc1350.html describes this protocol in detail. Server Core does provide support for this utility, but it's hidden deep within the directory structure. You'll likely find it in the \Windows\winsxs\x86_microsoft-windows-t..-deployment-package_31bf3856ad364e35_6.0.6001.16606_none_5ed3da618389cce9 or \Windows\winsxs\x86_microsoft-windows-t..-deployment-package_31bf3856ad364e35_6.0.6001.16606_en-us_5ed3da618389cce9 folder on your machine. This utility uses the following syntax:

```
TFTP [-i] host [GET | PUT] source [destination]
```

The following list describes each of the command line arguments.

-i   Specifies binary transfer mode (also called octet mode). This mode moves data byte by byte and doesn't perform any control character translation. Use binary mode to transfer nontext data such as graphics. The default mode, ASCII, converts the End of Line (EOL) characters to a carriage return for UNIX and a carriage return/line feed combination for personal computers. Use ASCII mode to transfer text files.

host   Specifies the host (remote) computer.

GET   Obtains a file from the host. This command transfers the file destination on the remote host to the file source on the local computer.

PUT   Sends a file to the host. This command transfers the file source on the local computer to the file destination on the remote host.

source   Specifies the file that you want to transfer.

destination   Specifies where to transfer the file.

Tracking the Network Path with the TraceRt Utility

The Trace Route (TraceRt) utility serves an important function by showing you the path between your machine and a remote machine. Essentially, this is a simpler form for the PathPing utility described in the "Tracing Transmission Paths with the PathPing Utility" section of the chapter. Unlike the PathPing utility, the TraceRt utility doesn't provide calculated network statistics, but it does show the time required between hops as shown in Figure 11.8. To obtain this kind of output, simply type **TraceRt** *Location* and press Enter.

FIGURE 11.8

Use TraceRt for quick connection checks between systems.

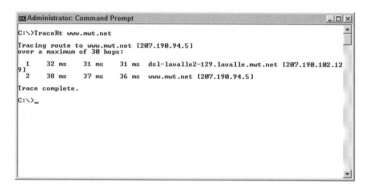

The TraceRt utility does have one significant advantage over the PathPing: it keeps trying to find a route even through multiple errors, which makes it valuable with troublesome routes. Using the TraceRt utility is also significantly faster than PathPing because you don't have to wait for it to calculate the statistics. This utility uses the following syntax:

```
tracert [-d] [-h maximum_hops] [-j host-list] [-w timeout]
[-R] [-S srcaddr] [-4] [-6] target_name
```

The following list describes each of the command line arguments.

-d Specifies that the utility not resolve addresses to hostnames. Using this command line switch can reduce the time required to trace a route. In addition, it can help you trace stubborn routes (those that won't provide a hostname). However, the information provided is less readable.

-h *maximum_hops* Defines the maximum number of hops the utility uses to search for the target. The PathPing utility automatically stops tracing the path when it reaches the specified number of hops. Using this option reduces the wait for long paths when you only need some of the path between your machine and the target.

-j *host-list* Specifies that the Echo Request messages used as part of defining the path between one point and another use the Loose Source Route option in the IP header with the set of intermediate destinations. The PING utility creates the list of servers that it outputs by extending the path between the source and destination by one machine for each call. The target machine, the one that's at the end of the line, receives an Echo Request message that requests that machine's name, which is why you receive a list of hosts as part of the output. This option lets the command use a number of intermediate routers to speed the process of defining the path between one machine and another. The results are less accurate, but you receive them faster.

-w *timeout* Specifies the number of milliseconds to wait for each reply. The default setting is 4,000 milliseconds.

-R   Tests the reverse route (from the target to your machine), as well, by adding a special routing header. You can only use this option with IPv6.

-S *srcaddr*   Specifies a source address to use so that you can test from a different client to the specified target. You can only use this option with IPv6. The default source address is the current machine.

-4   Forces TraceRt to use Internet Protocol Version 4 (IPv4) calls, even when the system normally uses IPv6.

-6   Forces PING to use Internet Protocol Version 6 (IPv6) calls, even when the system normally uses IPv4. Even though newer versions of Windows include some level of IPv6 support (see the "Working with IP Version 6" section of the chapter for details), most systems still use IPv4 and will do so for several more years.

Managing Windows in a New Way

Microsoft provides a lot of support for TCP/IP and it's no wonder that they do. The TCP/IP connection on your system is possibly the most important part of the server because it provides access to the outside world. Unfortunately, it's all too easy to misconfigure TCP/IP, which is why you need the utilities described in this chapter. This chapter helps you build these skills:

- Manage both IPv4 and IPv6 addresses
- Discover user information
- Obtain specific information about the system and its configuration
- Discover how the system routes information
- Perform network diagnostics
- Obtain network statistics
- Work with remote resources

Now that you know what utilities exist to work with TCP/IP, you'll want to spend some time working with them. The most important utilities are IPConfig and NetStat, so you should spend quite a bit of time working with them. These two utilities, when combined with a utility such as PING, PathPing, or TraceRt can solve as much as 90 percent of your networking problems. The other utilities described in this chapter help solve that other 10 percent, so you'll want to spend some time with them too.

You have a lot of other hardware installed on your system—the computing world doesn't exist solely of hard drives and network adapters. Chapter 12 discusses the somewhat paltry support that Microsoft provides for other hardware on your system. Even though these offerings aren't as robust as you might like, they do provide valuable services and you should try them out on your system.

Chapter 12

Managing Other Hardware

Previous chapters in this part have discussed a number of specific hardware issues, including the hard drive, network, and its support (low-level) software such as TCP/IP. Of course, your computer contains a lot more hardware. Even though the devices discussed in these previous chapters take center stage, you must also consider the other hardware components that make up your server and its connected devices. This chapter discusses the other devices, at least as far as Server Core provides support for them.

Server Core doesn't actually provide support for every piece of hardware on your system. In some cases, you'll need to obtain the support you need directly from the vendor or perhaps a third party. In some cases, a creative administrator has used a third-party solution to meet a need and found that it works after experimenting with it. These third-party solutions are always unsupported and Microsoft won't help you fix them when they fail. You'll find these solutions on online newsgroups in many cases. When you don't find what you need as a native component of Server Core, you'll need to obtain the required support elsewhere.

Unfortunately, you may not have a good hardware support option for some devices when working with Server Core. In many cases, the support software assumes that you have a graphical interface to use. For example, the temperature-sensing software that comes with many motherboards assumes that you have a standard graphical interface at your disposal. In many cases, the software still works, at least in a limited capacity, but in other cases, you'll need to search for a third-party alternative or wait until the vendor creates a new piece of software to work with Server Core.

NOTE Be sure you check the installation media that comes with the hardware for your system. Sometimes a vendor won't install command line tools automatically—assuming that you'll want to use the GUI instead. In other cases, the GUI product also includes a command line interface that you can use instead of the standard GUI. Verify that you actually have a problem before you look for solutions that you might not need.

In this chapter, you'll learn how to do the following:

- ◆ Configure line printers (those used with UNIX)
- ◆ Monitor memory
- ◆ Obtain general system information
- ◆ Use Notepad for various tasks
- ◆ Manage power settings
- ◆ Perform an unattended driver installation
- ◆ Manage Plug and Play settings

◆ Print from the command line

◆ Manage the system time

Working with Line Printers

Unless you're working with an older mainframe or UNIX setup, you probably won't ever run into a line printer. Line printer technology is outdated and not used all that often today. Today's modern equivalent isn't even a line printer; it's more likely a high-speed printer configured to provide the equivalent services. Of course, this might cause you to ask why there's a line printer topic in this chapter. It turns out that setting up a line printer is one of the ways you can share your printer (network or local) with a Linux machine. In fact, this technology is so embedded that some vendors like Hewlett-Packard provide print servers to provide Line Printer Daemon (LPD) services (see `http://h20000.www2.hp.com/bizsupport/TechSupport/Document.jsp?objectID=bpj02836` for details).

Windows provides a special LPD service to provide line printer support. The LPD service is an older TCP/IP service that you install with the Print Services for UNIX (found in the Other Network File and Print Services folder in the Windows Components Wizard dialog box). However, installing the server isn't enough. You'll need to configure the LPD service to provide a number of queues that users can use for printing. You can find an excellent procedure for performing the LPD configuration at `http://www.le.ac.uk/cc/dsss/docs/print-lpr.shtml`.

TIP If you're serious about providing Linux print services through an LPD server, you might want to use one of the better utilities on the market. A good starting product is the SDI LPD server found at `http://www.sdisw.com/LPD/default.htm`. This server provides a nice graphical interface that makes it easy to manage your print queues. In addition, because this product is shareware, you can try it before you buy it.

Once you have a printer configured to use LPD, you might wonder how to access it. The LPQ utility lets you see the status of the printer. The LPR utility lets you send output to the printer. Interestingly enough, these same utilities appear on both Macintosh and Linux systems, which is why these systems can access the LPD server on your Windows machine without problem. Both of these utilities work at the command line as described in the following sections.

NOTE You won't find the LPQ or LPR utilities in the normal location on a Server Core system. Look instead in the `\Windows\winsxs\x86_microsoft-windows-p..ting-lprportmonitor_31bf3856ad364e35_6.0.6001.16606_none_b409dc313dc8ecb7` folder of your hard drive for these executables. Except for the odd location, the utilities work the same as they do for older versions of Windows. Microsoft seems to be slating these utilities for departure since they don't appear in Vista at all.

Troubleshooting the Line Printer Daemon with the LPQ Utility

The Line Printer Queue (LPQ) utility provides status information that you can use to troubleshoot a LPD server. You can use this utility to display the status of each document in the queue. You may also use the LPD Print Service instead of this utility to obtain maximum functionality. This utility uses the following syntax:

```
LPQ  -Sserver -Pprinter [-1]
```

The following list describes each of the command line arguments.

-S*server* Defines the name or IP address of the server hosting the LDP service. You use the standard network name of the machine when working with Windows. Notice that there isn't any space between the -S command line switch and the server name. In addition, the command line switches for this utility are case sensitive; typing -s or /s isn't the same as typing -S.

-P*printer* Specifies the name of the LDP printer queue. This isn't the name of the printer, but the name of the printer entry you create as part of setting up an LPD server. The name you see in the Printers and Faxes folder is the same as the name of the LPD server queue for that printer.

-1 Displays the server information in verbose mode. This setting doesn't make much of a difference on Windows systems; you see the same information. However, you might see more information when accessing other platforms such as Linux. Note that this command line switch is a lowercase L.

Using the LPQ utility is relatively easy. For example, my machine's name is Main and I configured a LaserJet printer connection on it using the techniques described earlier in this section. Typing **LPQ -SMain -PLJ5** at the command prompt provides the display shown in Figure 12.1.

TIP There's nothing odd or strange about using an LPD server on Windows. Any printer you configure this way still provides the same management window as any other printer you connect to your machine or access from the network. You can use this GUI display to manage the print jobs in the queue. These features include all of the standard Windows features, such as changing job priority, pausing a job, or canceling all jobs. The only difference is the server used to service the print queue.

FIGURE 12.1
The LPQ utility tells you about the status of a selected printer queue on your machine.

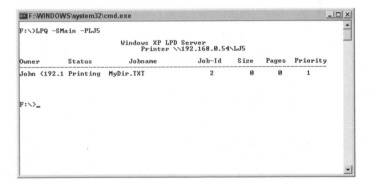

Sending a Print Job to a Printer with the LPR Utility

The Line Printer Request (LPR) utility sends a print job to the printer. When working at the command line, you'll normally send text files, but the LPR utility can also accommodate binary files and PostScript. You may also use the LPR Port Monitor instead of this utility to obtain the latest support. This utility uses the following syntax:

```
LPR -S server -P printer [-C class] [-J job] [-o option] [-x] [-d] filename
```

The following list describes each of the command line arguments.

-S*server*   Defines the name or IP address of the server hosting the LDP service. You use the standard network name of the machine when working with Windows. Notice that there isn't any space between the -S command line switch and the server name. In addition, the command line switches for this utility are case sensitive; typing -s or /s isn't the same as typing -S.

-P *printer_queue*   Specifies the name of the LDP printer queue. This isn't the name of the printer, but the name of the printer entry you create as part of setting up an LPD server. The name you see in the Printers and Faxes folder is the same as the name of the LPD server queue for that printer.

-C *class*   Defines the job classification to use for the burst page. You must define print jobs for the server to use this feature.

-J *job*   Defines the job name to print on the burst page. You must define print jobs for the server to use this feature.

-o *option*   Determines the type of the file. The default setting is a text file. The only standardized option value is a 1, which indicates a binary or PostScript file. The presence of this option doesn't mean that the printer can handle the file you send or that Windows won't strip control characters. Make sure you read the Microsoft Knowledge Base articles on this topic, such as the one found at `http://support.microsoft.com/kb/124735/EN-US/`, before you create binary print jobs.

-x   Enforces compatibility with SunOS4.1.x and prior version when working with a remote printer (you can read more about SunOS4.1.x and its successor at `http://www.sun.com/bigadmin/content/misc/solaris2faq.html`).

-d   Places this data file at the front of the print queue. The default is to place the data file at the end of the queue.

Generally, you won't need to use all of the LPR options. For example, you can print a text file on a Windows machine simply by specifying the server name, the print queue, and the name of the file as shown here:

```
LPR -SMain -PLJ5 MyDir.TXT
```

NOTE   Once you establish an LPD server on your system, you can use the associated printer as you would any other printer from Windows applications. Consequently, the LPR utility is like any other command line utility for printing—it lets you create basic output from the command line. However, LPD servers and their associated printers require special setup to pass control characters and other non-ASCII data. Make sure you understand and configure your LPD server setup before you use it for general application output.

Determining Memory Status with the Mem Utility

Many applications that execute at the command line have strict memory limitations. For example, you might try to run an old DOS application and find that it doesn't work as anticipated (or at all). In some cases, the application will tell you that it lacks sufficient memory, but in other cases, you need to diagnose the problem yourself using the Mem utility. This utility provides you with detailed information about the memory at the command prompt, which differs from the memory that Windows provides. The standard output shows the total amount of conventional memory, the amount of memory available to run applications, the amount of extended memory, and the amount of expanded memory. This utility uses the following syntax:

```
MEM [/PROGRAM | /DEBUG | /CLASSIFY]
```

The following list describes each of the command line arguments.

/PROGRAM or /P   Displays the status of programs currently loaded into memory. Use this command line switch to identify applications that you can remove to free memory. Figure 12.2 shows typical output when using this command line switch. Notice that the output lists every memory usage, including the memory used by the command processor for requirements such as the file handles and drives. The size column shows the memory usage for the application or other element in hexadecimal. The – Free – indicator in the Type column shows areas of free memory in the current command prompt.

NOTE   The programs loaded into memory for the command prompt aren't the same programs that are loaded into the Windows environment. The list of applications that you see when you view the Applications tab of the Windows Task Manager won't match those shown at the command prompt. The environments are separate. Windows treats the command prompt as a single black box entity, even though it's running one or more applications.

FIGURE 12.2

The program mode of the Mem utility describes the way applications use memory.

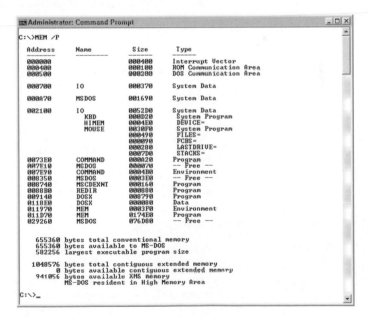

/DEBUG or /D   Displays the status of the programs, internal drivers, and other elements of the command prompt. Use this command line switch to identify potential problems at the command line prompt. The output from this command line switch looks like a very detailed version of the program output shown in Figure 12.2.

/CLASSIFY or /C   Displays the programs based on memory usage. Categorizes the programs by size, provides a list of memory in use, and displays the largest memory block available. Use this command line switch to check for potential problems in memory allocation. As shown in

Figure 12.3, the classify view is a little more readable than the other views and offers the memory allocation sizes in decimal. In addition, you can see the use of upper memory with greater ease.

TIP Not all older applications require more memory. A few older applications actually fail when they have too much memory. If your efforts to run the application fail when it has as much memory as possible, try reducing the available memory.

FIGURE 12.3
The Classify mode of the Mem utility categorizes application use of memory.

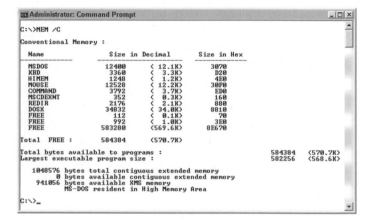

Obtaining General System Information with the MSInfo32 Utility

The Microsoft Information 32-bit (MSInfo32) utility made an initial appearance with Office products. In fact, that's why you'll still find it in the \Program Files\Common Files\Microsoft Shared\ MSInfo directory, rather than the more standard \Windows\System32 directory when working with older versions of Windows. Server Core provides its only copy of the utility in the \WINDOWS\ system32 directory. Interestingly enough, MSInfo32 is one of the few utilities that you can use in GUI mode. No, you can't save or export information directly from the GUI, but you can view the information. When working with Server Core, you must still save any information you want to save using the command line arguments.

NOTE You may need to make special provisions when using MSInfo to work with an older version of Windows. Because the MSInfo utility doesn't appear in the standard directory, you might find that it won't execute correctly at the command prompt. You might need to add one of the MSInfo utility paths to your setup to execute the application from anywhere at the command prompt. Of course, the utility will always execute when you're in the appropriate directory.

The main reason to use the MSInfo32 utility is to record a snapshot of the state of a system. The data includes everything from the kind of processor installed on the system to the applications running on it. In fact, you might be surprised at how much information this utility can record. Simply open the graphical portion of the utility, shown in Figure 12.4, to see the various information categories. Of course, you'll notice some missing categories as well. For example, Server Core doesn't

---

🌐 Real World Scenario

CHOOSING THE CORRECT UTILITY

It's not always important to use the command line utilities that come with Windows. In some cases, you'll find that you really want and need the features provided by a third-party application or by a utility that Microsoft has dropped. Many longtime Windows users will remember the WinMSD utility (see `http://support.microsoft.com/kb/q232848/` for details) that let you create system-level reports. The MSInfo32 utility replaces WinMSD. Even though the WinMSD executable still exists on your hard drive, it now displays a message telling you to use MSInfo32 instead.

Although Microsoft doesn't recommend that you download the actual WinMSD executable and use it with Windows XP and above, you'll find some substitutes on the Internet such as the WinMSDp command line utility found on the Petri.co.il Web site at `http://www.petri.co.il/download_free_reskit_tools.htm`. If you download this utility, make sure you address the security concerns in using it (see the Microsoft security bulletin at `http://www.microsoft.com/technet/security/bulletin/MS99-013.mspx` for details). The point is that using this utility might provide the interface that you really wanted to use instead of relying on Microsoft's choice for you, which is MSInfo32.

---

have an Internet Settings category because it doesn't support Internet Explorer. In fact, Server Core only supports these categories:

◆ Hardware Resources

◆ Components

◆ Software Environment

FIGURE 12.4
Use the MSInfo32 utility to obtain a snapshot of your system setup.

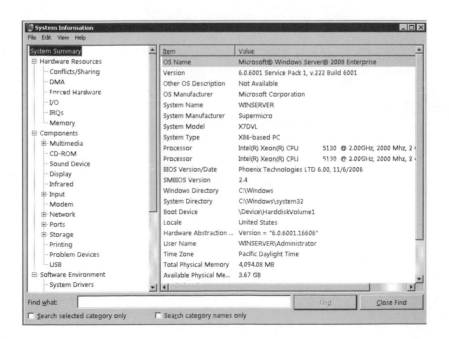

When you use the command line interface, the MSInfo32 utility records everything to a file on your system. You can use this file as an archive of the current system state and even use it to help set up another system to match the current system's setup. Administrators can use these snapshots to look for potential system problems by processing the resulting file through an application. This utility uses the following syntax:

```
MSInfo32 [Filename] [/pch] [/nfo Outfile] [/report Outfile]
[/category Catname] [/computer ComputerName] [/categories Catlist]
[/ShowCategories]
```

The following list describes each of the command line arguments.

Filename   Defines the Info (NFO) file, PCHealth XML file, or cabinet (CAB) file containing system information that you want MSInfo32 to open. The utility displays the file using the graphical interface. However, you could use this option to open a number of files that you regularly collect for viewing at the same time.

/pch   Opens the MSInfo32 utility in the history view. The history view displays changes to the system over time. For example, every time a piece of hardware experiences an address change, MSInfo32 records it for the history view.

/nfo Outfile   Outputs the current system state to the specified NFO file. The NFO file is actually in an XML format that you can examine using any application designed to work with XML. In fact, the XML formatting makes it quite easy to create a custom utility to extract only the information you need for a particular purpose.

NOTE   File output occurs in a silent mode. Even though the MSInfo32 utility returns immediately, that doesn't mean the output file is ready for use. MSInfo completes the task in the background so the user can continue working. Generally, you'll want to allow at least 10 minutes for the system to complete the task of outputting the file (more time is better).

/report Outfile   Outputs the current system state to the specified text file.

/category Catname   Opens MSInfo32 with the specified category selected. Use the /ShowCategories command line switch to open MSInfo with the category names displays, in place of the human-readable categories shown in Figure 12.4.

/computer ComputerName   Opens MSInfo32 with the information for the specified remote computer loaded in place of the local computer. You can also use this command line switch to generate reports for remote computers.

NOTE   Remote systems must have the Windows Management Instrumentation (WMI) service running to collect information. Otherwise, MSInfo32 will simply report that it can't collect the information.

/categories Catlist   Opens MSInfo32 with the specified categories in view. The utility hides all of the other categories. You can use this feature to reduce the amount of information you must wade through to locate the information you want. Add categories to the list by typing the category name with a plus sign (+) in front of it. A special category, All, displays all of the categories. Remove categories by typing the category name with a minus sign (–) in front of it. Use the /ShowCategories command line switch to open MSInfo with the category names displayed, in place of the human-readable categories shown in Figure 12.4. You can also use this command line switch to generate reports with only the selected categories included.

/ShowCategories   Opens MSInfo32 with the category names displayed in place of the standard human-readable names.

Performing a Formatted Printout with Notepad

Many people associate Notepad with a utility that you use in the Windows GUI, and that's where you use it most often. However, Notepad and many other applications have a hidden side. Unfortunately, you won't discover this hidden side by typing the command name followed by a /?. Notepad and other Windows applications won't provide you with any help for using them at the command line, yet this command line functionality still exists.

To locate such functionality, you must rely on the registry editor, RegEdit. To start this utility, type **RegEdit** at the command line and press Enter. At this point you need to look at the HKEY_CLASSES_ROOT hive. Locate the extension of the file that you want to work with. The example uses the .txt entry shown in Figure 12.5. The (Default) entry shown in the right pane contains the essential information; the file association. (For more information about file associations see the "Working with File Associations and Types" section of Chapter 14.)

FIGURE 12.5

Locate the extension of the file you want to print from the command line.

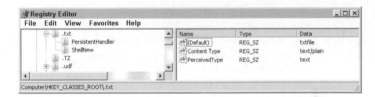

Now that you know the file association, locate its entry in the registry. Figure 12.6 shows the entries for the txtfile association. The entry you want is the command for the print command shown highlighted in the figure. Notice that this command calls on Notepad with an undocumented /p command line switch to perform the printing. The %1 after the command line switch is the name of the file. Consequently, if you want to print a text file at the command line using Notepad, you simply type **Notepad /p *filename*** and press Enter.

FIGURE 12.6

The file association provides clues as to how to use graphical utilities at the command line.

Managing Power Settings with the PowerCfg Utility

Some people associate the power configuration settings with how long their monitor stays on or how their UPS reacts to a power failure. However, power configuration encompasses a lot more ground that these simple configuration tasks. Even though you can change any power configuration using the graphical interface, the settings appear in disparate locations. Using the PowerCfg utility to manage the power configuration puts everything in one place. Of course, given the enormous job this utility has, it also has a complex command line. This utility uses the following syntax:

```
POWERCFG /LIST
POWERCFG /QUERY [GUID [SubGUID]] [/NUMERICAL]
POWERCFG /CHANGE GUID settings [/NUMERICAL]
POWERCFG /CHANGENAME GUID name [scheme_description]
POWERCFG /DUPLICATESCHEME GUID DESTINATION_GUID
POWERCFG /DELETE GUID [/NUMERICAL]
POWERCFG /DELETESETTING SUB_GUID SETTING_GUID
POWERCFG /SETACTIVE GUID [/NUMERICAL]
POWERCFG /GETACTIVESCHEME
POWERCFG /SETACVALUEINDEX SCHEME_GUID SUB_GUID SETTING_GUID
   SettingIndex
POWERCFG /SETDCVALUEINDEX SCHEME_GUID SUB_GUID SETTING_GUID
   SettingIndex
POWERCFG /HIBERNATE {ON|OFF}
POWERCFG /AVAILABLESLEEPSTATES
POWERCFG /DEVICEQUERY queryflags
POWERCFG /DEVICEENABLEWAKE devicename
POWERCFG /DEVICEDISABLEWAKE devicename
POWERCFG /EXPORT GUID [/FILE filename] [/NUMERICAL]
POWERCFG /IMPORT GUID [/FILE filename] [/NUMERICAL]
POWERCFG /LASTWAKE
POWERCFG /ALIASES
POWERCFG /SETSECURITYDESCRIPTOR {GUID | ACTION} SDDL
POWERCFG /GETSECURITYDESCRIPTOR {GUID | ACTION}
```

The following list describes each of the command line arguments.

/LIST, /L Lists the names of existing power schemes. You can see the same list in the Power Schemes tab of the Power Options Properties dialog box accessible through the Power Options applet of the Control Panel. This command line switch varies from the /Query command line switch that you can use to see the actual power scheme settings. You can use this command line switch to obtain a list of Globally Unique Identifiers (GUIDs) for the various power configurations as shown in Figure 12.7. Simply type **PowerCfg /L** and press Enter to obtain the information. The GUIDs are important in performing other power configuration tasks. Notice that the output places an asterisk (*) next to the currently selected power scheme.

FIGURE 12.7
Display the GUIDs for the current power configurations for use with other command line switches.

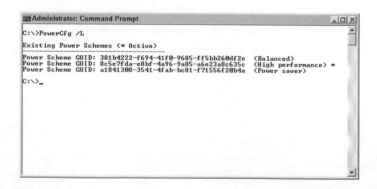

/QUERY [*GUID* [*SubGUID*]], /Q [*GUID* [*SubGUID*]]   Displays the configuration information for a specified power scheme. If you don't supply a power scheme, the utility displays all of the power schemes and their settings. The command line switch supplies the Name, Numerical ID, Turn off monitor (AC), Turn off monitor (DC), Turn off hard disks (AC), Turn off hard disks (DC), System standby (AC), System standby (DC), System hibernates (AC), System hibernates (DC), Processor Throttle (AC), and Processor Throttle (DC) fields as output. The AC fields specify the operating time when the system is on standard line current, while the DC fields specify the operating time when the system is on battery. Supply a GUID or subGUID to obtain particulars about a specific power scheme as shown in Figure 12.8. In this case, the output shows the High Performance power scheme. To access this scheme, you type **PowerCfg /Q 8c5e7fda-e8bf-4a96-9a85-a6e23a8c635c** and press Enter. However, let's say that you're only interested in the hard drive settings for the High Performance power scheme. In this case, you'd type **PowerCfg /Q 8c5e7fda-e8bf-4a96-9a85-a6e23a8c635c 0012ee47-9041-4b5d-9b77-535fba8b1442** and press Enter. The first GUID is for the High Performance power scheme and the second GUID is for the Hard Drive subGUID.

FIGURE 12.8
Use the power scheme GUIDs and subGUIDs to access information about them.

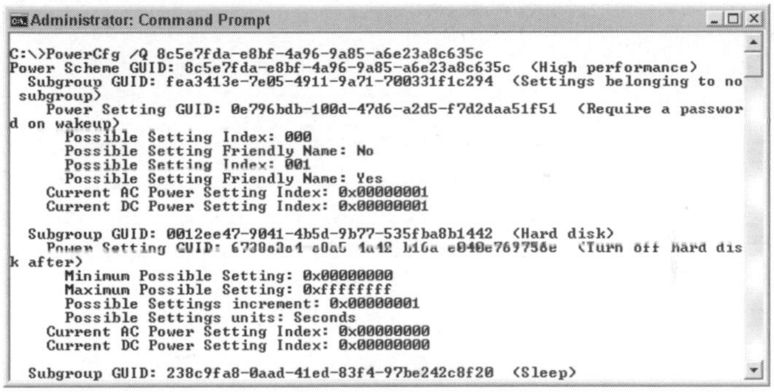

/DELETE *GUID*, /D *GUID*   Deletes the power scheme with the specified GUID.

/SETACTIVE *GUID*, /S *GUID*   Changes the active power scheme to the specified power scheme.

/CHANGE *GUID settings*, /X *GUID settings*   Modifies the settings for the specified power scheme. Changing a setting value to 0 disables that feature. You can change any of the power scheme settings individually using the command line switches that follow.

/monitor-timeout-ac *minutes*   Sets the monitor power-down time in minutes when the system is on AC power.

/monitor-timeout-dc *minutes*   Sets the monitor power-down time in minutes when the system is on battery.

/disk-timeout-ac *minutes*   Sets the hard drive power-down time in minutes when the system is on AC power.

/disk-timeout-dc *minutes*   Sets the hard drive power-down time in minutes when the system is on battery.

/standby-timeout-ac *minutes*   Sets the system standby time in minutes when the system is on AC power.

/standby-timeout-dc *minutes*   Sets the system standby time in minutes when the system is on battery.

/hibernate-timeout-ac *minutes*   Sets the system hibernation time in minutes when the system is on AC power.

/hibernate-timeout-dc *minutes*   Sets the system hibernation time in minutes when the system is on battery.

/processor-throttle-ac {NONE | CONSTANT | DEGRADE | ADAPTIVE}   Sets the processor-throttling feature when the system is on AC power.

/processor-throttle-dc {NONE | CONSTANT | DEGRADE | ADAPTIVE}   Sets the processor-throttling feature when the system is on battery.

/EXPORT *GUID* **[/FILE** *filename*], **/E** *name* **[/FILE** *filename*]   Exports the specified power scheme to a file. A file can contain only one power scheme, so you must always include the power scheme name. The /File command line switch defines the name of the file to use for storage. If you don't include this command line switch, the PowerCfg utility uses a default filename of Scheme.POW.

/IMPORT *GUID* **[/FILE** *filename*], **/I** *name* **[/FILEs**filename**]**   Imports the specified power scheme from a file. The file doesn't include a power scheme name, so you can give the power scheme any appropriate name. The /File command line switch defines the name of the file that contains the power scheme. If you don't include this command line switch, the PowerCfg utility uses a default filename of Scheme.POW.

/AVAILABLESLEEPSTATES, /A   Reports the sleep states available on the system. The PowerCfg utility supports four sleep states: S1 is a light sleep, S2 is a deeper sleep, S3 is the deepest sleep, and S4 is hibernation. Each successive sleep state reduces the power requirements of the system or device. However, deeper levels of sleep usually require longer wake-up periods as well. The PowerCfg utility tries to report the reason a system doesn't support a particular sleep state, but usually fails.

/DEVICEQUERY *queryflags*   Displays a list of devices that meet the criteria specified by the queryflags argument. You may use more than one query flag to narrow the list of returned devices. The number of devices that support particular power off and wake-up features on a modern system is amazing. However, you usually need to know how the devices will react when setting up a power critical device such as a laptop. For example, it doesn't help to place the devices in an S1 sleep level when most of them don't support that mode. The following list describes the query flags.

wake_from_S1_supported   Returns all devices that support waking the system from a light sleep.

wake_from_S2_supported   Returns all devices that support waking the system from a deeper sleep.

wake_from_S3_supported   Returns all devices that support waking the system from the deepest sleep state.

wake_from_any   Returns all devices that support waking the system from any sleep mode.

S1_supported   Lists devices that support light sleep states.

S2_supported   Lists devices that support deeper sleep states.

S3_supported   Lists devices that support the deepest sleep states.

S4_supported   Lists devices that support hibernation.

wake_programmable   Lists devices that a user can configure to wake from a sleep state.

wake_armed   Lists devices that are currently configured to wake from any sleep state.

all_devices   Returns a list of devices present in the system, even if they don't support any sleep mode or hibernation. This list only contains the device name.

all_devices_verbose   Returns a verbose list of devices, even if they don't support any sleep mode or hibernation. This list contains a wealth of information that varies by device. As a minimum, you'll receive the device name, the device identifier, and the sleep, wake, and hibernation modes it supports. Optional information includes whether you can program the device or configure it in some way.

/DEVICEENABLEWAKE *devicename*   Enables the specified device to wake the system from a sleep state. The device must provide programmable functionality. You can obtain a list of these devices using the /DEVICEQUERY wake_programmable command line switch.

/DEVICEDISABLEWAKE *devicename*   Disables a device from waking the system from a sleep state. You can obtain a list of devices currently set to wake the system using the /DEVICEQUERY wake_armed command line switch.

POWERCFG /CHANGENAME *GUID name* [*scheme_description*]   Modifies the name of the power scheme specified by GUID. Use the PowerCfg /List command to obtain a list of existing GUIDs. The name argument contains the new power scheme name. You can optionally change the power scheme description as well. Make sure you enclose any value that contains spaces in quotes.

POWERCFG /DUPLICATESCHEME *GUID* [*DESTINATION_GUID*]   Creates a new power scheme based on an existing power scheme. If you don't provide a destination GUID, the utility creates one for you automatically. Use the PowerCfg /List command to obtain a list of existing GUIDs.

POWERCFG /DELETESETTING *SUB_GUID SETTING_GUID*   Removes the specified power setting. You must provide both the subgroup GUID and the setting GUID as part of this call. Use the PowerCfg /Query command to obtain a list of both subgroup GUIDs and setting GUIDs.

POWERCFG /GETACTIVESCHEME   Displays the name and the GUID of the active power scheme.

POWERCFG /SETACVALUEINDEX *SCHEME_GUID SUB_GUID SETTING_GUID SettingIndex*   Sets a value associated with a particular power scheme when the system is powered by AC power. You must provide the power scheme GUID, subgroup GUID, setting GUID, and a setting value (normally a numeric or Boolean value). Use the PowerCfg /List command to obtain a list of power scheme GUIDs. Use the PowerCfg /Query command to obtain a list of both subgroup GUIDs and setting GUIDs.

POWERCFG /SETDCVALUEINDEX *SCHEME_GUID SUB_GUID SETTING_GUID SettingIndex*   Performs the same task as the /SETACVALUEINDEX command line switch, except when using DC power.

POWERCFG /LASTWAKE   Reports data about the last time the system returned from the sleep state. If the system hasn't ever returned from the sleep state, the call returns: Wake History Count - 0.

POWERCFG /ALIASES   Displays all power system aliases and their associated GUIDs. These entries aren't associated with the power scheme, subgroup, or setting, but generally refer to state information such as HIBERNATEIDLE or BATLEVELCRIT.

POWERCFG /SETSECURITYDESCRIPTOR {*GUID* | *ACTION*} *SDDL*   Sets the security descriptor associated with a particular power system component. Provide a GUID when you want to work with a power scheme. Use ActionSetActive, ActionCreate, or ActionDefault when you

want to modify a power system action. The SDDL variable must contain a security descriptor. You can learn more about SDDL at `http://msdn2.microsoft.com/en-us/library/aa379567`
`.aspx`. Use the `PowerCfg /GetSecurityDescriptor` call to see an example of an SDDL.

POWERCFG /GETSECURITYDESCRIPTOR {GUID | ACTION} Obtains the security descriptor associated with a particular power system component. Provide a GUID when you want to work with a power scheme. Use `ActionSetActive`, `ActionCreate`, or `ActionDefault` when you want to view a power system action.

Performing Unattended Driver Installation with the PnPUnattend Utility

The PnPUnattend utility provides helper services for unattended installations. You can also execute it from the command line to obtain information about installation progress and to create a log file of the installation. This utility uses the following syntax:

```
PnPUnattend.exe [/auditSystem] [/s] [/L]
```

The following list describes each of the command line arguments.

/auditSystem Performs an unattended driver installation.

/s Searches for the required driver installation information, without performing an install.

/L Creates a log file of any installation.

Managing PnP Setups Using the PnPUtil Utility

You can use the PnPUtil utility to perform a driver installation from the command line. In addition, the options let you remove or edit driver information based on the content of an INF file, which you must always provide. This utility uses the following syntax:

```
PnPUtil.exe [-f | -i] [-a | -d | -e ] <INFname>
```

The following list describes each of the command line arguments.

-f Forces the utility to perform the specified action (add, edit, or delete).

-i Performs a standardized installation when used with –a based on the INF content.

-a Adds the device driver specified by the INF file to the system. However, adding the device driver simply makes it available for installation. You must combine this command line switch with the –i command line switch to actually install the driver.

-d Deletes the device driver specified by the INF file from the system. The INF file normally has oem, followed by a number, followed by INF, such as `oem0.inf`. Deleting an OEM (Original Equipment Manufacturer) driver has the effect of uninstalling the device driver. You can obtain a list of OEM drivers using the –e command line switch.

-e Enumerates all of the third-party drivers currently installed on the system, but doesn't do anything with them. This is the only command line switch that doesn't require you to provide an INF filename.

INFname Provides the name of a file containing device driver information. You can use wildcard characters to specify multiple INF files.

Printing Data Files with the Print Utility

The Print utility represents the fastest and easiest way to send data to a printer for output. However, you don't have many choices when you use this technique. The only change you can make is to define the print device to use for output. Otherwise, the Print utility relies on all of the defaults that you assign to the printer. This utility uses the following syntax:

```
PRINT [/D:device] [[drive:][path]filename[...]]
```

The following list describes each of the command line arguments.

/D:*device* Specifies the device to use for output. The default setting uses the printer attached to LPT1.

drive Specifies the drive that holds the file for printing. The default is the current drive.

path Specifies the relative or absolute path of the file you want to print. The default is the current directory.

filename Specifies one or more files to send to the printer for output.

Managing the System Time with the W32Tm Utility

Time is a critical resource for most people and not just because there's too little of it. When your computer lacks proper time synchronization, your applications might not work as expected. Entries you make into remote databases suddenly bear the wrong timestamp. It's more than just inconvenient. The W32Tm utility helps you manage time on your system. You use it to set how Windows reacts to time events and to set your system up as a timeserver. This utility uses the following syntax:

```
w32tm [/register | /unregister ]
w32tm /monitor [/domain:<domain name>]
    [/computers:<name>[,<name>[,<name>...]]] [/threads:<num>]
    [/ipprotocol:<4|6>] [/nowarn]
w32tm /ntte <NT_time_epoch>
w32tm /ntpte <NTP_time_epoch>
w32tm /resync [/computer:<computer>] [/nowait] [/rediscover] [/soft]
w32tm /stripchart /computer:<computer> [/period:<refresh>] [/dataonly]
    [/samples:<count>] [/packetinfo] [/ipprotocol:<4|6>]
w32tm /config [/computer:<computer>] [/update]
    [/manualpeerlist:<peers>] [/syncfromflags:<source>]
    [/LocalClockDispersion:<seconds>] [/reliable:(YES|NO)]
    [/largephaseoffset:<milliseconds>]
w32tm /tz
w32tm /dumpreg [/subkey:<key>] [/computer:<computer>]
w32tm /query [/computer:<computer>] {/source | /configuration | /peers
    | /status} [/verbose]
w32tm /debug {/disable | {/enable /file:<name> /size:<bytes>
    /entries:<value> [/truncate]}}
```

The following list describes each of the standard command line arguments.

register Registers the current machine to run as a time service and adds the default configuration to the registry.

unregister Unregisters the current machine as a time service and removes all configuration information from the registry.

monitor Monitors a remote computer for time changes. This command line switch sets the local time to match the remote timeserver when you specify a domain. When used alone, this command switch reports monitoring statistics.

domain:*domain_name* Specifies which domain to monitor. If you don't supply a domain name or you haven't used the /computers command line switch, then the system uses the default domain. You may include this option more than once at the command line to create multiple time sources.

/computers:*name[,name[,name...]]* Specifies the computers you want to use for monitoring purposes on the domain. The command line switch may include multiple computers from the same domain. Separate each computer with a comma without a space between names. Prefix Primary Domain Controller (PDC) names with an asterisk (*). You may include this option more than once at the command line to create multiple time sources (once for each domain).

threads:*num* Determines the number of computers to analyze simultaneously. The default value is 3. You may specify any value between 1 and 50.

ntte *NT_time_epoch* Converts the specified Windows system time into a human-readable form.

/ntpte *NTP_time_epoch* Converts the specified Windows Network Time Protocol (NTP) time into a human-readable form.

/resync Causes a remote computer to resynchronize its clock. This command line switch also forces the remote computer to discard all error statistics and begin creating new ones.

/computer:*computer* Specifies the name of the target. If you don't specify this command line switch, the Win32Tm utility interacts with the local computer.

/nowait Forces the utility to return control of the command prompt immediately. Normally, the Win32Tm utility waits for the resynchronization process to complete before returning.

/rediscover Forces the utility to rediscover timeservers on the network before it performs the resynchronization process. Always use this command line switch when you've added a new timeserver to the network.

/soft Resynchronizes the system's clock without discarding the error statistics. Don't use this command line switch because Microsoft has disabled it. Keeping the current error statistics could cause the affected machine to update its clock incorrectly. Microsoft only provided this command line switch for compatibility purposes.

/stripchart Displays text output showing the time differential between the local computer and the specified computer. The display updates every 2 seconds unless you specify a different interval using the /period command line switch. The output never includes graphics, despite the presence of the /dataonly command line switch. The display continues to update with one entry per line at the command prompt until you press Ctrl+C. Using the /samples command line switch sets a specific number of updates so you don't have to press Ctrl+C to stop the utility.

/period:*refresh* Defines the strip chart update frequency in seconds.

/dataonly Displays only data in the output (this is the default and only output for Windows).

/samples:*count* Determines the number of samples to take before ending the strip chart.

/config   Configures the specified computer to use a particular time source. You can only use this command line switch to change the Windows time setup. Using the /config command line switch alone displays an error message. Contrast this command with the Net /Time utility described in the "Managing the Network with the Net Utility" section of Chapter 10.

/update   Notifies the target computer that the changes are complete and it should update the Windows time service. You must perform this configuration change for any of the settings discussed in this section to take effect.

/manualpeerlist:*peers*   Specifies one or more time service peers. Use spaces to define multiple peers. You may use a Domain Name System (DNS) name or an IP address to describe a peer. When using this command line switch with multiple peers, you must place the entire command line switch within quotes, not just the peer list.

/syncfromflags:*source*   Defines the sources to use for synchronization. You may specify multiple sources. The two valid sources include MANUAL (the list of peers supplied as part of a /manualpeerlist command line switch) and DOMHIER (relies on a domain controller, DC, within the domain hierarchy).

/LocalClockDispersion:*seconds*   Defines the accuracy of the local clock. Windows uses this rating as a means of compensating for errors when it can't locate a remote source.

/tz   Displays the local time zone settings. The output includes the time bias information, as well as settings for both standard and daylight savings time.

/dumpreg   Displays the Windows time settings located in the HKEY_LOCAL_MACHINE\SYSTEM\ CurrentControlSet\Services\W32Time key.

/subkey:key   Displays values associated with the specified subkey of the HKEY_LOCAL_ MACHINE\SYSTEM\CurrentControlSet\Services\W32Time key.

/ipprotocol:{4|6}   Chooses the IP version to use for the utility. You can choose between IP version 4 or IP version 6.

/nowarn   Prevents the display of warning messages. This feature is useful when you want to redirect the output to a file.

/packetinfo   Displays the NTP packet response message so that you can perform troubleshooting as required.

/reliable:{YES | NO}   Specifies whether this machine is a reliable time source. This setting only applies to domain controllers.

/largephaseoffset:*milliseconds*   Defines the difference between local and network time that W32Tm considers a spike. The utility registers errors whenever it encounters a large time spike and also attempts to correct the time differential.

/query   Displays information about the target computer's time source. You control the output by including one of the specific output command line switches (/source, /configuration, /peers, or /status) and the /verbose command line switch.

/source   Outputs the time source information for the specified computer. The default setting when not using an external time source is Local CMOS Clock.

/configuration   Outputs a considerable range of time source information including such specifics as the time source DLL.

/peers   Outputs a list of time source peers and their status.

/status   Outputs the Windows Time Service status. This information includes such useful statistics as the time of the last update and the poll interval.

/verbose   Augments the time service status information.

/debug   Enables or disables output of Windows Time Service information to a log.

/disable   Disables time service logging.

/enable   Enables time service logging.

/file:*name*   Specifies the name of a file to use for logging purposes.

/size:*bytes*   Specifies the maximum size of the time service log. When the log is full, Server Core begins removing the oldest entries and adding new entries. The time service uses a circular logging system so the log will never overflow.

/entries:*value*   Defines the list of entries that the log contains as numeric values. Unfortunately, Microsoft doesn't document these values, but the range is within the values from 0 to 300. Fortunately, the debugging mode works fine without this command line switch.

/truncate   Truncates an existing log file before making new entries. This command line switch ensures that the log doesn't contain any old entries when you start the debugging process.

Managing Windows in a New Way

Server Core provides a number of utilities for working with your other devices—those that don't constantly grab the headlines. Of course, this support is probably less than you'd like. For example, you won't find a utility for testing your display adapter completely or verifying the status of your hard drive controller. However, the support you do get helps you perform tasks such as setting up your power configuration. This chapter helps you build these skills:

- Configure line printers (Those Used with UNIX)
- Monitor memory
- Obtain general system information
- Use Notepad for various tasks
- Manage power settings
- Perform an unattended driver installation
- Manage Plug and Play settings
- Print from the command line
- Manage the system time

One of the configuration tasks that you probably haven't performed yet is to set up the power configuration. Make sure you use the information found in this chapter to perform that task. You don't want your server acting in an odd manner during the next power outage or turning off the hard drives when you need them most. It's also important to validate your time setup since so many Server Core security features rely on the correct time. You may find that you experience

Kerberos errors when you don't have the time set correctly. Using a timeserver on your own network or an external time source is always the best bet. The time services provided by the computer's BIOS are unfortunately inaccurate and you'll quickly find yourself battling a host of errors if you rely on the internal clock.

Chapter 13 begins a new part of the book. This part of the book helps you work with the applications you've set up on the server. The first chapter in this part, Chapter 13, helps you manage applications on your server. Consider this chapter the last physical setup chapter. When you leave this chapter, you should have a platform capable of supporting applications and Chapter 13 moves onto the task of actually getting those applications installed and supported.

Part 4

Working with the Software

Chapter 13

Managing Applications

You can manage applications at a number of levels in Server Core. Of course, you can install or remove user-level applications. The techniques for performing this task appear in the "Performing Application Installations" section of Chapter 3. This chapter looks at another level of application management. In this case, you'll discover the utilities that Microsoft provides for managing applications at the operating system level. Consequently, this chapter doesn't discuss user-level issues such as getting an editor to work. Instead of editors, you'll work with drivers, Component Object Model (COM) servers, and other low-level utilities.

Microsoft has changed how you work with operating system features in Server Core. It has actually divided the features that you can install into roles and features. A role is a major operating system component, such as acting as a Dynamic Host Configuration Protocol (DHCP) server. On the other hand, a feature augments the server in some way, such as providing support for BitLocker. The difference between the two kinds of add-ons is that one defines what the server can do and the other enhances the server functionality. In some cases, you'll find that you need to install certain features to ensure a role will work. Some roles rely on each other as well. Server Core provides input on how to perform the configuration properly.

You'll also want to discover how to work with error reports. Server Core includes a special utility for the task, ServerWEROptin. This utility is new for Server Core (you'll also find it in other versions of Windows Server 2008, but will likely work with the GUI to configure it). In most cases, providing error report information helps Microsoft create a better operating system without revealing any information about the sender—at least in theory.

NOTE I haven't personally taken the error reporting utilities apart, so I can't tell you with absolute certainty that the utilities are completely safe, but it seems to be in Microsoft's best interests to keep the information private. I tend to trust the error reporting features on servers used for general tasks, but not those containing mission critical information. It's a halfway approach, but at least Microsoft receives some information it can use to solve problems.

In this chapter, you'll learn how to do the following:

◆ Obtain driver and application information

◆ Manage applications

◆ Work with the Windows Package Manager

◆ Manage roles and features

◆ Manage COM servers

◆ Report errors

Obtaining Driver Information with the *DriverQuery* Command

The DriverQuery command displays a complete list of the drivers loaded on your system. Generally, you'll use this utility after you install the operating system to record the clean state of your system, and then after each major upgrade, including operating system service packs. By tracking the driver state of your system, you can determine when system errors are the result of faulty or incompatible drivers. This command uses the following syntax:

```
DRIVERQUERY [/S system [/U username [/P [password]]]] [/FO format]
[/NH] [/SI] [/V]
```

The following list describes each of the command line arguments.

/S *system* Specifies the remote system that you want to check. In most cases, you'll also need to supply the /U and the /P command line switches when using this switch.

/U [*domain*]*user* Specifies the username on the remote system. This name may not match the username on the local system. You'll need to supply a domain name when working with a domain controller.

/P [*password*] Specifies the password for the given user. You can provide the command line switch without specifying the password on the command line in cleartext. The system prompts you for the password. Using this feature can help you maintain the security of passwords used on your system.

/FO {TABLE | LIST | CSV} Defines the output provided by the utility. The table format is normally the easiest to view on screen. The table columns define the values for output, while each row contains one driver entry. The Comma Separated Value (CSV) output provides the best method for preparing the data for entry in a database. Use redirection (see the "Employing Data Redirection" section of Chapter 14 for details) to output the CSV data to a file and then import it to your database. The list format provides one data element per line. Each group of data elements defines one driver. The utility separates each driver by one blank line. Some people find the list format more readable when working in verbose mode since the table format requires multiple lines for each entry (the lines wrap).

/NH Forces the utility to display the data without a column header. You can only use this command line switch with the table and CSV formats. Omitting the header makes it easier to incorporate the data in a report or import it into a database.

/V Displays detailed data about each of the drivers. In addition to the standard output, the utility provides the driver description, start mode state, status, whether it accepts the stop command, whether it accepts the pause command, the size of the paged memory pool, the initial memory size, and the path to the driver file. This last column can provide you with helpful information about invasive drivers. Most standard drivers appear in the \Windows\System32\ or \Windows\System32\Drivers directory. You can't use this switch with the /SI command line switch.

/SI Provides details about driver signing. The information includes the device name, the information (INF) filename, whether Microsoft signed the driver, and the device driver manufacturer.

When used by itself, the DriverQuery utility provides a report about the local system that includes the module name, the display name (the name the user sees), driver type, and the date the vendor built the driver. The output is in a tabular format. The command line switches give you a great deal of flexibility as to the form of output and the content.

Installing Applications with the MSIExec Utility

The Microsoft Installer Executive (MSIExec) utility helps you install applications on a system. The application setup package must appear in a form that MSIExec can understand, which is normally a file with a Microsoft Installer (MSI) extension, although you'll see these files with an EXE extension as well. Generally, the MSI packages are robust enough that you can install them unattended after you test the application setup on a test machine. In fact, if you have many machines to set up, using this approach, coupled with automation, can save you considerable time. Unattended installations of tested application setups are an excellent choice for after hours scripting. This utility uses the following syntax:

```
msiexec /Option <Required Parameter> [Optional Parameter]
```

You can categorize the command line switches for MSIExec into several functional areas. Each area performs a specific Microsoft Installer task. The following list describes each of the command line installation options.

{/package | /i} {*Product.MSI* | *ProductGUID*}   Installs or configures the specified application. You can specify the application as an MSI package or as a GUID. When you use the GUID form, MSIExec looks for the application information in the registry and performs a configuration, rather than an installation. This installation option relies on the credentials of the current user.

/a *Product.MSI*   Performs an administrative installation. An administrative installation unpacks all of the files into a directory, normally on the network, and creates a smaller MSI file. Clients can then perform a local installation by accessing this directory on the network. Normally, you'll use this command line switch to create a centralized location from which to perform an installation for a number of machines. You'll specify the installation location using the TARGETDIR parameter.

/j{u | m} *Product.MSI* [{/t *TransformList* | /g *LanguageID*]   Advertises an application on a network. Use the /ju command line switch to advertise to the current user. The /jm command line switch advertises the application to all users on the network. Use the /jm command line switch when you need to install a package using elevated rights (privileges). The /t command line switch specifies a transform list used to advertise the product. A transform is a method of customizing the MSI database to meet specific needs. It's a property that you can specify at the command line using the TRANSFORMS parameter. For example, TRANSFORMS= ":1033" might select a file of advertising information in United States English based on a Locale Identifier (LCID) of 1033. You can also supply transforms as part of a Microsoft Transform (MST) file. The /g command line switch lets you specify a language identifier directly. The language is normally an LCID. You can find a list of common LCIDs at http://krafft.com/scripts/deluxe-calendar/lcid_chart.htm.

{/uninstall | /x} {*Product.MSI* | *ProductCode*}   Uninstalls a previously installed application. You can uninstall the product based either on the original installation package or on the product's GUID.

In addition to installation options, the MSIExec utility supports a number of display options. The following list describes each of these options.

/quiet   Installs the product without any user interaction. The product installs using the default arguments. However, you can override the arguments using parameters when the developer sets up the installation program correctly. For example, you can select an installation type, such as custom or typical, using the INSTALLLEVEL parameter. Make sure you check the product documentation for any custom parameters that the developer might create to address specific installation needs.

/passive   Performs an unattended installation. The setup program won't ask the user any questions, but the user still sees a progress bar. The progress bar gives the user some idea of how far the setup has progressed and indicates continued activity. An activity indicator is essential when the user knows about the installation. Otherwise, users may overwhelm your help desk with questions about why the application setup didn't complete (even though it would have if they'd simply given it time to complete).

/q[{n | b | r | f}]   Defines the user interface level. The interface level determines what the user sees during the application installation. Each of these levels has a specific meaning as described in the following list.

n   Conceals the user interface (no user interface).

b   Displays a basic user interface. Normally, this includes only the features required to install the application.

r   Displays a reduced user interface. The package developer defines the user interface setup, which is somewhere between the basic and the full display in complexity.

f   Displays the full user interface.

Once the installation has completed, you need to consider whether to restart the machine. The only time you need to restart the machine is when you need to replace a DLL or other system component that is in use. Generally, this type of update requires special programming for the setup routine and a discussion of the required programming techniques is outside the scope of this book. Here's the list of restart options.

/norestart   Performs the installation without a restart.

/promptrestart   Prompts the user for a restart when necessary.

/forcerestart   Forces the system to restart after the installation is complete.

An after hours installation might not go as planned. Consequently, you'll want to log any installation events so you can review the installation process later. It's important that you review the log even when it appears the installation occurred as predicted. A small error might not stop the installation from completing, but could stop the application from working as intended. The following list defines the command line switches for logging an installation.

/l[I] [w] [e] [a] [r] [u] [c] [m] [o] [p] [v] [x] [+] [!] [*] *LogFile*   Performs only the specified level of logging. You can combine multiple logging levels to obtain specific logging results. For example, using the /lia command line switch records all status messages and startup actions. The following list identifies the various logging levels that you can use.

i   Status messages

w   Nonfatal warnings

e   All error messages

a Startup of actions

r Action-specific records

u User requests

c Initial user interface parameters

m Out-of-memory or fatal exit information

o Out-of-disk-space messages

p Terminal properties

v Verbose output (you can only use this command line switch when you specify that you want all output by using the \1*v command line switch)

x Extra debugging information

+ Append to existing log file

! Flush each line to the log

* Log all information, except for v and x options

/log *LogFile* Performs a level of logging equivalent to the /1* command line switch.

The MSIExec utility can do more than simply install or remove applications. You can also use it to perform an update of the application. The following command line switches tell about the update options.

/update *Update1.MSP[;Update2.MSP]* Performs an update based on the content of one or more Microsoft Patch (MSP) files. Separate the individual MSP entries with a semicolon (;).

NOTE Some versions of MSIExec support a /p command line switch file updates where you supply the update package as the input argument. This form doesn't support multiple update packages and it doesn't provide a means of removing the patch. Use the /update command line switch if your version of MSIExec supports it. (The utility displays an error message when you attempt to use the /update command line switch with a version that doesn't support it.) The best way to determine the MSIExec version number isn't to use the MSIExec /? command. Check the MSI.DLL version number instead. When Microsoft performs an update, it usually updates MSI.DLL instead of MSIExec.EXE.

/uninstall *PatchCodeGuid[;Update2.MSP]* **/package** {*Product.MSI* | *ProductCode*} Removes an update based on the patch's GUID. You can remove additional, supplementary updates by supplying the MSP file.

If you've ever had an application act oddly and found that some small change in the system caused the error, you've wanted a repair option. Interestingly enough, the MSIExec option allows this action, even in cases where the product's installation interface doesn't supply the required functionality. Because it's easier to repair an application than to reinstall and configure it, you might try this option with any application that performs strangely. The following list describes the command line switch for repairing a faulty installation.

/f[p] [e] [c] [m] [s] [o] [d] [a] [u] [v] {*Product.MSI* | *ProductCode*} Repairs the product based on the original installation file or the product code. Use the original installation file for greater reliability in fixing an application. The following list describes the levels of repair that you can perform. You can combine multiple repair levels to achieve specific effects.

p Replaces a file only when the file is missing.

o Replaces a file when the setup program detects the file is missing or it finds another application has installed an older version of the file. This is the default action.

e Replaces a file when the setup program detects the file is missing or it finds another application has installed an equal or older version of the file.

d Replaces a file when the setup program detects the file is missing or it finds another application has installed a different version. This action replaces the file even when the file is newer than the one used by the application.

c Replaces a file when the setup program detects the file is missing or the file's checksum does not match the calculated value. This option often helps you locate and replace files tainted by viruses.

a Forces the setup program to reinstall all files.

u Updates all required user-specific registry entries.

m Updates all required computer-specific registry entries.

s Updates all existing shortcuts.

v Runs the setup program from a source media and caches the local package to the hard drive. This command line switch replaces the local package when it already exists.

You may have noticed more than a few references to properties in this section. Adding properties to the command line changes the way in which the MSI package unpacks. The properties that are available depend in part on the person who crafted the package, in part on the version of the Microsoft Installer used to create the package, and in part on your own personal requirements. The Windows Installer Property Reference at `http://helpnet.installshield.com/robo/projects/helplibdevstudio9/IHelpPropReference.htm` provides one of the most complete listings of properties you can use with Microsoft Installer. Of all these parameters, you'll use the special folder parameters, such as `TARGETDIR`, most often. To use a parameter at the command line, simply include the parameter name, followed by an equals sign (=), followed by the parameter value, such as `TARGETDIR="C:\Program Files\My Application"`. Always enclose parameters with spaces in quotes.

Accessing the Windows Package Manager with the PkgMgr Utility

The PkgMgr helps you service the operating system by installing and uninstalling both new packages and package updates. This utility uses the following syntax:

```
PkgMgr /ip [/m:Directory] /p:PackageName [/o:[BootPath]WinDirectory]
    [/n:Filename] [/s:Sandbox] [/quiet] [/norestart] [/l:LogFile]
PkgMgr /up [/m:Directory] /p:PackageName [/o:[BootPath]WinDirectory]
    [/n:Filename] [/quiet] [/norestart] [/l:LogFile]
PkgMgr /up PackageName [, PackageName...] [/o:[BootPath]WinDirectory]
    [/n:Filename] [/quiet] [/norestart] [/l:LogFile]
PkgMgr /iu PackageName [, PackageName...] [/o:[BootPath]WinDirectory]
    [/n:Filename] [/s:Sandbox] [/quiet] [/norestart] [/l:LogFile]
PkgMgr /uu PackageName [, PackageName...] [/o:[BootPath]WinDirectory]
    [/n:Filename] [/quiet] [/norestart] [/l:LogFile]
```

The following list describes each of the command line arguments.

PackageName   Specifies the name of the package that you want to work with.

/m:_Directory_   Specifies the location of the package. The default location is the current directory.

/p   Specifies the name of a single package.

/o:[_BootPath_]_WinDirectory_   Performs an offline action on the Windows image.

/n:_Filename_   Provides the name of a file that contains automated responses to installation requirements.

/s:_Sandbox_   Provides the name of a sandbox directory on the system where the application should extract files prior to checking them for viruses and other problematic code.

/quiet   Performs the required task without a user interface.

/norestart   Suppresses the restart at the end of the installation.

/l:_LogFile_   Logs all actions to the specified log file.

/ip   Installs one or more packages.

/up   Uninstalls one or more packages.

/iu   Installs a package update. The package must exist on the system or this command generates an error.

/uu   Uninstalls a package update. The original package and the package update must exist on the system or this command generates an error.

Adding and Removing Applications with the OCSetup Utility

Microsoft has changed the way that you manage Windows Server 2008. You now need to consider whether an option you want to add or remove is a role or a feature. A _role_ is a major part of the server, such as providing file services. On the other hand, a _feature_ augments basic server functionality. For example, the Telnet Client is a feature because it doesn't actually provide a new role for the server—it doesn't change the way in which you interact with the server in the same way that adding the File Services role does. This change affects both the graphical version of the product as well as Server Core. While you can use the Server Manager to add or remove roles and features when working with the graphical version, you must perform this task at the command line with working with Server Core. Needless to say, performing this task at the command line is more difficult than checking a box in a graphical utility. The following sections describe how to work with the OCSetup utility.

NOTE   You may have heard rumors about the amazing new ServerManagerCmd utility. This utility is no rumor and it really does work well. The only problem is that the ServerManagerCmd utility relies on the .NET Framework to do its work. At this time, Server Core won't have the required support installed as part of the product. Consequently, you must rely on the OCSetup and OCList utilities to perform setup tasks.

An Overview of the Server Core Roles and Features

Server Core provides fewer roles and features than the graphical version of Windows Server 2008. You can always list the roles and features that Server Core supports using the OCList utility described in the "Verifying Application and Role Status Using the OCList Utility" section of the chapter. Remember that roles define the major tasks you can perform with Server Core. Here's a list of the roles supported by the Enterprise Edition of Server Core.

- Active Directory Domain Services
- Active Directory Lightweight Directory Services (AD LDS)
- Dynamic Host Configuration Protocol (DHCP) Server
- DNS Server
- File Services
- Print Server
- Streaming Media Services
- Web Server (IIS)

Server Core also supports a number of standard features. Remember that a feature provides additional functionality, but doesn't change the major tasks you perform with Server Core. For example, installing Windows Backup adds to the functionality that Server Core provides, but it doesn't change the fact that your Server Core setup only provides file and print services. Here's the list of features supported by the Enterprise Edition of Server Core.

- Microsoft Failover Cluster
- Network Load Balancing
- Subsystem for UNIX-based Applications
- Windows Backup
- Multipath I/O
- Removable Storage Management
- Windows Bitlocker Drive Encryption
- Simple Network Management Protocol (SNMP)
- Windows Internet Naming Service (WINS)
- Telnet Client
- Quality of Service (QoS)

Because Server Core doesn't provide any support for the graphical installation utilities, you must use OCSetup to install or uninstall any of the roles or features. In a few cases, installing a role or feature will require a reboot, just as they do when working with the graphical version of Windows Server 2008. In addition, you may need to reboot the system when uninstalling a role or feature.

Considering the Server Core Default Settings

It's important to remember that Server Core has a default setup. No matter which edition of Server Core you install, you can count on it having certain characteristics when you complete the installation, which makes the task of working with roles and features considerably easier. Table 13.1

shows the default settings for a Server Core installation. Of course, you have already seen how to change many of these settings in previous chapters. For example, Chapter 1 tells you how to change the workgroup setting.

TABLE 13.1: Essential Windows Server 2008 Default Settings

SETTING NAME	DEFAULT SETTING	DESCRIPTION
Administrator Password	Blank	Provides default access to the system. The system is wide open when you start, so setting the password is a must-do item.
Computer Name	Random Value	Defines the computer's name on the network and provides the name others will use to access the computer. The random name that Microsoft provides will be hard to use.
Domain Membership	The computer is joined to a workgroup named WORKGROUP	Defines the computer's connectivity on the network. For a small company or a group within an enterprise, a workgroup may be fine, but most organizations will rely on a domain.
Windows Update	Off	Automatically updates the computer as needed. You need to turn on this feature after performing the initial update to ensure the server receives required updates.
Network Connections	Set to obtain their IP address using Dynamic Host Configuration Protocol (DHCP)	Using DHCP is a standard for domains because you must have a DHCP server to set up a domain. A workgroup with a shared Internet connection will also have a DHCP host. However, some workgroups will still require manual IP configuration.
Windows Firewall	On	Provides security for incoming and outgoing network traffic. The default Windows Firewall configuration is set to disallow any form of network traffic to ensure that no one can access the server while you configure it. Change this setting after initial server configuration, but before you attempt to download updates and fixes.
Roles	None Installed	Specifies the tasks that the server can perform. If you don't define any roles, the server looks more like a workstation than a server. In fact, it doesn't even make a good workstation.

Using the OCSetup Utility

Once you know the status of roles and features on your server and determine that you need to either install or uninstall a role or feature, you can use OCSetup to perform the task. This utility uses the following syntax:

```
OCSetup Component [/Uninstall] [/Passive] [/UnattendFile:Filename]
    [/Quiet] [/NoRestart] [/Log:Filename] [/X:Parameters]
```

The following list describes each of the command line arguments.

Component Specifies the name of the role or feature that you want to install. You must always provide a component name. The best way to obtain a component name is to use the OCList utility described in the "Verifying Application and Role Status Using the OCList Utility" section of the chapter. You can also use the OCList utility to ensure that you haven't already installed the component.

When you want to install a new component, all you need to do is provide the component name. For example, if you want to install Windows Backup, you'd type **OCSetup WindowsServerBackup** and press Enter. You won't actually see any messages unless OCSetup needs additional information. The command prompt returns to normal almost immediately after you enter the command. The only easy way to determine whether the installation is successful is to use the OCList utility to check the status.

/Uninstall Removes the specified component. For example, if you type **OCSetup WindowsServerBackup /Uninstall** and press Enter, OCSetup removes the Windows Backup feature. In many cases, removing a component requires a reboot. If you don't use the /NoRestart command line switch, Server Core assumes you want to restart the system immediately. For example, if you want to uninstall Windows Backup and don't want the server to reboot, then you must type **OCSetup WindowsServerBackup /Uninstall /NoReboot** and press Enter. Consequently, you must make sure you want to restart the system or you must use the /NoRestart command line switch.

/Passive Allows the installation or uninstallation tasks to progress without displaying any user messages. You still receive status messages.

/UnattendFile:Filename Defines the name of unattended installation file. You can use this file to perform multiple installs or uninstalls without entering the commands individually.

/Quiet Allows the installation or uninstallation tasks to progress without displaying any messages (user or status).

/NoRestart Prevents the system from restarting after performing an install or uninstall task, even if the task requires a restart. Although preventing the restart keeps users happy, it also means that the role or feature you've installed or uninstalled isn't complete. You can't use the role or feature until you manually restart the server.

/Log:Filename Defines an alternative location for the installation log. You won't normally want to use this command line switch.

/X:Parameters Defines any parameters needed to install a particular component successfully. If you don't provide the parameters, OCSetup queries you for them. The parameters depend on the component you want to install. Some components, such as Windows Backup, don't require any parameters at all.

Verifying Application and Role Status Using the OCList Utility

The OCList utility provides the means of determining the installation status of roles and features on your server. Since there isn't any other way of determining installation status, you need to use this utility to track component information. Always use this utility before you install or uninstall a role or feature to ensure the role or feature is actually in the state you expect. This utility doesn't have any command line switches. You simply type **OCList** and press Enter to obtain the status information, which may require a few seconds to appear on screen. Figure 13.1 shows typical output from the OCList utility.

FIGURE 13.1
Use the OCList utility to determine the status of roles and features on your server.

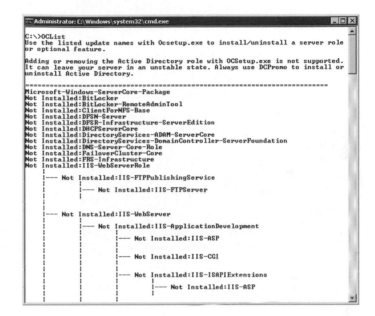

Adding and Removing Servers with the RegSvr32 Utility

Your machine has a wealth of Component Object Model (COM) servers installed on it. These servers perform a broad array of tasks too numerous to mention here. In all cases, these servers make a lot of registry entries; even a simple server makes a lot of entries and you won't want to add or delete them manually. Fortunately, the RegSvr32 utility makes it easy to add and remove COM server entries. This utility uses the following syntax:

```
RegSvr32 [/u] [/s] [/i[:Arguments] /n] Filename
```

The following list describes each of the command line arguments.

Filename   The name of the file that contains the COM server. In most cases, the file will have a DLL extension, but it could have a number of other extensions including EXE and OCX.

/u   Unregisters a server.

/s   Suppresses any informational messages. Using this option lets you create an installation batch file.

/i[:*Arguments*]   Calls a special function within the COM server named DllInstall. You may optionally pass command line arguments. The server vendor provides you with a list of command line arguments that you can pass the COM server.

/n   Suppresses the call to the standard DllRegisterServer function within the COM server. This special function normally registers the server for you, making all of the required registry entries. You can only use this command line switch with the /i switch.

Managing Compatibility Databases with SDBInst

The SDBInst utility helps you manage and maintain application databases. In fact, these databases often support application patches. Microsoft often uses the SDBInst utility to provide patches for all their products including Office and Windows. As an example of one of these patches (and there are many) check the Knowledge Base article at `http://support.microsoft.com/?kbid=328597`. Lest you think that this utility is a Microsoft invention, check the MySQL Web site at `http://dev.mysql.com/doc/maxdb/en/1f/906b3c12904d04e10000000a114084/content.htm`. You'll notice that not only does SDBInst have a place in other vendor application deployments, it exists on both the Windows and the Linux platforms (as shown by the instructions for both platforms on the Web site) as well.

The SDBInst program supports a special Solution Database (SDB) (or Support Database) file. Many vendors provide utilities for creating these files. For example, you'll find the instructions for producing SDB files using a utility from SoftwareBisque at `http://www.bisque.com/tom/Createown/SDB/sdb.asp`.

You can use SDBInst to install and uninstall SDB files. Uninstalling an SDB usually results in removing the patch that you applied to an application or operating system. This utility uses the following syntax (the first syntax installs a file, while the second uninstalls it):

```
SDBInst [-q] SDBFilename
SDBInst [-q] [-u SDBFilename] [-g GUID] [-p] [-n "Name"]
```

The following list describes each of the command line arguments.

-q   Forces the utility to rely on quiet mode. The utility doesn't display any dialog boxes to the user.

SDBFilename   Specifies the name of the SDB file that you want to install on the system.

-u SDBFilename   Specifies that you want to uninstall an SDB patch using a reference to the original SDB file.

-g GUID   Specifies that you want to uninstall an SDB patch using the GUID of the patch as defined in the registry.

-n "Name"   Specifies that you want to uninstall an SDB patch using the patch name. The patch name often appears in the Add or Remove Programs dialog box that you can access using the Add or Remove Programs applet in the Control Panel.

-p   Allows SDB files to contain patches.

Configuring Windows Error Reporting with ServerWEROptin

The ServerWEROptin utility lets you adjust error reporting for your Server Core setup. The default setting sends information about every error your server encounters automatically. Of course, you might not want Microsoft knowing about every error or you may simply not have this server connected to the Internet. In these and other situations, you'll want to adjust your error reporting strategy. You can learn more about the information Microsoft collects about your server at `http://go.microsoft.com/fwlink/?linkid=50163`. This utility uses the following syntax:

```
ServerWerOptin /q[uery] | /s[ummary] | /de[tailed] | /d[isable]
```

Unlike many other utilities in this book, all of the command line switches are mutually exclusive. You can only use a single command line switch. The following list describes each of the command line arguments.

/query   Displays the Windows error reporting status. For example, if you disable the error reporting, then the output says disabled. This command line switch also provides the latest URL you can use to learn more about this utility and the error reporting feature.

/summary   Configures the error reporting feature to send summary reports automatically. A summary report contains only the most basic error information and it's the safe option to use when you want to provide information to Microsoft, but want to keep the information you provide to a minimum. You set this level of error reporting by typing **ServerWEROptin /summary** and pressing Enter.

/detailed   Configures the error reporting feature to send the maximum amount of information to Microsoft. This is the option you should use on less critical servers that don't contain confidential information that you're concerned about compromising. Although Microsoft does guarantee your privacy, you'll still only want to use this option on less critical servers to prevent accidental data revelations. You set this level of error reporting by typing **ServerWEROptin /detailed** and pressing Enter.

/disable   Disables the error reporting feature on the server. This is the option to use if you have any doubts as to how Microsoft collects or uses the information you provide. It's also the option you should select if your server doesn't have an Internet connection. You set this level of error reporting by typing **ServerWEROptin /disable** and pressing Enter.

Managing Windows in a New Way

The focus of this chapter is operating system application management. You have discovered methods for installing and removing roles and features, as well as configuring the error reporting system. This chapter also helps you understand how to work with COM servers (to make them available to applications) and perform other critical software management tasks. This chapter helps you build these skills:

◆ Obtain driver and application information

◆ Manage applications

◆ Work with the Windows Package Manager

◆ Manage roles and features

◆ Manage COM servers

◆ Report errors

Now that you know how to install roles and features, you'll want to spend some time working with your server and configuring it to perform useful tasks. You'll also want to be sure that you configure the error reporting feature so it doesn't send more information to Microsoft than you intended. Many of these other utilities come into play as people begin using the server and noticing deficiencies. Even so, you can practice performing tasks such as registering COM servers. Trying to figure out how to perform these tasks in an emergency is going to be hard, so trying it out in advance is always a good idea.

Chapter 14 shows you how to manage data at the command line. This is one of the hardest tasks for administrators who are used to working with graphical utilities because Microsoft has done a very good job with its graphical utilities. Many administrators don't even realize that you can perform all of these tasks at the command line. Use Chapter 14 to discover how you'll perform all of those tasks that you once relied on Windows Explorer and other graphical utilities to perform.

Working with Data

Most administrators are used to relying on Windows Explorer to manage files on their system. However, Server Core doesn't provide this option. If you want to create, copy, delete, sort, rename, or perform other tasks with files, you must do it at the command line. Fortunately, you won't find a lack of utilities for performing this task in Server Core. In fact, you may be surprised at the number of ways in which you can interact with files because some of these techniques aren't available in the graphical interface. For example, you won't find a counterpart to the Sort utility in the graphical environment.

Of course, managing files also means working with them directly. This chapter shows you how to perform tasks such as compressing and expanding files, as well as outputting files to a device. You can also control how much of the file the server displays at the command line. All of these utilities make it easier to perform work with the files without actually installing any applications that may not work with Server Core.

One of the most interesting features that Server Core provides is full access to the Open Database Connectivity (ODBC) functionality. ODBC makes it possible to create a connection to a database, should an application on your server need it. Normally, administrators perform this administration using the Data Sources (ODBC) console found in the Administrative Tools folder of the Control Panel, but you'll find the command line alternative is quite capable as well.

In this chapter, you'll learn how to do the following:

- Manage files
- Compress and expand files
- Output files to a device
- Take ownership of files
- Manage file types and associations
- Work with the ODBC functionality

Comparing Two Files with the Comp Utility

Sometimes it's helpful to compare two files to determine what has changed or to verify that the files are precisely the same. A common use of this technique is to compare two text files. The files could contain anything from data to application settings. Another way to use this technique is to verify that no one has tampered with executable files. Viruses and other forms of intrusion often modify executable files. Just looking at the file isn't enough in many cases to verify the damage. However, keeping a known good copy of the file on an unmodifiable source, such as a CD, and using this simple comparison utility is often enough to detect the problem. It also provides you with a way of expunging the intruder from your executables by copying the known good executable from the CD (of course, you still have to consider registry entries and other ways intruders often use to rebuild themselves). This utility uses the following syntax:

```
COMP [data1] [data2] [/D] [/A] [/L] [/N=number] [/C] [/OFF[LINE]]
```

The following list describes each of the command line arguments.

data1 Specifies the source file. You can use wildcard characters to define multiple comparisons. For example, `*.DLL` compares every dynamic link library in the source directory against a DLL with the same name in the destination directory.

data2 Specifies the destination file. You can use wildcard characters to define multiple comparisons. However, the source and destination specifications must compare. If the source contains just one file, then the destination will also contain one file as well.

/D Displays the differences in decimal format (as numeric values for each character, whether or not there's an ASCII equivalent). This is the optimal setting when comparing binary or executable files.

/A Displays the differences as ASCII characters. This is the optimal setting when comparing text files of any type (including INI or other settings files and standard data files in XML or other format).

/L Displays the line numbers for differences. The Comp utility compares the two files line by line, where the carriage return (ASCII character 13), linefeed (ASCII character 10), or both designate the end of a line.

/N=number Performs a comparison of the specified number of lines in each file beginning with the first line.

/C Performs a case-insensitive comparison of the two files. Normally, Comp considers an uppercase letter different from a lowercase letter.

/OFF[LINE] Forces the Comp utility to compare files even when the files have the offline attribute set.

Copying Files with the *Copy* Command

The Copy command lets you create a copy of a file that exists in one directory into another directory. You can create copies on other drives, even drives that you map using Windows. In addition, this command works with nonfile devices such as the printer or keyboard. Generally, users rely on the functionality provided by Windows Explorer to move and copy files. However, the extensive list of command line switches provided by the Copy command makes it extremely flexible for use in batch commands. In addition, using some switches, such as the ASCII file transfer option for text files, can improve overall Windows copy performance. This command uses the following syntax:

```
COPY [/D] [/V] [/N] [/Y | /-Y] [/Z] [/L] [/A | /B ] source [/A | /B]
     [+ source [/A | /B] [+ ...]] [destination [/A | /B]]
```

The following list describes each of the command line arguments.

source Defines the source of the data that you want to copy. The source is usually a file, but you can use devices as a source of data. See the "Understanding Command Line Devices" sidebar for details. You can use wildcard characters to specify the filenames. See the "Working with Wildcard Characters" sidebar for details.

destination   Defines the output location for the data that you want to copy. The destination is usually a file, but you can use devices as a destination for data. See the "Understanding Command Line Devices" sidebar for details.

/A   Copies the file as ASCII text. Using this technique improves Copy command performance. However, using this command line switch with a binary file results in data loss.

/B   Copies the file in binary mode. Many files fall into the binary category, even though you might think they are standard text files. For example, a Word DOC file is a binary file because it contains control and other characters that won't transfer well using the /A command line switch.

/D   Decrypts the destination file. This special Windows command line switch decrypts files that are encrypted using Windows encryption features. If you don't use this command line switch, the destination remains encrypted.

/L   Copies a symbolic link to the target instead of the actual file pointed to by the symbolic link when the source is a symbolic link.

/N   Creates a destination file with an 8-character filename and a 3-character file extension. Use this command line switch when you must create destination files for older systems that rely on the DOS 8.3 naming convention. Avoid using this command line switch on files with long filenames unless you really do want to create a compatible file.

/V   Verifies the destination file is the same as the source file. Writing files with verification improves reliability at the cost of performance. Windows writes the destination and then performs a file comparison when using this command line switch.

/Y and /-Y   Suppresses or enforces the prompt for overwriting destination files with the same name as the destination file provided as input to the Copy command. Use the /Y command line switch in batch files where you know the batch file will overwrite an existing destination file. The /-Y command line switch is the default, so you never need to use it.

/Z   Copies files to network destinations in a restartable mode. If the network connection fails, the Copy command gives you the option of restarting the copy from the current file position. This command line switch makes it possible to copy large files using less reliable network connections.

One of the more important features of the Copy command is the ability to combine two files. For example, you might download a large file as two file fragments from an Internet site to reduce the problems associated with downloading a single large file. Combine the two file fragments to create a complete file by typing a plus sign (+) between source files like this:

```
COPY FilePart1 + FilePart2 CompleteFile
```

When the Copy command completes, CompleteFile will contain the sum of the two file fragments.

When using the Copy command with the console, you must add an end of file marker to the input by pressing Ctrl+Z. The end of file marker appears as ^Z on screen, which signifies it as control character 26. Pressing Enter after ^Z copies the file to the destination you indicate. The end of file marker doesn't appear when you send the resulting file to the console as output. Likewise, if you want a printer to output the partial page of data you sent to it, output a Ctrl+L character to it. You can see a complete list of standard control characters at http://www.cs.tut.fi/~jkorpela/chars/c0.html.

UNDERSTANDING COMMAND LINE DEVICES

You can access a number of devices from the command line. Some devices accept input, others output, and some accept both. These devices always reference a physical device of some type. In some cases, the device isn't attached to your machine, but it's accessible from your machine, such as a network printer. Many commands and utilities let you use a device in place of a drive letter as an argument. For example, the Copy command lets you use input from a device to create a file. You can also use a file as output to a device. Here's the standard list of command line devices.

CON The system console, which is the combination of keyboard and monitor used to access the computer system. Input comes from the keyboard and output goes to the monitor.

PRN The default printer. You must configure network printers to provide a port to support a command line device. The port appears on the Ports tab of the network printer's Properties dialog box. Even if your printer can provide bidirectional communication, the PRN device is only capable of output.

LPT1 through LPT4 The printer attached to the first through fourth printer (parallel) ports. The device need not physically attach to the parallel port; Windows can redirect the output to the physical device for you. You must configure network printers to provide a port to provide a command line device. The port appears on the Ports tab of the network printer's Properties dialog box. Even if your printer can provide bidirectional communication, the LPT devices are only capable of output.

AUX The auxiliary device; the one serviced by the first serial port (COM1). It's usually better to reference COM1 directly for readability in batch files. The AUX device is a holdover from the early days of DOS.

COM1 through COM4 The communication device attached to the first through fourth serial ports. Although standard outputs for this port include modems, you can connect printers as well. The serial port can act as both an input and an output device. You can configure network printers to use a COM port instead of an LPT port using the Ports tab of the network printer's Properties dialog box.

NUL The output doesn't go anywhere. The NUL(L) device is also known as the bit bucket.

**CLOCK$** This device is supposed to access the real-time clock. In reality, the device normally doesn't work in modern systems and Windows makes no effort to provide required redirection. You should avoid using the CLOCK$ device.

Removing Files with the *Del* and *Erase* Commands

The Del and Erase commands are functionally equivalent. The two commands started with different versions of DOS, but they perform the same task now: erasing files that you no longer need from the hard drive. Unlike the deletion that Windows performs, the files don't end up in the Recycle Bin; the deletion is permanent. These commands use the following syntax:

```
DEL [/P] [/F] [/S] [/Q] [/A[[:]attributes]] names
ERASE [/P] [/F] [/S] [/Q] [/A[[:]attributes]] names
```

The following list describes each of the command line arguments.

names Defines the file or directory names to remove from the hard drive. You can use wildcard characters to specify the filenames. See the "Working with Wildcard Characters" sidebar for details. Deleting a directory also deletes all of the files that the directory contains. Consequently, these commands can be exceptionally destructive.

/A Deletes files or directories based on their attributes. See the "Changing File and Directory Attributes with the Attrib Utility" section of Chapter 15 for details on working with attributes at the command prompt.

NOTE Server Core adds the L attribute for reparse points and the I attribute for nonindexed files. The I attribute is a little tricky because you see it when the file isn't indexed versus when it has the required feature such as when you use the other attributes. These new attributes help you work with new file system features.

/F Forces the deletion of files marked with the read-only attribute. Normally, the commands prompt the user to delete such files.

/P Prompts the user to delete every file. This command line switch provides a safety factor, but also increases the time required to delete files.

/Q Deletes files based on a wildcard specification without prompting the user first. Normally, the utilities prompt the user before deleting all of the files in a directory.

/S Deletes the specified files from all subdirectories. This command comes in handy when you want to remove all of the files with a given name on a hard drive. Windows often creates multiple copies of files; locating them all can be difficult.

WORKING WITH WILDCARD CHARACTERS

You might wonder how you can make your use of commands and utilities even more efficient. Most of these utilities will let you work with multiple files at once, but you need to know the secret of specifying multiple files. Wildcard characters let you specify a group of files or directories without naming each file or directory individually. There are two standard wildcard characters: * and ?. The asterisk (*) specifies any number of characters, while the question mark (?) specifies a single character. You can use the two wildcard characters in combination to create complex file specifications to locate just about any file.

Most people are familiar with the * character. Typing Dir S*.TXT at the command line locates every text file in the current directory that begins with an S. However, you can use the * in any location. For example, typing Dir *S*.TXT at the command line would locate any text file that contains an S in any part of its name. Likewise, typing Dir *S.TXT would locate any text file that contains an S at the end of its name. You can also use the * for the file extension. Typing Dir S.* locates any file with S as a filename, but with any file extension.

The ? is far more selective than the * and many people fail to recognize its value. For example, typing Dir S??.TXT at the command line will locate any text file with three characters in its filename that begins with the letter S. Consequently, this command will locate SUB.TXT and SUN.TXT, but not SUBST.TXT or RUN.TXT (notice that even though RUN.TXT contains three letters, it doesn't begin with an S). Like the *, you can use the ? wildcard character anywhere in the filename. For example, you can type Dir *.EX? to locate both compressed and uncompressed executable files in the current directory. Without the selectiveness of the ? wildcard, you might end up with files that you didn't really want to find.

Compressing Files with the Diantz and MakeCab Utilities

Most people assume that you need to use a third-party compression product to create file archives with Windows. Of course, the ZIP file format is the most popular solution, but there are other alternatives, such as the RAR format supported by WinRAR (`http://www.rarlab.com/`). However, you can use the cabinet (CAB) file format without buying a third-party utility. The only utility provided with newer Windows versions is MakeCAB. An older utility, Diantz, appears on the hard drive, but it calls MakeCAB. The CAB file appears in many places in Windows. For example, you'll find that Microsoft uses CABs to compress many application files on setup disks. In fact, there's even a Microsoft Cabinet Software Development Kit discussed at `http://support.microsoft.com/kb/310618/`. This utility uses the following syntax:

```
MAKECAB [/V[n]] [/D var=value ...] [/L dir] source [destination]
MAKECAB [/V[n]] [/D var=value ...] /F directive_file [...]
```

The following list describes each of the command line arguments.

source   Specifies the name of the file you want to compress. Unlike many Windows utilities, you can't use wildcards to create a file specification. Provide a source filename when you want to compress a single file or a directive file when you want to compress multiple files.

destination   Specifies the name of the destination file. When you specify a source file without a destination filename, the utility creates a file with an underscore that replaces the last letter of the file extensions. For example, when you type **MakeCAB NewFile.txt** and press Enter, the utility produces an output file with the name NewFile.tx_.

/F directive_file   Specifies the name of a Diamond Directive File (DDF) that contains instructions for creating complex archives. You can specify multiple files, some of which are compressed and others that aren't. Using a DDF, you can create an archive that spans multiple disks. The `MAKECAB.DOC` file in the \cabsdk\DOCS directory of the Microsoft Cabinet Software Development Kit tells how to create a DDF.

/D var=value   Defines variable settings for the MakeCAB utility. These variables control how MakeCAB works. For example, you can tell MakeCAB to create an archive without compressing any of the files by using the `COMPRESS=OFF` directive. You can find a complete list of variables and their associated values in section "4.2.2. Variable Summary" of the Microsoft Cabinet Software Development Kit.

/L dir   Specifies the directory to use to store the archive. The default setting uses the current directory.

/V[n]   Specifies a level of verbosity for the compression messages. The utility accepts any value between 1 and 3. The default setting is 1, which provides major messages and a completion message. The second verbosity level provides a list of files in the archive as the utility compresses them. The third verbosity level includes compression levels and other activities.

Modifying Files with the Edlin Utility

Edlin is a relic from a previous time. It actually predates the PC when it comes to the user interface because it edits files line by line. Someone who worked with a mainframe in the 1960s would probably feel right at home using Edlin, but most modern users won't. The important things to remember about Edlin are

◆ You can find it in every Microsoft operating system and some non-Microsoft operating systems as well.

◆ It uses the same interface everywhere you find it.

- ◆ The executable is extremely small and portable at 12 KB.

- ◆ It always works.

Figure 14.1 shows an example of how Edlin appears with a file loaded.

FIGURE 14.1

Edlin is an ancient editor that works in any environment.

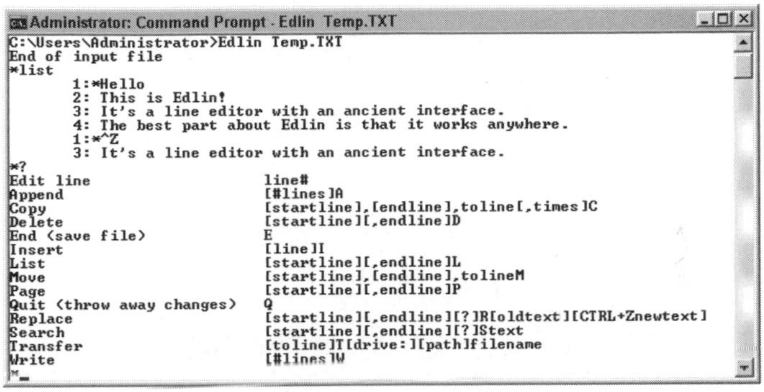

Figure 14.1 actually shows a number of Edlin features. The first line shows how to start Edlin by providing the name of the file you want to edit. Edlin can load any file, even binary files, if you provide the /B command line argument.

When you start Edlin, it doesn't display anything (yes, it's that primitive). You must type the List command and press Enter to show the content of the file, which you then edit one line at a time. Press Ctrl+Z to stop editing the text.

Typing a ? and pressing Enter displays the list of Edlin commands that comes next in Figure 14.1. Here's the one feature that I like about Edlin: it has a very capable search feature that doesn't assume anything about the file.

Finally, you type **Quit** and press Enter to end the editing session. Even though this editor works everywhere, you'll want to find a substitute such as the Edit utility described in the "Modifying Data Files with the Edit Utility" section of Chapter 5.

Repairing System Databases with the ESEnTUtl Utility

Windows has a number of associated databases. Of course, there's the main database, the registry, which contains all of the system, user, and application settings. However, Windows also contains a number of other databases that you don't normally hear about. These databases reside in Solution Database (SDB) files. Some of these databases record application setup. You'll find that they normally have a Setup.SDB filename. Other databases record service pack status and have names such as AppHelp.SDB, AppH_SP.SDB, DrvMain.SDB, MSIMain.SDB, and SysMain.SDB. Still other databases keep track of security or other system settings that don't appear in the registry such as SecEdit.SDB. In short, Windows hides a lot of information in places other than the registry. You can access all of these other databases using the Extensible Storage Engine Technology Utility (ESEnTUtl).

Not every SDB file on your hard drive is a database. To confuse matters, Microsoft also uses the SDB extension for some text-based files. For example, the Setup.SDB file for Visual Studio is a text-based file. You can read it using Notepad as shown in Figure 14.2. The text entries in this file can tell you a lot about the application, but the information isn't in a form that ESEnTUtl can manage. A true SDB file contains binary data.

FIGURE 14.2
Verify that an SDB file is actually a database before you use ESEnTUtl to manage it.

WARNING The ESEnTUtl utility is extremely powerful. Used incorrectly on the wrong file, it can wipe out security settings or make your system unbootable. Consequently, make sure you understand this utility completely before you use it. Always make a copy of any database before you modify it. Verify as many changes as possible against the Microsoft Knowledge Base before you make them.

The ESEnTUtl utility doesn't provide you with much help. In fact, you'll hardly find this utility mentioned at all in the Windows help file or many of the other Microsoft resources. One place you'll find it mentioned is the Microsoft Knowledge Base. Many Windows problems require you to use ESEnTUtl as a means of repair. The following list contains just a few examples from the Microsoft Knowledge Base (use the `http://www.google.com/search?hl=en&lr=&q=ESEnTUtl+site%3Asupport.microsoft.com&btnG=Search` Google search URL to obtain a complete list):

HOW TO: Use Ntdsutil to Manage Active Directory Files from the Command Line in Windows 2000 `http://support.microsoft.com/default.aspx?scid=kb;en-us;315131`

You receive an "Access is denied" error message when you install the Bluetooth stack and detect a Bluetooth device in Microsoft Windows XP Service Pack 2 `http://support.microsoft.com/?kbid=892891`

You cannot add a Windows component in Windows XP `http://support.microsoft.com/?id=884018`

Event ID 2108 and Event ID 1084 occur during inbound replication of Active Directory in Windows 2000 Server and in Windows Server 2003 `http://support.microsoft.com/default.aspx?scid=kb;en-us;837932`

The ESEnTUtl operates in several modes. Each mode performs a different task with the SDB file. Here's the syntax for each mode.

```
Defragmentation
     ESENTUTL /d <database name> [options]
Recovery
     ESENTUTL /r [options]
Integrity
     ESENTUTL /g <database name> [options]
Repair
     ESENTUTL /p <database name> [options]
Checksum
     ESENTUTL /k <database name> [options]
File Dump
     ESENTUTL /m[mode-modifier] <filename>
Copy
     ESENTUTL /y <source file> [options]
```

The options vary by mode. However, some options are common to all or most modes. Here's a list of the common options.

/8   Defines the database page size as 8 KB. Normally, ESEnTUtl detects the page size automatically. Use this option only when told to do so as part of a Microsoft Knowledge Base article or when you experience problems reading a database.

/o   Suppresses the Microsoft logo. You can use this option to create output for reports or as input to another database.

/s<Streaming Filename>   Sets the filename for streaming data output. The default setting is NONE. Use this switch when you want to send data to a destination using streaming data techniques, rather than a simple dump. This switch applies to the DEFRAGMENTATION, INTEGRITY, REPAIR, and FILEDUMP modes.

/t<Database Filename>   Sets the temporary database filename. The default setting is TEMPDFRG*.EDB. Normally, you won't need to change the database filename because ESEnTUtl already supports multiple temporary databases. This switch applies to the DEFRAGMENTATION, INTEGRITY, and REPAIR modes.

NOTE   Some of the modes use the same option switch for different purposes. Consequently, don't assume that the /f switch for the DEFRAGMENTATION mode performs the same task as the /f switch for the INTEGRITY mode.

Defragmentation removes excess space from the database and can improve system performance by reorganizing the database. The database becomes defragmented after long use because the system adds and removes entries without placing them in the optimal position (much as a hard drive becomes defragmented through use). The defragmentation-specific options include:

/f<file>   Sets the filename for streaming data defragmentation. The default setting is TEMPDFRG*.STM. Normally, you won't need to change this setting.

/i   Prevents ESEnTUtl from defragmenting the streaming file.

/p   Preserves the temporary database. Generally, ESEnTUtl deletes the temporary database once all of the changes are incorporated into the main database.

/b<Database *Filename*>   Creates a backup copy of the database prior to defragmentation using the specified filename. It's always a good idea to use this option so that you have another copy of the database should the defragmentation fail.

Recovery helps you overcome database errors. ESEnTUtl rebuilds the database using log entries. This is a typical feature of transactional databases where the database manager logs every action. The recovery-specific options include:

/l<*path*>   Defines the location of the log files used to recover the data. The default setting is the current directory. Normally, you don't need to change this setting because the log files usually appear in the same directory as the database.

/s<*path*>   Defines the location of any system files, such as the checkpoint file, required to perform the recover. The default location is the current directory. Normally, you don't need to change this setting because the system files usually appear in the same directory as the database.

/i   Ignores any mismatched or missing database attachments. However, by ignoring these missing elements, you risk database damage. Use this option only when the database is already damaged and the recovery is a last ditch effort at reconstruction.

/d[*path*]   Defines the location of database files. The default setting is the current directory. The default setting when you specify this option without a path is the directory originally logged in the log files, which may be different from the current directory.

Integrity checking verifies that the database is in an operational state and doesn't contain any structural errors. You can perform an integrity check when you suspect the database may contain errors, but don't want to perform any changes until you know that it does. The integrity-specific options include:

/f<*name*>   Defines the prefix to use for name of report files. The default setting uses the name of the database, followed by .integ.raw.

Repair mode actually changes the database. The most common repair simply removes the damaged entries. This action can result in various kinds of data loss that affect system operation. For example, you could lose some of the security settings for your system. Always make a backup of the database before you repair it. The repair-specific option includes:

/f<*name*>   Defines the prefix to use for the name of report files. The default setting uses the name of the database, followed by .integ.raw.

Checksum mode verifies that the file doesn't contain any bit-level errors. The checksum acts as a means of verifying the data itself is error free. Compare this check with an integrity check and you'll notice that the two provide complementary error checks. You should perform both checks on a database when you suspect that it contains errors. The CHECKSUM mode only supports the /8 and /o options.

File DUMP mode lets you view the content of the database in a nondestructive manner. It's the same as performing a query on any database. However, given the nature of these databases, the processing of querying content is slightly different. Instead of asking for the address of a customer or the number of widgets sold during the month of June, these queries obtain specifics about the database itself. The file dump–specific options include.

/t<*Table Name*>   Performs a database dump for a specified table only. Use a metadata dump to obtain a list of the tables within the database.

/v Provide verbose output for the specified command. Even though ESEnTUtl always accepts this option, some FILE DUMP mode modifiers can't provide additional information. For example, performing a file dump of the database header won't yield any additional results because the initial command always provides complete information.

In addition to options, the FILE DUMP mode supports a modifier that determines the kind of data it provides as output. You combine this modifier with the /m command line switch. For example, to dump the database header, you use the /mh command line switch. The following list describes the FILE DUMP modes:

H This is the default modifier. It obtains the database header information. The header contains a wealth of information about the database, such as the database type and an indication of whether it uses a streaming file. In addition, you can discover the last backup date and other essential maintenance information about the database. You can see a header dump by typing **ESENTUTL /mh SecEdit.SDB** in the \WINDOWS\security\Database folder and pressing Enter.

NOTE This book uses the \Windows folder because that's the most common setup for modern machines. However, your Windows folder might appear as \WinNT or something else depending on how you installed Windows. The universal method of accessing the Windows directory is to use \%WINDIR% for the \Windows directory and \%SYSTEM% for the \Windows\System32 directory. Because some utilities won't allow the use of environment variables, the book will use \Windows and \Windows\System as a consistent means of identifying these directories.

k A checkpoint file uses the CHK file extension. This file contains a checkpoint in the database transactions. The system writes each transaction to memory and log files first, and then commits them to the database. The reason for this system is twofold. First, writing the information to memory and a log file makes it possible to record transaction steps without changing the database, making it easier to commit and rollback transactions as needed. Second, using this approach makes it possible to write information to the database in the most efficient manner possible, which enhances overall system performance. The checkpoint is a reference to the transaction stream; it indicates that all of the transactions prior to the checkpoint appear in the database. Those after the checkpoint could appear in the database, but more likely appear in memory or in a log file. You can see a checkpoint by typing **ESENTUTL /mk EDB.CHK** in the \WINDOWS\system32\CatRoot2 folder and pressing Enter.

l A log file uses the LOG file extension and normally appears in the same folder as a CHK or SDB file. However, sometimes Windows places the log files in an associated folder, as is the case with the security logs. The log files contain a record of current transactions—either completed or in process. You can use the /r command line switch with a log file to roll back or reprocess transactions on the database. You can see a log file by typing **ESENTUTL /ml EDB.LOG** in the \WINDOWS\system32\CatRoot2 folder and pressing Enter.

m Metadata tells you about the content of a database. When you execute this command, you'll see a listing of the tables and indexes associated with the database, along with some statistical information about each entry. You can use this command to obtain a list of tables to use with other ESEnTUtl command line switches. You can see an example of metadata by typing **ESENTUTL /mm SecEdit.SDB** in the \WINDOWS\security\Database folder and pressing Enter.

s This modifier tells you how much space each of the tables and indexes within the database are using. You can use this command to determine whether you need to defragment the database using the /d command line switch. The best way to determine how much space the database should use is to defragment the database and use this command to take a snapshot of the defragmented size. When the database exceeds some threshold (normally 150 percent of the defragmented size), defragment the database and take another snapshot. You can see the size of the security database by typing **ESENTUTL /ms SecEdit.SDB** in the \WINDOWS\security\ Database folder and pressing Enter.

Copying lets you create another copy of a log file, streaming file, or database in a secondary location. The default utility settings copy the data from a source location to the current location, but you can change that behavior by using the /d command line switch as follows.

/d<Destination *Filename*>   Copies the file to the specified destination, rather than using the current directory and the same name as the source file.

Decompressing Files with the Expand Utility

The Expand utility lets you open the contents of a cabinet (CAB) file or compressed file and extract the contents. Generally, you use it to extract a missing file from a CD or other media, most notably Windows files. The advantage of using this utility is that you can use it with batch or script files to automate repair actions. An administrator can save time and effort using this approach for common repairs or repairs that must be made to a group of machines.

USING MODERN COMPRESSION TECHNIQUES

Computing constantly changes, but some command line utilities don't keep up. Either they work fine as is, or Microsoft simply decides to let a third party do the job. At one time, CAB files were the only form of compression widely available to Windows users. Today, third-party utilities, such as WinZIP (a shareware utility you can download and try before you buy), have largely replaced the need for this particular utility when working with CAB files. However, you must still use Expand when working with compressed files—those that have an underscore as part of their file extension. For example, you'd always use Expand to expand a file named MyApp.EX_ to MyApp.EXE. To make things easier for administrators, WinZIP has a command line add-in (http://www.winzip.com/prodpagecl.htm) that you can use much like the Expand utility for a much broader range of compressed file types. Even so, you'll still find that you need the Expand utility, in some cases, such as when you use the recovery console, simply because it's the only tool available.

You can use the Expand utility in one of several ways. The information you provide depends on the way in which you want to use the utility. This utility uses the following syntax:

```
EXPAND [-r] Source Destination
EXPAND -r Source [Destination]
EXPAND -D Source.cab [-F:Files]
EXPAND Source.cab -F:Files Destination
```

Essentially, you must always provide at least two kinds of information or make an assumption about the output of the utility. For example, if you supply the source filename and use the -r command line switch, Expand makes an assumption about the output filename based on the source filename. The following list describes each of the command line arguments.

Source   Name of the compressed file. The Expand utility works with single compressed files (those with an underscore in the file extension) and CAB files. It doesn't work with newer MSI, ZIP, or other compressed files.

Destination   Name of the uncompressed file when working with a single file. The destination folder for the uncompressed files when working with a CAB file.

-r   Renames the destination filenames based on the source filename. For example, when you supply MyApp.EX_ as the source filename, Expand automatically uses MyApp.EXE as the output filename. This option works by using the full name of the file that's embedded as part of the compressed file. (The XVI32 utility explored in the "Using XVI32 to View Files in Depth" section of Chapter 22 tells you how to view inside of a file.)

-D   Displays the list of files in the source file. When used with a single compressed file, you see only a single filename as output. CAB files normally contain multiple files.

-F:*Files*   Decompresses one or more selected files within a CAB file. You can specify multiple files by supplying wildcard characters. (See the "Working with Wildcard Characters" sidebar for details.) Don't use multiple copies of the -F command line switch to specify multiple discrete files. When you want to expand single files from a CAB file, you must use the Expand utility once for each file.

The Expand utility is extremely useful because it doesn't require a running copy of Windows to work. For example, you can use this utility from the Recovery Console where other third-party utilities will fail to work. Microsoft has created a Knowledge Base article to discuss the various scenarios for using the Expand utility at http://support.microsoft.com/default.aspx?scid=kb;en-us;888017.

Performing Advanced File Comparison with the FC Utility

The FC utility is a slightly advanced form of the Comp utility described in an earlier section. You can use it for the same types of activities, but perform a more flexible comparison of the two files. For example, this utility has a comparison mode specifically designed for binary files. This utility uses the following syntax (the first is for ASCII files; the second is for binary files):

```
FC [/A] [/C] [/L] [/LBn] [/N] [/OFF[LINE]] [/T] [/U] [/W] [/nnnn]
    [drive1:][path1]filename1 [drive2:][path2]filename2
FC /B [drive1:][path1]filename1 [drive2:][path2]filename2
```

The following list describes each of the command line arguments.

/A   Displays only the first and last lines for each set of differences. Normally, the FC utility (like the Comp utility) displays every line for a set of differences, making the output difficult to read when the files have a lot of differences.

/B   Performs a binary comparison of the two files. This means that the FC utility won't interpret control characters such as linefeed, carriage return, and end of file character (ASCII character 26) as it would when performing an ASCII comparison.

/C   Performs a case-insensitive comparison of the two files. Normally, FC considers an uppercase letter different from a lowercase letter.

/L   Performs an ASCII text comparison of the two files. This setting means that control characters become important in the comparison, as do the actual character meanings.

/LB*n*   Defines the maximum acceptable mismatches between the two files. When FC reaches *n*, it stops performing the comparison.

/N   Displays the line numbers for differences. The FC utility compares the two files line by line, where the carriage return (ASCII character 13), linefeed (ASCII character 10), or both designate the end of a line.

/OFF[LINE]   Forces the FC utility to compare files even when the files have the offline attribute set.

/T   Forces the FC utility to retain tabs within the output. Normally, it displays tabs using the default number of spaces (usually 8) between characters.

/U   Performs a Unicode comparison of the two files. Unicode character sets include additional characters to meet the needs of languages other than English. In addition, Unicode character sets often include characters designed to express both scientific and mathematical output.

/W   Compresses tabs and spaces for the purposes of comparison. You'd use this feature when comparing two data files where the content is important, but the manner of presentation isn't. Using this technique would let you compare the actual content of a raw data file against its formatted counterpart.

/*nnnn*   Specifies the number of consecutive lines that must match after a mismatch to continue the comparison. If the source and destination files don't compare more often than this number allows, then FC discontinues the comparison.

[*drive1:***][***path1***]***filename1***   Specifies the source file. You can use wildcard characters to define multiple comparisons. For example, *.DLL compares every dynamic link library in the source directory against a DLL with the same name in the destination directory.

[*drive2:***][***path2***]***filename2***   Specifies the destination file. You can use wildcard characters to define multiple comparisons. However, the source and destination specifications must compare. If the source contains just one file, then the destination will also contain one file as well.

Moving Files and Renaming Files and Directories with the *Move* Command

The Move command is functionally equivalent to copying a file or directory and then erasing it in the current directory. This command uses the following syntax:

```
Move one or more files:
MOVE [/Y | /-Y] [drive:][path]filename1[,...] destination
Rename a directory:
MOVE [/Y | /-Y] [drive:][path]dirname1 dirname2
```

The following list describes each of the command line arguments.

drive   Specifies the drive to use for the file or directory. The default is to use the current drive.

path   Specifies the absolute or relative path to use for the file or directory. The default is to use the current directory. However, you can specify an absolute or relative path as needed. See the "Understanding Absolute and Relative Paths" sidebar in Chapter 9 for additional details.

filename1   Defines one or more filenames to move. Separate multiple filenames using a comma.

destination   Defines the output location for the data that you want to copy. The destination can include a drive letter and path (absolute or relative). When working with a single file, you can also rename the file by specifying a different filename.

dirname1   Defines the source directory when moving a directory from one location to another. Moving a directory always moves any subdirectories and files that the directory contains. Generally, you can move directories to another location on the same drive, but you can't move directories to another drive. The Microsoft recommendation is to use Move only to rename directories.

dirname2   Defines the destination directory when moving a directory from one location to another.

/Y and /-Y   Suppresses or enforces the prompt for overwriting destination files with the same name as the destination file provided as input to the Move command. Use the /Y command line switch in batch files where you know the batch file will overwrite an existing destination file. The /-Y command line switch is the default, so you never need to use it.

Recovering Lost Files with the Recover Utility

The Recover utility provides a last ditch method of recovering files from a bad hard drive. Depending on the hard drive failure, you might be able to recover some files, but not others. For example, when the hard drive experiences a head crash, the files located within the damaged portions of the hard drive become unreadable because the media that contained the files is gone. However, files that aren't in the damaged section are unaffected; you can recover them in many cases. The Recover utility lets you move these undamaged files from the damaged drive to an undamaged drive. You'd normally use this utility after you had tried to recover the drive information using the ChkDsk command. This utility uses the following syntax:

```
RECOVER [drive:][path]filename
```

The following list describes each of the command line arguments.

drive   Specifies the drive to use as a source for file information.

path   Specifies the absolute path to use as a source for file information.

filename   Specifies the name of the file you want to recover. You must specify the name of a file and cannot use wildcards with this command. The utility performs a low-level search for the information on the hard drive. Consequently, this command can require a long time to run. When you want to search for multiple files, it's usually more efficient to create a batch file containing all of the filenames and let the computer work while you do something else.

WARNING   The Recover utility won't work with deleted files. In addition, it doesn't work if the File Allocation Table (FAT) is damaged in such a way that the utility can't discover the beginning file entry. Since most file systems provide a minimum of two FATs, it's unlikely that you'll lose the FAT.

Renaming a File with the *Ren* and *Rename* Commands

The Ren and Rename commands both let you rename files and directories (the Microsoft documentation only mentions files, but the commands do work with directories). Using these commands is definitely faster than renaming them manually using Windows Explorer when you have a lot of files to change. These commands use the following syntax:

```
RENAME [drive:][path]filename1 filename2
REN [drive:][path]filename1 filename2
```

The following list describes each of the command line arguments.

drive Specifies the drive to use for the file or directory. The default is to use the current drive.

path Specifies the absolute or relative path to use for the file or directory. The default is to use the current directory. However, you can specify an absolute or relative path as needed. See the "Understanding Absolute and Relative Paths" sidebar in Chapter 9 for additional details.

filename1 Defines the file or directory that you want to rename. You can use wildcard characters with this command. For example, if you want to rename all TXT files to have a TEXT extension, you'd type **REN *.TXT *.TEXT** and press Enter.

NOTE Unlike in Windows Explorer, the Ren and Rename commands won't constantly ask you about file extension changes. Although this means you'll spend less time clicking the Yes button, it also means that you could accidentally rename files that you didn't want to rename.

filename2 Defines the new file or directory name. If you use a wildcard character for filename1, then you generally have to use a wildcard character with this argument as well. When in doubt, always test the renaming strategy using sample files.

Performing Robust File Transfers with the RoboCopy Command

RoboCopy is a sort of super XCopy utility, in that you can copy a large number of files from one location to another. However, RoboCopy also provides a considerable number of file selection options and even job options, so that you can submit a copy requirement as a job. The source and destination can include Universal Naming Convention (UNC) paths, in addition to the standard paths. Unlike XCopy, you don't have to resort to odd logging methods because RoboCopy has them built in so you can see precisely what happened during the copying process. In addition, RoboCopy is forgiving in that it provides retry options to ensure a copy process has the best possible chance to succeed. This command uses the following command line syntax:

```
ROBOCOPY Source Destination [File [File]...] [Copy Options] [File Selection
Options] [Logging Options] [Retry Options] [Job Options]
```

WARNING The command line switches for RoboCopy aren't the same as the command line switches for XCopy. Consequently, you can't perform a simple search and replace in your batch or script files to use RoboCopy; you must completely rewrite the command.

The copying options define how RoboCopy performs copying tasks. For example, you might want to include all of the folders in the copied location, even those that are empty, so you'd use the /E command line switch. The following list describes each of the copy command line arguments.

/S Copies all files in the current directory, plus all subdirectories and their files except empty subdirectories. You can't use this command line switch to create an empty directory structure for a user or application; use the /E command line switch instead.

/E Copies all files in the current directory, plus all subdirectories and their files including empty subdirectories.

/LEV:*n* Copies only the top-level subdirectories specified by *n*. For example, if *n* is 3, then RoboCopy only copies three subdirectories down. If there's a fourth-level subdirectory, it won't appear in the copy.

/Z Copies the files using restartable mode. Using restartable mode means that you can restart the operation should an external force interrupt it. Normally, RoboCopy restarts an operation from the beginning with the retry options, but this command line switch restarts the copy with the failed file.

/B Copies files using backup semantics. When using this mode, you must have the backup right. Using backup semantics helps you overcome some obstacles where you might ordinarily receive an access denied error, such as copying a file for which you have only the write privilege. The resulting copy has all of the same Access Control List (ACL) entries as the original, so this feature doesn't cause a breach in security.

/ZB Attempts to perform the copy using restartable mode first (see the /Z command line switch) and then uses backup mode if restartable mode fails.

NOTE Using the /Z, /B, or /ZB command line switches can slow RoboCopy performance because the utility must perform additional file tracking as it makes a copy. However, the performance loss is more than overcome when working with unreliable network connections because you gain additional flexibility in handling troublesome files.

/EFSRAW Copies all of the encrypted files in the Encrypting File System (EFS) Read-After-Write (RAW) mode.

/COPY: *Copy_Flags* Defines which elements to copy from the source files to the destination files. For example, you might want to copy all of the owner information, but don't really care about the auditing information. The following list defines the copy flags.

- **D** Data
- **A** Attributes
- **T** Time stamps
- **S** Security (NTFS) ACLs
- **O** Owner info
- **U** Auditing info

/DCOPY:T Copies the directory time stamps. RoboCopy normally uses the current time for the time stamps.

/SEC Copies the files with all of the security information intact. This command line switch has the same effect as the /COPY:DATS command line switch.

/COPYALL Copies all of the file information with the files. This option makes a nearly mirror copy of the data from the source to the destination. Using this option is equivalent to using the /COPY:DATSOU command line switch.

/NOCOPY Performs a copy without copying any of the file data. This feature is useful with the /PURGE command line switch. You can also use it when checking for potential copy errors since the process is extremely fast when you don't copy the file data.

/SECFIX   Repairs the security information for a set of destination files. This option lets you update the security information without copying the file data, making the repair very fast. You can learn more about this feature in the Knowledge Base article at http://support.microsoft.com/kb/323275.

/TIMFIX   Repairs the time stamps for a set of destination files. This option lets you update the time stamps without copying the file data, making the change quite fast. This feature works very much like the /SECFIX command line switch, except it affects the time stamps, rather than security.

/PURGE   Deletes the files in the destination directory that no longer exist in the source folder. Consequently, the files in the destination directory match the files in the source directory after you use this command line switch.

WARNING   Use the /PURGE command line switch with extreme care. Even a small error in the command line arguments can delete a significant number of destination data. Whenever you use the /PURGE command line switch, the RoboCopy command removes any files that exist as part of the Extra file class. See the sidebar entitled, "An Overview of RoboCopy File Classes" for additional details.

/MIR   Creates a mirror image of the source directory in the destination directory. Using this command line switch is equivalent to combining the /E and /PURGE command line switches.

/MOV   Moves only the files in the source directory to the destination directory. RoboCopy deletes the files in the source directory after copying them to the destination directory.

/MOVE   Moves both files and subdirectories from the source directory to the destination directory. RoboCopy deletes the files and subdirectories in the source directory after copying them to the destination directory.

/A+:[RASHCNET]   Adds the requested attributes to the copied files. RoboCopy actually provides access to more attributes than the Attrib utility. The following list describes each of the attributes.

- ◆ R: Read-only
- ◆ A: Archive
- ◆ S: System
- ◆ H: Hidden
- ◆ C: Compress
- ◆ N: Nonindexed
- ◆ E: Encrypted
- ◆ T: Temporary
- ◆ O: Offline (/XA and /IA command line switches only)

TIP   NTFS actually supports a number of attributes that you can't readily access. You can find them discussed at http://www.febooti.com/products/filetweak/online-help/.

/A-:[RASHCNET]   Removes the requested attributes from the copied files. The meanings of the attributes are the same as the /A+ command line switch.

/CREATE   Creates a directory tree and zero-length files. You can use this feature when you need to copy the infrastructure from one location to another without copying the data.

/FAT   Removes the long filenames from the destination files. All the files appear using the 8.3 File Allocation Table (FAT) file system format.

/256   Turns off the long path support that RoboCopy provides. If RoboCopy detects a long path, it raises an error. The only time you'd need to use this feature is if the destination doesn't support long paths. For example, if you wanted to copy to an older system with DOS (or even some camera or flash drives), you would probably want to use this command line switch.

/MON:*n*   Monitors the source directory and performs a copy when more than *n* changes occur. Unlike XCopy, you can use RoboCopy to keep source and destination files synchronized automatically.

/MOT:*m*   Monitors the source directory and performs a copy after *m* minutes if RoboCopy detects a change. You can use this option to keep the number of copies under control for a high activity directory. RoboCopy uses a set amount of system resources, rather than using resources based on activity as the /MON:*n* command line switch does.

/RH:*hhmm-hhmm*   Defines the hours when RoboCopy can run. You can use this feature to ensure that copies only occur during nonpeak hours or after work. Use a 24-hour clock when defining the time range. For example, 1 p.m. is actually 1300.

/PF   Determines the RoboCopy run hours on a per file basis instead of checking at the beginning of each pass. This option does incur a performance penalty because RoboCopy must check to determine whether a copy is allowed for each file, but it does mean that the copying process will conform better to the hours set by the /RH command line switch.

/IPG:*n*   Determines the Inter-Package Gap (IPG) value in milliseconds (ms). A higher IPG frees bandwidth for other uses on slower network paths. A lower IPG helps RoboCopy perform better and accomplish tasks faster.

RoboCopy also provides a complex set of file selection options. These options determine which files actually appear in the destination directory. RoboCopy supports the following file selection option.

/A   Includes files with the archive attribute set. The operating system sets the archive attribute whenever anything changes a file. This option doesn't reset the archive attribute, which makes it useful when you want to create a backup of archived files later.

/M   Includes files with the archive attribute set. This option resets the archive attribute, so this is the command line switch to use when you use RoboCopy for backup purposes.

/IA:[RASHCNETO]   Includes only the files that have the requested attributes set. See the /A+ command line switch for details.

/XA:[RASHCNETO]   Excludes all of the files that have the requested attributes set. See the /A+ command line switch for details.

/XF *File* [*File*]...   Excludes any files that match the specified names or paths. The specifications can include wildcard characters.

/XD *Directory* [*Directory*]...   Excludes any directories that match the specified names or paths. The specifications can include wildcard characters.

/XC   Excludes Changed files. See the "An Overview of RoboCopy File Classes" sidebar for details on this file class.

/XN Excludes Newer files. See the "An Overview of RoboCopy File Classes" sidebar for details on this file class.

/XO Excludes Older files. See the "An Overview of RoboCopy File Classes" sidebar for details on this file class.

/XX Excludes eXtra files and directories. See the "An Overview of RoboCopy File Classes" sidebar for details on this file class.

/XL Excludes Lonely files and directories. See the "An Overview of RoboCopy File Classes" sidebar for details on this file class.

/IS Includes Same files. See the "An Overview of RoboCopy File Classes" sidebar for details on this file class.

/IT Includes Tweaked files. See the "An Overview of RoboCopy File Classes" sidebar for details on this file class.

/MAX:*n* Defines the maximum file size to include in bytes. Excludes any file larger than *n* bytes.

/MIN:*n* Defines the minimum file size to include in bytes. Excludes any file smaller than *n* bytes.

/MAXAGE:*n* Defines the maximum file age to include. Excludes any file older than *n* days old. You can also specify a date.

/MINAGE:*n* Defines the minimum file age to include. Excludes any file newer than *n* days old. You can also specify a date.

/MAXLAD:*n* Defines the maximum last access date to include. Excludes any file unused in *n* days. You can also specify a date.

/MINLAD:*n* Defines the minimum last access date to include. Excludes any file used in *n* days. You can also specify a date.

/XJ Excludes junction points for both directories and files (normally included with the results).

/FFT Assumes FAT File Times (FFT), which have a 2-second granularity.

/DST Compensates for one-hour daylight standard time (DST) time differences.

/XJD Excludes junction points for directories.

/XJF Excludes junction points for files.

Many command line utilities try an operation once and then fail if it doesn't succeed. RoboCopy continues to retry the task until you press Ctrl+C, in most cases, to stop the process manually (even RoboCopy gives up after 1 million retries). You can also tell RoboCopy how to react to failure conditions. The following list describes the retry options.

/R:*n* Modifies the number of retries on failed copies to *n*. The default setting is 1 million retries.

/W:*n* Defines the wait time between retries. The default setting is 30 seconds.

/REG Saves the /R:*n* and /W:*n* command line switches in the registry as default settings.

/TBD Tells RoboCopy to wait for sharenames To Be Defined (TBD). This command line switch addresses retry error 67.

Given everything that RoboCopy can do, you might not want to wait for it to accomplish a task. Consequently, RoboCopy provides logging options that you can use to output data to a permanent location. The following list describes the logging options.

/L   Provides a list of files only. RoboCopy doesn't copy, time stamp, or delete any files.

/X   Produces a report of all eXtra files, not just those selected.

/V   Produces verbose output, which includes skipped files.

/TS   Includes source file time stamps in the output.

/FP   Includes the full pathname of files in the output.

/BYTES   Prints the sizes of files in bytes.

/NS   Doesn't log file sizes.

/NC   Doesn't log file classes.

/NFL   Doesn't log filenames.

/NDL   Doesn't log directory names.

/NP   Doesn't display a progress indicator showing the percent copied.

/ETA   Shows the estimated time of arrival of copied files. This option is helpful when copying large files over slow networks.

/LOG:*file*   Outputs status to the log file and overwrites any existing log.

/LOG+:*file*   Outputs status to the log file and appends the information to any existing log.

/UNILOG:*file*   Outputs status to the Unicode log file and overwrites any existing log.

/UNILOG+:*file*   Outputs status to the Unicode log file and appends the information to any existing log.

/TEE   Outputs status to the console window, as well as the log file.

/NJH   Doesn't include a job header with the output.

/NJS   Doesn't include a job summary with the output.

/UNICODE   Outputs status using Unicode rather than ASCII characters.

You may want to use RoboCopy to perform complex tasks over the weekend or during a downtime. If you're using RoboCopy as one means of backup for your system, you might want to perform the task at night. In all of these situations, you'll want to create a RoboCopy job to perform the task. The following list describes the job options.

/JOB:*jobname*   Uses parameters from the named job file to perform a task. A job file is simply a list of RoboCopy and other commands that define what you want RoboCopy to do—a kind of script. The text file can contain any number of RoboCopy commands. You can also use the Set command to create local variables to hold values that you want RoboCopy to use (see the "Managing Environment Variables with the *Set* Command" section of Chapter 5 for details).

/SAVE:*jobname*   Saves the current command line arguments to the named job file. This is one of the easiest ways to create a job file for use with the /JOB command line switch.

/QUIT   Quits after processing command line so that you can view any arguments. This is a way to test jobs without actually performing the tasks that the jobs request.

/NOSD   Specifies that you haven't defined a source directory in the job file. RoboCopy uses the current directory.

/NODD   Specifies that you haven't defined a destination directory in the job file. RoboCopy uses the current directory.

/IF   Includes external files as part of the current job. This feature lets you concatenate multiple jobs together and perform them as a unit.

AN OVERVIEW OF ROBOCOPY FILE CLASSES

RoboCopy classifies files in several ways to make handling specific file conditions easier. The following list provides an overview of the RoboCopy file classes:

Lonely   A lonely file exists in the source directory, but not in the destination directory. If you perform an update copy using RoboCopy, the utility copies the file to the destination.

Tweaked   Tweaked files exist in both the source and destination directories. The file size and time stamp are the same. However, the attributes (those set with the Attrib utility) differ. You can fix this problem by specifically copying the attributes from the source to the destination. A standard copy won't affect the attributes when the file falls into this class.

Same   The source and destination files are the same in all respects.

Changed   The file exists in both the source and destination directories. The time stamp for both files is also the same. However, the file size differs. RoboCopy doesn't consider the status of the attributes when placing a file into this class.

Newer   The file exists in both the source and destination directories. The time stamp of the file in the destination directory is newer than the one in the source directory. RoboCopy doesn't consider the status of the file size or attributes when placing a file into this class.

Older   The file exists in both the source and destination directories. The time stamp of the file in the source directory is newer than the one in the destination directory. RoboCopy doesn't consider the status of the file size or attributes when placing a file into this class.

eXtra   An extra file exists in the destination directory, but not in the source directory. You can use the /PURGE command line switch to remove extra files. However, use the /PURGE command line switch with extreme care because a typo can cause RoboCopy to delete the entire destination directory.

Mismatched   The entry exists as a file in the source directory and as a folder in the destination directory. RoboCopy reports this problem in the output log, but doesn't attempt to fix it.

Replacing Existing Files with the Replace Utility

The Replace utility replaces a file in a destination folder with a file from a source folder. You can use it to copy files in a source folder to a destination without worrying and all of the usual warnings that Windows provides. The utility can also place unique files from the source folder into a destination folder. This utility uses the following syntax:

```
REPLACE [drive1:][path1]filename [drive2:][path2] [/A] [/P] [/R] [/W]
REPLACE [drive1:][path1]filename [drive2:][path2] [/P] [/R] [/S] [/W] [/U]
```

Notice that the two command lines use distinctly different command line switch sets. For example, you can't use the /A and the /S command line switches together. The following list describes each of the command line arguments.

drive1/drive2 Specifies the drive for the source and destination. The default is the current drive.

path1/path2 Specifies the absolute or relative path to use for the source and destination. The source must be different from the destination. The default is the current directory.

filename Defines the file or directory that you want to replace. You can use wildcard characters with this command. See the "Working with Wildcard Characters" sidebar for details.

/A Adds any new files to the destination directory. Normally, the Replace utility will only replace files. You cannot use this command line switch with the /S or /U switches.

/P Prompts the user for confirmation prior to replacing a file or adding a new file.

/R Replaces read-only files, as well as unprotected files. By default, the Replace utility only replaces standard read/write files.

/S Replaces all of the files in subdirectories of the destination directory. The Replace utility replaces all occurrences of the file. If a destination directory and a subdirectory both contain an instance of a file, the Replace utility replaces both instances of that file. You can't use this command line switch with the /A switch.

/W Waits for the user to insert a floppy disk or other removable media before beginning the replacement. Generally, you'd use this option as part of a batch file where the replacement requires more than one disk.

/U Replaces files that are older than the source files. When the destination files are the same age or newer than the source files, the Replace utility doesn't replace them. This command line switch is a safety feature that ensures you don't overwrite newer updates with older files.

Sorting File Content with the Sort Utility

The Sort utility is an amazing utility in that it can sort any text file. You can use this utility to perform analysis of output from other commands. For example, you could use it to perform a custom sort of a directory listing. The sort mechanism considers locale, so you can sort data based on a specific language. In addition, the Sort utility works on extremely large files, so you don't have to worry about getting halfway through a sort and having the sort fail. (Large sorts can take a while because the Sort utility writes any data that won't fit in memory to disk.) This utility uses the following syntax:

```
SORT [/R] [/+n] [/M kilobytes] [/L locale] [/REC recordbytes]
     [[drive1:][path1]filename1] [/T [drive2:][path2]] [/O
     [drive3:][path3]filename3]
```

The following list describes each of the command line arguments.

/+n Specifies the comparison character. The default is to use the first character of each line as a starting point. By using another character as a starting point, you can change the sort order of the data. For example, the Dir command won't let you sort a directory listing by time without first sorting it by date. If you're interested in sorting the listing by time, you could set the sort to use the time, /+13, as the starting point for the sort. This particular sort is handy because some vendors, including Microsoft, have used the time as a method of indicating the version number of their DLLs. Consequently, sorting by the time can provide a very fast indication of version number as long as you know what the time indicator means (vendors often provide this information in their knowledge bases).

NOTE There's no space between the /+ command line switch and the starting position of the sort. However, there's a space between the other command line switches and their arguments. Make sure you add or remove space as appropriate or the Sort utility will fail with an invalid command line switch error message.

/L[OCALE] *Local* Overrides the default system local, which is always the locale you selected for your Windows setup. Unfortunately, the only active override for Server Core is the C locale. The C locale provides a fast collating sort using binary differentiation, rather than language-specific sorting. Although this sort is quite fast, it might not always produce the results you need if your language uses diacritical marks. The sort is always case sensitive.

/M[EMORY] *Size* Defines the amount of memory in KB to use. Sort requires a minimum of 160 KB to perform its task. It's important to remember that the command window doesn't provide the same amount of memory as your machine contains. Generally, all modern machines have 640 KB of main memory available in the command window, with some memory used by command window components and some required by Sort itself. You can check the amount of available memory using the Mem utility (see the "Determining Memory Status with the Mem Utility" section of Chapter 12 for details). The only time you need to set the memory size is if Sort fails due to memory constraints. Sort uses 90 percent of available memory to maximize performance as a default.

/REC[ORD_MAXIMUM] *Characters* Defines the maximum number of characters in a record. The default size is 4,096 characters. However, you can specify up to 65,535 characters in a record. Larger record sizes use more memory for each record. Consequently, keeping the record size as small as possible will improve Sort efficiency.

/R[EVERSE] Reverses the sort order. Instead of sorting A to Z, the output appears in Z to A order. Likewise, Sort also reverses number order.

drive1 Specifies the drive for the sort input. The default is the current drive when you specify a filename.

path1 Specifies the absolute or relative path to use for the sort input. The default is the current directory when you specify a filename.

filename1 Defines the name of the file that you want to sort. If you don't provide a filename, Sort will use the standard input device, which is usually the keyboard for Windows, as the input. You can change the standard input by using redirection (see the "Employing Data Redirection" section of this chapter for details), but providing a filename normally provides faster results.

/T[EMPORARY] **[***drive2***:][***path2***]** Determines the directory used to hold the temporary files for the sort. Normally, you don't need to use this command line switch because it's easier to use the system temporary directory (the default) for storage. However, you might want to use this option if the current drive is low on storage space or you want to use a faster drive to hold the temporary data to promote faster sorting.

/O[UTPUT] **[***drive3***:][***path3***]***filename3*** Specifies the location of the output. You must provide a filename as a minimum when using this command line switch. The `drive3` and `path3` arguments let you place the file on a different drive and directory. If you don't specify this command line switch, the Sort utility sends the output to the standard output, which is the console.

Taking Ownership of Files with the TakeOwn Utility

Server Core provides a new method of taking ownership of a file using the TakeOwn utility. Given the importance that User Account Control (UAC) places on ownership for security reasons, using this utility could help you around some of the problems that UAC can create in user access. In some cases, you might find that you have to take ownership of a file to manipulate it effectively. The TakeOwn utility uses the following syntax.

```
TAKEOWN [/S system [/U [domain\]username [/P [password]]]] /F filename [/A] [/R
[/D prompt]]
```

The following list describes each of the command line arguments.

/S *system*   Specifies the remote system that you want to check. In most cases, you'll also need to supply the /U and the /P command line switches when using this switch.

/U [*domain*]*user*   Specifies the username on the remote system. This name may not match the username on the local system. You'll need to supply a domain name when working with a domain controller.

/P [*password*]   Specifies the password for the given user. You can provide the command line switch without specifying the password on the command line in cleartext. The system prompts you for the password. Using this feature can help you maintain the security of passwords used on your system.

/F *filename*   Specifies the object that you want to own. The object can be a file or directory. You can include a sharename when required. TakeOwn also lets you use wildcard characters to define the file or directory specification.

/A   Gives the Administrators group ownership of the object, instead of the current user (or the user whose credentials you supplied).

/R   Performs a recursive search for files meeting the file specification. TakeOwn searches the current directory first, and then all subdirectories.

/D *prompt*   Provides a default answer when the current user doesn't have the list folder permission for a particular directory. The acceptable answers are Y to take ownership of the directory or N to skip the directory.

Outputting Data Files with the *Type* Command

The Type command is a simple method of displaying the content of a file on screen. You use this command with text files; it won't display control codes in a readable form and stops displaying text when it sees an end of file character (ASCII 26). This command uses the following syntax:

```
TYPE [drive:][path]filename
```

The following list describes each of the command line arguments.

drive   Specifies the drive that holds the file for display. The default is the current drive.

path   Specifies the relative or absolute path of the file you want to display. The default is the current directory.

filename   Specifies the file you want to display on screen.

Many people combine the Type command with other commands and utilities to achieve special effects. In addition, you can use redirection to augment the functionality of the Type command. By using the correct redirection, you can use the Type command to send raw text to the printer reliably. The following sections describe data redirection and the use of the most common Type command partner utility, the More utility.

Employing Data Redirection

Data redirection is the process of sending data from one command or utility to another command or utility. You can also redirect command or utility output to a device (see the "Understanding Command Line Devices" sidebar in this chapter for details on standard devices) or a file. Redirection provides the means for sending output to a location other than the standard output device (the console), obtaining input from a device other than standard input (the keyboard), and using something other than the standard error device (usually the console) to report problems. The command line supports three forms of redirection: input, output, and pipe. Each requires use of specialized symbols.

One of the most common forms of redirection is the pipe and it uses the pipe symbol (|) that appears over the backslash on most keyboards. In fact, the pipe is much older than the PC and appears in the earliest Unix operating systems (see the history at http://www.linfo.org/pipes.html for details). The pipe accomplishes what its name implies; it acts as a pipe between small applications. You connect the applications using the pipe and data flows between the applications using the pipe. For example, you can temporarily connect the Dir command to the Sort command to create a customized directory output using a command like this:

```
Dir /A-D | Sort /+13
```

The resulting command obtains a listing of the current directory, without the directory entries and sorts them by the time column. Figure 14.3 shows the results of this command.

FIGURE 14.3
Combining commands and utilities makes the command prompt extremely flexible.

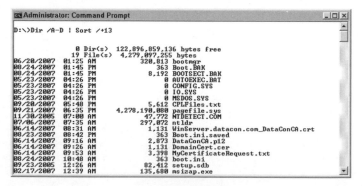

Redirection always works with a file or other streaming device. You never use redirection with another command. The two types of redirection are input and output, with output being the most commonly used. To output the results of a command such as Dir or Sort to a file, you use a greater than sign (>) or output redirection pointer. Windows clears the file if it exists and places the command output in it. However, you might want to place the results of several commands into a file. In this case, you use two greater than signs (>>). A double output redirection pointer always appends the output of a command to the existing file. Here's an example of sending the output of the Dir command to a file:

```
Dir *.TXT > MyFile.TXT
```

In this case, you'd end up with a file called MyFile.TXT that contains a list of all of the text files in the current directory.

Input relies on the less than symbol (<) or input redirection pointer. You can always use a file as input to a command that's expecting text or record data. In some cases, you can use file input to generate commands as well. The point is that a file or other streaming device acts as input. Although it's extremely uncommon, you also have access to a double input redirection pointer (<<). This symbol appends input to previous input for a command.

The combination of an output redirection pointer and an input redirection pointer can be the same as a pipe. Here's an example of the two forms of redirection used together:

```
Dir /A-D > MyFile.TXT
Sort /+13 < MyFile.TXT
```

In this case, the output of the Dir command appears in MyFile.TXT. The second command uses MyFile.TXT as input to the Sort command. The result is the same as the pipe example shown in Figure 14.3.

Although you can only include one redirection symbol on a command line, you can use as many pipes as needed to accomplish a task. This means that you can create a series of pipes to connect any number of commands and create some interesting command sequences. For example, you can combine the Dir, Sort, and More commands as shown here to provide output where you see one display at a time (see the "Using the More Utility" section for details on the More utility).

```
Dir /A-D | Sort /+13 | More
```

Using the More Utility

The More utility is one of the few utilities that you never use by itself. You always use this utility with some other utility or command. The More utility pauses the display so that you can see output that normally requires multiple screens to display. For example, you can combine the More utility with the Dir command to display the list of files in a directory one screen at a time. One of the most common uses of the More utility is to provide a means of paging output from the Type command. You can also use redirection to input files to the More utility; the implied partner in this case is the Type command. This utility uses the following syntax:

```
MORE [/E [/C] [/P] [/S] [/Tn] [+n]] < [drive:][path]filename
command-name | MORE [/E [/C] [/P] [/S] [/Tn] [+n]]
MORE /E [/C] [/P] [/S] [/Tn] [+n] [files]
```

The following list describes each of the command line arguments.

drive Specifies the drive that holds the file for display. The default is the current drive.

path Specifies the relative or absolute path of the file you want to display. The default is the current directory.

filename   Specifies the file you want to display on screen.

/E   Enables the More utility extended feature set. You'll find a discussion of these features later in this section.

/C   Clears the display prior to displaying a page. Normally, the More utility provides a continuous display, so you can scroll back and forth through the screen buffer.

/P   Expands form feed characters as displayable information, rather than reacting to them as an actual form feed.

/S   Removes excess blank lines from the display. The More utility squeezes multiple blank lines into a single blank line.

/T*n*   Changes the number of spaces for each tab. The default setting is 8 spaces.

NOTE   You can specify the command line switches in the MORE environment variable. For more information on using environment variables, see the "Managing Environment Variables with the *Set* Command" section of Chapter 5.

+*n*   Displays the first file starting at line *n*. This feature lets you continue displaying a file from a known position after stopping a display during a previous session.

files   Specifies a list of files to display. The More utility sends the files to the Type command in the order specified. It separates each file with a blank. You must provide the list of files as the last argument.

The More utility includes an extended mode that you enable using the /E command line switch. The extended mode provides additional functionality to make it easier to work with output files. For example, you can display a few additional lines to see part of a continuation of data in a file. The following list describes the extended mode commands, which you can type at the More prompt.

P *n*   Displays the next *n* lines of the file. Type the P command. You'll see a Lines prompt. Type the number of lines to display and press Enter.

S *n*   Skips the next *n* lines of the file (doesn't display them). Type the **S** command. You'll see a Lines prompt. Type the number of lines to display and press Enter.

F   Displays the next file in the list. If there's no next file, the More utility ends. This action doesn't necessarily end the previous application in the pipe. Press Ctrl+C to end the previous command (such as Type) as necessary.

Q   Quits the More utility without displaying any additional data. This action doesn't necessarily end the previous application in the pipe. Press Ctrl+C to end the previous command (such as Type) as necessary.

=   Shows the number of the current line of text. For example, if the More utility is currently displaying the 49th line in the file, you'll see Line: 49 as part of the More prompt.

?   Shows the list of extended commands.

<space>   Displays the next page of the file.

<enter>   Displays the next line of text in the file.

The More utility provides a simple prompt at the bottom of the command window for entering display commands. You can only move forward in a file, not backward. Whenever you enter a command, the More prompt extends to request any additional information. Figure 14.4 shows the More prompt after typing the P command. Notice that the prompt contains the Lines: entry, which lets you input the number of lines to display.

FIGURE 14.4
Using the More utility in extended mode makes it easy to manipulate the on-screen display.

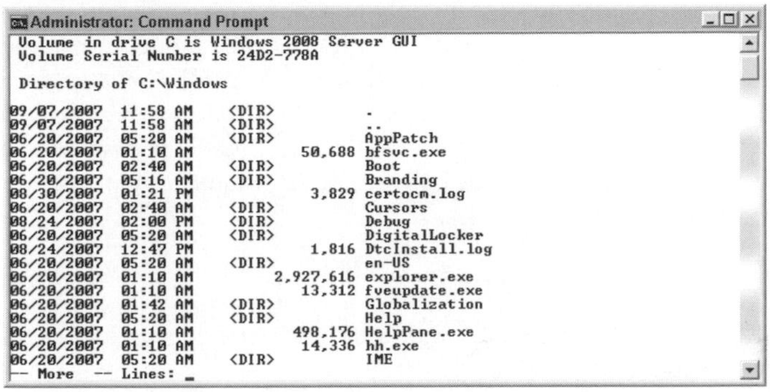

Validating File Operations with the *Verify* Command

The Verify command is very simple. It's an on or off setting that you use to tell the command processor how to interact with your files. Setting Verify on forces the command processor to check every file that it writes for errors before proceeding with the next file. However, using verify exacts a significant performance penalty, so the default setting is to have it off. The verify setting is a remnant from the early days of the PC when hard drives were less reliable than they are now. This command uses the following syntax:

```
VERIFY [ON | OFF]
```

Executing Verify by itself will display the current verify setting status. Generally, you'll keep the verify setting off unless you're copying files that require absolute verification. For example, you might want to use this setting when creating a disk for a presentation at work where errors aren't tolerated.

Performing Backups with the WBAdmin Utility

The WBAdmin utility provides you with considerably more functionality than NTBackup, you'll find that it's actually easier to use in many cases. Part of the ease of use comes from the modes that WBAdmin supports. You use a particular mode by typing WBAdmin followed by the mode keywords, such as START BACKUP. However, you'll also find that WBAdmin provides considerably fewer options than NTBackup. For example, you must back up an entire volume or mount point. The following list describes each of the modes.

START BACKUP   Starts the backup process. You'll need to provide backup information as command line arguments.

STOP JOB   Ends the current backup or recovery.

GET VERSIONS   Displays a list of backups that you can use for recovery purposes.

GET ITEMS   Displays a list of items found in a particular backup.

GET STATUS   Obtains the status of the current backup or recovery.

Three of the options are quite simple to use. Simply type the mode name and WBAdmin performs the required task without any additional input. For example, when you use the STOP JOB mode, WBAdmin stops the current backup or recovery without asking for any additional information. Since you can run only one job at a time, the process is quite simple.

The GET VERSIONS and GET STATUS modes also provide simple output. When working with GET VERSIONS, you see a list of backups you have performed. The information provided by this mode acts as input to the GET ITEMS mode where you have to supply a specific version. The GET STATUS mode simply shows the progress of the current backup or recovery.

The last two modes do require additional input from you. The following sections describe these two remaining modes.

START BACKUP

The START BACKUP mode lets you perform a backup of the system. This mode uses the following syntax:

```
WBADMIN START BACKUP -backupTarget:{TargetVolume | TargetNetworkShare}
-include:VolumesToInclude [-noVerify] [-quiet]
```

The following list describes each of the command line arguments.

-backupTarget:{TargetVolume | TargetNetworkShare}   Defines the location of the backup. You must provide a drive letter or a UNC path to a shared location on a network drive.

-include:VolumesToInclude   Defines the volumes or mount points that you want to back up. You can't define individual elements such as directories.

-noVerify   Performs the backup without a verify. Although this option is considerably faster, it's also quite risky because you don't know whether the backup is any good.

-quiet   Creates the backup without displaying the usual messages.

When you start a backup, the system retrieves any required volume information and then displays several messages unless you choose the -quiet option. After the backup starts, you'll see several status messages. The status messages continue until the backup is complete.

GET ITEMS

After you create a backup using the START BACKUP mode, you can use the GET VERSIONS mode to obtain a list of backups for your system. The version identifier is usually a date and time (GMT, not local). With the version identifier in hand, you can list the items in a backup. This mode uses the following syntax:

```
Usage: WBADMIN GET ITEMS -version:VersionIdentifier
[-backupTarget:{VolumeName | NetworkSharePath}]
[-machine:BackupMachineName]
```

The following list describes each of the command line arguments.

-version:VersionIdentifier   Defines the version identifier for the backup that you want to list. Use the Get Versions mode to obtain a list of versions.

-backupTarget:{VolumeName | NetworkSharePath}   Defines the backup target you want to use for listing purposes. This option is helpful when you use multiple backup targets.

-machine:BackupMachineName   Defines the machine you want to list. This option is helpful when you back up multiple machines in a single version.

Performing Bulk File Transfers with the XCopy Utility

The XCopy utility is one of the few that even Microsoft mentions regularly because it's so handy to have. You use the XCopy utility to perform bulk file transfers from anywhere on a local network to anywhere else on a local network. In addition to copying single files, XCopy can copy entire directory structures. It also has a wealth of command line switches so you have precise control over the copying process. This utility uses the following syntax:

```
XCOPY source [destination] [/A | /M] [/D[:date]] [/P] [/S [/E]] [/V]
      [/W] [/C] [/I] [/Q] [/F] [/L] [/G] [/H] [/R] [/T] [/U] [/K] [/N]
      [/O] [/X] [/Y] [/-Y] [/Z] [/B]
      [/EXCLUDE:Definition1[+Definition 2][+ Definition 3]...]
```

The following list describes each of the command line arguments.

TIP Server Core administrators should consider moving to the RoboCopy command to perform some tasks. You can find a description of the new RoboCopy utility in the "Performing Robust File Transfers with the RoboCopy Command" section of the chapter.

source Specifies which files to copy. You can use wildcard characters to define the file specification. See the "Working with Wildcard Characters" sidebar for details. The file specification can also include a drive and absolute or relative path.

destination Specifies the destination for the files. When working with a single file, you can also specify a new filename for the file.

/A Copies only the files with the archive attribute set. Copying the files doesn't change the attribute status, so you need to use the Attrib utility (described in the "Changing File and Directory Attributes with the Attrib Utility" section of Chapter 15) to change the archive bit. Some people use this particular feature to create a simple, but effective, backup utility. They send any changed files to a hard drive on another machine, and then clear the archive attribute. As an alternative, if you know the copying methodology works without flaw, you can use the /M command line switch.

/M Copies only the files with the archive attribute set. However, unlike the /A command line switch, this command line switch does reset the archive bit.

/D[:Month-Day-Year] Copies files changed on or after the specified date. When you leave out the date, then XCopy only copies the file when the date of an existing file in the destination is older than the source file. If the dates are the same or newer, then XCopy doesn't copy the file.

/EXCLUDE:Definition1[+Definition2][+ Definition3]... Excludes files or directories based on the strings you provide. For example, specifying .TXT as a string excludes all text files from the copy. On the other hand, specifying a string such as \MyDir excludes the entire \MyDir subdirectory from the copy. You can make strings ambiguous to describe a number of conditions. For example, including the string My would exclude files or directories with the word *My* in them as any part of the name, including the extension. You can create multiple excludes by separating each exclude string with a plus sign (+).

/P Prompts the user before creating each destination file.

/S Copies all files in the current directory, plus all subdirectories and their files except empty subdirectories. You can't use this command line switch to create an empty directory structure for a user or application; use the /E command line switch instead.

/E Copies all files in the current directory, plus all subdirectories and their files including empty subdirectories.

/V Verifies each new file as the system writes it. This command line switch overrides the system verify setting.

/W Waits for the user to insert a floppy disk or other removable media before beginning the copy process. Generally, you'd use this option as part of a batch file where the copying process requires more than one disk.

/C Forces XCopy to continue copying files even when an error occurs. Normally, XCopy stops when it encounters the first copy error.

/I Forces XCopy to assume the destination is a directory when the destination doesn't exist and you're copying more than one file. Otherwise, XCopy displays a message asking the user whether the destination is a file or a directory. This will cause a batch file to halt to wait for user participation.

/Q Copies the files without displaying the filenames. You can use this option in a batch file where you don't necessarily want the user bothered or aware of everything that's happening in the background.

/F Displays full source and destination filenames while copying, including both the drive and the path. Normally, XCopy displays only the filenames. This feature often comes in handy when diagnosing problems with complex batch files because it shows precisely where XCopy copies each file.

/L Displays a list of files that XCopy would copy, without actually copying them. This is a diagnostic mode where you can log the files and verify that the command line syntax produces the desired result.

/G Copies encrypted files to a destination that doesn't support encryption. This is a Windows-specific command line switch. The resulting destination files are unencrypted when you complete the copy, so using this command line switch can result in a security hole in your system.

/H Copies any files marked hidden or system. Normally, XCopy only copies the files without these attributes since hidden and system files are normally associated with operating system requirements (they aren't data files).

/R Forces XCopy to overwrite read-only files. Normally, XCopy won't overwrite read-only files to preserve their content.

/T Creates the directory structure, but doesn't copy any of the files. You can use this feature to create an empty directory structure for a new user or application without compromising data that might appear in an existing pattern directory structure. This command line switch won't include empty directories and subdirectories in the source. To include the complete directory structure in the destination, combine the /T and /E command line switches.

/U Copies only the source files that already exist in the destination. You could use this feature to perform updates on another system without compromising any unique files in the source system.

/K Copies all of the file and directory attributes. XCopy normally resets some of the attributes, such as read-only.

/N Creates a destination file with an 8-character filename and a 3-character file extension. Use this command line switch when you must create destination files for older systems that rely on the DOS 8.3 naming convention. Avoid using this command line switch on files with long filenames unless you really do want to create a compatible file.

/O Copies the file ownership and Access Control List (ACL) information. The ACL provides security for the file. If you don't use this command line switch, the destination system uses the default security settings for that system, which might not provide sufficient security for sensitive data.

/X Copies the file audit settings in addition to the file ownership and ACL information. File auditing monitors each file as Windows opens, closes, or modifies it. Using file auditing helps you track user and system activities, but does cause a performance hit.

/Y and /-Y Suppresses or enforces the prompt for overwriting destination files with the same name as the destination file provided as input to the XCopy command. Use the /Y command line switch in batch files where you know the batch file will overwrite an existing destination file. The /-Y command line switch is the default, so you never need to use it.

/Z Copies networked files in restartable mode. If the copy process stops for any reason, XCopy attempts to restart the file copy.

/B Copies a symbolic link to the target instead of the actual file pointed to by the symbolic link when the source is a symbolic link.

Working with File Associations and Types

Strictly speaking, you don't need to know anything about file associations or file types to work with files from the command prompt. However, Windows does need to know this information when working with files in the GUI. Whenever a user double-clicks a file, Windows looks up the file association based on the file extension, locates the file type information, and then executes an application to load the file based on what it finds. Consequently, knowing something about the file associations and types on your system is important, but it isn't something that you'll use from the command prompt.

Windows provides two commands for working with file associations and types. You use the Assoc command to determine and set the file associations. The file association connects a specific file type with an extension. The FType command defines the file type information. For example, you can specify what happens when a particular file type receives a request to open a file. The file types all rely on verbs, action words, to define specific tasks. The most common of these verbs are open and print, but depending on the file type, you might find many others.

The Assoc and the FType commands work together to show the relationships between file extensions and file types, and to allow you to modify these relationships. For example, an administrator could create a batch file to set up a user machine to use specific applications to handle certain kinds of files. The following sections describe these two commands.

Determining and Creating File Associations with the *Assoc* Command

The Assoc command can display or change the association between a file extension and a file type. For example, when you type **Assoc .TXT** and press Enter, the Assoc command responds with .TXT=txtfile on a Windows system using the default setup. This command uses the following syntax:

```
ASSOC [.ext[=[fileType]]]
```

The following list describes each of the command line arguments.

.ext Specifies the file extension that you want to assign or display. The file extension must begin with a period or the utility will fail. For example, you must type **.TXT** instead of TXT alone.

fileType   Specifies the file type to assign to the file extension. The file type must exist within the registry (create it if necessary using the FType command). Always place an equals sign between the file extension and type. For example, to associate the .TXT extension with the txtfile type, you'd type **Assoc .TXT=txtfile** and press Enter at the command line.

Determining and Creating File Types with the *FType* Command

The FType command can display the open verb action or set the action for this verb for any file type on your system. You can also use it to create new file types as needed to express a specific file requirement. The FType command only works with the open verb, not any of the other verbs (such as print) that the file type might contain. Even so, this command is invaluable in setting up a system quickly.

A file type always includes the file type name and the associated action. For example, if you type **FType txtfile** at the command prompt and press Enter, the FType command responds with txtfile=%SystemRoot%\system32\NOTEPAD.EXE %1 on a system using the default setup. In this case, txtfile is the file type. The action appears after the equals sign. The %SystemRoot% environment variable points to the Windows directory on your machine. The System32 directory contains many of the executable files including both EXEs and DLLs. The application that Windows starts to load is a text file in Notepad. The %1 after Notepad is a placeholder for the file. You can include as many placeholders as required by the application. The action can also include any command line switches that the application requires to handle the file type. This command uses the following syntax:

```
FTYPE [fileType[=[openCommandString]]]
```

The following list describes each of the command line arguments.

fileType   Specifies the name of the file type to display or change. Many common file types use the file extension followed by the word file as a name. For example, Windows normally associates a file with a .TXT extension with the txtfile file type.

openCommandString   Defines the action to take when a user double-clicks a file or otherwise requests that Windows open it. The action must include the application location and application name (including file extension). You may optionally include command line arguments, placeholders, and other application input as needed.

Working with ODBC Data Sources

Many people see Open Database Connectivity (ODBC) as old hat—technology that has gone the way of the dinosaur. However, this technology is still alive and well for many applications because it's so universal. You'll find that there are many more ODBC database drivers than any other type for Windows systems. Consequently, even though this technology is outdated, many developers still use it because ODBC is very reliable, available on just about any Windows system, and well understood. The following sections describe two ODBC command line topics.

NOTE   This discussion shows how to configure ODBC sources at the command line. It doesn't demonstrate how to create database applications based on those sources, nor does it tell you how to create a data source for a specific vendor product. Refer to a programming manual for your language of choice to discover how to work with ODBC data sources in an application. Your database product manual should contain information about how to configure the database for use with ODBC.

Configuring the ODBC Environment with the ODBCConf Utility

The ODBCConf utility helps you configure ODBC at the command line, rather than using the ODBC Data Source Administrator utility available in the Administrative Tools folder of the Control Panel—listed as the Data Sources (ODBC) console. You can use this utility to configure new data sources, check data source status, and perform other tasks on a remote machine from the command line. This utility uses the following syntax:

```
ODBCConf [/S] [/C] [/R] [/F Filename] [/E] [/L{n | v | d} Filename] [/A {Action}]
```

The following list describes each of the command line arguments.

/S   Prevents ODBCConf from displaying any error messages. Normally, it's a better idea to redirect the error message output to an error log when working with a remote system so that you can determine whether the actions succeeded.

/C   Forces ODBCConf to continue executing actions even if an action fails. This command line switch works well in situations where you need to perform multiple independent actions.

/R   Performs the requested actions after a system reboot.

/F *Filename*   Performs actions based on an input file. The response file contains a list of actions and all of the required input information. This option is often the best solution when you plan to perform a configuration on multiple machines or multiple times on the same machine.

/E   Erase the response file when the action completes. Use this command line switch with the /F switch.

/L{n | v | d} *Filename*   Sets the ODBCConf utility to output a log. You must provide a logging mode of (n)ormal, (v)erbose, or (d)ebug, along with a filename for the log. For example, /Lv MyLog.LOG would output a log in verbose mode to the MyLog.LOG file. The normal mode outputs the least information, while the debug mode outputs the most information. Using debug mode consumes considerable disk space and slows execution of any actions. You must use this command line switch to see any changes that ODBCConf makes since the utility doesn't display successful actions.

/A *{Action}*   Defines one or more actions to perform. The action must appear within curly brackets ({}).

The ODBCConf utility requires some type of action input to perform any task. You can provide a list of actions directly on the command line or you can use a response file. When working at the command line, you can include multiple /A command line switch entries. The ODBCConf utility executes these switches in order, so you must create the command line to reflect the required order. For example, you can't register a new Microsoft Data Access Components (MDAC) version until after you register its accompanying server. The following list describes each of the documented actions for the ODBCConf utility (some people have reported undocumented actions that I wasn't able to confirm).

REGMDACVERSION *Version*   Registers a new version of the MDAC as specified by the Version argument. Normally, Microsoft performs this task for you as part of installing the new MDAC on your machine.

SETFILEDSNDIR   Changes the File DSN directory to the specified value. The default setting is the \Program Files\Common Files\ODBC\Data Sources directory.

TIP Whenever you work with directory names that contain spaces, always enclose the directory name in double quotes. For example, to change the File DSN directory, you might type **ODBCConf /lv ODBCConf.log /a {SETFILEDSNDIR "F:\Program Files\Common Files\ODBC\ Data Sources"}**. Notice that the directory name is enclosed in double quotes so that the command line utility treats it as a single entity.

INSTALLDRVRMGR Installs a new driver manager.

INSTALLDRIVER *Configuration Path* Installs a new ODBC driver. The configuration argument is the configuration name, which you modify using the CONFIGDRIVER action. You must obtain this information from the database vendor. In fact, some vendors, such as Oracle, do provide files with all of the required information provided. The path is the location of the new driver.

INSTALLTRANSLATOR *Configuration Path* Installs a new code page translator. The configuration argument is a name that you use to reference the code page translator configuration. Modify the configuration using the CONFIGDRIVER action. You must obtain the configuration data from the database vendor. The path is the location of the new driver.

CONFIGDRIVER *Name Parameters* Configures a driver for use. The name argument is the name of the driver configuration supplied as part of an INSTALLDRIVER or INSTALLTRANSLATOR action. The parameters argument contains name value pairs that define the configuration for the driver. The name is followed by an equals sign, which is followed by the argument. You can use this action to configure an existing driver on the user's machine as long as you know the driver configuration name.

CONFIGDSN *Name {DSN | Attributes}* Creates a new user DSN entry that's accessible only by the current user. The name is the name of the driver supplied during installation. The DSN is the name of the DSN as it will appear in the ODBC Data Source Administrator utility. The attributes describe the information required to make the database connection. For example, a SQL Server DSN might include these arguments: `"SQL Server" "DSN=Northwind|Server= (Local)|Description=SQL Server|Database=Northwind||"`. In this case, the DSN uses the SQL Server configuration. The action creates a DSN named Northwind that uses the (Local) instance of SQL Server and the Northwind database.

CONFIGSYSDSN *Name {DSN | Attributes}* Creates a new system DSN entry that's accessible by everyone on a particular machine. In all other ways, this action works like the CONFIGDSN action.

REGSVR *Path* Registers a new MDAC server on the machine. The path argument specifies the location of the server DLL. You normally combine this action with the REGMDACVERSION action to register a new MDAC server.

Creating an ODBC Data Source at the Command Line

More than a few people have experienced problems using the ODBCConf utility because it often requires use of complex command line syntax. However, there's an easier way of adding an ODBC data source to a remote machine. Simply add the data source using a file DSN. These DSN files normally appear in the \Program Files\Common Files\ODBC\Data Sources folder of the remote system. Adding a DSN file automatically adds the DSN to the remote machine. (The application must take the file DSN into account or adding the DSN using this technique might not work.)

Although every database uses a different configuration strategy, the file DSN is always a text file with a DSN extension. It's essentially a form of INI (initialization or configuration) file. Here's an example file DSN for an Access database.

```
[ODBC]
DRIVER=Microsoft Access Driver (*.mdb)
UID=admin
UserCommitSync=Yes
Threads=3
SafeTransactions=0
PageTimeout=5
MaxScanRows=8
MaxBufferSize=2048
FIL=MS Access
DriverId=25
DefaultDir=G:\Access
DBQ=G:\Access\db1.mdb
```

Notice that this DSN includes such information as the database driver and the user identifier. It also includes the location of the Access database and other information to control access to it. You can easily create such a file using the ODBC Data Source Administrator utility, make any required changes to the text file for the remote system, and then copy it to the remote system's file DSN directory.

Managing Windows in a New Way

You'll work with data in many ways as an administrator. Data isn't just the files that users create—it's also the configuration files you use or any other form of information that someone or something creates. The information in this chapter helps you administer data. In most cases, you'll use other applications to create the data, but managing it is important. This chapter helps you build these skills:

- Manage files
- Compress and expand files
- Output files to a device
- Take ownership of files
- Manage file types and associations
- Work with the ODBC functionality

Now that you have the knowledge required to throw out Windows Explorer, you'll want to exercise your new freedom. Create a temporary directory on your server and fill it with copies of files that you won't need later. Try out the various commands and utilities in this chapter. Especially important is learning to use the utilities that perform a lot of tasks at once, such as RoboCopy. Although playing around with these new commands is fun, you also have a critical task to perform. If you haven't made a backup of your server already, now is the time to use the WBAdmin utility to do it. Even your test server has some value and you should take the time to back it up regularly, if for no other reason than to practice the techniques required to back up your production servers.

There is more to discover about files and directories. For example, you'll eventually want to check your hard drive for errors and set security on both the files and directories. Chapter 15 provides everything you need to know about these tasks and more.

Chapter 15

Managing Files and Directories

Files and directories are storage containers for data. In Chapter 14, you discovered many of the utilities that help you manage data. However, you haven't yet discovered the techniques for managing the storage containers that hold the data. Even a database manager relies on files to provide permanent data storage, so the information you find here applies even to complex data scenarios.

The files and directories on your hard drive require management. Normally, the application performs this management directly as part of performing its tasks. However, you may find the need to perform some management tasks manually. For example, a file may have a system or other attribute attached to it that won't allow you to move the file. Normally, you'd leave such a file alone, but you may find the need to move it, which means removing the attributes, moving the file, and reapplying the attributes.

All of the files and directories on your system appear as part of another container, the hard drive. You'll find most of the hard drive–related utilities in Chapter 9 of the book. However, this chapter contains a number of hard drive utilities that affect management of the files and directories. For example, when the hard drive encounters an error, the error affects the files and directories, so you'll find those management utilities in this chapter.

A final consideration for files and directories is security. Security consists of setting file and directory attributes known as Access Control Lists (ACLs) to control access. However, access control isn't always enough, so you must also perform file and directory monitoring. In many cases, someone with ill intent will leave fingerprints that will tell you about their activities. Monitoring is the only way to see the fingerprints these individuals leave behind.

In this chapter, you'll learn how to do the following:

- Manage file attributes and status information
- Perform hard drive maintenance related to files and directories
- Encrypt and compress file and directory entries on the hard drive
- Locate files based on various criteria
- Secure and monitor files and directories

Changing File and Directory Attributes with the Attrib Utility

The Attrib (attribute) utility lets you discover the attributes attached to a given file in an unambiguous way. Attributes are special notations that the file system makes about the folder or file. For example, when you modify a file, the file system sets the archive attribute, which tells your backup program that the file has changed. When the backup program makes a copy of the file, it resets the archive attribute. See the "Standard FAT and NTFS File Attributes" sidebar for additional details about attributes. This utility uses the following syntax:

```
ATTRIB [{+R | -R}] [{+A | -A }] [{+S | -S}] [{+H | -H}]
[drive:][path][filename] [/S [/D] [/L]]
```

The following list describes each of the command line arguments.

+ Sets an attribute.

- Clears an attribute.

R Modifies the read-only file attribute.

A Modifies the archive file attribute.

S Modifies the system file attribute.

H Modifies the hidden file attribute.

[drive:][path]*filename* Defines one or more files to modify or query. You can use wildcard characters to define the file specification. Specifying a file specification without any attribute changing command line switches displays the attributes for those files. Using Attrib by itself, without any file specification, displays the attributes for all files in the directory. This technique even displays system and hidden files.

/S Processes files that match the file specification in the current directory and all subdirectories.

/D Processes the directories as well as the files that match the file specification.

/L Processes the attributes of a symbolic link, rather than the symbolic link's target.

You can also use the Attrib utility to locate files with a specific attribute. It works much the same as the Dir (directory) command at the command prompt, but the focus is on the attributes, rather than other file or folder information. To test this command, open a command prompt in the root directory (the uppermost directory) of your C drive, type **Attrib *.*** at the command prompt, and press Enter. You'll see a list of all of the files in the root directory, along with their associated attributes. For example, many of the files will have an A for archive next to them. Some files, such as ntldr, will have the S (system), H (hidden), and R (read-only) attributes.

It's possible to view and change the attributes (except system) for a file using Windows Explorer. To change an attribute, right-click the file and choose Properties from the context menu. You'll see the file Properties dialog box. The Read-only and Hidden options on the General tab modify these attributes on the file. Click Advanced and you'll see the Advanced Attributes dialog box that contains the File Is Ready for Archiving option that controls the archive attribute. Although this method is aesthetically pleasing, you have to change the files one at a time. Using Attrib, you can change a number of files using a single command. For example, if you want to remove the system, hidden, and read-only attributes from every executable in a particular folder, you'd type:

```
Attrib -h -r -s *.EXE
```

Real World Scenario

STANDARD FAT AND NTFS FILE ATTRIBUTES

Everyone categorizes the data they create. For example, you might make a differentiation between data and executable files, and then further categorize the data by the application that created it. Categorizing files is important because the categorization process helps you define the file and specify what it does for you. The operating system categorizes files, too, and in a way that you can use to your advantage. By knowing how to use attributes, you can differentiate between files that the system uses (ones that you normally don't need to worry about) and those that you use.

A friend of mine was relating a story about another use for attributes. You use attributes as a means of determining how the operating system interacts with files. Many companies now enforce a policy of setting hidden files so they remain hidden, even in Windows. Otherwise, users will delete files they shouldn't, which is where this story began. It seems that one user deleted all of the "extraneous" files on her system to make room for more data files, files such as Command.COM, Config.SYS, and AutoExec.BAT. The next morning, the user complained that the system wouldn't boot. After restoring the system, the network administrator warned the user not to delete any more files. The next month, the user did the same thing all over again. It wasn't long before the company had a new "no delete" policy in place, which remains in force today for Windows users.

The File Allocation Table (FAT) file system used with DOS and older versions of Windows, the File Allocation Table 32-bit (FAT32) file system used with Windows 95 and above, and the Windows NT File System (NTFS) used with versions of Windows starting with Windows NT, rely on file attributes to identify particular file conditions. For example, the archive attribute shows that the file has changed since the last full backup. The command line utilities described in this book can't access all of these attributes directly. For example, even though some utilities can perform a task based on the offline attribute, none of them can manipulate this attribute in any significant way. All of the inaccessible attributes appear as part of NTFS. The following list describes the attributes that you can access using the command line utilities.

A   The operating system sets this attribute whenever a file or directory experiences a change. The attribute alerts backup applications to the need for creating a backup of the file under specific conditions. However, you can also use the attribute to monitor the system for unexpected changes. For example, unless you've recently updated a particular Windows DLL, the archive attribute should remain clear (unset). A change in the attribute status could indicate the activities of a cracker.

D   The directory attribute indicates that a file system entry is a directory, a container for other files and directories. You can use the directory in a number of ways—everything from mapping the structure of your hard drive to locating hidden entities on the hard drive. Many viruses now rely on hidden directories to store their data.

H   The hidden file attribute indicates that you normally can't see the file as part of a directory listing. The file still exists and the operating system can still access it. The original intent of the hidden attribute was to keep system and other sensitive files hidden from users who might accidentally modify or delete them. Windows generally makes this feature obsolete by showing all files, hidden or not, unless you set the operating system not to display them by selecting the "Do not show hidden files and folders" option on the View tab of the Folder Options dialog box. However, the hidden attribute still keeps files hidden from the view of command line utilities, so you need to know it exists.

R The read-only attribute ensures that you can't change, delete, or even move a file without seeing an error message. The read-only attribute commonly appears as part of operating system files. However, developers also use it with read-only data for applications and you might even see it in use for other purposes, such as license files. Windows does honor the read-only attribute, so you can't easily override the effects of this attribute no matter how you access the file.

S The system attribute marks a file as one that the operating system relies on to perform essential tasks. Generally, you don't want to change, delete, or modify files marked with this attribute—doing so could cause the operating system to freeze, refuse to boot, or behave erratically.

L Symbolic links are essentially pointers to a physical file or folder somewhere else on the drive, another local drive, or even a network drive. The symbolic link makes it unnecessary to track where a file or folder exists. Instead, you focus on the data itself. A directory entry marked as a symbolic link has no real content—just the pointer to the actual file or folder.

Determining File and Directory Status with the ChkDsk Utility

The ChkDsk utility has been around in various forms from the days of DOS—before Windows appeared on the scene. Of course, Microsoft keeps adding features to this utility and it now runs as part of Windows, instead of part of DOS, but the concept remains the same. You use ChkDsk to perform a basic check of the hard drive. In addition, you can optionally use it to recover lost clusters and attempt repairs on damaged clusters. This utility uses the following syntax:

```
CHKDSK [volume[[path]filename]]] [/F] [/V] [/R] [/X] [/I] [/C] [/L[:size]] [/B]
```

The following list describes each of the command line arguments.

/F Adds fixing media errors to the list of tasks to perform. This switch differs from /R, which recovers clusters lost when an application terminates unexpectedly.

/R Adds recovering lost clusters to the list of tasks to perform. Using this switch also adds the /F switch automatically.

/V Displays the full path and name of every file on the disk. Use this switch only on FAT- or FAT32-formatted drives.

/L [*Size*] Outputs the current size of the log file used to track drive activity when you use the /L switch alone. Including the optional log file size modifies the size of the log for the current drive. Theoretically, a larger log could help improve drive reliability, but in practice, the default size normally works well. Use this switch only on NTFS-formatted drives.

/X Forces the operating system to dismount a drive before performing a check. Dismounting the drive makes all drive resources unavailable, but also ensures uninterrupted access by ChkDsk, which can help improve the results of any tasks performed. The operating system must mount a drive before you can access the drive contents again. Use this switch only on NTFS-formatted drives.

/I Performs a less robust check of the drive indexes (the portion of the drive used to locate files). Normally, you won't use this switch when you want to check a drive for optimum performance. However, you can use this switch to reduce the time required to check the drive. Use this switch only on NTFS-formatted drives.

/C Skips checking cycles within the drive folders. When a folder contains cyclical references, damage to the files can result. Consequently, even though this switch does reduce the time to check the drive, you want to avoid using it because ChkDsk doesn't thoroughly check the drive otherwise. Use this switch only on NTFS-formatted drives.

/B Reevaluates bad clusters on the hard drive. If the cluster is readable, ChkDsk places it back into service. This option is only available on NTFS drives and using it also includes the /R command line switch.

To use ChkDsk to perform a basic check, type **ChkDsk** at the command prompt and press Enter. ChkDsk always assumes that you want to check the current drive. When you want to check a different drive, add the drive letter to the command. In addition, when you're working a FAT-formatted drive, you can specify a specific file. For example, you could type **ChkDsk C:\DRVSPACE.BIN** to check the DRVSPACE.BIN file on drive C.

NOTE You can't use ChkDsk directly on the Windows (boot) drive with either the /F or /R options because Windows needs access to specific files at all times. Use the ChkNTFS utility to repair the Windows drive. It's possible to use ChkDsk in the read-only mode to look for potential errors without fixing.

Performing Boot Time Disk Checks with the ChkNTFS Utility

Most of the hard drives used with Windows today rely on NTFS because it's more robust. It provides data encryption, extra security, and built-in file compression. In addition, NTFS is more reliable than the older FAT file system. (Even though you can't install Server Core on a FAT formatted drive, you can still use it to access FAT formatted drive, such as flash drives, so it's still important to know about the FAT file system.) However, NTFS also requires a little more care at times because it's more complex than FAT. The following sections describe how to use the ChkNTFS utility and how the associated AutoChk application enhances ChkNTFS at boot time.

Using the ChkNTFS Utility

The ChkNTFS utility works with ChkDsk to ensure your system remains problem free. You won't see the effects of this utility right away in most cases. This utility sets up your drive to use ChkDsk during the boot process, rather than after Windows has booted, to ensure you can gain full access to the drive. The drive repair can occur without Windows interference. When you select a drive for a scan, ChkNTFS says that it's dirty. Therefore, when you see that the drive isn't dirty, that means ChkNTFS hasn't scheduled it for a check. A drive can also become dirty when Windows detects an error on it. This utility uses the following syntax:

```
CHKNTFS volume [...]
CHKNTFS /D
CHKNTFS /T[:time]
CHKNTFS /X volume [...]
CHKNTFS /C volume [...]
```

To use ChkNTFS, you must provide a drive argument or one of the command line switches at a minimum. When you supply a drive argument, ChkNTFS tells you the drive format and determines whether Windows has scheduled it for a check. The following list describes each of the command line arguments.

volume   Determines the volume to check for errors. You can specify the volume using a drive letter followed by a colon, a mount point, or a volume name.

/D   Places all of the drives in the default state. You can use this switch to remove a drive from the checklist when you schedule the check. This switch won't reverse a mandatory check due to an error detected by Windows.

/T[:*Time*]   Tells how much time the utility allows before it begins the check sequence during boot time when you use this switch by itself. The automatic countdown lets you decide at boot time whether to run ChkDsk as planned. Supplying the optional time value modifies the countdown timer to give the user more or less time to make the ChkDsk decision. The default automatic countdown value is 10 seconds.

/X *Volume*   Excludes one or more drives from a check. You use this option when you set up the system to perform ChkDsk every time it boots. This is a one time switch—Windows excludes the drive for one boot cycle.

/C *Volume*   Schedules a drive for a check during the next boot cycle.

TIP   You don't have to use ChkNTFS to perform some tasks. For example, when you want to set up a drive for a scan, right-click the drive in Windows Explorer and choose Properties from the context menu. Select the Tools tab and click Check Now. You'll see a Check Disk dialog box. Check both of the repair options and click Start. When working with a boot drive, Windows Explorer displays an error saying that it couldn't complete the check. It then offers the chance to perform the check later during the next boot. Click Yes and Windows Explorer sets up the check.

Understanding How AutoChk Works with ChkNTFS

AutoChk is a non-Windows application; you can't run it from the command prompt. However, the utility does run during the boot process, which is when you'll see it at work. The AutoChk utility determines which volumes to check at boot time based on entries it finds in the registry. The HKEY_ LOCAL_MACHINE\SYSTEM\CurrentControlSet\Control\Session Manager key normally contains a value that indicates that AutoChk should check all volumes for the dirty bit (attribute), which means that they require a boot time check.

The dirty bit is an indicator. You can manually set the dirty bit by using the ChkNTFS utility or request that the system set it when using the ChkDsk utility on a drive that is locked. In addition, the system sets the dirty bit whenever one of a number of errors occurs. Finally, you can modify the registry so that AutoChk performs specific tasks whenever you boot the system. The Microsoft Knowledge Base article at http://support.microsoft.com/kb/q218461/ provides additional information on this topic.

It's important to note the correspondence between commands you enter at the command prompt using ChkNTFS and the corresponding change to the registry that results in AutoChk running during the boot process. For example, if you enter **ChkNTFS D: E: /X** at the command prompt, the system actually enters **Autocheck AutoChk /k:D /k:E** * into the registry. The /k AutoChk command line switch excludes the specified drive from checks during the boot process.

Encrypting Data with the Cipher Utility

The Cipher utility provides encryption status information about files and directories on your hard drive. It relies on the encryption capabilities built into NTFS and doesn't work with FAT-formatted drives. Windows registers encrypted files in the name of the current user, so the encryption is seamless. The only time you actually see the encryption at work is when you try to open files or directories encrypted by someone else. This utility uses the following syntax:

```
CIPHER [/E | /D | /C] [/S:directory] [/A] [/I] [/F] [/Q] [/B] [/H]
   [pathname [...]]
CIPHER /K
CIPHER /R:filename [/Smartcard]
CIPHER /U [/N]
CIPHER /W:directory
CIPHER /X[:efsfile] [filename]
CIPHER /Y
CIPHER /ADDUSER [/CERTHASH:hash | /CERTFILE:filename] [/S:directory]
   [/B] [/H] [pathname [...]]
CIPHER /REMOVEUSER /CERTHASH:hash [/S:directory] [/B] [/H]
   [pathname [...]]
CIPHER /REKEY [pathname [...]]
```

The following list describes each of the command line arguments.

pathname Defines the location of a file to encrypt or query. The pathname includes the drive, path, and filename. The pathname can include multiple files or directories; separate each file or directory with a space. You may also use wildcard characters with a pathname.

directory Defines an absolute or relative directory path. The directory can contain a drive when you use an absolute path. You can't specify a filename as part of the directory argument.

filename Defines a filename without a file extension. You can't include a drive or path as part of the filename. The filename can't contain wildcard characters.

efsfile Defines an Encrypting File System (EFS) path that can include a drive, path, and filename.

/A Performs tasks on files as well as directories. The file and its associated parent directory receive any changes you make to the file alone. The reason you want to change the parent directory is that an encrypted file can become decrypted when you modify it in a directory that you haven't encrypted. Microsoft recommends that you encrypt both the file and its parent directory. You also use this command line switch to encrypt just the file. For example, if you want to encrypt a file named NewFile.TXT, you'd type **Cipher /A /E /F NewFile.TXT** at the command prompt and press Enter.

/ADDUSER Adds a user as someone who can access an encrypted file. You must provide a credential for the user to use when accessing the file. Cipher makes it possible to use a certificate hash or a certificate file. When using a certificate file, Cipher accesses the certificate hash in the file and records it.

/B Aborts the encryption when encountering an error. By default, Cipher attempts to continue the encryption.

/C Displays information about the encrypted file.

/CERTFILE:filename Specifies the name of file that contains a hash for the user.

/CERTHASH:hash Provides the actual hash used to define security access for the user.

/D Decrypts the specified directories or files. When working with a directory, the directory is marked so the system won't encrypt files added to it afterward. You must include the /A command line switch to work with files.

/E   Encrypts the specified directories or files. When working with a directory, the directory is marked so that the system automatically encrypts any files added to it afterward. You must include the /A command line switch to work with files.

/F   Forces the encryption operation on all specified objects, even those that the system has already encrypted. Normally, the system skips any files that are already encrypted. You may have to use this switch when working with files in some instances.

/H   Forces the system to work with files (encrypt, decrypt, or query) that have the hidden or system attributes. Normally, the system skips files with these attributes.

/I   Forces Cipher to continue performing tasks even after it experiences an error. Normally, Cipher stops performing tasks when it encounters an error. Using this command line switch allows a batch file to continue processing files, even when some of the files failed to react as anticipated. You should redirect the output to a log file when using this option to track the errors and take any required remedial action when the task completes.

/K   Defines a new encryption key for the user running Cipher. You can't use any other command line switches with this command line switch. The system displays a message that includes the new key when you use this option. Save this thumbprint to a file so that you can use it to open files encrypted on one machine on another machine. The Microsoft Knowledge Base article at `http://support.microsoft.com/kb/295680/` describes this process in detail. Never let anyone see or use your encryption key because they can use the key to access your encrypted files.

/N   Prevents the system from updating keys used to encrypt files. Use this command line switch with the /U switch to locate all encrypted files on a local drive without actually performing any updates. Use redirection to place the list of encrypted files in a text file for later use.

/Q   Reports only essential information, such as errors, rather than general information including success messages.

/R   Generates an EFS recovery agent key and certificate. Cipher writes them to a PFX file (which contains the certificate and private key) and a CER file (that contains only the certificate). An administrator can use these files to add the certificate to another machine or as a means of recovering encrypted files on the current machine. The Microsoft Knowledge Base article at `http://support.microsoft.com/kb/887414` describes this process in detail.

/REKEY   Updates the specified files to use the current configured EFS key. This option uses the key associated with the current user account. The user must have the required access using the old key and also have a new current key. You use this option to update files before discarding an old key.

/REMOVEUSER   Removes a user from the list of users who can share a common encrypted file. You must supply the actual security hash value for the user. In addition, you must supply the Secure Hashing Algorithm 1 (SHA1) hash value for the certificate.

/S   Performs the requested tasks in the current directory and all subdirectories.

/Smartcard   Writes the recovery key and certificate to a smart card, rather than writing the information to a file. You use this option with the /R command line switch. This option requires that you install special hardware on your system, including a device for writing to smart cards.

/U   Touches all of the encrypted files on local drives. This action updates the user's encryption key or recovers the agent's key to the current keys, using any of the techniques described in this section (such as using the /K command line switch), if you've changed them. This command line switch fails with encrypted files that don't belong to the current user. However, it does list all of the encrypted files even if they belong to another user. Use this command line switch with the /N switch if you want to list the encrypted files without changing them.

/W Removes (wipes) data from the available unused disk space on the entire volume. You must use this option alone. You can specify any directory on the local hard drive. When working with a mount point, the Cipher utility removes the data from the remote drive. Use this option with care since it wipes out all data from deleted files, making recovery with most recovery tools impossible. The Microsoft Knowledge Base article at `http://support.microsoft.com/kb/315672/` provides details on how to perform this task safely.

/X Creates a backup of the current EFS certificate and keys into the specified file. If you supply the EFSFile input, the utility only backs up the current user's certificate. Otherwise, the utility backs up both the EFS certificate and any required keys.

/Y Displays your current EFS certificate thumbnail on the local PC.

When used by itself, the Cipher utility displays the current encryption state of files in the current directory. You can supply a directory without any other arguments to see the encryption state of files in other directories. The utility shows all encrypted files with an F and all unencrypted files with a U.

Compressing Data with the Compact Utility

One of the advantages of using NTFS is the file compression feature that it includes. Using file compression means that you can store more information on a single hard drive. In addition, due to the manner in which hard drives work, you can experience a small performance gain by using compression (compaction). This utility uses the following syntax:

```
COMPACT [/C | /U] [/S[:dir]] [/A] [/I] [/F] [/Q] [filename [...]]
```

The following list describes each of the command line arguments.

/C Compresses the specified files or directories. Using this command line switch on a directory marks it so that the system automatically compresses any files added afterward.

/U Uncompresses the specified files or directories. Using this command line switch on a directory marks it so that the system doesn't compress any files added afterward.

/S[:*dir*] Performs the specified tasks on the current directory or the directory included as an argument and all subdirectories. The default is the current directory.

/A Forces the system to work with files (compress, uncompress, or query) that have the hidden or system attributes. Normally, the system skips files with these attributes.

/I Forces Compact to continue performing tasks even after it experiences an error. Normally, Compact stops performing tasks when it encounters an error. Using this command line switch allows a batch file to continue processing files, even when some of the files failed to react as anticipated. You should redirect the output to a log file when using this option to track the errors and take any required remedial action when the task completes.

/F Forces the compression operation on all specified objects, even those that the system has already compressed. Normally, the system skips any files that are already compressed. You may have to use this switch when working with files in some instances.

/Q Reports only essential information such as errors, rather than general information including success messages.

filename Specifies the file or directory name to work with. You can use all of the standard wildcard combinations to specify multiple files or directories. See the "Working with Wildcard Characters" sidebar in Chapter 14 for details.

When used by itself, the Compact utility displays the current compaction state of files in the current directory, as shown in Figure 15.1. You can supply a directory without any other arguments to see the compaction state of files in other directories. The utility shows all compacted files with a C; all normal files have a space in place of the C. In addition to the compaction state, the standard output includes the actual file size, the compacted file size, and the compaction ratio. Unlike other utilities, Compact doesn't use a tabular format—each line contains a continuous entry that shows the information used to determine the compaction ratio. The bottom of the display shows the statistics for the directory including the number of compacted files, the actual and compacted size of all of the files, and the compaction ratio for the directory as a whole.

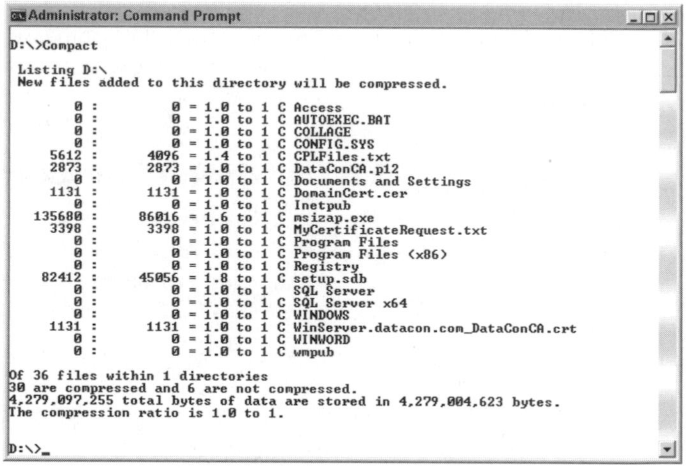

FIGURE 15.1

Use the Compact utility to discover how much space you save by using this feature.

Finding Files and Directories with the *Dir* Command

The `Dir` command offers a broad range of command line switches that makes looking for a file faster than you might think. Remembering all of the command line switches isn't necessarily easy, but you'll use some of them more often than you use others. In addition to command line switches, you can use wildcard characters to extend the functionally of the search. See the "Working with Wildcard Characters" sidebar in Chapter 14 for details on working with wildcard characters. This command uses the following syntax:

```
DIR [drive:][path][filename] [/A[[:]attributes]] [/B] [/C] [/D] [/L]
[/N] [/O[[:]sortorder]] [/P] [/Q] [/R] [/S] [/T[[:]timefield]] [/W]
[/X] [/4]
```

The following list describes each of the command line arguments.

/A[[:]*attributes*] Displays files with the specified attributes. An attribute defines the file system characteristics of a file. For example, a file with a hidden attribute isn't visible from the command prompt unless you use the /AH command line switch. You can also exclude a file with a specific attribute from the search by adding the minus (-) sign in front of the attribute. For example, specifying the /-AD switch would exclude directories from the output. See the sidebar, "Standard FAT and NTFS File Attributes" for a list of the command line attributes you can check from the command line.

/B   Removes the heading and summary information from the output. You can use this feature to prepare a directory listing for a batch file or a script. It also comes in handy when you want to prepare a list of files for a report.

/C   Displays the thousand separator in file sizes, which is the default for most systems. This feature makes the file sizes easier to read. Use the /-C command line switch to remove the thousand separator from the file sizes.

/D   Displays the file output in a wide list format. Generally, this feature allows the display to hold more filenames at the expense of additional information, such as the file size. The Dir command sorts the list by column.

/L   Displays the output using lowercase characters. Generally, the Dir command displays the filenames using uppercase or mixed case characters. A mixed case character display is standard for the Windows command window.

/N   Displays files using the long list format where filenames appear on the far right of the display. This is the default setting for the Windows command window.

/O[[:]*sortorder*]   Lists the directory in a sorted order. Generally, Windows sorts the directory by name. Normally, the Dir command sorts items in ascending order. You can sort in descending order by adding a minus (-) sign to the command line switch. For example, /-AD would sort the directory in descending date order. You can use any of the sort orders for the output.

    E By extension (alphabetic)

    D By date/time (oldest first)

    G Group directories first

    N By name (alphabetic)

    S By size (smallest first)

/P   Pauses the output after each screen of information.

/Q   Displays the file owner information in addition to the standard file output.

/R   Displays the alternate data streams in a file. Previously, Windows only displayed the main data stream. Server Core lets you view the alternative data streams that many developers use to hide data from view.

/S   Displays the files in the specified directory and all subdirectories. Each subdirectory has a separate header unless you specify the /B command line switch.

/T[[:]*timefield*]   Determines which time field appears in the listing. The Dir command always uses the visible time field for sorting. The default setting shows the last modified date. Here are the time field values you can use.

    C Creation

    A Last Access

    W Last Written

/W Displays the file output in a wide list format. Generally, this feature allows the display to hold more filenames at the expense of additional information, such as the file size. The Dir command sorts the list by row.

/X Displays the short names generated for non-8.3 filenames (those used for DOS). The Dir command uses the same format as provided by the /N command line switch with the short name inserted in front of the long name. The display contains blanks for any long filenames that don't have an associated short filename.

/4 Displays the years with four digits. This is the default setting for the Windows command line.

 **Real World Scenario**

FINDING DATA FILES QUICKLY

It's no secret that people have trouble finding their data files. You also won't find many people who will say that Microsoft has done a good job of making it easier to find data files. Third-party utilities for locating information on your hard drive abound because Microsoft hasn't lived up to people's needs or expectations. Unfortunately, these third-party utilities also come with hidden security problems, making people wary of using them. In short, it appears that you can choose between not finding what you need or turning over the security of your system to someone else. However, I have a third alternative, one that works well and doesn't compromise security.

At one time, Microsoft did do a reasonable job of helping you find the data files that you need. The only problem is that they never updated the utilities that performed these tasks with a graphical interface, so you must use them at the command line. For example, judicious use of the Dir command will help you locate any file that you can name or identify by its attributes. For example, if you can't find a file based on the name because you don't remember it, don't worry; the Dir command can help you locate it based on the date you created it or on the file size and I guarantee that it works far better than Windows Explorer.

Of course, sometimes you don't know anything about a file except that it contains a certain reference. That's when I use the FindStr utility. You can search any file with it, not just data files, and locate the strings you want. I've even used this utility to find executables on my hard drive based on a prompt I remembered. In short, you already have the tools you need to find anything on your hard drive.

Locating Information in Files with the Find and FindStr Utilities

The Find and FindStr utilities both locate files based on their content. The Find utility is less capable than FindStr, in most cases. The Find utility uses the following syntax:

```
FIND [/V] [/C] [/N] [/T] [/OFF[LINE]] "string"
    [[drive:][path]filename[...]]
```

The following list describes each of the command line arguments.

/V Displays all of the lines that don't contain the specified string.

/C Displays a count of the lines containing the specified string, but not the actual location.

/N Displays the line number of each occurrence of the specified string within the file.

/I Ignores the case of the characters when searching for the string. Normally, the Find utility will treat Cat, CAT, and cat as different strings.

/OFF[LINE] Processes all of the specified files, even if they have the offline attribute set.

string Defines the text string that you want to find. The Find utility doesn't allow the use of regular expressions, so you can only locate strings based on their actual content.

[drive:][path]*filename* Defines the files to search for the specified string. You can use wildcard characters to define the file specification.

NOTE If you don't specify a path, the Find utility searches the text typed at the prompt or piped from another command. This feature means that you could use Find to perform tasks such as locating a particular file based on size in a directory listing (as an example). You can use redirection to let Find locate particular data in the output of any command or utility.

There's one use for Find that isn't found in FindStr—you can use Find to determine just the number of occurrences of the search string in the target file using the /C switch. This particular feature and the smaller size of Find make it useful for scripting tasks where FindStr is overkill.

The easiest way to use FindStr is to define a simple string and make the call. FindStr looks in all of the files in the current folder for any words in the string. For example, typing **FindStr "Hello World"** *.* at the command prompt and pressing Enter causes the FindStr utility to look for the individual words *Hello* and *World* in all files in the current folder. The FindStr utility uses the following syntax:

```
FINDSTR [/B] [/E] [/L] [/R] [/S] [/I] [/X] [/V] [/N] [/M] [/O]
[/P] [/F:file] [/C:string] [/G:file] [/D:dir list] [/A:color
attributes] [/OFF[LINE]] strings [[drive:][path]filename[...]]
```

The following list describes each of the command line arguments.

/B Matches the search string against the beginning of the line.

NOTE Some of the FindStr features are line related. A line of text or other data ends when FindStr encounters a special carriage return (character number 13) and line feed (character number 10) combination. When looking at a text file, you see one line of text separated from another by white space. The carriage return and line feed combination causes the white space. In DLLs and other unreadable files, there's no need for lines of text, so the carriage return and line feed combination appear irregularly, if at all. This means the lines are much larger and could include the entire file.

/E Matches the search string against the end of the line.

/L Interprets the search strings literally. This means you no longer have access to regular expressions, and you also don't have to escape the special characters.

/R Defines the search string as a regular expression. See the "Using Regular Expressions at the Command Prompt" sidebar for additional information.

/S Looks for the search string in the specified files in the current directory and all subdirectories. When you use this command line switch in the root directory of a hard drive, you can search the entire hard drive for a search string. Because FindStr actually looks in every file, you'll find this process can take a long time.

/I   Performs a case-insensitive search. Normally, FindStr differentiates between *Hello* and *hello*—using this command line switch changes that behavior so the two capitalizations are treated the same.

/X   Prints only the lines that match the search string exactly.

/V   Prints only the lines that don't contain an exact match.

/N   Prints the line number before each line that matches. This option helps you find the line faster in a text editor that supports line numbering.

/M   Prints only the filenames of files that contain a match. You can redirect the output from FindStr to a file to use as an input for a script or other additional processing.

/O   Prints the character offset of the matching text in each line. This option helps you find the text faster in text editors that provide column number support.

/P   Tells FindStr to skip files that contain nonprintable characters, such as executable files. Given that most data files now contain nonprintable characters, you should probably avoid using this option unless you know the data appears in pure text files.

/F:*File*   Reads the list of files to process from a file. You can also supply a value of "/" to type the names of the files to check at the command line.

/C:*String*   Performs a literal search with the search string. For example, normally when you type "**Hello World**" as the search string, FindStr looks for the words separately—lines containing either *Hello* or *World* will match. However, when you specify this option, FindStr only matches lines that contain the whole term, *Hello World*. This is actually one of the most useful command line switches for finding just about any information. Let's say you have a series of Word documents that you're using as help file and that you're looking for the Accessing Widgets header. You could type **FindStr /M /C:"Accessing Widgets" *.DOC** and press Enter to locate the required header. FindStr will print out a list of the files that contain the text you want to locate. However, let's say that you want to locate any mentions of this topic in the text instead of seeing just the headers. You could then modify the command line and type **FindStr /M /I /C:"Accessing Widgets" *.DOC** and press Enter to perform a case insensitive search.

/G:*File*   Reads the list of search strings to look for from a file. You can also supply a value of "/" to type the search strings at the command line.

/D:*Directories*   Defines a list of directories to search. You must separate each directory entry with a semicolon.

/A:*ColorAttribute*   Tells FindStr to display the filenames using colors. You must provide two hexadecimal (base 16) values from 0 through F (these values are the same as 0 through 15 decimal). The first value is the background color and the second is the text color. This switch doesn't affect display of the matching text color, which relies on the current background and foreground colors of the command prompt.

/OFF[LINE]   Processes all of the specified files, even if they have the offline attribute set.

strings   Defines one or more text strings that you want to find. Use regular expressions (the /R command line switch) to locate text based on wildcards.

[drive:][path]*filename*[...]   Defines one or more files to search for the specified string. You can use wildcard characters to define the file specification.

USING REGULAR EXPRESSIONS AT THE COMMAND PROMPT

The true power of FindStr and other advanced text manipulation command line utilities is that you can create specialized strings using a concept called regular expressions. A regular expression defines how to look for a string, rather than precisely which string to find. Regular expressions can contain the special characters described in the following list.

. (Period)   Provides a placeholder for any single character. For example, "w.ll" could represent the words *wall*, *well*, or *will*.

* (Asterisk)   Represents 0 or more occurrences of the previous character or class. For example, "to*" could represent the words *to* or *too*, or simply the letter *t*. (Because the asterisk can represent 0 occurrences of a letter, "to*" can find just the letter t because that's all that's left when you have 0 occurrences of the letter o.)

^ (Circumflex)   Represents a character or class at the beginning of a line. For example, "^Hello" would find the word in the line *Hello World*, but not in the line *George said, Hello*.

$ (Dollar sign)   Represents a character or class at the end of the line. For example, "World$" would find the word in the line *Hello World*, but not in the line *World Peace*.

[Characters]   Contains a character class (set of characters) from which FindStr selects. For example, "w[ai]ll" will match the words *wall* and *will*, but won't match *well*.

[^Characters]   Contains a character class (set of characters) that FindStr won't select. For example, "w[^ai]ll" will match the word *well*, but won't match the words *wall* or *will*.

[Character-Character]   Specifies a range of characters that FindStr will use for selection. For example, "[a-z]" selects all characters *a* through *z*, but not numbers or special symbols.

\Character   Tells FindStr to use the character literally, rather than as a special character. Programmers call this process escaping the character. For example, "z**" locates terms that begin with *z* followed by 0 or more asterisks within the file.

\<Characters   Locates the characters when they appear at the beginning of a word. For example, "\<we" locates the words *welcome* and *well*, but not the word *owe*.

Characters\>   Locates the characters when they appear at the end of a word. For example, "we\>" locates the word *owe*, but not the words *welcome* and *well*.

Using regular expressions lets you create complex search patterns that reduce search time and ensure good results. For example, you could create a telephone number search pattern using the search string "(...)...-...." assuming that your telephone numbers always include an area code and are formatted using the method shown. I've actually used this search pattern to locate telephone numbers hidden in DLLs.

Changing File and Directory Access with the ICACLS Command

Server Core places a significant new emphasis on security. Given the current computing environment, the emphasis is welcome. However, the new emphasis requires a new security utility as well. The ICACLs command replaces the older CACLs utility used in previous versions of Windows. Besides the information found in this chapter, you can find usage information for the ICACLS command in the "Setting Security" section of Chapter 3. This new command has an interesting array of command line syntaxes as shown here:

```
ICACLS Name /Save ACLFile [/T] [/C] [/L] [/Q]

ICACLS Directory [/Substitute SidOld SidNew [...]] /Restore ACLFile
[/C] [/L] [/Q]

ICACLS Name /SetOwner User [/T] [/C] [/L] [/Q]

ICACLS Name /FindSID SID [/T] [/C] [/L] [/Q]

ICACLS Name /Verify [/T] [/C] [/L] [/Q]

ICACLS Name /Reset [/T] [/C] [/L] [/Q]

ICACLS Name [/Grant[:r] SID:Permission[...]]
        [/Deny SID:Permission [...]]
        [/Remove[:g|:d]] SID[...]] [/T] [/C] [/L] [/Q]
        [/SetIntegrityLevel Level[...]]
```

The following list describes each of the command line arguments.

Name   Provides the name of an ACL to work with when using the ICACLs utility. For example, if you type **ICACLs C:** and press Enter, you'll see the Discretionary Access Control List (DACL) for the root folder of the C drive. Figure 15.2 shows typical output from this command. The /Grant command line switch explains the meanings of the letters after each user or group entry. Notice that some entries appear twice. For example, the Administrators group has modify access (M) in the first entry and object inherit (OI), container inherit (CI), inherit only (IO), full (F) access rights in the second. The first entry shows the Administrators group rights to the current folder, while the second shows the Administrators group rights to subfolders and files.

FIGURE 15.2

Supplying only a filename or directory displays the DACL for that filename or directory.

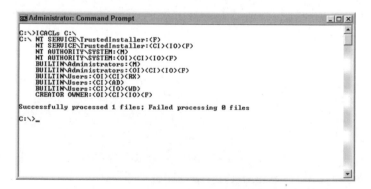

/Save   Stores all of the ACLs for the matching names into an ACL file for later use with the /Restore option. For example, if you type **ICACLs C:\ /Save MyAcls.TXT** and press Enter, you'll save all of the DACLs for the root directory of the C drive to a file named MyAcls.TXT.

ACLFile   Provides the name of a file used to store all of the ACLs.

/T   Changes the ACLs of the specified files or directories in the current directory and all sub-directories.

/C   Ignores access denied errors by moving to the next file or next action.

/Q   Performs the task in quiet mode. The utility doesn't display any success messages. You'll normally use this feature in a batch file to ensure the batch file user isn't bothered by messages. However, you won't want to use this feature while testing your batch file or performing tasks manually because this command line switch hides important status messages.

/L   Processes the ACLs of a symbolic link, rather than the symbolic link's target.

Directory   Defines a directory used to perform a task.

/Substitute *SidOld SidNew* **[...]**   Specifies that the command should substitute an old Security Identifier (SID) with the value of a new SID.

/Restore   Restores the content of an ACL file to either an old or new SID.

/SetOwner   Changes the owner of the specified items.

User   Defines the name of a user who is the subject of a particular task.

/FindSID   Locates all of the names that contain an ACL that mentions the specified SID.

SID   Specifies an SID to used to perform a task. The SID may appear in either friendly name form or numerical form. Append an asterisk (*) to the beginning of the SID when you use the numerical form.

/Verify   Locates all of the files that have security problems. The two specific checks verify that the file doesn't have an ACL that isn't in canonical form and that the ACL lengths are consistent with ACE counts. The ICACLs utility preserves the canonical order of the ACEs within an ACL. It follows this form:

- ◆ Explicit denials
- ◆ Explicit grants
- ◆ Inherited denials
- ◆ Inherited grants

/Reset   Replaces any custom file ACLs with the default inherited ACL. This action resets the file's security to a known state of accessibility.

/Grant[:r] *SID:Permission*   Grants the specified user the rights defined by the combination of an SID and associated permission. When you include the :r argument, the granted rights replace those the user currently holds. Otherwise, the new rights are in addition to those that the user already possesses. The Permission variable is actually a mask that you can specify in one of two forms: simple and specific. You can't mix the types in a single use of the utility. Here's the list of simple rights that you can assign.

- ◆ F (full access)
- ◆ M (modify access)
- ◆ RX (read and execute access)
- ◆ R (read-only access)
- ◆ W (write-only access)

Here's a list of the specific rights that you can assign.

- ◆ D (delete)
- ◆ RC (read control)
- ◆ WDAC (write DAC)
- ◆ WO (write owner)
- ◆ S (synchronize)
- ◆ AS (access system security)
- ◆ MA (maximum allowed)
- ◆ GR (generic read)
- ◆ GW (generic write)
- ◆ GE (generic execute)
- ◆ GA (generic all)
- ◆ RD (read data/list directory)
- ◆ WD (write data/add file)
- ◆ AD (append data/add subdirectory)
- ◆ REA (read extended attributes)
- ◆ WEA (write extended attributes)
- ◆ X (execute/traverse)
- ◆ DC (delete child)
- ◆ RA (read attributes)
- ◆ WA (write attributes)

When working with directories, you may also assign inheritance rights to the security settings. Inheritance rights apply to either simple or specific rights. Here's the list of inheritance rights.

- ◆ (OI) (object inherit)
- ◆ (CI) (container inherit)
- ◆ (IO) (inherit only)
- ◆ (NP) (don't propagate inherit)

/Deny *SID:Permission* Defines the specified user the rights defined by the combination of an SID and associated permission. When the system adds the specified deny ACE, it also removes any associated grant ACE that may appear in the user's list of rights. See the /Grant command line switch for an explanation of permissions.

/Remove[:[g|d]] *SID* Removes all occurrences of the specific SID within an ACL. When you add the :g argument, the system removes all grant ACEs associated with the SID. When you add the :d argument, the system removes all deny ACEs associated with the SID. The default action removes both grant and deny ACEs.

/SetIntegrityLevel *Level*[...]   Adds an integrity ACE to all of the matching files. You specify the integrity level as L (low), M (medium), or H (high). This option also accepts the inheritance options of CI (container inherit) and OI (object inherit) when working with directories.

You may have noticed in Figure 15.2 that the Administrators group doesn't have full access to the root directory. This is the default setting for Windows Server 2008, even the Server Core version. Having this limitation in place does protect the drive from viruses, rootkits, and adware to an extent, but can also prove encumbering when working at the command line as Server Core demands. Use these steps to remove this restriction.

1. Type **Takeown /A /F C:** and press Enter. This command takes ownership of C:\ for the Administrators group. You must take ownership or any attempt to change the access rights for administrators will fail.

2. Type **ICACLs C:\ /Grant:r Administrators:F /T /C** and press Enter. This command tells the ICACLs command to change the rights for C:\. The /Grant command line switch replaces the current rights for administrators (notice the :r entry) with full access. The /T command line switch indicates that the ICACLs is supposed to perform this replacement for all subdirectories and files and that it should ignore any errors it experiences. Figure 15.3 shows typical results from executing this command. The Administrators group now has full access to the root directory, however, you don't have full access yet, even if you are a member of the Administrators group. Notice that you still don't have access to the Program Files or Windows directories. That's because Microsoft places additional restrictions on these folders.

FIGURE 15.3
Change your rights to the root directory so you can perform administrative tasks.

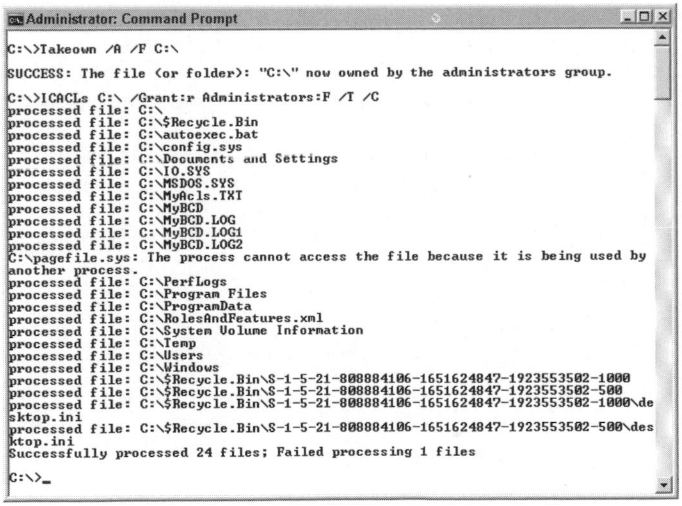

3. Type **Takeown /A /F C:\Windows** and press Enter.

4. Type **ICACLs C:\Windows /Grant:r Administrators:F /T /C** and press Enter. This particular step can take a long time to complete. Make sure you wait long enough before you assume something has gone wrong—in fact, just go get a cup of coffee while you're waiting.

5. Type **Takeown /A /F "C:\Program Files"** and press Enter (make sure you include the double quotes or the command won't work).

6. Type **ICACLs "C:\Program Files" /Grant:r Administrators:F /T /C** and press Enter. At this point, you should have the access required to perform administrative tasks (with the caveat that your system is also more exposed to possible outside attack).

7. Log off the system and log back in. This act replaces your personal ACL with the new one you created for the Administrators group.

Detecting Shared Open Files with the OpenFiles Command

The OpenFiles command helps you track open shared files on any system of a network. This utility has a number of purposes, but the most important is to ensure that a system has no shared files open before shutting it down. Even though Windows performs an orderly shutdown on the server, the client may have data stored in a local cache that could get lost when the server shuts down. You could also use this utility to look for signs of unwanted intrusion (either locally or from a remote source). A shared file that you can't account for could indicate the activities of a cracker or a disgruntled employee. The OpenFiles utility has three modes of operation, DISCONNECT, QUERY, and LOCAL, which are discussed in the sections that follow.

Disconnect

This mode disconnects a user or closes a file. You can use this mode to force a closure. In some cases, you might find this necessary when an application terminates abnormally and leaves the file in an uncertain state. This mode uses the following syntax:

```
OPENFILES /Disconnect [/S system [/U username [/P [password]]]]
{[/ID id] [/A accessedby] [/O {Read | Read/Write | Write}]}
[/OP openfile]
```

The following list describes each of the command line arguments.

WARNING   Always disconnect users or close files with care. Pursue every other possible means of disconnecting the user or closing the file before you use the DISCONNECT mode. Disconnecting users or closing files using this technique may corrupt the data file or cause the application to lose data because this method doesn't consider any of the data that appears in the application cache.

/S *system*   Specifies the remote system that you want to check. In most cases, you'll also need to supply the /U and the /P command line switches when using this switch.

/U *[domain\]user*   Specifies the username on the remote system. This name may not match the username on the local system. You'll need to supply a domain name when working with a domain controller.

/P *[password]*   Specifies the password for the given user. You can provide the command line switch without specifying the password on the command line in cleartext. The system prompts you for the password. Using this feature can help you maintain the security of passwords used on your system.

/ID *id*   Specifies the identifier of the file to disconnect. You may use the * wildcard to disconnect all currently shared files by identifier. Use the OPENFILES /Query mode to obtain the list of files currently open on the system, including the file identifier.

/A *username*   Disconnects all files opened by a particular user as specified by username. You can use the * wildcard to disconnect all currently shared files by username. Use the OPENFILES /Query mode to obtain the list of files currently open on the system, including the username.

/O {Read | Read/Write | Write}   Closes all files opened in a particular mode. The valid values include read, read/write, and write. You can use the * wildcard to disconnect all currently shared files by open mode. Use the OPENFILES /Query /V mode to obtain the list of files currently open on the system, including the open mode. Note that the standard display doesn't include the open mode, so you must specify the /V command line switch.

/OP *openfile*   Disconnects all open file connections created by a particular open filename. You can use the * wildcard to disconnect all currently shared files by filename. Use the OPENFILES /Query mode to obtain the list of files currently open on the system, including the name of the open file.

Query

Use this mode to obtain a list of the files currently open on a system. This mode uses the following syntax:

```
OPENFILES /Query [/S system [/U username [/P [password]]]]
[/FO {TABLE | LIST | CSV}] [/NH] [/V]
```

The following list describes each of the command line arguments.

/S *system*   Specifies the remote system that you want to check. In most cases, you'll also need to supply the /U and the /P command line switches when using this switch.

/U *[domain\]user*   Specifies the username on the remote system. This name may not match the username on the local system. You'll need to supply a domain name when working with a domain controller.

/P *[password]*   Specifies the password for the given user. You can provide the command line switch without specifying the password on the command line in cleartext. The system prompts you for the password. Using this feature can help you maintain the security of passwords used on your system.

/FO {TABLE | LIST | CSV}   Defines the output provided by the utility. The table format is normally the easiest to view on screen. The table columns define the values for output, while each row contains one driver entry. The CSV output provides the best method for preparing the data for entry in a database. Use redirection (see the "Employing Data Redirection" section of Chapter 14 for details) to output the CSV data to a file and then import it to your database. The list format provides one data element per line. Each group of data elements defines one driver. The utility separates each driver by one blank line. Some people find the list format more readable when working in verbose mode since the table format requires multiple lines for each entry (the lines wrap).

/NH   Forces the utility to display the data without a column header. You can only use this command line switch with the table and CSV formats. Omitting the header makes it easier to incorporate the data in a report or import it into a database.

/V   Displays detailed file information. The standard display includes the file identifier, accessed by information, file type, and filename complete with path. The extended information provided by this command line switch includes the hostname (server), number of locks, and the mode used to open the file (read, read/write, or write).

Local

This mode uses the following syntax:

```
OPENFILES /Local [{ ON | OFF }]
```

The following describes the command line argument.

{ ON | OFF }   Enables or disables the "maintain objects list" system global flag. The state of this flag determines whether the system tracks the state of local file handles. Enabling this flag adds overhead, which reduces performance, and also lets you track the status of shared files on your system. Calling the OPENFILES /Local mode without using this command line switch at all displays the current flag status, which is disabled on Windows systems.

Finding Files and Directories with the Where Utility

The Dir command provides you with a directory listing based on simple command line switches and wildcard characters. It's done the job for many years and is probably still the command of choice when you need to perform most file searches. The Where utility adds complex pattern matching to the search. The purpose of this command is to augment the features that Dir already provides. This command uses the following syntax:

```
WHERE [/R dir] [/Q] [/F] [/T] pattern...
```

The following list describes each of the command line arguments.

/R   Searches all of the subfolders for a given pattern starting from the specified directory. This option works the same as the /S command line switch used with other versions of Windows.

/Q   Performs the search in quiet mode. The utility only returns the exit code of the search. The valid exit codes include:

- ◆ 0: Search is successful
- ◆ 1: Search is unsuccessful
- ◆ 2: Other failures (such an incorrect syntax) caused the search to fail

/F   Displays the matched filename in double quotes. This feature makes it easier to parse the output when you place it in a file using redirection, rather than display it on screen.

/T   Displays the file size, last modified date, and time for all of the matched files. Normally, the Where utility displays only the filename.

pattern...   The pattern can include the * (asterisk) and ? (question mark), just as you'd use them with the Dir command. In addition, you can use environment variables by using the $EnvVariable:SearchCriteria pattern and a specific path using the Path:SearchCriteria pattern. These alternative search patterns let you look for data in ways that you can't using the Dir command. Here are some examples of all four search techniques:

```
Search for all DLLs in the current folder:
Where *.DLL
```

```
Search for all four letter DLLs beginning with the A in the current
folder:
Where A???.DLL

Search for all DLLs in the Path environmental variable:
Where $Path:*.DLL

Search for all DLLs in the C:\Programs and C:\Windows\System32 folder:
Where "C:\Program Files;C:\Windows\System32:B*.DLL"
```

Managing Windows in a New Way

The directories and files on your system act as storage containers for your data. If you don't secure the storage containers, then the data is at risk. It's akin to leaving the cookie jar open and not expecting anyone to grab a cookie, or two, or even the whole jar. The techniques described in this chapter help you secure the containers that hold your data, manage those containers to ensure they remain useful, and even perform repairs on the containers as needed. This chapter helps you build these skills:

◆ Manage file attributes and status information

◆ Perform hard drive maintenance related to files and directories

◆ Encrypt and compress file and directory entries on the hard drive

◆ Locate files based on various criteria

◆ Secure and monitor files and directories

Windows Explorer does provide useful functionality in that you can learn quite quickly who has access to a particular file or directory. However, the graphical interface can actually hide security holes in plain sight because people don't actually view the information that Windows Explorer provides until it's too late. The ICACLS command described in this chapter is an essential tool for securing your system and it pays to review the security you have in place at least.

This chapter also presents myriad other tools to help you manage the storage containers on the hard drive. One of my personal favorites is the FindStr utility because it can help you find data inside files faster than Windows Explorer ever could and with greater accuracy than Windows Explorer provides. Sometimes Microsoft does get something right and in this case, it's a utility. You'll want to spend time working with all of the utilities in this chapter because they're essential tools and unlike many of the commands and utilities in this book, you'll use these commands and utilities regularly to perform administrative work.

Chapter 16 shows how to perform another kind of configuration. In this case, you'll examine techniques you can use to configure the system. Even though you'll use these tools rarely, they're essential because they present the only way to accomplish the task. In fact, you may be surprised to learn that you'll use these tools in the graphical version of Windows Server 2008 as well because it doesn't provide a graphical tool to perform these tasks either. Chapter 16 is a chapter that you'll reference every once in a while, but you'll be glad it's here when you need it.

Chapter 16

Configuring the System Setup

Your system requires certain configuration and monitoring that isn't part of any application or the hardware, but part of the operating system itself. This chapter discusses three requirements that you'll always perform at the command line because there isn't any other way to perform these tasks. In fact, you'll probably use the information from this chapter even when working with the graphical version of Windows Server 2008. For example, you don't have any graphical means of changing the boot configuration in Windows Server 2008, you must use the BCDEdit utility.

In this chapter, you'll learn how to do the following:

◆ Manage the boot configuration using the BCDEdit command

◆ Access the WinPE network installer using the NetCfg utility

◆ Obtain system configuration information using the SystemInfo utility

Managing the Boot Configuration with the BCDEdit Command

The Boot Configuration Data Store Editor (BCDEdit) command is a powerful replacement for the BootCfg utility provided with previous versions of Windows. The main reason for the replacement is that Microsoft has significantly changed the boot cycle to accommodate new technologies such as BitLocker. The BCDEdit utility relies on commands, as do many utilities in Windows, but you access the commands from the command line, rather than using an interactive environment as you would when working with other utilities such as Telnet. You specify one or more commands in sequence to obtain specific results from BCDEdit. Consequently, this utility doesn't use a precise command line syntax, nor do the commands appear in any specific order. Here are the commands that you can use with their associated options.

/bootdebug [*ID*] {On | Off}   Turns boot debugging on or off. When you specify an identifier, the switch affects the specified application. You can use this command on any entry, but it only affects boot applications. If you specify this command without an identifier, the system sets boot debugging for the operating system loader.

NOTE   You can obtain a list of common identifiers by typing **BCDEdit /? ID** at the command line. The resulting list shows the common identifiers that could appear in the boot configuration, not those that actually do appear. Use the BCDEdit /enum command to display the identifiers that do appear as part of the configuration.

/bootems [*ID*] {On | Off}   Turns on or off Emergency Management Services (EMS) for the specified entry. When you specify an identifier, the switch affects the specified application. You can use this command on any entry, but it only affects boot applications. If you specify this command without an identifier, the system sets EMS for the operating system loader.

/bootsequence *ID* [...] [{/addfirst | /addlast | /remove}] Modifies the boot sequence. Use a single identifier with the /addfirst and /addlast options to add an identifier to the beginning or end of the boot sequence. Use the /remove option to remove the identifiers from the boot sequence.

[/store *Filename*] /copy *ID* /d *Description* Copies the specified identifier. The /d option specifies the description that you want assigned to the copy of the identifier. You may optionally store the copy in a different file using the /store option, which must appear in front of the /copy command.

/create [*ID*] /d *Description* [{/application *AppType* | /inherit [*AppType*] | /inherit DEVICE | /device}] Creates a new identifier. You can optionally specify an identifier for the new entry. The /d option provides a description of the new entry. The /application option creates a new application entry of one of the following types: BOOTSECTOR, OSLOADER, RESUME, or STARTUP. The /inherit option creates an inherit entry, one that's inherited by other entries. If you don't specify an application type, then any application can inherit the entry. The allowable inherit entry types include BOOTMGR, BOOTSECTOR, FWBOOTMGR, MEMDIAG, NTLDR, OSLOADER, and RESUME. The /inherit DEVICE option creates a special inherit entry that's only inherited by device options. The /device option creates a new device options entry.

NOTE The type information associated with the data store defines the format of the entry and how it affects the boot process. For example, an OSLOADER entry lets you load other operating systems. These options appear as part of the boot menu. Use the BCDEdit /? TYPES command to display a complete list of entry types. Add the type name to the command line and you'll see specific help for that type.

/createstore *Filename* Creates a new file that contains a boot configuration data store.

/dbgsettings [*DebugType* [DEBUGPORT:<port>] [BAUDRATE:*BAUD*] [CHANNEL:*Channel*] [TARGETNAME:*TargetName*] /start *StartPolicy* /noemux] Changes the debugger settings. Don't confuse this setting with /bootdebug, which chooses the items to debug. This setting affects the specified debugger type: SERIAL, 1394, or USB. Use the DEBUGPORT and BAUDRATE settings for serial port debugging, the CHANNEL setting for 1394 debugging, and the TARGETNAME setting for USB debugging. The /start option defines how the device starts and you can use these settings: ACTIVE, AUTOENABLE, or DISABLE. The /noemux option tells the kernel mode debugger to ignore any user-mode exceptions.

/debug [*ID*] {On | Off} Turns on or off kernel mode debugging. When you specify an identifier, the switch affects the specified Windows boot loader. You can use this command on any entry, but it only affects Windows boot loader entries. If you specify this command without an identifier, the system sets kernel mode debugging for the current boot loader.

/default *ID* Specifies the entry to use as the default boot manager. When the timer runs out, the system automatically boots the selected entry.

[/store *Filename*] /delete *ID* [/f] [/cleanup | /nocleanup] Deletes the specified entry from the data store. Use the /f option to ensure BCDEdit deletes the entry; otherwise, it won't delete well-known entries. The /cleanup option ensures that the deleted item is removed from the display order. This option also removes any entries that reference the deleted entry. The /cleanup option is the default—you must specify /nocleanup when you don't want the deleted entry removed from the display order. You may optionally delete entries in a different file using the /store option, which must appear in front of the /delete command.

[/store *Filename*] /deletevalue [*ID*] *DataType* Deletes a data element from an entry in the boot configuration. The data type corresponds to one of the standard types you obtain using the BCDEdit /? TYPES command. When you specify an identifier, the switch affects the specified entry. If you specify this command without an identifier, the system deletes an entry for the current boot loader. You may optionally delete entries in a different file using the /store option, which must appear in front of the /deletevalue command.

/displayorder *ID* [...] [{/addfirst | /addlast | /remove}] Modifies the entry display order. Use a single identifier with the /addfirst and /addlast options to add an identifier to the beginning or end of the display order. Use the /remove option to remove the identifiers from the display order.

/ems [*ID*] {On | Off} Turns on or off Emergency Management Services (EMS) for the specified boot entry. When you specify an identifier, the switch affects the specified boot entry. You can use this command on any entry, but it only affects boot entries. If you specify this command without an identifier, the system sets EMS for the current boot entry.

/emssettings {BIOS | EMSPORT:*Port* EMSBAUDRATE:*BAUDRate*} Defines the global EMS settings. This command doesn't enable or disable EMS for any particular boot entry—it simply defines how EMS communicates. The BIOS option lets EMS rely on the BIOS configuration to determine how to react. This setting only works when your BIOS provides EMS support. The EMSPORT and EMSBAUDRATE settings affect serial port support and you shouldn't use them with the BIOS option.

[/store *Filename*] /enum [{*EntryType* | *ID*}] [/v] Lists the contents of the data store. The /enum command can list all of the entries, a specific entry, or entries of a particular type. The types you can list include ACTIVE, FIRMWARE, BOOTAPP, BOOTMGR, OSLOADER, RESUME, INHERIT, and ALL. The /v option displays the entry GUIDs, rather than the well-known values. You may optionally list entries in a different file using the /store option, which must appear in front of the /enum command (see Figure 16.1).

/export *Filename* Exports the system's data store to an external file. This is an essential part of any work you do with the boot configuration. Always export the current boot configuration to a file so that you can restore it if your changes don't work. To export the book configuration, type **BCDEdit /Export C:\ThisConfig.TXT** and press Enter. If you later find that the changes you made don't work, you can use the /Import command line switch to import the old file. It's important to remember that you can boot the distribution media and open a command prompt to execute this command, so it's possible to recover from bad boot configurations, even if the server won't boot properly.

/import *Filename* Imports the entries found in an external file into the system data store. You must use the \Export command line switch to create an external data store before you can use this file. To import a data store that you created previously, type **BCDEdit /Import C:\ThisConfig.TXT** and press Enter.

FIGURE 16.1

The /enum command outputs the contents of the current data store.

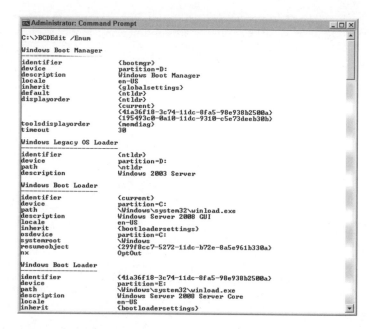

[/store *Filename*] /set [*ID*] *DataType Value* Changes the value of an entry to a new value. When you specify an identifier, the command affects the specified entry. If you specify this command without an identifier, the system sets values for the current boot entry. You may optionally change entries in a different file using the /store option, which must appear in front of the /set command.

The /set command is the one that you'll use most often because it lets you make changes. The easiest and safest way to use this command is to create an enumeration of the current data store by typing **BCDEdit /Enum** and pressing Enter (see Figure 16.1 for typical output). Once you know the specifics of the data store, you can set values. For example, if you want to set the Description property for the Windows Legacy OS Loader entry shown in Figure 16.1, you might type **BCDEdit /Set {ntldr} Description "Windows 2003 Server - 64 Bit"** and press Enter. Notice that you provide an identifier for the boot partition, {ntldr}. The name of the property is Description. The value for that property is "Windows 2003 Server - 64 Bit". You must encase any properties that contain spaces in quotes. Whenever you make a change, always verify it by typing **BCDEdit /Enum** and pressing Enter. Make only one change at a time and verify each change.

/store [*Filename*] Defines the data store to which other commands in the stream apply. You can't use this command with the /createstore command. If you don't include a filename, the commands affect the system store.

/timeout *Timeout* Changes the time that the boot manager waits for the user to make a selection before booting the default entry. The default setting is 30 seconds.

/toolsdisplayorder *ID* [...] [{/addfirst | /addlast | /remove}] Modifies the tools display order when displaying the tools menu during the boot sequence. Use a single identifier with the /addfirst and /addlast options to add an identifier to the beginning or end of the tools display order. Use the /remove option to remove the identifiers from the tools display order.

Now that you have a better idea of the commands you can use with BCDEdit, it's time to look at what passes for command line syntax. This utility uses the following syntax:

```
BCDEdit <Command> [<Command>...] [/? [TOPICS] [ID] [TYPES [{BOOTAPP |
BOOTMGR | BOOTSECTOR | CUSTOMTYPES | FWBOOTMGR | MEMDIAG | NTLDR |
OSLOADER | RESUME}]] [FORMATS]] [/enum] [/v]
```

The following list describes each of the command line arguments.

/?   Obtains help about the specific command.

TOPICS   Displays a list of detailed help topics, which includes the commands, standard identifiers, data types, and other command line options.

ID   Displays a list of well-known identifiers for the operating system. For example, the {bootmgr} entry refers to the Windows Boot Manager entry.

TYPES [{BOOTAPP | BOOTMGR | BOOTSECTOR | CUSTOMTYPES | FWBOOTMGR | MEMDIAG | NTLDR | OSLOADER | RESUME}]   Displays help information about configuration entry types. Using TYPES alone displays a list of the available types. Using TYPES with a specific entry, such as TYPES BOOTAPP, displays the type information for that entry.

FORMATS   Displays information about the type information formatting rules.

/enum   Lists the entries in a store.

/v   Displays verbose information for the specified command. The amount of additional information varies by command.

Accessing the WinPE Network Installer with the NetCfg Utility

The NetCfg utility provides access to the Windows Pre-installation Environment (WinPE). Using this deployment environment can save you considerable time and effort as described at http://www.microsoft.com/licensing/sa/benefits/winpe.mspx. Learn more about WinPE at http://www.microsoft.com/technet/windowsvista/deploy/winpe.mspx. This utility uses the following syntax:

```
netcfg [-v] [-e] [-winpe] [-l <full-path-to-component-INF>]
    -c {p | s | c} -i <comp-id>
netcfg [-v] -winpe
netcfg [-v] -q <comp-id>
netcfg [-v] [-e] -u <comp-id>
netcfg [-v] -s {a | n}
netcfg [-v] -b <comp-id>
```

The following list describes each of the command line arguments.

WARNING   You must pass the arguments in the order shown in the syntax or the command may fail. It's always a good idea to use the order shown in the syntax examples, but when using the NetCfg utility the order is essential.

-v   Displays verbose information about the specified task. The amount and type of information depends on the command that you're executing.

-e   Uses servicing environment variables during package installation and uninstallation.

-winpe   Installs the TCP/IP, NetBIOS, and Microsoft Client for Windows pre-installation environment. To use this feature, type **NetCfg -v -winpe** and press Enter. Even though the verbose command line switch is optional, you'll want it in this case to see precisely how the installation proceeds. In addition, make sure you have signed drivers for all of the installation features or you'll see a list of error messages as the system tries to perform the install.

-l *Full-Path-To-Component-INF*   Specifies the location of the INF file that contains the package installation instructions. To install a driver or product that relies on an INF file, type **NetCfg** *MyProd.***INF** (where MyProd is the filename of the INF file) and press Enter.

-c {p | s | c}   Defines the class of the package you want to install: protocol, service, or client.

-i *CompID*   Installs the specified package. Use the –s command line switch to obtain a list of component identifiers. For example, if you type **NetCfg -c p -i ms_netbt** and press Enter, you would install the WINS Client(TCP/IP) Protocol. Notice that you must specify the type of package you want to install using the -c command line switch. In this case, you're installing a protocol, so you use the p value.

-q *CompID*   Queries the installation status of the specified package. Use the –sn command line switch to obtain a list of component identifiers. For example, if you type **NetCfg -v -q ms_msclient** and press Enter, you obtain the installation status of the Client for Microsoft Networks.

-u *CompID*   Uninstalls the specified package. Use the –s command line switch to obtain a list of component identifiers. For example, if you type **NetCfg -u ms_netbt** and press Enter, you would uninstall the WINS Client(TCP/IP) Protocol.

-s {a | n}   Displays the specified component types where a is adapters and n is network components. For example, if you type **NetCfg -sa** and press Enter, you may see a list of adapters, as shown in Figure 16.2.

FIGURE 16.2
Display a list of component types using the -sa or -sn command line switches.

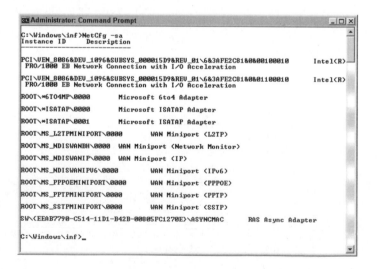

-b *CompID*   Shows the binding paths for the specified component. Use the −sn command line switch to obtain a list of component identifiers. When you see the output, it will contain a number of adapter identifiers such as pci\ven_8086&dev_1096. Use the −sa command line switch to determine which adapters appear in the list.

Getting System Configuration Information with the SystemInfo Utility

The SystemInfo utility lets you query the system for configuration information. The purpose of this utility is to provide a quick overview of the system configuration, not the detailed information that other utilities, such as MSInfo32 (described in Chapter 3) provide. One of the more important outputs of this utility is the hot fixes section, which provides you with a complete list of the hot fixes applied to the system (something you can't easily find out using other utilities). This utility uses the following syntax:

```
SYSTEMINFO [/S system [/U username [/P [password]]]] [/FO
{TABLE | LIST | CSV}] [/NH]
```

The following list describes each of the command line arguments.

/S *system*   Specifies the remote system that you want to check. In most cases, you'll also need to supply the /U and the /P command line switches when using this switch.

/U *[domain\]user*   Specifies the username on the remote system. This name may not match the username on the local system. You'll need to supply a domain name when working with a domain controller.

/P *[password]*   Specifies the password for the given user. You can provide the command line switch without specifying the password on the command line in cleartext. The system prompts you for the password. Using this feature can help you maintain the security of passwords used on your system.

/FO {**TABLE** | **LIST** | **CSV**}   Defines the output provided by the utility. The table format is normally the easiest to view on screen. The table columns define the values for output, while each row contains one driver entry. The CSV output provides the best method for preparing the data for entry in a database. Use redirection (see the "Employing Data Redirection" section of Chapter 14 for details) to output the CSV data to a file and then import it to your database. The list format provides one data element per line. Each group of data elements defines one driver. The utility separates each driver by one blank line. Some people find the list format more readable when working in verbose mode since the table format requires multiple lines for each entry (the lines wrap). Figure 16.3 shows an example of the output you'd see if you typed **SystemInfo /FO List** and pressed Enter. This is one command where you may want to use output redirection. For example, if you type **SystemInfo /FO List > MySysInfo.TXT** and press Enter, the output will appear in a file named MySysInfo.TXT.

/NH   Forces the utility to display the data without a column header. You can only use this command line switch with the table and CSV formats. Omitting the header makes it easier to incorporate the data in a report or import it into a database.

FIGURE 16.3
Use the SystemInfo utility to obtain basic information about a system.

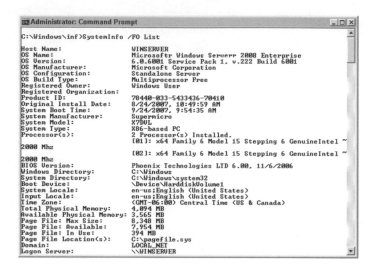

Managing Windows in a New Way

Managing your system is an important part of the administrative tasks you perform. Knowing all the details about your system helps you see when something is going wrong or someone is trying to gain unwanted access. You won't use the utilities in this chapter very often, but it's very important to know they exist when you have specific configuration issues to address. This chapter helps you build these skills:

♦   Manage the boot configuration using the BCDEdit command

♦   Access the WinPE network installer using the NetCfg utility

♦   Obtain system configuration information using the SystemInfo utility

Of the three commands and utilities described in this chapter, the BCDEdit command is the most dangerous because a wrong move can prevent your system from booting. However, it's also the most essential utility because there isn't any graphical replacement for it. Even an administrator for the graphical version of Windows Server 2008 will need this utility. The best thing you can do right now is use BCDEdit to create a backup of your configuration information using the /Export command line switch. Make sure you work with the other utilities as well. For example, you can export the output of the SystemInfo utility to a file using redirection and save it for future use, such as comparing your system's ideal state to its current state.

Connectivity is an important issue for servers because without connectivity no one can use the server resources. Chapter 17 provides a discussion about connectivity in Server Core and shows how you can ensure everyone can connect to your machine. Of course, you have already started this process as part of the "Configuring the Server for Initial Use" section of Chapter 1 (and many of the other chapters so far in the book), but Chapter 17 provides a complete view of everything that Server Core offers for your configuration needs.

Chapter 17

Creating System Connections

Connections are an essential part of any network and as an administrator you already know that better than anyone. This chapter explores several kinds of connections. Remote management connections help you manage the server. You can use FTP connections to allow file uploads and downloads. Terminal Server connections let users and administrators access the server from a remote location as if they're working with their local computer. It's also the basis for many other features, such as Remote Desktop, a significant aid for administrators who have a lot of machines to manage (see the "Configuring the Server for Initial Use" section of Chapter 1 for details on Remote Desktop configuration). Remote Access Server (RAS) is the long time standby for dial-up and other older server connection solutions. Finally, Telnet is a management aid that has been around before Windows.

All of these connections have one thing in common—they allow someone to connect to the server. The technique used to access the server determines the technology you use to make the connection, but the result is the same—access to server resources. Since a server exists solely to provide resources, this chapter is one of the more important chapters in the book.

In this chapter, you'll learn how to do the following:

◆ Perform remote system management

◆ Manage FTP servers

◆ Configure and manage Terminal Server

◆ Configure and manage Remote Access Server

◆ Use Telnet to obtain access to remote systems

Remote System Management

In many cases, you'll need to create remote connections before you can perform some types of maintenance tasks. Many of the utilities described in this book provide a method for creating a remote connection, but not necessarily a connection where you can manipulate objects as well as run utilities. In addition, some utilities don't provide a remote connection feature. Even though the Remote Desktop does open the potential for a security breach, you can generally keep security under control by ensuring you create a secure connection. The following sections describe utilities you can use to perform remote system management.

NOTE Unlike the graphical version of Windows Server 2008, Server Core doesn't support Internet Connection Sharing (ICS). One of the prerequisites for using ICS is the Shared Access service. You can see this service by typing **SC Query SharedAccess** and pressing Enter at a command line in the graphical version. When you look for this same service in Server Core, you'll find that it's missing. Microsoft may eventually enable this service, but in the meantime, you can't use ICS within Server Core. As an alternative to using ICS, you can always set up a dedicated router on your network—one that hopefully includes a hardware firewall.

Creating Remote Connections with the MSTSC Utility

The Microsoft Terminal Server Connection (MSTSC) utility provides remote connectivity using the Remote Desktop feature introduced in Windows XP. The utility relies on a Remote Desktop Connection (RDP) file to create the connection in most cases. You must have administrator privileges to use this utility. This utility uses the following syntax:

```
mstsc.exe {ConnectionFile | /v:server} [/console] [/f] [/w:width /h:height] [/public]
  [/span]
mstsc.exe /edit"ConnectionFile"
mstsc.exe /migrate
```

The following list describes each of the command line arguments.

ConnectionFile Specifies the RDP file you want to use to create the connection.

/v:server Specifies the name of a remote computer. You can use this feature in place of an RDP file when you don't have an RDP defined.

/console Connects to the console session of the specified Windows 2000 server.

/f Starts the Remote Desktop session in full-screen mode. Using this feature overcomes issues that you might encounter displaying the remote computer's desktop in a window.

/w:width Specifies the width of the Remote Desktop window.

/h:height Specifies the height of the Remote Desktop window.

/edit Opens the specified RDP file for editing.

/migrate Migrates older connection files that you created with the Client Connection Manager in older versions of Windows to the new RDP file format.

/public Runs the session in public mode. When a session runs in public mode, Terminal Server doesn't save any of the private user data. For example, it won't save the user's registry settings. In addition, Terminal Server won't make use of any private user data within the session. Consequently, you might find that some application settings are missing.

/span Matches the local and remote computer screen sizes and spans multiple computer screens when required to perform the match. When working with spanned computer screens, the screens must all have the same height and you must align them vertically. Microsoft places a maximum resolution restriction of $4,096 \times 2,048$ pixels on this mode.

⊕ Real World Scenario

USING REMOTE DESKTOP TO BEST ADVANTAGE

Don't assume that the MSTSC utility and Remote Desktop as a whole are simple ways to create a connection. Yes, you can create a connection and even make it secure, but the Microsoft documentation for the graphical portion of this utility leaves a lot to the imagination. Fortunately, a third party has stepped in to make it easier to create useful connections with MSTSC. You can find the first of the graphical interface articles on the PETRI.co.il site at http://www.petri.co.il/add_a_new_rdp_listening_port_to_terminal_server.htm. The related articles section at the bottom of the Web page leads you to a wealth of additional information, including download instructions for RDP Version 5.2.

In general, this is a client-to-server connection. The only problem is that Windows 2000 Server doesn't know about Remote Desktop, so it might appear at first that MSTSC is useless. Fortunately, you can add an RDP listening port, which makes the Windows 2000 Server completely accessible. It's tips like this that the PETRI.co.il Web site excels in providing. You may also want to go to the Microsoft Knowledge Base (http://support.microsoft.com/search/?adv=1) to check for Server Core specifics as they become available.

Setting Up a Telephony Client with the TCMSetup Utility

Use this utility to set up or disable the Telephony Application Programming Interface (TAPI) client. Despite its name, TAPI helps the system create a number of connection types, so correct setup is important. For example, this setup can define physical connectivity to the corporate Private Branch Exchange (PBX). You must use this utility to perform some setups, such as designating a Windows 2000 server as a resource for TAPI clients. This utility uses the following syntax:

```
tcmsetup [/r] [/q] [/x] /c Server [Server...]
tcmsetup [/q] /c /d
```

The following list describes each of the command line arguments.

/r Disables automatic server discovery. Only the servers that you specify with this command appear as TAPI resources.

/q Prevents the utility from displaying message boxes. Use this feature with batch files to prevent the system stopping to wait for user input.

/x Specifies that TAPI relies on connection-oriented callbacks. Use this feature on heavy traffic networks where packet loss is high. The default setting uses connectionless callbacks, which offer better efficiency at the expense of reliability.

/c Defines this request as a client setup. You must include this command line switch.

Server Specifies one or more remote servers to use as TAPI service providers. You must specify a minimum of one server. The client uses the server's lines and telephones for communication. The client must appear within the same domain as the server or in a domain that has a two-way trust relationship with the client's domain. Separate each of the servers in a multiple server listing with a space.

/d   Clears the list of remote TAPI servers. Disables the TAPI client by preventing it from using TAPI service providers that appear on remote servers. The command also prevents automatic discovery of TAPI servers. You must use this utility to reenable TAPI services on the client.

Performing Remote Windows Management with the WinRM Utility

The Windows Remote Management (WinRM) utility helps you manage a remote system from the command line. This utility is Microsoft's implementation of the WS-Management protocol, which provides a secure method of connecting local and remote computers using a Web service. You can learn more about the WS-Management protocol at http://msdn2.microsoft.com/en-us/library/aa384470.aspx. This utility uses the following general syntax:

```
winrm OPERATION RESOURCE_URI [-SWITCH:VALUE [-SWITCH:VALUE] ...]
    [@{KEY=VALUE[;KEY=VALUE]...}]
```

The WinRM utility provides access to a number of operations (or commands) that combine with a resource Uniform Resource Identifier (URI) to perform tasks on the remote machine. The command line syntax for each of the operations is as follows:

```
winrm g[et] RESOURCE_URI [-SWITCH:VALUE [-SWITCH:VALUE] ...]
set RESOURCE_URI [-SWITCH:VALUE [-SWITCH:VALUE] ...]
    [@{KEY="VALUE"[;KEY="VALUE"]}] [-file:VALUE]
winrm c[reate] RESOURCE_URI [-SWITCH:VALUE [-SWITCH:VALUE] ...]
    [@{KEY="VALUE"[;KEY="VALUE"]}] [-file:VALUE]
winrm d[elete] RESOURCE_URI [-SWITCH:VALUE [-SWITCH:VALUE] ...]
winrm e[numerate] RESOURCE_URI [-ReturnType:Value] [-Shallow]
    [-BasePropertiesOnly] [-SWITCH:VALUE [-SWITCH:VALUE] ...]
winrm i[nvoke] ACTION RESOURCE_URI [-SWITCH:VALUE [-SWITCH:VALUE] ...]
    [@{KEY="VALUE"[;KEY="VALUE"]}] [-file:VALUE]
winrm id[entify]  [-SWITCH:VALUE [-SWITCH:VALUE] ...]
winrm quickconfig [-quiet] [-transport:VALUE]
```

The following list describes each of the command line arguments.

g[et]   Obtains management information.

s[et]   Modifies the management information. You can also specify this operation as put.

c[reate]   Defines new instances of management resources.

d[elete]   Removes an instance of a management resource.

e[numerate]   Lists the instances of the specified management resource.

i[nvoke]   Executes a method on a management resource.

id[entify]   Determines whether WinRM or another compatible WS-Management implementation is running on a remote machine.

quickconfig   Configures the local machine to accept WS-Management requests from other machines.

RESOURCE_URI   Specifies the URI of the management resource. For example, if you want to obtain the current WS-Management configuration, you would query the winrm/config URI. You could access the Spooler service using the wmicimv2/Win32_Service?Name=spooler URI. WinRM supports a number of common URIs that you can discover by typing **winrm help uris** and pressing Enter.

-SWITCH:VALUE   Specifies a switch and value pair that modifies the performance of the specified operation. The common switches appear later in this section of the chapter. Type **winrm help switches** and press Enter to obtain the complete list of switches.

@{KEY="VALUE"[;KEY="VALUE"]}   Defines an argument and its associated value. The argument can control the operation of the management resource or configure the management resource in some way. For example, typing **winrm set winrm/config @{MaxEnvelopeSizekb="100"}** would change the maximum envelope size for the local copy of WinRM. The key and value pair must appear within curly braces ({}) and be preceded by an at (@) sign. You can incorporate multiple settings in one request by separating them with a semicolon (;).

-file:VALUE   Specifies the name of a file containing key and value pairs. See the @{KEY="VALUE" [;KEY="VALUE"]} entry for details. The file simply makes it easier to provide the data at the command line.

-ReturnType:{Object | EPR | ObjectAndEPR}   Determines the return type of the data. The Object return type provides a listing of the object. The End Point Reference (EPR) return type provides information about the resource URI and selectors for the specified instance. The ObjectAndEPR type returns both an object listing and the EPR data.

-Shallow   Enumerates only the instances of the base class as specified by the resource URI. Otherwise, the utility returns both the base class and derived classes.

-BasePropertiesOnly   Enumerates only those properties associated with the base class specified by the resource URI. The utility ignores this command line argument when you specify the -Shallow command line argument.

ACTION   Executes the particular method (action) on the object specified by the resource URI. You specify any method arguments using key/value pairs.

-quiet   Performs the configuration without prompting for confirmation. This switch is useful when you want to configure WinRM in the background.

-transport:VALUE   Performs a quick configuration of the specified transport. The utility currently supports HTTP and HTTPS as transports. The utility defaults to using HTTP as the transport.

Most of the operations accept a number of switches that help define how the operation performs its tasks. The following list describes the common switches.

-timeout:MS   Defines the timeout in milliseconds for the successful completion of a command (otherwise, the system keeps retrying the command without limit). This switch limits the duration of a particular operation.

-skipCAcheck   Specifies that the certificate issuer need not be a trusted root authority when working with a remote system using HTTPS. Use this switch when accessing a system that has a self-issued certificate, such as a server on your LAN or a machine attached to your WAN. Never use this switch when working with a system that you don't trust.

-skipCNcheck   Specifies that the certificate common name (CN) of the server need not match the hostname of the server. Using this switch is a significant security risk, even for local servers. Generally, it's better to self-issue a certificate with all of the correct information in place.

-dialect:VALUE   Determines the dialect of the filter expression for enumeration or fragment. For example, if you want to use a Windows Management Instrumentation (WMI) Query Language (WQL) formatted filter, then you would specify -dialect:http://schemas.microsoft .com/wbem/wsman/1/WQL. Likewise, if you want to use an XML Path (XPath) Language query, you'd specify `-dialect:http://www.w3.org/TR/1999/REC-xpath-19991116`. The default filtering relies on WQL as described for the `-filter` command line switch.

`-filter:`*VALUE*   Defines a filter used to limit the amount of data returned by a query. The filter looks very much like a SQL statement, but relies on the filtering dialect you choose. The default filtering dialect is WQL, where you choose objects based on WMI. For example, if you wanted to locate the BITS service on a system, you'd type `winrm enum wmicimv2/* -filter:"select * from win32_service where Name=\"BITS\" "`. Figure 17.1 shows the results of issuing this command.

`-fragment:`*VALUE*   Defines the section within the instance XML that you want to update or retrieve for a given operation. WinRM requires that you supply the name of the object and the fragment particulars as an object method. For example, to retrieve the description of the BITS service, you would type `winrm get wmicimv2/Win32_Service?name=BITS -fragment: Description/text()`.

`-options:{`*KEY*`="`*VALUE*`"[;`*KEY*`="`*VALUE*`"]}`   Defines arguments used for provider-specific needs. You must consult the documentation for your provider to use this switch. If you need to provide a null value, use `$null` as the input.

`-SPNPort`   Specifies a port number to append to the Service Principal Name (SPN) of the remote service. The utility uses the SPN for authentication purposes when using Negotiate or Kerberos authentication.

`-encoding:{utf-8 | utf-16}`   Defines the encoding used to transmit data to and from the remote system. The default option is `utf-16`.

`-f[ormat]:{xml | pretty | text}`   Specifies the output format of the data. The default setting is `text`, which is the human-readable form shown in Figure 17.1. The `xml` setting outputs pure XML without any white space. Using the `pretty` setting outputs XML with white space to make the data more readable.

Accessing a System with the WinRS Utility

The Windows Remote Shell (WinRS) utility helps you execute commands on a remote system. This utility doesn't support interaction, which means that the command you supply has to provide all required information. The console displays the results of any command you execute. This utility uses the following syntax:

```
winrs [-r[emote]:ENDPOINT] [-un[encrypted]] [-u[sername]:USERNAME
    -p[assword]:PASSWORD] [-t[imeout]:SECONDS] [-d[irectory]:PATH]
    [-env[ironment]:STRING=VALUE] [-noe[cho]] [-nop[rofile]] COMMAND
```

The following list describes each of the command line arguments.

-r[emote]:*ENDPOINT* Specifies the endpoint (the target of the command) using either an URL or a NetBIOS name. The default setting uses LOCALHOST for all commands.

-un[encrypted] Specifies that the utility won't encrypt messages to the remote system. This feature is helpful for diagnosing problems with the setup. However, it also represents a security problem because all communication takes place as cleartext. The default setting encrypts all data using NTLM or Kerberos keys.

-u[sername]:*USERNAME* Provides the username to the remote system. If you don't supply this command line switch, the remote system prompts you for a username and password. You must use this command line switch with the -password command line switch.

-p[assword]:*PASSWORD* Provides the user's password to the remote system. If you don't supply this command line switch, the remote system prompts you for a username and password. You must use this command line switch with the -username command line switch.

-t[imeout]:*SECONDS* Determines the maximum time that the command will execute in seconds. This command line switch acts as a safety feature when working with a remote system that may not respond. The default setting doesn't place any limit on the time the command can execute.

-d[irectory]:*PATH* Specifies the starting location for the command. If you don't specify this command line switch, the command begins execution in the location specified by the %USERPROFILE% environment variable.

-env[ironment]:*KEY=VALUE* Defines an environment variable to use when executing the command. You must supply the environment variables as key/value pairs. Each command line switch can only specify one environment variable, so you must use multiple instances of this command line switch to provide multiple environment variables to the remote system.

-noe[cho] Sets echo off. Using this command line switch ensures that user answers to remote prompts don't appear on the local system. The default setting leaves echo on so the user can see any input provided.

-nop[rofile] Forces the remote system to execute the command without loading the user's profile on that system. You must use this command line switch when the user issuing the command isn't a local administrator on that system. Otherwise, the command will fail even if it would normally succeed.

COMMAND Specifies any command that you want to execute on the remote system. The command must appear as it would at the local command prompt. You may use any command that the remote system can execute at the command prompt.

TIP   If you find that the remote command has stalled and you need to terminate it, press Ctrl+C or Ctrl+Break. As with the local system, pressing these key combinations will terminate the command.

Managing FTP Servers with the FTP Utility

The File Transfer Protocol (FTP) utility is one of the easiest ways of transferring files to literally any system. FTP is a standardized protocol that just about every operating system platform supports. In addition, FTP appears in more forms than just about any other protocol. For example, you can use FTP from Internet Explorer or Firefox with equal ease. However, the FTP utility lets you perform file transfers at the command prompt, so you can use it even if the host system isn't operating quite right. This utility uses the following syntax:

```
FTP [-v] [-n] [-i] [-d] [-g] [-s:<Filename>] [-a] [-w:<Buffer_Size>]
    [-x:sendbuffer] [-r:recvbuffer] [-b:asyncbuffers] [-A] [-?]
    [<Host>]
```

FTP uses case-sensitive switches. For example, –A isn't the same as –a. In addition, you must use the – (minus) sign and not the / (slash) when typing command line arguments. You need to type the command with these requirements in mind. Most of these switches also appear in the interface, so you can modify the behavior after you start the application. The following list describes each of the command line arguments.

-v   Disables the display of remote server responses. It comes in handy if you want the download to progress in the background without disturbing your foreground task.

-n   Disables auto-logon on initial connection.

-i   Removes interactive prompting during multiple file transfers. This enables you to automate the file transfer process.

-d   Displays all FTP commands passed between the client and server. This enables you to debug script files.

-g   Disables filename globbing (essentially, wildcard expansion), which permits the use of wildcard characters in local filenames and pathnames.

-s:*Filename*   Replaces <Filename> with the name of a text file containing FTP commands. In essence, this switch enables you to create a script for your FTP download. Use this switch instead of redirection (>).

-a   Tells FTP to use any available interface when creating a connection to the host.

-w:*Buffer_Size*   Changes the data transfer buffer size. The default size of 4,096 bytes normally works well. However, you might want to decrease the buffer size if you experience errors on a connection or use a larger buffer size for local connections. A large buffer is more efficient, but you lose less data for each damaged packet when working with a small buffer.

-A   Logs in as an anonymous user. Note that this is the only switch typed in uppercase.

-?   Displays online help. Note that, at the time of this writing, there are typos in both the Help and Support Center document and the application-supplied help.

-x:*sendbuffer*   Overrides the default send buffer size of 8,192 bytes.

-r:*recvbuffer*   Overrides the default received buffer size of 8,192 bytes.

-b:*asyncbuffers*   Overrides the default number of asynchronous buffers (3 is the default).

Host   Provides name or address of the host you want to connect to for a file download.

The FTP utility provides a surprising array of commands you can use after you run the utility. There really are too many to list here, but you can get a list easily enough. All you need to remember is one command: the question mark (?). If you type a question mark, you see a list of all the things you can do with FTP.

Working with Terminal Server

Microsoft originally released Terminal Server with Windows NT 4.0, and it's been around in various forms ever since. Terminal Server provides Windows functionality by using a mainframe model. The client acts as a terminal for the server that has all of the applications the client needs to run. Using this model, the client can run Windows even if it doesn't provide the functionality required to do so. You can find Terminal Server resources at `http://technet.microsoft.com/en-us/windowsserver/terminal-services/default.aspx`.

Make sure you check out the new Query utility if you're using Vista. This new utility helps you discover details about Terminal Server and its associated users, processes, and sessions.

TIP   You may find that you need to change the Server Core IP address to allow access to other machines on the network. For example, the IP address for the Local Area Connection may default to 169.254.54.55. Discover the current address by typing `NetSH Interface IP Show Config` and pressing Enter. Once you determine that the connection IP address is incorrect for your network, use the NetSH utility again to set the address correctly. For example, if you want to set the Local Area Connection IP address to 192.168.0.1, then you'd type `NetSH Interface IP Set Address "Local Area Connection" Static 192.168.0.1 255.255.255.0` and press Enter (where the first number is the IP address and the second number is the subnet mask). Adding a third IP entry allows you to define a default gateway when necessary. After you make the required change, you must shut down the system and restart it for the change to take effect.

This chapter doesn't teach you how to use Terminal Server. However, it does show you how to use a number of utilities to access, query, and manage this important resource. The following sections describe the command line utilities that you'll use when working with Terminal Server.

TIP   When you display help for many of the utilities described in this section, you'll see the Terminal Server command that the utility executes. For example, the QAppSrv utility executes the QUERY TERMSERVER command. The utilities don't provide access to all of the Terminal Server commands because you don't need to use all of them from the command line. However, you can find an easy-to-use list of these commands on the Web site at `http://www.robvanderwoude.com/termserv.html`.

Locating Terminal Servers with the QAppSrv Utility

The QAppSrv utility displays a list of all of the application terminal servers on a network. If you use this utility without any arguments, it searches the network for a terminal server and displays its name. Running this utility is the same as using the QUERY TERMSERVER command from within Terminal Server. This utility uses the following syntax:

```
QAppSrv [servername] [/DOMAIN:domain] [/ADDRESS] [/CONTINUE]
```

The following list describes each of the command line arguments.

servername   Specifies the Terminal Server to query.

/DOMAIN:*domain*   Displays information for the specified domain. The default setting displays information for the current domain.

/ADDRESS   Displays the network and node addresses for the Terminal Servers on the network.

/CONTINUE   Forces the utility to display all of the servers without pausing after each screen of information.

Obtaining Processes with the QProcess Utility

The QProcess utility displays information about Terminal Server processes. It's the same as running the QUERY PROCESS command from within Terminal Server. The output of this utility includes the username, session name, session identifier, process identifier, and user. This utility uses the following syntax:

```
QProcess [* | processid | username | sessionname | /ID:nn |
programname] [/SERVER:servername] [/SYSTEM]
```

Notice that you may only specify one of the process identifiers. For example, if you include a session name, you can't include the program name. The following list describes each of the command line arguments.

*   Displays all of the visible processes.

processid   Displays the specified process.

username   Displays all processes that belong to a particular user.

sessionname   Displays all of the processes running within a particular session name.

/ID:*nn*   Displays all of the processes running within a particular session identifier.

programname   Displays all of the processes associated with a particular application.

/SERVER:*servername*   Specifies the terminal server to query. The default is the current server.

/SYSTEM   Displays process information for system purposes.

Getting Session Information with the QWinSta Utility

Use this utility to obtain information about the various sessions running on a system. It's the same as running the QUERY SESSION command from within Terminal Services. The utility outputs the session name, username, session identifier, session state, session type, and the device used to create the session. The device information is blank for the local session. This utility uses the following syntax:

```
QWinSta [sessionname | username | sessionid] [/SERVER:servername]
[/MODE] [/FLOW] [/CONNECT] [/COUNTER]
```

Notice that you may only specify one of the session identifiers. If you provide a session name, then you can't provide a username as well. The following list describes each of the command line arguments.

sessionname   Specifies the name of the session to query.

username   Specifies the name of the user to query.

sessionid   Specifies the numeric identifier of the session to query.

/SERVER:*servername* Specifies the terminal server to query. The default is the current server.

/MODE Displays the current line settings. In this case, the output changes to show the session name, session state, device used to access the system, session type, device baud rate, device parity, device data bits, and device stop bits.

/FLOW Displays the current flow control settings. In this case, the output changes to show the session name, session state, device used to access the system, session type, and the flow control settings.

/CONNECT Displays the current connect settings. In this case, the output changes to show the session name, session state, device used to access the system, session type, and the connection settings.

/COUNTER Displays the current Terminal Services counters information. In addition to the standard information, the output includes the total sessions created, total sessions disconnected, and total sessions reconnected.

Terminating a Session with the Reset Utility

Use this utility to reset a session. In this case, the system disconnects the user from the system and receives a message to that effect. If you simply want to reset the session to a known good state, use the RWinSta utility instead. This utility uses the following syntax:

```
RESET [sessionname | sessionid] [ /server:server name] /v
```

Notice that you may only specify one of the session identifiers. If you provide a session name, then you can't provide a session identifier as well. The following list describes each of the command line arguments.

sessionname Specifies the name of the session to reset.

sessionid Specifies the numeric identifier of the session to reset.

/SERVER:*servername* Specifies the terminal server to reset. The default is the current server.

/v Displays additional information about every action that the utility takes to reset the session. This information varies by session.

Resetting the Hardware and Software with the RWinSta Utility

This utility resets the subsystem hardware and software to a known state. You use it when a session has experienced non-recoverable errors. It's the same as running the RESET SESSION command from within Terminal Services. This utility uses the following syntax:

```
RWinSta {sessionname | sessionid} [/SERVER:servername] [/V]
```

Notice that you may only specify one of the session identifiers. If you provide a session name, then you can't provide a session identifier as well. The following list describes each of the command line arguments.

sessionname Specifies the name of the session to reset.

sessionid Specifies the numeric identifier of the session to reset.

/SERVER:*servername* Specifies the terminal server to reset. The default is the current server.

/V Displays additional information about every action that the utility takes to reset the session. This information varies by session.

Monitoring Other Sessions with the Shadow Utility

Use this utility to monitor another Terminal Server session. This utility uses the following syntax:

```
SHADOW {sessionname | sessionid} [/SERVER:servername] [/V]
```

Notice that you may only specify one of the session identifiers. If you provide a session name, then you can't provide a session identifier as well. The following list describes each of the command line arguments.

sessionname   Specifies the name of the session to monitor.

sessionid   Specifies the numeric identifier of the session to monitor.

/SERVER:*servername*   Specifies the terminal server to monitor. The default is the current server.

/V   Displays additional information about every action that the utility takes to monitor the session. This information varies by session.

Attaching a User Session with the TSCon Utility

Use this utility to attach a user session to an existing Terminal Server session. This utility uses the following syntax:

```
TSCON {sessionid | sessionname} [/DEST:sessionname] [/PASSWORD:pw] [/V]
```

Notice that you may only specify one of the session identifiers. If you provide a session name, then you can't provide a session identifier as well. The following list describes each of the command line arguments.

sessionname   Specifies the name of the session to monitor.

sessionid   Specifies the numeric identifier of the session to monitor.

/DEST:*sessionname*   Connects the current user session to the specified destination Terminal Service session.

/PASSWORD:*pw*   Specifies the password of the user who owns the identified session.

/V   Displays additional information about every action that the utility takes to connect to the Terminal Services session. This information varies by session.

Disconnecting an Active Session with the TSDiscon Utility

Use this utility to disconnect from an existing Terminal Services session. The Terminal Services session continues to run after you disconnect from it. This utility uses the following syntax:

```
TSDISCON [sessionid | sessionname] [/SERVER:servername] [/V]
```

Notice that you may only specify one of the session identifiers. If you provide a session name, then you can't provide a session identifier as well. The following list describes each of the command line arguments.

sessionname   Specifies the name of the session to disconnect.

sessionid   Specifies the numeric identifier of the session to disconnect.

/SERVER:*servername* Specifies the terminal server to disconnect from. The default is the current server.

/V Displays additional information about every action that the utility takes to disconnect from the session. This information varies by session.

Ending Processes with the TSKill Utility

Use this utility to end a Terminal Services process. This utility uses the following syntax:

```
TSKILL processid | processname [/SERVER:servername] [/ID:sessionid | /A] [/V]
```

Notice that you may only specify one of the process identifiers. If you provide a process name, then you can't provide a process identifier as well. The following list describes each of the command line arguments.

processid Specifies the numeric identifier of the process to terminate.

processname Specifies the name of the process to terminate.

/SERVER:*servername* Identifies the server that is running the process. The default setting is the current server. You must include either the /ID or /A command line switch when using this command line switch and a process name to terminate a session.

/ID:*sessionid* Identifies the session under which the process is running.

/A Ends this process for all sessions.

/V Displays detailed information about the processes that the utility terminates.

Shutting Down Terminal Server with the TSShutDn Utility

Use this utility to shut down Terminal Server in a controlled manner. The users receive a message stating the server shutdown time. In addition, you can use this utility to reboot the server. For some odd reason, Vista doesn't support this utility and Microsoft doesn't provide an alternative. This utility uses the following syntax:

```
TSSHUTDN [wait_time] [/SERVER:servername] [/REBOOT] [/POWERDOWN]
[/DELAY:logoffdelay] [/V]
```

The following list describes each of the command line arguments.

wait_time Determines the number of seconds the system waits after user notification to terminate all user sessions and shut down the Terminal Server. The default setting is 60 seconds.

/SERVER:*servername* Specifies the name of the server to shut down. The default setting shuts down the current server.

/REBOOT Reboots the server after all the user sessions terminate. The server restarts and ends up in a known good state.

/POWERDOWN Powers the Terminal Server down. The host system remains running.

/DELAY:*logoffdelay* Specifies the number of seconds to wait after logging off all connected sessions. The delay provides time for applications to complete any required tasks. The default setting is 30 seconds.

/V Displays detailed information about all of the actions the utility performs to shut down the Terminal Server.

Working with Remote Access Server

The Remote Access Server (RAS) provides dial-up connectivity to your server from a remote location. Some people might think that dial-up connectivity and the other services that RAS provides belong to a bygone age, but most large organizations actually rely on a mixed environment in which dial-up is still an essential part of the picture. For example, the ComputerWorld article at `http://www.computerworld.com/hardwaretopics/hardware/story/0,10801,106776,00.html` points out some amazing mixed environment statistics. Microsoft also takes this need seriously by providing a special area on their Web site for general networking and RAS needs at `http://www.microsoft.com/technet/community/en-us/networking/default.mspx`.

TIP Even though the Windows NT resources that Microsoft provides might seem outdated, RAS really hasn't changed much from that early version of Windows. For example, the vast majority of the information in the RAS Reference at `http://www.microsoft.com/resources/documentation/windowsnt/4/server/reskit/en-us/net/sur_ras.mspx` is just as useful today as when Microsoft first put it together. (Modems have admittedly gotten faster, but the concepts remain the same.)

The following sections describe the RAS-specific tools included with Windows. However, these utilities aren't the end of the story. To manage RAS functionality you must become familiar with the NetSH utility. You'll find a discussion of this utility in the "Scripting Networking Solutions with the NetSH Utility" section of Chapter 6. Finally, Microsoft provides many tools such as RASSrvMon (RAS Server Monitor) that aren't available with Windows. You can download these tools at `http://www.microsoft.com/downloads/details.aspx?FamilyID=9d467a69-57ff-4ae7-96ee-b18c4790cffd`.

Dialing Out with the RASDial Utility

Use the RASDial utility to determine the current RAS status, as well as dial out to a RAS server. Use the RASDial utility by itself to determine the current RAS status. The output displays any connections you've made. This utility uses the following syntax:

```
RASDial entryname [username [password|*]] [/DOMAIN:domain]
    [/PHONE:phonenumber] [/CALLBACK:callbacknumber]
    [/PHONEBOOK:phonebookfile] [/PREFIXSUFFIX]
RASDial [entryname] /DISCONNECT
RASDial
```

The following list describes each of the command line arguments.

entryname Specifies an entry from the RAS phonebook (PBK file) entry. The utility uses the default PBK file located in the \Windows\System32\RAS directory unless you specify a different PBK file using the /PHONEBOOK command line switch. Always place entry names that contain spaces in quotes. You may also elect to use a telephone number that doesn't appear in the phonebook by using the /PHONE command line switch.

***username*[{ *password* | *}]** Specifies the username used to connect to the remote system. In many cases, you'll also need to supply a password to create the connection. If you supply an asterisk (*) for the password, RAS prompts you for the password. Using this technique reduces the possibility of someone compromising your password. Instead of seeing the password in plaintext at the command prompt, anyone viewing your display simply sees a series of asterisks in the prompt dialog box.

/Domain:*domain* Specifies the user's domain on the remote machine. If you don't specify a domain, the system uses the last value of the Domain field in the Connect To dialog box.

/Phone:*phonenumber* Substitutes the specified telephone number for the one in the RAS phonebook entry. You can use this feature to dial one-time telephone numbers for support or other reasons.

/Callback:*callbacknumber* Substitutes the specified callback telephone number for the one in the RAS phonebook. The callback number is the one that the server calls to re-create a connection after it verifies your user information. Many remote systems use callbacks as a security measure to ensure they reach a valid user. Your user account must allow you to specify a different callback number in order for this feature to work.

/Phonebook:*phonebookfile* Specifies an alternative RAS phonebook (PBK) file. You can use this alternative phonebook to hold personal or specialized numbers. The default phonebook appears in the \Windows\System32\RAS directory under your username.

/PrefixSuffix Applies the current TAPI location dialing settings to the telephone number. You set up these options using the Phone and Modem Options applet found in the Control Panel. The system doesn't use these options by default; you must specifically turn them on for dialing outside of your current location.

/Disconnect Disconnects an existing RAS connection. You may optionally specify a particular entry name when you have multiple RAS connections in use.

Accessing Dial-Up Networking with the RASPhone Utility

Use the RASPhone utility to create entries in your RAS phonebook. Each entry specifies a kind of connection. The four major connection types include dial-up to a private network, connecting to a private network through the Internet using a Virtual Private Network (VPN), connecting directly to another computer using a serial, parallel, or infrared port, and connecting to a network using broadband. The discussion in this section doesn't tell you how to use the graphical utilities to create such a connection; it concentrates on the command line interface. Using RASPhone by itself displays the graphical interface. This utility uses the following syntax:

```
RASPhone [-f file] [[{-e | -d | -h | -r}] entry]
RASPhone [-f file] -a [entry]
RASPhone [-f file] -l{a | d | e | h | r} [link]
```

The following list describes each of the command line arguments.

-f *file* Defines the full path to the RAS phonebook (PBK) file. The path can include a drive, relative or absolute path, and a filename.

-e Displays the dialog box required to edit the specified entry. The dialog box varies by entry type.

-d Displays the dial-up dialog box for creating a connection to the remote resource.

-h Disconnects the specified remote connection without displaying a dialog box.

-r Deletes the specified entry from the RAS phonebook without displaying a dialog box. Note that this task is permanent; you can't undelete a RAS phonebook entry and must create it from the beginning if you accidentally delete it.

entry Specifies an entry from the RAS phonebook (PBK file) entry. The utility uses the default PBK file located in the \Windows\System32\RAS directory unless you specify a different PBK file using the /PHONEBOOK command line switch. Always place entry names that contain spaces in quotes. You may also elect to use a telephone number that doesn't appear in the phonebook by using the /PHONE command line switch.

-a Displays the New Connection Wizard that you use to create a new entry. This wizard relics on a graphical interface; you can't create entries at the command line.

-l{a | d | e | h | r} Performs any of the specified command line tasks to a dial-up short-cut file instead of the RAS phonebook.

link Specifies the full path to the dial-up link shortcut file. The path can include a drive, relative or absolute path, and a filename.

Communicating with Telnet

Telnet provides low-level access to other machines using a standardized protocol and connection. This section describes the command line interface for the Windows version of Telnet, which varies a little from the interface other platforms use. This section won't tell you how to perform management tasks.

 Real World Scenario

OLD DOESN'T MEAN OUTDATED

Some people will view the utilities in some parts of this book as antiquated relics from an earlier time. However, these time-tested utilities are often your best means of managing a system, especially when you can use your knowledge on multiple machines. Telnet is an older utility that predates Windows. In addition to your Windows installation, you'll find Telnet on just about every other operating system. The utility is low level, but quite useful. Many administrators rely on this tool to perform configuration tasks, access a frozen server from a remote location, check routers, and generally perform tasks that you can't easily perform using a graphical utility.

You'll find a number of Telnet-related files that don't include any type of user interface in the \Windows\System32 folder. These support files provide additional Telnet functionality. For example, the TlNtSess.EXE file controls the Telnet session. You can obtain an overview of how these other files affect Telnet under Windows on the Microsoft site at http://technet2.microsoft.com/windowsserver/en/library/566bc823-b916-40cf-a0c0-1dedffaebeb11033.mspx.

NOTE Server Core doesn't install any Telnet support by default. You must install the Telnet functionality using the OCSetup utility found in the "Adding and Removing Applications with the OCSetup Utility" section of Chapter 13.

Administrating Telnet with the TLNTAdmn Utility

The Telnet Administrator utility helps you control Telnet sessions on your machine. You access it using the TLNTAdmn utility. If you use TLNTAdmn alone, you'll see a display of the current server status, as shown in Figure 17.2. Adding start, stop, pause, or continue to the command line controls the Telnet service state. Note that these commands only work if you set Telnet to manual or automatic mode—the command fails if you disable the Telnet service.

FIGURE 17.2

Use the TLNTAdmn utility to display the status of your Telnet server.

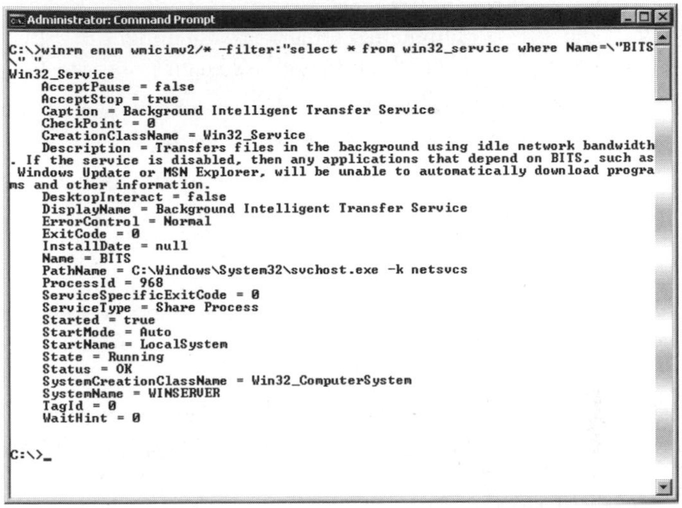

The TLNTAdmn utility includes three user-specific commands. Use the -s switch with an optional session identifier to display the user status information. Each user entry includes the user ID, name, remote connection point, and logon time. The idle time column is a good indicator of who has gone to lunch with their Telnet connection intact. Use the -m switch with a session identifier to send the user a message. The third user option is the -k SessionIdentifier switch. Use it to end a user session. This utility uses the following syntax:

```
TLNTAdmn [ComputerName] [-u user [-p password]] start | stop | pause |
continue | -s sessionid | -k sessionid | -m sessionid message | config
config_options
```

The following list describes each of the command line arguments.

ComputerName   Specifies the name of a remote computer. The default setting uses the local computer.

-u user   Specifies the name of the user account used to execute command. The default setting relies on the user account for the currently logged in user.

-p password   Specifies the user password.

start   Starts the Telnet service. This option only works when the service is set to automatic or manual. You can't start a disabled service.

stop   Stops the Telnet service.

pause   Pauses the Telnet service. A pause is temporary when compared to a stop. Don't use pause when you actually mean to stop the service.

continue   Continues the service from a pause.

-s sessionid   Lists information about the specified session.

-k sessionid   Terminates the specified session. Exercise care in using this option since a terminated session could cause data loss. Generally, you'll use this as a last resort. Try sending a message to the user first to shut down the session from the client side or physically end the session from the client terminal yourself.

-m *sessionid message*   Sends a message to the specified session. Make sure you place any message within quotes. Otherwise, the utility sends just the first word of the message to the remote terminal and then displays an error message.

config *config_options*   Changes the server configuration. Use one or more configuration options to change the way in which the server works.

Telnet provides a number of configuration options. Each of these configuration options controls an aspect of the way in which Telnet works. Change the server configuration carefully because some options can cause connection errors or make the server unavailable to users who need it. The following list describes each of the configuration options.

dom = *Domain*   Sets the default domain for checking usernames. If you're using a peer-to-peer configuration, then the only domain is your machine. The only time you can set this to another domain is if you have a Windows server set up as a domain controller.

ctrlakeymap = **<Yes|No>**   Sets the mapping of the ALT key to Ctrl+A when on. This is the default setting. This setting doesn't affect the VTNT terminal, but does affect other terminal types. See RFC 884 (`http://www.faqs.org/rfcs/rfc884.html`) for a list of standard Telnet terminal types.

timeout = *hh:mm:ss*   Determines how long the Telnet server waits before it logs out a user automatically. You must include the colons between the hours, minutes, and seconds. In addition, if you want to set a value to 0, then include a 0 on the command line. For example, if you want to set the timeout value to 30 minutes, type **TLNTADMN config timeout = 0:30:00** at the command line.

timeoutactive = **{Yes | No}**   Enables idle session timeout counter. Whenever a session reaches the timeout value, the Telnet server disables it automatically.

maxfail = *Attempts*   Sets the maximum number of login failure attempts before disabling the user account. Telnet won't allow disabled user accounts to connect.

maxconn = *Connections*   Determines the maximum number of connections the Telnet server accepts. Note that the Microsoft documentation states that you can accept a maximum of two sessions. This is incorrect. Using this configuration option allows you to accept the maximum number of connections your machine can handle.

port = *Number*   Changes the connection port number. It's always a good idea to change this number to something other than the default to help thwart crackers. Of course, if you leave the port open and use poor security, someone will still get in.

sec = **[+/-]NTLM [+/-]PASSWD**   Determines the acceptable security (authentication) mechanisms. Allowing NTLM enables the user to log in using their default Windows username and password.

mode = **{Console | Stream}**   Controls how the server reacts to control character input. Always use console mode to ensure users can use applications such as EDIT.

Executing Commands Remotely with the Telnet Utility

The Telnet utility manages Telnet sessions at the command prompt. You'll start the Telnet client at a command prompt by typing **Telnet** and pressing Enter. Telnet displays a Welcome message, the escape character, and a Microsoft Telnet prompt. This utility uses the following syntax:

```
TELNET [-a][-e escape char][-f log file][-1 user][-t term][host [port]]
```

The following list describes each of the command line arguments.

-a Performs an automatic logon using the currently logged on username and password. This option works about the same as the -l option except you don't have to specify the username. Windows XP and above ignore this option if you have NTLM security enabled. It automatically logs on using the currently logged on username and password.

NOTE The Windows XP and above versions of Telnet sets Windows NT LAN Manager (NTLM) authentication on by default. This means that it will always attempt to log on using the currently logged on username and password. Using this option makes access somewhat automatic. All you need to do is type `Telnet HostName` at the command prompt and Telnet connects you, if you have proper rights. However, this option has two unfortunate side effects. The first is that you can't specify another username and password to log onto the system. The second is that the NTLM option appears to interfere with operation of some Telnet clients. You can turn off this feature using the TLNTAdmn utility described in the "Administrating Telnet with the TLNTAdmn Utility" section of the chapter.

-e Modifies the escape character used to enter the Telnet client prompt from a remote session. Telnet defaults to Ctrl+], which is a good choice because it isn't used by anything else.

-f *Filename* Sets the filename for client-side logging. Using this option also turns client-side logging on. Client-side logging doesn't track the commands you type at the Telnet prompt; they only record what you've done at the remote terminal connection. For example, if you type a `Dir` command at the remote prompt, you'll see the `Dir` command and results in the log. However, you won't see the command used to open the connection because that occurs at the Telnet prompt.

-l *Username* Specifies the username to log in with on the remote system. You can't specify a password at the command line, so you still have to provide a password before the session will start. Windows XP and above ignores this option if you have NTLM security enabled. It automatically logs on using the currently logged on username and password.

-t *TerminalType* Specifies the terminal type used for command processing and text display. Telnet supports the VT100, VT52, ANSI, and VTNT terminal types. The terminal type determines the characteristics of the session. It dates back to a time when people accessed mainframes using utilities such as Telnet. Using the default ANSI terminal usually works fine. Telnet remembers your preferred terminal type from session to session.

TIP The default terminal type of ANSI does work fine for most connections, especially those with a mainframe. However, the ANSI terminal type causes problems when you run certain Windows XP character mode utilities. Any utility that has a display and a functional menu system will likely require you to use the VTNT terminal. For example, if you normally use the EDIT command to work with text files, you'll want to use the VTNT terminal.

HostName [PortNumber] Specifies the hostname or IP address of the remote computer. You may optionally specify a service name or port number. The only time you need to specify a port number is to access a service other than Telnet or if the Telnet administrator changes the port number.

Managing Windows in a New Way

You'll find many pointers for working with communications under Server Core. A server is all about communication and getting communications to work right is essential. Of course, with all of the communications that a server supports, there isn't a simple answer to some requirements. One of the issues pointed out is that you may not find every piece of support you require in Server Core. Many companies rely on ICS to provide Internet access to a workgroup and this option isn't available in Server Core. This chapter helps you build these skills:

- Perform remote system management
- Manage FTP servers
- Configure and manage Terminal Server
- Configure and manage Remote Access Server
- Use Telnet to obtain access to remote systems

Most of the programs discussed in this chapter require practice on your part. You won't get much work done with the FTP utility until you've worked with it for a while. The same holds true for working with RAS and Telnet. Since you'll find use for these utilities for general management tasks, as well as a means to troubleshoot problems in an emergency, it's a good idea to work with them using a test setup. In this case, you'll actually want to set up a client system and a server so that you can see how communications work over a network. Trying to learn these applications on a single system can provide a less than real world experience.

Chapter 18 moves onto the task of monitoring your server. Monitoring is important for many reasons. For example, you need to ensure that the performance of your system remains consistent and you can't do that without performing some level of monitoring. You'll also use monitoring to detect existing or potential hardware failures, as well as the activities of outsiders who don't have your best interests in mind. In short, Chapter 18 is an essential maintenance chapter—it describes the monitoring tasks you must perform to have a healthy server.

Chapter 18

Monitoring System Events and Performance

Monitoring your server is an essential task. You need to monitor it in a number of ways. When you perform automated tasks, you need to ensure the tasks complete as anticipated. You'll also need to check the event logs for events that have occurred on your system. This is one place where using the Event Viewer console is more convenient, but you can also perform the task from the command line when necessary. The goal is to make sure you understand what the system is doing.

The performance of your system is important as well. If the system doesn't perform well, then users will complain. Performance is more than simple speed. A system that performs well has good security, is reliable, and completes tasks quickly. Unless you include all three goals in your performance strategy, your system is doomed to perform poorly at some point.

Monitoring also means knowing what others are doing with the server. You must not only check for external sources of corruption but also internal sources. Corruption can come in many forms. Of course, the forms of corruption that grab the headlines include viruses, adware, and stolen data. However, corruption could mean entering the wrong data into a database or configuring an application incorrectly. Any data issue that prevents your server from providing the level of performance it's designed to provide is corruption. This chapter helps you understand monitoring from a number of perspectives.

In this chapter, you'll learn how to do the following:

◆ Document system status information

◆ Create, delete, and view events

◆ Create, delete, and view event triggers

◆ Record and manage system performance information

◆ Work with performance logs

◆ Work with performance counters

Recording System Status Information

Making a permanent record of system status information is important, especially when an error occurs. Windows uses the term *event* to indicate a change. Events aren't necessarily errors. In fact, some events are informational, while others are simply warnings. Windows also provides a number of other events, such as security events where it performs an audit of the security on a system. Generally, though, you'll only consider three kinds of events: informational, warning, and errors. The following sections describe the utilities for working with system events.

USING EVENT LOGS EFFECTIVELY

Windows records all events in the event log. You can use the Event Viewer console in the Administrative Tools folder of the Control Panel to view the events. The standard logs for events are Application, Security, and System. Unfortunately, many users don't know the event logs exist and administrators don't find time to use them. In many cases, someone will call me in to look at their system and I find the answers I need to fix the error right in the event log that they failed to review. In fact, I'm amazed at how often the event log entry tells me what action to take or at least provides enough specifics that I can research the repair in the Microsoft Knowledge Base.

Educating yourself about the event log and understanding how to use it effectively are important. You can learn more about the event log in general on the Microsoft Web site at http://technet2.microsoft.com/windowsserver/en/library/9930c8f1-54ed-4d07-afa6-bc3c597bbe9c1033.mspx.

However, effective event log usage goes even further. As you begin writing your own applications (even batch file applications), consider adding event log entries to one of the standard logs or use a special log for the purpose. The Code Project article (http://www.codeproject.com/dotnet/evtvwr.asp) shows how to add new event logs using registry entries. You'll also want to review the MSDN "EventLog Key" article at http://msdn2.microsoft.com/en-us/library/aa363648.aspx.

Managing System Events with the EventCreate Utility

The EventCreate utility adds a new event log entry. You can send an event log entry to any current log, including any custom log that you create. In fact, this utility can create event log entries with the same complexity and level of information that any application can create. This utility uses the following syntax:

```
EVENTCREATE [/S system [/U username [/P [password]]]] /ID eventid
[/L logname] [/SO srcname] /T {ERROR | WARNING | INFORMATION} /D description
```

Notice that you must provide the /ID, /T, and /D command line switches. The following list describes each of the command line arguments.

/S *system* Specifies a remote system. You can use any connected system to store the event log entries. Some administrators send event log entries to a central location to ensure someone sees them. The remote system must allow the required access.

/U *[domain\]user* Defines the user context for executing the command. The user context is important because not every user has access to the event log. In addition, the user context appears as part of the event log entry.

/P *[password]* Provides a password for the user context. The utility prompts you for the password (when necessary) if you don't include it on the command line. In most cases, supplying the password when prompted is safer from a security perspective than including this information on the command line or as part of a batch file entry.

/L *logname* Determines the name of the log to use for the event entry. The three standard logs found on every Windows machine are Application, Security, and System. Many machines include additional event logs installed by applications that the system uses.

/T {ERROR | WARNING | INFORMATION}   Specifies the kind of event to create. Even though the Windows event log accepts other event types, the only three acceptable types are error, warning, and information. These three types reflect three levels of severity, with information being the least severe and error being the most severe.

/SO *source*   Defines the source of the event. You can use any string as the source. However, providing a meaningful application identifier is usually the best idea. Given that you'll use this feature from the command line, you might simply want to use "Command Line" as your source. When working with a batch file, use the batch filename as the source. Scripts and other forms of automation should use the script or application name.

/ID *id*   Specifies the event identifier for the event. The identifier is a number between 1 and 1,000. Whenever practical, provide specific numbers for specific events. For example, you might assign a value of 500 to all file errors. The event identifier lets you sort the events in a manner other than type or source, so you should also keep this in mind when you create the event identifier list for your application.

/D *description*   Provides an event description. The description should tell the viewer what happened to cause the event, the event effects, and any other pertinent information the viewer might need to resolve event problems caused by the event. Even informational events should include significant event information. For example, you might record that your application started, found no work to do, and terminated. Even though the application didn't experience an error, the information is still important to someone who expected your application to complete useful work.

NOTE   The event log accepts several additional pieces of information that you can't add using the EventCreate utility. The event category requires that you register a specialized DLL to handle the category information. Given that you probably won't add the required DLL for a batch file application, Microsoft left this particular entry out. An event can also register data that amplifies the event description. The lack of support for this feature is regrettable because you could use it to create better event log entries. However, you can overcome this problem by providing a detailed description and possibly including the data as part of the description, rather than as a separate entry.

Triggering System Events with the EventTriggers Utility

One of the problems with the event log is that it can quickly become clogged with information—more information than many network administrators want to wade through to locate a particular event of importance. Starting with Windows XP, you can set an event trigger on the event log. When an event log entry matching the criteria you specify appears, you can tell the EventTriggers utility to perform any number of tasks—anything from sending an email message to running a particular application (batch files included).

The interesting part about using event triggers is that you can track problems occurring on any system (local or remote) with greater ease. Although you might want to look at all of those informational messages in the event log at some point, the SQL Server error message is the one that you really want to know about the second it occurs. The SQL Server message is an example of an event log entry that you want to track using an event trigger. Of course, the entry could just as easily be from any other application. For example, you might want to know when the Windows Time Service fails to find an online time synchronization source.

The EventTriggers utility provides three modes of operation: Create, Delete, and Query. Each one of these modes controls a particular aspect of working with event triggers. The following sections discuss these three modes of operation and show how you use them to manage event triggers on your system.

CREATE

Before you can use event triggers, you have to create them. The Create mode helps you add new event triggers. Each event trigger reacts to a separate event in the event log, so you need one event trigger for each event log entry that you want to monitor. This mode uses the following syntax:

```
EVENTTRIGGERS /Create [/S system [/U username [/P [password]]]] /TR
triggername /TK taskname [/D description] [/L log] { [/EID id]
[/T type] [/SO source] } [/RU username [/RP password]]
```

The following list describes each of the command line arguments.

/S *system* Specifies a remote system. You can use any connected system to store the event log entries. Some administrators send event log entries to a central location to ensure someone sees them. The remote system must allow the required access.

/U *[domain\]user* Defines the user context for executing the command. The user context is important because not every user has access to the event log. In addition, the user context appears as part of the event log entry.

/P *[password]* Provides a password for the user context. The utility prompts you for the password (when necessary) if you don't include it on the command line. In most cases, supplying the password when prompted is safer from a security perspective than including this information on the command line or as part of a batch file entry.

/TR *triggername* Defines a human-readable name to associate with the event trigger. Using names such as MyTrigger probably won't work well. It's important to create a descriptive name that you'll recognize easily. Make sure you make the name unique by adding some elements for the event log entry that it monitors. For example, WinMgmtWarning63 would be a good name for an event generated by the Windows management service at the warning level for event identifier number 63.

/L *log* Specifies the Windows event log to monitor. The three common logs include Application, System, and Security. The DNS Server and Directory logs commonly appear on servers. You can also specify any custom log. You can use wildcard characters to define the log name. The default value is "*" (without the quotes), which is all of the event logs on the specified machine.

/EID *id* Specifies which Event ID to monitor in the event log. This value is application specific, so you need to know which Event ID an application will use for a particular requirement.

/T *type* Specifies the Event Type to monitor in the event log. The valid values include ERROR, INFORMATION, WARNING, SUCCESSAUDIT, and FAILUREAUDIT. The SUCCESSAUDIT and FAILUREAUDIT only appear in security logs.

/SO *source* Specifies the Event Source to monitor in the event log. The Event Source varies by application and by entity performing a task. For example, the system can just as easily generate an event that a user can generate. Unless you want to monitor the activities of a specific entity, you should refrain from supplying this command line switch.

/D *description*   Specifies the Description to monitor in the event log. Using this command line switch makes the event trigger very specific. In fact, the event trigger becomes so specific that you might miss events. Use this particular command line switch with caution and only in cases where you know exactly which message you want to receive.

/TK *taskname*   Defines the name of the task to perform when the event trigger fires. Generally, this is the name of an application (including any required command line switches), batch file, script, or other executable entity. For example, you can tell Outlook to send you a message about the event using Outlook's command line switches to generate an email.

/RU *username*   Defines the user account to use to run the task. Use " " (two quotes) for the system account. The default username is the current username or the name used to access the remote system with the /U command line switch.

/RP *password*   Defines the password for the task user account. The EventTriggers utility ignores this value when working with the system account. Supply a value of "*" (without the quotes) or none when you want the EventTriggers utility to prompt for a password.

DELETE

Use the Delete mode to remove any event triggers you no longer need. This mode uses the following syntax:

```
EVENTTRIGGERS /Delete [/S system [/U username [/P [password]]]] /TID id
[/TID id1 [...[/TID idn]]]
```

The following list describes each of the command line arguments.

/S *system*   Specifies a remote system. You can use any connected system to store the event log entries. Some administrators send event log entries to a central location to ensure someone sees them. The remote system must allow the required access.

/U *[domain\]user*   Defines the user context for executing the command. The user context is important because not every user has access to the event log. In addition, the user context appears as part of the event log entry.

/P *[password]*   Provides a password for the user context. The utility prompts you for the password (when necessary) if you don't include it on the command line. In most cases, supplying the password when prompted is safer from a security perspective than including this information on the command line or as part of a batch file entry.

/TID *id*   Specifies the Trigger Identifier to remove from the list of event triggers. Every time you create a new event trigger, the system assigns it an identifier. You can see this identifier by using the Query mode. This command line switch accepts the * wildcard, which deletes all of the event triggers on the system.

QUERY

The Query mode displays a list of all of the event triggers on a system. You can use this list for real-time work with the event triggers. However, by changing the format, you can also use this mode to add the event triggers to a database for later reference. This mode uses the following syntax:

```
EVENTTRIGGERS /Query [/S system [/U username [/P [password]]]] [/FO
{TABLE | LIST | CSV}] [/NH] [/V]
```

The following list describes each of the command line arguments.

/S *system*   Specifies a remote system. You can use any connected system to store the event log entries. Some administrators send event log entries to a central location to ensure someone sees them. The remote system must allow the required access.

/U *[domain\]user*   Defines the user context for executing the command. The user context is important because not every user has access to the event log. In addition, the user context appears as part of the event log entry.

/P *[password]*   Provides a password for the user context. The utility prompts you for the password (when necessary) if you don't include it on the command line. In most cases, supplying the password when prompted is safer from a security perspective than including this information on the command line or as part of a batch file entry.

/FO {TABLE | LIST | CSV}   Defines the output format for this mode. The default output is a tabular view. The table columns define the values for output, while each row contains one event trigger entry. The CSV output provides the best method for preparing the data for entry in a database. Use redirection (see the "Employing Data Redirection" section of Chapter 14 for details) to output the CSV data to a file and then import it to your database. The list format provides one data element per line. Each group of data elements defines one event trigger. The utility separates each event trigger by one blank line. Some people find the list format more readable when working in verbose mode since the table format requires multiple lines for each entry (the lines wrap).

/NH   Specifies that the EventTriggers utility shouldn't display the column headers. You can use this option when creating pure content for reports or other needs. The EventTriggers utility accepts this command line switch only when using the table and CSV formats.

/V   Outputs additional information about each event trigger. The default output includes the trigger identifier, event trigger name, and the name of the task the event trigger performs. The additional information includes the hostname, the event trigger query (the arguments used to trigger it), the description information, and the username used to run the task.

Managing Event Information with the WEvtUtil Utility

The WEvtUtil utility helps you monitor the event logs on a system. This utility replaces the other utilities provided in earlier versions of Windows. You might wonder about this change, until you begin looking at the Server Core event log setup, which is very complex. (The new event logs are a significant change from past versions of Windows that have contained the same few logs.) The WEvtUtil utility has the flexibility required to work with Server Core's complex event log setup. This utility uses the following syntax:

```
WEvtUtil COMMAND [ARGUMENT [ARGUMENT] ...] [/OPTION:VALUE [/OPTION:VALUE] ...]
```

It helps to discuss WEvtUtil command line arguments as commands and common options (with associated arguments). The following list describes each of the commands (the short name appears first, followed by the long name in parentheses).

el (enum-logs)   Displays a list of all of the logs on the system.

gl (get-log) *Logname*   Obtains configuration information about a specific log. You must provide the fully qualified name of the log that you want to work with. For example, if you want to know about the Backup log, you must provide the fully qualified name of Microsoft-Windows-Backup. Use the el command to obtain a list of fully qualified names.

sl (set-log) *Logname* **[/***Option***:***Value* **[/***Option***:***Value***]** **...]** Changes the configuration of a log file. You can supply option/value pairs or use an XML file to make the changes. The WEvtUtil utility accepts either short or long option names. When using an XML file, you must supply the /c option. The following list describes the option/value pairs used to configure a log (the long names appear in parentheses after the option).

/e:{True | False} (enabled) Enables or disables the log. The default value is true to enable the log.

/i:{System | Application | Custom} (isolation) Defines the log isolation mode: system, application, or custom. In addition, the mode identifies the other logs with which the log shares a session, which means these other logs have write permission for the target log. Use the System mode when a log affects that system as a whole. The resulting log shares a session with the System log. The Application mode is the option to use with general applications. Logs in this class share a session with the Application log. The Custom mode is for private logs that you don't want to share a session with any other log. You must use the /ca option to define security for custom logs.

/lfn:*Value* **(logfilename)** Provides the full path to the physical location of the log on the hard drive.

/rt:{True | False} (retention) Determines whether the log retains existing entries when the log becomes full. When you set the log retention mode to True, the log retains earlier entries when the log becomes full and discards all new entries. The default value of false discards older entries in favor of new ones.

/ab:{True | False} (autobackup) Performs an automatic backup of the log when it reaches maximum size. You must set the retention value to true using the /rt option when using this feature.

/ms:*Value* **(maxsize)** Specifies the maximum log size in bytes. The maximum log size in Server Core is 1,048,576 bytes (1,024 KB). Log files are always multiples of 64 KB, so Server Core rounds any value you provide to a multiple of 64 KB.

/l:*Value* **(level)** Defines the log level filter (normally critical, error, warning, information, or verbose). You may use any valid level value. This feature is only applicable to logs with a dedicated session (which means that the isolation mode is normally custom). You can remove a level filter by setting the value to 0.

/k:*Value* **(keywords)** Defines the log keyword filter (common keywords include Audit Failure, Audit Success, Classic, Correlation Hint, Software Quality Monitoring (SQM), Windows Diagnostics Infrastructure (WDI) Context, and WDI Diag). The value can include any valid 64-bit keyword mask. This feature is only applicable to logs with a dedicated session (which means that the isolation mode is normally custom).

/ca:*Value* **(channelaccess)** Defines the access permission for an event log. You must provide a valid security descriptor defined using the Security Descriptor Definition Language (SDDL). You can learn more about SDDL at `http://msdn2.microsoft.com/en-us/library/aa379567..aspx`.

/c:*Value* **(config)** Defines a path to a configuration file. The configuration file contains log file settings in the form of an XML file. When using this feature, you must not specify the `logname` command line argument because this value is ready as part of the configuration file. Here's a typical example of a configuration file.

```xml
<?xml version="1.0" encoding="UTF-8"?>
<channel name="Application" isolation="Application"
        xmlns="http://schemas.microsoft.com/win/2004/08/events">
  <logging>
    <retention>true</retention>
    <autoBackup>true</autoBackup>
    <maxSize>9000000</maxSize>
  </logging>
  <publishing>
  </publishing>
</channel>
```

Notice that the `<channel>` element includes the log filename as Application and an isolation level (/i) of Application. The logging options appear as part of the `<logging>` element. Each child element name is the long name for an option. For example, the `<retention>` element corresponds to the /rt command line argument. You can add other configuration options to the log, such as the publishing options.

ep (enum-publishers) Displays a list of event publishers. The list can be quite long, so you'll normally want to redirect the output to a text file.

gp (get-publisher) *PublisherName* **[/OPTION:VALUE [/OPTION:VALUE] ...]** Obtains specific event publisher configuration information. The output includes such helpful information as a publisher help link and the name of the DLL used to create event entries. This argument also supports the following options (the long names appear in parentheses after the option).

  /ge:{True | False} (getevents) Obtains metadata for the events that this publisher will raise, in addition to the standard data.

  /gm:{True | False} (getmessage) Obtains the actual messages that the event entries will use instead of the message ID.

  /f:{XML | Text} (format) Determines the output format of the data. The default setting is Test. When you use XML, the output appears as an XML file that you can view using any XML viewer (making the output considerably easier to understand).

im (install-manifest) *Manifest* Installs an event manifest. The manifest can contain multiple publishers and logs. You can obtain an overview of event manifest instrumentation at http://msdn2.microsoft.com/en-gb/library/aa385227.aspx.

um (uninstall-manifest) *Manifest* Removes the specified event manifest from the system.

qe (query-events) *Path* **[/OPTION:VALUE [/OPTION:VALUE] ...]** Outputs event information from a log or log file. The path argument normally contains the name of the log. However, if you use the /lf option, then you must provide the physical path to the event log file. This argument also supports the following options (the long names appear in parentheses after the option).

  /lf:{True | False} (logfile) Specifies that the path argument contains a physical path to a log file, rather than a log filename.

/sq:{True | False} (structuredquery) Specifies that the path argument contains a path to a file that contains a structure query.

/q:Value (query) Provides an XPath query to filter the events read from the log. The utility returns all of the events when you don't provide this option. You can't use this option with the /sq option.

/bm:Value (bookmark) Specifies a path to a file that contains a bookmark from a previous query. Using a bookmark lets you continue a previous query.

/sbm:Value (savebookmark) Specifies a path to a file that the utility uses to store a bookmark for the current query. The bookmark file extension should be XML.

/rd:{True | False} (reversedirection) Defines the direction in which the utility reads events. The default setting of true returns the most current events first.

/f:{XML | Text} (format) Determines the output format of the data. The default setting is Test. When you use XML, the output appears as an XML file that you can view using any XML viewer (making the output considerably easier to understand).

/l:LCID (locale) Provides a locale string that defines the locale used to output text information. This option is only available when you use the /f option to print events in text format.

/c:Number (count) Defines the maximum number of events to read. If you combine this switch with the bookmark feature, you can read a segment of the event log at a time.

/e:RootElementName (element) Defines a root element name to use to produce well-formed XML.

gli (get-log-info) Path Outputs information about the specified log. The path argument normally contains the name of the log. However, if you use the /lf option, then you must provide the physical path to the event log file. This argument also supports the following options (the long names appear in parentheses after the option).

/lf:{True | False} (logfile) Specifies that the path argument contains a physical path to a log file, rather than a log filename.

epl (export-log) Path TargetFile [/OPTION:VALUE [/OPTION:VALUE] ...] Exports a log to the specified target file. The path argument normally contains the name of the log. However, if you use the /lf option, then you must provide the physical path to the event log file. This argument also supports the following options (the long names appear in parentheses after the option).

/lf:{True | False} (logfile) Specifies that the path argument contains a physical path to a log file, rather than a log filename.

/sq:{True | False} (structuredquery) Specifies that the path argument contains a path to a file that contains a structure query.

/q:Value (query) Provides an XPath query to filter the events read from the log. The utility returns all of the events when you don't provide this option. You can't use this option with the /sq option.

/ow:{True | False} (overwrite) Overwrites the contents in any existing target file without confirmation when set to True. The default setting is False.

al (archive-log) LogFile [/OPTION:VALUE [/OPTION:VALUE] ...] Archives an exported log—the log entries remain in place, but the utility outputs a copy of all existing log entries. You can create a log using either the `export-log` or `clear-log` commands. This argument also supports the following options (the long names appear in parentheses after the option).

> **/l:*LCID* (locale)**   Provides a locale string that defines the locale used to output text information. This option is only available when you use the `/f` option to print events in text format.

cl (clear-log) *LogName* [/*OPTION:VALUE*]   Clears the specified log. This command differs from archiving in that the utility actually clears the log entries instead of leaving them in place. This argument also supports the following option (the long names appear in parentheses after the option).

> **/bu:*Filename* (backup)**   Creates a backup of the log before clearing it. You must specify a backup filename with an EVTX extension. (Don't use the EVT extension used with previous version of Windows because the file formats aren't compatible.)

Most of the commands use common options. The options are in addition to the special options discussed as part of the commands. The following list describes each of the options.

NOTE   There are some differences between the WEvtUtil options and the options used by other utilities, even though many of them perform the same function. For example, the familiar /S command line switch (for remote system) is now the /r command line switch. Be careful when making assumptions about the options for this utility.

/r:*System* (remote)   Specifies a remote system. You can use any connected system to store the event log entries. Some administrators send event log entries to a central location to ensure someone sees them. The remote system must allow the required access.

/u:[*domain*]*user* (username)   Defines the user context for executing the command. The user context is important because not every user has access to the event log. In addition, the user context appears as part of the event log entry.

/p:*Password* (password)   Provides a password for the user context. The utility prompts you for the password (when necessary) if you don't include it on the command line. In most cases, supplying the password when prompted is safer from a security perspective than including this information on the command line or as part of a batch file entry.

/a:{Default | Negotiate | Kerberos | NTLM} (authentication)   Specifies the kind of authentication to use for the remote location. The default value is Negotiate. Using a specific value can improve security when the remote machine offers multiple authentication options.

/uni:{True | False} (unicode)   Specifies that the utility should display all output in Unicode when set to True.

Working with Performance Information

No matter what you do with your system, at some point, you'll want to know how it's performing. Performance data generally takes two forms. The static variety acts as a long-term record of the performance of your system as a whole. You can use it to track the performance of your system over time. The dynamic variety shows the current performance of your system. You can use it to check for changes in system status, look for positive gains after optimization, and even use it to troubleshoot your system (such as when a network card fails to deliver the throughput you anticipated).

UNDERSTANDING THE IMPORTANCE OF PERFORMANCE

Some people just aren't race fans; they don't care how well something is performing as long as it eventually gets the job done. They have no need for speed. However, performance monitoring is considerably more important than simply having bragging rights about your system speed. You don't need to be a race fan to gain something important from performance monitoring.

One of the tasks I perform after I set up a new system is to obtain and store a baseline performance evaluation. The purpose of this stored data is to provide a baseline for comparison later—after the system has operated for a while. When someone complains that their system no longer works as it did when it was new, I use the performance baseline I created to find out where the problem lies. For example, an inordinate level of network traffic might clue me into the activities of a cracker or a load of adware on the system. High error levels might tell me that a piece of hardware is beginning to fail. Both hard drives and network adapters are famous for providing this heads-up information before they become unusable. In short, performance isn't necessarily about speed; you can use performance statistics to learn more about your system and to fix it faster.

Unlike many of the utilities discussed in this chapter, you can perform setups using the command line utilities, but actual monitoring usually occurs using the Performance console found in the Administrative Tools folder of the Control Panel. This chapter focuses on the command line tasks—those parts of performance monitoring that other books tend to ignore. However, you'll need to augment this information with a usage guide for the Performance console. This book won't tell you how to use the graphical interface. The following sections describe the command line interface in detail.

Adding Performance Counters with the LodCtr Utility

Performance monitoring relies on the existence of counters. A counter is a special piece of code that counts something. The count might reflect the number of times a user accesses a file or makes a network request. No matter what the counter monitors, it provides output that the various performance monitoring applications can use to report performance data. In many cases, the performance counters appear as part of the application, so they're available from the moment you install the application. However, you can also obtain external counters. The LodCtr utility loads a counter into the system so that you can access it from performance monitoring software. This utility uses the following syntax:

```
LODCTR [\\computername] FileName
LODCTR /S:<IniFileName>
LODCTR /R:<IniFileName>
```

The following list describes each of the command line arguments.

computername   Specifies the name of a remote computer. You must have access to the computer through Windows. This utility doesn't provide any means of specifying a username or password for the remote computer.

FileName   Defines the name of a file that contains the initialization data for a counter. The INI file normally contains the name of the DLL with the counter code, counter definitions (such as the human-readable name and any required help text), and the explanation text for an extensible counter DLL.

IniFileName   Defines the name of an initialization file that contains counter registration information. This file lets you save and restore counter settings on a single machine or to move counter settings from one machine to another. The registration strings generally include the First Counter, First Help, Last Counter, and Last Help information for each of the counters. You'll also see a [PerfStrings_009] section that includes a list of all of the performance counter strings by number.

WARNING   Even though the documentation for this utility seems to say that the utility produces a REG (registry) file, the file isn't a registry script. If you try to install the file using the RegEdit utility, the RegEdit utility displays an error. In fact, the file does appear in the INI file format and you should probably give it an INI file extension, rather than the REG file extension Microsoft recommends.

/S   Saves the performance counter registry strings to the specified file.

/R   Restores the performance counter registry string from the specified file.

Managing Performance Logs and Alerts with the LogMan Utility

The Windows performance monitoring software includes the capability of creating performance logs and of creating alerts. The logs act as a historical record of the data the performance monitoring software collects. The alerts can perform tasks based on the current system performance. For example, if a system is low on memory or other resources, you can use an alert to send a message to the administrator to fix the problem. This utility uses the following syntax:

```
LogMan VERB <collection_name> [options]
```

Notice that you must supply a verb, which is an action for the utility to perform. The verb has no slash as a command line switch would have; simply type the word by itself. The following list describes each of the verbs for this utility.

create {counter | trace}   Creates a new counter or trace collection. The kind of entry you create determines its location in the Performance console. A counter appears within the Counter Logs folder, while a trace appears within the Trace Logs folder.

start   Starts an existing collection. This action sets the begin time to manual.

stop   Stops an existing collection. This action sets the end time to manual.

delete   Deletes an existing collection. None of the collection information remains; you can't undo this action.

query {*collection_name* | *providers*}   Queries a collection or provider. Typing **query** by itself displays a list of collections that includes the collection name, the collection type (counter or trace), and the collection status. When you supply a collection name, the display includes the name, type, status, start mode (normally manual), stop mode (normally manual), output filename, the run as information (username), and the counters monitored by the collection (such as \Process(_Total)\% Processor Time). If you use the provider's keyword, you'll see a list of registered providers and their associated GUID.

update   Updates an existing collection of properties. You specify the existing collection name, along with the new properties that you want to use. Whenever an existing property conflicts with a new property, the new property overrides the existing property value.

You combine verbs with a collection name and one or more command line switches to perform tasks with LogMan. The following list describes each of the command line arguments.

collection_name Defines the name of the collection to use. The collection name is the name that you assign to the counter or trace when you create it. This is the same name that appears in the Performance console.

-s *computer* Performs the task on a remote system. The default setting uses the local system.

-config *filename* Provides a file containing a list of settings to use in place of command line options. Using this feature lets you repeat setups with greater ease. In addition, creating the sometimes complex command line setups this utility requires is difficult. Using a configuration file reduces the work you'll need to perform at the command line.

-b *M/d/yyyy h:mm:ss*[{ *AM* | *PM* }] Defines the starting time for the collection. Collection continues until the specified ending time (see the -e command line switch) or you manually end the collection process using the stop verb. The default setting uses the current day and time. You can input times using a 24-hour clock. When specifying a time based on a 12-hour clock, add the ~AM or ~PM option.

-e *M/d/yyyy h:mm:ss*[{ *AM* | *PM* }] Defines the ending time for the collection. The default setting uses the current day and time. You can input times using a 24-hour clock. When specifying a time based on a 12-hour clock, add the ~AM or ~PM option.

-m [start] [stop] Modifies the collection to use a manual start or stop, rather than relying on a scheduled beginning or ending time.

-[-]r Repeats the collection daily at the specified begin and end time when used with a single dash. Using a double dash removes the daily collection feature. This command is only valid for begin and end times specified on the same day, month, and year.

-o { *Filename* | *DSN!Log* } Specifies the output information for the collection. You can use an output file by specifying a path and filename. As an alternative, you can specify a SQL database (for any vendor that supports SQL) by including the Open Database Connectivity (ODBC) DSN and the log set name within the SQL database. (See the "Working with ODBC Data Sources" section of Chapter 14 for information on configuring ODBC from the command line.) The default setting is to use a file with the same name as the performance collection and a BLG extension for counters or an ETL extension for traces.

-f { *Bin* | *Bincirc* | *CSV* | *TSV* | *SQL* } Defines the log format for the output. You can choose between binary, circular binary, CSV, Tab Separated Value (TSV), and Structured Query Language (SQL).

-[-]a Appends data to the existing log file when used with a single dash. Overwrites the existing log file when used with a double dash. The default setting is to overwrite the existing log file.

-[-]v [*nnnnnn* | *mmddhhmm* **]** Attaches versioning information (either a number or the current date) to the end of the log filename when used with a single dash. Removes the versioning information when used with a double dash.

-[-]rc *Filename* Runs a command after the system closes the log when used with a single dash. Disables running a command when used with a double dash. The commands always run in the foreground (so the user can see them).

-[-]max *Size* Defines the maximum log file size in megabytes when used with a single dash. When the log file exceeds the maximum size, the system stops collecting data even if other command line arguments specify a longer collection time. This command line switch specifies the number of records when used with a SQL output. Removes the log file size restriction when used with a double dash.

-[-]cnf [[[hh:]mm:]ss] Creates a new file when the specified time elapses or the file reaches the maximum file size when used with a single dash. Removes the collection time restriction when used with a double dash.

-c *CounterPath* [*CounterPath...*] Specifies one or more performance counters to collect. Each performance counter has a path that begins with the counter object, specific counter, and finally the instance. Consequently, the \Process(_Total)\% Processor Time counter path would collect the _Total instance of the % Processor Time counter found in the Processor object. Make sure you place each counter path in double quotes. The counter path can include wildcard characters. Here's a list of acceptable counter path formats.

\\machine\object(parent/instance#index)\counter

\\machine\object(parent/instance)\counter

\\machine\object(instance#index)\counter

\\machine\object(instance)\counter

\\machine\object\counter

\object(parent/instance#index)\counter

\object(parent/instance)\counter

\object(instance#index)\counter

\object(instance)\counter

\object\counter

-cf *Filename* Specifies a file containing a list of performance counters to collect. Each counter path must appear on a separate line.

-si [[hh:]mm:]ss Defines the sample interval (how often the system samples the counter) for the collection.

-ln *logger_name* Specifies the logger name for event trace sessions. The default logger name is the same as the collection name.

-[-]rt Runs the event trace session in real-time mode instead of a file when used with a single dash. Runs the event trace session using a log file.

-p *provider* [*flags* [*level*]] Defines a single provider to use as a source of data. The system providers usually include the Windows Kernel Trace and ACPI Driver Trace Provider. Installed providers commonly include ASP.NET Events, MSSQLSERVER Trace, and .NET Common Language Runtime. You can also specify nonsystem providers. Use the LogMan Query Providers option to obtain a list of providers for the current system.

-pf *Filename* Specifies a file containing a list of providers to use as part of an event trace. Each provider must appear on a separate line.

-[-]ul Runs the event trace session in user mode when used with a single dash. The system can only report on a single provider when running in user mode. Runs the event trace session in kernel mode when used with a double dash.

-bs *Value*   Specifies the event trace session buffer size in kilobytes.

-ft <[[hh:]mm:]ss>   Defines the interval for flushing the event trace session buffer from memory to disk.

-nb *Minimum Maximum*   Defines the minimum and maximum number of event trace session buffers.

-fd   Flushes all of the active buffers for an existing event trace session to disk.

-[-]u *[user [password]]*   Defines a user account and password to use when running the collection. Using * as the password input causes the LogMan utility to prompt you for the password. Entering the password at a prompt means that other people won't see it at the command line or within a batch file.

-rf *[[hh:]mm:]ss*   Runs the collection for the specified time.

-y   Answers yes to all questions without prompting. This feature lets you set up counters and traces within a batch file without worrying about interruptions.

-ets   Sends commands to event trace sessions without saving or scheduling.

-mode *trace_mode [trace_mode ...]*   Specifies advanced event session logger mode values, which can include globalsequence, localsequence, or pagedmemory. The globalsequence option forces the event trace logger to add a sequence number to every event it logs even if the entries are in different logs. The localsquence option adds sequence numbers to every event logged to a specific event trace. The sequence number might appear in another log, but all sequence numbers within a specific log are unique. The pagedmemory option forces the event logger to use paged memory, rather than non-paged memory, for its internal buffer allocations. Although using paged memory can slow event logger performance, it can also enhance system performance as a whole.

Not all of the command line switches work with all of the verbs. You need to know which command line switches to use with each verb. With that requirement in mind, here are a few LogMan examples.

```
LogMan create counter perf_log -c "\Processor(_Total)\% Processor Time"
LogMan create trace trace_log -nb 16 256 -bs 64 -o c:\logfile
LogMan start perf_log
LogMan update perf_log -si 10 -f csv -v mmddhhmm
LogMan update trace_log -p "Windows Kernel Trace" (disk,net)
```

Viewing the Results of Changes with the PerfMon Utility

PerfMon was the performance monitoring utility of the past. Windows 2000 represents a sort of transition point where you can use PerfMon or the Performance console. However, starting with Windows XP, the Performance console is the main event and PerfMon has taken a background role. Now all that this utility does for you is open the Performance counter with settings that you saved from Windows NT 4.0. In other words, you can see the same counters as you did in Windows NT 4.0, but the application displaying them differs. Consequently, the command line switches that you see here won't reflect what you used in the past. This utility uses the following syntax:

```
PerfMon [Filename] [/HTMLFILE:ConvFilename Filename]
```

The following list describes each of the command line arguments.

Filename   Specifies a file containing Windows NT 4.0 PerfMon settings to adjust the display in the Performance console.

ConvFilename   Specifies a file containing Windows NT 4.0 converted files. You may use the chart (.PMC), report (.PMR), alert (.PMA), and log (.PML) files from a Windows NT 4.0 setup.

/HTMLFILE   Displays the archived PerfMon files that you converted from a Windows NT 4.0 system. You must supply both the converted filename as well as the settings file used to config-ure the Performance console.

Reconfiguring Performance Logs with the ReLog Utility

Use this utility to create new performance logs from existing performance logs. The new logs can use a different sample rate. In addition, you can use this utility to convert a log from one format to another. You can use this utility to convert Windows NT 4.0 logs, including the compressed log for-mat. This utility uses the following syntax:

```
ReLog <filename [filename ...]> [options]
```

The following list describes each of the command line arguments.

filename   Specifies the names of one or more files that you want to convert.

-a   Appends the output to an existing binary file.

-c *CounterPath* **[***CounterPath* **...]**   Defines one or more counters to filter from the input log. The output log contains the remaining counters. Each performance counter has a path that begins with the counter object, specific counter, and finally the instance. Consequently, the \Process(_Total)\% Processor Time counter path would collect the _Total instance of the % Processor Time counter found in the Processor object. Make sure you place each counter path in double quotes. The counter path can include wildcard characters. Here's a list of accept-able counter path formats.

```
\\machine\object(parent/instance#index)\counter

\\machine\object(parent/instance)\counter

\\machine\object(instance#index)\counter

\\machine\object(instance)\counter

\\machine\object\counter

\object(parent/instance#index)\counter

\object(parent/instance)\counter

\object(instance#index)\counter

\object(instance)\counter

\object\counter
```

-cf *Filename*   Specifies a file containing a list of performance counters to collect. Each counter path must appear on a separate line.

-f { Bin | Bincirc | CSV | TSV | SQL }   Defines the log format for the output. You can choose between binary, circular binary, CSV, TSV, and SQL.

-t value   Changes the sampling rate by writing every *n*th record into the output file. For example, if the original file contains one record for each second, specifying a value of two would change the sampling rate to one every other second. The default setting writes every record into the output.

-o { Filename | DSN!Log }   Specifies the output information for the collection. You can use an output file by specifying a path and filename. As an alternative, you can specify a SQL database (for any vendor that supports SQL) by including the ODBC DSN and the log set name within the SQL database. (See the "Working with ODBC Data Sources" section of Chapter 14 for information on configuring ODBC from the command line.) The default setting is to use a file with the same name as the performance collection and a BLG extension for counters or an ETL extension for traces.

-b M/d/yyyy h:mm:ss[{ AM | PM }]   Defines the starting time for the collection. Collection continues until the specified ending time (see the -e command line switch) or you manually end the collection process using the stop verb. The default setting uses the current day and time. You can input times using a 24-hour clock. When specifying a time based on a 12-hour clock, add the ~AM or ~PM option.

-e M/d/yyyy h:mm:ss[{ AM | PM }]   Defines the ending time for the collection. The default setting uses the current day and time. You can input times using a 24-hour clock. When specifying a time based on a 12-hour clock, add the ~AM or ~PM option.

-config Filename   Specifies a configuration filename that contains all of the command line options.

-q   Lists all of the performance counters found in the input file. You can use this list to create input for the -c or -cf command line switches.

-y   Answers yes to all questions without prompting. This feature lets you set up counters and traces within a batch file without worrying about interruptions.

Tracking Performance with the TypePerf Utility

You don't have to use the graphical interface to view performance data in real time. The TypePerf utility provides continuously updated performance data in a command window in text format. The display updates at the specified rate until you press Ctrl+C to stop it. This utility uses the following syntax:

```
TypePerf <counter [counter ...]> [options]
TypePerf -cf <filename> [options]
TypePerf -q [object] [options]
TypePerf -qx [object] [options]
```

The following list describes each of the command line arguments.

counter   Specifies one or more performance counters to display. Each performance counter has a path that begins with the counter object, specific counter, and finally the instance. Consequently, the \Process(_Total)\% Processor Time counter path would collect the _Total instance of the % Processor Time counter found in the Processor object. Make sure you place each counter path in double quotes. The counter path can include wildcard characters. Here's a list of acceptable counter path formats.

```
\\machine\object(parent/instance#index)\counter

\\machine\object(parent/instance)\counter

\\machine\object(instance#index)\counter

\\machine\object(instance)\counter

\\machine\object\counter

\object(parent/instance#index)\counter

\object(parent/instance)\counter

\object(instance#index)\counter

\object(instance)\counter

\object\counter
```

-f { Bin | Bincirc | CSV | TSV | SQL }   Defines the log format for the output. You can choose between binary, circular binary, CSV, TSV, and SQL.

-cf *Filename*   Specifies a file containing a list of performance counters to collect. Each counter path must appear on a separate line. The default for the TypePerf utility is CSV.

-si [[*hh:*]*mm:*]*ss*   Defines the sample interval (how often the system samples the counter) for the collection. The default is 1 second.

-o { *Filename* | *DSN!Log* }   Specifies the output information for the collection. You can use an output file by specifying a path and filename. As an alternative, you can specify a SQL database (for any vendor that supports SQL) by including the ODBC DSN and the log set name within the SQL database. (See the "Working with ODBC Data Sources" section of Chapter 14 for information on configuring ODBC from the command line.) The default setting is to use a file with the same name as the performance collection and a BLG extension for counters or an ETL extension for traces. The default output is STDOUT (the display).

-q [*object*]   Lists the installed counters. If you want to see the counters for a specific object, include the object name (such as Process). This command line switch doesn't list counter instances.

-qx [*object*]   Lists the installed counters with instances. If you want to see the counters for a specific object, include the object name (such as Process).

-sc *samples*   Defines the number of samples to collect. The default setting collects samples until you press Ctrl+C.

-config *Filename*   Specifies a configuration filename that contains all of the command line options.

-s *computer*   Performs the task on a remote system. The default setting uses the local system.

-y   Answers yes to all questions without prompting. This feature lets you set up counters and traces within a batch file without worrying about interruptions.

Removing Performance Counters with the UnlodCtr Utility

The UnlodCtr utility unloads counters from memory. This utility uses the following syntax:

```
UNLODCTR [\\computername] driver
```

The following list describes each of the command line arguments.

computername Specifies the name of a remote computer. You must have access to the computer through Windows. This utility doesn't provide any means of specifying a username or password for the remote computer.

driver Defines the name of the driver that you want to unload. Unloading a driver removes all its entries from the registry.

Managing Windows in a New Way

Server Core provides a number of helpful monitoring tools. These tools help you perform basic monitoring tasks on any server. For example, creating, reading, and acting on event log entries should be part of the daily tasks you perform when working with the server. You should also regularly monitor your server for performance issues that could represent any of a number of problems, including outside intrusions. Of course, these tools are basic. As the complexity of your server increases, you need to consider getting third-party tools to augment the tools that Server Core provides. This chapter helps you build these skills:

- Document system status information
- Create, delete, and view events
- Create, delete, and view event triggers
- Record and manage system performance information
- Work with performance logs
- Work with performance counters

Practice is the only way to learn how to use these tools. Start simple by monitoring the event logs and checking the performance of your system. As your skill increases, move on to creating your own event logs and loading custom performance counters. Once you understand how these tools work, begin adding event log entries to your batch and script files so that the system automatically records problems with any automation you use. Consider creating automation to check the performance of your system. Scripts that read the output of performance monitoring tools and alert you to specific conditions are a good addition to your administrator toolbox. All this said, make sure you also discover how to use the graphical tools from a remote machine to monitor Server Core. This is one situation where using the graphical tools is helpful because they present the output in several forms (some of them graphical).

If you promote your Server Core installation to a domain controller, you'll need to know how to work with Active Directory at the command line. Server Core automatically installs Active Directory as part of the domain controller promotion, so you don't really have a choice about learning about Active Directory should you choose to use Server Core as a domain controller. Chapter 19 provides you with the details of working with Active Directory at the command line in Server Core.

Chapter 19

Configuring Directory Services

Active Directory is the data storage container for modern Windows networks of any size. One or more domain controllers provide support for the Active Directory database, which is a hierarchical, object-based data store. Using Active Directory has centralized data storage needs for most companies by providing a single replicated data store for all settings of any type. The data need not appear on a single machine, but you access it as if it does appear in one location. Active Directory contains all settings for every kind of object on the network—everything from users to workstations. By knowing which objects to access, you can learn anything you want about the network and perhaps more than you knew was available before you began your search. Of course, you need the proper rights to access the data. Unlike previous storage technologies, Active Directory does provide a significant amount of security to protect the vast store of data it contains.

NOTE The Active Directory support you can expect from Windows varies by the version that you're using. None of the workstation versions of Windows, including Windows XP and Vista, ships with Active Directory tools, but you can use many of the tools in these environments. See the article at `http://technet2.microsoft.com/windowsserver/en/library/767c4008-46c1-4684-85a8-ff7f25cd6d551033.mspx` for the workstation support details on these tools. When working with Windows 2000, you basically receive support using ADSIEdit, DSQuery, and NTDSUtil. All of the other tools discussed in this chapter require a Windows 2003 or Windows Server 2008 (graphical or Server Core version) setup, access to a Windows 2003 or Windows Server 2008 machine, or that you download and install the Active Directory tools supplied with Windows 2003 or Windows Server 2008.

Because of everything it does, Active Directory is quite complex. You don't want to make a mistake when editing it, which means performing actions consistently. Microsoft provides a number of utilities to help you maintain Active Directory. This chapter doesn't discuss the graphical utilities, but you'll actually find that the command line utilities are more powerful and provide better access to Active Directory than the graphical utilities in most cases. More importantly, the command line utilities in this chapter let you script Active Directory actions so that you can perform a number of tasks using simple command line entries that are difficult to use incorrectly. You can perform Active Directory automation equally well using batch files, scripts, or even full-fledged applications.

Working with Active Directory in newer versions of Windows carries some extra baggage. Vista and Windows Server 2008 users will have to observe a few additional precautions when working with these utilities.

♦ You must open an administrator command prompt to use these utilities. (Server Core users automatically get an administrator command prompt.) To open an administrator command line, right-click the Start ➢ Programs ➢ Accessories ➢ Command Prompt entry and choose Run as Administrator from the context menu.

◆ You must ensure you have full access to the server. Remember that Vista and Windows Server 2008 (either version) treat any network drive as the Internet zone until such time as you change the zone to the Trusted zone. You typically need to have Trusted zone access to the network drive to work with Active Directory.

◆ As with any other version of Windows, you must have administrative privileges to work with Active Directory in Vista or Windows Server 2008. In some cases, you might have to provide access to a resource specifically in your name to manipulate it.

The sections that follow begin with descriptions of a few helpful command line utilities. The chapter progresses to looking at specific kinds of objects and showing how you can manipulate them. Finally, the chapter discusses how you can work with users, groups, and computers.

In this chapter, you'll learn how to do the following:

◆ Manage Active Directory using the WMIC NTDomain alias

◆ Create, list, edit, move, manage, and delete Active Directory objects

◆ Maintain the directory services database using the NTDSUtil utility

◆ Manage users, groups, and computers

Managing Directory Services Using the WMIC NTDomain Alias

As with many WMIC commands (see the "Configuring Server Core Using the WMIC Command" section of Chapter 3 for details), the NTDomain alias supports the ASSOC, CREATE, DELETE, GET, LIST, and SET actions. You use these actions just as you would for any other alias. The important issue is that you can obtain Active Directory information using the NTDomain alias for the local machine. Remember that WMIC is essentially a local configuration command and not a global settings command. You'll use the other utilities in this chapter to perform global tasks.

NOTE It's important to remember that you can't use WMIC to promote your server to a domain controller. You also can't use the OCSetup utility to perform the task. The correct utility to perform a promotion is the DCPromo utility. To use the DCPromo utility, simply type **DCPromo** at the command line and press Enter. If you want to use advanced options with DCPromo, include the /adv command line switch. When you have an answer file to use with the DCPromo utility, include the /answer:*Filename* command line switch, where *Filename* is the name of the file you want to use. You can learn about how DCPromo works at http://technet2.microsoft .com/windowsserver/en/library/8faf4c77-4a89-4167-b6b4- f29cc8f2fd381033.mspx.

When working with the CREATE action, you only have access to the DomainGuid property. The system automatically generates a Domain Globally Unique Identifier (GUID) when you promote the system to a domain controller. If you're using the system only for a local network, the GUID provided should be unique. Even though the GUID should be unique everywhere, there is a small chance that you could find it repeated due to the technique used by the Open System Foundation (OSF) algorithm of basing part of the GUID on the Media Access Control (MAC) address of the Network Interface Card (NIC) in your server. Consequently, when working with very large networks in multiple countries, you may want to use the CREATE action to install a new Universally Unique

Identifier (UUID), which is guaranteed to provide a unique number. You can see the structure of a GUID at http://msdn2.microsoft.com/en-us/library/aa373931.aspx. If you don't have any other means of generating a UUID, you can use the tool found at http://www.famkruithof.net/uuid/uuidgen. To use this feature, type **WMIC NTDomain CREATE DomainGuid="*5d694368-7041-11dc-8314-0800200c9a66*"** (where you supply your own UUID) and press Enter.

You may eventually need to remove some properties from the domain configuration. Of course, verify these properties exist first by typing **WMIC NTDomain GET** and pressing Enter. Once you determine which property you need to delete, it's a good idea to use interactive mode to do it. For example, if you decide to delete the current DomainGuid property value, type **WMIC NTDomain DELETE /INTERACTIVE:DomainGuid** and press Enter. Always use interaction mode because the WMIC utility shows you what you're deleting before you delete it. If you've selected the wrong property, press **N** to stop the deletion. The list of available properties for the NTDomain alias include:

Caption	DSDnsForestFlag
ClientSiteName	DSGlobalCatalogFlag
CreationClassName	DSKerberosDistributionCenterFlag
DcSiteName	DSPrimaryDomainControllerFlag
Description	DSTimeServiceFlag
DnsForestName	DSWritableFlag
DomainControllerAddress	InstallDate
DomainControllerAddressType	Name
DomainControllerName	NameFormat
DomainGuid	PrimaryOwnerContact
DomainName	PrimaryOwnerName
DSDirectoryServiceFlag	Roles
DSDnsControllerFlag	Status
DSDnsDomainFlag	

The GET and LIST actions work much as you expect them to—nothing has changed for this alias from Chapter 3. Because there's only one entry for the NTDomain alias (since there is only one server), the LIST format can work better than using GET. The only available writeable property for SET is the Roles property. Since there is no CALL action associated with this alias, your configuration options are limited, but you can still get a lot of information about the domain at the command line.

Creating New Objects Using the DSAdd Utility

The DSAdd utility adds new objects to Active Directory. Each object requires different input to create the object. The DSAdd utility supports the following common objects.

- computer
- contact
- group
- ou (organizational unit)
- user
- quota

🌐 Real World Scenario

GRAPHICS AND THE COMMAND LINE OFTEN WORK TOGETHER

Just because you're focusing on the command line doesn't mean you won't ever need to work with a graphical utility. This book doesn't discuss the main graphical utility for editing Active Directory, the Active Directory Services Interface Editor (ADSIEdit). The ADSIEdit utility can come in quite handy, though, even when you're working at the command line. For example, you can use it when you're creating a script to ensure you get the Lightweight Directory Access Protocol (LDAP) statement for selecting an object correct. Instead of figuring out the LDAP by hand, you can simply copy and paste it for the object you want to select from ADSIEdit. Interestingly enough, ADSIEdit is another one of those graphical tools that works for the most part in Server Core, so you can use this graphical tool for management purposes by starting it from the command line.

I've been using ADSIEdit for a wealth of needs over the years. For example, it appears in my book, *.NET Development Security Solutions* (Sybex, 2003), because it's a necessary tool for developers. You can find a number of articles, tutorials, and reference guides for ADSIEdit online. For example, you can find a great overview of ADSIEdit on Microsoft TechNet at `http://technet2.microsoft.com/WindowsServer/en/Library/ebca3324-5427-471a-bc19-9aa1decd3d401033.mspx`. You'll find a great tutorial article about ADSIEdit on the ExhangeIS Web site at `http://exchangeis.com/blogs/exchangeis/archive/2005/08/09/48.aspx`. If you're working with Windows 2003, make sure you check out the Windows 2003-specific information about ADSIEdit at `http://www.computerperformance.co.uk/w2k3/utilities/adsi_edit.htm`.

All of these objects require some basic input to obtain the data. For example, you can expect to provide a username. The following list provides the common inputs for each of the objects.

ObjectDN   Specifies the distinguished name for the object that you want to add. In most cases, the command line syntax for the objects appear with the object name, such as `ComputerDN` for the computer object's distinguished name. Every object requires a distinguished name so the distinguished name is one of the few pieces of required information you must provide. If you don't supply the distinguished name on the command line, the utility attempts to obtain the distinguished name using the standard input (StdIn) device, which can include the keyboard, a redirected file, or as piped output from another command. Always end the standard input with the Ctrl+Z character.

-desc *Description*   Determines the object description. Always enclose arguments that contain spaces within quotes. Because most descriptions contain spaces, you can reduce errors by always enclosing descriptions in quotes.

{-s *Server* | -d *Domain*}   Connects to the specified remote server or domain (not both). You must have the required rights to access the server or domain. The default settings rely on the domain controller for the logon domain. If you aren't logged into a domain, the utility attempts to use the logon server. When a logon server isn't available, the utility uses the local machine or registers an error that Active Directory isn't installed.

-u *UserName*   Specifies the name of the user account to use to log onto a remote server. The default setting relies on the user account of the currently logged on user. The username can take several forms, as shown in the following list.

   UserName   The account name such as GeorgeS.

   Domain\UserName   The domain name combined with the username, such as `MyDomain\GeorgeS`.

User Principal Name (UPN) The UPN version of the username that includes the fully qualified domain, such as GeorgeS@MyDomain.MyCompany.com.

-p {Password | *} Specifies the user password. The utility prompts you for a password when you provide the asterisk (*) in place of the actual password. Using this second option is actually better from a security perspective because the prompt dialog box replaces your password with asterisk. Using the command line option displays your password in plaintext.

-q Places the utility in quiet mode. The utility doesn't output any information to the command line.

{-uc | -uco | -uci} Specifies that the input or output data is in Unicode format. The following list describes each of these Unicode options.

-uc Specifies a Unicode format for both input and output when using a pipe (|).

-uco Specifies a Unicode format for output when using a pipe (|) or file.

-uci Specifies a Unicode format for input when using a pipe (|) or file.

computer

The computer object adds a new computer to Active Directory. This object uses the following syntax:

```
dsadd computer ComputerDN [-samid SAMName] [-desc Description]
    [-locLocation] [-memberof GroupDN ...] [{-s Server | -d Domain}]
    [-u UserName] [-p {Password | *}] [-q] [{-uc | -uco | -uci}]
```

The following list describes each of the command line arguments.

-samid SAMName Defines the SAM account name for the computer.

-loc Location Specifies the physical location of the computer.

-memberof GroupDN ... Defines the group membership of the computer you want to add. The input argument is the distinguished name of a group. You may specify more than one group. Separate the group distinguished names with spaces.

contact

The contact object adds a new contact to Active directory. A contact is someone who exists outside of the company and doesn't have access to the network. This object uses the following syntax:

```
dsadd contact ContactDN [-fn FirstName] [-mi Initial] [-ln LastName]
    [-display DisplayName] [-desc Description] [-office Office]
    [-tel PhoneNumber] [-email Email] [-hometel HomePhoneNumber]
    [-pager PagerNumber] [-mobile CellPhoneNumber] [-fax FaxNumber]
    [-iptel IPPhoneNumber] [-title Title] [-dept Department]
    [-company Company] [{-s Server | -d Domain}] [-u UserName]
    [-p {Password | *}] [-q ] [{-uc | -uco | -uci }]
```

The following list describes each of the command line arguments.

-fn FirstName Specifies the contact's first name.

-mi Initial Specifies the contact's middle initial.

-ln LastName Specifies the contact's last name.

-display DisplayName Determines the contact's display name (the name you see when you access the contact entry).

-office *Office*   Defines the physical office location of the contact.

-tel *PhoneNumber*   Specifies the contact's landline business telephone number.

-email *Email*   Specifies the contact's email address.

-hometel *HomePhoneNumber*   Specifies the contact's home telephone number. Normally, this entry is for a landline telephone, but could also contain a secondary cellular telephone number.

-pager *PagerNumber*   Specifies the contact's pager telephone number and any required special codes.

-mobile *CellPhoneNumber*   Specifies the contact's cellular telephone number.

-fax *FaxNumber*   Specifies the contact's facsimile telephone number.

-iptel *IPPhoneNumber*   Specifies the contact's Internet Protocol (IP) telephone number.

-title *Title*   Specifies the contact's business title.

-dept *Department*   Defines the department in which the contact works.

-company *Company*   Specifies the contact's company name.

group

The group object adds a new group to Active Directory. This object uses the following syntax:

```
dsadd group GroupDN [-secgrp {yes | no}] [-scope {1 | g | u}]
    [-samid SAMName] [-desc Description] [-memberof Group ...]
    [-members Member...] [{-s Server | -d Domain}] [-u UserName]
    [-p {Password | *}] [-q] [{-uc | -uco | -uci}]
```

The following list describes each of the command line arguments.

-secgrp {yes | no}   Determines whether the utility adds the group as a security group (yes) or as a distribution group (no). The default setting adds the group as a security group.

-scope {1 | g | u}   Determines the group scope. The scopes include local (l), global (g), and universal (u). Mixed mode domains don't support the universal scope. The default setting is global.

-samid *SAMName*   Specifies the SAM name for the group. You must supply a unique value. The utility creates a SAM name for the group from the distinguished name when you don't supply this value.

-memberof *Group* **...**   Defines the group membership of the group you want to add. The input argument is the distinguished name of a group. You may specify more than one group. Separate the group distinguished names with spaces.

-members *Member* **...**   Defines the membership of this group. All objects that have membership in this group have the same rights as this group.

ou (Organizational Unit)

The ou object adds a new organizational unit to Active Directory. This object uses the following syntax:

```
dsadd ou OrganizationalUnitDN [-desc Description]
    [{-s Server | -d Domain}] [-u UserName] [-p {Password | *}] [-q]
    [{-uc | -uco | -uci}]
```

This object doesn't support any specialized command line arguments.

user

The user object adds a new user to Active Directory. A user is someone who has actual access to the network and generally works for the company. This object uses the following syntax:

```
dsadd user UserDN [-samid SAMName] [-upn UPN] [-fn FirstName]
    [-mi Initial] [-ln LastName] [-display DisplayName]
    [-empid EmployeeID]
    [-pwd {Password | *}] [-desc Description] [-memberof Group ...]
    [-office Office] [-tel PhoneNumber] [-email Email]
    [-hometel HomePhoneNumber] [-pager PagerNumber]
    [-mobile CellPhoneNumber] [-fax FaxNumber] [-iptel IPPhoneNumber]
    [-webpg WebPage] [-title Title] [-dept Department]
    [-company Company] [-mgr Manager] [-hmdir HomeDirectory]
    [-hmdrv DriveLetter:] [-profile ProfilePath] [-loscr ScriptPath]
    [-mustchpwd {yes | no}] [-canchpwd {yes | no}]
    [-reversiblepwd {yes | no}] [-pwdneverexpires {yes | no}]
    [-acctexpires NumberOfDays] [-disabled {yes | no}]
    [{-s Server | -d Domain}] [-u UserName] [-p {Password | *}]
    [-q] [{-uc | -uco | -uci}]
```

The following list describes each of the command line arguments.

-samid *SAMName*   Defines the SAM account name for the user.

-upn *UPN*   Defines the UPN version of the username that includes the fully qualified domain such as GeorgeS@MyDomain.MyCompany.com.

-fn *FirstName*   Specifies the user's first name.

-mi *Initial*   Specifies the user's middle initial.

-ln *LastName*   Specifies the user's last name.

-display *DisplayName*   Determines the user's display name (the name you see when you access the contact entry).

-empid *EmployeeID*   Specifies the employee identifier. This is a text field, so you can use any form of identifier you want.

-pwd {Password | *}   Defines the user's password. Using a default password and requiring the user to reset it on first access to the network is always the most secure choice for creating a password (see the -mustchpwd command line switch for details). If you supply an asterisk (*), the system prompts you for the password.

-memberof *Group* ...   Defines the group membership of the user you want to add. The input argument is the distinguished name of a group. You may specify more than one group. Separate the group distinguished names with spaces.

-office *Office*   Defines the physical office location of the contact.

-tel *PhoneNumber*   Specifies the user's landline business telephone number.

-email *Email*   Specifies the user's email address.

TIP   You can use the $username$ token to your advantage when creating scripts with this utility. This token can replace the user's name for the -email, -hmdir, -profile, and -webpg arguments. For example, you can specify the user's home directory as -hmdir\users\ $username$\home.

-hometel *HomePhoneNumber* Specifies the user's home telephone number. Normally, this entry is for a landline telephone, but could also contain a secondary cellular telephone number.

-pager *PagerNumber* Specifies the user's pager telephone number and any required special codes.

-mobile *CellPhoneNumber* Specifies the user's cellular telephone number.

-fax *FaxNumber* Specifies the user's facsimile telephone number.

-iptel *IPPhoneNumber* Specifies the user's Internet Protocol (IP) telephone number.

-webpg *WebPage* Specifies the user's Web page URL.

-title *Title* Specifies the user's business title.

-dept *Department* Defines the department in which the contact works.

-company *Company* Specifies the user's company name.

-mgr *ManagerDN* Defines the user's manager using a distinguished name.

-hmdir *HomeDirectory* Defines the user's home directory. The home directory is where the user stores data and begins any computing session. When you supply the home directory using a UNC path, the utility requires that you also supply a drive letter for mapping this path using the -hmdrv command line switch.

-hmdrv *DriveLetter:* Defines the user's home directory drive letter. The utility maps the drive letter to the user's directory path on the server.

-profile *ProfilePath* Defines the user's profile path.

-loscr *ScriptPath* Defines the user's logon script path.

-mustchpwd {yes | no} Forces the user to change their password during the next logon when set to yes. The default setting is no, which means the user doesn't need to change their password.

-canchpwd {yes | no} Specifies whether the user can change their password. The default setting of yes allows the user to change their password. You must set this argument to yes when you use the -mustchpwd command line switch. Always force the user to change the password for a new account or after resetting the account.

-reversiblepwd {yes | no} Determines whether the system stores the password using reversible encryption. The default setting of no prevents the user from using reversible encryption. Always set this argument to no to improve system security.

-pwdneverexpires {yes | no} Determines whether the user's password expires based on a system policy. The default setting of no forces the user to change the password regularly. Always set this argument to no to improve system security.

-acctexpires *NumberOfDays* Specifies the number of days after today when the user's account expires. A value of 0 sets the account to expire at the end of today. A positive value sets the account to expire in the future. A negative value sets the account to expire in the past. You can't set the account to never expire using this argument.

-disabled {yes | no} Specifies whether the user account is disabled. The default setting of yes disables the account for use. You must specifically enable the account by setting this argument to no.

quota

The quota object creates a quota specification for Active Directory. The quota specification determines the maximum number of directory objects that a given security principal can hold. This object uses the following syntax:

```
dsadd quota -part PartitionDN [-rdn RelativeDistinguishedName]
    -acct Name -qlimit Value [-desc Description]
    [{-s Server | -d Domain}] [-u UserName] [-p {Password | *}] [-q]
    [{-uc | -uco | -uci}]
```

The following list describes each of the command line arguments.

-part *PartitionDN* Specifies the distinguished name of the directory partition that receives the quota. If you don't supply the distinguished name on the command line, the utility attempts to obtain the distinguished name using the standard input (StdIn) device, which can include the keyboard, a redirected file, or as piped output from another command. Always end the standard input with the Ctrl+Z character.

-rdn *RelativeDistinguishedName* Specifies the relative distinguished name of the quota that you want to create. If you don't specify this command line switch, the utility sets it to Domain_AccountName using the domain and account name of the security principal specified by the -acct command line switch.

-acct *Name* Specifies the security principal (user, group, computer, or InetOrgPerson) to whom the quota specification applies. You may use a distinguished name as input for this command line argument. The command line argument also accepts the security principal information in the form Domain\SAMAccountName.

-qlimit *Value* Specifies the number of directory objects that the security principal can own within the specified partition. Provide a value of -1 to specify an unlimited quota.

Listing Objects Using the DSGet Utility

The DSGet utility obtains information about existing Active Directory objects. The DSGet utility supports the following common objects.

- computer
- contact
- group
- ou (organizational unit)
- server
- user
- subnet
- site
- quota
- partition

The objects all use the same basic command line. You must supply a distinguished name for the object you want to access, followed by the items you want to display, and ending with any security-related information to access a remote machine. See the "Creating New Objects Using the DSAdd Utility" section of the chapter for a description of the distinguished name and security command line switches. This utility uses the following syntax for each of the supported objects:

```
dsget computerComputerDN... [-dn] [-samid] [-sid] [-desc] [-loc]
    [-disabled] [{-s Server | -d Domain}] [-u UserName]
    [-p {Password | *}] [-c] [-q] [-l] [{-uc | -uco | -uci }]
    [-part PartitionDN [-qlimit] [-qused]]
dsget computerComputerDN [-memberof [-expand]]
    [{-s Server | -d Domain}] [-u UserName] [-p {Password | *}] [-c]
    [-q] [-l] [{-uc | -uco | -uci }]
dsget contactContactDN... [-dn] [-fn] [-mi] [-ln] [-display]
    [-desc] [-office] [-tel] [-email] [-hometel] [-pager] [-mobile]
    [-fax] [-iptel] [-title] [-dept] [-company]
    [{-s Server | -d Domain}] [-u UserName] [-p {Password | *}] [-c]
    [-q] [-l] [{-uc | -uco | -uci }]
dsget groupGroupDN... [-dn] [-samid] [-sid] [-desc] [-secgrp]
    [-scope] [{-s Server | -d Domain}] [-u UserName]
    [-p {Password | *}] [-c] [-q] [-l] [{-uc | -uco | -uci }]
    [-part PartitionDN [-qlimit] [-qused]]
dsget groupGroupDN [{-memberof | -members }] [-expand]
    [{-s Server | -d Domain}] [-u UserName] [-p {Password | *}] [-c]
    [-q] [-l] [{-uc | -uco | -uci}]
dsget ouOrganizationalUnitDN... [-dn] [-desc]
    [{-s Server | -d Domain}] [-u UserName] [-p {Password | *}] [-c]
    [-q] [-l] [{-uc | -uco | -uci}]
dsget serverServerDN... [-dn] [-desc] [-dnsname] [-site]
    [-isgc] [{-s Server | -d Domain}] [-u UserName] [-p {Password | *}]
    [-c] [-q] [-l] [{-uc | -uco | -uci }]
dsget serverServerDN [{-s Server | -d Domain}] [-u UserName]
    [-p {Password | *}] [-c] [-q] [-l] [{-uc | -uco | -uci}]
    [-topobjowner Display]
dsget serverServerDN [{-s Server | -d Domain}] [-u UserName]
    [-p {Password | *}] [-c] [-q] [-l] [{-uc | -uco | -uci}]
    [-part PartitionDN]
dsget userUserDN... [-dn] [-samid] [-sid] [-upn] [-fn] [-mi] [-ln]
    [-display] [-empid] [-desc] [-office] [-tel] [-email]
    [-hometel] [-pager] [-mobile] [-fax] [-iptel] [-webpg] [-title]
    [-dept] [-company] [-mgr] [-hmdir] [-hmdrv] [-profile] [-loscr]
    [-mustchpwd] [-canchpwd] [-pwdneverexpires] [-disabled]
    [-acctexpires] [-reversiblepwd] [{-uc | -uco | -uci}]
    [-part PartitionDN [ qlimit] [-qused]]
dsget subnetSubnetDN... [-dn] [-desc] [-loc] [-site]
    [{-s Server | -d Domain}] [-u UserName] [-p {Password | *}] [-c]
    [-q] [-l] [{-uc | -uco | -uci}]
dsget site SiteCN... [-dn] [-desc] [-autotopology] [-cachegroups]
    [-prefGCsite] [{-s Server | -d Domain}] [-u UserName]
    [-p {Password | *}] [-c] [-q] [-l] [{-uc | -uco | -uci}]
```

```
dsget quotaObjectDN... [-dn] [-acct] [-qlimit]
   [{-s Server | -d Domain}] [-u UserName] [-p {Password | *}] [-c]
   [-q] [-l] [{-uc | -uco | -uci}]
dsget partitionObjectDN... [-dn] [-qdefault] [-qtmbstnwt]
   [-topobjowner Display] [{-s Server | -d Domain}] [-u UserName]
   [-p {Password | *}] [-c] [-q] [-l] [{-uc | -uco | -uci}]
```

The following list describes each of the display arguments and unique command line switches in alphabetical order.

-acct   Displays the distinguished names of accounts that have quotas assigned.

-acctexpires   Displays the object's account expires status.

-autotopology   Displays the object's Internet topology generation status. A value of yes means that the system automatically generates the topology for specified sites.

-c   Reports any errors encountered when displaying the object, but continues to the next object in the argument list when you specify number objects. The default action is to stop displaying data when the utility encounters the first error.

-cachegroups   Displays the object's universal group membership caching status. A value of yes means that logons don't check the global catalog.

-canchpwd   Displays the objects that can change password status. A value of yes means the user can change the password.

-company   Displays the object's company.

-dept   Displays the object's department.

-desc   Displays the object's description.

-disabled   Displays the object's account disabled status. When the utility returns yes, the object's account is disabled.

-display   Displays the object's display name.

-dn   Displays the object's distinguished name.

-dnsname   Displays the object's DNS hostname.

-email   Displays the object's email address.

-empid   Displays the object's employee identifier.

-expand   Displays the object's complete group membership by recursively expanding each group. The expansion continues until the utility reaches the end of the group listing no matter on how many levels the groups are nested.

-fax   Displays the object's facsimile telephone number.

-fn   Displays the object's first name.

-hmdir   Displays the object's home directory. The home directory can include either a standard or a UNC path.

-hmdrv   Displays the mapped drive associated with the object's home directory.

-hometel   Displays the object's home telephone number.

-iptel   Displays the object's IP telephone number.

-isgc   Displays the object's global catalog status—yes when it's a global catalog and no when it isn't.

-l   Displays the entries in a list format. The default setting displays the entries in a table format.

-ln   Displays the object's last name.

-loc   Displays the object's physical location.

-loscr   Displays the object's logon script path.

-memberof   Displays the object's group association. You can't use this argument when specifying multiple objects as input.

-members   Displays the object's list of members.

-mgr   Displays the object's manager's distinguished name.

-mi   Displays the object's middle initial.

-mobile   Displays the object's cellular telephone number.

-mustchpwd   Displays the object's must change password status. A value of yes means the user must change the password during the next logon.

-office   Displays the object's physical office location.

-pager   Displays the object's pager number.

-part *PartitionDN*   Connects to the specified directory partition. You must use a distinguished name to specify the directory partition.

-prefGCsite   Displays the name of the preferred global catalog site used to refresh universal group membership caching for the object's domain controller.

-profile   Displays the object's profile path.

-pwdneverexpires   Displays the object's password never expires status. A value of yes means the password never expires.

-qdefault   Displays the default quota that applies to any security principal creating an object in the directory partition. An unlimited quota displays as -1.

-qlimit   Displays any effective quota associated with an object that appears within the specified object.

-qtmbstnwt   Displays the percentage to use when reducing the tombstone object count during a quota usage calculation.

-qused   Displays the amount of quota that the object has used within the specified directory partition.

-reversiblepwd   Displays the object's reversible password status. A value of yes means that user can use a password with reversible encryption.

-samid   Displays the object's SAM account name.

-scope   Displays the object's group scope—local (l), global (g), or universal (u).

-secgrp   Displays the object's security group status—yes for a security group and no for a distribution group.

-sid   Displays the object's SID.

-tel   Displays the object's business telephone number.

-title   Displays the object's title.

-topobjowner [*Display*]   Displays a sorted list of the number objects that each security principal (users, computers, security groups, and InetOrgPersons) owns. The utility sorts the list with the largest owner first. You can specify the number of security principals to display as the argument for this command line switch. Displays all of the object owners by supplying a value of 0. The default setting displays 10 security principals.

-upn   Displays the object's UPN.

Editing Existing Objects Using the DSMod Utility

The DSMod utility modifies existing objects within Active Directory. Each object requires different input to modify the object. The DSMod utility supports the following common objects.

- computer
- contact
- group
- ou (organizational unit)
- user
- quota

All of these objects require some basic input to obtain the data. For example, you can expect to provide a username. The following list provides the common inputs for each of the objects. See the "Creating New Objects Using the DSAdd Utility" section of the chapter for a description of the distinguished name and security command line switches. The arguments for modifying an object are essentially the same as the arguments for adding an object with the following exceptions. (Refer to the "Creating New Objects Using the DSAdd Utility" subsections for details on individual objects.)

-c   Reports any errors encountered when modifying the object, but continues to the next object in the argument list when you specify number objects. The default action is to stop displaying data when the utility encounters the first error.

-disabled {Yes | No}   Changes the object's account disabled status. Setting the object's disabled status to Yes means that the object can't log onto the network.

Moving Existing Objects Using the DSMove Utility

The DSMove utility moves or renames a single object. When moving an object, you can change the location to anywhere in the current domain. This utility uses the following syntax:

```
dsmove ObjectDN [-newname NewName] [-newparent ParentDN]
    [{-s Server | -d Domain}] [-u UserName] [-p {Password | *}] [-q ]
    [{-uc | -uco | -uci}]
```

See the "Creating New Objects Using the DSAdd Utility" section of the chapter for a description of the distinguished name and security command line switches. The following list describes each of the command line arguments.

-newname *NewRDN*   Renames the objects using the specified relative distinguished name.

-newparent *ParentDN*   Specifies the new parent of the object. Giving the object a new parent moves it within the object hierarchy. You must supply a distinguished name for the new parent.

Managing Active Directory with the DSQuery Utility

The Directory Services Query (DSQuery) utility helps you to obtain information about Active Directory content. For example, you can obtain a complete list of the computers attached to the network or the names of the users who rely on the network. Each kind of data requires that you use a specific object type or the asterisk (*) for all object types. The following list shows the most common objects (those supported by the utility).

◆ computer

◆ contact

◆ group

◆ ou (organizational unit)

◆ site

◆ server

◆ user

◆ quota

◆ partition

◆ * (all objects)

All of these objects require some basic input to obtain the data. For example, you can expect to provide a username. The following list provides the common inputs for each of the objects.

{StartNode | forestroot | domainroot | ObjectDN} Determines the node where the search starts. You can specify a node's distinguished name, or use one of the default starting nodes that include forestroot (forest root) or domainroot (domain root). Searching in the forest root means that the utility performs a global catalog search of all the domain controllers. Only the quota object uses the Object Distinguished Name variable, which defines the distinguished name of the object to use as a starting point for searches. The default setting is domainroot.

-o {dn | rdn | samid | upn} Specifies the output format for the list of entries the search obtains. Not every object can use every output format. For example, when you search the contact object, you can't use the samid output. See the individual object descriptions for additional details. The default setting relies on the dn format. The following list describes the common formats.

dn Displays the distinguished name for each entry.

rdn Displays the relative distinguished name for each entry. A relative distinguished name only shows the path from the starting point to the current location in the Active Directory hierarchy.

samid Displays the Security Access Manager (SAM) account name for each entry.

upn Displays the User Principal Name (UPN) for each entry. This output only applies to the user object.

-scope {subtree | onelevel | base} Defines the scope of the search. The scope determines how far down the hierarchy the utility searches for the specified object. The subtree option searches the subtree root and the specified start node. The onelevel option searches the immediate children (one level down the hierarchy) of the start node only. The base option searches the single object represented by the start node. When working with the forest root node, you can only perform a subtree search. The default search scope is subtree.

-name *Name* Searches for the object with the specified name. You can use the asterisk (*) to signify wildcard searches. For example, A* would search for all objects beginning with the letter A, while *ing would search for objects that end with "ing." You can also combine wildcards. For example, A*ing would search for objects that begin with "A" and end with "ing."

-desc *Description* Searches for an object with a specific description. As with the -name argument, you can use wildcard characters as part of the search criteria. Always enclose arguments that contain spaces within quotes. Because most descriptions contain spaces, you can reduce errors by always enclosing descriptions in quotes.

{-s *Server* | -d *Domain*} Connects to the specified remote server or domain (not both). You must have the required rights to access the server or domain. The default settings rely on the domain controller for the logon domain. If you aren't logged into a domain, the utility attempts to use the logon server. When a logon server isn't available, the utility uses the local machine or registers an error that Active Directory isn't installed.

-u *UserName* Specifies the name of the user account to use to log onto a remote server. The default setting relies on the user account of the currently logged on user. The username can take several forms as shown in the following list.

> **_UserName_** The account name such as GeorgeS.

> **_Domain\UserName_** The domain name combined with the username such as MyDomain\GeorgeS.

> **User Principal Name (UPN)** The UPN version of the username that includes the fully qualified domain such as GeorgeS@MyDomain.MyCompany.com.

-p {*Password* | *} Specifies the user password. The utility prompts you for a password when you provide the asterisk (*) in place of the actual password. Using this second option is actually better from a security perspective because the prompt dialog box will replace your password with asterisks. Using the command line option displays your password in plaintext.

-q Places the utility in quiet mode. The utility doesn't output any information to the command line.

-r Searches using recursive techniques. A recursive search follows all referrals in children of the starting object, which means that you'll see all potential results for a particular search. However, recursive searches can consume considerable resources and require additional time to complete. The default setting doesn't perform a recursive search.

-gc Performs the search using the Active Directory global catalog, which means searching the entire forest. The default search only searches the current domain. A global catalog search locates objects that meet the search criteria across the entire network, but requires more resources and additional time to complete.

-limit *NumberOfObjects* Determines the number of objects that the utility returns for the specified search. Limiting the number of objects that the utility returns can enhance performance and use resources more efficiently. Setting this argument to 0 returns all of the objects. The default setting returns the first 100 objects.

{-uc | -uco | -uci} Forces the utility to output the results or input arguments in Unicode. The following list describes each of these Unicode options.

-uc Specifies a Unicode format for both input and output when using a pipe (|).

-uco Specifies a Unicode format for output when using a pipe (|) or file.

-uci Specifies a Unicode format for input when using a pipe (|) or file.

TIP Use the pipe (|) to transfer data between Active Directory utilities. In fact, you can use the output of one search as input to a second search to create complex searches.

Even though the basic concepts are the same for each object, the individual objects present small differences in the manner in which you query them. The following sections describe these common objects and tell how you can access them.

computer

The computer object locates computers on the network that match the search criteria. A computer can serve any purpose in this case—everything from a server to a workstation. This object uses the following syntax:

```
dsquery computer [{StartNode | forestroot | domainroot}]
    [-o {dn | rdn | samid}] [-scope {subtree | onelevel | base}]
    [-name Name] [-desc Description] [-samid SAMName]
    [-inactive NumberOfWeeks] [-stalepwd NumberOfDays] [-disabled]
    [{-s Server | -d Domain}] [-u UserName] [-p {Password | *}] [-q]
    [-r] [-gc] [-limit NumberOfObjects] [{-uc | -uco | -uci}]
```

The following list describes each of the special command line arguments.

-samid *SAMName* Searches for computers that have the specified SAM account name.

-inactive *NumberOfWeeks* Searches for computers that have been inactive for the specified number of weeks. In this case, the system measures activity by logons to the domain. Consequently, even if someone uses a computer daily, the system considers it inactive until the user logs into the domain.

-stalepwd *NumberOfDays* Searches for computers that have not changed their password for the specified number of days.

-disabled Searches for computers that have disabled accounts. The reason the system disabled the account isn't important.

contact

The contact object locates all contacts in Active Directory that match the specified search criteria. Note that this object doesn't support the samid option for the -o command line switch. This object uses the following syntax:

```
dsquery contact [{StartNode | forestroot | domainroot}] [-o {dn | rdn}]
    [-scope {subtree | onelevel | base}] [-name Name]
    [-desc Description] [{-s Server | -d Domain}] [-u UserName]
    [-p {Password | *}] [-q] [-r] [-gc] [-limit NumberOfObjects]
    [{-uc | -uco | -uci}]
```

This object doesn't support any specialized command line arguments.

group

Use the group object to locate all groups that match the specified search criteria. In some cases, this object fails to find the group because you haven't specified the group criteria correctly. Use the asterisk (*) object when group searches fail to locate the groups you want to find. This object uses the following syntax:

```
dsquery group [{StartNode | forestroot | domainroot}]
    [-o {dn | rdn | samid}] [-scope {subtree | onelevel | base}]
    [-name Name] [-desc Description] [-samid SAMName]
    [{-s Server | -d Domain}] [-u UserName] [-p {Password | *}] [-q]
    [-r] [-gc] [-limit NumberOfObjects] [{-uc | -uco | -uci}]
```

The following describes the special command line argument.

-samid *SAMName*   Searches for groups that have the specified SAM account name.

ou (Organizational Unit)

The ou object locates all organizational units that match the specified search criteria. In some cases, this object fails to find the organizational unit because you haven't specified the group criteria correctly. Use the asterisk (*) object when ou searches fail to locate the organizational unit you want to find. Note that this object doesn't support the samid option for the -o command line switch. This object uses the following syntax:

```
dsquery ou [{StartNode | forestroot | domainroot}] [-o {dn | rdn}]
    [-scope {subtree | onelevel | base}] [-name Name]
    [-desc Description] [{-s Server | -d Domain}] [-u UserName]
    [-p {Password | *}] [-q] [-r] [-gc] [-limit NumberOfObjects]
    [{-uc | -uco | -uci}]
```

This object doesn't support any specialized command line arguments.

site

The site object searches for a site that matches the specified search criteria. A site normally specifies a location or region versus the domain used to provide a logical separation of computers despite location. Note that this object supports a limited range of command line arguments. It doesn't support a starting node selection or a scope. In addition, it doesn't support the samid option for the -o command line switch. This object uses the following syntax:

```
dsquery site [-o {dn | rdn}] [-name Name] [-desc Description]
    [{-s Server | -d Domain}] [-u UserName] [-p {Password | *}] [-q]
    [-r] [-gc] [-limit NumberOfObjects] [{-uc | -uco | -uci}]
```

This object doesn't support any specialized command line arguments.

server

The server object locates all servers (rather than all machines) that match the specified search criteria. This object doesn't support a starting node selection or a scope. In addition, it doesn't support the `samid` option for the -o command line switch. This object uses the following syntax:

```
dsquery server [-o {dn | rdn}] [-forest] [-domain DomainName]
    [-site SiteName] [-name Name] [-desc Description]
    [-hasfsmo {schema | name | infr | pdc | rid}] [-isgc]
    [{-s Server | -d Domain}] [-u UserName] [-p {Password | *}] [-q]
    [-r] [-gc] [-limit NumberOfObjects] [{-uc | -uco | -uci}]
```

The following list describes each of the command line arguments.

-forest   Searches for all domain controllers (server objects) that are part of the current forest.

-domain *DomainName*   Searches for all server objects that are part of the specified domain. You must use the DNS name of the domain controller. Don't use this command line switch when you want to display all of the domain controllers within the current domain since this is the default setting.

-site *SiteName*   Searches for all of the domain controllers (server objects) that appear as part of the specified site.

-hasfsmo {schema | name | infr | pdc | rid}   Searches for the domain controller that holds the requested operations master role. The following list describes each role.

schema   Specifies the schema master of the forest.

name   Specifies the domain-naming master of the forest.

infr   Specifies the infrastructure master of the forest.

pdc   Specifies the PDC of the domain specified by the -domain command line switch or the current domain when you don't specify a domain.

rid   Specifies the Relative Identifier (RID) master of the domain specified by the -domain command line switch or the current domain when you don't specify a domain.

-isgc   Searches for all Global Catalog (GC) servers in the scope specified by the -forest, -domain, or -site command line switches. If you don't specify any of the command line switches that the utility uses to define a scope, the utility locates all GC servers in the current domain.

user

The user object locates all users in Active Directory that match the specified search criteria. In some cases, this object fails to find the group because you haven't specified the group criteria correctly. Use the asterisk (*) object when group searches fail to locate the groups you want to find. This object uses the following syntax:

```
dsquery user [{StartNode | forestroot | domainroot}]
    [-o {dn | rdn | upn | samid}] [-scope {subtree | onelevel | base}]
    [-name Name] [-desc Description] [-upn UPN] [-samid SAMName]
    [-inactive NumberOfWeeks] [-stalepwd NumberOfDays] [-disabled]
    [{-s Server | -d Domain}] [-u UserName] [-p {Password | *}] [-q]
    [-r] [-gc] [-limit NumberOfObjects] [{-uc | -uco | -uci}]
```

The following list describes each of the command line arguments.

-upn *UPN*   Searches for users with the specified UPN.

-samid *SAMName*   Searches for users that have the specified SAM account name.

-inactive *NumberOfWeeks* Searches for users that have been inactive for the specified number of weeks. In this case, the system measures activity by logons to the domain. Consequently, even if someone uses a computer daily, the system considers the user inactive until they log into the domain.

-stalepwd *NumberOfDays* Searches for users that have not changed their password for the specified number of days.

-disabled Searches for users that have disabled accounts. The reason the system disabled the account isn't important.

quota

The quota object locates quota specifications that match the specified search criteria. The quota specification determines the maximum number of directory objects a given security principal can own in a particular directory partition. Note that this object doesn't support the samid option for the -o command line switch. Use spaces to separate multiple distinguished names in an argument. In addition, you can't specify a scope or name. This object uses the following syntax:

```
dsquery quota {domainroot | ObjectDN} [-o {dn | rdn}] [-acct Name]
    [-qlimit Filter] [-desc Description] [{-s Server | -d Domain}]
    [-u UserName] [-p {Password | *}] [-q] [-r] [-gc]
    [-limit NumberOfObjects] [{-uc | -uco | -uci}]
```

The following list describes each of the command line arguments.

-acct *Name* Forces the utility to locate quota specifications assigned to the specified security principal (user, group, computer, or InetOrgPerson). You may use a distinguished name as input for this command line argument. The command line argument also accepts the security principal information in the form Domain\SAMAccountName.

-qlimit *Filter* Defines the search in terms of a quota specification. This command line argument tends to filter the output and reduce the number of responses you must search to locate a particular entry. The utility reads any filter you provide with this argument as a string. Always use quotes around the argument. Any range values you provide must also appear within the quotes, such as -qlimit "=99". Use a value of "-1" to locate quotas without any limit.

partition

The partition object locates partitions within Active Directory that match the specified search criteria. The search features of this object are somewhat limited. You don't have access to the starting node, the samid option for the -o command line switch, the scope, the object name, or object description. This object uses the following syntax:

```
dsquery partition [-o {dn | rdn}] [-part Filter]
    [{-s Server | -d Domain}][-u UserName] [-p {Password | *}] [-q] [-r]
    [-gc] [-limit NumberOfObjects] [{-uc | -uco | -uci}]
```

The following describes the command line argument.

-part *Filter* Defines a filter for partition objects by specifying a common name (CN).

* (All Objects)

The * object differs from all of the other objects discussed in this section. First, you can use the * object to search for any other object in Active Directory. Second, this object relies on the LDAP to locate items in Active Directory, rather than using the more direct approach the other objects provide. Some of the arguments are still the same as for other objects. For example, you can still choose a starting point for a search. This object uses the following syntax:

```
dsquery * [{ObjectDN | forestroot | domainroot}]
    [-scope {subtree | onelevel | base}] [-filter LDAPFilter]
    [-attr {AttributeList | *}] [-attrsonly] [-l]
    [{-s Server | -d Domain}] [-u UserName] [-p {Password | *}] [-q]
    [-r] [-gc] [-limit NumberOfObjects] [{-uc | -uco | -uci}]
```

The following list describes each of the command line arguments.

-filter *LDAPFilter* Defines a search filter that relies on LDAP. The utility searches for the specified object using the LDAP filter in place of directly accessible values, such as an object name. The default filter of (objectClass=*) returns all Active Directory objects. An LDAP filter consists of object name and value pairs. For example, a filter value of (&(objectCategory=Person) (sn=smith*)) locates a person with any form of the name of smith.

-attr {*AttributeList* | *} Defines the attributes that should appear as part of the result set. For example, you might want to know the first and last names of persons that you locate in Active Directory, but not their addresses. Separate each attribute name in the list using a semicolon. Make sure you surround the attribute list with quotes. If you specify an asterisk (*), the utility returns all attributes for the requested object. The utility automatically outputs the data in a list format when you use this option, even if you don't specify the -l command line switch. The default attribute list value is the distinguished name of the selected object.

-attrsonly Outputs only the attribute types present for the objects in the result set. The utility doesn't output any of the object values. The default setting displays both the attribute type and the associated value.

-l Displays the output in a list format. The default setting displays the output in a tabular format.

Deleting Objects Using the DSRm Utility

The DSRm utility removes the specified object from Active Directory. The action is a one-way process; you can't undo it. This utility uses the following syntax:

```
dsrm ObjectDN... [-subtree  [-exclude ]] [-noprompt ]
    [{-s Server | -d Domain}] [-u UserName] [-p {Password | *}] [-c ]
    [-q ] [{-uc | -uco | -uci}]
```

See the "Creating New Objects Using the DSAdd Utility" section of the chapter for a description of the distinguished name and security command line switches. The following list describes each of the command line arguments.

-subtree [-exclude] Specifies that the utility should delete both the object and all objects within the object's subtree. Adding the -exclude command line switch excludes the object defined by the ObjectDN argument from deletion (essentially deleting the subtree). The default setting deletes only the object specified by the ObjectDN argument.

-noprompt Forces the utility to perform all deletions without prompting you. Normally, the utility prompts you to approve each deletion as a safety precaution.

Managing the Active Directory Database with the NTDSUtil Utility

The Windows NT Directory Services Utility (NTDSUtil) is an interactive utility, for the most part, so you won't use it with a batch file very often. However, by entering the correct command at the command prompt, you can get to the correct area of this utility quickly. This utility uses the following syntax:

```
NTDSUtil [{Command | Stream}]
```

The following list describes each of the command line arguments.

NOTE   Because this is an interactive command-processing environment, the chapter won't discuss NTDSUtil in detail. However, you can find a wealth of tutorials online for this utility. For example, you'll find an excellent tutorial for the novice on the ComputerPerformance site at http://www.computerperformance.co.uk/w2k3/utilities/windows_ntdsutil.htm.

Command   Specifies an optional starting point for executing commands in the interactive environment. Here's a list of standard commands that NTDSUtil understands.

Authoritative restore   Restores the Directory Information Tree (DIT) database.

Domain management   Prepares the system to create a new domain.

Files   Manages the NTDS database files.

Help   Displays help information about the selected management function. The help you see depends on the commands you issued previously. See the Stream command line argument entry for details.

IPDeny List   Manages the LDAP IP deny list. This list determines the machines that can access Active Directory remotely.

LDAP policies   Manages the LDAP protocol policies.

Metadata cleanup   Removes old metadata from the system. This feature includes removing old objects off decommissioned servers.

Popups {On | Off}   Enables or disables popups.

Quit   Ends a particular command level. You must issue multiple Quit commands, one for each level. See the Stream command line argument entry for an example. Entering the Quit command at the NTDSUtil prompt always exits the application.

Roles   Manages the NTDS role owner tokens.

Security account management   Manages the security account database. This command line switch also searches for and removes duplicate SID entries in the security account database.

Semantic database analysis   Analyzes the database looking for semantic errors.

Stream   Specifies multiple commands that NTDSUtil should execute as a stream. The commands must appear as a single string with each command separated with a space. For example, you can obtain help about the roles task by typing **NTDSUtil Roles Help Quit Quit** at the command line and pressing Enter. First, the NTDSUtil prompt appears, where the utility enters the Roles command. Second, at the Flexible Single Master Operations (fsmo) maintenance prompt, the utility enters the Help command. Third, the utility enters the Quit command to exit the fsmo maintenance prompt. Fourth, the utility enters Quit again to exit the NTDSUtil and the command prompts.

Working with Users, Groups, and Computers

It's time to start working with all of the utilities you've seen so far in the chapter to create short scripts that help you get things done quickly at the command line. In many cases, you could type these scripts at the command prompt, but trying to remember the precise syntax could prove difficult. It's better to place the commands in a batch file or create an interactive script to use them. The following sections describe specific topics, but you can use these examples to create a wealth of other scripts.

 Real World Scenario

KEEPING SCRIPTS SIMPLE

Many people create batch files and scripts that perform so many tasks that the code becomes too complicated to understand. The problem is feature creep. If one feature sounds good, two features must be better, and three features beyond compare. Unfortunately, despite the bad example set by many shrink-wrap application vendors, more features aren't always better. In fact, a simple single function script often works better than a script that can perform multiple tasks. Single function scripts and batch files are easier to debug and understand.

Of course, this brings up the question of remembering so many command lines that you don't really gain any benefit from all of those single function script or batch files. That's where menu systems come in handy. The "Using the *Choice* Command" section of Chapter 5 describes a very simple technique for accessing all of your batch or script files from a menu. All you need to do is create the script or batch file, and then call it from your menu. You now have all of the advantages of a multi-feature batch or script file without any of the pain.

Obtaining a User's Logon Name

Sometimes you'll receive a help desk ticket where the user expects that you'll know their logon name, despite the fact that you have several thousand users to track. In many cases, without the logon name, you can't do much for the user. Of course, you could always track down the user and ask them for the information, but there's an easier way to obtain the information for Active Directory users. The following script displays the logon name for a user based on the last name that you pass.

```
DSQUERY USER -name %1 | DSGET USER -samid -display
```

In this case, the input you provide is the user's last name. The DSQuery User object sends the user information to the DSGet User object using a pipe (|). The DSGet utility, in turn, looks up the user's SAM identifier and provides it as output on the command line. (When more than one user has the same last name, you'll see a list of all of the associated logon names, but at least the list is shorter than starting from scratch.)

Obtaining a User's Full Name

Sometimes a user will provide you with their email address and a logon name and that's it. What you really want is the user's full name so that you can understand their needs better by looking up their association with the company. When this problem occurs, you can still look up the user information using Active Directory. Simply use the script shown here.

```
DSQUERY USER -samid %1 | DSGET USER -samid -display
```

In this case, the input you provide is the user's logon name. The DSQuery User object sends the user information, based on a SAM identifier search, to the DSGet User object using a pipe (|). The DSGet utility outputs the user's full name. Note that there's normally more than one way to accomplish a task. If you're using an older version of Windows or a system that doesn't have Active Directory installed, you can achieve the same results using this script.

```
NET USER %1 | FIND /I " name "
```

In this case, you pass the user's logon name to the Net utility. This utility outputs all of the information about the user to the Find utility using a pipe (|). The Find utility, in turn, locates just the name entries.

Discovering User Group Membership

Many support problems revolve around security. One of the most common security problems is a lack of group membership. The user attempts to perform a task that is under the purview of a specific group and the user doesn't belong to that particular group. Unfortunately, all that the user has told you is that the task is impossible to perform and the boss really needs the task completed today. Rather than play 20 questions trying to discover the user's group membership, you can use this simple script to obtain the information from Active Directory.

```
DSQUERY USER -samid %1 | DSGET USER -memberof -expand
```

In this case, you pass the user's logon name to the DSQuery User object. The DSGet utility receives the output from DSQuery through a pipe (|). The DSGet User object then displays the group membership for the user and expands the information so you get all of the details.

Resetting a User's Password

One of the tasks that administrators love least, yet perform most often, is resetting a user's password. Those users who don't keep their password recorded on a sticky note next to their monitor are prone to forgetting them. After a long weekend or a holiday, the administrator's office suddenly fills with users who have no clue as to what their password is. You could use a graphical utility to reset those passwords one at a time (wasting an entire morning as a result) or you can use this simple script to reset the password based on the user's logon name.

```
DSQUERY USER -samid %1 | DSMOD USER -pwd "newpassword"
```

In this case, the DSQuery User object obtains the user's information based on the logon name and passes it to the DSMod utility through a pipe (|). The DSMod User object uses the -pwd command line switch to change the user's password to newpassword. You could extend this script by passing a second argument to the batch file, but it really isn't necessary because the reader will need to change the password anyway.

NOTE   Make sure you turn off echo when working with scripts that will reveal password information, even when this information is a default setting as shown here. You don't want someone peering over your shoulder to see a password that should remain private. As an alternative, you can always replace the password string with an asterisk (*). The utility will prompt you to provide a password at the appropriate time. Anything you type will appear as a series of asterisks on screen.

Displaying a List of Hostnames

Anyone working on a large network will attest to the difficulty of remembering all of the hostnames. Even if you work on the network every day, you'll run into a server that you don't work with very often and find yourself scratching your head to remember the hostname. Rather than look up the name using a graphical utility, where you could spend more than a few minutes trying to find the hostname you need, you can obtain a quick list from Active Directory using the following script.

```
FOR /F "tokens=2 delims==," %%H IN ('DSQUERY Server') DO @ECHO.%%H
```

The focus of this script is the DSQuery Server command, which outputs a list of all of the domain controllers. The rest of the script simply processes the output of the DSQuery Server command so that you see the hostnames. Notice how the script uses an at (@) sign in front of the Echo command so that all you see is the hostnames. It's important to include the @ sign as needed to keep the output of your scripts readable.

Managing Windows in a New Way

This chapter has provided you with an overview of the tasks you can perform on Active Directory, which is the centralized storage scheme for modern Windows networks. When you use these utilities at the command prompt, you'll find that you save considerable time performing tasks when compared to using the graphical utilities. Active Directory relies heavily on objects to store data. For example, you can create a user object that contains specific information about the users on your network. The object remains the same for each user, but each object instance contains unique information about a particular user. This chapter helps you build these skills:

◆   Manage Active Directory using the WMIC NTDomain alias

◆   Create, list, edit, move, manage, and delete Active Directory objects

◆   Maintain the directory services database using the NTDSUtil utility

◆   Manage users, groups, and computers

Now it's your turn to work with Active Directory. Because Active Directory is such a large and complex database, you don't want to experiment with a production system—one that you rely on to get your work done. The best thing you can do is set up a test server that you can use to work out details about your Active Directory setup and practice using the command line utilities described in this chapter. Use the test server to test your batch files and scripts as well. The thing to remember is that you won't lose your job if the test server goes down due to a poorly conceived Active Directory change. Causing the production server to lose data or even freeze is another story.

Chapter 20 begins a new part of the book that focuses on working with users. It's important to set up user accounts properly and ensure that the user feels at home when using the computer. Chapter 20 begins that process by showing how to create and manage user accounts. You've already discovered some of the essentials of user management in Chapter 15, but Chapter 20 takes the process significantly further so that you can provide full system functionality to users who need it.

Part 5

Working with the User

Chapter 20

Managing System Users

When a user occupies a single machine, security isn't much of a problem because the user can't go anywhere. However, when the user starts working with network resources, problems can occur because now the activity isn't restricted to the local machine. Anything the user does on the server can have dire consequences. When multiple users interact on multiple machines with shared resources, the problems of any kind of a security glitch mount exponentially. If you were to spend too much time thinking about it, you could go crazy.

Fortunately, Server Core provides a number of techniques for managing users on the system. You can audit user activities, set security for the user, manage the user through group polices, verify the user's session information, and even check the user's login information. All of these features of Server Core make it easier to create a secure environment when you employ them fully. This chapter discusses the various user security tools that you can use at the command line.

In this chapter, you'll learn how to do the following:

◆ Audit, monitor, and configure user security information

◆ View and manage group policies

◆ Obtain and manage session status information

◆ Obtain user login and identity information

Auditing User Access with the AuditPol Utility

The AuditPol utility helps you manage audit policies. Auditing is the process of monitoring user or other object successes and failures with the current system. For example, you could monitor every time the user fails to log into the system properly. The AuditPol utility supports the following modes of operation.

Get   Displays the current audit policy.

Set   Modifies the audit policy.

List   Displays a list of selectable audit policies.

Backup   Saves the current audit policy to a file.

Restore   Restores a saved audit policy from a file.

Clear   Restores the audit policy to a known state (no audit policy at all).

Remove   Removes the per-user audit policy for the specified user.

The following sections describe each of these modes in detail.

Get

The Get mode displays the audit policy for the current or specified user. This mode uses the following syntax:

```
AuditPol /Get [/user:<username>|<{sid}>]
[/category:*|<name>|<{guid}>[,:<name>|<{guid}>...]]
[/subcategory:<name>|<{guid}>[,:<name>|<{guid}>...]]
[/option:{CrashOnAuditFail | FullPrivilegeAuditing | AuditBaseObjects |
AuditBaseDirectories}] [/sd] [/r]
```

The following list describes each of the command line arguments.

/user:{*username | SID*}   Specifies the user account to query. You can provide either the username or the SID. Add the domain (domain\username) to qualify the username in a domain setting. You must use either the /category or /subcategory option with this option. The utility queries the system audit policy when you don't supply a username.

/category:{* | *name | GUID*}[, {*name | GUID*}...]   Specifies one or more categories to query. You can query all of the categories by using an asterisk (*) in place of a specific category name. The utility lets you identify a category using its name or GUID. Separate multiple category entries using commas and enclose any category name with a space or other special symbol in double quotes. An example of a category is System.

/subcategory:{*name | GUID*}[, {*name | GUID*}...]   Specifies one or more subcategories to query. The utility lets you identify a subcategory using its name or GUID. Separate multiple subcategory entries using commas and enclose any category name with a space or other special symbol in double quotes. You don't have to specify both category and subcategory—using subcategory alone is sufficient. An example of a subcategory is Security System Extension.

/sd   Retrieves the security descriptor used to delegate access to the audit policy. You can't use this option with any other option—it must appear separately.

/option:{CrashOnAuditFail | FullPrivilegeAuditing | AuditBaseObjects | AuditBaseDirectories}   Retrieves the state (policy) for the specified option. You can't use this option with any other option—it must appear separately.

/r   Displays the output in CSV format.

Set

The Set mode changes the audit policy for the current or specified user. This mode uses the following syntax:

```
AuditPol /set
[/user[:<username>|<{sid}>][/include][/exclude]]
[/category:<name>|<{guid}>[,:<name>|<{guid}>...]]
   [/success:<enable>|<disable>][/failure:<enable>|<disable>]
[/subcategory:<name>|<{guid}>[,:<name>|<{guid}>...]]
   [/success:<enable>|<disable>][/failure:<enable>|<disable>]
[/option: {CrashOnAuditFail | FullPrivilegeAuditing | AuditBaseObjects |
AuditBaseDirectories} /value:<enable>|<disable>]
```

The following list describes each of the command line arguments.

/user:{*username* | *SID*}   Specifies the user account to set. You can provide either the username or the SID. Add the domain (domain\username) to qualify the username in a domain setting. You must use either the /category or /subcategory option with this option. The utility queries the system audit policy when you don't supply a username.

/include   Forces the system to generate an audit as part of the per-user policy even if the audit isn't specified by the system audit policy. This option is the default. You use this option with the /user option.

/exclude   Forces the system to suppress an audit as part of the per-user policy even if the audit is specified by the system audit policy. This option isn't honored for users who are members of the Administrators local group. You use this option with the /user option.

/category:{*name* | *GUID*}[, {*name* | *GUID*}...]   Specifies one or more categories to set. The utility lets you identify a category using its name or GUID. Separate multiple category entries using commas and enclose any category name with a space or other special symbol in double quotes. An example of a category is System.

/subcategory:{*name* | *GUID*}[, {*name* | *GUID*}...]   Specifies one or more subcategories to set. The utility lets you identify a subcategory using its name or GUID. Separate multiple subcategory entries using commas and enclose any category name with a space or other special symbol in double quotes. You don't have to specify both category and subcategory—using subcategory alone is sufficient. An example of a subcategory is Security System Extension.

/success {Enable | Disable}   Sets the success auditing for the associated category or subcategory. Use Enable or Disable to start or end success auditing.

/failure {Enable | Disable}   Sets the failure auditing for the associated category or subcategory. Use Enable or Disable to start or end failure auditing.

/option:{CrashOnAuditFail | FullPrivilegeAuditing | AuditBaseObjects | AuditBaseDirectories} /value {Enable | Disable}   Sets the state (policy) for the specified option. You can't use this option with any other option—it must appear separately. Always include the /value option to enable or disable the option.

/sd   Sets the security descriptor used to delegate access to the audit policy. You can't use this option with any other option—it must appear separately. The security descriptor must include a Discretionary Access Control List (DACL) specified using the Security Descriptor Definition Language (SDDL).

List

Use the List mode to obtain a list of possible users, categories, or subcategories, rather than the audit settings. For example, if you use the /user option alone, you'll see a list of users that have audit policies set, rather than the user's settings. This mode uses the following syntax:

```
AuditPol /list
[/user|/category|/subcategory[:<categoryname>|<{guid}>|*] [/v] [/r]
```

The following list describes each of the command line arguments.

/user   Displays a list of users who have audit policies set.

/category   Displays a list of categories whether or not they have audit policies set.

/subcategory[:{*categoryname* | *GUID* | *} Displays a list of subcategories when you supply a category name or associated GUID. Use the asterisk (*) to display a list of all subcategories regardless of category.

/v Outputs additional information depending on the list you display. This option displays the SID for users and the GUID for both categories and subcategories.

/r Displays the output in CSV format.

Backup

The Backup mode lets you make a backup of the current audit policy. This mode uses the following syntax:

```
AuditPol /backup /file:<filename>
```

The following describes the command line argument.

/file:*Filename* Specifies the name of the file you want to use for the backup.

Restore

The Restore mode restores an audit policy you previously saved to a file. This mode uses the following syntax:

```
AuditPol /restore /file:<filename>
```

The following describes the command line argument.

/file:*Filename* Specifies the name of the file you want to restore.

Clear

The Clear mode clears the audit policies for all users on the system. This mode uses the following syntax:

```
AuditPol /clear [/y]
```

The following describes the command line argument.

/y Suppresses the prompt that asks whether you're sure you want to clear all of the audit policies.

WARNING Use the Clear mode with care because you'll remove all the audit policies and the process isn't reversible. The best policy is to make a backup before you use this option.

Remove

The Remove mode clears the per-user audit policy for the specified users. This mode uses the following syntax:

```
AuditPol /remove [/user[:<username>|<{sid}>]] [/allusers]
```

The following list describes each of the command line arguments.

/user:{*username* | *SID*} Specifies the user account to change. You can provide either the username or the SID. Add the domain (domain\username) to qualify the username in a domain setting. You must use either the /category or /subcategory option with this option. The utility queries the system audit policy when you don't supply a username.

/allusers Removes the per-user audit policies for all users. This option is equivalent to using the Clear mode from a user perspective. However, the audit policy options remain intact.

Configuring Profiles with the CMStP Utility

Use this utility to install or remove a Connection Manager Service Profile (CMStP). The Connection Manager provides access to a number of specialized user connections. For example, the Connection Manager could allow access to a Virtual Private Network (VPN). You can find a description of this and related technologies at http://www.windowsitpro.com/Windows/Article/ArticleID/4981/4981.html. This utility uses the following syntax:

```
ServiceProfileFileName.exe /q:a /c:"cmstp.exe
ServiceProfileFileName.inf [/nf] [/ni] [/ns] [/s] [/su] [/u]"
cmstp.exe [/nf] [/ni] [/ns] [/s] [/su] [/u]
    "[Drive:][Path]ServiceProfileFileName.inf"
```

The two syntaxes are completely different. This utility allows these two forms of access for managing profiles. The following list uses Syntax 1 and Syntax 2 to reference these two command line syntaxes since the command line arguments differ for each and describe each of the command line arguments.

ServiceProfileFileName.exe Specifies the name of the installation package that contains the profile that you want to install. This argument appears as part of Syntax 1. Notice that Syntax 1 actually relies on the installer package to call this utility, rather than calling the utility directly.

/q:a Specifies that the installer package should install the profile without prompting the user. The CMStP utility still displays the installation succeeded message. This argument appears as part of Syntax 1.

[Drive:][Path]ServiceProfileFileName.INF Specifies the configuration file that contains instructions for installing the profile. The CMStP utility assumes the information (INF) file appears in the same directory as the installer package when using Syntax 1, so you can't use the drive and path arguments as part of Syntax 1. You should, however, include the drive and path arguments as part of Syntax 2 unless the INF appears in the current directory.

/nf Prevents the CMStP utility from installing the support files.

/ni Prevents the CMStP utility from creating a desktop icon. All newer versions of Windows ignore this command line switch since they create a desktop shortcut (see the /ns command line switch); it's only valid with Windows NT 4.0 and the Windows 9x versions.

/ns Prevents the CMStP utility from creating a desktop shortcut. All newer versions of Windows use this command line switch.

/s Specifies that the installer package should install or uninstall the profile without prompting the user. In addition, the installer package won't display verification or success messages.

/su Specifies that the installer package should install the profile for a single user (the currently logged in user) rather than for all users. You can only use this command line switch with versions of Windows XP and newer.

/u Uninstalls the service profile.

Obtaining Group Policy Results with the *GPResult* Command

Use this command to obtain the Resultant Set of Policy (RSoP) for a particular user on a system. This command considers all of the security settings for both the computer and the user and creates a resultant policy—the policy that actually affects the user's security setup on the system. Microsoft provides a wealth of articles on RSoP. For example, you can see how RSoP affects Internet Protocol Security (IPSec) assignments at `http://technet2.microsoft.com/windowsserver/en/library/ 35675107-c728-47cd-8ad9-bfd2d5e7fe0a1033.mspx`. You'll also find an excellent article on planning and logging RSoP at `http://www.windowsnetworking.com/articles_tutorials/Resultant-Set-Policy-Planning-Logging.html`. This command uses the following syntax:

```
GPRESULT [/S system [/U [domain\]user [/P [password]]]]
[/SCOPE {USER | COMPUTER}] [/USER [domain\]targetuser] [/V | /Z]
```

The following list describes each of the command line arguments.

/S *system* Specifies the remote system that you want to check. In most cases, you'll also need to supply the /U and the /P command line switches when using this switch.

/U [*domain***]user** Specifies the username on the remote system. This name may not match the username on the local system. You'll need to supply a domain name when working with a domain controller.

/P [*password***]** Specifies the password for the given user. You can provide the command line switch without specifying the password on the command line in cleartext. The system prompts you for the password. Using this feature can help you maintain the security of passwords used on your system.

/USER [*domain***]targetuser** Displays RSoP data for the specified user. You can check the information of users in other domains by including the user domain.

/SCOPE {*USER* | *COMPUTER***}** Specifies the scope of the output. You can display the user or computer information separately. The utility displays both user and computer information when you omit this command line switch.

/V Displays verbose information about the user or computer. The amount of additional information you receive varies by system. The utility displays detail-specific settings that have a precedence of 1.

/Z Displays superverbose information about the user or computer. The amount of additional information you receive varies by system. The utility displays detail-specific settings that have a precedence of 1 or higher. Using this command line switch lets you see whether a setting is set in multiple places.

TIP Much of the Microsoft documentation leads you to believe that this utility is useless without having Active Directory installed. However, even without Active Directory, you can discover security information about a user with this utility. For example, you can verify that the system views the workstation as stand-alone, check the user's group participation, and verify local policies for the user.

Managing Group Policies with the GPUpdate Utility

The Group Policy Update (GPUpdate) utility lets you update the group policies on a computer. Use this utility as a replacement for the now obsolete /refreshpolicy command line switch for the

SecEdit utility. Using this utility ensures that essential group policy changes appear on a computer, especially systems that are on 24 hours per day. This utility uses the following syntax:

```
GPUpdate [/Target:{Computer | User}] [/Force] [/Wait:<value>]
[/Logoff] [/Boot] [/Sync]
```

The following list describes each of the command line arguments.

/Target:{*Computer | User*}   Specifies that the utility updates only user or computer policy settings. The default is to refresh both user and computer policy settings.

/Force   Reapplies all policy settings, even those that haven't changed. Normally, the utility only applies new settings. This command line switch ensures that the system has all of the current policies, even if a policy was accidentally changed.

/Wait:*value*   Determines the number of seconds the utility waits for policy processing to finish. The default setting is 600 seconds. You can cause the utility to end immediately by using a value of 0. A value of –1 forces the utility to wait indefinitely for the policy processing to complete. Use the –1 option when you want to ensure the policies are in place before rebooting the system. Policy processing continues in the background even if the utility ends.

/Logoff   Forces the system to log off after the utility finishes refreshing the system policies. Using this option ensures the user sees the new policy settings. You must use this feature to install client-side extension policies that don't refresh in the background, but do refresh when the user logs in. For example, you'll need to use this technique for software installation and folder redirection policies. The utility ignores the command line switch when there aren't any policies that require a logoff to implement.

/Boot   Forces a reboot for situations similar to the /Logoff command line switch. However, this command line switch affects those policy updates that require a reboot, rather than a simple logoff. As with the /Logoff command line switch, the utility ignores this command line switch when there aren't any policies that require a reboot.

/Sync   Performs the next foreground policy application synchronously (possibly reducing the update time required for group policies). Foreground policy applications occur at computer boot and during user logon. You can specify this command line switch with the /Target command line switch to synchronize updates for just the user or just the computer policies. The utility ignores the /Force and /Wait command line switches when you use this command line switch.

Obtaining Session Status Information with the Query Utility

Query provides four different modes that help you discover information about Terminal Server. This utility falls more in line with Microsoft's latest strategy for working with Terminal Server, so you should use it whenever possible in new scripts and batch files. The following sections tell you about the process, session, user, and Terminal Server (TermServer) modes.

PROCESS

The PROCESS mode helps you discover information about Terminal Server processes. Every application creates a process when it runs, so this information focuses on the applications that Terminal

Server is running. The output information includes the username, session name, session identifier (ID), Process Identifier (PID), and image (application) name. This mode uses the following syntax:

```
QUERY PROCESS [* | processid | username | sessionname | /ID:nn |
programname] [/SERVER:servername]
```

The following list describes each of the command line arguments.

*   Displays all of the visible processes.

processid   Displays process information for the specified PID.

username   Displays all of the processes belonging to a particular user. You'll always find processes belonging to your personal account, local account, network service account, and local service account.

sessionname   Displays all of the processes running in a particular session. The two default sessions are console and services.

/ID:*nn*   Displays all of the processes running within a particular session. You'll always see two sessions. Session 0 works with the services sessions and session 1 works with the console sessions.

programname   Displays all of the sessions associated with a particular program name. If multiple people are using the same application, you'll see one session for each user.

/SERVER:*servername*   Enumerates the specified processes on a particular Terminal Server. If you don't have rights to access the Terminal Server, you'll see a security error message. If the server isn't running Vista, Windows Server 2008 Full version, or Server Core, you'll likely see an "Error Enumerating Processes" message.

SESSION

The SESSION mode tells you about the sessions running on Terminal Server. Depending on what command line options you use, you can obtain a wealth of session information. The default settings provide the session name, username, session identifier, session state, connection type, and connection device. This mode uses the following syntax:

```
QUERY SESSION [sessionname | username | sessionid] [/SERVER:servername]
[/MODE] [/FLOW] [/CONNECT] [/COUNTER]
```

The following list describes each of the command line arguments.

sessionname   Displays all of the processes running in a particular session. The two default sessions are console and services.

username   Displays all of the processes belonging to a particular user. You'll always find processes belonging to your personal account, local account, network service account, and local service account.

sessionid   Displays all of the processes running within a particular session. You'll always see two sessions. Session 0 works with the services sessions and session 1 works with the console sessions.

/SERVER:*servername*   Enumerates the specified processes on a particular Terminal Server. If you don't have rights to access the Terminal Server, you'll see a security error message. If the server isn't running Vista, Windows Server 2008 Full version, or Server Core, you'll likely see an "Error Enumerating Processes" message.

/MODE   Displays the current line settings. The output changes to include several new columns including the session name, state, device, type, baud, parity, data bits, and stop bits.

/FLOW   Displays the current flow control settings. The output changes to include several new columns including the session name, state, device, type, and flow control.

/CONNECT   Displays the current connection mode. The output changes to include several new columns including the session name, state, device, type, and connection type.

/COUNTER   Displays three counter settings that include total sessions created, total sessions disconnected, and total sessions reconnected.

USER

The USER mode displays information about users logged into Terminal Server. The output information includes the username, session name, session identifier, session state, idle time, and logon time. This mode uses the following syntax:

```
QUERY USER [username | sessionname | sessionid] [/SERVER:servername]
```

The following list describes each of the command line arguments.

username   Displays all of the processes belonging to a particular user. You'll always find processes belonging to your personal account, local account, network service account, and local service account.

sessionname   Displays all of the processes running in a particular session. The two default sessions are console and services.

sessionid   Displays all of the processes running within a particular session. You'll always see two sessions. Session 0 works with the services sessions and session 1 works with the console sessions.

/SERVER:*servername*   Enumerates the specified processes on a particular Terminal Server. If you don't have rights to access the Terminal Server, you'll see a security error message. If the server isn't running Vista, Windows Server 2008 Full version, or Server Core, you'll likely see an "Error Enumerating Processes" message.

TERMSERVER

The TERMSERVER mode outputs information about Terminal Server. The information you receive depends on the Terminal Server you query and the command line options you select. This mode uses the following syntax:

```
QUERY TERMSERVER [servername] [/DOMAIN:domain] [/ADDRESS] [/CONTINUE]
```

The following list describes each of the command line arguments.

servername   Specifies the name of the Terminal Server. The system must be running Terminal Server. The Query utility won't return any information, even if you have Terminal Server installed, unless Terminal Server is running at the time of the query.

/DOMAIN:*domain*   Specifies the domain to search for Terminal Servers. The Query utility assumes that you want to query the current domain.

/ADDRESS   Adds network and node address information to the output.

/CONTINUE   Displays all of the Terminal Server information as continuous output, rather than pausing after each screen. Use this option when you plan to redirect the output to a file.

Obtaining User Login Information with the QUser Utility

The QUser utility provides quick access to user login information. The information you receive includes the username, session name, session identifier, state, amount of idle time, and the login time. You can use this utility to quickly find orphaned logins (sessions that are started, but never ended even though the user has stopped using the session). This utility uses the following syntax:

```
QUSER [username | sessionname | sessionid] [/SERVER:servername]
```

The following list describes each of the command line arguments.

username   Specifies the login name of the user you want to query.

sessionname   Specifies the name of the session you want to query. The default session name is Console.

sessionid   Specifies the number of the session you want to query.

/SERVER:*servername*   Provides the name of a server. The default setting queries the local machine.

Discovering User Identity with the WhoAmI Utility

Discovering who you are in relation to other elements of the system is important. A username is only part of your identity. For example, the system also knows about an SID and your group affiliations. The WhoAmI utility provides information about the current user based on input criteria. Using this utility alone displays just the username. This utility uses the following syntax:

```
WHOAMI [/UPN | /FQDN | /LOGONID]
WHOAMI { [/USER] [/GROUPS] [/PRIV] } [/FO {TABLE | LIST | CSV}] [/NH]
WHOAMI /ALL [/FO {TABLE | LIST | CSV}] [/NH]
```

The following list describes each of the command line arguments.

/UPN   Displays the user's name in User Principal Name (UPN) format. Use this option in a domain setting.

/FQDN   Displays the user's name in Fully Qualified Distinguished Name (FQDN) format. Use this option in a domain setting.

/USER   Displays the username and SID.

/GROUPS   Displays the user's group affiliations. Each group entry includes the group name, type (such as well-known group or alias), group SID, and group attributes (such as mandatory group, enabled by default, and enabled group).

/PRIV   Displays the user's privileges. Each privilege entry includes the privilege name, description, and state (enabled or disabled).

/LOGONID   Displays the SID that represents the user's logon identification.

/ALL   Displays the username, user's group affiliations, user's privileges, and logon identifier.

/FO {TABLE | LIST | CSV}   Defines the output provided by the utility. The table format is normally the easiest to view on screen. The table columns define the values for output, while each row contains one driver entry. The CSV output provides the best method for preparing the data for entry in a database. Use redirection (see the "Employing Data Redirection" section of Chapter 14 for details) to output the CSV data to a file and then import it to your database. The list format provides one data element per line. Each group of data elements defines one driver. The utility separates each driver by one blank line. Some people find the list format more readable when working in verbose mode since the table format requires multiple lines for each entry (the lines wrap).

/NH   Forces the utility to display the data without a column header. You can only use this command line switch with the table and CSV formats. Omitting the header makes it easier to incorporate the data in a report or import it into a database.

Managing Windows in a New Way

Managing users—determining who they are and what they're doing, is part of the way you maintain control over the server. As long as you can track user activities, at least to an extent, you can discover the sometimes terrifying activities of users on your server. In some cases, the users aren't even trying to do anything wrong, but the results can be the same—a server with reduced capacity, loss of security, loss of reliability, adware, viruses, and a vast array of issues too large to write about in a single chapter. This chapter helps you build these skills:

◆ Audit, monitor, and configure user security information

◆ View and manage group policies

◆ Obtain and manage session status information

◆ Obtain user login and identity information

The best way to learn how to use these utilities is to track your own activities. You already know what you're doing, so it's easier to see how the utilities work. Once you gain confidence using the utilities, work with someone else. Try using the utilities to track what they're doing. The combination of both activities should help build your skills quickly. After you're sure that you understand the utilities completely, you can begin using them as part of batch files and scripts. For example, you can use the output of the WhoAmI utility to determine the user's identity and perform tasks based on that identity.

Chapter 21 takes you through the next step of the process of managing users. A secure system is an essential part of the user environment. If the user can't trust the environment, then you'll begin observing behaviors that tend to make the problem worse, rather than better. A computer network relies on trust, which means providing the security that the user requires.

Chapter 21

Securing the System

The secure system, the one without any intrusion and without any security holes, is an illusion. It isn't possible to create such a system because humans will always find a way to overwhelm or overcome any security measure you put in place. To employ an old cliché, it's easier to destroy than build. You as a builder are at a disadvantage from the outset and the nefarious individual who wants to rob you of everything your system can provide knows it. Fortunately, the situation isn't hopeless. You can protect yourself from all but the most determined individual and with a little practice; you can even track the determined individual's forays into your system.

Server Core provides many interesting new features to help you secure your system. None of the users, including the administrator, run at the administrator level, which makes it much tougher for someone to use your account to do their dirty deeds on your system. The hard drive is locked down, making it harder to get into areas that no one should tamper with. You have the standard security that Windows has always provided to protect the system—all you need to do is ensure you actually use it. Finally, you have the utilities described in this chapter.

The utilities that Microsoft provides to secure your system are adequate. No, you won't find any bells and whistles with these utilities. These utilities lack automation and you'll have to remain diligent in using them. However, with a good security plan and diligence, it's possible to keep your system safe.

In this chapter, you'll learn how to do the following:

◆ Protect your system from viruses, adware, and other sources of contamination

◆ Manage and terminate applications as necessary

◆ Convert event logs into a usable format

Virus and External Intrusion Protection

Before you read anything else in this section, it's important to understand that most versions of Windows don't provide a virus checker in the purest sense of the term, but the Malicious [Software] Removal Tool (MRT) comes very close. You won't find any utility to block spyware or adware in earlier versions of Windows either. Server Core does provide rudimentary virus, spyware, and adware protection.

In addition, even though Windows XP SP2 and above do provide a firewall, some industry pundits consider it weak at the very least. For one thing, the firewall doesn't do a good job checking both incoming and outgoing data. The firewall in Server Core is significantly stronger and includes two-way protection.

In some people's minds, these three items are the end of any virus and intrusion protection requirement on a system and they'll stop reading this section immediately. However, virus and intrusion protection only begins with these three types of utilities; you really do need more protection and you need to perform some tasks manually if you want to keep your system safe, rather than constantly cleaning up the aftermath of a successful attack.

The utilities in the sections that follow represent a next step. They aren't the final word in virus and external intrusion detection, but they help. You'll want to combine these utilities with other utilities described throughout the book. The point of these particular utilities is that they specialize in helping you maintain better control over your system. These utilities are relatively easy to use and complement the functionality of the three major applications that most people rely on exclusively to safeguard their systems.

VERIFYING DRIVER SAFETY WITH THE SIGVERIF UTILITY

Many people aren't overly concerned about the unsigned drivers on their systems. After all, the driver seems to do its job. However, drivers work at the lowest level of the operating system and you can't judge their performance solely on how they work from a user perspective. You must hold drivers to a higher standard than applications if you want to keep your system safe. A signed driver might not provide absolute safety from the vagaries of viruses and external intrusion, but it's generally better equipped to keep your system safe. At least a third party has verified that the driver meets specific standards of construction.

The SigVerif utility helps you locate drivers that lack a signature. It uses a graphical interface, so you won't find detailed coverage of it in this book. However, you can start this utility at the command prompt and store the results in a file for later analysis. The point is that this utility locates any unsigned driver on your system so you can request signed versions from the hardware vendors that put your system together. You can read more about this utility at `http://www.windowsitpro.com/Article/ArticleID/7918/7918.html`.

Removing Viruses with the BlastCln Utility

The Blast Clean (BlastCln) utility helps you locate and remove two common viruses on your system, Blaster and Nachi. Microsoft updates the BlastCln utility monthly through the Windows Update service. In fact, you've probably run this utility every time you visited Windows Update without really knowing it because this utility appears on the list every month. However, you might want to check your machine more often than once a month to ensure it remains clean. In addition, running the utility as part of Windows Update doesn't provide you with a detailed report of any potential infestations on your system. Running the utility from the command prompt using the /V command line switch does provide additional information. You can learn a little more about this utility from the Knowledge Base article at `http://support.microsoft.com/?kbid=833330`. This utility uses the following syntax:

```
BlastCln [/v] [/u] [/f] [/z] [/q]
```

The following list describes each of the command line arguments.

/v Displays additional information about the virus checking process. Generally, the output tells you that the utility is checking services, processes, the registry, and the hard drive for specific filenames. When the utility doesn't find any evidence of either Blaster or Nachi, it tells you that it's stopping the tool.

/u   Performs the virus check using unattended mode. The user doesn't see any evidence that the utility is running.

/f   Forces other applications to quit when the computer shuts down after the utility has cleaned up either a Blaster or Nachi infection.

/z   Prevents a restart of the system after the BlastCln utility installation is complete.

/q   Performs the virus check using quiet mode. The user doesn't see any evidence that the utility is running and the utility doesn't request any user interaction when it detects a virus.

Detecting and Removing Malicious Software with the MRT Utility

The MRT helps you remove common malicious software from your system. You can find a description of this utility in the Knowledge Base article at http://support.microsoft.com/?id=890830. It's important to review this Knowledge Base article relatively often because Microsoft updates it each month with the list of viruses that MRT can detect. If you're an administrator, make sure you check the deployment instructions in the Knowledge Base article at http://support.microsoft .com/kb/891716. When used alone, the MRT utility displays a graphical interface the user can use to clean a system. This utility uses the following syntax:

```
MRT [/Q] [/N] [/F] [/F:Y]
```

The following list describes each of the command line arguments.

/Q   Forces the utility to run in quiet mode, which means the user won't see the usual graphical interface.

/N   Performs virus detection only; the utility doesn't clean up any viruses that it finds.

/F   Forces the utility to perform an extended scan of the system. The extended scan requires considerably more time, but can help you locate virus files, registry settings, and hidden directories in addition to the usual memory check.

/F:Y   Forces the utility to perform an extended scan of the system. In addition, the utility automatically cleans up any viruses that it finds.

Verifying System Files with the SFC Utility

The System File Scan (SFC) utility can help you keep viruses at bay by ensuring you have the correct version of the system files on your system. Viruses often replace system files with patched versions that contain the virus code. Hitchhiking on an existing system file makes it less likely that someone will remove the virus and ensures the virus gets a chance to run, so virus writers are motivated to use system files whenever they think they can. This utility uses the following syntax:

```
SFC [/SCANNOW] [/VERIFYONLY] [/SCANFILE=<file>] [/VERIFYFILE=<file>]
[/OFFWINDIR=<offline windows directory>
/OFFBOOTDIR=<offline boot directory>]
```

NOTE   The syntax of the SFC utility presented in this chapter is specific to Vista, Windows Server 2008 Full version, and Server Core. The syntax is completely different from older versions of SFC that you find in products such as Windows XP. The older windows products use a command line that looks like this: SFC [/SCANNOW] [/SCANONCE] [/SCANBOOT] [/REVERT] [/PURGECACHE] [/CACHESIZE=x]. If you need this and other older versions of the command line for Windows administrative, get *Windows Administration at the Command Line* (Sybex, 2007).

The following list describes each of the command line arguments.

/SCANNOW Scans all of the protected system files immediately and repairs any damage it finds. The utility normally relies on the content of the \WINDOWS\system32\dllcache folder to make repairs to the system files. However, it can also use the Server Core DVD, the content of service pack folders, or even online sources when necessary. In many cases, you'll want to verify the files using the /VERIFYONLY command line switch before you do a repair using this command line switch.

/VERIFYONLY Verifies all of the protected system files immediately and works much the same as the /SCANNOW option. However, this option doesn't perform any repairs. Even so, it provides you with a report of system file reliability. To use this option, type **SFC /VERIFYONLY** and press Enter. You'll see the utility work in stages as shown in Figure 21.1.

FIGURE 21.1
Verify that your system files are reliable and repair them only as needed.

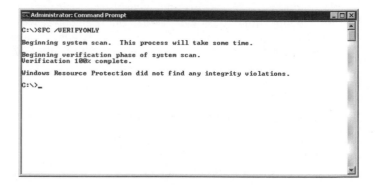

/SCANFILE=*File* Scans the specified file and repairs any damage. You must provide the full path to the file.

/VERIFYFILE=*File* Verifies the specified file, but doesn't repair any damage. You must provide the full path to the file.

/OFFBOOTDIR=*Directory* Performs offline repair of the specified boot directory.

/OFFWINDIR=*Directory* Performs offline repair of the specified Windows directory.

Verifying Drivers with the Verifier Utility

The Verifier utility performs general driver verification on your system through the Driver Verifier. Driver vendors are supposed to use this utility to ensure their drivers don't make illegal system calls or cause system corruption. You can use Verifier to ensure you do have good drivers loaded on your system and that a virus hasn't modified the driver files on your machine. Most of the drivers on your machine appear in the \WINDOWS\system32\drivers folder and have a SYS file extension. This utility uses the following syntax:

```
verifier /standard /driver NAME [NAMF ...]
verifier /standard /all
verifier [/disk] [ /flags FLAGS ] /driver NAME [NAME ...]
verifier [/disk] [ /flags FLAGS ] /all
verifier /querysettings
verifier /volatile /flags FLAGS
verifier /volatile /adddriver NAME [NAME ...]
```

```
verifier /volatile /removedriver NAME [NAME ...]
verifier /reset
verifier /query
verifier /log LOG_FILE_NAME [/interval SECONDS]
```

The following list describes each of the command line arguments.

/standard   Performs a standard check of the specified drivers during the next boot cycle. The standard check includes the Special Memory Pool, Forcing Interrupt Request Level (IRQL) Checking, Memory Pool Tracking, I/O Verification (but not the enhanced version), Deadlock Detection, and DMA Verification checks. Technically, every driver on your machine should be able to pass a standard check. The driver vendor should provide you with information about any drivers that won't pass the Verifier checks.

/driver *NAME* [*NAME* ...]   Checks one or more drivers with a specific name during the next boot cycle. Use this command line option to check one or two specific drivers, rather than checking all of the drivers on the machine. Separate each driver name with a space. You can't use wildcard characters to define a filename specification.

/all   Verifies all of the drivers on the machine.

/flags *FLAGS*   Performs a specific check using the tests defined by the supplied bit flags. For example, if you want to check both special pool checking and force IRQL checking, then you would supply a flag value of 00000011b (binary) or 3 (decimal). You can specify the flag values in hexadecimal by preceding the flag value with 0x. The following list describes each of the flags.

   Bit 0   Special Pool Checking

   Bit 1   Force IRQL Checking

   Bit 2   Low Resources Simulation

   Bit 3   Pool Tracking

   Bit 4   I/O Verification

   Bit 5   Deadlock Detection

   Bit 6   Enhanced I/O Verification

   Bit 7   DMA Verification

/querysettings   Displays a summary of the nonvolatile Driver Verifier settings. These options include the options you have selected and the list of drivers selected for verification.

/volatile   Forces a change to the Driver Verifier volatile settings. These changes take effect immediately, rather than during the next boot cycle. The settings last until you reboot the machine, so they aren't permanent. You can only perform the Special Memory Pool, Forcing IRQL Checking, and Low Resources Simulation checks when using volatile settings.

/adddriver *NAME* [*NAME* ...]   Adds the specified driver to the volatile driver list. Separate each driver name with a space. You can't use wildcard characters to define a filename specification.

/removedriver *NAME* [*NAME* ...]   Removes the specified driver from the volatile driver list. Separate each driver name with a space. You can't use wildcard characters to define a filename specification.

/reset   Clears all of the Driver Verifier settings. The Driver Verifier won't verify any drivers during the next boot cycle.

/query Displays a list of the current Driver Verifier activity.

/log *LOG_FILE_NAME* **[/interval** *SECONDS***]** Creates a log file with the specified name. At specific intervals, the log records the Driver Verifier statistics. The default logging interval is 30 seconds. You can specify the logging interval using the /interval command line switch. The utility won't stop when you issue this command at the command prompt. To stop the recording process and regain control of the command prompt, press Ctrl+C.

/disk Enables the Disk Integrity Verification option after the next system boot. This option is only available for Windows 2003 and above.

Configuring Local Security Policies with the SecEdit Utility

The Security Edit (SecEdit) utility helps you analyze and manage security policies on your system. This utility uses the following syntax:

```
secedit /analyze /db FileName [/cfg FileName] [/overwrite]
[/log FileName] [/quiet]
secedit /configure /db FileName [/cfg FileName ] [/overwrite]
[/areas Area1 Area2 ...] [/log FileName] [/quiet]
secedit /export [/db FileName] [/cfg FileName]
[/mergedpolicy] [/areasArea1 Area2 ...] [/log FileName] [/quiet]
secedit /import /db FileName.sdb /cfg FileName [/overwrite]
[/areas Area1 Area2 ...] [/log FileName] [/quiet]
secedit /validate FileName
secedit /GenerateRollback /CFG FileName /RBK SecurityTemplatefilename
 [/log FileName] [/quiet]
```

The following list describes each of the command line arguments.

/analyze Provides performance analysis of the security policy on a system by comparing it to the settings in a database.

/db *FileName* Specifies the database used to perform the analysis, configuration, or other tasks.

/cfg *FileName* Specifies a security template to import into the database before the utility performs a task. You can create a security template using the Security Template Microsoft Management Console (MMC) snap-in.

/overwrite Overwrites any existing database entries before the utility imports the security template. Otherwise, the utility adds the settings in the security template to the existing database.

/log *FileName* Specifies the file to use for logging purposes. The log receives the status of the configuration process. If you don't specify this command line switch, the utility uses the SCESrv.LOG file located in the \WINDOWS\security\logs folder.

/quiet Performs the analysis without displaying any comments.

/configure Performs a security configuration based on the content of the specified security database.

/areas *Area1 Area2* ... Specifies the security areas to manage. If you don't include this command line switch, the utility manages all security areas. You can specify multiple areas by separating each area with a space. The following list contains the valid security areas.

SECURITYPOLICY   Defines the user security policy, which includes account policies, audit policies, event log settings, and security options.

GROUP_MGMT   Defines the restricted group settings.

USER_RIGHTS   Defines the user rights assignments to system objects.

REGKEYS   Defines the registry permissions.

FILESTORE   Defines the file system permissions.

SERVICES   Defines the system service settings.

/export   Exports the security settings to a database file.

/mergedpolicy   Creates a merged database file that includes both local and domain security settings.

/import   Imports the security settings from a database file. You can use a template file to provide overrides for settings in the database.

/validate *FileName*   Validates the contents of a security template. Use this option to reduce syntax-induced errors.

/GenerateRollback   Generates a security rollback based on the content of a security rollback template. The system offers you the opportunity to create a rollback template when you apply a security update to the system. This rollback template returns the system to the state it was in before the security update.

/RBK *SecurityTemplatefilename*   Specifies the name of the file that contains the security rollback template.

Working with General Applications

Most users live for general applications. Word processors, spreadsheets, graphics, productivity enhancers, and other applications all serve the user's needs in some way. Of course, the operating system also runs applications and you'll find more than a few services and other low-level tasks running. In fact, even a well-maintained system will run 25 or more tasks and most run far more. Most users have no idea which applications are running on their systems, but using the utilities in this book, you can discover what those applications are, who's running them, and what the application is supposed to do. The following sections describe three helpful utilities for managing applications on your system.

Terminating Tasks with the *TaskKill* Command

You have a number of ways to kill tasks on a system, but sometimes you have to kill a task by remote control or use the command line to do it. The TaskKill command fulfills both needs. It lets you maintain control over a system, even if you have to use a network connection to do it. This command uses the following syntax:

```
TASKKILL [/S system [/U username [/P [password]]]] { [/FI filter]
[/PID processid | /IM imagename] } [/F] [/T]
```

The following list describes each of the command line arguments.

/S *system*   Specifies the remote system that you want to check. In most cases, you'll also need to supply the /U and the /P command line switches when using this switch.

/U *[domain\]user* Specifies the username on the remote system. This name may not match the username on the local system. You'll need to supply a domain name when working with a domain controller.

/P *[password]* Specifies the password for the given user. You can provide the command line switch without specifying the password on the command line in cleartext. The system prompts you for the password. Using this feature can help you maintain the security of passwords used on your system.

/FI *Filter* Filters the output information from the utility. The filters can become complex, so read the text that appears after this list for additional information. Table 21.1 describes the filter criteria.

TABLE 21.1:   An Overview of TaskKill and TaskList Filters

FILTER	DESCRIPTION	COMPARISON OPERATORS	VALID VALUES
STATUS	Use this filter to locate any applications that are no longer responding so that you can manually end them.	eq, ne	Running or Not Responding
IMAGENAME	Use this filter to locate a particular application in the list based on its filename.	eq, ne	The executable filename
PID	Use this filter to locate a particular instance of an application when there's more than one copy of the application running.	eq, ne, gt, lt, ge, le	Process Identifier
SESSION	Unless you're using a sharing application such as Terminal Services, this filter is useless because every application running is for the current session.	eq, ne, gt, lt, ge, le	The session number
SESSIONNAME	Unless you're using a sharing application such as Terminal Services, this filter is useless because every application running is for the current session.	eq, ne	The name of the session

TABLE 21.1: An Overview of TaskKill and TaskList Filters *(CONTINUED)*

FILTER	DESCRIPTION	COMPARISON OPERATORS	VALID VALUES
CPUTIME	Use this filter to locate applications that have just started or have been running a long time. For example, you might notice a sudden drop in system performance and can use this filter to locate applications that have just started to help determine which application might have caused the performance problem.	eq, ne, gt, lt, ge, le	The amount of time that the application has used the CPU in hours, minutes, and seconds since the session has started
MEMUSAGE	Sometimes you have more applications loaded than the system can comfortably support. Use this filter to locate applications that you can end or possible candidates for removal from the system.	eq, ne, gt, lt, ge, le	The amount of memory the application uses in kilobytes
USERNAME	Use this filter to separate applications that the user starts from those the system starts.	eq, ne	The name of the user who started the application
SERVICES	Use this filter to locate the application hosting a particular service on the system.	eq, ne	A service name
WINDOWTITLE	Use this filter to locate a particular application based on the name it displays to the user.	eq, ne	The name the application displays to the user on the title bar
MODULES	Use this filter to locate applications based on the modules they use. You can use this filter to help locate a variety of problems, including DLL conflicts (when two applications use the same DLL, but they each need a different DLL version).	eq, ne	The filenames of any modules that an application uses

/PID *processid* Specifies the Process Identifier (PID) of the process that you want to terminate.

/IM *imagename* Specifies the image name (application name) of the process that you want to terminate. You can use wildcard characters to terminate multiple applications.

/F Forces the process to terminate. Using this option can cause data loss by terminating an application before it has saved any changes the user had made.

/T Terminates the process and any processes started by the process. The `TaskKill` command removes all of the processes that the application creates. This is the best option to use for an application that has frozen because there isn't any guarantee the application will clean up after itself.

Listing Applications and Services with the *TaskList* Command

The `TaskList` command provides a lot more information than Task Manager, but it's also harder to use. You can use `TaskList` to find specific information about services and applications running on your system. For example, you can determine which services are running or perhaps locked up (not responding). To get a display similar to the one shown in Task Manager, type **`TaskList`** at the command prompt and press Enter. You'll see a list of the standard applications running on your system as shown in Figure 21.2.

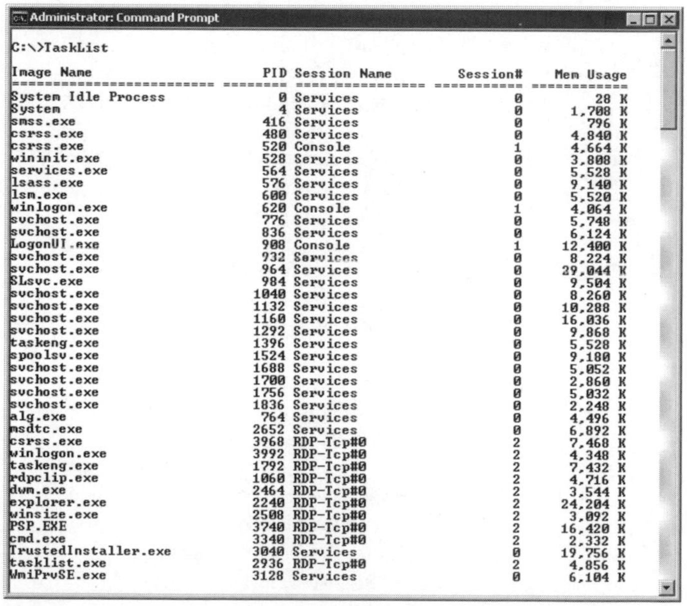

```
Administrator: Command Prompt

C:\>TaskList

Image Name                     PID Session Name        Session#    Mem Usage
========================= ======== ================ =========== ============
System Idle Process              0 Services                   0         28 K
System                           4 Services                   0      1,708 K
smss.exe                       416 Services                   0        796 K
csrss.exe                      480 Services                   0      4,840 K
csrss.exe                      520 Console                    1      4,664 K
wininit.exe                    528 Services                   0      3,808 K
services.exe                   564 Services                   0      5,528 K
lsass.exe                      576 Services                   0      9,140 K
lsm.exe                        600 Services                   0      5,520 K
winlogon.exe                   620 Console                    1      4,064 K
svchost.exe                    776 Services                   0      5,748 K
svchost.exe                    836 Services                   0      6,124 K
LogonUI.exe                    908 Console                    1     12,400 K
svchost.exe                    932 Services                   0      8,224 K
svchost.exe                    964 Services                   0     29,044 K
SLsvc.exe                      984 Services                   0      9,504 K
svchost.exe                   1040 Services                   0      8,260 K
svchost.exe                   1132 Services                   0     10,288 K
svchost.exe                   1160 Services                   0     16,036 K
svchost.exe                   1292 Services                   0      9,868 K
taskeng.exe                   1396 Services                   0      5,528 K
spoolsv.exe                   1524 Services                   0      9,180 K
svchost.exe                   1688 Services                   0      5,052 K
svchost.exe                   1700 Services                   0      2,860 K
svchost.exe                   1756 Services                   0      5,032 K
svchost.exe                   1836 Services                   0      2,248 K
alg.exe                        764 Services                   0      4,496 K
msdtc.exe                     2652 Services                   0      6,892 K
csrss.exe                     3968 RDP-Tcp#0                  2      7,468 K
winlogon.exe                  3992 RDP-Tcp#0                  2      4,348 K
taskeng.exe                   1792 RDP-Tcp#0                  2      7,432 K
rdpclip.exe                   1060 RDP-Tcp#0                  2      4,716 K
dwm.exe                       2464 RDP-Tcp#0                  2      3,544 K
explorer.exe                  2240 RDP-Tcp#0                  2     24,204 K
winsize.exe                   2508 RDP-Tcp#0                  2      3,092 K
PSP.EXE                       3740 RDP-Tcp#0                  2     16,420 K
cmd.exe                       3340 RDP-Tcp#0                  2      2,332 K
TrustedInstaller.exe          3040 Services                   0     19,756 K
tasklist.exe                  2936 RDP-Tcp#0                  2      4,856 K
WmiPrvSE.exe                  3128 Services                   0      6,104 K
```

FIGURE 21.2
Obtain a list of the standard tasks running on your system.

As you can see, the `TaskList` command provides the same information as the GUI tool. You see the same columns as usual. Use the `/FI` command line switch to modify the appearance of the list, especially the order, when necessary. This command uses the following syntax:

```
TASKLIST [/S system [/U username [/P [password]]]] [/M [module] | /SVC
| /V] [/FI filter] [/FO format] [/NH]
```

The following list describes each of the command line arguments.

/S *system* Specifies the remote system that you want to check. In most cases, you'll also need to supply the /U and the /P command line switches when using this switch.

/U [*domain*]*user* Specifies the username on the remote system. This name may not match the username on the local system. You'll need to supply a domain name when working with a domain controller.

/P [*password*] Specifies the password for the given user. You can provide the command line switch without specifying the password on the command line in cleartext. The system prompts you for the password. Using this feature can help you maintain the security of passwords used on your system.

/M [*Module*] Displays a list of applications that require the specified support module. Most applications require use of one or more modules (usually DLLs) for support. When you use this switch alone, TaskList displays a list of every module used by every loaded application. It's quite a list, so you'll probably want to redirect the output to a file using the > or >> redirection symbols and adding a filename. The switch also lets you optionally specify a specific module name. You can use this option to determine which applications require a specific module to execute. Often, this process can help you understand why a particular application glitches when another application is loaded (sometimes they rely on a shared module, but each application requires a different version of that module). You can't use this command line switch with either the /V or /SVC command line switches.

/SVC Displays a list of services supported by each of the SVCHOST.EXE entries in the task list. You'll find that each SVCHOST.EXE entry supports one or more services. This is probably one of the most important command line switches for this command because it shows you how services are working on your system. To use this command line switch, type **TaskList /SVC** and press Enter. You'll see a list of standard applications and services as shown in Figure 21.3. Compare this output to Figure 21.2 and you'll notice that the Services column replaces the Session Name, Session #, and Mem Usage columns. You can't use this command line switch with either the /V or /M command line switches.

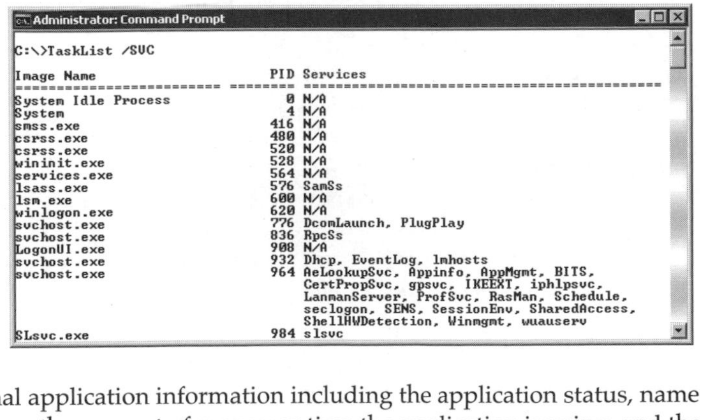

FIGURE 21.3

List all of the services running on your system so you can see how the services work.

```
Administrator: Command Prompt

C:\>TaskList /SVC

Image Name                     PID Services
========================== ======== =============================================
System Idle Process              0 N/A
System                           4 N/A
smss.exe                       416 N/A
csrss.exe                      480 N/A
csrss.exe                      520 N/A
wininit.exe                    528 N/A
services.exe                   564 N/A
lsass.exe                      576 SamSs
lsm.exe                        600 N/A
winlogon.exe                   620 N/A
svchost.exe                    776 DcomLaunch, PlugPlay
svchost.exe                    836 RpcSs
LogonUI.exe                    900 N/A
svchost.exe                    932 Dhcp, EventLog, lmhosts
svchost.exe                    964 AeLookupSvc, Appinfo, AppMgmt, BITS,
                                   CertPropSvc, gpsvc, IKEEXT, iphlpsvc,
                                   LanmanServer, ProfSvc, RasMan, Schedule,
                                   seclogon, SENS, SessionEnv, SharedAccess,
                                   ShellHWDetection, Winmgmt, wuauserv
SLsvc.exe                      984 slsvc
```

/V Displays additional application information including the application status, name of the user running the process, the amount of processor time the application is using, and the name of the application window. You might be surprised at how many of the applications listed the system runs on your behalf or to maintain Windows. One of the most useful columns for optimization purposes is Window Title, which tells you the human-readable name of the application. The connection between the executable and window names can help you locate viruses, adware, and spyware on your system. The /V command line switch puts out so much information that the standard table format is nearly useless. Consequently, you should use the /FO command line switch to use the list format. However, this makes the list too long to use. To obtain the best output, type **TaskList /V /FO LIST | More** and press Enter. You'll see a list format output that scrolls as needed as shown in Figure 21.4. You can't use this command line switch with either the /SVC or /M command line switches.

FIGURE 21.4

You must use a number of switches for the verbose output.

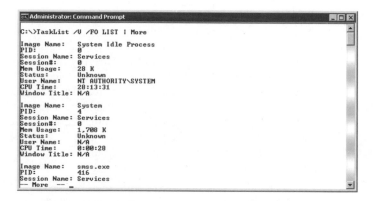

/FI *Filter* Filters the output information from the command. The filters can become complex, so read the text that appears after this list for additional information. Table 21.1 describes the filter criteria. Filters are essential in some cases, especially when working with the /V command line switch. For example, if you want verbose information about the applications you're using, you can type **TaskList /V /FO LIST /FI "USERNAME eq Administrator"** and press Enter. Notice that you must enclose the filter criteria in quotes. In this case, you're telling the system to filter by username where the username equals Administrator. Of course, you'll use your name when trying out this command line on your machine. Figure 21.5 shows typical output from this command.

/FO {TABLE | LIST | CSV} Defines the output provided by the command. The table format is normally the easiest to view on screen. The table columns define the values for output, while each row contains one driver entry. The CSV output provides the best method for preparing the data for entry in a database. Use redirection (see the "Employing Data Redirection" section of Chapter 14 for details) to output the CSV data to a file and then import it to your database. The list format provides one data element per line. Each group of data elements defines one driver. The command separates each driver by one blank line. Some people find the list format more readable when working in verbose mode since the table format requires multiple lines for each entry (the lines wrap).

/NH Forces the command to display the data without a column header. You can only use this command line switch with the table and CSV formats. Omitting the header makes it easier to incorporate the data in a report or import it into a database.

FIGURE 21.5
Filtering helps you
locate the information
you need faster.

Converting Event Trace Logs with the TraceRpt Utility

The TraceRpt utility converts the binary data in the event trace logs for the system into a format that you can use for permanent database storage or other needs. This utility uses the following syntax (the first syntax is for data stored in files, while the second is for real-time data conversion):

```
TraceRpt filename [filename ...] [options]
TraceRpt -rt <session_name [session_name ...] [options]
```

The following list describes each of the command line arguments and options.

filename   Specifies one or more Event Trace Log (ETL) files to process.

-rt   Performs real-time processing instead of converting a file.

session_name   Specifies the session to track in real time.

-o [*filename*]   Specifies the output file for the ETL data. The output is in CSV format. The default filename is dumpfile.csv.

-summary [*filename*]   Specifies a summary report text file. The output is in CSV format. The default filename is summary.txt.

-report [*filename*]   Specifies a text output report file for the ETL data. The default filename is workload.txt.

-config *filename*   Specifies the name of a settings file that contains the required command options.

-y   Answers yes to all of the utility questions without prompting the user.

-f {XML | HTML}   Defines the output format of the report. The output format defines what you see on screen.

-of {CSV | EVTX | XML}   Specifies the dump format (the format when outputting to a file). The default output is XML.

-df Filename   Provides a Microsoft-specific counting and reporting schema file.

-int Filename   Specifies the name of a file to use to dump the interpreted event structure.

-rts   Places a raw time stamp in the event trace header. You can use this option with the −o option, but not with the −report or −summary options.

-tmf Filename   Specifies the name of a Trace Message Format (TMF) definition file. The TMF file contains instructions for parsing and interpreting binary data. You can discover more about the structure and contents of the TMF definition file at http://msdn2.microsoft.com/en-gb/library/ms797950.aspx.

-tp Value   Defines the TMF file search paths. As with any other path, you can separate multiple paths using the semicolon (;).

-i Value   Defines the provider image path. A provider is the originator of an event log. Learn more about providers at http://msdn2.microsoft.com/en-gb/library/ms797953.aspx. The Program Database (PDB) file that matches the provider is located in the symbol server. Details of the PDB appear at http://msdn2.microsoft.com/en-gb/library/ms797956.aspx. As with any other path, you can separate multiple paths using the semicolon (;).

-pdb Value   Defines the symbol server path. As with any other path, you can separate multiple paths using the semicolon (;).

-gmt   Converts that Windows Software Trace Preprocessor Payload (WPP) time stamps to Greenwich Mean Time (GMT) time. You can learn more about the WPP at http://msdn2.microsoft.com/en-gb/library/ms793164.aspx.

-rl {1 | 2 | 3 | 4 | 5}   Sets the system report level. The default level is 1. A higher report level includes more information in the report.

-lr   Creates a less restrictive report. The utility uses a best match system for events that don't match the event schema.

-export [Filename]   Exports the event schema to a file. The default filename is Schema.MAN. You can optionally provide a different filename.

Managing Windows in a New Way

For some administrators, security is a few settings changes and that's about it. A server secured using this approach won't discourage anyone. In order to provide a secure environment, you must monitor it, manage the applications running on the server, and ensure the user really is writing a report and not digging into a restricted directory. Even though the Microsoft tools are a bit inconvenient and a tad weak, they do work. This chapter helps you build these skills:

◆ Protect your system from viruses, adware, and other sources of contamination

◆ Manage and terminate applications as necessary

◆ Convert event logs into a usable format

Now that you know about the tools that Microsoft provides for monitoring your system, you need to consider how to employ them. As with the utilities described in Chapter 20, you'll want to monitor your own account first. Make sure you use a test system because you definitely don't want to kill tasks on a production system unless you have to. Once you feel comfortable with your skills, test them out on a colleague. You'll find that figuring out what someone else is doing is harder than monitoring yourself. Of course, the big difference between the tools in this chapter, and those you used in Chapter 20, is that you'll never use these tools in a batch file or script. Always make sure you monitor the system personally and take actions based on what you see.

Chapter 22 begins a new section on third-party utilities. You'll find that the Internet abounds with third parties who want to help you overcome the deficiencies in Microsoft's tools. Chapter 22 shows a few of the tools you can use to make the command line a little easier to work with. Unlike the graphical tools you may have used in the past, these tools do work with Server Core because they aren't graphical in the usual sense (despite some of them having a bit of a graphical appearance). Even if these tools don't appeal to you, they show you what's available so you can find just the right tool online.

Part 6

Helpful Third-Party Utilities

Chapter 22

Obtaining Command Prompt Enhancers

You might have noticed by now that Microsoft has packed Windows with tools that you can use at the command prompt. In fact, until you begin working with these tools, you might feel that they answer every possible need. However, after working at the command prompt for a while, you might find yourself wishing for a few additional tools or perhaps some additional features for existing tools. For example, many people feel that the XCopy utility works fine, but they'd like it to have some additional flexibility so they could use it as a quick backup application. This chapter contains descriptions of some of the third-party tools that you can use to answer these needs. These command prompt enhancers provide you with the added functionality you need to perform some advanced tasks.

In this chapter, you'll learn how to do the following:

◆ Use XVI32 to view files in depth

◆ Move data with Send To Toys

◆ Check file integrity using FCIV

◆ Get the better XCopy with XXCopy

◆ Work with shell extensions using ShellExView

◆ Examine processes using Process Explorer

Using XVI32 to View Files in Depth

You won't work at the command line for very long before you discover a need to look inside files. For example, you might need to check a file to determine whether it really is a graphic image or an executable in disguise. You need to perform this check without executing the file and viewing the image with a graphics application might not tell you what you want to know. What you really need is a program that works along the same lines as the Debug utility described in the "Examining, Modifying, and Debugging Files with the Debug Utility" section of Chapter 5, but with a better interface. The XVI32 utility lets you look inside files and it also provides a great deal of functionality in a graphical package. Figure 22.1 shows a typical view of the XVI32 utility. In this case, the application is showing the content of the `_Default.pi_` file.

Real World Scenario

WORKING WITH FILE EXTENSIONS

Windows attempts to hide file extensions and simply show you an icon to identify files. In fact, the lack of file extensions has prompted some industry leaders to warn of viruses and other problems that users encounter when they maintain the Microsoft default of hiding file extensions. Some people use this feature to make one file look like another and you could end up opening an executable instead of the text file that you thought you were opening. Nevertheless, the command line has no lack of file extensions. People who haven't worked at the command line before are shocked by the number of file extensions they see. The fact that the command prompt lacks any form of familiar icon makes things worse because you don't have any visual aid in determining the purpose or function of a particular file extension. You could inadvertently trash your system by deleting the wrong file or by running another.

The FILExt Web site at `http://filext.com/` can help you overcome the problem of figuring out what task a file performs based on its file extension. This Web site contains descriptions of thousands of file extensions. In fact, you might be surprised at the amount of information this Web site provides. For example, you can discover the Multipurpose Internet Mail Extensions (MIME) type of the file, so you know how applications such as your browser and email reader view it. You can also find identifying information for the file, such as the fact that executable files have the letters MZ as the first two characters within the file. Even if someone gives the file another name, you can use these letters as a potential means of finding the executable.

FIGURE 22.1

Use the XVI32 utility to look inside files on your machine without executing their content.

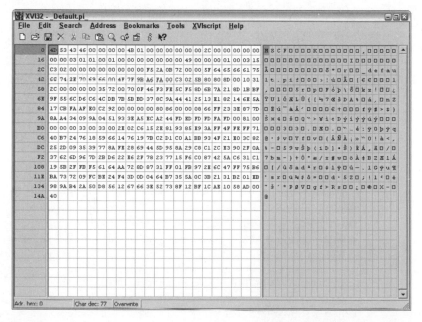

Because Microsoft compressed the file shown in Figure 22.1 as a CAB file, the file begins with the letters MSCF for Microsoft Compressed File. You can see the hexadecimal numbers in the left pane and the associated characters in the right pane. Look at the third row down and you'll see the preserved name (_default.pif) of this file in the right pane near the left side and continuing down to the fourth line. If you changed the filename entry, the expanded file would have a different name, whatever you typed. Of course, you have a limit of using the same amount of space as the original filename unless you want to get into some complex editing.

The same file compressed with a utility such as WinZIP begins with the letters PK. The WinZIP file would also include a catalog of filenames. The internals of most files contain information that lets you know more about how the system views the file. You can use this information to detect tampering and to see when a file has a different file extension than it really should. Some people have used applications such as this one to look for additional information inside files. For example, developers often leave interesting comments inside files that you can only see using a utility such as XVI32.

NOTE If you like XVI32, you should check the author's other freeware tools at `http://www.chmaas.handshake.de/delphi/freeware/freeware.htm`. You may find tools such as Name to Clipboard and BatMaker are exactly what you need to make your command line experience better.

The XVI32 utility is freeware, so all you need to do is download it from `http://www.chmaas .handshake.de/freeware/xvi32/xvi32.htm` and start using it. You don't have to install this program; simply unpack it into a directory on your machine. According to the utility's author, even developers at Microsoft use this utility. Even if they didn't, XVI32 has a lot to offer. You can search a file using a string or a hexadecimal number. The utility counts the number of times that a particular string or number appears in the file. You can even perform a global search and replace. The XVI32 utility comes with its own scripting language so that you can automate tasks as needed. The tools let you perform tasks such as encoding or decoding numbers, changing the character conversion table (so the right pane meets specific conversion needs), and even calculating the Cyclic Redundancy Code (CRC) of a file so you can easily detect changes in it.

 Real World Scenario

CREATING A SEND TO CONTEXT MENU ENTRY FOR ANY APPLICATION

Many administrators know the secret of using the Send To menu to their advantage. For example, one administrator told me that she uses the Send To menu for a number of tasks. In one case, she has two shortcuts to send a database used with their company's macros to both the network and a satellite office any time she updates it. The system downloads the macros to the user's PC using the login script so they always have an updated copy of the macros. This administrator goes on to say that she has several other Send To menu items that she uses to copy files to servers in both offices. In short, the Send To context menu can provide a considerable time savings.

Like many utilities, the XVI32 utility is handiest when you make it available as part of the Send To context menu that appears when you right-click a file in Windows Explorer. To make XVI32 available from this menu, locate your personal Send To folder at \Documents and Settings\<User Name>\ SendTo. Right-click any blank area within this folder and choose New ➤ Shortcut from this menu. Follow the steps in the Create Shortcut wizard to create a shortcut to the XVI32.EXE file. (Since the XVI32 utility doesn't have an installation program, you'll find the executable wherever you decompressed the archive; other applications normally appear in your \Program Files folder under the application or vendor name.) Adding the shortcut adds the XVI32 entry to the Send To context menu. Right-clicking any file and choosing the XVI32 entry automatically sends that file to XVI32 for display.

One of the most impressive features of XVI32 is that it doesn't choke on huge files. You can open files of significant length without worrying about data corruption or an error message. In fact, the author tells you that XVI32 can easily support a 60 MB file and offers a freeware random file generator for the purpose named `RndFileC.EXE`. Most people never need to open such a huge file, but it's nice to know that the functionality is available when you need it.

Moving Data with Send To Toys

Many people are completely unaware of the functionality provided by the Send To context menu on their machine. Once people become aware of this feature, they quickly become addicted and never want to return to manually moving data to applications. In fact, with a proper setup on the Send To context menu, you can almost throw away the File ➤ Open command on many applications. The "Creating a Send To Context Menu Entry for Any Application" sidebar in this chapter tells you how to add any application to the Send To context menu. Unfortunately, this technique only works for applications. If you want to send a file to the Clipboard, for example, you're simply out of luck. The Send To Toys 2.4 utility overcomes this particular problem. You can download this utility at `http://fileforum.betanews.com/detail/Send_To_Toys/1011999707/1`. The current version performs these and other tasks as described in the following list.

◆ Output data to a Control Panel applet.

◆ Remove a file by sending it to the Recycle Bin.

◆ Send any shortcut or application to the Quick Launch area of the Taskbar. The Quick Launch area lets you execute your most common applications quickly. However, you could also place a batch file or script in the Quick Launch area to work at the command line more effectively.

◆ Send any file to the Clipboard so that you can use its content directly. You can also save the data using a specific name so that you can include multiple entries on the Clipboard (you'll need to use the Clipboard Viewer to see them). In addition, you can send the output of any command to the Clipboard instead of seeing the result on screen.

◆ Send a file to the `\Windows\System32` folder. For a command prompt user, this feature means that you can create a file anywhere, and then move it to the system folder for execution with any of the command line utilities described in the book.

◆ Output the filename to the command prompt. This option lets you copy a file from its current location to the command prompt where you're working. You can additionally force the use of `COMMAND.COM` (the old DOS command interpreter) in place of `CMD.EXE`. This feature is possibly the most helpful for people who work at the command prompt regularly because you no longer have to move things manually.

To give you an idea of how many options this utility adds to your Send To menu, look at Figure 22.2. The figure on the left shows my original Send To menu setup. Notice that it already includes a number of application entries, along with the standard Windows entries and a few entries added by third-party products such as WinZIP. The menu on the right shows the updated context menu with the Send To Toys features added.

TIP The FileForum Web site has a wealth of utilities you can download to perform specific tasks. FileForum is one of the Web sites that you might have to search using Google (see the "Finding the Third-Party Utilities That You Want" sidebar in this chapter for details) because it offers so many great utilities. If you only want to view the utilities available for tweaking your system, check out the URL at `http://fileforum.betanews.com/browse/SystemUtilities/Tweaking`.

FIGURE 22.2

The main reason to use Send To Toys is to obtain new Send To context menu entries.

The feature that many people like best about this product is that you can use it to configure the Send To menu. Simply select the Send To Toys applet in the Control Panel and you'll see the Send To Toys dialog box shown in Figure 22.3. The Send To tab lets you add and remove items from the Send To menu without using the technique described in the "Creating a Send To Context Menu Entry for Any Application" sidebar. The Folders tab tells how to treat files when you move them. It defines where the file is moved and how the system reacts to the move (such as opening the folder where the file resides). The Clipboard Settings tab defines how the utility interacts with the Clipboard. For example, you can decide whether to place the entire file path on the Clipboard, or just the filename. You can also decide how to wrap filenames that contain spaces (or whether to wrap them at all). The default setting relies on quotes, but you can use any character desired.

FIGURE 22.3

You can also use the Send To Toys utility to configure the Send To context menu with greater ease.

Checking File Integrity Using FCIV

Most network administrators are deeply concerned about the damage caused by crackers, viruses, adware, spyware, and errant applications. In fact, the errant application causes considerably more damage than most administrators know or will admit to when asked. The important issue is to realize that damage does take place and have some method for detecting it. The File Checksum Integrity Verifier (FCIV) from Microsoft creates a cryptographic hash (essentially a fingerprint) for the files you specify. Use the utility as soon as you install the system or perform an update to create a set of fingerprints for every system file. When you suspect that something has changed outside your direct purview, you can run the utility again and compare the output to look for changes. You can obtain this tool from the Microsoft Knowledge Base at `http://support.microsoft.com/kb/841290/`.

Besides using this utility to track the fingerprints of your files for your own use, you can use it create a cryptographic hash for other people. When you send someone a file through email, they have no idea whether someone else has intercepted the message and changed the file. Perhaps this third party added a virus. The person receiving the file won't know who added the virus to the file, but they'll blame you. Supplying a hash value for each file as part of your upload assures the recipient that they can check and validate the attachment.

Other utilities do provide a form of file integrity. However, the majority of these utilities rely on a CRC, which is an insecure method of determining file validity because CRC doesn't always detect changes. The FCIV utility relies on the Message Digest 5 (MD5) or Secure Hashing Algorithm 1 (SHA-1) hashing methods. Using either of these two methods is very secure because every file generates a different result. Consequently, if someone as much as changes the case of a letter inside the file, you know about it. This utility uses the following syntax:

```
FCIV  -add {file | dir [-r] [-type file ...] [-exc dir ...] [-wp] [-bp basepath]}
[{-md5 | -sha1 | -both}] [-xml db]
FCIV -list [{-md5 | -sha1 | -both}] -xml db
FCIV -v {file | dir} [-bp basepath] [{-md5 | -sha1 | -both}] [-xml db]
```

The following list describes each of the command line arguments.

-add Adds a new entry to a database. If you don't specify the -xml command line switch, the utility sends the output to the display. You can redirect this output to a text file for inclusion with an email message when desired.

-list Displays a list of the verification entries in a database. You must supply a database name using the -xml command line switch.

-v Verifies a file or directory against the content of a verification database. The verification process returns 0 for success or 1 for failure, so you can use this utility within a batch file or script to perform complex verification checks.

{file | dir} Specifies an individual file or directory to check. When working with a directory, you can specify additional options as defined in the following list.

-r Performs recursive checks of all subdirectories. This command line switch performs the same tasks as the /s command line switch provided with many other utilities.

-type file ... Defines the type of file you want to include in the database. For example, if you specify **-type *.exe**, the utility only adds executable files to the database. You can include this command line switch multiple times. If you included **-type *.exe -type *.txt** on the command line, the utility would include both executable and text files.

-exc *file* **...** Specifies a file that contains a list of directories that you don't want to include as part of the database. Place one directory specification per line in the file. Add a blank line to the end of the list.

-wp Creates a database without including the path information. Normally, the utility includes the full path of every file.

-bp *basepath* Creates a database without including the base path information. For example, if the full path to a file is C:\MyFiles\Files1\Temp.TXT and you use **-bp C:\MyFiles** as the command line switch, the output displays Files1\Temp.TXT. This option is especially useful when the source and destination directories for a verification aren't the same.

{-md5 | -sha1 | -both} Specifies the hashing algorithm used for the file or directory. The default setting relies on the MD5 hashing algorithm. You can learn more about the MD5 hashing algorithm at http://www.ietf.org/rfc/rfc1321.txt and the SHA-1 algorithm at http://www.itl.nist.gov/fipspubs/fip180-1.htm. The -both command line switch generates one hash for each standard so that you end up with two hashes per file.

-xml *db* Defines the name of a file used to store the hashes for each file in XML format.

The output from this program is a table showing the hashes for each file in your specification. For example, if you specify that you want the hash of a particular directory and that you want to use both hashing methods, you might see output similar to that shown in Figure 22.4. The MD5 hash appears first, followed by the longer SHA-1 hash. The full path to each file appears last.

FIGURE 22.4
Even though it looks like gibberish, the hash values uniquely identify each file.

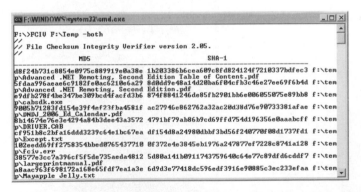

You can send the output from the utility to an XML file. The XML format is the only option that the utility offers for storing the hashes in an easily used form. It's possible to open the XML file in Internet Explorer to see how it looks. Figure 22.5 shows a typical example. Notice how each file appears as part of a <FILE_ENTRY> element. The name and hashes appear as child elements.

When you perform a verification, the utility outputs a simple success message of "All files verified successfully." However, when the verification fails, you'll see a list of entries that didn't match. You'll see a list of modified files that includes the original hash value and the new hash value. The hash values aren't actually important. What's important is that you can use them to detect changes in files.

FINDING THE THIRD-PARTY UTILITIES THAT YOU WANT

Believe me when I say that you won't ever test all of the command line–oriented third-party utilities on the market. In fact, if you test even a fraction of them fully, you'll do well. Of course, this lack of testing time means that you have to find the utility you want sooner than later. Magazines often provide great reviews of shareware, but finding those reviews can be difficult. Many magazine search engines leave a lot to the imagination.

Fortunately, Google provides a great search engine. However, if you just enter search terms in Google, you're unlikely to locate the utility you want. The selection of keywords and focusing the search is critical. Always place the most important words for your search first. For example, placing the word *shareware* first usually guarantees that you'll see the try-before-you-buy items first in Google. In addition, use special search terms as needed. I find the *site:* search term one of the most useful that Google provides. The *site: word*, followed by the site domain, such as *www.microsoft.com* (don't include the protocol in this case), performs a detailed search on Microsoft's Web site and ignores everything else. Using these techniques, you can search magazine Web sites for detailed reviews of the utilities you want.

FIGURE 22.5
The FCIV offers only the XML data format to save the hashes for you.

Getting the Better XCopy with XXCopy

Magazines often provide valuable resources for the administrator who works at the command line by making you aware of certain problems. For example, the article titled, "Windows Tips: Safer Backups—The Long and Short of It," at `http://www.pcworld.com/howto/article/0,aid,41242,00 .asp` makes you aware of a problem with using XCopy or XCopy32 for creating a backup of your system. The article goes on for several pages, but the short version is that these utilities sometimes don't make a perfect copy due to the way that Windows handles long filenames. Although XCopy usually works fine for moving an application from one location to another, you might not want to use it to back up all of that sensitive information on your hard drive. It's not that XCopy will damage the data, but it could damage the filenames.

In many cases, the article tells you about the problem and perhaps provides a quick fix or two, but doesn't go any further. What you end up with is a good understanding of the problem, but no real solutions. However, there are the bright spot articles that also provide a solution and this article is one of them. Along with the article, you can download the XXCopy utility from the PC World Web site at `http://www.pcworld.com/downloads/file_description/0,fid,7995,00.asp`. If you want to work directly with the originator of the XXCopy utility, go to their Web site at `http://www.xxcopy.com/index.htm`. In fact, it's a good idea to go to the vendor Web site to obtain the most current version of this utility.

The XXCopy utility comes in a number of flavors. All of these flavors support the standard XCopy syntax described in the "Performing Bulk File Transfers with the XCopy Utility" section of Chapter 14. Consequently, any batch file or script that relies on XCopy can use XXCopy today. In addition to these standard command line switches, you have the option of using all of the XXCopy command line switches. The freeware version has 160 command line switches alone. The /? command line switch displays the most common XXCopy command line switches, but doesn't even begin to display them all. Go to the Web site at `http://www.xxcopy.com/xxcopy01.htm` to obtain a complete listing of the command line switches.

Individuals can obtain and use a freeware version of the standard XXCopy utility without paying anything. Of course, the vendor is hoping that individuals will see the value of XXCopy and want to purchase the XXCopy Pro version. Any commercial entity must purchase the XXCopy Pro version to have a valid license. You can obtain a trial version of this version at `http://www.xxcopy.com/index.htm#testdrive`.

Working with Shell Extensions Using ShellExView

Anyone who uses Windows has used a shell extension, but it's likely that you don't know anything about it. A shell extension is a COM object that extends Windows in some way. For example, when you install WinZIP on a system, it installs several shell extensions. Clicking a ZIP file produces a new context menu that contains options for working with shell extensions. In addition, you'll see new WinZIP options for general files and even as part of the Send To menu. In most cases, these shell extensions behave properly and add to the functionality of the system.

However, every time you add something new to the operating system, especially a feature that's constantly monitoring what you do in order to display a context menu, you incur a performance penalty. When the addition provides something valuable, the performance penalty is usually worthwhile. Once you add enough items, though, you begin to see a significant performance penalty and have no idea of how to fix it. Unfortunately with shell extensions, Windows doesn't provide any means of fixing the problem and manually patching the registry is certain to cause problems. That's where ShellExView comes into play. You can use this utility to not only view the shell extensions installed on your system (you probably have no idea of how many there are) but also manage the shell extensions so you get both functionality and performance. You can download this utility at `http://www.nirsoft.net/utils/shexview.html`.

This utility is incredibly easy to use. After you download it, you can unpack it and start working immediately. Figure 22.6 shows the initial window for this utility. As you can see, this newly formatted and updated system contains 235 shell extensions (just think about how many an older system has accumulated). The utility tells you the extension name, whether it's disabled, how it modifies Windows, a description, version, product name, company, whether it appears as part of My

Computer (Computer in Vista and Windows Server 2008), the desktop, or the Control Panel, file-name, Class Identifier (CLSID), file and CLSID creation times, whether this is a Microsoft product, the file specifications the product affects, file attributes, and file size. In short, everything you could possibly want to know about the shell extension. Unfortunately, the window doesn't display everything in a convenient form. Double-click an entry to see everything as a single form.

FIGURE 22.6
Most Windows systems include hundreds of shell extensions, some of which you won't need.

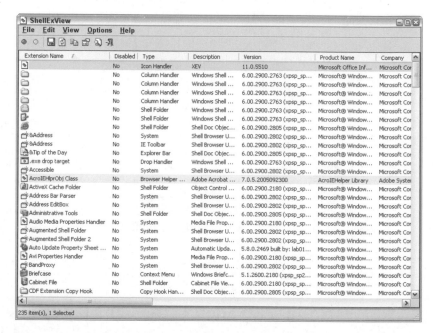

Knowing as much as you do now about the various shell extensions, you can start to decide which extensions to disable. The utility helps you with this process by highlighting shell extensions that you've already disabled, from vendors other than Microsoft, or of a suspicious nature. You also have the descriptions and the purpose of the shell extensions to consider. Highlight any suspect or less than useful shell extension and click Disable Selected Items to remove it from system use. This action doesn't remove the shell extension completely, it simply makes the shell extension unusable.

If you find later that you don't want to keep the shell extension, you can get rid of it by using the RegSrv32 utility described in the "Adding and Removing Servers with the RegSvr32 Utility" section of Chapter 13. Simply locate the server file using the Filename column of the window.

WARNING   Make sure any COM object you remove from the system doesn't provide services that you need. Very often, a single file includes a number of shell extensions. Unregistering one of them unregisters them all. You can register the COM object again by using the RegSvr32 utility when you make a mistake.

The interesting part about the ShellExView utility from a command line perspective is that you can also use it to find information about a system. Unfortunately, the vendor doesn't document the required command line switches as part of a /? command line switch for the product. However, you can find a listing of them in the vendor Web site and in this book. Here are the current ShellExView command line switches.

/stext *Filename*   Saves the current list of shell extensions to a regular text file.

/stab *Filename*   Saves the list of shell extensions to a tab-delimited text file that you can import into a database. Using this option makes it possible for an administrator to create a list of shell extensions for every machine on the network. Unfortunately, to obtain the listing for another machine, you need to use Terminal Server or Remote Desktop to access the machine. This utility doesn't include any remote system connectivity features.

/stabular *Filename*   Saves the list of shell extensions into a tabular text file. You could use this option to create reports.

/shtml *Filename*   Saves the list of shell extensions to an HTML file in tabular format. The resulting file is a nicely formatted Web page that you can view in any browser.

/sverhtml *Filename*   Saves the list of shell extensions to an HTML file in list format. The resulting file is a nicely formatted Web page that you can view in any browser.

/xml *Filename*   Saves the list of shell extensions into an XML file. This is actually the most versatile format. Not only can you save the resulting file into a database, you can also use eXtensible Stylesheet Language Transformation (XSLT) to translate it into a number of other forms, such as a Web page. The use of XSLT makes it possible to create any output document you might need.

/NoLoadSettings   Runs ShellExView using the default application settings. Normally, ShellExView saves the previous settings so it appears as it did when you last used it.

Examining Processes Using Process Explorer

Windows does provide you with process information, but it isn't always enough. Right-click the Taskbar and choose Task Manager from the context menu to see the Windows Task Manager dialog box. The Processes tab of this dialog box provides an overview of the processes on your system. Server Core provides additional tabs that provide more information than previous versions of Windows. For example, you'll find a complete list of services currently running on your system on the Services tab. The TaskList command described in the "Listing Applications and Services with the *TaskList* Command" section of Chapter 21 provides even more information, but it still might not be enough. That's where Process Explorer comes into play. If you want a very detailed description of the processes running on your system, you can obtain it using Process Explorer. You can download Process Explorer from http://www.microsoft.com/technet/sysinternals/utilities/ProcessExplorer.mspx.

 Real World Scenario

PERFORMING A WINDOWS MEMORY DIAGNOSTIC

Not every utility you need to run your system efficiently works at the command line. You might have a memory problem with your machine, but current Windows technology usually doesn't tell you about it. Consequently, you'll run into odd data errors and weird, unexplainable, application glitches. The events seldom repeat because memory usage changes minute by minute on a Windows machine. You don't see a pattern because the operating system constantly changes the content of memory in response to application requests. An application request could result in the operating system storing some data in the paging file and moving other data into memory from the paging file.

In most cases, the software that supposedly tests memory from within Windows does a very poor job and many administrators resorted to maintaining a DOS boot partition on disk or using boot disks to test memory using a DOS-based utility in the past. Because DOS doesn't constantly change memory, it's possible to test memory completely with a DOS utility, even though it isn't possible to do so from Windows. To overcome the problems of testing memory in Windows, Microsoft recently released a Windows Memory Diagnostic. You can download this utility from http://oca.microsoft.com/en/windiag.asp.

The Windows Memory Diagnostic is a low-level tool. You actually place it on a 3.5-inch floppy disk or a CD and use that media to boot your system. The reason that you have to use this approach is that you can't actually test memory inside Windows—at least not with any accuracy. People in the know have said this for years and Microsoft has finally acknowledged the fact by releasing this utility. The reason that this utility is so important is that many people do have memory problems on their system that cause all kinds of hard-to-trace problems. Because memory can fail through use, it's important to test systems regularly for memory problems. Even though this utility doesn't run at the command line, as an administrator you should have this utility (or one like it) because you never know when a memory problem will ruin your day.

TIP   An interesting bit of information about Process Explorer is that Microsoft heavily supports it. A visit to the Web page shows a list of related tools that you might want to explore, along with a list of Microsoft Knowledge Base articles that relate to Process Explorer and its use.

Process Explorer is ready to use when you extract it from the ZIP drive. In fact, this very simple utility includes the application, help file, and license file. The main window shows a hierarchical display of the executables running on your system, as shown in Figure 22.7.

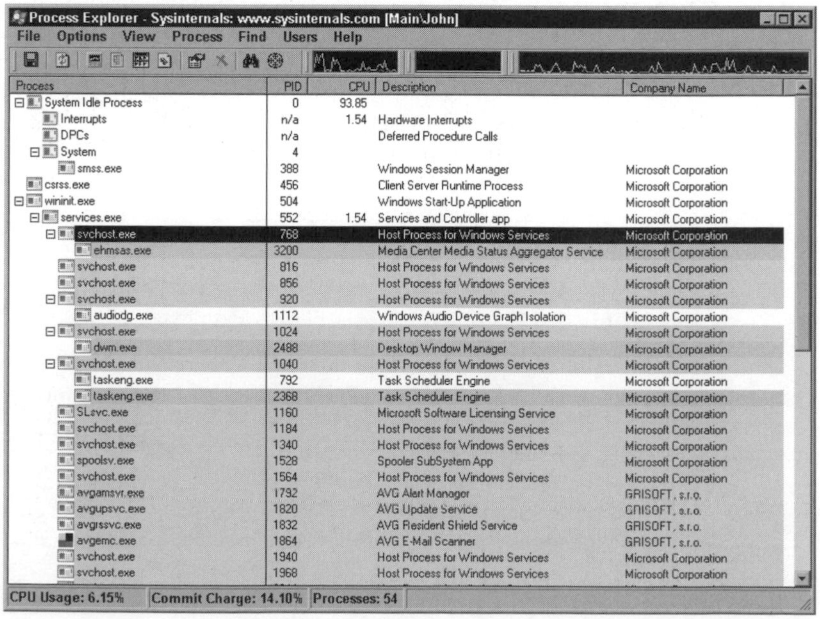

FIGURE 22.7
Process Explorer provides extremely detailed information about the processes on your system.

The hierarchical display shows the relationships between executables so you have a better idea of how the executable is loaded and started. Figure 22.7 shows only part of what you can expect from this utility. You'll find a wealth of options on the View menu to display yet more information. The Process menu contains options for managing processes, such as changing their priority or killing them when needed. The Find menu helps you locate a particular executable on the list.

When you double-click an entry, you see a properties dialog box like the one shown in Figure 22.8. This dialog box tells you everything the system knows about the process. In fact, when you choose the Threads tab, you'll likely see a dialog box telling you that you can obtain more information about the process by installing the Windows debug server. The point is that you can drill down into the innermost secrets of virtually any process using Process Explorer, but those with less experience may find the amount of information overwhelming.

FIGURE 22.8

Use Process Explorer to learn the innermost details of the processes running on your system.

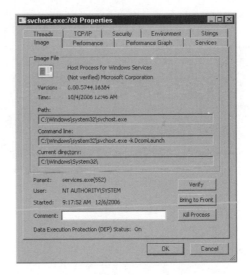

NOTE Many utilities in this book require administrator privileges when used in Server Core. Process Explorer will ask for privilege elevation the moment you start it. You can't run this utility in any version of Windows without an administrator account.

Managing Windows in a New Way

This chapter has provided you with a glimpse of the many command line enhancers available on the market today. The command line has been around for well over 20 years now, so you won't find any lack of third-party utilities. In fact, the trick is often more along the lines of finding just the right utility, rather than one that will do the job adequately. This chapter provides you with some ideas on what is available for you at the command prompt. Utilities such as XXCopy take a simple idea and make it into something far more useful. However, you might find that you need to look at files in depth quite often, which makes a utility such as XVI32 incredibly helpful. A good administrator has an entire toolbox packed with utilities such as these to address specific needs. This chapter helps you build these skills:

◆ Using XVI32 to view files in depth

◆ Moving data with Send To Toys

◆ Checking file integrity using FCIV

◆ Getting the better XCopy with XXCopy

◆ Working with shell extensions using ShellExView

◆ Examining processes using Process Explorer

Now it's time for you to begin building your toolbox. Try out the utilities in this chapter. However, don't stop with these utilities. Check online to see what other utilities you can discover. A tool that happens to work fine for me might not address your needs. In fact, these differences in needs spawned the large third-party industry in command line tools. Everyone has different needs; you need to discover what yours are by trying out a number of utilities and seeing which ones work best for you.

Although these utilities enhance your command line experience in some way, they don't all work at the command line. For example, the XVI32 utility has a graphical interface and you'll never actually use it at the command line. Chapter 23 focuses on the command line itself. You'll find tools that make the command line itself easier to use in Chapter 23. For example, you'll discover a method for shutting down a system faster after you perform maintenance on it. You'll also find a friendlier, graphical replacement for the command line. Yes, you'll still run batch files and use commands, but the interface itself is better and you'll find that you have more control over the entire command line interface.

Chapter 23

Increasing Productivity at the Command Line

Many utilities increase your overall efficiency when working with Windows. In general, anything that affects Windows will likely affect your performance at the command line as well, even if the effect is marginal or only environmental. However, to get the most out of the command line, you really need to improve the command line itself. That's where the utilities in this chapter come into play. These utilities are unlikely to affect anything you do with Windows as a whole, but they do affect your command line efficiency.

In this chapter, you'll learn how to do the following:

◆ Obtain additional information with ToggIt command line helper

◆ Use Quick Shutdown to end a session fast

◆ Create a friendlier interface with PromptPal

◆ Get a more functional command line with WinOne

◆ Automate email using sendEmail

◆ View XML files using XML Notepad 2007

 Real World Scenario

CONSIDERING OTHER REMOTE MANAGEMENT OPTIONS

This book is packed with a number of remote management options that come with Windows. You should also consider the remote management options that you can obtain free online. Microsoft provides one such remote management utility with the Windows Server 2008 Full version—Server Manager. Using Server Manager you can perform all kinds of interesting tasks from a remote location such as installing and removing both roles and features. You can obtain an overview of Server Manager and the features it provides at http://www.microsoft.com/windowsserver2008/servermanagement .mspx. You can find additional Server Manager resources at http://technet2.microsoft.com/ windowsserver2008/en/servermanager/default.mspx.

Microsoft is heavily promoting Server Manager as one of the best ways to manage your server, but it doesn't come with Server Core and you can't use it within Server Core even if you install it. Using Server Manager directly on your workstation won't work either. Of course, you could always go to the system that has Windows Server 2008 Full Version installed on it, assuming that you have this operating system installed. Unfortunately, using one server to manage another isn't very practical. The best solution is to download the Windows Server 2008 Resource Kit, which will have a copy of Server Manager that you can use on your client machine.

Once you install the Resource Kit version of Server Manager on your workstation, you'll have another option for remote management of Server Core. Server Manager still can't answer every need, however. You still need to perform the initial setups for Server Core as described in this book. Anyone who wants to manage Server Core from a remote location using Server Manager will still need an account on the Server Core system and you'll still have to perform all of the tasks to make remote management possible. In short, you'll still end up spending some amount of time at the command line to use Server Core.

Obtaining Additional Information with ToggIt Command Line Helper

The ToggIt Command Line Helper is a kind of a super help utility that makes it easier for you to remember command line syntax for network and hardware-related commands. The vendor originally designed the utility as a study aid for administrators obtaining their certification, but that isn't any reason you can't use it for other tasks. You can download this utility from a number of places online, but the safest location is the ToggIt Web site at `http://www.toggit.com/`. You can also obtain it from the NoNags site at `http://www.nonags.com/nonags/cl.html`. When you visit the NoNags Web site, you should also view some of the other command line utilities.

WARNING You'll run into a lot of buyer beware scenarios when working with software on the Internet. Sometimes, a piece of software that looks completely innocent can trash your system. The ToggIt Command Line Helper brought this point home to me recently. You can download this utility from a number of locations online. The URL provided in this chapter is one of the safer locations. The software itself is freeware, so no one should ask you to buy it. One of the locations that I tried to use to download this software had added a shell around the actual utility. The shell asked me to install a piece of adware in exchange for using this free utility. The deception started with the first page of the installation program where the vendor simply asked me to agree to the licensing agreement without telling me anything about that agreement. Only by opening the licensing agreement and reading it before I went forward was I spared the frustration of uninstalling some very nasty adware later. Always read the licensing agreement before you start an installation. Make sure you understand what the vendor expects from you.

The basic ToggIt Command Line Helper interface looks like a nicer form of the standard command line prompt, as shown in Figure 23.1. The interface includes a menu with predefined commands. To use a particular command, select it from the menu. In addition, you can type commands directly in the Type Command to Execute field that appears directly below the menus.

FIGURE 23.1

The ToggIt Command Line Helper provides a nicer command line interface and helpful menus.

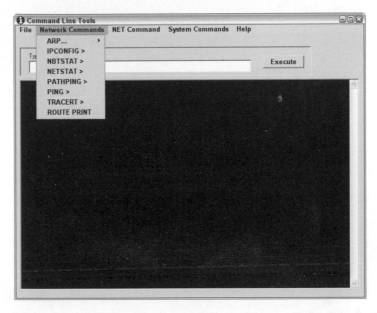

Many of the commands that the ToggIt Command Line Helper supports execute directly. For example, when you select the Mem /C command from the System Commands ➤ Mem menu, the utility automatically executes the command and displays the result as shown in Figure 23.2. However, when you select the Net Use command from the Net Command menu, the utility displays the prompt shown in Figure 23.2. In this case, you need to provide additional information before you can execute the command. The utility prompts you for the information. Simply type the values and click Execute.

FIGURE 23.2

Sometimes you need to provide additional information before executing a command.

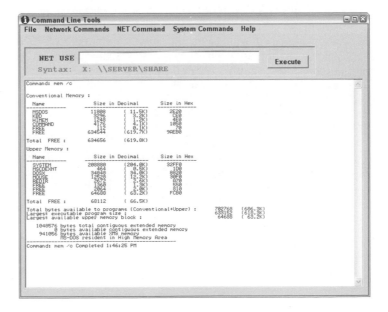

Although the ToggIt Command Line Helper is limited, it does provide some useful functionality for someone who needs the required commands. Theoretically, you could use this utility as a support tool. Simply have a user access the utility and read the information it provides. Because you aren't expecting the user to perform any complicated task (just select a menu entry), things will normally work as expected.

 Real World Scenario

WHEN NOT ENOUGH IS TOO MUCH

There's a danger that many people disregard when it comes to utilities of any sort. Too many utilities can become a liability, rather than a help. Digging through the accumulation of utilities becomes a chore and requires time that you won't normally have in an emergency. Keeping all of those utilities updated and paying for licenses when necessary adds to the problem. It all comes down to a problem of priorities—deciding which utilities you really need to get your work done and which are just added weight.

Of course, you want to try out new utilities and discard those that don't work as intended. In some cases, clutter is simply a matter of not getting rid of utilities that failed to meet expectations. Fortunately, you have an easy and convenient way of locating utilities that you don't really use. Simply use the Dir command. You can specify that you want to see only EXE files. Use the /TA command line switch to change the time field to the last access date. Add the /OD command line switch so that you can see which utilities you haven't accessed for a long time. By using this technique, you can clean up your list of utilities very quickly and keep your toolbox fit and trim.

Using Quick Shutdown to End a Session Fast

The Quick Shutdown (QSD) tool helps you perform a system shutdown interactively or from the command line. You could use this tool to perform a specific kind of shutdown from a batch file or script after performing a maintenance action. In most respects, QSD is simply a more functional version of the ShutDown utility provided with Windows XP and above. To use the interactive form of this utility, simply look for the icon in the Taskbar tray. You can download this tool at http://www.winutility.com/qsd/. This utility uses the following syntax:

```
qsd.exe [-f] [-s] [-r] [-l] [-h] [-d] [-k] [-e:x:]
```

The following list describes each of the command line arguments.

-f   Forces all of the running applications to exit immediately, instead of giving them time to save their data. You can use this feature when you need to shut down the computer for emergency reasons, such as a circuit meltdown. However, using this option may mean data loss. Make sure the emergency is real.

-s Shuts down the computer normally. All of your applications will have time to save data and settings. This option results in a power down of the computer. If you simply need to reboot the computer to add new drivers or DLLs, then use the -r command line switch instead.

-r Reboots the computer. The computer will go through an entire soft boot cycle. After the boot process completes, you can log back into the system and resume computing.

-l Logs the current user off the system. The machine doesn't reboot. You can accomplish some types of file replacement installations simply by logging off the existing user and asking them to log back into the system. This feature also lets you create batch files where you switch between users to accomplish specific tasks.

-h Places the computer in hibernation mode. The system remains on and the user remains logged into the system. The system restores the current setup when the user performs the task required to remove the system from the hibernate state, such as moving the mouse or pressing a button on the keyboard.

-d Places the computer in standby mode.

-k Locks the workstation. The user is still logged into the system, but has to supply a username and password to unlock the workstation. You would use this feature when the user goes to lunch or to a meeting.

-e:x: Ejects removable media from the system. You must supply the letter of the drive to eject.

 Real World Scenario

NOT ALL UTILITIES RUN AS EXPECTED

The command line as it appears in most versions of Windows is the same command line that originally appeared in DOS. (Vista, Windows 2008 Full version, and Server Core do place additional security restraints on the command line.) Yes, the command line today supports additional utilities, but even the old DOS utilities are available on Windows. In short, apparently nothing is new. However, appearances can be deceiving. The Windows command line doesn't rely on the older command processor, Command.EXE; it relies on a new command processor, CMD.EXE, instead. In addition, the Windows command line does provide access to a wealth of new utilities and it places limitations on how utilities work. The limitations are going to cause you grief when working with some utilities.

In order to provide a safe environment for your applications to run, the Windows command line must make some assumptions about the utilities. For example, a utility can't use certain low-level function calls because they would interrupt other applications or make the environment unusable. Unfortunately, Microsoft doesn't display a message box every time a utility violates one of these rules. The only thing that will happen is that the utility will fail—apparently for no reason at all. The only way for you to ensure that the utility works as anticipated is to view Microsoft's rules and then ensure the utility doesn't violate any of them. You can find a list of these rules at http://support.microsoft.com/default.aspx?scid=kb;en-us;Q314106.

Creating a Friendlier Interface with PromptPal

The PromptPal utility replaces the command line with a friendlier interface. You can download this utility from the Web site at http://www.promptpal.com/. This utility does require a full installation, unlike many of the utilities described so far in this chapter. In addition, the program you download from the Web site is a 30-day trial version. However, if you spend much time working at the command prompt, you'll find that your return on investment is substantial when you consider the time you'll save. Figure 23.3 shows the PromptPal interface, which looks almost nothing like the Windows command prompt you used in the past.

FIGURE 23.3

PromptPal supports an interface that makes working at the command prompt fun.

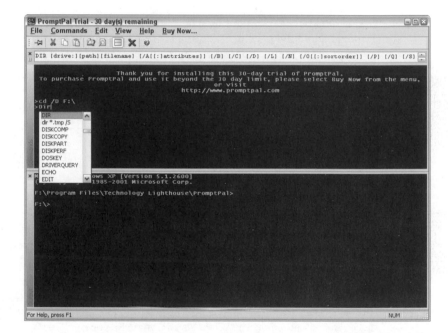

The utility sports a two-pane interface. The upper pane is where you type your commands; the lower pane shows the results. Using this approach means that you can always see the command you typed and the result it produced with equal ease. However, that's only where the extended functionality starts. Whenever you start typing a command, PromptPal displays a list of matching commands, eliminating most typing errors. In addition, it displays the longer versions of that command that you typed in the past as shown directly below the DIR entry in Figure 23.3. The full command syntax appears in the bar directly below the menu as shown in the figure. Consequently, you don't have to try to remember all of those command line switches. When you type a command line switch, PromptPal displays the entire list, along with the meaning behind each command line switch, as shown in Figure 23.4 (the figure shows the explanation list, truncated for space considerations in the book).

PromptPal includes a wealth of configuration choices. You can change the appearance of the display in a number of ways. Any display change you can make with a regular command prompt is also available in PromptPal (which means you can display a green background with red letters if you want). However, the most important configuration option appears in Figure 23.5. This configuration option lets you add new commands to PromptPal, edit existing definitions, and remove commands you don't want to use from the list. Consequently, the help you receive from PromptPal is completely configurable.

FIGURE 23.4
PromptPal helps
you remember all of
those command line
switches and their
meanings.

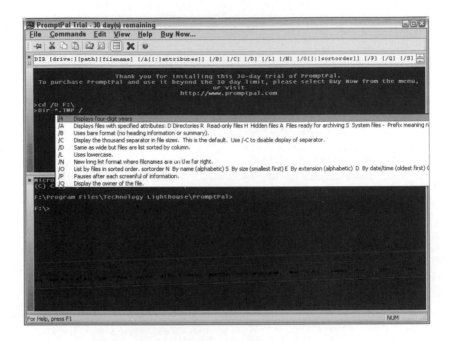

FIGURE 23.5
Add, edit, or delete
commands as needed
in PromptPal.

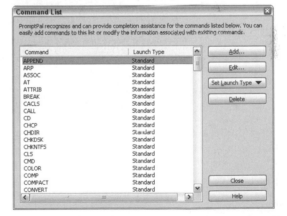

Getting a More Functional Command Line with WinOne

The WinOne utility is more along the lines of a look and feel command line prompt enhancement. What you receive is a far nicer interface than Windows provides for the command prompt, along with many options for modifying the interface. You can download this utility at http://www .winone.com.au/. Figure 23.6 shows how this utility appears on screen. Although you can't see it in the book, WinOne provides a significant amount of color coding that makes working with command or utility output significantly easier, especially for tabular items.

Real World Scenario

WORKING IN MIXED ENVIRONMENTS

Many administrators work in mixed environments today, so it's not surprising that they look for software that has the same functionality in as many environments as possible. PromptPal and WinOne look, more than any other utility in this chapter, like they bring the Windows command line much closer to the functionality of the Linux command line environment (CLE). Many administrators feel that the Linux CLE is much more intuitive than the Windows version, even if the commands aren't necessarily the same. If you work in both the Windows and Linux environments, you might want to use these utilities to bring the two environments closer.

Working in a mixed environment can be difficult. Although this book doesn't provide much Linux information, a few books on the market do. One of the best books for learning more about working in a mixed environment is *Windows and Linux Integration* by Jeremy Moskowitz and Thomas Boutell (Sybex, 2005).

FIGURE 23.6
WinOne provides a nicer look and feel than the basic command prompt that Windows provides.

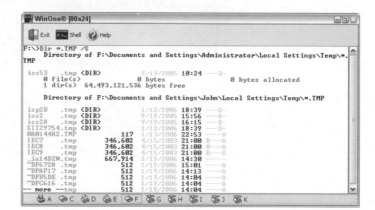

In addition, WinOne includes its own batch language that you can compile. The batch applications can include special dialog boxes, so you have an opportunity to combine the advantages of the command line with a graphical interface. The book doesn't include an example of this batch language because you can probably do better by using standard batch development techniques and a batch file compiler. Chapter 7 discusses batch and script file compilers in greater detail.

TIP   Even though this chapter doesn't discuss them, you'll find a wealth of shrink-wrap (commercial) products on the market to enhance the command line. Many of them started as shareware, but moved on to full commercial vendors and now provide only a product demonstration for free. You can find some of these utilities on software brokering Web sites such as BMTMicro at http://www.bmtmicro.com/BMTCatalog/win/02system.html. For example, the 4NT utility on this Web site is an excellent command interpreter replacement that has a long history. Many of you might have heard of it as 4DOS.

Automating Email Using sendEmail

The sendEmail program is interesting because it originally appeared on the Linux platform, not on Windows. Essentially, sendEmail is a Simple Mail Transfer Protocol (SMTP) agent, so you don't have to rely on any external application to use it. You do need an SMTP server, which the send-Email application assumes is on Localhost unless you specify otherwise. Make sure you download the Windows version of the utility at `http://caspian.dotconf.net/menu/Software/SendEmail/`.

The really interesting feature of this product, though, is that you can use it to send an email to anyone from the command prompt, a batch file, or a script (the Web page makes it appear that you need to use Practical Extraction and Report Language or PERL, which also works of course, but isn't a requirement). Consequently, an administrator who needs to monitor a host of network machines can do so effectively simply by checking email. This utility uses the following syntax:

```
sendEmail -f ADDRESS  [-t ADDRESS [ADDRESS ...]] [-u SUBJECT] [-m
    MESSAGE] [-s SERVER[:PORT]] [-a   FILE [FILE ...]] [-cc ADDRESS
    [ADDRESS ...]] [-bcc ADDRESS [ADDRESS ...]] [-xu USERNAME [-xp
    PASSWORD]] [-l  LOGFILE] [-v [...]] [-o NAME=VALUE]
sendEmail —help TOPIC
```

Of these arguments, you must provide the -f command line switch as a minimum. You must also provide at least one recipient using the -t, -cc, or -bcc command line switches. Finally, even though you don't absolutely have to provide it, you should include a message body using the -m or -o command line switches. You can also type the message using the standard input device (STDIN). The following list describes each of the command line arguments.

-f *ADDRESS* Defines the address of the sender. If you're using this utility to report system progress or errors, you can use the user's address and machine name for the address. For example, using an address of "John, Main<JMueller@mwt.net>" tells you that the user's name is John and that the machine name is Main. You must still provide a return address, which can be your own email address or the user's email address.

NOTE Newer Windows systems with built-in firewall support might block the sendEmail utility. Unfortunately, you'll just see an odd error message; neither the utility nor Windows will tell you what is really happening to the email. Make sure you set your firewall to allow sendEmail to transmit the message using whatever port you select. The default port for this utility is 25, but you can change the standard port using the -s command line switch.

-t *ADDRESS [ADDRESS ...]* Defines one or more addresses to receive the email message. These email addresses appear in the To field of the message. You can also send the email to addresses in the CC field using the -cc command line switch and the BCC field using the -bcc command line switch.

-u *SUBJECT* Defines the message subject. Make sure you place the message subject in quotes when it contains spaces. Any other argument with spaces also requires quotes.

-m *MESSAGE* Defines the message body. The message body can contain anything that you can place in a standard message, including HTML. However, at some point, this utility becomes more cumbersome than helpful for complex messages and you should consider switching to a full-fledged email application.

-s *SERVER[:PORT]* Specifies the SMTP server. Don't include a protocol with the SMTP server argument—include only the full server name such as `smtp.myserver.com`. The default server is Localhost. You may also specify a port number to use when contacting the server. The default setting is the standard SMTP port of 25.

-a *FILE [FILE ...]* Adds one or more file attachments to the email message. You can use this option to send complex test data.

-cc *ADDRESS* **[***ADDRESS* **...]** Defines one or more carbon copy recipients. These addresses appear in the CC field of the message.

-bcc *ADDRESS* **[***ADDRESS* **...]** Defines one or more blind carbon copy recipients. Even though these email addresses receive the message, they won't appear as part of either the To or CC fields. Instead, you'll normally see a default entry, such as Undisclosed-Recipient.

-xu *USERNAME* Specifies the username for SMTP server authentication. You may not require this input with public servers.

-xp *PASSWORD* Specifies the user's password for the SMTP server account. You normally must provide a username with the -xu command line switch to use this option.

-l *LOGFILE* Specifies a log file to use to record email events.

-v **[...]** Forces the utility to provide additional information about email events. Use this command line switch multiple times for added verbosity.

-q Forces the utility to restrict any email event output. The user won't see any messages at the command line. You can use this option to ensure a background process doesn't disturb the user.

-o *NAME=VALUE* Defines special email processing requirements. This book doesn't describe the email header in detail. However, the following list provides a short description of the various properties that this utility makes available.

message-file=*FILE* Specifies the message relies on a file, rather than a standard body, as the means of sending information.

message-header=*EMAIL_HEADER* Defines one or more special headings for the email message.

message-format=raw Specifies that the utility will send the email using a raw, prebuilt message.

message-charset=*CHARSET* Defines the character set used by the email message.

reply-to=*ADDRESS* Defines the address to use for replies. The default setting uses the address in the From field of the message for replies. This option provides an alternative to the default.

timeout=*SECONDS* Determines how long the utility, servers, and other elements of the mail transfer system wait for a successful email transmission.

TIP You can find a host of Web sites that describe the email message header online. If you want to understand the email process better and the tools required when working with email headers, look at the Tracking E-mail site at http://www.expita.com/header1.html.

–help *TOPIC* Obtains additional help about a particular topic. Even though you can use the /? command line switch to obtain general help, you can obtain a wealth of additional information by using this command line switch. The following list describes the additional topics.

addressing Explains the various addressing and related options.

message Explains the message body input and related options.

misc Contains all of the miscellaneous topics that don't fit under any other heading.

networking Explains all of the networking options, such as selecting a server using the -s command line switch.

output Explains the logging and other output options.

Real World Scenario

CONSIDERING MULTIPLATFORM REQUIREMENTS

You might not think that a book on the Windows command line would merit much thought about working on other platforms, but it does. Most administrators today don't have the luxury of just working with Windows or any other individual platform for that matter. Most companies now have multiple platforms for various tasks and the use of more than one platform isn't going to change. In fact, the problem promises to become worse, not better, as time progresses, for administrators.

The sendEmail application is a command line utility that just happens to run at the command line on multiple systems. Any time you can find a single software application that runs on multiple platforms, it's a good idea to check it out. Using the same software on multiple platforms means that you can leverage the work you perform on one platform on all of the other platforms as well. You'll reduce errors and the need for complex training in multiple packages. In some cases, you'll even be able to use the applications you create on multiple platforms because the software that your applications access is the same on every platform.

Unfortunately, software that runs on more than one platform is still the exception and not the rule. In addition, most multiplatform software runs on two platforms; software that runs equally well on three or more platforms is rare. Software that runs precisely the same on three or more platforms is even rarer, but it does exist for specific needs. If your network has an odd combination of mainframe, Linux, Windows, and Macintosh, you probably won't find a lot of software to meet your command line needs, but you should still look. When you find someone who has two of your platforms covered, try to convince them to cover the other platforms too. Multiple platform networks are here to stay—any software you can find that runs equally well on all of those platforms makes your job easier.

Viewing XML Files Using XML Notepad 2007

Microsoft started using XML in Windows XP, but if you've noticed anything in the other chapters of this book, Server Core makes significant use of XML. In many cases, the files don't even have an XML extension. Microsoft uses a wealth of file extensions for XML files today. Any configuration file is likely to use XML. You'll also find that many log files and even some lower-level operating system data files all rely on XML. With this change in mind, you really need a good XML utility to work at the command line, but many of the free products on the market come up lacking. XML Notepad provides a decent level of XML support and you'll find that it works just fine for most, if not all, command line administration needs. You can obtain this utility at http://www.microsoft .com/downloads/details.aspx?familyid=72D6AA49-787D-4118-BA5F-4F30FE913628.

NOTE   Microsoft has produced a number of versions of XML Notepad. Old versions of XML Notepad won't install in Server Core. You must download and install XML Notepad 2007 from the Web site provided in this section in order to obtain a working copy of XML Notepad. Even XML Notepad 2006 fails to install in Server Core.

After you install XML Notepad, the setup program automatically opens an HTML page containing information about XML Notepad. You'll typically find this file at C:\Program Files\XML Notepad 2007\Readme.htm. One of the links opens a sample XML folder. In this folder you'll find the Basket.XML file that appears in Figure 23.7. Right-click the file in Windows Explorer and choose Edit with XML Notepad to open the file.

FIGURE 23.7
XML Notepad provides a safe editing environment for your XML files.

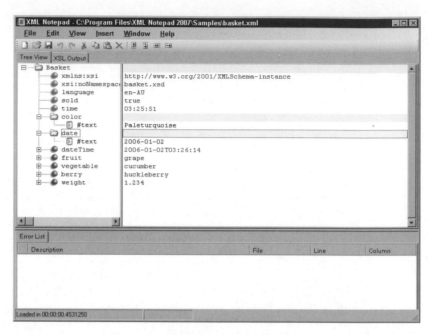

The XML Notepad display color codes entries by type and includes special icons to identify various types. For example, value entries appear with a special icon to differentiate them from elements.

You add a new entry by selecting it from the Insert menu. As an alternative, you can add new entries by right-clicking an existing entry and choosing the entry type from the context menu. In both cases, the new entry appears as a child of the currently selected entry in the left pane. You type a value for the new entry in the right pane. When you make a mistake in creating an entry, such as not adhering to a restriction in an XSD file, XML Notepad provides an entry in the bottom pane. Double-clicking the error entry takes you to that position in the file.

If your file has an XSLT processing instruction, you can view the output by clicking the XSL Output tab. The RSS.XML file provides a sample of this XML Notepad feature. You can change XSL files by clicking the ellipses button (...) and choosing another XSL file in the Open dialog box. Click Transform to display the transformed XML file.

One of the more interesting features of XML Notepad is the ability to compare two XML files. Begin by loading the primary XML file into XML Notepad. Choose View ➤ Compare XML Files to display an Open dialog box. Select the secondary XML file and click Open. You'll see an XmlDiff window open that has a complete comparison of the two files. This feature is helpful when performing configuration tasks where you want one machine to have some, but not all, of the settings of another machine or you need to check XML files for damage.

Managing Windows in a New Way

This chapter has addressed efficiency at the command line. It considers the matter of making you more efficient at the command line when you have manual tasks to perform. The utilities in this chapter all affect the command prompt in some way. For example, when you use PromptPal, what you actually create is a better interface for working at the command line. Anything you can do to make the environment easier from your perspective is a plus that you shouldn't avoid. This chapter helps you build the following skills:

◆ Obtain additional information with ToggIt command line helper

◆ Use Quick Shutdown to end a session fast

◆ Create a friendlier interface with PromptPal

◆ Get a more functional command line with WinOne

◆ Automate email using sendEmail

◆ View XML files using XML Notepad 2007

The utilities in this chapter are just a small sampling of what is available online. In some cases, these utilities won't meet any of your needs and you'll wonder why I included them in the book. The important issue is to obtain the utilities that do meet your particular needs, which are going to be very personal in this case. The way you work at the command line determines which utilities you need. Of course, you have many other ways to become more efficient at the command line. Don't forget to use automation and after hours tasking as required. Sometimes, it's more a matter of balancing all of the efficiency methods, rather than focusing on a single way to work faster and with greater ease.

Chapter 24 begins a new topic that most of you are going to find extremely interesting—running IIS 7 under Server Core. The amazing thing is that you can do so much without any kind of graphical interface. About the only application type you can't support is ASP.NET. Chapter 24 gets you started with IIS 7 and Chapter 25 completes the topic for Server Core.

Part 7

Working with IIS 7

Chapter 24

Installing and Configuring IIS

One of the newest features in Windows Server 2008, including Server Core, is Internet Information Server (IIS) 7. If Server Core had a Graphical User Interface (GUI), you'd quickly see that a lot has changed for IIS. In fact, you'd be pretty amazed at the changes, including extensive built-in support for the .NET Framework. However, given that Server Core doesn't support a GUI or the .NET Framework, what you'll mainly notice is a lack of functionality. You can support static content and scripted pages using Server Core, but you can't provide the significant dynamic content provided by ASP.NET (at least, not without help—Appendix A contains one suggestion for fixing this oversight).

Fortunately, you do have full Active Server Pages (ASP), Common Gateway Interface (CGI) (including the new FastCGI), and PHP: Hypertext Preprocessor (PHP) (originally known as Personal Home Page) support at your disposal, which means you can still create some interesting applications. In addition, Server Core provides full Internet Server Application Programming Interface (ISAPI) support, which means you can also use custom ISAPI modules and filtering.

Installing and configuring IIS using the GUI can be a challenge, but you can usually figure out the next step with a little help. Trying to perform an installation and configuration from the command line is a different story. One of the reasons I chose to include IIS in this book is that it represents one of the more confusing and complex configuration tasks in Server Core. What you really need is a GUI, but you don't have it.

This chapter helps you install IIS, configure a basic Web site, and add content to that Web site. When you can perform these tasks, you can begin using the Web site for something productive. You can use the resulting Web site for any static content, including all of those forms your company uses, standard HTML, dynamic content based on scripts, and a number of other content types such as file downloads. In fact, you can even use the Web site for streaming media—you just can't use it for ASP.NET. The limitation may not even be noticeable for many smaller organizations or large organizations that don't need all of the bells and whistles for the company intranet.

In this chapter, you'll learn how to do the following:

◆ Install IIS

◆ Create a basic Web site

◆ Add content

Performing the IIS Installation

Before you can do anything with IIS on a remote system, you need to install it. Because you lack a GUI installation tool, you might be tempted to use the OCSetup utility described in the "Adding and Removing Applications with the OCSetup Utility" section of Chapter 13. However, IIS requires the use of services, so you can't install it using OCSetup—you use the PkgMgr utility described in the "Accessing the Windows Package Manager with the PkgMgr Utility" section of Chapter 13 instead. The following sections describe how to perform various kinds of IIS installations.

WHAT IS MISSING FROM SERVER CORE?

It's important to know what you won't find in Server Core when working with IIS so that you don't expect to find something that isn't there. Beside ASP.NET support and lack of .NET Framework support, you won't find support for these features:

◆ IIS-ASPNET

◆ IIS-NetFxExtensibility

◆ IIS-ManagementConsole

◆ IIS-ManagementService

◆ IIS-LegacySnapIn

◆ IIS-FTPManagement

◆ WAS-NetFxEnvironment

◆ WAS-ConfigurationAPI

These features generally relate to a GUI feature or a .NET feature. Consequently, if you use IIS on Server Core in the way in which Microsoft originally intended, you probably won't even notice these missing features.

NOTE You may want to perform some installation tasks from a remote location such as your client machine. Unfortunately, the remote administration service that handles HTTP remote administration and delegated administration relies on the .NET Framework. In addition, IIS 7 won't allow you to use the IIS 6 administration utilities found in products such as Windows XP. Consequently, you can't perform remote administration tasks using the standard methods you may have used in the past. Fortunately, you can modify the CONFIG files that IIS 7 relies on from a remote location. You'll find a discussion of these and other administration topics in Chapter 25.

Performing a Standard Installation

A standard installation provides you with basic functionality that you can use to build a Web site. The result isn't a complete Web site, but you can access the resulting Web site and begin using it to create something usable. Of course, you'll want to verify any IIS components that you already have installed on the system using OCList. The entry that you want to find is IIS-WebServerRole and it should say Not Installed. Once you verify that you haven't installed the IIS Web Server role, you can use the following steps to install it.

1. Type `PkgMgr /IU:IIS-WebServerRole;WAS-WindowsActivationService;WAS-ProcessModel` and press Enter to perform a default installation. Remember that you'll see the hourglass icon for a few seconds, and then nothing. To actually determine whether you have installed anything, you must use OCList.

NOTE If you want to perform a complete installation of absolutely every IIS feature, you'll need a long command line to do it. Type `PkgMgr / IU:IIS-WebServerRole;IIS-WebServer;IIS-CommonHttpFeatures;IIS-StaticContent;IIS-DefaultDocument;IIS-DirectoryBrowsing;IIS-HttpErrors;IIS-HttpRedirect;IIS-ApplicationDevelopment;IIS-ASP;IIS-CGI;IIS-ISAPIExtensions;IIS-ISAPIFilter;IIS-ServerSideIncludes;IIS-HealthAndDiagnostics;IIS-HttpLogging;IIS-LoggingLibraries;IIS-RequestMonitor;IIS-HttpTracing;IIS-CustomLogging;IIS-ODBCLogging;IIS-Security;IIS-BasicAuthentication;IIS-WindowsAuthentication;IIS-DigestAuthentication;IIS-ClientCertificateMappingAuthentication;IIS-IISCertificateMappingAuthentication;IIS-URLAuthorization;IIS-RequestFiltering;IIS-IPSecurity;IIS-Performance;IIS-HttpCompressionStatic;IIS-HttpCompressionDynamic;IIS-WebServerManagementTools;IIS-ManagementScriptingTools;IIS-IIS6ManagementCompatibility;IIS-Metabase;IIS-WMICompatibility;IIS-LegacyScripts;IIS-FTPPublishingService;IIS-FTPServer;WAS-WindowsActivationService;WAS-ProcessModel` and press Enter to perform a complete installation.

2. Type **OCList** and press Enter. Locate the IIS-WebServerRole entry. It should now show Installed, as shown in Figure 24.1. As you look through the list, you'll notice that several other features are also installed, including these items.

   ♦ IIS-ApplicationDevelopment

   ♦ IIS-CommonHttpFeatures

   ♦ IIS-DefaultDocument

   ♦ IIS-DirectoryBrowsing

   ♦ IIS-HealthAndDiagnostics

   ♦ IIS-HttpCompressionStatic

   ♦ IIS-HttpErrors

   ♦ IIS-HttpLogging

   ♦ IIS-Performance

   ♦ IIS-RequestFiltering

   ♦ IIS-RequestMonitor

   ♦ IIS-Security

   ♦ IIS-StaticContent

   ♦ IIS-WebServer

   ♦ IIS-WebServerManagementTools

- ◆ IIS-WebServerRole

- ◆ WAS-ProcessModel

- ◆ WAS-WindowsActivationService

Unfortunately, it doesn't install most of the subfeatures. For example, IIS-ApplicationDevelopment includes IIS-ISAPIFilter, but this feature isn't installed, so you must install it separately. You also won't have access to features such as IIS-ASP for scripted page support. Some features, such as IIS-DefaultDocument, do appear twice in the list. Don't worry, this condition is normal.

FIGURE 24.1
The initial installation only provides support for a few IIS features.

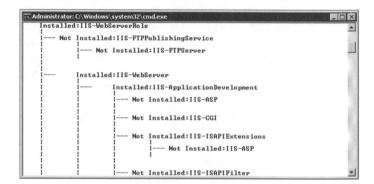

3. Verify the W3Svc is running by typing **SC Query W3Svc** and pressing Enter. You should also verify that the system has set the W3Svc to start automatically by typing **SC QC W3Svc** and press Enter. The service queries should appear as shown in Figure 24.2. Notice that STATE property is set to RUNNING and the START_TYPE property is set to AUTO_START.

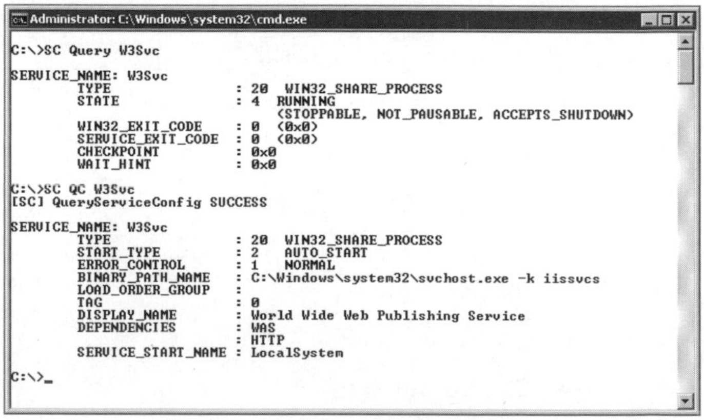

FIGURE 24.2
Verify that the W3Svc service is running properly after the installation.

4. Open an entry in the firewall to ensure that you can contact the server by typing **NetSH AdvFirewall Firewall Set Rule Group="World Wide Web Services (HTTP)" New Enable=Yes** and pressing Enter. The NetSH utility should tell you that it has updated the rule.

5. Verify the status of the firewall rule by typing `NetSH AdvFirewall Firewall Show Rule Name="World Wide Web Services (HTTP Traffic-In)"` and pressing Enter. You'll see output similar to that shown in Figure 24.3. Notice that the Enabled property is set to Yes and that the Action property is set to Allow. Now that you have everything set up, it's time to test the Web site from a client.

FIGURE 24.3
Check the status of the firewall setting.

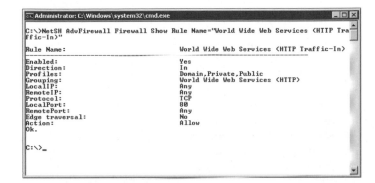

6. On the client, open a copy of your favorite browser. Type the name of your server in the Address field and press Enter. You should see a display like the one shown in Figure 24.4.

FIGURE 24.4
Your Web site is installed at this point, but not ready for use.

Adding Support for ASP

If you want to install support for ASP, all you need is a little longer command line than when you perform a standard installation. You would type `PkgMgr /IU:IIS-WebServerRole;IIS-WebServer;IIS-CommonHttpFeatures;IIS-StaticContent;IIS-DefaultDocument;IIS-DirectoryBrowsing;IIS-HttpErrors;IIS-ApplicationDevelopment;IIS-ASP;IIS-ISAPIExtensions;IIS-HealthAndDiagnostics;IIS-HttpLogging;IIS-LoggingLibraries;IIS-RequestMonitor;IIS-Security;IIS-RequestFiltering;IIS-HttpCompressionStatic;IIS-WebServerManagementTools;WAS-WindowsActivationService;WAS-ProcessModel` and press Enter at the command line at Step 1.

Of course, if you have already performed the standard installation, you'd type `PkgMgr /IU:IIS-ASP;IIS-ISAPIExtensions;IIS-LoggingLibraries` and press Enter at the command line instead. ASP support includes full ISAPI functionality because you can't have one without the other. After you complete the installation, verify that the system has ASP support installed using the OCList utility. Figure 24.5 shows the results when you update a standard installation to include ASP support. Notice that the IIS-ISAPIExtensions feature is actually a parent of the IIS-ASP feature, so you must install both as shown in the command line for this example.

FIGURE 24.5
Adding ASP support means supporting ISAPI as well.

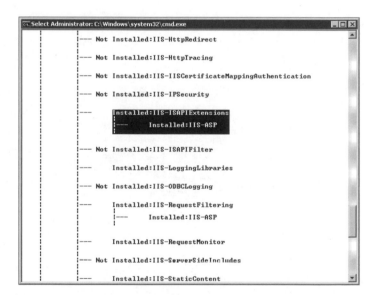

Adding Support for PHP and FastCGI

PHP isn't a stand-alone product when working with IIS. You must install a third-party product in order to obtain PHP support on IIS 7. The product that most people recommend for use with IIS appears on the PHP Web site at http://www.php.net/downloads.php. Unless you want to perform a lot of extra steps, you'll normally want to obtain the Windows version of PHP in ZIP format found at http://us3.php.net/get/php-5.2.4-win32-installer.msi/from/a/mirror. Since you can't download the file directly using Server Core, download it using a client machine and copy it to a folder to which you have access on Server Core. The following steps will help you install and configure both PHP and FastCGI support for Server Core once you have the Microsoft Installer (MSI) file downloaded (you perform all of these steps at the Server Core console).

1. Type **PkgMgr /IU:IIS-CGI;IIS-ISAPIExtensions;IIS-LoggingLibraries** and press Enter.

2. Verify the IIS-CGI installation succeeded using the OCList utility. You should see results similar to those shown in Figure 24.6.

FIGURE 24.6
Verify that you have added CGI support to the server.

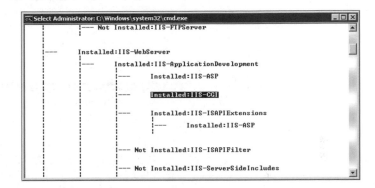

3. Use the CD command to change directories to the root directory.

4. Type **MD PHP** and press Enter to create a storage directory for the PHP files.

5. Use the ICACLS utility to provide yourself with shared access to the folder. For example, you might type **ICACLs C:\PHP /grant:r YourName:(F) /T /C** and press Enter to give yourself access.

6. Extract the files from the ZIP file and move them to the C:\PHP folder of the Server Core installation from your client machine.

7. Add the IIS executable directory to your path statement so that you can create the required handler mappings for both PHP and FastCGI by typing **PATH=%PATH%;C:\Windows\System32\INetSrv** and pressing Enter.

8. Type **AppCmd Set CONFIG /section:system.webServer/fastCGI /+[fullPath='C:\PHP\PHP-CGI.EXE']** and press Enter to add the FastCGI support.

TIP The AppCmd utility is a new utility for Server Core. You'll find it described in the "Using the AppCmd Utility" section of Chapter 25. This utility makes it easier to perform IIS 7 configuration tasks from the command line. Of course, you always have the option of modifying the configuration files directly. This technique appears in the "Modifying the Config Files" section of Chapter 25. Basic configuration is easier to perform with the AppCmd utility, so that's why you'll see it used exclusively in this chapter.

9. Type **AppCmd Set CONFIG /section:system.webServer/handlers /+[name='PHP-FastCGI',path='*.php',verb='*',modules='FastCgiModule',scriptProcessor='C:\PHP\PHP-CGI.EXE',resourceType='Either']** and press Enter to add the FastCGI handler for PHP files.

10. Type **AppCmd List CONFIG /section:system.webServer/fastCGI** and press Enter to verify the support entry. Type **AppCmd List CONFIG /section:system.webServer/handlers** and press Enter to verify the handler entry. You should see results like those shown in

Figure 24.7. Notice the PHP-FastCGI entry in the handler list and verify that this entry matches your entry.

11. Type **Copy PHP.INI-Recommended PHP.INI** and press Enter to copy the standard initialization file. At this point, the default PHP configuration is in place. You must perform any additional configuration using the standard PHP configuration you'd use on any other machine.

12. Test your PHP installation by loading a PHP file.

FIGURE 24.7
Verify that you have added both FastCGI support and a PHP handler.

Configuring a Basic Web Site

When you start working with IIS 7, the only Web site you have available is the Default Web Site. If you're performing testing and discovering how certain configuration features work, using the Default Web Site works fine. However, you'll eventually want to use some of the techniques described in Chapter 25 to add other features to your Web server. This section describes a few of the tasks you might want to perform on a basic Web site to begin testing and working with the Server Core version of IIS 7.

The configuration information for a Web server appears in the \Windows\System32\inetsrv\ config folder in a series of CONFIG files. You can edit these files using something as simple as Notepad because the CONFIG files are text formatted as XML. Generally speaking, using Notepad is a painful process because you must remember arcane syntax. Using Notepad is also error prone because you may leave out formatting requirements for the XML accidentally. If you really must edit the files by hand, then use a product such as XML Notepad 2007 to ensure you format the XML correctly. Figure 24.8 shows a typical view of the ApplicationHost.CONFIG file.

FIGURE 24.8
Use the XML
Notepad 2007 utility
to view and edit the
IIS CONFIG files
manually.

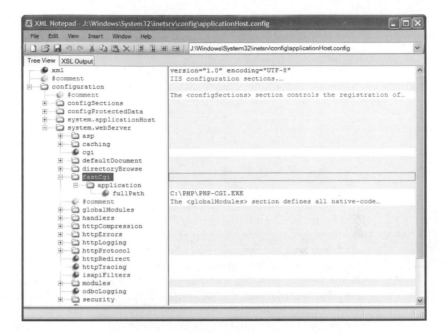

The preferred editor for IIS in Server Core is AppCmd because it ensures that the entries you make are correct. However, using AppCmd can be a challenge because it isn't very helpful in telling you how to make the entries. Viewing the CONFIG files using XML Notepad can provide you with a great deal of information. When you open the `ApplicationHost.CONFIG` file, you can begin to see some of the reason for the command line syntax for the AppCmd utility described in the "Adding Support for PHP and FastCGI" section of the chapter. Even though the command line doesn't say anything about XML formatting, you can see that the AppCmd utility provides the correct formatting automatically. When you type **AppCmd Set CONFIG /section:system.webServer/fastCGI /+[fullPath='C:\PHP\PHP-CGI.EXE']** and press Enter, the AppCmd utility creates the entry shown in Figure 24.8. It creates a new element named `fastCGI`, adds an `application` element to it with a value named `fullPath` that is set to C:\PHP\PHP-CGI.EXE.

Although you won't discover the full functionality of AppCmd in this chapter, it's helpful to know a few of the tasks you can perform with it almost immediately. The CONFIG object is the one that you'll use most when you perform an initial configuration because it provides access to the Web server configuration information. You can also use it to gain access to the default Web site. For example, if you type **AppCmd List CONFIG /section:DirectoryBrowse** and press Enter, you'll see the current `DirectoryBrowse` setting, which controls the user's ability to browse the file entries on the Web server. As shown in Figure 24.9, the default setting is `False`. However, if you want to change this setting, you can type **AppCmd Set CONFIG /section:DirectoryBrowse /enabled:True** and press Enter. The AppCmd utility will let you know that the item has changed as shown in Figure 24.9. When you type **AppCmd List CONFIG /section:DirectoryBrowse** and press Enter a second time, you'll see the changed setting shown in Figure 24.9.

FIGURE 24.9
The AppCmd utility provides you with a safe way to modify the CONFIG file settings.

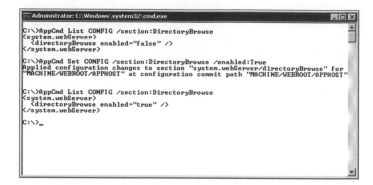

Now, let's say that you want the default setting for DirectoryBrowse set to False for the Web server, but True for the Default Web Site. In this case, you must specify the name of the Web site you want to change, so you'd type **AppCmd Set CONFIG "Default Web Site" /section:DirectoryBrowse /enabled:True** and press Enter. The name of the Web site is Default Web Site. Of course, you'd use the name of whatever Web site you want to change. You can verify that the Web server and the Default Web Site have different settings. First, type **AppCmd List CONFIG /section:DirectoryBrowse** and press Enter to check the Web server. Second, type **AppCmd List CONFIG "Default Web Site" /section:DirectoryBrowse** and press Enter to check the Default Web Site. Figure 24.10 shows the results you'd see. Notice that the Web server and Default Web Site entries differ.

FIGURE 24.10
You can change settings at any level you want using AppCmd.

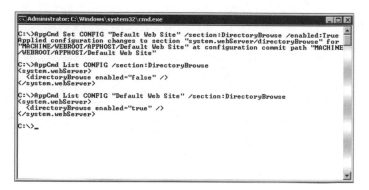

The configuration process works for any setting you want to change. Let's say you want to check the status of logging for the server. You can type **AppCmd List CONFIG /section:Log** and press Enter to perform this task. The default settings enable both the centralBinaryLogFile and centralW3CLogFile files. Both logs appear in the %SystemDrive%\inetpub\logs\LogFiles folder. If you want to use only the W3C log file format and you want to place the files in the D:\IISLogs folder, you'd use a three step process to make the change:

1. Type **AppCmd Set CONFIG /section:Log /centralBinaryLogFile.enabled:False** and press Enter. Notice that you specify the section as Log, the object as centralBinaryLogFile, and the attribute as enabled. The value of the enabled is False. You separate the attribute from the value with a colon in this case (or you'll see an error).

2. Type **AppCmd Set CONFIG /section:Log /centralW3CLogFile.directory:"D:\IISLogs"** and press Enter. As with the `enabled` attribute, you separate the `directory` attribute from the `D:\IISLogs` value using a colon. Notice that you must enclose the directory within double quotes, especially if the directory name contains any spaces.

3. Verify the results by typing **AppCmd List CONFIG /section:Log** and pressing Enter. Always verify the results of any changes you make. Figure 24.11 shows typical results from this task.

FIGURE 24.11

Configure the log files as needed on your server, but always verify the results.

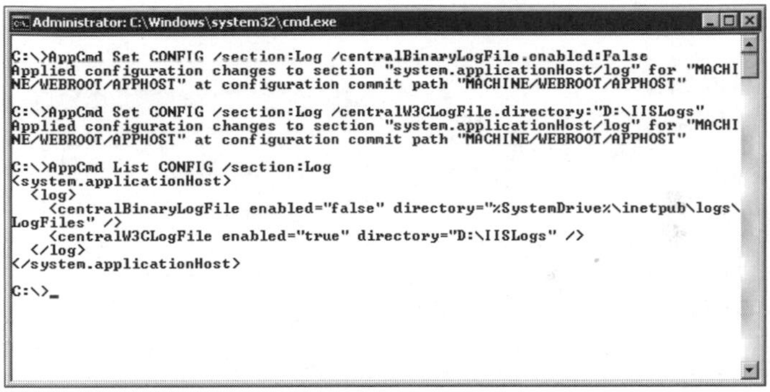

TIP Remember to use the question mark (?) as your guide for additional information when working with the AppCmd utility. In many cases, AppCmd will tell you what to type next. For example, when you type **AppCmd Set CONFIG /Section:?** and press Enter, you see a complete list of all of the available sections. Choose a section, such as Log, type **AppCmd Set CONFIG /Section:Log /?** and press Enter. AppCmd shows you a complete list of the attributes you can change for the Log section. If you enter an incorrect value for an attribute, such as a string in place of a Boolean value, then AppCmd tells you about the error. Of course, AppCmd won't know when you've entered an incorrect value of the correct type, such as the wrong directory.

A final basic configuration task to consider is adding or removing entries from collections. A collection is a list of items that belong to a particular object. For example, a Web site can have a number of default documents. If you want to list all of the default documents for a Web site, such as the Default Web Site, type **AppCmd List CONFIG "Default Web Site" /Section:DefaultDocument** and press Enter. You'll see results similar to those shown in Figure 24.12.

FIGURE 24.12

List collections of items on your server to see items such as default documents.

You don't actually want to have the IISStart.HTM file as part of the Default Web Site unless you plan to use it for something. Consequently, removing this file as part of your configuration is important. To remove a file, you must specify its position in the list. This file appears in the fifth position, but the list is zero based, so you refer to it as value number 4 (the first item in the list if value number 0). Type **AppCmd Set CONFIG "Default Web Site" /Section:DefaultDocument /-Files.[@4]** and press Enter. Notice that you place a minus sign (–) in front of Files to indicate that you want to remove this entry. Validate the change by typing **AppCmd List CONFIG "Default Web Site" /Section:DefaultDocument** and pressing Enter. Figure 24.13 shows the results of this change. Notice that the figure shows that the change affects only the Default Web Site and not the Web server itself.

FIGURE 24.13

Remove items from a list using a zero-based item number.

Sometimes you need to add an item to a collection. You can specify the position in which to add it as part of the addition. The position is important because it determines the order in which IIS 7 looks for the item. For example, when working with a default document, IIS 7 would look for Default.HTM as the first default document using Figure 24.13 as an example. IIS 7 would work its way through the list and look for Index.HTML last. If you want to add a document named Welcome.HTML as the first document in the list, you'd type **AppCmd Set CONFIG "Default Web Site" /section:DefaultDocument /+Files.[@Start,value=ÔWelcome.HTML']** and press Enter. In this case, you use a plus sign (+) to tell AppCmd that you want to add an element to the list. The square brackets ([]) show how to add the item. You specify a position that can include a number (@1), @Start, or @End, followed by the attributes and their values. In this case, the attribute name is value and the value is Welcome.HTML. As always, verify the results of the command by typing **AppCmd List CONFIG "Default Web Site" /Section:DefaultDocument** and pressing Enter. Figure 24.14 shows the results of this change.

FIGURE 24.14

Add new items using an index or keywords such as Start and End.

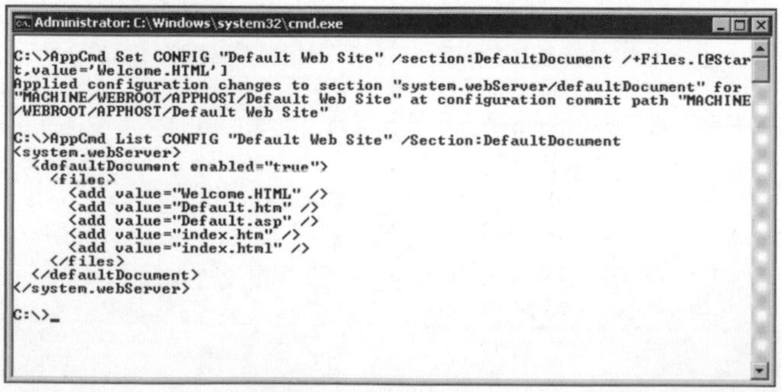

Adding Content

At some point, you'll want to add content to your Web site. You can perform this task directly in the \inetpub\wwwroot folder of the Default Web Site. For example, you can use the XCopy utility to copy existing content from one machine to another. Make sure you use the /S or the /E command line switch to obtain all of the content for the Web site. The /E command line switch ensures that you copy any empty folders that you may have supplied to hold data.

As with any other Web server, any applications that you provide on the server can add content to the Web site. These applications can also store and manage data for you and perform any other tasks that you might normally expect them to do. Just because Server Core relies on a command line interface, doesn't mean that you should expect anything less from it in the way of content.

Generally speaking, you'll want to produce content for the Web site using applications on your client system and then move it to the server for testing. This practice probably doesn't vary any from the techniques you already use to work with Web content. Of course, you can't use a database to hold content for your Web site if you plan to keep Server Core self-contained. However, Server Core can access a database on another server and use the information that server provides to create a Web page.

IIS 7 can support any content for which you have an executable in the form of a CGI application or an ISAPI extension. In order to use the content, you must create a mapping using the AppCmd utility. The "Adding Support for PHP and FastCGI" section of the chapter shows how to create a mapping. You must first register the handler and then create a mapping between the file extension and the handler. Of course, you can't use any managed executables without third-party support. The lack of managed executable support is the reason that IIS 7 doesn't natively support ASP.NET applications in Server Core.

Managing Windows in a New Way

Creating a Web site using Server Core isn't as straightforward as clicking a few items in a GUI utility. You'll have to use the commands that you've learned about throughout this book to get the task done. However, you also gain a number of benefits from using Server Core. For example, your Web sites will consume considerably fewer resources. Your server doesn't require the latest hardware to get the job done either because Server Core consumes fewer resources. It's even possible that you'll notice a pleasant change on your electrical bill because you don't need as much power to use Server Core as a Web server. This chapter helps you build these skills:

- ◆ Install IIS
- ◆ Create a basic Web site
- ◆ Add content

Now that you know the basics about IIS on Server Core, it's time to put them into practice. Although you can't set up an ASP.NET site without using a third-party product such as Mono (http://www.mono-project.com/Main_Page), you can still create both static and scripted Web sites. Try using the procedures in this chapter to set up your own IIS server on Server Core. Test it out and you'll like what you see. The performance will be quite perky and you'll find that you can support a lot of users with very little machine.

This chapter has introduced IIS 7 from a Server Core perspective to you. Of course, you don't have anything configured as of yet and will need to do so for a truly useful Web site. Chapter 25 helps you take the next step in working with IIS on Server Core by demonstrating techniques you can use for configuration. Part of the configuration requires that you use new command line utilities that you haven't seen in past chapters. You'll also need to work with the XML-based configuration files, so it may be a good time to break out that copy of XML Notepad 2007 that you read about in Chapter 23.

Chapter 25

Managing IIS

Most of the time you spend with IIS 7 involves some type of configuration or other management task. The basics described in Chapter 24 will probably garner you a test setup and let you start on your production system, but they're not complete instructions for building a Web server. This chapter adds to the information found in Chapter 24. It builds your knowledge so you can manage IIS on Server Core. This chapter almost completely ignores the graphical interface, however, because describing it would require another book.

Microsoft does provide some special features on Server Core that make your work considerably easier. You met one of the utilities in Chapter 24, AppCmd. This particular utility makes working at the command line considerably easier. Interestingly enough, AppCmd isn't a default part of the Windows Server 2008 graphical version. You can, however, use AppCmd just as easily with the graphical version of the product as you can with Server Core. The second utility, W3WP, does come with all versions of Windows that support IIS 7, but you'll probably use it more when working with Server Core than you will with other versions of Windows.

This chapter also discusses a number of configuration files that you can use to change how IIS 7 works. These configuration files are precisely the same no matter which version of Windows you use to host IIS 7. Consequently, it's possible to configure an IIS 7 setup using the GUI, and then move it over to Server Core. You'll still need to make some changes in most cases, but the number of changes should be small.

In this chapter, you'll learn how to do the following:

◆ Use a client system to manage the server

◆ Work with the AppCmd utility

◆ Work with the W3WP utility

◆ Modify the CONFIG files directly

Working from the Client

Working with IIS 7 from the client presents some special challenges. The IIS 6 utilities that come with Windows XP and older versions of Windows won't work with IIS 7. In addition, the GUI utilities for IIS 7 supplied with Vista won't work with Server Core because Server Core doesn't provide the required .NET Framework support. Therefore, it might seem as if your chances of working with IIS 7 from a client are limited. Of course, there are ways to overcome most problems and you do have options for working with IIS 7 from the client.

The first choice you have for working with IIS 7 from the client is to rely on Remote Desktop. If you plan to use the command line for management tasks, this is actually the best choice. You won't have to fight with the command line over rights or other issues that can plague you when you work from the command line on the client. Of course, you can always use any command line command or utility that does support a remote connection directly from the client command line. Be sure that Server Core grants you appropriate rights to complete the task when you use a remote connection.

A second choice for working with IIS 7 from the client is to install Windows PowerShell on the client. All of the Windows PowerShell commands include a `-computer` command line switch that you can use to access the remote system. If you have the appropriate rights on the remote system using your current account, all you need to provide is the `-computer` command line switch because Windows PowerShell will log you into the remote system automatically. However, if you don't have the appropriate rights, then you can use `Get-Credential` command to obtain the proper credentials and pass them to the server. Of course, using Windows PowerShell currently represents a significant increase in complexity.

TIP The current version of Windows PowerShell (1.0) has some limitations when it comes to remoting. You often have to perform extra work to accomplish a specific task and not all cmdlets work as well as they should on a remote system. Microsoft plans to fix many of these issues in Windows PowerShell 2.0 and add some other goodies as well. You can read more about these proposed updates at `http://searchwinit.techtarget.com/originalContent/0,289142, sid1_gci1270125,00.html`. If you do use Windows PowerShell, make sure you get the 2.0 update when it becomes available.

A third choice is to configure the Server Core IIS setup using a machine with GUI capabilities. You can then move the required CONFIG files to Server Core. The "Modifying the CONFIG Files" section of this chapter tells you about the CONFIG files. Even if the two servers don't have precisely the same configuration, you can still get the configuration close enough that you can perform some modifications to the CONFIG files using either the AppCmd utility or an XML file editor such as XML Notepad.

A fourth choice is to modify the CONFIG files directly from the client system. You can create a share on the server, use the ICACLs utility to set security properly, and then map a drive to it. Windows Explorer provides the access you require to the server and the CONFIG files it contains. Now you can open the CONFIG files on the client using a product such as XML Notepad as if the file were local to your machine.

The four options provide you with some good ideas for working with Server Core from the client. Using these four techniques, you can create any setup you require. Of course, there are probably other ways to perform the task as well. When working with Server Core, creativity is the key word. You're working with a stripped down version of the operating system that gives you some significant advantages, but you must find ways to overcome some of the connectivity disadvantages and, of course, the lack of a functional GUI for configuring applications.

Using the AppCmd Utility

The AppCmd utility is the command line utility used to manage every aspect of IIS 7. You've already seen this utility used in several places in Chapter 24. However, Chapter 24 only shows the CONFIG object and AppCmd has a lot more to offer. This utility uses the following syntax:

```
APPCMD (command) (object type) [<identifier>] [</parameter1:value1 ...>]
```

Each of these entries provides a complex data entry. The following sections describe each of these entries in detail. AppCmd provides vast capabilities, so it's important to work with this utility for a while using a test system so that you can see the results of any configuration tasks you perform.

An Overview of the Object Types

The commands that you can use are directly related to the object type you choose to use. However, AppCmd supports an assortment of general commands that meet most needs. While a command specifies the kind of task to perform, the object type determines how to apply the command. For example, you might want to apply the command to the CONFIG object. The identifier determines which Web site to work with. If you don't provide an identifier, any task you perform applies to the Web site as a whole. Finally, some tasks require that you provide input parameters (arguments). Here are the object types that the AppCmd utility supports.

APP   Performs management tasks with applications. You can add, delete, and list applications. In addition, you can change the application configuration using the `Set` command. IIS 7 comes with one default application, APP "Default Web Site/" (applicationPool:DefaultAppPool), which you can see by typing **AppCmd List APP** and pressing Enter. The default information only shows the application name and its associated application pool. If you want see a complete listing, type **AppCmd List APP /text:*** and press Enter.

APPPOOL   Manages the application pools used to run each application. IIS 7 creates worker processes for each application in an application pool. You can create as many application pools as needed to ensure applications perform as expected and don't interfere with other applications. IIS 7 comes with a single application pool, the DefaultAppPool. When an error does occur and the applications within a particular application pool fail, the system normally starts a new worker process and gracefully terminates the existing worker process in a process called *recycling*. You can manually recycle an application pool to fix errors immediately by typing **AppCmd Recycle APPPOOL "DefaultAppPool"** and pressing Enter (where DefaultAppPool is the name of the application pool you want to fix). You'll see a success message when the recycling process completes.

BACKUP   Backs up and restores data on your server. You can also delete backups you no longer need and configure backups to meet specific needs. The default settings perform backups automatically, so if you have used IIS 7 for any length of time you can type **AppCmd List BACKUP** and press Enter to see a list of the backups. To restore a backup, you must know the name of a backup on your system. For example, typing **AppCmd Restore BACKUP "CFGHISTORY_0000000006"** and pressing Enter restores the backup entitled, CFGHISTORY_0000000006. If you want to restore the backup without stopping the server first, include the `/stop:false` command line switch.

CONFIG   Performs general configuration of the server and individual Web sites. You can see a wealth of examples for this object in Chapter 24.

MODULE   Installs, uninstalls, and manages server modules. IIS 7 uses a modular approach to working with server components. You don't have to install all of the modules that IIS 7 provides to obtain certain levels of functionality. In addition, IIS 7 only loads the modules it actually needs to perform a task. Chapter 24 tells you about the default modules that IIS 7 installs. Don't confuse the `Install` and `Uninstall` commands with the `Add` and `Delete` commands. You use the `Install` and `Uninstall` commands to add or remove modules. The `Add` and `Delete` commands configure modules you already have installed. You can also install or uninstall modules using the PkgMgr utility as described in Chapter 24.

REQUEST   Monitors HTTP requests for your system. This object has only one command, List. You use it to obtain a list of current HTTP requests for the server. You can only use this object for monitoring purposes—it doesn't let you add or delete requests.

SITE   Manages the virtual sites on your server. IIS 7 comes with one virtual site installed, the Default Web Site. You can use the commands associated with this object to add or remove sites, start or stop them, configure them, or provide a detailed listing of configuration information. The default output information of the List command is usually inadequate for learning anything about the site—it only includes the virtual site name, identifier, bindings, and state. If you really want to know as much about the sites as possible, type **AppCmd List SITE /text:* >** **SiteConfiguration.TXT**. The SiteConfiguration.TXT file contains complete statistics about the sites on your server. Remember that you can specify a site if you don't need to know about all of the sites on your server. For example, type **AppCmd List SITE "Default Web Site" /text:*** and press Enter to learn about the Default Web Site. It's also possible to work with sites using their URL. For example, type **AppCmd List SITE http://localhost /text:*** to discover everything about the Default Web Site by accessing it using its URL. Sometimes you need specific information. In this case, you can specify the information you want to see using the /text command line switch. For example, type **AppCmd List SITE /text:limits.maxBandwidth** and press Enter to see the maximum bandwidth for each site.

TRACE   Manages the failed request trace logs. IIS 7 doesn't configure any trace logs by default because this is a debugging object. Consequently, you must first configure a trace log before you can do anything with it. After some time, the trace log will have entries in it. You use the List command to see all of the trace logs you have created on the server. The Inspect command lets you see the content of the logs. For example, if you want to configure a trace log for the Default Web Site for all ASP requests that take more than 60 seconds, you would type **AppCmd Configure** **TRACE "Default Web Site/" /enablesite** and press Enter to enable tracing on the Web site (which is turned off by default). You would then type **AppCmd Configure TRACE "Default Web** **Site/" /enable /path:*.ASP /timeTaken:"00:01:00"** and press Enter to create the trace log. Notice that you must supply the Default Web Site path, not the Default Web Site name (which is why the example includes a completing backslash). AppCmd also lets you use an URL as input to the command. The following list describes the special command line switches for this object.

/enablesite   Enables the Failed Request Event Buffering feature on the site.

/disablesite   Disables the Failed Request Event Buffering feature on the site.

/enable   Enables (adds, when necessary) a log file for a particular Failed Request Event Buffering rule. The rule specifies what kind of monitoring to perform. For example, you can specify a particular path. You can enable monitoring for all requests by supplying the asterisk (*) instead of a specific path.

/disable   Disables (removes) a Failed Request Event Buffering rule.

/path:*Pathname*   Defines the path that you want to use for debugging purposes. You can use any valid filename specification and include wildcard characters as needed for the *Pathname* variable. If you decide that you want to monitor all paths, then use the asterisk (*) by itself.

/areas:*Provider/Area[,Provider/Area...]*   Defines the areas of interest for a trace log. These areas help determine what the trace log tracks. This command line switch lets you include multiple entries. Examples of common areas include ASP/ (note that there isn't an area in this case), ASPNET/Infrastructure, ASPNET/Module, ASPNET/Page, ASPNET/ AppServices, ISAPI Extension/ (note that there isn't an area in this case), WWW Server/ Authentication, WWW Server/Security, WWW Server/Filter, WWW Server/StaticFile, WWW Server/CGI, WWW Server/Compression, WWW Server/Cache, WWW Server/ RequestNotifications, WWW Server/IISGeneral, and WWW Server/All. In order to use a particular provider, you must register in the `system.webServer/tracing/ traceProviderDefinitions` section of the `ApplicationHost.CONFIG` file. The default setting is to add all of the providers and areas defined for the current system.

/verbosity:{Ignore | CriticalError | Error | Warning}   Determines the amount of information that IIS 7 records about entries in the trace log. The Ignore setting provides the least amount of information, while the Warning setting provides the most information. The default verbosity is Error.

/timeTaken:*Timespan*   Determines how long IIS waits to make an entry in the trace log, even when the request eventually succeeds. This setting helps you track down requests that require too much time to complete. Even if there isn't anything wrong with your server, you can use this setting to monitor the performance of the Web site under a normal load. You must define either the `/timeTaken` or the `/statuscodes` arguments to create a functional entry.

/statuscodes:*CodesAsInt*   Defines the status codes that the trace log will track. For example, you might not be interested in tracking the 200 (success) messages. You can see a list of the standard HTML codes at `http://www.w3.org/Protocols/rfc2616/rfc2616-sec10 .html`. This command line switch is inclusive. You can't use it to exclude the 200 messages, but you can use it to include the 500 messages. The default status codes include 500,400,401, and 403. You must define either the `/timeTaken` or the `/statuscodes` arguments to create a functional entry.

VDIR   Creates, removes, and manages virtual directory entries for the server. The default setup includes a root directory for the Default Web Site. When adding a new virtual directory, you normally include an application name, path within the Web site, and physical path. For example, if you want to add a new virtual directory with the name MyVDir that has a physical path of C:\Temp, you would type **AppCmd Add VDIR /app.name:"Default Web Site/" /path: /MyVDir /physicalpath:C:\Temp** and press Enter. The VDIR object is often used with other commands. For example, if you type **FOR /F %f IN ('AppCmd List VDIR /text:physicalPath') DO DIR %f** and press Enter, you'll receive a directory listing for each of the virtual directories on the server.

WP   Monitors the worker processes currently executing on the server. You can only list the worker processes—you can't add or delete worker processes. If you find that a particular worker process is frozen or otherwise incapacitated, use the `APPPOOL Recycle` command to fix the problem.

You provide an object type every time you want to perform a task. For example, if you want to create a virtual directory for a Web site, then you must use the VDIR object. The CONFIG object is the one that you'll use most often when you initially set up a server, as described in Chapter 24.

An Overview of the General Command Line Switches

The AppCmd utility also supports a number of general command line switches that work with every object type. These general command line switches modify how AppCmd performs a task in some way. The following list describes each of these general command line switches.

/?   Displays context sensitive help that depends on the content of any other command line arguments. For example, if you type **AppCmd /?** and press Enter, you'll see a listing of the object types and general command line switches. However, if you type **AppCmd CONFIG /?** and press Enter, you'll see a list of commands the that CONFIG object supports. When you type **AppCmd List CONFIG /?** and press Enter, you'll see examples of how to use the List command with the CONFIG object.

/text:{ * | *value*}   Specifies the preferred output information. When you include the asterisk (*), the command outputs all available information about the object. You can also specify a value that reflects a particular entry for the object. For example, if you want to display just the maximum bandwidth for each of the Web sites on the server, you'd type **AppCmd List SITE /text:limits.maxBandwidth** and press Enter.

/xml   Outputs the information as XML instead of pure text. Seeing the information in this format helps you locate the correct entries in the CONFIG file when modifying files by hand. In addition, you can ensure you typed a command correctly when you see blank output. For example, when you type **AppCmd List APP /XML** and press Enter, you'll see XML output such as this for the default setup.

```
<?xml version="1.0" encoding="UTF-8"?>
<appcmd>
    <APP path="/"
         APP.NAME="Default Web Site/"
         APPPOOL.NAME="DefaultAppPool"
         SITE.NAME="Default Web Site" />
</appcmd>
```

/in or -   Accepts input from the standard input device in XML format. You can use this feature to transfer information from one application to another in XML format.

/config[:*]   Displays the configuration information for the selected object. Adding the asterisk (*)provides all of the configuration information, including inherited information, rather than a summary. For example, if you type **AppCmd List APP /config** and press Enter, you'll see the following output for the default configuration (notice that this output lacks the XML header provided with the /xml command line switch, but it also includes additional configuration information).

```
<application path="/">
  <virtualDirectoryDefaults />
  <virtualDirectory
    path="/"
    physicalPath="%SystemDrive%\inetpub\wwwroot" />
  <virtualDirectory path="/MyVDir" physicalPath="C:\Temp" />
</application>
```

/metadata   Displays the configuration metadata for the selected object.

/commit:{app | parent | url | apphost | webroot | machine}   Determines where AppCmd saves configuration changes that you make. In most cases, you'll never use this command line switch on Server Core. When Microsoft eventually adds ASP.NET support, you may use it to configure some ASP.NET features. The TechNet article at http://technet2.microsoft.com/windowsserver2008/en/library/30884867-a56d-4f31-8143-be0f35a30f8d1033.mspx describes these commands in detail. Note that you normally combine this command line switch with a /section command line switch and an attribute argument.

/debug   Displays debugging information for each of the commands that you type. For example, when you type **AppCmd List APP /debug** and press Enter, you see an additional line of output that includes INFO (timetaken:31, hresult:00000000, objects:1). The time taken to perform the task is in milliseconds. The hresult value tells you whether there are any errors (a value of 0 indicates no errors). The object's value tells you how many objects participated in the command.

WORKING WITH THE APPCMD COMMANDS

The AppCmd utility provides a number of basic commands that you can use with particular objects. The purpose is essentially the same in each case. For example, the Create command creates a new instance of a particular object and you can use the List command to display a list of all of the objects of that type. Table 25.1 shows which commands you can use with each object.

TABLE 25.1:   Available Commands for Each Object

COMMAND	APP	APP-POOL	BACKUP	CON-FIG	MOD-ULE	REQUEST	SITE	TRACE	VDIR	WP
ADD	X	X	X		X		X		X	
CLEAR				X						
CONFIGURE								X		
DELETE	X	X	X		X		X		X	
INSPECT								X		
INSTALL					X					
LIST	X	X	X	X	X	X	X	X	X	X
LOCK				X						
MIGRATE				X						
RECYCLE		X								
RESET				X						
RESTORE			X							
SEARCH				X						
SET	X	X		X	X		X		X	
START		X					X			
STOP		X					X			
UNINSTALL					X					
UNLOCK				X						

Now that you have a basic idea of which commands are available, you'll want some additional information on how to use them. The following list describes each of the commands and helps you understand what they do. See Chapter 24 for additional examples of how to use these various commands.

Add Adds a new object or a new object entry. The goal of the Add command is to add a new entry to the configuration file for an existing object. When you need to add a new object, you'll normally rely on another command such as Configure or Install.

Clear Clears a configuration setting without actually removing it. This command comes in handy when you need to remove the values associated with a configuration entry, without deleting it. For example, if you type **AppCmd Clear CONFIG "Default Web Site/" -section: defaultDocument** and press Enter, you'll clear the default documents associated with the Default Web Site. You must provide a defaultDocuments section, but it need not contain any document entries.

Configure Adds or removes trace log entries. See the TRACE object entry in the "An Overview of the Object types" section of the chapter for details.

Delete Removes an existing object or object entry. The goal of the Delete command is to remove an entry in the configuration file for an existing object.

Inspect Displays the content of trace log entries. See the TRACE object entry in the "An Overview of the Object Types" section of the chapter for details.

Install Adds a new module to the server. You can also achieve this goal using the PkgMgr utility. See the MODULE object entry in the "An Overview of the Object Types" section of the chapter for details.

List Outputs information about the requested object. The information is based on the XML data contained within the CONFIG files for the Web site or server. Many of the examples in this chapter tell you how to work with the List command because it can tell you how to work with a particular object.

Lock Makes it impossible to change a configuration entry.

Migrate Creates a backup of the configuration settings for a server. This command isn't the same as performing a data backup using the BACKUP object. While the BACKUP object works with the Web site data, this command works with the Web site settings.

Recycle Resets the specified application pool to ensure that all worker threads are working as intended. See the APPPOOL object entry in the "An Overview of the Object Types" section of the chapter for details.

Reset Sets a configuration setting to its default setting. This command is contrasted with the Clear command, which makes the configuration setting blank. For example, if you clear the default document settings, then the Web site won't have any default documents associated. However, resetting the configuration adds the default documents found in IIS when you first install it.

Restore Restores a previous backup when working with BACKUP object. See the BACKUP object entry in the "An Overview of the Object Types" section of the chapter for details.

Search Locates a particular configuration setting within the CONFIG file.

Set   Modifies an existing object or object entry. The goal of the Modify command is to change an entry in the configuration file for an existing object. AppCmd will always tell you whether the changes you make are successful.

Start   Starts an application pool or Web site so that it can perform useful work. As soon as the application pool or Web site is running, the associated application or Web site will begin responding to user requests (this action can require several seconds to complete).

Stop   Stops an application pool or Web site. Any applications or Web sites that rely on the object will cease to respond to user requests.

Unlock   Makes it possible to change a previously locked configuration entry.

Uninstall   Removes a module from the server. You can also achieve this goal using the PkgMgr utility. See the MODULE object entry in the "An Overview of the Object Types" section of the chapter for details.

Using the W3WP Utility

Normally, you won't worry about launching a worker process at all—you'll let IIS do it. However, the World Wide Web Worker Process (W3WP) utility can help you launch a worker process manually. The only times you'd need this utility are to determine why a worker process isn't working properly or to perform a remote execution from the command line (rare). This utility uses the following syntax:

```
W3WP -debug [-s <site id>]
W3WP -h [Application Host File] [-w <Root Web.CONFIG File>]
     [-in <Instance Name>]
```

The following list describes each of the command line arguments.

-debug   Use this argument to launch a worker process using the default application host configuration file. The default settings use the default Web site (site ID 1). You can modify this behavior using the -s argument.

-s SiteID   Defines the site identifier to use for launching the worker process. Getting the right site identifier is important. The easiest way to find this number is to choose the Web site in the Connections pane of the Internet Information Services (IIS) Manager. Click Advanced Settings in the Actions pane and you'll see the Advanced Settings dialog box. The site identifier appears in the ID field. You can also locate this information in the \Windows\System32\inetsrv\config\ ApplicationHost.CONFIG file. The information appears in the configuration\system .applicationHost\sites element as one of the site element entries.

-h [ApplicationHostConfigurationFilename]   Launches a worker process using the specified application host configuration filename. If you don't specify a filename, then the utility uses the default Web site (site ID 1).

-in InstanceName   Defines the instance name to use. The default setting uses HWC- followed by the process identifier (PID) for the worker process. Consequently, when the instance has a PID of 1001, you'll see a name of HWC-1001 for it.

-w RootWebConfigurationFilename   Defines the root Web configuration file to use when launching the worker process.

Modifying the CONFIG Files

IIS 7 relies on a number of configuration (CONFIG) files. You'll find that it includes configuration files for the Web site as a whole and individual configuration files for each Web site your server supports. Normally, you'll use a GUI utility to change the CONFIG files or work with the AppCmd utility, rather than change these files directly. However, in some cases, you'll need to perform direct edits of the CONFIG files to achieve specific goals. For example, you can't easily modify the verbosity of area entries for a trace log using AppCmd—you must set the verbosity using a direct CONFIG file entry. The following sections describe each of the CONFIG files you need to consider when working with IIS 7.

Understanding the *Web.CONFIG* File

The Web.CONFIG file appears more than once on your server. In fact, you'll see one Web.CONFIG file for each Web site and application. Every virtual directory includes a Web.CONFIG file as well. In fact, you'll run into the Web.CONFIG file so often, it's easy to become confused. The sections that follow describe some of the issues you need to consider when working with Web.CONFIG, tell you the easiest way to make the changes, and describe some of the most common elements that you'll modify.

NOTE IIS 7 doesn't use the metabase and it has a considerable number of other changes too. You may find that old tools and utilities don't work as they once did. Make sure you check out the list of breaking changes in IIS 7 at http://www.iis.net/default.aspx?tabid=2&subtabid=25&i=1236&p=2. If your application requires FrontPage extensions, make sure you check out the fix for this issue at http://www.iis.net/articles/view.aspx/IIS7/Deploy-an-IIS7-Server/Installing-IIS7/Install-FrontPage-Server-Extensions.

UNDERSTANDING THE CONFIGURATION FILE HIERARCHY

IIS starts out with basic settings. These settings don't appear in any of the standard folders for the Web site. You'll find them in the \Windows\Microsoft.NET\Framework\v2.0.50727\CONFIG\ folder on your system, which is the starting point for all of the Web.CONFIG settings. When you need to make a server-level setting change, you must open the server-level Web.CONFIG file to do it. Any settings you make in this Web.CONFIG file affect every other level unless you provide a specific override at that level.

TIP If you ever make a mistake in the Web.CONFIG file for the Web server that completely disables the Web server (or, at least, damages it in such a way that fixes are difficult), you'll find a Web.CONFIG.Default file in the \Windows\Microsoft.NET\Framework\v2.0.50727\CONFIG\ folder on your system. Copy this file to the Web.CONFIG file. Don't simply rename the Web.CONFIG.Default file because you won't have a backup for later. Using this approach resets the server to defaults—you'll lose all of your settings, but you'll regain access to the server and be able to restart it. Use this technique as a last ditch fix for severe configuration problems.

The next level is the Web site. The root folder for the Web site contains the Web site settings. The default Web site settings appear in the \inetpub\wwwroot folder. Any other Web site you create has a Web.CONFIG file in its root folder. Any changes you make to these files affect the entire Web site, including all applications, unless you specifically override them at the folder or application level. These changes also override any settings you define at the Web server level. The important point is that these files affect the next level in the Web server hierarchy, even though they don't appear at the next level in the Windows folder hierarchy. The two hierarchies are different and it's important not to confuse them.

Folders and applications come next. When a folder or application appears within the Windows folder hierarchy, it's easy to determine that folder's or application's position in the Web server hierarchy as well. However, folders and applications can rely on virtual directories. When you use a virtual directory for the folder or application, the Web.CONFIG file appears in the root folder of that virtual directory. Again, even though the Windows hierarchy differs from the Web server hierarchy, the Web server hierarchy is the one that matters. Folder and application Web.CONFIG file settings always override those of the Web site and the Web server.

AN OVERVIEW OF THE *WEB.CONFIG* ELEMENTS

It's time to put a number of puzzle pieces together to obtain a better understanding of how things work with the Web.CONFIG file. The important issue to remember is that only changed items appear in the Web.CONFIG file. For example, if you create a trace log entry for the Default Web Site using the AppCmd utility (type **AppCmd Configure TRACE "Default Web Site/" /enable /path:*.ASP /timeTaken:"00:01:00" /verbosity:Warning** and press Enter to see this example), Web.CONFIG file for the Default Web site will look like Listing 25.1.

LISTING 25.1:   Creating a CONFIG File Entry for a Trace

```xml
<?xml version="1.0" encoding="UTF-8"?>
<configuration>
    <system.webServer>
        <tracing>
            <traceFailedRequests>
                <add path="*.ASP">
                    <traceAreas>
                        <add provider="WWW Server"
                            areas="Authentication,Security,
                                Filter,StaticFile,CGI,Compression,
                                Cache,RequestNotifications,Module"
                            verbosity="Verbose" />
                        <add provider="ASP"
                            areas="" verbosity="Verbose" />
                        <add provider="ISAPI Extension"
                            areas="" verbosity="Verbose" />
                    </traceAreas>
                    <failureDefinitions timeTaken="00:01:00"
                                    verbosity="Warning" />
                </add>
            </traceFailedRequests>
        </tracing>
    </system.webServer>
</configuration>
```

The XML for this example points out a reason that you might want to edit the CONFIG file manually. Notice that the /verbosity command line switch sets the verbosity attribute in the <failureDefinitions> element. Microsoft doesn't provide a way to change the verbosity setting for each of the providers. These settings include General, Critical Errors, Errors, Warnings, Information, and Verbose.

You'll find additional reasons to modify the settings directly as you work with IIS to configure your Web site. Microsoft provides a complete listing of the various Web.CONFIG elements at http://msdn2.microsoft.com/en-us/library/ms228147(VS.80).aspx. You'll also want to view the entries at http://msdn2.microsoft.com/en-us/library/1fk1t1t0(VS.80).aspx. The default settings for the Web server include these elements:

location Determines whether the administrator can override the settings provided as child elements. The default value is True. Any elements contained within this element are subject to the override setting. You can learn more about this element at http://msdn2.microsoft.com/en-us/library/b6x6shw7(VS.80).aspx.

system.net Determines the basic settings for Internet applications. The most common child element is defaultProxy, which determines the proxy used to handle HTTP requests. You can learn more about this element at http://msdn2.microsoft.com/en-us/library/6484zdc1.aspx or http://msdn2.microsoft.com/en-US/library/aa309410(VS.71).aspx.

system.web Defines the settings for the ASP.NET application environment. For example, this element contains child elements that control both authorization and compilation of ASP.NET applications. You can learn more about this element at http://msdn2.microsoft.com/en-us/library/dayb112d.aspx or http://msdn2.microsoft.com/en-us/library/dayb112d(VS.71).aspx.

The Web server settings tend to define the big picture—how the Web server reacts with all of the Web sites and the applications they contain by default. Once you move past the Web server, to the Web site, you'll see other elements. The two default elements are system.web and system.webServer. The system.web entries tend to define the ASP.NET application environment in more detail.

The system.webServer settings are the root entries for the IIS 7 configuration. These settings control the Web server engine and modules. In some cases, these settings used to appear in the binary database that IIS used to hold metadata, but these settings all appear in XML form now. For example, this is where you'll find the default document, directory browsing, failed request tracing, and the handler mappings. You can learn more about this element at http://msdn2.microsoft.com/en-us/library/ms689429.aspx.

There aren't any default elements for folders and applications. The elements you see depend on the configuration requirements of the folder or application. In many cases, folders won't require any settings at all. Applications generally require settings to perform tasks. The system.webServer element contains a defaultDocument child element that has the default document for the application, as shown in Figure 25.1. Because this is an ASP.NET application, the default document is default.aspx, as shown in the figure. The Visual Studio environment automatically changes this entry as needed to match the default document set by the developer.

The configuration element normally contains a system.web element as a minimum. Notice the comments shown in Figure 25.1. These comments provide instructions that help you modify the entries correctly. For example, the compilation element normally contains a debug attribute that determines whether the application is using a debug or release compilation. This same setting appears in the graphical interface as part of the .NET Compilation pane. You change it using the Debug property.

FIGURE 25.1
Applications normally contain some default elements designed to make them work.

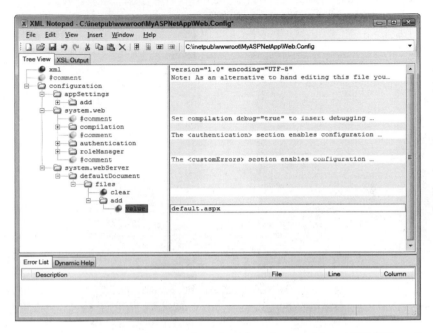

In many instances, applications also contain an authentication element. Most ASP.NET applications rely on forms authentication, so you'll see the mode attribute set to Forms. The other valid options include None, Windows, and Passport. The interesting part about this setting is that it includes the Passport option, which doesn't appear in the Authentication pane. However, it doesn't include the basic or digest authentication options, which do appear in the Authentication pane of the graphical tool, so there isn't a one-to-one correlation between the graphical tool and the Web.CONFIG file.

When you choose the basic or digest options, the mode attribute contains the Windows option. Of course, this makes it impossible to know where the basic and digest settings actually appear since IIS 7 does rely on XML for all settings. It turns out that implementing basic or digest security requires additional entries that you'll find in the \Windows\System32\inetsrv\config\ApplicationHost .CONFIG file (see the "Working with the *ApplicationHost.CONFIG* File" section of the chapter for details on working with this file).

Working with the *ApplicationHost.CONFIG* File

The \Windows\System32\inetsrv\config\ApplicationHost.CONFIG file contains a number of settings that don't appear in the individual Web.CONFIG files. The Web.CONFIG files normally contain managed settings, while the ApplicationHost.CONFIG file contains native code settings of various sorts. For example, when you use basic or digest authentication, the settings appear in the ApplicationHost.CONFIG file, rather than the Web.CONFIG file, as shown in Figure 25.2.

FIGURE 25.2
The ApplicationHost
.CONFIG file normally
contains native code
settings.

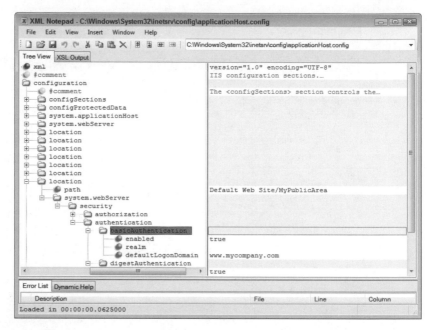

Even though the file appears quite complex, you can break the `ApplicationHost.CONFIG` file into five major areas. Once you know which area to view for a particular kind of data, working with the file becomes considerably easier. The following list describes each of the major areas.

configSections The `configSections` element defines the sections within the configuration file. You'll never need to change anything in this element because IIS depends on a specific configuration to accomplish tasks and you'll use other means to configure custom applications.

configProtectedData The `configProtectedData` element contains the security provider information for the system. You normally won't need to change this information unless you obtain a third-party provider (there aren't any available for IIS 7 at the time of this writing). If you do obtain a third-party provider, it's likely that the provider's installation program will make all of the appropriate entries for you. In sum, you probably won't need to change the settings in this element.

system.applicationHost The `system.applicationHost` element is a configured section—one that doesn't necessarily have to appear by default, but you'll normally see it. This element contains a number of interesting configuration options that include the application pools, custom metadata, listener adapters, log file settings, and some Web site settings. A number of these settings are impossible to set using the graphical utilities. For example, you can't set the log file settings using the graphical interface, but you can set them quite easily using the settings in this file. The Web site settings include the Web site bindings, failed request logging, and application location information.

system.webServer The `system.webServer` element is a configured section—one that doesn't necessarily have to appear by default, but you'll normally see it. Many of these entries look like they came directly from the graphical interface. For example, you'll find the CGI settings here, as well as the default Web page and directory browsing settings for the Web server as a whole. Some settings aren't available from the graphical interface. For example, you can set up ODBC logging using elements contained within this element. One of the performance options you'll want to check is caching. You can enable or disable caching for the Web server as a whole or for the kernel.

location   Every time you create a new location in IIS, IIS creates a new `location` element to hold it. The `location` element contains a `path` attribute as a minimum that describes the location. For example, you'll find an entry for the Default Web Site in the list. Every application, virtual directory, or folder with special settings appears in the list. A common child element is `system .webServer`. This element may contain any number of child elements or no child elements at all. The elements you see depend on the special settings for the location. When working with an application, it's common to see elements for setting the security, default directory, and handlers.

Working with the *Administration.CONFIG* File

The `\Windows\System32\inetsrv\config\Administration.CONFIG` file contains administrative settings for the server. For example, you'll configure the actual list of administrators here and define the list of administrator providers you want to use, as shown in Figure 25.3. As with the `ApplicationHost.CONFIG` file, the `Administration.CONFIG` file contains a number of required entries that you probably won't change, including the `configSections` element.

FIGURE 25.3
The Administration .CONFIG file contains administrative settings.

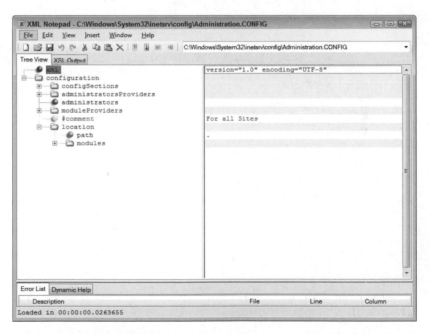

The main item of interest is the `moduleProviders` element. It contains a list of modules that IIS uses to perform useful work. You can't access these providers from the graphical interface—they affect IIS at a relatively low level. IIS sorts them by server and ASP.NET modules. As with the security profiles, the modules you use must appear in the GAC. You can add new modules by registering the module in the GAC using the GACUtil utility and then adding the appropriate entry to the `moduleProviders` element.

Simply adding an add element to the `moduleProviders` element won't make the provider accessible to the server. You must link the provider to a particular location, which is where the `location` element comes into play in this file. When you open the `location` element, you'll find that it contains a `modules` element that has a list of modules for that location. You simply refer to the name of the element you created in the `moduleProviders` element. When you remove an element from this list, the server no longer uses the module provider for that particular location, but it remains configured for use later. The default IIS setup only includes one location, the Web server itself.

Managing Windows in a New Way

This chapter has demonstrated how to perform a number of the configuration tasks required to make your basic IIS server fully functional. Normally, you'll begin working with the server through the client. When you can't obtain the proper results by working through the client, fill in the gaps using the AppCmd and W3WP utilities because they check your entries for errors. When all else fails, modify the CONFIG files directly. You should use this as your last option because the potential for error is high.

◆ Use a client system to manage the server

◆ Work with the AppCmd utility

◆ Work with the W3WP utility

◆ Modify the CONFIG files directly

Now that you have a better idea of how IIS 7 works from the command line, you'll want to begin configuring your test server to perform advanced tasks. Make sure you focus on structure first so that you can ensure you have all of the proper security in place. Work in a top-down fashion by setting up sites first and virtual directories second. Make sure you set all of the required security using the standard Windows security features (see Chapters 15, 20, and 21 for details). Add content once you have the site structure configured and have all of the required security in place.

Chapters 24 and 25 have shown you what IIS 7 looks like from the command line. Of course, that's the only view you get within Server Core. However, Microsoft has created some great graphical tools that these chapters couldn't discuss. My book, *Microsoft IIS 7: Implementation and Administration* (Sybex, 2007), provides full coverage of the IIS 7 most people see. This book also contains a considerable number of additional tips for working at the command line, so you'll want to add it to your library when you have to perform advanced configuration tasks. Although having my IIS 7 book is a great idea, the content of these two chapters are really all you need to configure a basic Web server on Server Core.

Congratulations! You've come to the last chapter of the book. What you see in this book is my experiences with Server Core, those of the various editors, and those of the beta readers. Obviously, Server Core is a complex product and your experiences may differ from ours—we all learn from experience. If you want to share your experiences with me, please contact me at `JMueller@mwt.net`. I always want to hear about your experiences, good, bad, or indifferent. Let me know what you think of the book as well. I always incorporate reader comments into the next edition of the book, so your input will help me create a better book. Make sure you also review the appendices. Appendix A provides you with 52 handy tips (one for each week of the year) for making your Server Core experience better. Appendix B and C provide two different ways to view every command and utility in this book. You'll find that they make it very easy to find just the command or utility you want. Finally, Appendix D provides best practices you should consider employing when you work with Server Core.

Appendices

Appendix A

52 Indispensable Command Line Tricks and Techniques

This appendix contains 52 helpful hints that you can use to work at the command line more efficiently and successfully. There's one tip for each week of the year. As you continue working at the command line, build batch files and scripts, and discover new commands and utilities that Microsoft has hidden there, you'll discover just how much of a resource the command line can be. Now that I've shared my tips with you, I'd love to hear about any tips you might have. Write me at JMueller@mwt.net to share them with me.

1. Always test new scripts and batch files using a test machine. Verify that the script or batch file works as anticipated before you test it on production machines. Even after you test scripts and batch files, provide additional monitoring while the script or batch file is new to allow potential bugs to surface.

2. Consider learning to use batch files for automation before you move on to scripts. Many automation tasks don't require scripts to succeed. Batch files are a very simple and easily understood way to add automation to the command line.

3. Third-party utilities are a tempting way to make the command line more accessible. However, it's usually a better idea to determine whether Windows provides a command or utility to accomplish the task first. Even if the Windows command or utility won't accomplish the task in the manner in which you want to accomplish it, the exercise of working with the command or utility will help you select third-party products with a greater potential for success.

4. Use the PushD and PopD utilities to save and restore directories as needed while working at the command line. These two utilities can save you considerable typing time. Use these utilities to create batch files that move between directories as needed to perform work. In many cases, you'll find that this feature makes it considerably easier to perform complex tasks with less typing because you don't have to type the full path to every file.

5. Environment variables come in three forms. The first is system variables that affect all computer users. The second is user variables that affect a single user permanently. You can find the first and second forms listed in the Environment Variables dialog box accessible by clicking Environment Variables on the Advanced tab of the System Properties dialog box. The third environment variable form is the temporary variables you create at the command line using the Set command.

6. Always use the most current version of a utility when possible. For example, even though many people are familiar with the older WinMSD utility, the MSInfo32 utility replaces it in Windows XP and above. Generally, you'll find that the newer utilities provide added functionality and reliability.

7. There aren't any absolutes when working at the command line. Sometimes you must break the rules in order to devise a reliable and secure method of automating a task. For example, even though the SchTasks utility is newer and more functional than the AT utility, you'll find that the AT utility often works better in batch files because of its simplicity. In this case, even though the SchTasks utility is more functional, the AT utility can produce a better batch file as long as you don't need the features the SchTasks utility provides.

8. Use after hours scripting carefully. Restrict after hours scripting to those tasks that actually require it. For example, an application, command, or utility that requires exclusive access to a database is a good candidate for after hours scripting. Don't use after hours scripting for any application, command, or utility that is unreliable or presents security risks.

9. Remember that a command is an internal feature of the command processor or another executable environment, such as the FTP application. A utility is an external, freestanding application. Even though commands and utilities are both executable code, commands depend on the resources of their enabling environment.

10. Even though a utility exists, that doesn't mean you should use it. For example, Microsoft disables the Messenger service by default in newer versions of Windows because crackers can use it to gain access to your system. However, the Msg utility requires access to the Messenger service. Unless you want to create a security hole in your system, refrain from using the Msg utility except where the network has no outside access.

11. Remember, this book documents a number of command and utility features that don't appear as part of the command or utility help, the local Windows help, or even the Windows Resource Kit. Some of these additions come from third-party Web sites (the sites appear in the book whenever possible). Some come from reader input for past books. Still other information comes from my personal experimentation. If you find a feature that doesn't work or you locate a feature that I should know about, contact me at JMueller@mwt.net.

12. More people use JavaScript than use VBScript. You can use both scripting languages (and many others) at the command line. However, if you're learning a new scripting language and want to obtain the maximum benefits from your efforts, JavaScript is by far the more popular of the two scripting languages. Not only can you use it with ease for work at the command line, you'll also find it in use on many Web sites. JavaScript is also standardized across multiple platforms, which means it's conceivable that an application you create can run equally well on a Macintosh or a Linux system as it does on your Windows system. Of course, you must use standards-based programming techniques to obtain this level of cross-platform support.

13. Always document your batch files using the REM command. The batch file you document might require modifications later and you don't want to spend hours relearning how the batch file works. Make things easier for yourself; use lots of comments to document your batch files.

14. The RunDll32 utility is possibly the most powerful single utility on your system because you can use it to access code within any DLL that provides a list of public calls. For example, you can use the RunDll32 utility to shut down the system or display a message box on screen. The number of tasks you can perform is only limited by the number of DLLs installed on the system.

15. Look in the `\Windows\System32` folder for executables. These executables often provide helpful utilities that Microsoft or a third party installs for you. To check whether the executable is a usable utility, type **`ExecutableName /?`** and press Enter to see any help it provides. No help file usually means that it isn't a utility.

16. One focus of Microsoft with Server Core is improved security. Consequently, many commands and utilities that work fine with older versions of Windows appear with reduced functionality in Server Core. You may also find yourself using the RunAs utility more often to support command line development. Of course, Server Core includes many new commands and utilities as well.

17. Sometimes, it's hard to figure out how to change the registry to obtain a particular effect in Server Core. Having relied on graphical utilities for many years, most administrators don't know what's going on in the registry. In some cases, you can cheat by loading a hive from another system that has the configuration you want. Use the File ➢ Load Hive command to perform this task. Compare the registry on Server Core with the registry hive from the other machine to see which changes you need to make in order to obtain the desired result.

18. Microsoft continuously updates the commands and utilities for Windows. Make sure you perform regular system updates to ensure you have access to the latest command and utilities. When you do obtain an updated piece of software, spend time learning its new features. The time you spend will pay off in greater productivity later.

19. Always configure the command window to meet your viewing needs. In addition, you can change settings, such as color, to add aesthetic appeal to the command line. Always remember that the system saves your settings based on title, so a command window with a different title can have different settings.

20. The SET command is a powerful feature that many people don't use effectively. A SET command can store any data you require at the command prompt. For example, you can easily use it to store numeric information as well as paths to files and user information. Generally, you'll use the SET command to store short information sequences.

21. Use temporary files to store large amounts of cumbersome data. You can also use a temporary file as a kind of database. Parse through the temporary file using the FOR /F command format. For example, with the proper code, you can use a directory listing as a means for locating and deleting temporary files on your machine.

22. Because Server Core is a command line–only interface, you'll want to be sure that you configure your command line for optimum performance. Be sure you set scripting to use CScript, rather than WScript. Add color to the display to make it look nicer. Use fonts that are appealing and gentle on the eyes. Anything you can do to make the command prompt better is a real plus in Server Core.

23. Right-clicking doesn't accomplish much in Server Core. Remember that you'll access the built-in GUI items by pressing Ctrl+Alt+Del. When you want to try a graphical utility, make sure you start it using the command line. In many cases, you'll find that the utility has command line switches you can use to make the startup work better—such as loading files and configuring settings so you don't need to perform these tasks using the GUI every time you start the utility.

24. Always assume that every application, batch file, script, command, and utility on your system is going to fail. Try to list every possible failure mode, even when you think that such a failure mode is unlikely. Provide for the detection, recovery, and workaround for each failure mode so that the software continues to run, rather than failing gracefully.

25. The Microsoft Knowledge Base at `http://support.microsoft.com/default.aspx?scid=fh;EN-US;KBHOWTO` is the greatest help for the command line user. Often, Microsoft document changes and new software appear here long before you see them anywhere else. In fact, you can find material here that you won't find anywhere else.

26. The only good time to compile your script file is after you've tested it thoroughly. In most cases, you can use third-party utilities to obtain a native executable file.

27. The DS utilities, such as DSQuery, provide you with extensive access to Active Directory. Even though these utilities don't appear as part of a standard Windows installation, you can install them from a server that supports them. Using the various DS utilities, you can add, delete, query, edit, and get Active Directory objects.

28. Redirection is an important part of working at the command line at any time. You can redirect both input and output using the redirection symbols. For example, instead of displaying a directory listing at the command prompt, you can send it to a file instead. By placing the output in a file, you can perform sequential processing of the individual file entries.

29. The XCopy command is the most versatile method of copying bulk data from one location to another. If you need to copy just a few files in the same directory, use the Copy command for greater efficiency (it executes more quickly than XCopy does). Avoid using older commands such as `DiskCopy` because Microsoft designed them in an era when floppies were the main form of data transfer from one machine to another.

30. Rely on the TypePerf utility to track performance characteristics at the command line. Use PerfMon when you need to perform long-term performance tracking or require use of the graphical performance monitoring interface that Windows supplies.

31. Use automation with great care. Always test the applications, batch files, and scripts you intend to automate before you let them run unmonitored. Never automate unreliable applications, batch files, or scripts.

32. Remember to use the `AutoExec.NT` and `Config.NT` files to modify the application execution environment. You can perform any task in `AutoExec.NT` that you would with a standard batch file.

33. Many applications don't use the registry to store settings anymore. Look for files with extensions such as CONFIG and INI to locate the settings in these newer applications. In some cases, the file will simply have an XML extension or you may find it contains XML or textual information that looks like configuration settings. User-specific settings generally appear in the `\Documents and Settings\`*UserName*`\Application Data\`*ApplicationName* directory (where UserName is the name of the user and ApplicationName is the name of the application).

34. Keep in mind that you have multiple methods for performing remote access tasks at the command line. Many people immediately think about using Terminal Server for remote tasks, but many utilities provide direct machine access through command line arguments. Use the direct access method when you only require the services of a single utility. Remember that newer versions of Windows also include Remote Desktop, but that you must make registry changes to systems in some cases to use this technique. You can also rely on older technologies to perform remote tasks, such as Telnet. In short, don't limit yourself to one technique for remote access; use the technique that works best for a particular scenario.

35. Killing tasks using utilities such as TaskKill might seem like a good idea when the system isn't responding as anticipated. However, a seemingly frozen application may simply be performing a task in the background, so it's important to wait before you kill the task. Always assume that killing a task will result in data loss of some kind. In addition, killing the task might not revive the system; you could still end up having to reboot the system to restore its responsiveness.

36. Assume that someone is going to break into your system and cause significant damage to it, because someone almost certainly will. Treat security as a barrier that keeps honest people honest. A determined cracker will always find a way in, so your only defense is to rely on monitoring and constant maintenance to detect the intrusions when they occur.

37. One of the essential issues to remember about working with scripts is that they can use any registered object on the machine. In addition to the special WScript object, a script can access any other object on the system, such as the media player. All you need to remember is the CreateObject() method used to create new objects based on existing system classes.

38. Make sure you use the OCList utility to determine which features are installed on Server Core. You don't have any other utility you can use for the task since Server Core doesn't provide a GUI. Use the OCSetup utility to add new roles and features to your server as needed. These utilities are new to Server Core, so you'll have to make special note of them.

39. Use wildcard characters to create file specifications when you need to process more than one file with a single command. Some commands and utilities don't support wildcard characters at all. However, most utilities support at least the asterisk (*) wildcard and many support the single character question mark (?) wildcard character as well. Some utilities support exotic string specification techniques and you should employ these wildcard character combinations whenever possible.

40. Most commands and utilities support the /? command line switch when you need help. However, some don't support this standard. When you find a utility that doesn't support the /? command line switch, try the /help command line switch instead. You can also try the Help command to obtain information about the command or utility.

41. Remember that using pipes to connect Active Directory utilities together is one of the most powerful techniques for working with Active Directory. Using a pipe makes it possible to perform tasks with Active Directory without knowing the names of the object in advance. In addition, you can perform tasks on object sets, such as a group of users.

42. Remember that you can only use static and scripted content when setting up a Web server with IIS 7 in Server Core. Because Server Core doesn't support the .NET Framework (at least as of this writing) you can't run ASP.NET applications directly in IIS. However, there are some interesting discussions taking place on using Mono (http://www.mono-project.com/), a .NET Framework substitute, to run ASP.NET applications on Server Core. You can find some helpful instructions here: http://www.gotmono.net/Default.aspx?pageindex=5 &pageid=27 and here: http://ajaxwidgets.com/Blogs/thomas/how_to_run_an_asp_ net_2_0_webs.bb.

43. Always consider the security issues of using any application, command, or utility. Never automate an application, command, or utility that presents a potential security problem. For example, applications, commands, or utilities that require administrative privileges often present a significant security risk that you won't want to leave open for crackers to exploit.

44. Never assume that users will perform any particular task. For example, even if you send a message across the network to close all open files on your system before you perform a maintenance task, you still need to verify that users have followed through by using the OpenFiles utility. The OpenFiles utility tells you about any open files on your system, giving you peace of mind when you perform the maintenance task.

45. Always run applications using the lowest number of rights that you can. Logging in with administrator rights for every task is an open invitation to cracker invasion. If you need to run a task that requires temporary extended rights, then use the RunAs utility to perform the task. The RunAs utility lets you execute just one command using Administrator rights, rather than using Administrator rights all of the time.

46. Remember that Server Core doesn't provide access to the common dialog boxes, which means that many of your favorite utilities won't work. You may be able to open a file with a particular utility and view it, but you won't be able to save any changes because the utility will lack the required common dialog box support. Applications that provide their own custom dialog boxes will work fine.

47. Scripting languages are more powerful than batch files because they include better flow control. In addition, you can possibly compile a script for better execution speed. However, with power comes complexity. Creating a script is an order of magnitude more complex than working with batch files.

48. Don't assume a limitation in a Windows graphical utility necessarily translates to the command line. For example, most people realize that Windows Explorer does a very poor job of finding content on your system. In fact, it does such a poor job that many people have resorted to third-party products to locate information on their systems. However, a combination of the Dir command and the FindStr utility can help you locate any information on your system for free and often faster than these third-party utilities can perform the task. Of course, you need to know how to use these command line utilities to take advantage of this command line feature that works far better than its Windows counterpart does.

49. The system creates a number of environment variables for you. For example, you'll find that the OS environment variable tells you whether you're using Windows as an operating system (preventing people from using batch files intended for the Windows environment on a DOS system). You can always list the environment variables on your system using the SET command. Simply type **SET** and press Enter to see the list.

50. Create custom versions of AutoExec.NT and Config.NT for applications that require them. The custom versions can use different settings to ensure that the application runs as anticipated. You specify these custom files using the Windows PIF Settings dialog box that you access by clicking Advanced on the Program tab of the application's Property dialog box.

51. Use the error level output of commands and utilities to detect errors in batch files. An IF ERRORLEVEL command can detect the error. A simple GoTo command can redirect the flow of the batch file to an error-handling section, and then redirect program flow for another attempt at the failed command or utility. Using this looping approach helps you create a certain level of error handling and fault tolerance even in batch files. Make sure you record all error information possible in an output file.

52. The command line is like the submerged part of an iceberg. Few people see it, many people don't know about it, yet it exists and it comprises the greater part of the Windows operating system. Every time you think that a graphical utility will replace the command line, look again because someone will find a way to automate it with a batch file or script.

Appendix B

Alphabetical Command List

This appendix provides you with an alphabetical listing of all of the commands and utilities found in the book. You can use Table B.1 as a quick reference guide to make it easier to locate a particular command or utility. Given that the book provides you with details on using 225 different commands and utilities, locating a particular entry can prove difficult, which is why I included this appendix. If you can't find the command or utility you want, try the topical listing found in Appendix C. Please contact me at JMueller@mwt.net if you think you've found a command or utility that appears in the default Server Core (not Windows 2008 Server Full version please) installation that doesn't appear in this book. I'll be more than happy to document it in the next edition of the book.

TABLE B.1:   Alphabetical Reference to Commands and Utilities

COMMAND OR UTILITY NAME	CHAPTER	SECTION
ANSI.SYS	5	Using ANSI.SYS to Control the Environment
Append	9	Opening Remote Directories with the Append Utility
ARP	11	Managing the Address Resolution Protocol with the ARP Utility
Assoc	14	Determining and Creating File Associations with the *Assoc* Command
AT	8	Working with the AT Utility
Attrib	15	Changing File and Directory Attributes with the Attrib Utility
AuditPol	20	Auditing User Access with the AuditPol Utility
AutoChk	15	Understanding How AutoChk Works with ChckNTFS
BCDEdit	16	Managing the Boot Configuration with the BCDEdit Command
BlastCln	21	Removing Viruses with the BlastCln Utility
Call	5	Using the *Call* Command
CD	9	Determining the Current Directory and Changing Directories with the *CD* and *ChDir* Commands

TABLE B.1:   Alphabetical Reference to Commands and Utilities *(CONTINUED)*

COMMAND OR UTILITY NAME	CHAPTER	SECTION
Change	6	Changing Logons, Ports, and Users with the Change Utility
CHCP	5	Set the Code Page Number with the CHCP Utility
ChDir	9	Determining the Current Directory and Changing Directories with the CD and *ChDir* Commands
ChgLogon	6	Enabling or Disabling Session Logons with the ChgLogon Utility
ChgPort	6	Listing COM Port Mappings Using the ChgPort Utility
ChgUsr	6	Modifying the Install Mode with the ChgUsr Utility
ChkDsk	15	Determining File and Directory Status with the ChkDsk Utility
ChkNTFS	15	Performing Boot Time Disk Checks with the ChkNTFS Utility
Choice	5	Using the *Choice* Command
Cipher	15	Encrypting Data with the Cipher Utility
Clip	5	Redirecting Command Line Output to the Clipboard with the Clip Utility
CLS	5	Clearing the Display with the *CLS* Command
CMD	5	Using the CMD Switches
CmdKey	5	Managing Usernames and Passwords with CmdKey
CMStP	20	Configuring Profiles with the CMStP Utility
Color	5	Changing Screen Colors with the *Color* Command
Comp	14	Comparing Two Files with the Comp Utility
Compact	15	Compressing Data with the Compact Utility
COMRepl	3	Replicating COM+ Applications with the COMRepl Utility
Convert	9	Converting FAT Partitions to NTFS with the Convert Utility
Copy	14	Copying Files with the *Copy* Command
CScript	6	Running Scripts with the CScript and WScript Utilities
Date	5	Working with the System Date Using the *Date* Command

TABLE B.1:   Alphabetical Reference to Commands and Utilities *(CONTINUED)*

COMMAND OR UTILITY NAME	CHAPTER	SECTION
Debug	5	Examining, Modifying, and Debugging Files with the Debug Utility
Defrag	9	Improving Disk Access Performance with the Defrag Utility
Del	14	Removing Files with the *Del* and *Erase* Commands
Diantz	14	Compressing Files with the Diantz and MakeCab Utilities
Dir	15	Finding Files and Directories with the *Dir* Command
DiskComp	5	Comparing the Contents of Disks with the DiskComp Utility
DiskCopy	5	Copying One Disk to Another with the DiskCopy Utility
DiskPart	9	Managing Partitions with the *DiskPart* Command
DiskPerf	9	Managing Disk Performance with the DiskPerf Utility
DiskRAID	9	Managing RAID Setups Using the DiskRAID Utility
DosKey	5	Tracking Command Line Actions with the DosKey Utility
DosX	5	Adding DPMI Support Using the DosX Utility
DriverQuery	13	Obtaining Driver Information with the *DriverQuery* Command
DSAdd	19	Creating New Objects Using the DSAdd Utility
DSGet	19	Listing Objects with the DSGet Utility
DSMod	19	Editing Existing Objects Using the DSMod Utility
DSMove	19	Moving Existing Objects Using the DSMove Utility
DSQuery	19	Managing Active Directory with the DSQuery Utility
DSRm	19	Deleting Objects Using the DSRm Utility
Echo	5	Using the *Echo* Command
Edit	5	Modifying Data Files with the Edit Utility
Edlin	14	Modifying Files with the Edlin Utility
EMM.SYS	5	Controlling the Expanded Memory EMM Entry
Erase	14	Removing Files with the *Del* and *Erase* Commands
ESEnTUtl	14	Repairing System Databases with the ESEnTUtl Utility

TABLE B.1:   Alphabetical Reference to Commands and Utilities *(CONTINUED)*

COMMAND OR UTILITY NAME	CHAPTER	SECTION
EventCreate	18	Managing System Events with the EventCreate Utility
EventTriggers	18	Triggering System Events with the EventTriggers Utility
Exe2Bin	5	Converting Executables with the Exe2Bin Utility
Exit	5	Using the *Exit* Command
Expand	14	Decompressing Files with the Expand Utility
FC	14	Performing Advanced File Comparison with the FC Utility
Find	15	Locating Information in Files with the Find and FindStr Utilities
FindStr	15	Locating Information in Files with the Find and FindStr Utilities
Finger	11	Discovering User Information with the Finger Utility
FltMC	9	Managing the File System with the FltMC Utility
For	5	Using the *For* Command
ForFiles	5	Using the ForFiles Utility
Format	5	Formatting a Disk with the Format Utility
FSUtil	9	Monitoring the File System with the *FSUtil* Command
FTP	17	Managing FTP Servers with the FTP Utility
FType	14	Determining and Creating File Types with the *FType* Command
GetMAC	10	Getting the Media Access Control Information with the GetMAC Utility
Goto	5	Using the *Goto* Command
GPResult	20	Obtaining Group Policy Results with the *GPResult* Command
GPUpdate	20	Managing Group Policies with the GPUpdate Utility
GrafTabl	5	Enable Graphics Character Support with the GrafTabl Utility
Graphics	5	Printing Command Line Graphics with the Graphics Utility
Help	5	Obtaining Command Line Help with the Help Utility
HIMEM.SYS	5	Controlling Extended Memory with *HIMEM.SYS*
Hostname	11	Getting the Local Hostname with the Hostname Utility

TABLE B.1: Alphabetical Reference to Commands and Utilities *(CONTINUED)*

COMMAND OR UTILITY NAME	CHAPTER	SECTION
ICACLS	15	Changing File and Directory Access with the *ICACLS* Command
If	5	Using the *If* Command
IPConfig	11	Managing the Internet Protocol with the IPConfig Utility
iSCSICli	9	Working with iSCSI Using the iSCSICli Utility
Label	9	Managing Volume Labels with the Label Utility
LH	5	Saving Memory Using the *LH* Command
LoadFix	5	Load Older DOS Applications with the LoadFix Utility
LodCtr	18	Adding Performance Counters with the LodCtr Utility
LogMan	18	Managing Performance Logs and Alerts with the LogMan Utility
Logoff	5	Terminating a Session Using the Logoff Utility
LPQ	12	Troubleshooting the Line Printer Daemon with the LPQ Utility
LPR	12	Sending a Print Job to a Printer with the LPR Utility
MakeCab	14	Compressing Files with the Diantz and MakeCab Utilities
MD	9	Creating Directories with the *MD* and *MkDir* Commands
Mem	12	Determining Memory Status with the Mem Utility
MkDir	9	Creating Directories with the *MD* and *MkDir* Commands
MKLink	9	Creating Symbolic Links and Hard Links with the *MKLink* Command
Mode	5	Configuring System Devices with the Mode Utility
MOFComp	3	Administering Managed Object Format Files with the MOFComp Utility
More	14	Using the More Utility
MountVol	9	Mounting a Volume with the MountVol Utility
Move	14	Moving Files and Renaming Files and Directories with the *Move* Command
MRInfo	11	Obtaining Multicast Router Information with the MRInfo Utility
MRT	21	Detect and Remove Malicious Software with the MRT Utility
MSCDexNT	5	Adding CD Support with MSCDexNT Utility

TABLE B.1:   Alphabetical Reference to Commands and Utilities *(CONTINUED)*

COMMAND OR UTILITY NAME	CHAPTER	SECTION
MSIExec	13	Installing Applications with the MSIExec Utility
MSInfo32	12	Obtaining General System Information with the MSInfo32 Utility
MSTSC	17	Creating Remote Connections with the MSTSC Utility
NBTStat	11	Getting NetBIOS over TCP/IP Status with the NBTStat Utility
Net	10	Managing the Network with the Net Utility
NetCfg	16	Accessing the WinPE Network Installer with the NetCfg Utility
NetDiag	11	Performing Network Diagnostics with the NetDiag Utility
NetSH	6	Scripting Networking Solutions with the NetSH Utility
NetStat	11	Getting Network Statistics with the NetStat Utility
Notepad	12	Performing a Formatted Printout with Notepad
NSLookup	11	Tracking Servers with the NSLookup Utility
NTDSUtil	19	Managing the Active Directory Database with the NTDSUtil Utility
NW16	5	Adding NetWare Support with the NW16 and VWIPXSPX Utilities
OCList	13	Verifying Application and Role Status Using the OCList Utility
OCSetup	13	Adding and Removing Applications with the OCSetup Utility
ODBCConf	14	Configuring the ODBC Environment with the ODBCConf Utility
OpenFiles	15	Detecting Shared Open Files with the *OpenFiles* Command
Path	9	Setting and Viewing Application Paths with the *Path* Command
PathPing	11	Tracing Transmission Paths with the PathPing Utility
Pause	5	Using the *Pause* Command
PerfMon	18	Viewing the Results of Changes with the PerfMon Utility
PING	11	Checking Connections with the PING Utility
PkgMgr	13	Accessing the Windows Package Manager with the PkgMgr Utility
PnPUnattend	12	Performing Unattended Driver Installation with the PnPUnattend Utility
PnPUtil	12	Managing PnP Setups Using the PnPUtil Utility

TABLE B.1:   Alphabetical Reference to Commands and Utilities *(CONTINUED)*

COMMAND OR UTILITY NAME	CHAPTER	SECTION
PopD	9	Storing and Retrieving Directories with the *PushD* and *PopD* Commands
PowerCfg	12	Managing Power Settings with the PowerCfg Utility
Print	12	Printing Data Files with the Print Utility
Prompt	5	Using the *Prompt* Command
PushD	9	Storing and Retrieving Directories with the *PushD* and *PopD* Commands
QAppSrv	17	Locating Terminal Servers with the QAppSrv Utility
QProcess	17	Obtaining Processes with the QProcess Utility
Query	20	Obtaining Session Status Information with the Query Utility
QUser	20	Obtaining User Login Information with the QUser Utility
QWinSta	17	Getting Session Information with the QWinSta Utility
RASDial	17	Dialing Out with the RASDial Utility
RASPhone	17	Accessing Dial-Up Networking with the RASPhone Utility
RD	9	Removing a Directory with the *RD* and *RmDir* Commands
Recover	14	Recovering Lost Files with the Recover Utility
ReDir	5	Installing the Network Redirector Using the ReDir Utility
RegEdit	4	Starting and Configuring the Registry Editor
RegIni	4	Scripting Registry Entries with the RegIni Utility
RegSvr32	13	Adding and Removing Servers with the RegSvr32 Utility
RegTLib	3	Managing Type Libraries with the RegTLib Utility
ReLog	18	Reconfiguring Performance Logs with the ReLog Utility
Rem	5	Using the *Rem* Command
Ren	14	Renaming a File with the *Ren* and *Rename* Commands
Rename	14	Renaming a File with the *Ren* and *Rename* Commands
Replace	14	Replacing Existing Files with the Replace Utility
Reset	17	Terminating a Session with the Reset Utility

TABLE B.1:   Alphabetical Reference to Commands and Utilities *(CONTINUED)*

COMMAND OR UTILITY NAME	CHAPTER	SECTION
RmDir	9	Removing a Directory with the *RD* and *RmDir* Commands
RoboCopy	14	Performing Robust File Transfers with the *RoboCopy* Command
Route	11	Manipulating the Network Routing Tables with the Route Utility
RPCPing	11	Checking Connections Using RPC with the RPCPing Utility
RSM	9	Managing Removable Storage with the RSM Utility
RunAs	6	Impersonating a User with the RunAs Utility
RWinSta	17	Resetting the Hardware and Software with the RWinSta Utility
SC	3	Controlling Services with the *SC* Command
SCHTasks	8	Managing Tasks with the *SCHTasks* Command
SCRegEdit	4	Working with the SCRegEdit Script
SDBInst	13	Managing Compatibility Databases with SDBInst
SecEdit	21	Configuring Local Security Policies with the SecEdit Utility
ServerWEROptin	13	Configuring Windows Error Reporting with ServerWEROptin
Set	5	Managing Environment Variables with the *Set* Command
SetVer	5	Defining Application Compatibility with the SetVer Utility
SetX	5	Managing Environment Variables with the SetX Utility
SFC	21	Verifying System Files with the SFC Utility
Shadow	17	Monitoring Other Sessions with the Shadow Utility
Shift	5	Using the *Shift* Command
ShutDown	3	Shutting Down the System with the *ShutDown* Command
SLMGR	3	Managing Activation with SLMGR
Sort	14	Sorting File Content with the Sort Utility
SRDiag	3	Saving and Restoring System Restore Data with the SRDiag Utility
Start	5	Executing Applications Using the *Start* Command
Subst	9	Associating a Folder to a Drive with the Subst Utility

TABLE B.1: Alphabetical Reference to Commands and Utilities *(CONTINUED)*

Command or Utility Name	Chapter	Section
SxsTrace	3	Tracing WinSxs Behavior with the SxsTrace Utility
SystemInfo	16	Getting System Configuration Information with the SystemInfo Utility
TakeOwn	14	Taking Ownership of Files with the TakeOwn Utility
TaskKill	21	Terminating Tasks with the *TaskKill* Command
TaskList	21	Listing Applications and Services with the *TaskList* Command
TCMSetup	17	Setting Up a Telephony Client with the TCMSetup Utility
Telnet	17	Executing Commands Remotely with the Telnet Utility
TFTP	11	Managing Files with the TFTP Utility
Time	5	Working with the System Time Using the *Time* Command
TimeOut	5	Using the TimeOut Utility
Title	5	Changing the Command Window Title with the *Title* Command
TLNTAdmn	17	Administrating Telnet with the TLNTAdmn Utility
TraceRpt	21	Converting Event Trace Logs with the TraceRpt Utility
TraceRt	11	Tracking the Network Path with the TraceRt Utility
Tree	9	Displaying a Directory Structure with the Tree Utility
TSCon	17	Attaching a User Session with the TSCon Utility
TSDiscon	17	Disconnecting an Active Session with the TSDiscon Utility
TSKill	17	Ending Processes with the TSKill Utility
TSShutDn	17	Shutting the Terminal Server Down with the TSShutDn Utility
Type	14	Outputting Data Files with the *Type* Command
TypePerf	18	Tracking Performance with the TypePerf Utility
UnlodCtr	18	Removing Performance Counters with the UnlodCtr Utility
Ver	5	Determining the Operating System Version with the *Ver* Command
Verifier	21	Verifying Drivers with the Verifier Utility
Verify	14	Validating File Operations with the *Verify* Command

TABLE B.1: Alphabetical Reference to Commands and Utilities *(CONTINUED)*

COMMAND OR UTILITY NAME	CHAPTER	SECTION
Vol	5	Getting Volume Information with the *Vol* Command
VSSAdmin	9	Managing the Volume Shadow Service with the VSSAdmin Utility
VWIPXSPX	5	Adding NetWare Support with the NW16 and VWIPXSPX Utilities
W32Tm	12	Managing the System Time with the W32Tm Utility
WaitFor	5	Using the WaitFor Utility
WBAdmin	14	Performing Backups with the WBAdmin Utility
WEvtUtil	18	Managing Event Information with the WEvtUtil Utility
Where	15	Finding Files and Directories with the Where Utility
WhoAmI	20	Discovering User Identity with the WhoAmI Utility
WinMgmt	3	Interacting with the WBEM Server with the WinMgmt Utility
WinRM	17	Performing Remote Windows Management with the WinRM Utility
WinRS	17	Accessing a System with the WinRS Utility
WMIC	3	Configuring Server Core Using the WMIC Command
WScript	6	Running Scripts with the CScript and WScript Utilities
XCopy	14	Performing Bulk File Transfers with the XCopy Utility

Appendix C

Topical Command List

This appendix provides you with a topical (categorical) listing of all of the commands and utilities found in the book. You can use Tables C.1 through C.14 to locate commands and utilities by topic (category). If you can't find the command or utility you want, try the alphabetical listing found in Appendix B. Please contact me at JMueller@mwt.net if you think you've found a command or utility that appears in the default Server Core (not Windows 2008 Server Full version please) installation that doesn't appear in this book. I'll be more than happy to document it in the next edition of the book.

TABLE C.1: Active Directory Related Commands and Utilities

COMMAND OR UTILITY NAME	CHAPTER	SECTION
DSAdd	19	Creating New Objects Using the DSAdd Utility
DSGet	19	Listing Objects with the DSGet Utility
DSMod	19	Editing Existing Objects Using the DSMod Utility
DSMove	19	Moving Existing Objects Using the DSMove Utility
DSQuery	19	Managing Active Directory with the DSQuery Utility
DSRm	19	Deleting Objects Using the DSRm Utility
NTDSUtil	19	Managing the Active Directory Database with the NTDSUtil Utility

TABLE C.2: Application Management Related Commands and Utilities

COMMAND OR UTILITY NAME	CHAPTER	SECTION
COMRepl	3	Replicating COM+ Applications with the COMRepl Utility
Exe2Bin	5	Converting Executables with the Exe2Bin Utility
LoadFix	5	Load Older DOS Applications with the LoadFix Utility

TABLE C.2:   Application Management Related Commands and Utilities *(CONTINUED)*

COMMAND OR UTILITY NAME	CHAPTER	SECTION
OCSetup	13	Adding and Removing Applications with the OCSetup Utility
ODBCConf	14	Configuring the ODBC Environment with the ODBCConf Utility
PkgMgr	13	Accessing the Windows Package Manager with the PkgMgr Utility
RegEdit	4	Starting and Configuring the Registry Editor
RegTLib	3	Managing Type Libraries with the RegTLib Utility
SetVer	5	Defining Application Compatibility with the SetVer Utility
Start	5	Executing Applications Using the *Start* Command

TABLE C.3:   Batch File and Script Related Commands and Utilities

COMMAND OR UTILITY NAME	CHAPTER	SECTION
AT	8	Working with the AT Utility
Call	5	Using the *Call* Command
Choice	5	Using the *Choice* Command
Clip	5	Redirecting Command Line Output to the Clipboard with the Clip Utility
CLS	5	Clearing the Display with the *CLS* Command
CmdKey	5	Managing Usernames and Passwords with CmdKey
Color	5	Changing Screen Colors with the *Color* Command
CScript	6	Running Scripts with the CScript and WScript Utilities
Date	5	Working with the System Date Using the *Date* Command
DosX	5	Adding DPMI Support Using the DosX Utility
Echo	5	Using the *Echo* Command
EventCreate	18	Managing System Events with the EventCreate Utility
EventTriggers	18	Triggering System Events with the EventTriggers Utility

TABLE C.3: Batch File and Script Related Commands and Utilities *(CONTINUED)*

COMMAND OR UTILITY NAME	CHAPTER	SECTION
Exit	5	Using the *Exit* Command
For	5	Using the *For* Command
ForFiles	5	Using the ForFiles Utility
Goto	5	Using the *Goto* Command
GrafTabl	5	Enable Graphics Character Support with the GrafTabl Utility
Graphics	5	Printing Command Line Graphics with the Graphics Utility
If	5	Using the *If* Command
LH	5	Saving Memory Using the *LH* Command
Logoff	5	Terminating a Session Using the Logoff Utility
Mode	5	Configuring System Devices with the Mode Utility
More	14	Using the More Utility
MSCDexNT	5	Adding CD Support with MSCDexNT Utility
MSInfo32	12	Obtaining General System Information with the MSInfo32 Utility
Net	10	Managing the Network with the Net Utility
NetSH	6	Scripting Networking Solutions with the NetSH Utility
Path	9	Setting and Viewing Application Paths with the *Path* Command
Pause	5	Using the *Pause* Command
PopD	9	Storing and Retrieving Directories with the *PushD* and *PopD* Commands
Prompt	5	Using the *Prompt* Command
PushD	9	Storing and Retrieving Directories with the *PushD* and *PopD* Commands
Rem	5	Using the *Rem* Command
RunAs	6	Impersonating a User with the RunAs Utility
SCHTasks	8	Managing Tasks with the *SCHTasks* Command
SCRegEdit	4	Working with the SCRegEdit Script
Set	5	Managing Environment Variables with the *Set* Command

TABLE C.3: Batch File and Script Related Commands and Utilities *(CONTINUED)*

COMMAND OR UTILITY NAME	CHAPTER	SECTION
SetX	5	Managing Environment Variables with the SetX Utility
Shift	5	Using the *Shift* Command
Start	5	Executing Applications Using the *Start* Command
Time	5	Working with the System Time Using the *Time* Command
TimeOut	5	Using the TimeOut Utility
Title	5	Changing the Command Window Title with the *Title* Command
Ver	5	Determining the Operating System Version with the *Ver* Command
Vol	5	Getting Volume Information with the *Vol* Command
WaitFor	5	Using the WaitFor Utility
WhoAmI	20	Discovering User Identity with the WhoAmI Utility
WScript	6	Running Scripts with the CScript and WScript Utilities

TABLE C.4: Command Line Related Commands and Utilities

COMMAND OR UTILITY NAME	CHAPTER	SECTION
ANSI.SYS	5	Using ANSI.SYS to Control the Environment
CHCP	5	Set the Code Page Number with the CHCP Utility
Clip	5	Redirecting Command Line Output to the Clipboard with the Clip Utility
CLS	5	Clearing the Display with the *CLS* Command
CMD	5	Using the CMD Switches
Color	5	Changing Screen Colors with the *Color* Command
Date	5	Working with the System Date Using the *Date* Command
DosKey	5	Tracking Command Line Actions with the DosKey Utility
EMM.SYS	5	Controlling the Expanded Memory EMM Entry
EventCreate	18	Managing System Events with the EventCreate Utility

TABLE C.4: Command Line Related Commands and Utilities *(CONTINUED)*

COMMAND OR UTILITY NAME	CHAPTER	SECTION
EventTriggers	18	Triggering System Events with the EventTriggers Utility
Help	5	Obtaining Command Line Help with the Help Utility
HIMEM.SYS	5	Controlling Extended Memory with *HIMEM.SYS*
Mode	5	Configuring System Devices with the Mode Utility
More	14	Using the More Utility
MSInfo32	12	Obtaining General System Information with the MSInfo32 Utility
Notepad	12	Performing a Formatted Printout with Notepad
Path	9	Setting and Viewing Application Paths with the *Path* Command
PopD	9	Storing and Retrieving Directories with the *PushD* and *PopD* Commands
PushD	9	Storing and Retrieving Directories with the *PushD* and *PopD* Commands
RunAs	6	Impersonating a User with the RunAs Utility
Set	5	Managing Environment Variables with the *Set* Command
SetX	5	Managing Environment Variables with the SetX Utility
Time	5	Working with the System Time Using the *Time* Command
Title	5	Changing the Command Window Title with the *Title* Command
TraceRpt	21	Converting Event Trace Logs with the TraceRpt Utility
Ver	5	Determining the Operating System Version with the *Ver* Command
Vol	5	Getting Volume Information with the *Vol* Command

TABLE C.5: Diagnostics Related Commands and Utilities

COMMAND OR UTILITY NAME	CHAPTER	SECTION
Debug	5	Examining, Modifying, and Debugging Files with the Debug Utility
EventCreate	18	Managing System Events with the EventCreate Utility
EventTriggers	18	Triggering System Events with the EventTriggers Utility

TABLE C.5: Diagnostics Related Commands and Utilities *(CONTINUED)*

COMMAND OR UTILITY NAME	CHAPTER	SECTION
NetDiag	11	Performing Network Diagnostics with the NetDiag Utility
PathPing	11	Tracing Transmission Paths with the PathPing Utility
PING	11	Checking Connections with the PING Utility
RPCPing	11	Checking Connections using RPC with the RPCPing Utility
RWinSta	17	Resetting the Hardware and Software with the RWinSta Utility
ServerWEROptin	13	Configuring Windows Error Reporting with ServerWEROptin
SFC	21	Verifying System Files with the SFC Utility
SRDiag	3	Saving and Restoring System Restore Data with the SRDiag Utility
SystemInfo	16	Getting System Configuration Information with the SystemInfo Utility
TaskKill	21	Terminating Tasks with the *TaskKill* Command
TaskList	21	Listing Applications and Services with the *TaskList* Command
Telnet	17	Executing Commands Remotely with the Telnet Utility
TraceRpt	21	Converting Event Trace Logs with the TraceRpt Utility
WBAdmin	14	Performing Backups with the WBAdmin Utility
WEvtUtil	18	Managing Event Information with the WEvtUtil Utility
WinRM	17	Performing Remote Windows Management with the WinRM Utility

TABLE C.6: Disk Management Related Commands and Utilities

COMMAND OR UTILITY NAME	CHAPTER	SECTION
Append	9	Opening Remote Directories with the Append Utility
AutoChk	15	Understanding How AutoChk Works with ChckNTFS
CD	9	Determining the Current Directory and Changing Directories with the *CD* and *ChDir* Commands
ChDir	9	Determining the Current Directory and Changing Directories with the *CD* and *ChDir* Commands
ChkDsk	15	Determining File and Directory Status with the ChkDsk Utility

TABLE C.6:   Disk Management Related Commands and Utilities *(CONTINUED)*

COMMAND OR UTILITY NAME	CHAPTER	SECTION
ChkNTFS	15	Performing Boot Time Disk Checks with the ChkNTFS Utility
Convert	9	Converting FAT Partitions to NTFS with the Convert Utility
Defrag	9	Improving Disk Access Performance with the Defrag Utility
DiskPart	9	Managing Partitions with the *DiskPart* Command
DiskPerf	9	Managing Disk Performance with the DiskPerf Utility
DiskRAID	9	Managing RAID Setups Using the DiskRAID Utility
Format	5	Formatting a Disk with the Format Utility
iSCSICli	9	Working with iSCSI Using the iSCSICli Utility
Label	9	Managing Volume Labels with the Label Utility
MD	9	Creating Directories with the *MD* and *MkDir* Commands
MkDir	9	Creating Directories with the *MD* and *MkDir* Commands
MKLink	9	Creating Symbolic Links and Hard Links with the *MKLink* Command
MountVol	9	Mounting a Volume with the MountVol Utility
Move	14	Moving Files and Renaming Files and Directories with the *Move* Command
Path	9	Setting and Viewing Application Paths with the *Path* Command
RD	9	Removing a Directory with the *RD* and *RmDir* Commands
Replace	14	Replacing Existing Files with the Replace Utility
RmDir	9	Removing a Directory with the *RD* and *RmDir* Commands
RSM	9	Managing Removable Storage with the RSM Utility
Subst	9	Associating a Folder to a Drive with the Subst Utility
TakeOwn	14	Taking Ownership of Files with the TakeOwn Utility
Tree	9	Displaying a Directory Structure with the Tree Utility
VSSAdmin	9	Managing the Volume Shadow Service with the VSSAdmin Utility
WBAdmin	14	Performing Backups with the WBAdmin Utility
Where	15	Finding Files and Directories with the Where Utility

TABLE C.7:   File Management Related Commands and Utilities

COMMAND OR UTILITY NAME	CHAPTER	SECTION
Assoc	14	Determining and Creating File Associations with the *Assoc* Command
Attrib	15	Changing File and Directory Attributes with the Attrib Utility
Cipher	15	Encrypting Data with the Cipher Utility
Comp	14	Comparing Two Files with the Comp Utility
Compact	15	Compressing Data with the Compact Utility
Copy	14	Copying Files with the *Copy* Command
Del	14	Removing Files with the *Del* and *Erase* Commands
Diantz	14	Compressing Files with the Diantz and MakeCab Utilities
Dir	15	Finding Files and Directories with the *Dir* Command
DiskComp	5	Comparing the Contents of Disks with the DiskComp Utility
DiskCopy	5	Copying One Disk to Another with the DiskCopy Utility
Edit	5	Modifying Data Files with the Edit Utility
Edlin	14	Modifying Files with the Edlin Utility
Erase	14	Removing Files with the *Del* and *Erase* Commands
Expand	14	Decompressing Files with the Expand Utility
FC	14	Performing Advanced File Comparison with the FC Utility
Find	15	Locating Information in Files with the Find and FindStr Utilities
FindStr	15	Locating Information in Files with the Find and FindStr Utilities
FltMC	9	Managing the File System with the FltMC Utility
FSUtil	9	Monitoring the File System with the *FSUtil* Command
FType	14	Determining and Creating File Types with the *FType* Command
ICACLS	15	Changing File and Directory Access with the *ICACLS* Command
MakeCab	14	Compressing Files with the Diantz and MakeCab Utilities
Move	14	Moving Files and Renaming Files and Directories with the *Move* Command
Notepad	12	Performing a Formatted Printout with Notepad

TABLE C.7:   File Management Related Commands and Utilities *(CONTINUED)*

COMMAND OR UTILITY NAME	CHAPTER	SECTION
OpenFiles	15	Detecting Shared Open Files with the *OpenFiles* Command
Print	12	Printing Data Files with the Print Utility
Recover	14	Recovering Lost Files with the Recover Utility
Ren	14	Renaming a File with the *Ren* and *Rename* Commands
Rename	14	Renaming a File with the *Ren* and *Rename* Commands
Replace	14	Replacing Existing Files with the Replace Utility
RoboCopy	14	Performing Robust File Transfers with the *RoboCopy* Command
SFC	21	Verifying System Files with the SFC Utility
Sort	14	Sorting File Content with the Sort Utility
TFTP	11	Managing Files with the TFTP Utility
Type	14	Outputting Data Files with the *Type* Command
Verify	14	Validating File Operations with the *Verify* Command
Where	15	Finding Files and Directories with the Where Utility
XCopy	14	Performing Bulk File Transfers with the XCopy Utility

TABLE C.8:   Hardware Configuration Related Commands and Utilities

COMMAND OR UTILITY NAME	CHAPTER	SECTION
Change	6	Changing Logons, Ports, and Users with the Change Utility
ChgPort	6	Listing COM Port Mappings Using the ChgPort Utility
DriverQuery	13	Obtaining Driver Information with the *DriverQuery* Command
LPQ	12	Troubleshooting the Line Printer Daemon with the LPQ Utility
LPR	12	Sending a Print Job to a Printer with the LPR Utility
MRInfo	11	Obtaining Multicast Router Information with the MRInfo Utility
PnPUnattend	12	Performing Unattended Driver Installation with the PnPUnattend Utility

TABLE C.8:   Hardware Configuration Related Commands and Utilities *(CONTINUED)*

COMMAND OR UTILITY NAME	CHAPTER	SECTION
PnPUtil	12	Managing PnP Setups using the PnPUtil Utility
PowerCfg	12	Managing Power Settings with the PowerCfg Utility
RWinSta	17	Resetting the Hardware and Software with the RWinSta Utility
Verifier	21	Verifying Drivers with the Verifier Utility

TABLE C.9:   Networking Related Commands and Utilities

COMMAND OR UTILITY NAME	CHAPTER	SECTION
ARP	11	Managing the Address Resolution Protocol with the ARP Utility
Finger	11	Discovering User Information with the Finger Utility
FTP	17	Managing FTP Servers with the FTP Utility
GetMAC	10	Getting the Media Access Control Information with the GetMAC Utility
Hostname	11	Getting the Local Host Name with the Hostname Utility
ICACLS	15	Changing File and Directory Access with the *ICACLS* Command
IPConfig	11	Managing the Internet Protocol with the IPConfig Utility
LPQ	12	Troubleshooting the Line Printer Daemon with the LPQ Utility
LPR	12	Sending a Print Job to a Printer with the LPR Utility
MRInfo	11	Obtaining Multicast Router Information with the MRInfo Utility
MSTSC	17	Creating Remote Connections with the MSTSC Utility
NBTStat	11	Getting NetBIOS over TCP/IP Status with the NBTStat Utility
Net	10	Managing the Network with the Net Utility
NetCfg	16	Accessing the WinPE Network Installer with the NetCfg Utility
NetDiag	11	Performing Network Diagnostics with the NetDiag Utility
NetSH	6	Scripting Networking Solutions with the NetSH Utility
NetStat	11	Getting Network Statistics with the NetStat Utility

TABLE C.9:   Networking Related Commands and Utilities *(CONTINUED)*

COMMAND OR UTILITY NAME	CHAPTER	SECTION
NSLookup	11	Tracking Servers with the NSLookup Utility
NW16	5	Adding NetWare Support with the NW16 and VWIPXSPX Utilities
PathPing	11	Tracing Transmission Paths with the PathPing Utility
PING	11	Checking Connections with the PING Utility
ReDir	5	Installing the Network Redirector Using the ReDir Utility
Route	11	Manipulating the Network Routing Tables with the Route Utility
RPCPing	11	Checking Connections using RPC with the RPCPing Utility
Telnet	17	Executing Commands Remotely with the Telnet Utility
TraceRt	11	Tracking the Network Path with the TraceRt Utility
VWIPXSPX	5	Adding NetWare Support with the NW16 and VWIPXSPX Utilities

TABLE C.10:   Remote Access Related Commands and Utilities

COMMAND OR UTILITY NAME	CHAPTER	SECTION
QAppSrv	17	Locating Terminal Servers with the QAppSrv Utility
QProcess	17	Obtaining Processes with the QProcess Utility
RASDial	17	Dialing Out with the RASDial Utility
RASPhone	17	Accessing Dial-Up Networking with the RASPhone Utility
Reset	17	Terminating a Session with the Reset Utility
Telnet	17	Executing Commands Remotely with the Telnet Utility
TLNTAdmn	17	Administrating TelNet with the TLNTAdmn Utility
TSCon	17	Attaching a User Session with the TSCon Utility
TSDiscon	17	Disconnecting an Active Session with the TSDiscon Utility
TSKill	17	Ending Processes with the TSKill Utility
TSShutDn	17	Shutting the Terminal Server Down with the TSShutDn Utility

TABLE C.10:   Remote Access Related Commands and Utilities *(CONTINUED)*

COMMAND OR UTILITY NAME	CHAPTER	SECTION
WinRM	17	Performing Remote Windows Management with the WinRM Utility
WinRS	17	Accessing a System with the WinRS Utility

TABLE C.11:   Server Configuration Related Commands and Utilities

COMMAND OR UTILITY NAME	CHAPTER	SECTION
BCDEdit	16	Managing the Boot Configuration with the *BCDEdit* Command
COMRepl	3	Replicating COM+ Applications with the COMRepl Utility
Convert	9	Converting FAT Partitions to NTFS with the Convert Utility
ESEnTUtl	14	Repairing System Databases with the ESEnTUtl Utility
MOFComp	3	Administering Managed Object Format Files with the MOFComp Utility
MSIExec	13	Installing Applications with the MSIExec Utility
Net	10	Managing the Network with the Net Utility
NetSH	6	Scripting Networking Solutions with the NetSH Utility
OCList	13	Verifying Application and Role Status using the OCList Utility
OCSetup	13	Adding and Removing Applications with the OCSetup Utility
PkgMgr	13	Accessing the Windows Package Manager with the PkgMgr Utility
RegEdit	4	Starting and Configuring the Registry Editor
RegIni	4	Scripting Registry Entries with the RegIni Utility
RegSvr32	13	Adding and Removing Servers with the RegSvr32 Utility
RegTLib	3	Managing Type Libraries with the RegTLib Utility
SC	3	Controlling Services with the *SC* Command
SCRegEdit	4	Working with the SCRegEdit Script
SDBInst	13	Managing Compatibility Databases with SDBInst
ShutDown	3	Shutting Down the System with the *ShutDown* Command

TABLE C.11:   Server Configuration Related Commands and Utilities *(CONTINUED)*

COMMAND OR UTILITY NAME	CHAPTER	SECTION
SLMGR	3	Managing Activation with SLMGR
SRDiag	3	Saving and Restoring System Restore Data with the SRDiag Utility
SxsTrace	3	Tracing WinSxs Behavior with the SxsTrace Utility
TCMSetup	17	Setting Up a Telephony Client with the TCMSetup Utility
TLNTAdmn	17	Administrating TelNet with the TLNTAdmn Utility
W32Tm	12	Managing the System Time with the W32Tm Utility
WinMgmt	3	Interacting with the WBEM Server with the WinMgmt Utility
WMIC	3	Configuring Server Core Using the WMIC Command

TABLE C.12:   Session Management Related Commands and Utilities

COMMAND OR UTILITY NAME	CHAPTER	SECTION
ChgLogon	6	Enabling or Disabling Session Logons with the ChgLogon Utility
Logoff	5	Terminating a Session using the Logoff Utility
Query	20	Obtaining Session Status Information with the Query Utility
QUser	20	Obtaining User Login Information with the QUser Utility
QWinSta	17	Getting Session Information with the QWinSta Utility
Reset	17	Terminating a Session with the Reset Utility
Shadow	17	Monitoring Other Sessions with the Shadow Utility

TABLE C.13:   System Monitoring Related Commands and Utilities

COMMAND OR UTILITY NAME	CHAPTER	SECTION
AuditPol	20	Auditing User Access with the AuditPol Utility
BlastCln	21	Removing Viruses with the BlastCln Utility

TABLE C.13: System Monitoring Related Commands and Utilities *(CONTINUED)*

COMMAND OR UTILITY NAME	CHAPTER	SECTION
EventCreate	18	Managing System Events with the EventCreate Utility
EventTriggers	18	Triggering System Events with the EventTriggers Utility
FltMC	9	Managing the File System with the FltMC Utility
FSUtil	9	Monitoring the File System with the *FSUtil* Command
LodCtr	18	Adding Performance Counters with the LodCtr Utility
LogMan	18	Managing Performance Logs and Alerts with the LogMan Utility
Mem	12	Determining Memory Status with the Mem Utility
MRT	21	Detect and Remove Malicious Software with the MRT Utility
MSInfo32	12	Obtaining General System Information with the MSInfo32 Utility
NetStat	11	Getting Network Statistics with the NetStat Utility
OCList	13	Verifying Application and Role Status using the OCList Utility
OpenFiles	15	Detecting Shared Open Files with the *OpenFiles* Command
PerfMon	18	Viewing the Results of Changes with the PerfMon Utility
QProcess	17	Obtaining Processes with the QProcess Utility
ReLog	18	Reconfiguring Performance Logs with the ReLog Utility
SystemInfo	16	Getting System Configuration Information with the SystemInfo Utility
TaskList	21	Listing Applications and Services with the *TaskList* Command
TypePerf	18	Tracking Performance with the TypePerf Utility
UnlodCtr	18	Removing Performance Counters with the UnlodCtr Utility
WhoAmI	20	Discovering User Identity with the WhoAmI Utility

TABLE C.14:   User Management Related Commands and Utilities

COMMAND OR UTILITY NAME	CHAPTER	SECTION
AuditPol	20	Auditing User Access with the AuditPol Utility
Change	6	Changing Logons, Ports, and Users with the Change Utility
ChgLogon	6	Enabling or Disabling Session Logons with the ChgLogon Utility
ChgUsr	6	Modifying the Install Mode with the ChgUsr Utility
CmdKey	5	Managing Usernames and Passwords with CmdKey
CMStP	20	Configuring Profiles with the CMStP Utility
GPResult	20	Obtaining Group Policy Results with the *GPResult* Command
GPUpdate	20	Managing Group Policies with the GPUpdate Utility
ICACLS	15	Changing File and Directory Access with the *ICACLS* Command
Net	10	Managing the Network with the Net Utility
QProcess	17	Obtaining Processes with the QProcess Utility
QUser	20	Obtaining User Login Information with the QUser Utility
SecEdit	21	Configuring Local Security Policies with the SecEdit Utility
Shadow	17	Monitoring Other Sessions with the Shadow Utility
WhoAmI	20	Discovering User Identity with the WhoAmI Utility

Appendix D

Listing of Best Practices

Most administrators are used to following best practices when working with the Windows GUI. There are principles you follow to ensure you get the right results, at least most of the time. Likewise, when you work at the command line, there are best practices you can follow to ensure you get good results, at least most of the time. This appendix tells you about the best practices I've created while working at the command over the last 20 years. These are time-tested techniques you can use to obtain good results. They won't always provide perfect results; only practice on your part will produce the perfect results you seek, but they'll help considerably. I'd love to hear your best practices as well—feel free to contact me at JMueller@mwt.net.

Always Verify the Data

It always pays to verify the data you're going to use with a command or utility. Unlike the GUI environment, the command line environment doesn't ever provide you with a list of acceptable choices. Consequently, you may find that something very small can product very bad results. For example, you may have two employees and one is named Newman, while the other is named Neumann. The difference of two characters can make a huge difference. When working with a GUI, you'd probably see both names and choose the right one or ask someone if you weren't sure. When working at the command line, you may not ever know that both names exist. That's why you always want to verify any data you use.

Get the data in written form whenever possible. Obtaining it in a form that you can cut and paste to the command line is even better. Not only does such a practice save you typing time, but doing so makes it considerably more difficult to make a mistake. Typos are understandably a significant source of problems at the command line. Anything you can do to verify data before you complete a command is a plus. Copying and pasting are essential parts of working at the command line.

TIP   To copy any text in a GUI window, highlight the text and then press Ctrl+C. To paste the text from the clipboard into the command line window, right-click the command line window and choose Paste from the context menu. It's also possible to move information in the other direction. In this case, right-click the command line window and choose Mark from the context menu. Highlight the text you want to copy and then press Enter. To paste the text into any GUI window, place the cursor at the insertion point and press Ctrl+V.

Real Administrators Use Help

This book contains 225 commands and utilities. These are the commands and utilities that you find in a standard Server Core Enterprise Edition setup. Interestingly enough, you'll probably find the vast majority of these commands and utilities in other editions too. Add to these commands and utilities the commands and utilities that come with any applications you install, and it's pretty easy to see that you aren't going to memorize them all.

Unfortunately, some administrators don't want to admit that they lack a photographic memory and attempt to execute commands without looking at the help the command provides. No, this help isn't enough to help you learn how to use the command or utility in most cases, but it's enough to jog the memory of an experienced administrator. All you need to do is type the name of the command followed by the /? command line switch and the command will output help information for you.

Although this top-level help is enough to understand simple commands such as Dir, it's not enough to understand complex utilities such as WMIC. In this case, you have to drill down to the level of help you need. You can start by typing **WMIC /?** and pressing Enter to obtain a list of aliases. Once you decide on something like the CPU alias, type **WMIC CPU /?** and press Enter to see the list of actions you can perform. After you decide on an action, such as GET, type **WMIC CPU GET /?** and press Enter to obtain the information you need about the GET action for the CPU alias. Of course, you can always save yourself a lot of time and simply look up the help for WMIC in this book (see Appendix B for an alphabetical list of commands and utilities).

Test Your Theories on a Test System

Nothing is so unforgiving as the command prompt when it comes to experimentation. You can completely trash your hard drive in a matter of seconds and may not even realize it. It's possible to kill groups, eliminate users, remove applications, destroy data wholesale, and completely ruin your career without a single word of warning from the command line.

This isn't the place to test out something without realizing that things can go horribly wrong very quickly. In fact, the reason that many administrators moved from the command line to the GUI is to avoid such errors, but you don't have that choice when working with Server Core, so you have to work safely at all times. To try anything new, always use a test system that is configured like your real server. You'll appreciate the safety net that such an arrangement provides the first time you have to reformat the test machine drive due to unforeseen complications.

Write absolutely everything down as you test a new process. Don't use a file on the server to store this information—it may not be there in a few moments. If you don't have a secondary machine you can use, then write down your procedure on paper. Verify everything you write down to make sure you wrote it correctly. Execute a command only after you verify that you have written it down correctly and used help to ensure you have formatted the command correctly. If something does go horribly wrong, having a written record can make it possible for someone to help you fix the problem. Even if you can't get help, at least you know not to try that command line syntax again. In some cases, you have to be willing to fail in order to make progress. Of course, the safety net of your test system makes such failure nonfatal (but still aggravating).

Even after you create a complete procedure that works in every way, test it several more times on the test system before you begin using it in a production environment. Otherwise you may find that the procedure isn't as bug free as you anticipated.

Use Batch Files, Scripts, and Written Procedures

Documentation of all sorts will save you time and effort. A single command or utility probably won't do everything you want. Consequently, you need some method of documenting the command or utility sequence that helps you accomplish useful work on your server. Batch files, scripts, and written procedures all provide useful ways to record sequences that you'll use more than once.

Of course, you'll want to make sure that you write these items in a way that makes it easy to figure out what you did the next time you need to perform the task. Add copious comments to batch files and scripts to ensure they are documented fully. Make sure your comments are useful. Place an emphasis on what something does, why you did it that way, and how to work with it. Otherwise, the information you save is useless. Writing things down has a number of additional benefits that you should consider as part of the payback for the work you'll perform.

◆ Any time you write something down, it makes it easier to perform the task again and it also reduces the time required to do it.

◆ You'll perform the task with fewer mistakes.

◆ The documentation also makes it possible for someone working for you to accomplish the task when you're not available—such as when you're home watching the game over the weekend and really don't want to hear about the latest network failure.

◆ You can document precisely what you have done when you do need outside help in fixing a problem.

◆ Approved procedures tend to reduce the risk of making the problem worse.

The one thing to avoid is using someone else's batch file, script, or written procedure without testing it first, especially if the item was written for another system. Yes, the information can be helpful, but your system is different from the one for which the batch file, script, or written procedure was designed. Differences between systems can cause significant damage, so you have to know that this external information is actually going to work. Of course, you don't want to reinvent the wheel either. Getting information from someone else can often help you create your own custom solution faster.

Make Backups

Before you begin any major configuration exercise on your server, make a backup. It seems like obvious advice, but administrators often fail to take it. They think that a little configuration job won't cause much trouble until they're picking up the pieces later. You should already have a good backup program in place because your server contains valuable data. If you aren't backing up your server regularly (regularly is defined as at least once a day and probably more often than that), then you're already setting yourself up for a major surprise at the worst possible moment. Don't cause that moment to occur by performing a task on a server that hasn't been backed up for the last month.

Try to perform any configuration tasks as soon as possible after the backup completes so that a disaster will cause as little loss as possible. In fact, if you can perform the tasks before anyone starts working with the server, you'll likely have better results.

Perform User-Specific Changes during Downtime

Some changes you make to a user account affect the user immediately; other changes wait until the next time the user logs into the system. Think about this issue for a moment and you'll figure out that this scenario can create instabilities. The user is likely to become unhappy because their account won't work as anticipated. In fact, the account can become unstable. In a worst case scenario, the instabilities could cause system crashes and data loss (this scenario is rare, but you always have to work as if you'll be the unlucky individual who has it happen to them). If you can't make the changes before the user gets into work, specifically have the user log out of the system, perform the configuration task, and ask the user to log back in. Using this approach will reduce user frustration.

The same approach also applies to a group. Many group level changes can cause instabilities in the affected accounts. Normally, you'll want to make group changes when everyone is logged out to ensure that the changes take effect the next time the users of the group log back into the system.

TIP   Some users are invariably going to cheat. It's possible to stand behind the user, watch them log out, and then go back to your office to perform the reconfiguration while they log back into the system. Inevitably the user will call back sometime later saying they were logged out, yet the instabilities that they're telling you about can only occur if they were logged in while you made the required account changes. If this occurs, have the user log back out and back into the system again.

Glossary

This book includes a glossary so that you can find terms and acronyms easily. It has several important features you need to know about. First, every nonstandard acronym in the entire book appears here. I have left out common acronyms. (The glossary does exclude common acronyms such as units of measure and most file extensions because these terms are easy to find in other sources and most people know what they mean.) This way, there isn't any doubt that you'll always find everything you need to use the book properly.

Second, these definitions are specific to the book. In other words, when you look through this glossary, you're seeing the words defined in the context in which they're used in this the book. This might or might not always coincide with current industry usage since the computer industry changes the meaning of words so often.

WHAT TO DO IF YOU DON'T FIND IT HERE

While this glossary is a relatively complete view of the words and acronyms in the book, you'll run into situations when you need to know more. No matter how closely I look at terms throughout the book, there's always a chance I'll miss the one acronym or term that you really need to know. In addition to the technical information found in the book, I've directed your attention to numerous online sources of information throughout the book and few of the terms the Web site owners use will appear here unless I also chose to use them in the book. Fortunately, many sites on the Internet provide partial or complete glossaries to fill in the gaps:

Acronym Finder `http://www.acronymfinder.com/`

Free Online Dictionary Of Computing (FOLDOC) `http://nightflight.com/foldoc/`

Microsoft Encarta `http://encarta.msn.com/`

Microsoft Security Glossary `http://msdn2.microsoft.com/en-us/library/ms950397.aspx`

More Microsoft Glossaries `http://www.winlexic.com/more_microsoft_glossaries.htm`

TechEncyclopedia `http://www.techweb.com/encyclopedia/defineterm.jhtml?term=COM`

Webopedia `http://webopedia.internet.com/`

Merriam-Webster Online `http://m-w.com/`

yourDictionary.com `http://www.yourdictionary.com/`

Some entries in this list are quite specialized. For example, the Microsoft Security Glossary discusses the Microsoft view of security terms. You can find other Microsoft Glossaries listed at `http://www.microsoft.com/resources/glossary/default.mspx`. If you still don't find what you need, try the Microsoft Search page at `http://search.microsoft.com/`, type the word **glossary**, add a specific area such as network, and click Go.

A

Access Control Entry (ACE)

Defines the object rights for a single user or group. Every ACE has a header that defines the type, size, and flags for the ACE. Next comes an access mask that defines the rights a user or group has to the object. Finally, there's an entry for the user's or group's Security Identifier (SID).

Access Control List (ACL)

Part of the Windows-based operating system security Application Programming Interface (API) used to determine both access and monitoring properties for an object. The ACL originally appeared in Windows NT. Each ACL contains one or more Access Control Entries (ACEs) that define the security properties for an individual or group. There are two major ACL groups: Security Access Control List (SACL) and Discretionary Access Control List (DACL). The SACL controls Windows auditing feature. The DACL controls access to the object.

ACE

See Access Control Entry

ACL

See Access Control List

Active Directory (AD)

A method of storing machine, server, and user configuration within Windows versions, starting with Windows 2000. Active Directory supports full data replication so that every domain controller has a copy of the data. This is essentially a special purpose database that contains information formatted according to a specific schema. Active Directory is designed to make Windows more reliable and secure, while reducing the work required by both the developer and administrator for application support and distribution. The user benefits as well since Active Directory fully supports roving users and maintains a full record of user information, which reduces the effects of local workstation downtime.

AD

See Active Directory

Address Resolution Protocol (ARP)

A method of computing the specific address of any entity on any Transmission Control Protocol/Internet Protocol (TCP/IP) network. The network driver sends out a broadcast message asking which piece of hardware is associated with a particular IP address. If a piece of hardware responds with a combination of its IP address and hardware identification number, then the network driver makes the association. This technique is normally used with devices such as Small Computer System Interface (SCSI) host adapters, where using the SCSI ID is much easier than using the 48-bit Ethernet hardware address.

ARP

See Address Resolution Protocol

ASR

See Automated System Recovery

Asynchronous Transfer Mode (ATM)

A data transfer method that relies on packets (cells) of a fixed size. The cell size used with ATM is smaller than used with older technologies, which enhances network efficiency by reducing the number of padding characters required to create complete cells. An ATM network typically transfers data at 25 to 622 Mbps. Most ATM services use one of four types of transmission. The Constant Bit Rate (CBR) service uses a constant stream that's equivalent to working with a leased line. The Variable Bit Rate (VBR) service varies the stream as needed to accommodate bursts in activity. This is a good option for voice and video-conferencing. The Available Bit Rate (ABR) service guarantees a minimum constant bandwidth, but allows bursts when the network is otherwise unused. The Unspecified Bit Rate (UBR) service is a low cost alternative that doesn't guarantee a specific bandwidth. This is a good option for file transfers and other tasks that can tolerate delays.

ATM

See Asynchronous Transfer Mode

Attribute

An attribute expresses some feature peculiar to an object. When referring to a database, each field has an attribute that expresses what type of information it contains, the length of the field, the field name, and the number of decimals. When referring to a display, the attribute expresses pixel color, intensity, and position. In programming, an attribute can also specify some type of object functionality, such as the method used to implement security.

Automated System Recovery (ASR)

A Windows technology that stores enough system information to recover from a number of system failures, such as an application installation that doesn't succeed well. ASR attempts to cover every contingency and does very well in recovering from many errors, but doesn't recover from every potential system error.

C

CAB

See Cabinet File

Cabinet File (CAB)

1. A compressed-format file similar to ZIP files used to transfer code and data from one location to another. For example, many Web sites use the CAB file to download applications to a user system using a browser as the intermediary. Use the Compress utility to create the file and the Expand utility to decompress the file. 2. A single file created to hold a number of compressed files. A related set of cabinet files can appear within a folder. During application installation, the compressed files in a cabinet are decompressed and copied to an appropriate directory for the user.

CACL

Change Access Control List

CI

See Container Inherit

Clear to Send (CTS)

A serial port signaling line that indicates the Data Communications Equipment (DCE), such as a modem, can receive data from the Data Terminal Equipment (DTE), such as a computer.

Comma Separated Value (CSV)

A type of text database file where the data fields are separated from one another using commas. Each carriage return/line feed combination (new line) creates a new record. Many applications can retrieve CSV files and convert them to other database representations.

Command Line

The input area allocated for entering instructions executed by the command processor. The operating system provides a standard prompt where you begin typing the instruction. In most cases, the prompt remains unavailable until the instruction completes.

Container Inherit (CI)

Signifies that this particular user inherited the Access Control Entry (ACE) from a parent directory.

Cracker

A hacker (computer expert) who uses their skills for misdeeds on computer systems where they have little or no authorized access. A cracker normally possesses specialty software that allows easier access to the target network. In most cases, crackers require extensive amounts of time to break the security for a system before they can enter it. Some sources call a cracker a black hat hacker.

CRC

See Cyclic Redundancy Code

Cryptographic Service Provider (CSP)

A specialty company that deals in certifying the identity of companies, developers, or individuals on the Internet. This identification check allows the company to issue an electronic certificate, which can then be used to conduct transactions securely. Several levels of certification are normally provided within a specific group. For example, there are three levels of individual certification. The lowest merely verifies the individual's identity through an Internet email address; the highest requires the individual to provide written proof along with a notarized statement. When you access a certified site or try to download a certified document such as a component, the browser displays the electronic certificate on screen, allowing you to make a security determination based on fact.

CSP

See Cryptographic Service Provider

CSV

See Comma Separated Value

CTS

See Clear to Send

Cyclic Redundancy Code (CRC)

A technique used to ensure the reliability of information stored on any media, transported across network cabling, or sent from one place to another using other techniques. It uses a cyclic calculation to create a numeric check number. The computer performs the same calculation when it retrieves the data and compares it to the CRC. If the two match, there's no data error. Otherwise, the sender must transmit the data again or the recipient must reconstruct it. If neither the sender nor the recipient can reconstruct the data, the system registers an error and informs the user of the data loss.

D

DACL

See Discretionary Access Control List

Data Set Ready (DSR)

A serial port signaling line that indicates that the Data Communications Equipment (DCE), such as a modem, is turned on.

Data Stream

One of several methods to send or access information that resides either in local or remote storage. A data stream consists of a series of bits taken from any location within a data storage unit (such as a file). The information can flow continuously (as in an Internet transfer for music) or in blocks (as occurs when reading data from a file on the local hard drive). The reading and writing sequence need not use blocks of any given size and the transfer often works with individual bits rather than characters or words.

Data Terminal Ready (DTR)

A serial port signaling line that indicates that the Data Terminal Equipment (DTE), such as a computer, is turned on.

DDF

See Diamond Directive File

Defragmenting

1. The process of organizing files on a storage media so that the file system can access each sector of the file sequentially. Defragmenting the file improves overall system performance by reducing the head movement of the hard drive. 2. The process of organizing and cleaning the Windows registry. The defragmentation application reorders the entries for faster access and locates entries that the system no longer requires. In most cases, the application removes the extraneous entries with user permission to enhance registry performance. In addition, the registry exists in multiple physical locations on the hard drive, which become physically fragmented. However, since Windows locks the registry files, standard defragmentation doesn't reorganize these files, so this process normally includes physical disk file organization as well.

DHCP

See Dynamic Host Configuration Protocol

Diamond Directive File (DDF)

Similar to an INF (information) or BAT (batch) file, the DDF provides instructions to a CAB (cabinet) creation utility such as DIANTZ for compressing one or more files into a single storage file. CAB files are normally used to distribute data locally, using a CD or other similar type of media, or remotely, through an Internet or other server connection. The DDF can also list files needed for a complete installation, but stored in other locations. Normally, these missing files already appear on the user's computer, so downloading them again would waste time. The DDF makes it possible to download them only as needed.

Directory

A logical unit of storage for most forms of media. Directories provide a means of separating files into different locations based on type or use. Using directories makes it easier to locate data and use applications.

Directory Information Tree (DIT)

All or part of the Active Directory database. A Directory Service Agent (DSA) can contain all or part of the Active Directory database. Each DSA has its own DIT. All of the DSA database pieces, when combined, form all of the data for Active Directory for a particular domain, but an individual DSA may contain only part of the database. In Active Directory, the top of the Active Directory database information tree is an object of the DomainDNS class that contains the Domain Controller object.

Discretionary Access Control List (DACL)

A Windows security component. The DACL controls access to an object. You can assign both groups and individual users to a specific object.

Disk Quota

A limit placed on the amount of hard drive space that a user can rely on to hold data. Many administrators use disk quotas to keep hard disk resource usage under control. In a shared environment, disk quotas ensure that each user receives a fair share of the available disk space.

Distributed Link Tracking (DLT)

A service that monitors all of the links on the system. The type of link can include file, shortcut, and Object Linking and Embedding (OLE), among others. The main purpose of the service is to detect and fix broken links so they don't damage the system or its data. For example, when a user changes the name of a linked file, the system updates the links so they point to the correct file again.

DIT

See Directory Information Tree

DLL

See Dynamic Link Library

DLT

See Distributed Link Tracking

DNS

See Domain Name System

Domain Name System (DNS)

An Internet technology that allows a user to refer to a host computer by name rather than using its unique IP address.

DOS Protected-Mode Interface (DPMI)

A method of accessing extended memory from a DOS application using the eXtended Memory Manager (XMM) that Microsoft introduced for Windows 3.0. The main feature of DPMI is that it provides a means of protecting the extended memory using a method that Windows understands.

DPMI

See DOS Protected-Mode Interface

DSR

See Data Set Ready

DTR

See Data Terminal Ready

Dynamic Host Configuration Protocol (DHCP)

A method for automatically determining the IP address on a TCP/IP connection. A server provides this address to the client as part of the setup communications. Using DHCP means that a server can use fewer addresses to communicate with clients and that clients don't need to provide a hard-coded address to the server. You must configure your server to provide these services.

Dynamic Link Library (DLL)

A specific form of application code loaded into memory by request. It's not a stand-alone executable like an EXE file. A DLL does contain one or more discrete routines that an application may use to provide specific features. For example, a DLL could provide a common set of file dialogs used to access information on the hard drive. More than one application can use the functions provided by a DLL, reducing overall memory requirements when more than one application is running. DLLs have a number of purposes. For example, they can contain device-specific code in the form of a device driver. Some types of COM objects also rely on DLLs

E

ECMA

See European Computer Manufacturer's Association

EFI

See Extensible Firmware Interface

EFS

See Encrypting File System

EMM

See Expanded Memory Manager

EMS

See Expanded Memory Specification

Encapsulated PostScript (EPS)

A graphics file format used by the PostScript language. PostScript is a page description language that uses text to define the elements of a drawing. Like all vector graphic formats, PostScript allows infinite scaling and provides better resolution characteristics than bitmapped graphics. Use of PostScript requires an interpreter on every machine where the language is used.

Encrypting File System (EFS)

A component of the Windows NT File System (NTFS) that performs encryption and decryption of files in a transparent manner. The user that originally encrypted the file can access it seamlessly, but any other user is denied access. The user must mark the file as encrypted to use this feature.

End Of File (EOF)

The physical or logical end of a file. In text files, the end of file is the control character 26 or ^Z. In database files, the end of file marker is a logical element that depends on the database in use. Other file types have similar end of file markers.

End of Line (EOL)

The character or characters that define the end of a line of text within any data source on a computer system. The PC relies on the line feed (character 10) and carriage return (character 13) control character combination. A UNIX system uses only the carriage return character, while a Macintosh uses the line feed character.

Environment Variable

An operating system–supported means of storing temporary data in memory. The data appears as name value pairs and the operating system can access the variable by name or as a value (in expanded form). The expanded form of an environment variable appears within percent signs (%) such as %PATH%. The user can set, view, and clear environment variables at the command line using the Set command. The environment variable settings also appear on the Environment Variables dialog box that the user can access through the Environment Variables button on the Advanced tab of the System Properties dialog box.

EOF

See End Of File

EOL

See End of Line

EPS

See Encapsulated PostScript

European Computer Manufacturer's Association (ECMA)

A standards committee originally founded in 1961. ECMA is dedicated to standardizing information and communication systems. For example, they created the ECMAScript standard used for many Web page designs today. You can also find ECMA standards for product safety, security, networks, and storage media.

Expanded Memory Manager (EMM)

A device driver such as EMM386.EXE that provides expanded memory services on an 80386 and above equipped machine (which definitely includes all modern machines). An application accesses expanded memory using a page frame or other memory-mapping techniques from within the conventional or upper memory area (0 to 1,024 KB). The EMM usually emulates expanded memory using extended memory managed by an eXtended Memory Manager (XMM) such as HIMEM.SYS, which provides access to the eXtended Memory Specification (XMS) memory. An application must change the processor's mode to protected mode to use XMS.

Expanded Memory Specification (EMS)

A method (specification) for older DOS and console applications to access memory outside of the 640 KB conventional memory area. This specification defines one method of extending the amount of memory that a processor can address from the conventional memory area. It uses an area outside of system memory to store information. An Expanded Memory Manager (EMM) provides a window view into this larger data area. The old 3.2 EMS specification requires a 64 KB window in the Upper Memory Block (UMB). The newer 4.0 specification can create this window anywhere in conventional or UMB memory.

eXtended Memory Specification (XMS)

A device driver that emulates expanded memory by using extended memory (the memory above the 1 MB limit imposed by DOS). The original version of this specification (developed by Quarterdeck) appeared in 1986. It allowed an 80286 or above processor to access up to 64 KB of extended memory from within the conventional memory area by enabling the A20 address line. This specification makes it possible to multitask from within DOS by freeing more application memory. In 1990, Microsoft revised its HIMEM.SYS driver with the release of Windows 3.0. The scope of XMS memory increased to multitask Windows applications. Versions of Windows starting with Windows NT don't require HIMEM.SYS

to provide access to extended memory, but the DOS applications run by these versions of Windows do, so newer versions of Windows make a version of HIMEM.SYS available for these applications.

Extensible Firmware Interface (EFI)

A standard method of providing boot information to the operating system that replaces the Basic Input/Output System (BIOS). The information that EFI provides includes platform specifics such as hardware configuration, boot setup, and runtime service calls. The operating system and its loader receive all of this information prior to starting the boot cycle.

eXtensible Markup Language (XML)

1. A method used to store information in an organized manner. The storage technique relies on hierarchical organization and uses special statements called tags to separate each storage element. Each tag defines a data attribute and can contain properties that further define each data element. 2. A standardized Web page design language used to incorporate data structuring within standard HTML documents. For example, you could use XML to display database information using something other than forms or tables. It's actually a lightweight version of Standard Generalized Markup Language (SGML) and is supported by the SGML community. XML also supports tag extensions that allow various parts of a Web-based application to exchange information. For example, once a user makes a choice within a catalog, that information could be added to an order entry form with a minimum of effort on the part of the developer. Since XML is easy to extend, some developers look at it as more of a base specification for other languages, rather than a complete language.

eXtensible Stylesheet Language (XSL)

A technology that separates the method of presentation from the actual content of either an eXtensible Markup Language (XML) or Hypertext Markup Language (HTML) page. The XSL document contains all of the required formatting information so that the content remains in pure form. This is the second style language submitted to the World Wide Web Consortium (W3C) for consideration. The first specification was for Cascading Style Sheets (CSS).

XSL documents use an XML-like format. This term is also listed as eXtensible Style Language by some sources.

eXtensible Stylesheet Language Transformation (XSLT)

The language used within the eXtensible Style Language (XSL) to transform the content provided in an eXtensible Markup Language (XML) file into a form for display on screen or printing. An XSL processor combines XML content with the formatting instructions provided by XSLT and outputs a new document or document fragment. XSLT is a World Wide Web Consortium (W3C) standard.

F

FAT

See File Allocation Table

Fault Tolerance

The ability of an object (application, device, or other entity) to recover from an error. For example, the fault tolerance provided by a transaction server allows a network to recover from potential data loss induced by a system or use failure. Another example of fault tolerance is the ability of a Redundant Array of Inexpensive Disks (RAID) system to recover from a hard drive failure.

FFT

File Allocation Table (FAT) File Times

File Allocation Table (FAT)

The method of formatting media used by DOS and other operating systems. This technique is one of the oldest formatting methods available. There have been several different versions of FAT based on the number of bits used to store disk locations. The original form was 12 bits, which was quickly followed by the 16-bit version used by many computers today. A 32-bit version of FAT, also called FAT32, was introduced with the OEM Service Release 2 (OSR2) version of Windows 98. The 32-bit version of FAT stores data more efficiently on the large hard drives available on today's computers. FAT also appears on

many other media, such as the memory cards used for cameras.

File Replication Service (FRS)

A service used to copy file system policies and logon scripts for Windows. In addition, this service can copy content as needed between servers with the assistance of the Distributed File System (DFS).

Firewall

Hardware or software (or a combination of both) used to prevent unauthorized access to a private network. The firewall can use any of a number of techniques to detect unauthorized packets and deny access to them. Some firewalls not only check incoming packets but outgoing packets as well. There are many types of firewalls including packet filter, application gateway, proxy server, and circuit-level gateway. For maximum protection, the proxy server normally works best in a hardware configuration.

Fully Qualified Domain Name (FQDN)

The combination of a host and domain name, including the top-level domain name. For example, `www.microsoft.com` is a Fully Qualified Domain Name (FQDN). In this case, www is the host, microsoft is the second-level domain, and com is the top-level domain.

FQDN

See Fully Qualified Domain Name

FRS

See File Replication Service

G

Globally Unique Identifier (GUID)

A 128-bit number originally used to identify a Component Object Model (COM) object within the Windows registry. Microsoft now uses the GUID wherever a system requires a unique identifier. When working in COM, the system uses the GUID to find the object definition and allow applications to create instances of that object. However, the system can use the GUID for other purposes as well. GUIDs can include any kind of object, even nonvisual elements.

In addition, some types of complex objects are actually aggregates of simple objects. For example, an object that implements a property page will normally have a minimum of two GUIDs: one for the property page and another for the object itself.

GUID

See Globally Unique Identifier

H

Hacker

An individual who works with computers at a low level (hardware or software), especially in the area of security. A hacker normally possesses specialty software or other tools that allows easier access to the target hardware or software application or network. The media defines two types of hackers, which includes those that break into systems for ethical purposes and those that do it to damage the system in some way. The proper term for the second group is crackers (see Cracker for details). Some people have started to call the first group "ethical hackers" or "white hat hackers" to prevent confusion. Ethical hackers normally work for security firms that specialize in finding holes in a company's security. However, hackers work in a wide range of computer arenas. For example, a person who writes low-level code (like that found in a device driver) after reverse engineering an existing driver is technically a hacker. The main emphasis of a hacker is to work for the benefit of others in the computer industry.

Hard Link

A connection between two files. The new file is a pointer to the existing file. In essence, the system creates another directory entry to a single file. The file continues to exist until the system removes all of the directory entries pointing to it. Any change an object makes to the content of the new file also appears within the existing file, and vice versa.

Hierarchical Storage Manager (HSM)

Manages the user's data storage hierarchy. A hierarchy might consist of several hard drives, a compact disk (CD), digital video disc (DVD), and tape drive.

High Memory Area (HMA)

The first 64 KB area of memory beyond the 1 MB boundary that the processor can access in real mode on an 80286 or above processor. The system accesses this memory area by activating the A20 memory line.

HMA

See High Memory Area

HSM

See Hierarchical Storage Manager

HTTP

See Hypertext Transfer Protocol

HTTPS

See Hypertext Transfer Protocol Secure Sockets

Hypertext Transfer Protocol (HTTP)

One of several common data transfer protocols for the Internet. HTTP normally transfers textual data of some type. For example, the Hypertext Markup Language (HTML) relies on HTTP to transfer the Web pages it defines from the server to the client. The eXtensible Markup Language and Simple Object Access Protocol (SOAP) also commonly rely on HTTP to transfer data between client and server. It's important to note that HTTP is separate from the data it transfers. For example, it's possible for SOAP to use the Simple Mail Transfer Protocol (SMTP) to perform data transfers between client and server.

Hypertext Transfer Protocol Secure Sockets (HTTPS)

A secure form of Hypertext Transport Protocol (HTTP) that relies on the Secure Sockets Layer (SSL) encryption technology to transfer data.

I

ICACL

Improved Change Access Control List

IDE

See Integrated Development Environment

IGMP

See Internet Group Multicast Protocol

IIS

See Internet Information Server

Integrated Development Environment (IDE)

The development environment used to write application code. An IDE provides all of the tools needed to write an application using one or more specialized editors. The IDE normally includes support for development language help, access to any tools required to support the language, a compiler, and a debugger. Some IDEs include support for advanced features such as automatic completion of language statements and balloon help showing the syntax for functions and other language elements. Many IDEs also use color or highlighting to emphasize specific language elements or constructs.

Internet Group Multicast Protocol (IGMP)

Controls the remote systems that receive a packet based on the RFC1112 specification. IGMP keeps neighboring multicast routers informed of the host group memberships present on a particular local network. To support IGMP, every level 2 host must join the all-hosts group (address 224.0.0.1) on each network interface at initialization time and must remain a member for as long as the host is active.

Internet Information Server (IIS)

Microsoft's Web server that runs under the Windows operating system. IIS includes all of the standard Web server features including File Transfer Protocol (FTP) and Hypertext Transfer Protocol (HTTP), along with both mail and news services in older versions of the product. The latest version of IIS concentrates on developer requirements and doesn't provide mail and news services.

Internet Packet Exchange (IPX)

A peer-to-peer communication protocol based on the Internet Protocol (IP) portion of the TCP/IP pair. IPX is a security datagram protocol used for connectionless communication. It offers superior functionality to IP, but never became popular because it's a proprietary Novell technology.

Inter-Packet Gap (IPG)

The distance, measured in milliseconds, between packets on a TCP/IP network.

IPG

See Inter-Packet Gap

IPX

See Internet Packet Exchange

L

LCID

See Locale Identifier

LDAP

See Lightweight Directory Access Protocol

Lightweight Directory Access Protocol (LDAP)

A set of protocols used to access directories and is based on a simplified version of the X.500 standard. Unlike X.500, LDAP provides support for TCP/IP, a requirement for Internet communication. LDAP makes it possible for a client to request directory information like email addresses and public keys from any server. In addition, since LDAP is an open protocol, applications need not worry about the type of server used to host the directory.

Line Printer Daemon (LPD)

A special application that provides printing services.

Line Printer Queue (LPQ)

A special application that provides spooling services for print jobs sent from a client to a print service. The application normally places the print job on a local hard drive until the printer can output it.

Line Printer Remote (LPR)

The client-side software used to make requests of a remote print server using TCP/IP as the protocol. The LPR protocol normally appears as part of a UNIX setup, but also appears on operating systems such as Windows.

Locale Identifier (LCID)

A number that uniquely identifies a country, language, or other nationalistic information. An application, online resource, or data manager uses the LCID to provide specific information, services, or resources in a form that the user can understand. For example, many applications support more than one language and the application would use the LCID to change the prompts to match the user's language.

LPD

See Line Printer Daemon

LPQ

See Line Printer Queue

LPR

See Line Printer Remote

M

MAC

See Media Access Control

Master File Table (MFT)

A file that contains information about all of the directories and files on the associated hard drive. The current MFT implementation uses the first sixteen 1,024-byte records in the file to tell the operating system about itself. Afterward, each record contains information about a file or directory. The records tell the operating system how to retrieve the files or interact with the directory. For example, the records contain file permissions, the name and size of the file, the date and time the operating system created it, and the date and time any operating system object modified it.

Master File Table Zone (MFT Zone)

The physical location of the Master File Table (MFT) on a hard drive.

MDAC

See Microsoft Data Access Components

Media Access Control (MAC)

The unique address assigned to every Network Interface Card (NIC) that identifies each node on a network. The MAC layer is at the data link control (DLC) layer of the OSI reference model for networks. It directly interacts with the network media, which means that each type of network will have a different MAC that identifies the nodes on that network. The MAC layer also referred to the DLC layer on some networks.

Memory Fragmentation

A type of memory bottleneck that occurs when an operating system is left running for an extended time. The allocation and deallocation of memory by applications can leave pockets of memory too small to handle typical application requests, even though there's more than enough memory to handle the request. The result of memory fragmentation is a loss of performance due to increased disk thrashing as the operating system moves data from physical memory to the hard drive and back again.

MFT

See Master File Table

MFT Zone

See Master File Table Zone

Microsoft Data Access Components (MDAC)

A set of components designed to make data access easier. MDAC is actually a software development kit (SDK) that includes components, sample code, headers, libraries, and other elements that allow the developer to use newer Microsoft technologies such as Object Linking and Embedding-Database (OLE-DB).

Microsoft Database Engine (MSDE)

A miniature form of SQL Server that enables developers to create test database applications. This term also appears as Microsoft Desktop Engine and Microsoft Data Engine in various references. Microsoft designed this engine for use by one person, usually the developer, although you can potentially use it for up to five people. The developer accesses MSDE through a programming language Integrated Development Environment (IDE) or using command line utilities. In some cases, MSDE also provides access to a remote copy of SQL Server. Some third-party products, such as MSDE Query, provide a Graphical User Interface (GUI) for MSDE.

Microsoft Installer (MSI)

1. A technique for installing applications within Windows that allows later removal even if the system configuration has changed. This technique also provides support for additional vendor information, partial installations, multiple configurations, and installation recovery. 2. A file format containing instructions for installing Windows applications. The file is actually a database that contains specialized instructions and data in a specific format that's read by the Microsoft installer application.

Microsoft Message Queuing Services (MSMQ)

A technology that enables a developer to create applications that rely on asynchronous data transfer. The data passed between client and server is recorded in a message and stored in a local or remote queue until the recipient can process it. A local listener alerts the affected application component to the presence of the message in the queue. A player interprets the content of the message for the application component so that the application component can react to it. The asynchronous application support provided by MSMQ has a number of useful applications including disconnected application support and load balancing.

MIME

See Multipurpose Internet Mail Extensions

Modifier

An addition that changes the way that a command, utility, interface, programming instruction, or other computer technology works. When used with a command or a utility, a modifier changes the way a command line switch works, the way the application processes data, the way the user perceives or interacts with the data, or the way the application outputs information. When used with a programming instruction, a modifier can change the internal workings of the instruction or provide amplifying information to the instruction. Modifiers typically augment the computer technology in some way,

rather than define the precise workings of the technology.

MSDE

See Microsoft Database Engine

MSI

See Microsoft Installer

MSMQ

See Microsoft Message Queuing Services

Multipurpose Internet Mail Extensions (MIME)

The standard method for defining the content of Internet messages. This standard allows computers to exchange objects, character sets, and multimedia using email without regard to the computer's underlying operating system. MIME is defined in the Internet Engineering Task Force (IETF) Request for Comment (RFC) 1521 standard.

N

NCSA

National Center for Supercomputing Applications

Network Time Protocol (NTP)

A technique for synchronizing computer time with a time source. NTP is a standardized technology based on RFC1305.

NTFS

See Windows New Technology File System

NTLM

See Windows NT LAN Manager Security

NTP

See Network Time Protocol

O

Object Inherit (OI)

Signifies that the Access Control Entry (ACE) reflects a right inherited by the file and not a user.

ODBC

See Open Database Connectivity

OEM

See Original Equipment Manufacturer

OI

See Object Inherit

Open Database Connectivity (ODBC)

One of several methods for exchanging data between Database Management Systems (DBMSs). In most cases, this involves three steps: installing an appropriate driver, adding a source to the Data Sources (ODBC) applet in the Control Panel, and using specialized statements, such as Structured Query Language (SQL), to access the database. The precise functionality and configuration requirements of ODBC depend on the ODBC driver used to create the connection.

Open System Interconnection Reference Model (OSI)

A theoretical seven layer protocol model of network connectivity commonly used to teach how network protocols interact. Data is passed from one layer to the next until the sender physically transmits it to another machine. The reverse process takes place when the data arrives at the receiving machine, unwrapping layer after layer of protocol information, until the data appears in its original form. The OSI reference model was originally supposed to unite all network models, but proprietary formats prevented full acceptance by vendors and the OSI reference model became a teaching tool instead. (The X.400 and X.500 standards are directly based on the OSI reference model.) The seven OSI reference model layers include application, presentation, session, transport, network, data link, and physical.

Original Equipment Manufacturer (OEM)

Used to identify manufacturers that produce some type of PC hardware. In this case, hardware can include anything from individual chips to entire systems. For example, a vendor that designs and builds display adapters is considered an OEM. An OEM is normally responsible for writing device drivers and other software required to use the hardware it sells.

OSI

See Open System Interconnection Reference Model

P

Path Maximum Transmission Unit (PMTU)

A standardized method that two Transmission Control Protocol (TCP) peers can use to discover the size of the Internet Protocol (IP) Maximum Transmission Unit (MTU). This feature helps the peers maximize performance by using the largest packet size to transmit data between them.

PBK

See Phonebook File

PDC

See Primary Domain Controller

Phonebook File (PBK)

A file containing the telephone numbers and other information for user contacts stored in various applications including Microsoft Office and Outlook Express.

PID

See Process Identifier

PIF

See Program Information File

PIM

See Protocol Independent Multicast

Pipe

A method of transferring data from one process to another. When used with a command line utility, the user types the pipe symbol (|) to represent the connection between two commands or utilities. Pipes usually provide a streamed data transfer, but can also perform block transfers depending on the capabilities of the processes.

PMTU

See Path Maximum Transmission Unit

Primary Domain Controller (PDC)

The Windows server responsible for tracking changes made to the domain accounts and storing them in the directory database (usually Active Directory with newer versions of Windows). In addition, the PDC provides user authentication and other services. A domain has one PDC. Windows 2000 and above doesn't have an actual PDC. Instead, newer Windows servers use Active Directory as the authentication database. All Domain Controllers (DCs) are equal with regard to functionality However, many utilities and applications that work with a PDC also work with the Windows 2000 setup.

Process Identifier (PID)

A numeric value associated with a process running on a specific machine. Every process has a unique PID, making it possible to locate a specific process, even if multiple copies of a single application are running on the machine. The PID is used by a wide variety of monitoring applications. It's also used to access an application or as a means of identification when terminating an errant application.

Program Information File (PIF)

A means of storing application configuration settings as a separate file. Windows automatically looks at the configuration settings when you execute the corresponding application and makes any required environment changes. The PIF usually includes various memory settings along with the application's command path and working directory.

Protocol Independent Multicast (PIM)

Defines the type of routing the server uses.

R

RAS

See Remote Access Server

RCP

Remote Copy Protocol

Ready to Send (RTS)

A serial port signaling line that indicates the Data Terminal Equipment (DTE), such as a computer, is ready to send data to the Data Communications Equipment (DCE), such as a modem.

Relative Identifier (RID)

An Active Directory term that denotes the unique part of a Security Identifier (SID) for an object. The RID ensures that each SID is truly unique, even when other objects have the same name or other attributes. A RID is always a number that's drawn from a pool of numbers. No two SIDs have the same number.

Remote Access Server (RAS)

An optional Windows service that allows an outside entity (such as a user) to create a connection into the server from a remote location. Generally, the outside entity uses this service to access server resources such as files or applications. An outside entity can access this service in a variety of ways, including as a callback mechanism.

Remote Installation Services (RIS)

A Windows 2000 and higher feature that allows administrators to install a copy of Windows on a remote client system without physically visiting the client machine. This feature is part of the Remote Operating System Installation feature in Windows 2000. Microsoft has added extended forms of this feature to all versions of Windows since Windows 2000.

Remote Procedure Call (RPC)

One of several techniques for accessing a procedure or a method (some code) within another application. RPC is designed to look for the application first on the local workstation and then across the network at the applications stored on other workstations.

Resource Reservation Protocol (RSVP)

A set of network rules that allows an object (usually an application or a service) to request the resources it needs to run from the server in advance, which ensures that the network administrator can manage resource usage and that the operating system can plan ahead for application requirements. This is an especially important feature for resource hungry applications like multimedia or Voice Over IP (VOIP).

Resultant Set of Policy (RSoP)

Defines the rights of a particular object based on all of the security entries for that object in an Access Control List (ACL) attached to an operating system resource. For example, a user inherits rights from groups and the parent directory, and has personal rights to a file. Whether the user gains access to the file depends on the result of comparing all of those sources of rights.

RID

See Relative Identifier

RIS

See Remote Installation Services

Rivest Shamir Adleman algorithm (RSA)

An authentication technology named after its creators that relies on a private-public key pair to create a set of credentials. The credentials are then used as a means of identification for logging into various network resources. Using this methodology allows for secure data transmission as well as user-oriented features like one password logon to the network.

RPC

See Remote Procedure Call

RSA

See Rivest Shamir Adleman algorithm

RSHD

Remote Shell Daemon

RSoP

See Resultant Set of Policy

RSVP

See Resource Reservation Protocol

RTS

See Ready to Send

S

SACL

See Security Access Control List

SAM

See Security Access Manager

Script

A type of simple interpreted application, productivity enhancer, or automated data manipulator developed using a macro or simplified programming language. Most operating systems support at least one scripting language. You'll also find scripting capability in many higher-end applications such as Web browsers and word processors. Scripts are normally used to write small utility type applications rather than large-scale applications that require the use of a compiled language. In addition, many script languages are limited in their access of the full set of operating system features.

SCM

See Service Control Manager

Secure Hashing Algorithm 1 (SHA-1)

The mathematical basis for encrypting and decrypting data used with the Digital Signature Standard (DSS) introduced by the National Institute of Standards and Technology (NIST). DSS also relies on Digital Signature Algorithm (DSA) to provide the digital signature functionality.

Security Access Control List (SACL)

One of several specialized Access Control Lists (ACL) used to maintain object integrity. This list controls Windows' auditing features. Every time a user or group accesses an object and the auditing feature for that object is turned on, Windows makes an entry in the audit log.

Security Access Manager (SAM)

A service that manages a database containing information about an object (such as a user) and its security settings. Some sources also call this service the Security Accounts Manager. In either case, the security database normally appears within a special hive of the registry. Windows secures this hive using the Registry Editor to make it difficult to access. The SAM can also use alternative input sources such as Active Directory.

Security Identifier (SID)

The part of an access token that identifies the object throughout the network; it's the same as having an account number at a bank or other organization. The identifier is unique. The access token that the SID identifies tells what groups the object belongs to and what privileges the object has.

Sequential Packet Exchange (SPX)

The part of the IPX/SPX protocol pair that guarantees delivery of a message sent from one node to another. Think of SPX as the postal clerk that delivers a certified letter from one place to another. In network terms, each page of the letter is called a packet. SPX delivers the letter one page at a time to the intended party.

Service Control Manager (SCM)

The part of Windows that controls the various services loaded to provide background support. The SCM starts, stops, pauses, and continues services, as well as providing service status information. The SCM is also part of the load-balancing technology used by Windows servers. When a client makes a DCOM call to the load-balancing router, it's the SCM that actually receives the request. The SCM looks up the component in the load-balancing router table, then makes a DCOM call to one of the servers in the application cluster to fulfill the request. The server in the application cluster creates an instance of the request object, then passes the proxy for it directly to the client. At this point, the server and the client are in direct communication; the router is no longer needed.

SHA-1

See Secure Hashing Algorithm 1

Shell Extension

A special application that gives some type of added value to the operating system interface. Many shell extensions provide added functionality by working with a specific file type or provide increased user access by offering additional commands. In most cases, the application must register itself with the registry before the operating system will recognize it.

SID

See Security Identifier

Simple Mail Transfer Protocol (SMTP)

One of the most commonly used protocols to transfer text (commonly mail) messages between clients and servers. This is a stream-based protocol designed to allow query, retrieval, posting, and distribution of mail messages. Normally this protocol is used in conjunction with other mail retrieval protocols such as point of presence (POP). However, not all uses of SMTP involve email data transfer. Some Simple Object Access Protocol (SOAP) applications have also relied on SMTP to transfer application data.

Simple Network Management Protocol (SNMP)

A network protocol (originally designed for the Internet) used to manage devices from different vendors. The protocol originally appeared in the 1980s and relies on Protocol Data Unit (PDU) messages to transmit requests. SNMP-compliant devices, known as agents, respond to these requests by sending information from Management Information Bases (MIBs) to the requestor.

Smart Card

A type of user identification used in place of passwords. The smart card contains an encrypted chip that provides the user identification information; most smart cards are about the size and shape of a credit card. The use of a smart card makes it much harder for a third party to break into a computer system using stolen identification. However, a lost or stolen smart card still provides user access. The most secure method of user identification is biometrics.

SMTP

See Simple Mail Transfer Protocol

SNMP

See Simple Network Management Protocol

Sparse File

A file that allocates a lot of space on a hard drive, but actually uses very little of that space. For example, a data cache might allocate 1 MB of hard drive space, but only use a few KB of that space to hold data. The system allocates the space because it could require it to keep applications running, but the system doesn't need all of the space all of the time. A sparse file is a type of reservation system where the system reserves hard drive space for a future need.

SPX

See Sequential Packet Exchange

SQL

See Structured Query Language

Structured Query Language (SQL)

Language used by most Database Management Systems (DBMSs) to exchange information; also used by DBMSs as their native language. SQL provides a method for manipulating data controlled by the DBMS. It defines which tables to use, determines what information to get from the table, and resolves how to sort the information. A typical request will include the name of the database, table, and columns needed for display or editing purposes. SQL can filter a request and limit the number of rows using special features. Developers also use SQL to manipulate database information by adding, deleting, modifying, or searching records. The IBM research center designed SQL between 1974 and 1975. Oracle introduced the first product to use SQL in 1979. SQL originally appeared on mainframe and minicomputers. Today it's a favorite language for most PC DBMSs as well. There are many versions of SQL.

Symbolic Link

A pointer to a physical file or folder somewhere else on the drive, another local drive, or even a network drive. The symbolic link makes it unnecessary to track where a file or folder exists. Instead, you focus on the data itself. A directory entry marked as a symbolic link has no real content—just the pointer to the actual file or folder.

T

Tab Separated Value (TSV)

A type of text database file where the data fields are separated from one another using tabs. Each carriage return/line feed combination (new line) creates a new record. Many applications can retrieve TSV files and convert them to other database representations.

TAPI

See Telephony Application Programming Interface

TCP/IP

See Transmission Control Protocol/Internet Protocol

TDR

See Time Domain Reflectometer

Telephony Application Programming Interface (TAPI)

A set of DLLs and other system resources used by applications to interact with various types of communication equipment. Developers can use TAPI to create communication applications or applications that use communications to provide services such as help. The TAPI service provides functionality for dial-up services such as modems and faxes. Windows also uses it for networking services such as Internet connectivity no matter what form the connectivity takes (dial-up, broadband, digital subscriber line, and so on).

Time Domain Reflectometer (TDR)

A special device that detects and analyzes cabling problems by sending a signal through the cable and measuring the return signal. Unlike a resistance check, a TDR can measure partial breaks, stress fractures, and other conditions that a technician can't see using visual inspection.

Time-to-Live (TTL)

An Internet Protocol (IP) packet entry that controls the lifetime of the packet. The router forwards the datagram when the TTL in the IP header is greater than the TTL threshold for the interface. This value limits the distances that packets can travel.

Token

The representation of data, an object, database element, programming syntax, or other information using a code word, phrase, number, or object. For example, in programming, a token could represent a statement, punctuation mark, argument, or other syntactical element. Users often receive tokens describing their rights as part of the security features of an operating system. Networks also use tokens to control data flow and perform other tasks.

Transmission Control Protocol/Internet Protocol (TCP/IP)

A standard communication line protocol (set of rules) developed by the United States Department of Defense. The protocol defines how two devices talk to each other. TCP defines a communication methodology where it guarantees packet delivery and also ensures the packets appear at the recipient in the same order they were sent. IP defines the packet characteristics.

TSV

See Tab Separated Value

TTL

See Time-to-Live

U

UAC

See User Account Control

UDP

See User Datagram Protocol

UMB

See Upper Memory Block

UNC

See Universal Naming Convention

Unicode Character

A double byte (16-bit) character used to represent more than the character set used by the English language. Unicode character sets are standardized by international convention. Advanced operating systems such as Windows and Linux normally rely on Unicode for enhanced language support and consistent data handling. Older versions of Windows, such as Windows 98, rely on the American Standard Code for Information Interchange (ASCII), an 8-bit code that works well only for English. Unicode is the standard character set used by newer versions of Windows, although all versions of Windows can still use ASCII characters when needed for compatibility purposes.

Uniform Resource Identifier (URI)

A generic term for all names and addresses that reference objects on the Internet. A URL is a specific type of URI. See Uniform Resource Locator (URL).

Uniform Resource Locator (URL)

A text representation of a specific location on the Internet. URLs normally include the protocol (http:// for example), the target location (World Wide Web or www), the domain or server name (mycompany), and a domain type (com for commercial). (Many URLs don't include the www portion of the address anymore.) It can also include a hierarchical location within that Web site. The URL usually specifies a particular file on the Web server, although there are some situations when a Web server will use a default filename. For example, asking the browser to find `http://www.mycompany.com`, would probably display the `DEFAULT.HTM` or `INDEX.HTM` file at that location. The actual default filename depends on the Web server used. In some cases, the default filename is configurable and could be any of a number of files. For example, Internet Information Server (IIS) offers this feature, so the developer can use anything from an HTM, to an ASP, to an XML file as the default.

Universal Naming Convention (UNC)

A method for identifying network resources without specifying a local resource such as a drive letter. In most cases, a user will employ this convention with drives and printers, but the user can also apply it to other types of resources. A UNC normally includes a server name followed by a device name in place of a locale identifier. For example, a user might refer to a disk drive on a remote machine as "\\AUX\ DRIVE_C." The advantage of using UNC is that the resource name won't change, even if the user's local device mappings do.

Universally Unique Identifier (UUID)

Another name for a Globally Unique Identifier (GUID). The two terms are interchangeable. The UUID is part of the Distributed Computing Environment (DCE) standardized by the Open Software Foundation (OSF), while Microsoft created the GUID acronym.

Update Sequence Number (USN)

Provides a persistent log of all of the changes made to the files on the system. As users add, delete, and modify files and directories, the Windows NT File System (NTFS) makes an entry in the USN. Each volume has a separate USN. The main use of the USN for administrators is to check the changes made to one or more files. Using the USN is more efficient than relying on time stamps and the administrator receives more information as well.

Upper Memory Block (UMB)

The area of memory between 640 KB and the 1 MB boundary. IBM originally set aside this area of memory for device ROMs and special device memory areas. Various memory managers, including the one supplied with Windows, let you load applications and device drivers in this area to free more memory in the lower 640 KB area.

URI

See Uniform Resource Identifier

URL

See Uniform Resource Locator

User Account Control (UAC)

A Windows security feature that increases security by reducing the chance that an application can perform any act on the user's behalf, without the user's knowledge. This feature first appeared as part of Windows Vista. The operating system displays a dialog box asking permission to perform the required task. When the user answers yes, the system performs a privilege elevation that allows the task to progress.

User Datagram Protocol (UDP)

Provides the means for applications to exchange individual packets of information over an IP network. UDP uses a combination of protocol ports and IP addresses to get a message from one point of the network to another. More than one client can use the same protocol port as long as all clients using the port have a unique IP address. There are two types of protocol ports: well-known and dynamically bound. The well-known port assignments use the ports numbered between 1 and 255. When using dynamically bound port assignments, the requesting applications queries the service first to see which port it can use. Unlike TCP/IP, UDP/IP provides very few error recovery services, making it a fast way to deliver broadcast messages and performing other tasks where reliability isn't a concern.

USN

See Update Sequence Number

UUID

See Universally Unique Identifier

V

Valid Data Length (VDL)

The length of the valid data within a file, rather than the actual file length as indicated by an End of File (EOF) marker.

VDL

See Valid Data Length

VDS

See Virtual Disk Service

Virtual Disk Service (VDS)

Device drivers that provide specialized disk support on Windows. This service is normally associated with a Redundant Array of Inexpensive Disks (RAID) setup.

Virtual Terminal Windows NT (VTNT)

An emulation of the Telnet Terminal Type Option standard specified in RFC884. The VTNT emulation supports a remote Telnet console session by transmitting display coordinates and character attributes using structures defined in the Microsoft Console Application Programming Interface (API).

Volume Shadow Service (VSS)

A service that tracks changes to individual files on the system. The system can use the shadowed information to restore the previous state of the file.

VSS

See Volume Shadow Service

VTNT

See Virtual Terminal Windows NT

W

WAS

See Web Process Activation Service

WBEM

See Web-Based Enterprise Management

Web-Based Enterprise Management (WBEM)

A technique for managing computers and other devices using Web-based tools, rather than traditional desktop applications originally introduced by Microsoft.

Web Process Activation Service (WAS)

Lets the operating system automatically activate COM+ applications as required, which means the system uses resources more efficiently, but that you also lose a certain level of control over the application process. When using WAS, the application executes as part of an Internet Information Server (IIS) process for library COM+ applications or as a DLLHost.exe process for server COM+ applications.

Wildcard Character

A special character used to represent one or more letters, numbers, punctuation characters, or other special characters. For example, the Dir (directory) command can use the asterisk (*) to represent any number of characters and the question mark (?) to represent a single character. Applications also use wildcard characters. For example, word processors often use wildcard characters to help you search for strings. Programming languages implement a complex wildcard character scenario called regular expressions used to match patterns in strings such as a telephone number.

Windows Management Interface (WMI)

A Windows service and interface that helps an administrator or developer remotely monitor, control, and configure workstations or servers. This particular technology falls into the agent category and is very common on many network operating systems. An agent (special files executing on the client machine) allows the server to gain access to client machine resources and configuration information. Obviously, only machines that have the agent installed are accessible to the requestor.

Windows New Technology File System (NTFS)

The method of formatting a hard disk drive used by Windows NT/2000/XP/2003/2008, Server Core, and Vista. While it provides significant speed advantages over other formatting techniques, only these newer versions of the Windows operating system and applications designed to work with that operating system can access a drive formatted using this technique. Windows 2000 uses NTFS5, a version of this file system designed to provide additional features, like enhanced security. Each newer version of Windows from Windows XP to Windows Server 2008 (including Server Core) provides an updated version of NTFS that includes additional features. An older version of Windows usually can't read a newer version of NTFS than Microsoft designed it to use.

Windows NT LAN Manager Security (NTLM)

A security scheme based on a challenge/response scenario. The server challenges the client, which must then provide an appropriate username and password. If the username and associated password are found in the server's security list for the service that the client has requested, then access to the service is granted. This security scheme is relatively easy to break and has been replaced by more reliable security schemes like Kerberos in later versions of Windows.

Windows Side-by-Side Execution (WinSxS)

A technology for maintaining multiple versions of DLLs on a system so that each application can use the version of the DLL it requires.

WinSxS

See Windows Side-by-Side Execution

WMI

See Windows Management Interface

X

XML

See eXtensible Markup Language

XML Schema Definition (XSD)

The portion of the eXtensible Markup Language (XML) specification that defines data types and other data elements. Most browsers and other applications use XSD to verify the XML document. XSD is also related to a Web site containing such information by use of XML parsers. A designer can create a custom XSD for use with a particular application.

XMS

See eXtended Memory Specification

XSD

See XML Schema Definition

XSL

See eXtensible Stylesheet Language

XSLT

See eXtensible Stylesheet Language Transformation

Index

Note to the reader: Throughout this index **boldfaced** page numbers indicate primary discussions of a topic. *Italicized* page numbers indicate illustrations.